Cambridge Studies in Chinese History, Literature and Institutions
General Editors
Patrick Hanan and Denis Twitchett

STATE AND SCHOLARS IN T'ANG CHINA

Dr McMullen's book takes as its subject the main academic
agencies of the T'ang dynasty in China (A.D. 618–906). It
shows how they provided the context for much of the
scholarly writing that survives from the dynasty, and how
the attitudes of the intellectual elite towards them
changed in the three centuries of T'ang rule. Institutions
concerned with education, with interpreting the
Confucian canons, with state ritual, official history,
literary composition and the public examinations for
which the T'ang is famous all functioned relatively
successfully in the first half of the dynasty. After the An
Lu-shan rebellion of 755, however, they were much less
effective. Scholarly life did not surrender its state centred
orientation, but became more devolved and independent
of the official institutions. Private and unofficial writing
increasingly supplanted in importance the official
compilations of the first half of the dynasty.

State and Scholars
in T'ang China

DAVID McMULLEN

St John's College, Cambridge

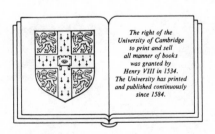

The right of the
University of Cambridge
to print and sell
all manner of books
was granted by
Henry VIII in 1534.
The University has printed
and published continuously
since 1584.

CAMBRIDGE UNIVERSITY PRESS

CAMBRIDGE

NEW YORK   NEW ROCHELLE

MELBOURNE   SYDNEY

Published by the Press Syndicate of the University of Cambridge
The Pitt Building, Trumpington Street, Cambridge CB2 1RP
32 East 57th Street, New York, NY 10022, USA
10 Stamford Road, Oakleigh, Melbourne 3166, Australia

© Cambridge University Press 1988

First published 1988

Printed in Great Britain at the University Press, Cambridge

British Library cataloguing in publication data
McMullen, David
State and scholars in T'ang China. –
(Cambridge studies in Chinese history, literature and institutions).
1. Learning and scholarship – China – History
I. Title
001.2'0957 AZ791

Library of Congress cataloguing in publication data
McMullen, David.
State and scholars in T'ang China.
(Cambridge studies in Chinese history, literature, and institutions)
Bibliography: p. 379
1. China – Intellectual life – 221 B.C.–960 A.D.
2. Learning and scholarship – China – History.
3. China – History – T'ang dynasty, 618–907.
I. Title. II. Series.
DS747.42.M36 1987   951'.01   87-9411

ISBN 0 521 32991 4

CE

CONTENTS

ACKNOWLEDGEMENTS

In the course of writing this book, I have become indebted to colleagues and friends in many places. I owe my greatest debt to Professor E.G. Pulleyblank (University of British Columbia) who, as Professor of Chinese at Cambridge, supervised my doctoral thesis, and who has continued to show me kindness since. His contribution to our understanding of T'ang intellectual history has been enormous, and the following pages will reveal my debt to the framework that his publications in this field have provided. He also read through an early draft of my own study and offered concise, perceptive and kindly advice.

This book is the indirect result of Professor D.C. Twitchett's (Princeton University) request to me to contribute a chapter on T'ang Confucianism for the second of the two volumes devoted to the Sui and T'ang dynasties in *The Cambridge History of China*. Professor Twitchett has listened sympathetically to my views, and after reading an early draft gave me invaluable help and advice. Many other friends and colleagues have read drafts and made helpful comments; they include Dr Paul Smith (Haverford College), Ms Bettine Birge (Columbia University), Dr Michael Quirin (University of Bonn) and my Cambridge colleagues Dr Michael Loewe and Dr T.H. Barrett (now Professor of Chinese History at the School of Oriental and African Studies, University of London).

In 1980, I was able, with the help of a grant from the Japan Foundation for the Promotion of Science, to stay for several months at the Research Institute of Humanistic Studies at Kyoto University. There my friend Professor Tonami Mamoru helped me with suggestions for reading and by answering innumerable queries. I went from Japan to China, and with the support of the Chinese Academy of Social Sciences was able to visit the places about which I had read so much. I owe a particular debt to the late Professor Wang Chung-lo at Shantung University for the help he gave me and for his kindness in making a large collection of original rubbings available to me there. The study of the institutional, intellectual and literary history of T'ang China has been changed greatly by publications in this field since I embarked on this project. No aspect of the T'ang Confucian tradition that I have attempted to summarise has been without major contributions in recent years. The work on T'ang verse by Professor Stephen Owen, the late Professor Howard Wechsler's recently published work on seventh-century state ritual, Professor Charles Hartman's study of Han Yü and Professor Barrett's exploration of the thought of Li Ao have all altered the way in which future scholars will think about the subjects concerned. I also owe a special debt to Professor Twitchett for letting me see and cite from a draft of the first section of his forthcoming book *The writings of official historiography under the T'ang*. These studies have put our knowledge of T'ang intellectual, scholarly and literary history on a new footing.

Dr Helen Dunstan (Australian National University) and my brother Dr James McMullen (Oxford University) both set aside their own programmes to make detailed and helpful comments on the penultimate draft of this book. Its completion also owes beyond measure to the patience and help of my wife Sally. But developing an overview of the Confucian learned tradition for the three centuries of the T'ang dynasty still presented a challenge, and I am, despite the help that I have had, entirely responsible for the form and content of the account that follows.

1

INTRODUCTION

For more than two millennia, successive dynasties in China associated
their rule with the world view, ethical priorities and institutions
advocated by Confucianism. No system of thought, either native or
foreign, challenged the pre-eminence of Confucianism in administration or education; none was so consistently promoted throughout
society. The reasons for this remarkable record of continuity were
complex and varied. Among them, one important factor was the ability
of Confucianism to adapt in response to new political and social
realities, while retaining an essential core.

All Confucians in Chinese history emphasized that the ethical values
and canonical texts of their tradition were constant. But they also
implied that other elements, from institutional and ritual directives to
psychological and philosophical ideas, were capable of re-interpretation and evolution. In T'ang (A.D. 618–907) and pre-T'ang times,
official historians considered the tradition principally in terms of
successive institutional measures affecting its prosperity. From the
Sung (A.D. 960–1279) onwards, Neo-Confucians gave priority to
writing down and anthologizing the doctrinal ideas of successive
teachers. In recent decades, modern scholars, detached from the
political and social imperatives of the tradition, have developed this
long standing insight of continuous change. They have made evolution
in the tradition the theme of important analyses at both the intellectual
historical and the social level, and have contributed greatly to modern
understanding of the role of Confucianism in Chinese history and its
legacy to the China of today.

Implicit in much pre-modern documentation of the Confucian tradition, and explicit in almost all recent scholarly exploration of it, has
been the view that, from the establishment of the Han empire in 206
B.C. until the end of the imperial era in A.D. 1911, the history of
Confucianism divides into two very different periods. The first of these
covers the two great early empires, the classical empire of the Han

(206 B.C.–A.D. 220) and the late medieval empire of the T'ang. Under the Former Han (206 B.C.–A.D. 8), the ethical teaching of original Confucianism and Confucian ideas on statecraft were integrated with the speculation of the cosmological school of the late pre-Ch'in period and with current Legalist and Taoist ideas on political control. The main feature of the resulting system was an elaborate and comprehensive series of functioning correlations between Confucian ethical norms and the physical elements of the universe. This system interpreted and justified most activities of imperial dynastic government, and brought under the state's purview the scholarly activities associated with state ritual, history and literature. First elaborated by the New Text scholar Tung Chung-shu for the great emperor Wu ti (r. 140–87 B.C.), this view of the world underwent modification under the Later Han. There followed a period of some four centuries when China was politically either weakened or divided, and when the rival teachings of Buddhism and Taoism spread at all levels of society. During the period of disunion (A.D. 317–589), Confucianism as a state ideology, depending as it did on stable and effective imperial rule, was to some extent in abeyance. Then under the Sui (589–618) and the T'ang, China was politically reunified, and the Confucian educated court scholars of the late sixth and early seventh centuries reinterpreted the ideology of the Han period to justify the late medieval imperial state.

The second main period in the history of the Confucian tradition, the Neo-Confucian era, extends from the end of the T'ang until the foundation of the Republic, and it coincides with what some scholars have seen as the pre-modern age in Chinese social history. Neo-Confucianism retained and refined the original ethical teaching of Confucius and many elements of early imperial Confucianism. But Chinese society of the late imperial period was generally richer, and education was more widespread. Scholars in the creative mainstream of the tradition lived in a much less court-centred milieu than their medieval predecessors. They typically addressed their teaching to their own circles of disciples rather than directly to the emperor and his policy-making agencies. They emphasized local government and society as much as the court and central government. Their outlook on man was more universal. They developed a much more analytical and speculative approach, particularly to problems of philosophy and psychology. They also formulated new perspectives in history, literature and other learned disciplines.

Neo-Confucianism in its many forms had important antecedents in the second half of the T'ang,[1] but dominated scholarly life only from the Northern Sung (960–1127). It was given its classic formulation by the great scholastic philosopher Chu Hsi (1130–1200). Parts of Chu Hsi's system were adopted as state orthodoxy by the later empires, the Southern Sung (1127–1279); Yüan (1279–1368); the Ming (1368–1644); and the Ch'ing (1644–1911). Chu Hsi's version of Neo-Confucianism exerted a powerful influence on education, on the public examination system and on the conventional outlook of the mandarinate. But throughout the late imperial period, the Neo-Confucian tradition retained its vitality and continued to evolve.

Because of its greater critical sense and its more elaborate metaphysics, from early in its history, Neo-Confucianism developed a selective attitude to the long history of the Confucian tradition. To mainstream Neo-Confucians, the teaching of the sages Confucius (551–479 B.C.) and Mencius (371–289 B.C.) contained the essential truth of their system. But from the time of Mencius until the eleventh century, the true way had not been properly taught or understood. In this view, the Confucianism of the medieval period was lacking both in doctrinal precision and in fidelity to the moral principles that Confucius and Mencius had formulated. Since they had understood the truth only imperfectly, T'ang Confucians and their writings were less worthy of study and emulation than the sage teachers of antiquity or than the ideas of Neo-Confucians themselves. Modern scholarly research, in turn, has tended to follow Neo-Confucianism in focussing primarily on the classical period of Confucius and Mencius and on the later, Neo-Confucian tradition. It has established that, despite what has been characterized as its perenniality, Neo-Confucian thought was by no means necessarily the 'negative, inhibitory ethic' that some of its critics have attacked it as being.[2] Rather, it was often intellectually creative, and expressive of a variety of evolving social and political interests. Relative neglect of the medieval Confucian tradition has had the result, however, that in Western languages, comparatively few important books and articles have treated the Confucian tradition of the late medieval empires, the Sui and the T'ang.

This book attempts an overview of the Confucian scholarly tradition of the T'ang period, in the conviction that, despite Neo-Confucian disapproval, this too was a time when the tradition was vital, adaptable and historically interesting. Though T'ang Confucians lacked both the Neo-Confucian intellectual range and Neo-Confucian concern for precision in doctrine, many of the scholarly activities and institutional and political issues in which they were involved were not substantially different from those of their successors. Confucian canonical texts,

Confucian orientated scholarly projects, the Confucian state ritual programme and Confucian ideals of administration all played an important part in the lives of T'ang scholars, just as they did in the tradition of later periods. But the learned tradition and the political ideals that concerned T'ang scholars were, the surviving documentation strongly suggests, analyzed, promoted and developed above all in the context of the higher levels of official life, mainly in the learned and advisory institutions of the central bureaucracy at Ch'ang-an. In the following pages, therefore, the main learned agencies of the central government at the capital are used as a framework. These institutions concerned principally education, canonical scholarship, the state ritual programme, official history writing and literary activities. Each of these subjects is allocated a separate chapter, which traces over the dynasty the scholarly activities that each involved. The main concern of this book is to outline the changes in attitude that took place among scholars in these fields.

For much of the dynasty, the institutions associated with these activities dominated Confucian scholarly life. They were the most productive and successful bodies of their kind that China had seen. It was the political milieu provided by these agencies and by the central bureaucracy as a whole that, in the early and middle T'ang, gave Confucian education and learning its special quality. When this milieu deteriorated, the Confucian ethical system and ritual programme that had been integral to it in turn lost its vitality. Confucians in the second half of the dynasty therefore developed new attitudes in each of these learned activities. The re-appraisal that they made of the nature of the state they served and of their own role as individuals in society forms a second theme in each of the chapters that follow.

The scholars who served during part or all of their careers in these academic posts or agencies were members of a community which, though very frequently divided over political and scholarly issues, accepted many of the same basic assumptions. An attempt is therefore made to show that, small though this community was in comparison with the educated community of later periods, its characteristic attitudes were not formulated only by the better known figures of T'ang Confucianism, men like the exegetical scholar K'ung Ying-ta, the scholar minister Wei Cheng, the historian and critic Liu Chih-chi or the Confucian polemicist Han Yü. Rather, the political and scholarly language of T'ang Confucianism was usually shared by significant numbers of the scholarly elite.

T'ang Confucian scholars wrote and compiled voluminously. The sources for the history of T'ang Confucianism that survive today represent only a small fraction of what they produced. The main primary writings from which this account is drawn comprise the official compendia, on institutions and the ritual programme, that T'ang scholars themselves compiled, and the anthologies of literature that they assembled and edited. The official histories that were compiled in the course of the dynasty and that attained their present form soon after the end of the T'ang have provided a major source. Unofficial institutional compendia compiled under the T'ang, and major collections of documents preserved in the compilations of the Sung period have also survived. Less institutional material has also provided essential information. Individual literary collections form the most important category at this less formal level; but verse anthologies and collections of anecdotes and reminiscences also sometimes provide vivid glimpses into the T'ang scholarly world. The large numbers of epitaphs that have been unearthed in the course of this century, particularly in the vicinity of Pei-mang shan near Lo-yang, the favoured burial ground for officials and their families, provide a body of evidence that often integrates strikingly with transmitted sources.

Confucians in the late medieval empires

Many of the factors that made late medieval Confucianism distinct from Neo-Confucianism are to be understood in the light of changes in the political and social status of the tradition. The roles that members of the Confucian-orientated scholarly elite played, or expected to play, in the public service to which their tradition committed them evolved as much between the second half of the T'ang and the Sung as during any period until the West breached China's isolation. The Sui and T'ang dynasties, reunifying and centralizing the Chinese political world after three centuries of disunion, were successors to a sequence of states based in the north. Originally in the fourth and fifth centuries largely non-Chinese, these states had in the course of time become more and more sinicized. By the end of the Northern Wei (386–535), as the result of a programme of sinicization undertaken piecemeal mainly in the late fifth century,[3] they claimed the sanction of Chinese tradition for most of their civil governmental activities. The scholars of the Confucian canonical tradition who competed to serve these dynasties and to promote Confucian values and institutions in their administrations were members of a Chinese social elite with long traditions of Confucian learning.[4] In time, other, semi-Chinese, aristocratic families had joined this elite, so that by the time of the reunification, it was heterogeneous in its origins. Its members also inter-married extensively, and in its lower echelons it merged increasingly with less eminent local elite families.[5] But in the seventh and eighth centuries, under the reunified empire, the members of this scholarly aristocracy had a common commitment to the Confucian learned tradition, were acutely aware of their status and traditions and shared their dedication to official service.

Like Confucians throughout the imperial era, the aristocratic scholars who made up this elite in the early T'ang had knowledge and skills that were considered indispensable to dynastic rule. They were experts in the only ideological tradition that could legitimize and strengthen the entire edifice of dynastic government. They cited not only the ideals they held to have been realized in the canonical Chou period (*c.* 1121–249 B.C.) but also precedents from the Han dynasty, an age that exemplified in more immediate and concrete ways the practicability and grandeur of dynastic control of all China. They were expert also in post-Han precedents in civil government, particularly in the organization of the canonically sanctioned state ritual programme, and in the history of the literary tradition. Some were learned in criminal law, and in relatively technical fields, such as calendrical science, *yin-yang* theory, and astrology, which also provided essential sanctions for dynastic power.

Despite the fact that emperors often brought them into the centre of the political arena, however, these early seventh-century Confucian orientated scholars did not exert an all-powerful political influence. They were, rather, only one element in the competitive milieu over which emperors presided. Their recommendations were often in conflict with the interests of the military class, to which both the Sui and the T'ang emperors were deeply committed, and which were almost certainly politically more powerful than most surviving sources suggest.[6] Confucian scholars were forced to compete for the emperor's patronage and resources against representatives of the rival teachings of Buddhism and Taoism, the religious appeal of which they could not match. There were, also, cultural forces in court and in society which they resisted. The most important to them, perhaps, because it had been so central to the identity of their predecessors in the period of disunion, was what they saw as the harmful effect of the sybaritic courtly literary milieu of the conquered southern dynasties.

In bureaucratic terms, moreover, the position of these Confucian orientated scholars was far from unassailable. There was often a conflict between their values and ideals and the practices of the

bureaucracy of which they formed a part. Much of the persistence with
which they addressed the emperor on political and ritual issues is to be
understood as their attempt to expand their influence and persuade
high authority of their own reading of history and their own view of
the world. They sometimes had careers as general service officials, and
their upholding of the Confucian interest then depended mainly on
promotion to the very senior posts in the central government. Or else
they operated at a slightly lower level, in the scholarly agencies at the
capital, within what was by the early seventh century a firmly established but politically rather restricted tradition of academic activity.
These agencies were broadly of two kinds: advisory or consultative
colleges, and permanent institutions in the regular bureaucracy. Advisory colleges were set up by individual sovereigns to supply prompt
scholarly advice, to house libraries, execute scholarly commissions,
and even to supply company for literary entertainment. Depending as
they did on the favour of individual emperors, the proximity of these
colleges to the source of political power guaranteed that they commanded prestige; but it also made them especially liable to changes in
standing and fortune. Some lapsed into obscurity, or came to exist on
paper only. But in the T'ang, the most effective of them came to be
politically far more influential than the permanent academic or educational bodies in the bureaucracy.

These permanent institutions, the second category of scholarly body,
originated in almost all cases as far back as the Han dynasty. They
dealt with the range of learned activities that were justified in
Confucian terms. The most important of them adminstered the official
education system, which had been, even in the period of disunion,
overwhelmingly Confucian in orientation; the state's ritual programme, again sanctioned by the Confucian canons; official history
writing; literary activities on behalf of the state; and the collecting and
editing of books, again all activities justified by appeal to Confucian
authority.

The early T'ang aristocratic scholars appointed to both these categories of institution worked under the direction of high authority, that
is of the emperor and the chief ministers. Typically, scholars were
appointed to *ad hoc* scholarly commissions to undertake specific
projects, and were automatically rewarded on completing them. They
also participated, often vigorously, in political life, mainly by submitting policy recommendations on issues where their learning and
command of precedent were needed. In their scholarly roles, they
often wrote at great length, but they tended in their approach to be

both conservative and compilatory. Many of their works involved selecting from existing sources. In the expression that was often used in commendation of them, these works required a 'balanced adjudication' (*che chung*) of a range of inherited materials.[7] The scope of their writing was largely suggested by tradition, by the scope of the compilations that preceding dynasties had commissioned. The results were intended to have definitive status in the official world to which they were addressed. But almost paradoxically, late medieval official scholarship also embodied one of the central and permanent features of the long tradition of official compilatory scholarship in imperial China: the recognition and documentation of recent change. Official scholars, directed by high authority, tried to retrieve and survey the immediate as well as the remoter past. Their ideal was comprehensiveness; but at the same time they expressed the political, or even the religious, priorities of the authorities they served.

Though certainly Confucian in orientation, these scholars did not make concepts of doctrinal orthodoxy the basis for either scholarly or political activity, as their Sung successors were to do. Ideas drawn from the Confucian canons often formed the basis of their political positions; but scholars used the canons in this way typically to justify individual policy recommendations, rather than as part of a sharply defined and internally consistent body of doctrine. If they wrote theoretically, it tended to be in specific contexts, and their more theoretical statements resembled the 'ideas bound to occasions'[8] seen as characteristic of more primitive societies. There was almost none of the Neo-Confucian emphasis on the unity of all experience, or the search for enlightenment in Confucian terms. Much of their writing was addressed to the sovereign and the court. Their court-centred outlook led them to emphasize the role of the emperor. They adduced the traditional cosmological framework of imperial dynastic rule, inherited from the Han, to stress the grandeur of imperial rule and the responsibility of the emperor.

This tradition of official scholarship had developed over the period of disunion more in the conquered south than in the victorious north. To some extent after the reunification of 589, the position of Confucian scholars in the central government still reflected a process of sinicization. The newly founded and ambitious houses of Sui and T'ang were catching up, as it were, on the more sophisticated, but discredited, south. The relatively primitive cultural atmosphere and soldierly vigour of the early T'ang court and Ch'ang-an were important factors in its patronage of Confucian scholars, helping to shape the practical outlook of the first T'ang emperors towards the learned world.[9]

The aristocratic scholar community from which official scholars were drawn formed an identifiable group in late medieval society. Scholars were distinct by virtue of their education in the Confucian canons and in historical and philosophical texts. They also knew exegetical literature and had command of the verse tradition. The role that this body of knowledge played in defining them as a community is evident from stories in which those who betrayed ignorance of it provoked savage hilarity.[10] But their identity as a group was reinforced by other factors. They were distinguished by their social style and by their dress.[11] Even in the eighth and ninth centuries, they remained 'book-men' (*shu sheng*). Some of the most famous, when they reached high level posts in the general bureaucracy, or when, as they were apt to do, they put forward strategic or military advice, were rebuked for bookishness or lack of practical experience.[12]

Seventh- and eighth-century scholars were, however, politically highly ambitious and unassailably convinced of the correctness of their view of the T'ang dynastic state. They reminded the sovereign, referring to a famous incident in Han history, that though the empire had been won on horseback, it could not be governed on horseback.[13] They hoped to control not only the general civil administration down to local level, but the military side of the state as well. A few, in lives of exceptional energy and activity, attained the ideal of combining successful general service careers with management of academic projects. Their 'talents combined military and civil' (*ts'ai chien wen wu*), and they 'went out as generals and came in as chancellors' (*ch'u chiang ju hsiang*), and directed academic programmes as well.[14]

By the second half of the seventh century, despite the instability of politics in the immediate court, the fabric of civil government was strong enough to permit developments that increased the political influence of these scholars, and indeed reinforced the position of the Confucian tradition as the state ideology for the rest of the imperial era. These developments took place first in the evolving bureaucracy and particularly through its recruitment process, the justly famous T'ang examination system, and secondly among the community of men set apart by education and life style from which officials were drawn.

The examination system, growing in sophistication in the late seventh and eighth centuries, functioned more and more to identify an intellectual and literary elite that commanded great prestige within officialdom and in literate society beyond it. As examination graduates monopolized the administration of the most important of the examinations, this elite consolidated its influence within the bureaucracy. In the course of the political conflicts of the early eighth century, it extended its influence over the most prestigious civil posts in the central government and over all its scholarly and literary operations. The official scholars who served in the academic agencies did not now represent a narrowly defined hereditary aristocracy so much as a self-perpetuating community that was given cohesion by a common experience of education and office, and by common attitudes to learning. Within this community, there was diversity in social background, usually deriving from regional differences or differences of family history and origins. Scholars differed from one another significantly in their private commitment to the supra-mundane faiths of Buddhism and Taoism. Important divisions were also brought about by factional competition, individual political ambition and intellectual temperament. In a few cases, individual officials acted politically in ways that seriously betrayed the interests of their fellows, to be eliminated from the scholar community, and condemned in its documentation with a thoroughness that still causes surprise. But on the whole, eighth-century official scholars formed a socially homogeneous group, whose many interconnections were copiously documented in their writings.

Service under the dynasty, in this period of stability, carried enormous prestige. It provided a road to wealth and status, and many of the scholars whose names recur in the following pages acquired in the course of their serving careers estates, property and large libraries. But scholarly office was not simply a route to material success. T'ang Confucianism could not have retained its vitality if it had not also appealed to the altruistic and idealistic in successive generations of officials. Service to the state was also the focus of ideals that might involve high principles of duty and self-sacrifice. The bureaucracy was governed by ethical laws that had priority over the individuals to whom they applied. The notion of the 'public weal' that modern sociology has seen as central to the early Chinese bureaucracy was very conspicuous in the writings of T'ang scholars.[15] The idea that their public duty had priority over their private interests was read out from the Confucian canons and was repeated in many contexts, including those provided by the scholarly agencies. Office and rank were, in the phrase repeated by some of the most distinguished of the scholar ministers of the dynasty, 'public vessels' (*kung ch'i*), and were not to be allocated on the basis of private favours.[16] In the examination system, in state ritual and in the compilation of the dynastic history, the principle of 'impartiality' (*kung*) was especially conspicuous. The term 'public vessel' represented one of many T'ang ideals that provided given names in the dynasty.[17] Though the concept of the public or general good was sometimes adduced in circumstances in which the self-interest of those who cited it is transparent,[18] it nonetheless represented a central ideal in the political life of T'ang officials.[19]

The ideals of the scholar community as a separate group were also particularly clearly expressed in one of the honours systems that T'ang scholars themselves administered to reward officials who were considered to have served the dynasty well. Deceased officials of the third degree and above were given canonization titles, single or double character designations that were related to the quality of their service. Allocation of canonizations, like the operation of all of the dynasty's status systems, was highly political. Nonetheless the virtues that the system commended stood for the ideals of T'ang officialdom as a whole. Such qualities as uprightness (*chen*), loyalty (*chung*), calmness (*an*), and control (*chieh*) provided canonization titles. But it is clear from surviving comments on the system that the most coveted designation of all was that of *wen*, meaning literary, sophisticated or refined. In the T'ang some 23 scholars are recorded as receiving the single character designation of *wen*, and some 33 *wen* in combination with another character.[20] These were the dynasty's most successful men of learning, many of them household names in the scholar community. The achievements of most are mentioned in the chapters that follow.

T'ang political and military success reached its climax in the third and fourth decades of the eighth century. After the outbreak of the An Lu-shan rebellion in the autumn of 755, the loss of the capitals and the campaigns that followed, the dynasty was unable to re-establish its former power. Loss of central power was accompanied by profound changes in economic and social structure. The provincial administrations, now wealthier and much more powerful in relation to the court, were often dominated by men whose backgrounds might be military or otherwise non-Confucian. The social composition of the bureaucracy as a whole became more fluid, and the power of the descendants of the pre-T'ang aristocracy was further reduced.[21] The position of Confucian-orientated scholars in the second half of the dynasty did not, however, change completely. They held the same offices, for the establishment of posts in the academic agencies at Ch'ang-an remained remarkably stable, at least on paper. Many of the attitudes to which their predecessors had subscribed in the early T'ang, especially those concerned with dynastic power, persisted and became conventionalized. For the scholar community, the court and central government institutions were still the focus of ambition, and the submission of policy recommendations a central commitment. Official service under the dynasty retained immense status. To 'ascend to be among the immortals', or to 'mount the blue sky', that is to succeed in the official career, remained a general ambition.[22] The examination process continued to command great prestige. Examination graduates maintained their position as an elite within the bureaucracy, particularly in the advisory colleges, and in certain other metropolitan scholarly posts. The central bureaucracy became more sophisticated in its attitudes, and even more aware of its past. But it was also more divided by political factions, and administratively much less effective than in the period before the rebellion.

Because the late eighth- and ninth-century state was so much less solvent, it was no longer possible to reward academic commissions on the pre-rebellion scale. Far fewer official scholarly compilations were initiated. Academic office now very seldom led to the sort of productivity that the seventh and early eighth centuries had seen. The compilatory tradition in scholarship that had flourished spectacularly at the height of the dynasty was now continued mainly on unofficial initiative. The results were sometimes close in form to state commissioned works, and they might also, on submission to the throne, be officially recognized. But some of these works showed a sense of distance from high authority and a critical spirit that had been absent from much of the official scholarship of the first half of the dynasty.

Scholars at the close of the eighth century and the start of the ninth documented their own lives and attitudes to a rare degree of detail. Their surviving correspondence, essays and verse, the main source for their outlook, far exceed in quantity those of their forebears earlier in the dynasty. In their unofficial writings, some of them played down the cosmological dimension of the state that had been a central theme in the public writings of their seventh- and early eighth-century predecessors. Instead, they typically emphasized their own administrative experience and political concerns. They also reinterpreted among themselves the political, literary and, for the first time for several centuries, the doctrinal ideas of Confucianism. Occasionally, their unofficial ideas were expressed in official scholarly operations. The views of some influenced the examinations, which they themselves still largely controlled. But on the whole, as the ninth century wore on, the official academic system showed an increasing inability either to continue its former role or to adapt.

In a longer perspective, therefore, this sequence of great political success and prosperity, followed, in the post-rebellion period, by decentralization and instability, changed particularly the unofficial outlook of serving officials. It provided the context in which there began to take place the significant shift of emphasis within the Confucian scholarly tradition that has enabled modern scholars to trace in the second half of the eighth and in the ninth century the origins of the transition into the Neo-Confucian era.

The institutional background

Academic officials on *ad hoc* scholarly commissions, in the advisory colleges, or in the scholarly agencies of the regular bureaucracy produced most of the scholarly writing that survives from the first half of the dynasty. Much surviving unofficial comment on the learned tradition from all periods of the dynasty may be related to these bodies or to individual scholarly posts. No T'ang organ of government was ever static; all were subject to changes, if not in organization and function, then at least in standing or prestige, and the academic institutions were no exception. But a prefatory account of the T'ang academic agencies should describe their place in the bureaucracy in structural rather than evolutionary terms, and should characterize the general category of surviving literature that each produced. The basis for the following brief summary is the *Liu tien* (*Government regulations*). Completed in 738 or 739, this was an official institutional compendium which defined the central and provincial administrative organization of the T'ang at the time of the dynasty's greatest prosperity, and which came to be recognized as one of the dynasty's most important productions of official normative scholarship.[23] The function of offices prescribed in the *Liu tien* is confirmed by sections on institutions in the two compendia on government that survive from the early ninth century, the *T'ung tien* (*Comprehensive compendium*)[24] and the *Hui yao* (*Gathering of essentials*)[25] and by the monographs on offices and posts in the two official T'ang histories, the *Chiu T'ang shu* (*Old T'ang history*)[26] and the *Hsin T'ang shu* (*New T'ang history*).[27] Rescripts of appointment to particular scholarly posts,[28] and 'wall-records' (*t'ing pi chi*), for particular academic premises,[29] mostly from the late eighth or early ninth centuries, supplement these general accounts.

The T'ang scholarly and educational bodies were not a uniform series of equal status or size. The division between the elite advisory colleges on the one hand and the long standing institutions in the regular bureaucracy on the other was partly one of prestige. But it also reflected a distinction in function. The advisory colleges were intended to fulfil loosely defined aims; those of the regular bodies were more precise. The responsibilities of the advisory colleges might in practice include some of those formally belonging to the regular bodies, each of which discharged a more discrete scholarly or educational role. The advisory colleges were staffed by scholars whose basic offices were elsewhere in the central bureaucracy at the capital. Most of the regular academic bodies, on the other hand, provided those appointed to them with their basic offices. In addition to these two categories of scholarly agency, there were certain individual posts in the regular bureaucracy for which special intellectual ability and literary skill were required. Those that commanded the most prestige were the tenures in the central secretariat that involved attending the emperor in an advisory capacity; the grand counsellors, monitors, omissioners, remembrancers and diarists were the most important. Posts concerned with the politically fraught activity of composing imperial rescripts demanded a high degree of learning and intellect. Tenures involving the administration of the examination system also required proven scholarly and literary competence.

The establishment of advisory colleges was caused partly by the need to honour a tradition extending back into the period of disunion, but also because the sovereign needed, in times of both crisis and stability, a small, highly selected group of trusted scholars who would offer advice based on history and precedent. In the phrase much used of this sort of body, their purpose was to 'provide comprehensively for casual consultation' (*pei ku wen*). This was a central obligation, and an ideal to which T'ang scholars very frequently referred.[30] These colleges also supplied the company for entertainment or literary diversion. Though outside the regular establishment of advisory officials attendant on the emperor, they were not 'kitchen cabinets'. As euphuistic titles like Hung-wen kuan (College for the amplification of literature) or Ch'ung-wen kuan (College for the exaltation of literature) suggest, they were associated with the tradition of Confucian learning and statecraft, and with Confucian ideals of learning and refinement. The identification that they acquired with skill in literary composition was another of the reasons for their standing before the emperor.

In T'ang times, scholars recognized that a succession of institutions fell into the general category of advisory college, and that each newly founded college tended to some extent to eclipse its predecessors.[31] Those founded at the height of the dynasty's prosperity, in the reign of Hsüan tsung, were the most successful and important. But certain organizational features recurred in these agencies. They generally consisted of between eighteen and twenty-four scholars holding office at three ranks:[32] a chief minister, especially from the late K'ai-yüan and T'ien-pao periods on, was appointed to the senior rank as a concurrent tenure. The middle rank was filled by middle echelon officials whose basic posts were often in the regular academic bodies or in the crown prince's extensive establishment, while the junior rank was used for junior metropolitan officials, usually examination graduates of good social and intellectual standing. These colleges had their own support staff and libraries. Two were required to operate a teaching facility for the sons of high ranking officials or royal princes. Almost all of them, once founded, continued to exist, at least nominally, until the end of the dynasty.

Three such colleges were entered in the *Liu tien*: the first, the Hung-wen tien or Hung-wen kuan was founded originally in 621 as the Hsiu-wen kuan (College for the cultivation of literature), and was subject to a number of name changes.[33] This college was administered by the grand secretary of the chancellery. It had an important library and a support staff, and accepted thirty-eight students, preparing them for examinations (*chien shih*). Scholars of the Hung-wen kuan, according to the *Liu tien*, were entitled to take part in discussions about changes in regulations or ritual questions. The college lasted throughout the dynasty.

The Ch'ung-wen kuan, founded in 639, was a similar but less prominent institution, with a similar responsibility for preparing students, in this case 15 to 20, for examinations. It was formally a part of the crown prince's establishment, and again lasted into the ninth century.[34] Another body of this kind was the exotically named K'ung ho fu (Academy for the riding of cranes), which existed for a brief period under the empress Wu. Presumably because of its association with her and with her corrupt favourites, the *Liu tien* omits all reference to this college.[35] In scholarly terms much the most productive advisory college at the time the *Liu tien* was compiled was, however, the Chi-hsien yüan (College of assembled wise men), founded in 725 by Hsüan tsung, the dynasty's greatest imperial patron of scholarship. Together with a precursor institution that it replaced, the Chi-hsien yüan was the object of his special favour. Assigned to the department of affairs of state, it was supervised by a chief minister.

It had a 'confidential official' (*nei kuan*) as its deputy, and an establishment of sixteen scholars at its inauguration. Its total establishment therefore comprised eighteen, the number that, perhaps because it provided a graphic pun on Li, the T'ang dynastic surname, seems to have been considered particularly appropriate to an agency closely identified with the emperor. Hsüan tsung's hope that this college would 'shed lustre on the histories' (*kuang shih ts'e*) was amply fulfilled; the *Liu tien* itself was only one of the thirty or so compilations its scholars produced.[36]

Finally, one of the most celebrated of all T'ang institutions, the Han-lin yüan (College of assembled brushes), founded in 738, was also initially in the category of these advisory colleges.[37] Its functions in the first instance were less formal than those of the Chi-hsien yüan, but its ascent to great political power after the An lu-shan rebellion again derived in part from the fact that the composition of imperial rescripts became one of its responsibilities. The Han-lin therefore differed from the Chi-hsien yüan in that officials appointed to it produced not the official compilations, codes, commentaries and anthologies that the Chi-hsien yüan scholars compiled so successfully, but rather collections of imperial rescripts. The Han-lin was the last advisory college to be founded in the dynasty. In 781, a proposal to set up another with thirty scholars and its own premises, as part of the emperor Te tsung's determined effort to restore the dynasty to its pre-rebellion greatness, lapsed.[38]

The function of rescript writing, requiring a close relationship with the emperor, played a central role in increasing the influence of scholars in the bureaucracy. Other posts in the central secretariat that were associated with rescript writing and that therefore also generated substantial amounts of writing were those of the grand secretaries (*chung-shu she jen*). At fifth degree first class, theirs were by no means the most senior scholarly offices in the central administration. Their posts were also subject to much more evolution, in terms of political function, than the posts in the specialist academic institutions. The grand secretaries, of whom there were six, held office in the central secretariat and enjoyed enormous prestige in officialdom. Though holders of an office with confidential duties, they were allowed by custom, as Han-lin rescript writers were, to compile their own collections of the rescripts they composed. Such collections, often with laudatory prefaces by fellow scholars, were respected in all periods of the dynasty.[39]

By the time the *Liu tien* was completed, the office of grand secretary had begun to contribute significantly to the increasing power of the scholarly elite within the bureaucracy in another, quite different way. From 736, when their political role was made subject to restrictions, it became conventional to second one of the grand secretaries after his three-year tenure to direct the regular annual examinations at the capital, usually as vice-president of the board of rites.[40] Grand secretaries were usually themselves examination graduates, and this convention in turn enabled them to recruit to the bureaucracy scholars who shared their own outlook. In this way, they perpetuated and increased the power of the scholarly elite within the bureaucracy.

All these appointments, whether as scholars in the main advisory colleges or as grand secretaries in the central secretariat, brought those concerned near the centre of political power, or at least into social and political contact with high authority. Most of the academic bodies in the second category, those in the regular bureaucracy, however, did not usually enjoy this sense of involvement with the political centre. Indeed T'ang sources sometimes explicitly characterize them as being removed from the political mainstream. The fact that they saw much less evolution over the dynasty is an indication of their relative distance from the central political arena. There were four principal institutions involved: the state academy directorate (*kuo-tzu chien*); the court of sacrifices (*t'ai-ch'ang ssu*); the imperial library (*pi-shu sheng*); and, an exception in being more politically involved, the history office (*shih kuan*).

Of these, the scholarly body with the closest connection with the Confucian tradition was the state academy directorate, or, in the term often archaistically applied to it, the grand academy (*t'ai hsüeh*).[41] This, the main educational institution, was one of five directorates in the central administration, and was the only academic body to be sited outside the imperial city (*huang ch'eng*), the great enclosed precinct in which most of the central government bodies were located. It was staffed by a president (*chi chiu*), traditionally a Confucian scholar of repute, whose rank, third degree second class, made him in formal terms one of the highest ranking of all academic officials. The president had administrative and ceremonial duties, but little real political power. He had, for example, no formal part in examining and selecting for official service the students in the directorate for whose instruction he was responsible. Below the president were two vice-presidents (*ssu yeh*), again traditionally respected Confucian scholars. Below them were the erudits (*po shih*) and assistant instructors (*chu chiao*) of the six schools (*liu kuan*) which were located in the directorate's premises.

Of these six constituent schools, three, the T'ai hsüeh (Great school), with an enrolment of 500, the Kuo-tzu hsüeh (School for the sons of state), with 300 and the Ssu-men hsüeh (School of the four gates) with 1,300 students, were concerned with instruction in Confucian canonical texts. Each had its own precinct, with a gateway, court and hall. Each drew pupils from a different group. The Kuo-tzu hsüeh enrolled mainly sons and grandsons of third-degree officials and above; the T'ai hsüeh, sons of fathers and grandfathers of the fifth degree and above; and Ssu-men hsüeh, sons of fathers and grandfathers of the seventh degree and above and commoners of great ability.

The other three schools, for law (*lü*), orthography (*shu*) and mathematics (*suan*), specialized in the disciplines for which they were named. A seventh school, the College for the amplification of literature (Kuang-wen kuan), was added in 750, some years after the compilation of the *Liu tien*.[42] The T'ai hsüeh and Ssu-men hsüeh each had six erudits and six assistant instructors, and the Kuo-tzu hsüeh five of each. The rank of erudits in the Kuo-tzu hsüeh was fifth degree first class, and that of assistant instructors, sixth degree first class. In the T'ai hsüeh and Ssu-men hsüeh it was slightly lower. After 662, the entire directorate was duplicated at the T'ang dynasty's second or alternative capital of Lo-yang, but with smaller enrolments.

The main function of the state academy directorate was to prepare students for the annual examinations held at the capital. By the time of the *Liu tien*, the most important of these were the *chin shih* and the *ming ching*, but there were also less important examinations, taken in much smaller numbers, for the specialist schools. The ideal standard for the directorate's staff, by which their performance was assessed, was that 'their instruction should have method and the students should complete their syllabus'.[43] The *Liu tien*, in prescribing the syllabus taught, mentions only the Confucian canons and commentaries. It seems likely, therefore, that the directorate did not provide formal teaching in literary composition or in dissertation writing, two major components of the *chin shih*, the regular examination that came to command most prestige. This in turn helps explain the relatively low reputation of the teaching provided by the directorate. Instruction was given, according to the *Liu tien*, very formally, with regular internal examinations to monitor progress. Spare time was devoted to calligraphy; playing the lute (*ch'in*), and archery were permitted, other entertainments were not. Board was provided from state funds.

The directorate had another major function which was defined by the *Liu tien*: its premises housed the principal shrine to Confucius and to those exemplars of the Confucian commentarial tradition whom the dynasty officially honoured. This shrine and its iconography formed the model for a system of Confucian temples with schools attached, which existed at prefectural, county, and at one period under Hsüan tsung, village levels empire-wide. The *Liu tien* does not specify another central responsibility of the directorate, that of determining and preserving the definitive text of the Confucian canons. It was, however, in this connection that in the early T'ang scholars appointed to it produced a substantial volume of important scholarship.

The second regular bureaucratic institution that had important Confucian scholarly functions was the court of sacrifices.[44] This, the first of the nine courts of the central administration, had extensive premises in the imperial city and its own library or records department. It was concerned with implementing the dynasty's massive ritual programme, and was therefore the institution that lay behind much of the great volume of writing on state ritual that survives from the T'ang. It was headed by a president, whose rank, third degree first class, was a single class higher than that of the president of the state academy directorate. The title of president was sometimes conferred on leaders of diplomatic missions to non-Chinese states, since this was a role sanctioned by traditional ideas of state ritual.[45] Beneath the president were two vice-presidents, also commanding prestige. These senior posts were supported by a number of relatively humble offices with specific ritual duties, like those of assistants (*ch'eng*), grand invocators (*t'ai chu*), ushers and heralds.

The posts in the court of sacrifices that carried specifically scholarly responsibilities, however, were those of its four erudits (*po shih*).[46] At seventh degree third class, their rank was comparable to that of their counterparts in the state academy directorate. Their duty was to ensure that there was a scholarly basis for changes proposed in state rituals. The ideal was that the directives they supplied should, 'with every movement be consonant with the canons.'[47]

The court's erudits had another major responsibility: they were instrumental in operating the T'ang system of canonizations.[48] According to the *Liu tien*, 165 of these designations existed. They constituted one of the most important of the four posthumous status systems that the dynasty operated, the other three being burial near an imperial mausoleum, installation in the form of spirit tablets (*shen chu*) in the imperial ancestral temple, and conferment of posthumous office. A canonization that the erudits proposed might be disputed, and this resulted in a small but interesting genre of bureaucratic writing, the 'canonization discussion' (*shih i*). The *Liu tien* also mentions a system for the private canonization of exemplars or teachers by their followers, that had at least semi-official status, and examples are recorded in official and unofficial sources.[49]

The court of sacrifices also had an educational role. The *Liu tien* stipulates a quota of 370 acolytes, of whom 260 were attached to the two dynastic ancestral temples and 110 served at the suburban altars. Acolytes were the sons of officials of the sixth grade and below. They started service at the age of about twelve. Their apprenticeship entitled them to take examinations leading to official status. Their status and function in relation to the students at the state academy directorate became controversial in the course of the dynasty. In the early eighth century, as a result of the empress Wu's determination to promote the female interest in the bureaucracy, there were also girl acolytes.[50] A medical school, with a fixed syllabus and provision for examinations, was also attached to the court; it is mentioned in the *Liu tien*, and in other institutional sources, but, as a specialist institution, is barely documented in unofficial writings.[51]

A third important scholarly institution was the history office (*shih kuan*). Its premises were next to the chancellery (*men-hsia sheng*), at first to its north, then after the completion of a large palace structure on its site, to the south of the chancellery building. Its establishment of scholars was small when compared with that of the state academy directorate. But it was an 'inner office' (*chin shu*), closely associated with political power, and its academic and political prestige was greater than that of the directorate and of other permanent bodies with scholarly functions in the regular bureaucracy. This was because from the emperor and the higher bureaucracy down to the scholar community generally, all had a keen interest in the dynastic history, the scholarly monument that was its purpose to produce. In pre-T'ang times the compilation of imperially commissioned dynastic histories had been allocated either to individually chosen scholars or to the bureau of compositions, a department of the imperial library, and the history office was the most important innovation that the T'ang made in terms of state-managed scholarship[52].

The *Liu tien* states that the history office was staffed by scholars whose basic offices were held elsewhere, and that it was responsible for the final stages of compiling the 'veritable records' (*shih lu*) of successive reigns, which were then to be stored in the inner imperial library. At least in the eighth and ninth centuries, there were normally very few historian compilers (*shih kuan hsiu chuan*), probably between two and four.[53] Their production of veritable records involved a complex process of information collecting from court and provincial administrations. The court officials principally concerned were the diarists (*ch'i-chü she-jen; ch'i-chü lang*) who attended the emperor and recorded his actions and pronouncements.[54] Despite their relatively low rank, these posts belonged to a group of tenures that commanded high prestige. With the counsellors, monitory officials, omissioners and remembrancers, they were called 'officials in attendance' (*kung-feng kuan*), were appointed by direct imperial order and may even have had a special position in formal assemblies of the whole court.[55] Their attendance and participation in inner court discussions and production of 'court diaries' (*ch'i-chü chu*) made them representatives before the emperor of the high ideals of the scholar community, and their role was politically very sensitive.[56] Already by the time of the compilation of the *Liu tien*, both emperors and chief ministers had interfered with and compromised the independence of their records. As a result of their political exposure, the diarists gave rise to Confucian-orientated protest and comment throughout the dynasty.

Other branches of the central and provincial administration forwarded a range of information to the history office. The *Liu tien* specifies astrological and climatic events; changes in the arrangement of the imperial ancestral temple; developments in state ritual and music; military events; changes in criminal law, in institutions and in administrative geography. Scholars in two other bodies, the secretaries of the bureau of merit assessments (*k'ao kung ssu*) and the erudits of the court of sacrifices, prepared or vetted material for the biographies of deceased officials of the third grade and above.[57] Individual officials, too, might propose that particular events be mentioned in the official record. Of the *shih lu* for successive T'ang reigns, only one is extant, that for the six-month reign of Shun tsung in 805. Its attribution to the famous Confucian scholar Han Yü has meant that this brief history has been much analyzed.[58] Other *shih lu* survive only in the form of very brief quotations. They were, however, edited into the dynastic history (*kuo shih*), which, spanning an increasing number of reigns, was up-dated at irregular but politically significant intervals in the course of the dynasty. The dynastic history in turn formed the basis of the extant official accounts, the *Chiu T'ang shu* and the *Hsin T'ang shu*.

A final specialist academic institution with a long history of high prestige was the imperial library, also known archaistically as the 'three pavilions' (*san ko*) and referred to by other names. In Sui and

T'ang times, the imperial library had an outer and an inner department. The outer department, sited in the imperial city, was storeyed, had elaborate fittings and commanded a good view of the landscape beyond Ch'ang-an. It was headed by a director, whose rank, third degree second class, was one class below that of the director of the court of sacrifices. Though this was not a 'strategic post' (*yao chü*), 'gentlemen with a love of learning sought to have it'.[59] Below the director were two deputy directors, while the junior officials in the library, the collators (*chiao shu lang*) and correctors (*cheng tzu*), were traditionally very junior officials, usually examination graduates, who had literary and intellectual ability and political connections.[60] These junior posts seem to have involved only light duties, and so gave those appointed to them the chance to be active politically and to lay the basis for their future careers. Though other official libraries and some of the advisory colleges had collator posts, those at the imperial library were the most coveted.

The main functions of the imperial library were to 'supervise matters concerning the books and illustrations of the state', to build up its collections and compile and update catalogues to it. The library, at least until the foundation of the Chi-hsien yüan, was thus the definitive repository of the dynasty's books. It therefore provided the basis for the official bibliographies that were compiled at irregular intervals in the seventh and eighth centuries. Very large anthologies of *belles lettres* that the emperor commissioned were also based on its holdings.

The director of the imperial library was also in charge of the bureau of compositions (*chu tso chü*). This agency had the duty of composing texts for inscription and prayers for use in ritual observances. By the time of the compilation of the *Liu tien*, it had lost some of its earlier prestige and also the association it had had up to the early eighth century with the compilation of the dynastic history.[61] The highest officials in this bureau were two secretaries who held the rank of fifth degree third class. There were six subordinate posts, which were comparable to the junior posts in the imperial library, in that they were allocated to young officials of ability and promise, usually again examination graduates.[62] The bureau of astrology, (*t'ai shih chü* or *ssu t'ien t'ai*) was a second agency that for most of the T'ang was subordinate to the imperial library. Its officials, however, had specialist skills and were probably less easily transferred to other posts in the academic bureaucracy.[63]

The state academy directorate, court of sacrifices, history office and imperial library were the main academic bodies in the regular bureaucracy. Other scholarly posts, for example those attached to the crown prince's extensive household, did not in themselves produce scholarly literature that has survived in any quantity. But there remained one more major scholarly operation, the examinations, that resulted in a large and varied body of documentation. The examination system involved all the learned disciplines mentioned so far: canonical scholarship, knowledge of state ritual, historical knowledge and composition skills. It was of enduring concern to T'ang scholar officials, and, as in later periods of Chinese history, provoked a great deal of very keen criticism and comment. It registered, though often less than straightforwardly, the changes that took place in the outlook of Confucian orientated scholars over the dynasty.

There were by the late K'ai-yüan period three main categories of examination, each with its own purpose and scope. First the board of rites (*li pu*), or before it up to 736 the bureau of merit assessments,[64] conducted what were called 'regular examinations' (*ch'ang k'o*). These were held, in humiliating and uncomfortable conditions, in a special compound at the capital, annually rather than every third year as in the late imperial period. The examination that commanded most prestige was the *chin shih*.[65] This examination, as it stabilized in the reign of Hsüan tsung, comprised three sections: first a test of rote knowledge of the Confucian canons, secondly a test of composition skills, and finally a series of dissertations. For the purpose of the first section of the *chin shih* and other regular examinations, the canons were listed in a series of nine, and were classified into major, the *Li chi* (*Record of ritual*) and the *Tso chuan* (*Spring and autumn annals with the chronicle of Tso*); medium, the *Mao shih* (*Book of odes*), *I li* (*Ritual directives*) and *Chou li* (*Ritual of Chou*); and minor, the *Chou i* (*Book of changes*), the *Shang shu* (*Book of documents*), *Kung-yang chuan* (*Tradition of Kung-yang*) and *Ku-liang chuan* (*Tradition of Ku-liang*). Up to 737, *chin shih* candidates were required to know one minor canon. From 737, knowledge of a major canon was demanded. Knowledge of the approved or 'established' commentaries for the canon concerned, as well as the main text, was necessary. The second section of the *chin shih* took the form of a test of skill in literary composition, usually involving a poem (*shih*) and a rhymeprose (*fu*), on a prescribed topic and to prescribed rhymes. Finally there was a section for 'dissertations on contemporary problems' (*shih wu ts'e*), containing five main questions, which were divided into multiple sub-questions, each of which required a few sentences of comment from candidates.

The quota of successful candidates for the *chin shih* was very low, probably between two and three per cent of the thousand or so candidates participating annually, and in the course of the dynasty the competition for it became intense.[66] By the late T'ang, it had already become the examination that displaced all others in terms of prestige. It had also become the most important institutional process through which members of the scholarly elite selected their own successors. The very restricted numbers admitted to the *chin shih* degree had an important function in identifying this elite and in increasing its political and social cohesion. The ascendancy in prestige of the *chin shih*, which had already started by the time the *Liu tien* was compiled, had a distorting effect on the documentation that has survived for the T'ang examination system as a whole. The records of composition topics set, the candidates' compositions themselves, and dissertation questions and answers survive in much greater numbers for the *chin shih* than for other examinations. The anecdotal literature relating to the *chin shih* is also more abundant. Of its three sections, only that involving rote knowledge of the Confucian canons is not now represented in surviving documentation. Even so, only a minute fraction of the writing generated by the *chin shih* has survived.

The other principal doctoral examination, therefore, the *ming ching*, is much less fully documented than the *chin shih*, although its pass quota was higher and the number of candidates for it larger.[67] The *ming ching* by K'ai-yüan times consisted primarily of tests of rote knowledge of the Confucian canons, probably again with officially established commentaries if not formally included then at least taken into account. The same classification of the canons into major, medium and minor used for the *chin shih* was used for the *ming ching*. Candidates could either take two canons, one major and one minor; or two medium canons; or three, one major, one medium and one minor. From 681, the examination took the form of 'context questions' (*t'ieh*) which required that candidates, having been shown a phrase of the text they had prepared, reproduce the passage that followed. Candidates were also required to answer dissertation questions, usually on the meaning of the canons and these were sometimes written, but usually oral. Only a handful of *ming ching* dissertation questions survives;[68] no examination answers are extant, nor are there any model or specimen answers. The same relative poverty of documentation surrounds the variant forms of the *ming ching* that were introduced after the An Lu-shan rebellion period in response to reformist demands.

Regular examinations were also held in the specialist topics, law, orthography and mathematics, taught in the state academy directorate, and in the medical curriculum taught in the court of sacrifices.[69] As specialist branches of learning, these subjects commanded relatively little prestige, and the politically and intellectually able avoided them. The examinations in them are, in consequence, extremely poorly documented. At best, the names of a handful of successful candidates survive. An examination for child prodigies (*t'ung-tzu k'o*) is also sparsely documented.

The second main category of recruitment test, inferior in prestige to the *chin shih*, was the decree examination (*chih k'o*).[70] In theory, decree examinations were held *ad hoc*, that is when the emperor identified the need for officials in any of a wide range of categories, skills, or moral worth. In practice, at least in certain periods of the dynasty, they were held fairly regularly. If the regular examinations were the particular preserve of the scholarly bureaucracy, decree examinations, at least at some periods, had a more than nominal association with the imperial interest. In the K'ai-yüan period, for example, Hsüan tsung used them to recruit talented military personnel, a category of official to whom the scholarly bureaucracy was, if not sectionally hostile, at least apathetic. They were also used independently of the official school system to select civil officials. They were held to be considerably less demanding than the regular examinations. In 729, while the *Liu tien* was being compiled, a president of the state academy directorate objected to the easier syllabus and larger numbers admitted by decree examinations, when compared with the much more demanding *ming ching* and *chin shih*, for which the directorate's students were prepared.[71]

The procedure for decree examinations was standard: a decree was issued in the name of the emperor asking for those in specified categories to come to the capital for participation in an examination. The following year, the examination, usually involving a series of dissertation questions with multiple sub-questions, was held. The elaborate edicts announcing decree examinations expressed the hope that 'not a particle of skill should be left out' (*p'ien shan pu i*). Particularly in the second half of the dynasty, the highly critical tenor of some answers means that this category of examination registered changing attitudes to the state probably better than others. Decree examinations are also comparatively well documented, at least in certain periods of the dynasty. Despite their lower prestige, some very famous scholar ministers were recruited through them.

The third category of selection test was one that, in contrast to the *chin shih* and *ming ching*, which merely conferred official status (*ch'u shen*), led immediately to appointment. These 'higher doctoral examinations' comprised two tests, held annually. The first was the *po hsüeh hung tz'u*, which when it attained its definitive form consisted of a rhymeprose, a poem and an essay. The second, the *pa ts'ui*, include model judgements (*p'an*) on hypothetical legal cases. In both cases numbers of questions and answers survive, sometimes from the brushes of officials who later became famous.[72]

Finally, and quite distinct from the recruitment examinations and the *hung t'zu* and *pa ts'ui*, were selection and promotion tests for those of the sixth rank and below, conducted by the bureau of merit assessments.[73] Officials competing for promotion took part in tests that assessed them under four headings: speech, appearance, writing and ability in 'judgements' (*p'an*). Enormous numbers of *p'an* were written for these examinations; thousands survive, to account, at one estimate, for no less than one twentieth of the total number of extant short prose pieces from the dynasty.[74] They are another source through which attitudes may be seen to have evolved, though one that, because of the obscurity and allusive quality of the language in which they are written, has been explored rather little.

The great proportion of Confucian-orientated scholarly literature that survives from the first half of the T'ang was produced in the context provided by these institutions and operations. Dominant though they were, however, it should already be clear that they did not account for the totality of seventh- and early eighth-century scholarly writing. Throughout the dynasty, high authority, in the name of the emperor, also fulfilled its ideological role as the centre of scholarly activity by providing a more general mechanism for the recognition of scholarly or literary enterprise. Scholars outside the immediate academic institutions were encouraged to submit writings for imperial inspection and approval. From early in the dynasty, the submission of such independent writings, some of which survive, was recognized as a route to office, or to promotion within the official hierarchy.[75] Scholars, whether in general service or in academic office, also frequently submitted policy memorials and took part in policy debates, recording their contributions. Their more directly political writings often concerned learned issues and involved invoking the Confucian canons. These political submissions are therefore also an aspect of the scholarly life of their community.

Categories of scholarly writing
Viewed as a series, the institutions of the T'ang bureaucracy that produced Confucian-orientated scholarly literature may be divided into

those like the advisory colleges and the examination system which did not specialize in particular disciplines, and the regular bureaucratic institutions that ran discrete academic operations. These operations comprised four principal non-technical subjects: canonical scholarship; state ritual scholarship; the compilation of the dynastic history; and the production of bibliographical catalogues and large literary anthologies.[76] In a number of different scholarly contexts, the T'ang learned world recognized these four disciplines as separate activities. They were represented by separate divisions or sub-divisions in the official bibliographical scheme, by which the imperial library, the Chi-hsien library and the crown prince's library were arranged, and which the *Liu tien* itself described.[77] Canonical scholarship, history and literary anthologies formed three of the four divisions into which all written work, apart from Buddhist and Taoist material, was classified. Prescriptive state ritual scholarship, the responsibility primarily of the court of sacrifices, was a discrete sub-division of the history division.[78] In official histories also, each of these four categories was allocated separate space: the biographies of canonical scholars, historians and literary men each formed separate groups in the biographical section of the dynastic history, while state ritual was the subject of a separate monograph.[79] Official sources also referred to 'school officials' (*hsüeh kuan*); 'ritual officials' (*li kuan*); 'historian officials' (*shih kuan*); and 'literary scholars' (*wen shih*). This compartmentalization fails only in the case of the imperial library, which had responsibilities wider than a simple correlation with the *belles-lettres* division or the literary biographies section of the dynastic history would suggest. In turn, the term 'literary scholar' was the only one of the four not used with reference to specific academic agencies. Even here, however, appointment to the library was associated with skill in composition, especially of verse.[80]

T'ang official scholars' classificatory, compendious approach to organizing knowledge, however, did not necessarily involve rigid specialization on the part of the individuals engaged in it. Throughout the dynasty, there were many examples of official scholars who were active in all four disciplines. They might also compile works in important fields of learning not described in this book, such as genealogy,[81] the calendar[82] or criminal law.[83] Many scholars, in the course of general service careers, held posts in most of the specialist academic institutions, besides conducting the examinations. They were helped by the flexibility of the T'ang system of office holding, by the relatively short tenures that were usual, though not invariable,[84] in most of the regular scholarly bodies apart from the history office, and by the system of concurrent tenures. This enabled, for example, a scholar holding a basic office in the court of sacrifices to work on the dynastic history, or the holder of a general service post in the central bureaucracy to be a rescript writer. The system of *ad hoc* commissions, used for the great majority of official compilations, also drew personnel from the full range of academic institutions and even occasionally from general service posts in the metropolitan area.

Despite this impressive flexibility, however, the basic lines of demarcation between the disciplines were formally maintained at the institutional and bibliographical levels, with results that were important to the long term evolution of the Confucian scholarly tradition. These categories therefore, integral to T'ang official scholarship as they were, offer a scheme by which the tradition may be surveyed, one that does not do violence to the attitudes of T'ang scholars themselves.

The periodization of T'ang scholarship in this study conforms to that of T'ang political and social history. There were three distinct phases. The first is that of the foundation, the reigns of Kao tsu and T'ai tsung. In this period, high authority, the emperor and his chief ministers, directed a great deal of the scholarly activity. Imperial domination of the learned world and official scholars' co-operation with the emperor were at their most effective. On the other hand, the unofficial world in which the community of official scholars lived is barely documented at all in surviving sources. The second phase is bounded by the accession of Kao tsung in 649 and the outbreak of the An Lu-shan rebellion in 755. The Chou interregnum, lasting from 690 till 705, falls in the middle of this period. In this century, sovereigns still dominated the academic agencies, commissioned works and intervened in controversies. The state institutions, as a result, remained the centre of activity for most scholars. But unofficial sources, especially verse but also prose, begin to provide an independent picture of the values and attitudes of the scholar community. The final period begins with the rebellion of 755, and runs on to the closing decades of the dynasty. Post-rebellion emperors, even the most powerful of them, no longer provided the centre of the scholarly and intellectual world, and the creative developments were now mainly private or unofficial. A large amount of unofficial writing survives from this period, especially from the last two decades of the eighth century and the first thirty years of the ninth. This third period is therefore one of complex change in the political and intellectual climate, and during it some scholars formulated views that contrast sharply with those of their predecessors nearly two centuries before.

2

THE SCHOOL SYSTEM AND THE CULT OF CONFUCIUS

Official scholars in the early and mid T'ang periods saw the prosperity or decline of the Confucian tradition in terms of a number of quite concrete institutional and ritual provisions. The most important of these, identified since the Later Han period (A.D. 25–220),[1] comprised the preservation of the definitive text of the Confucian canons; the promotion of the cult to Confucius and its main ritual, the *Shih-tien*; and the well-being of the official school system at metropolitan and provincial levels. Less important, but no less traditional, aspects included ennobling successive generations of the lineal descendants of Confucius, the K'ung clan; imperial visits to Ch'ü-fu, the traditional site of Confucius's grave; and the maintenance of the temple for Confucius at Yen-chou, in the ancient state of Lu, 'between the Chu and the Ssu [rivers]', where he had taught.

The first of these provisions, relating to the state's role in preserving the text of the canons and to the commentarial tradition, is so essential to an account of T'ang Confucianism that it will be considered separately (Chapter 3). But provision of an official institutional framework for education in the Confucian canons and a cult of Confucius was also, with certain qualifications, a major issue in T'ang Confucianism. It is true that the state school system was never as important in the political arena as other academic operations, such as the state ritual programme or the dynastic history. To most members of the scholarly elite, education and training for the official career was primarily a private or domestic matter. The official education system offered their sons, through its system of quotas of candidates for the regular examinations, administrative rather than educational advantages. But the official schools and the cult of Confucius provided an easily identified public cause, sanctioned by canonical authority and by pre-T'ang institutional practice. Not least because of imperial interest in the schools and their rituals, both were relatively well documented. Attitudes towards them also changed significantly in the course of the dynasty. This evolution, moreover, was parallelled in all the discrete areas of the learned tradition with which this book is concerned.

In the first reigns of the dynasty, the Confucian cult and education system are documented mainly by official material, regulations drafted or encoded, edicts requiring expansion, and records of performances of *Shih-tien* rituals of homage to Confucius. This was a period when the resources of the dynasty, the ambitions of emperors and the aspirations of the scholar community were all largely compatible, and when expansion of official education by fiat from the political centre caused no obvious difficulties. Towards the end of the seventh century, however, developments in the court meant that the school system ceased to prosper in this way. Scholars submitted memorials requesting repair or reform of schools. In this period, their approach remained public and official, and there is little indication of any private or unofficial analysis of the status and function of the schools. In the early eighth century the schools were fully staffed and enrolled; but their effectiveness in educational terms is difficult to determine.

In the second half of the T'ang the political and financial weakness of the dynasty meant that the empire-wide school system was in constant need of reform. Promotion of education brought no immediate political rewards, either to the emperor and his ministers or to individual scholar officials. Posts in the provincial education system, in the T'ang as in other periods of Chinese history, lacked prestige. Scholar officials in prefectural or county posts sometimes reformed or re-established local schools. But it is probable that the effect of their initiatives, like their tenure of office in any locality, was in most cases short-term. The benefits that were claimed for reform of both the metropolitan and provincial systems in the eighth and ninth centuries amount to little more than intangible improvements in the mores of officialdom and of the people, to be described in high-flown and imprecise language. Only the education of the crown prince, self-evidently a special case, was a live political issue and a rallying point for scholars' views throughout the dynasty.

The low standing of the official system in the political world of the post-rebellion period led a minority of official scholars in the late eighth century radically to redefine education ideals. A new theme, one that appears in different ways in all areas of Confucian-orientated writing, is detectable. Some middle- and lower-ranking scholar officials now implied that education did not depend on state institutions, or the prosperity of Confucianism simply on the maintenance of the state cult. They analysed instruction as an individual undertaking, since it was in the private context that was most meaningful to them. They put more urgent emphasis on the revival of Confucian values in society than on the state-maintained schools or the state cult of Confucius. Their comments suggest a climate of thought very different from that at the start of the dynasty.

The reigns of Kao tsu and T'ai tsung

Both founding emperors of the T'ang, Kao tsu and T'ai tsung, emphatically endorsed the idea that knowledge of the Confucian canons and respect for the values they contained should be promoted. They claimed in their official pronouncements that they had assumed power and restored administration after a period of militarism and harsh government.[2] They also endorsed the conventional perspective that saw a much longer term decline since the early Chou dynasty, the age held to have produced the Confucian canons. Kao tsu stated that, 'The texts of Confucianism have all been burnt and the teaching of [the duke of] Chou and of Confucius has lapsed and is no longer cultivated.'[3] T'ai tsung affirmed commitment to 'the way of [the sage emperors] Yao and Shun and [the duke of] Chou and Confucius', rather than to Buddhism or Taoism, suggesting that it was as important to good administration 'as wings to birds or water to fish'.[4] He also held that the balance between civil (*wen*) and military (*wu*) values should be redressed in favour of the civil, and that now was the time to 'lay down the military and cultivate the civil',[5] and restore Confucianism.

The scholars whom T'ai tsung promoted to ministerial rank in the Chen-kuan period (627–49) were equally concerned to promote Confucian teaching and to emphasize its moral priorities. They compared their age unfavourably with that of the Han, when, they believed, statesmen had cited the canons to solve contemporary problems.[6] The scholar-minister Wei Cheng (580–643, canonized *Wen-chen*) in the preface to the biographies of Confucian exegetes of the Sui, written between 629 and 636 (Ch. 5, pp. 165–7), exclaimed, 'How great is Confucianism as a teaching; how copious the benefits it brings to living beings ... It is the very root and source of good administration and moral reform; it opens the ears and eyes of all humanity.'[7] This was a period of expansion for Confucian state education. New political and social stability and the dynasty's need for qualified personnel combined with institutional measures to make a connection between official education and the official career that was probably firmer at this time than at any other period in the dynasty.

The revival of the cult of Confucius

High flown expressions of commitment to the expansion of Confucian education like these, conventional in T'ang times at the head of edicts or the prefaces to official compilations, introduced a series of practical measures. Like so many initiatives by high authority affecting the T'ang scholarly tradition, these were not taken as a concerted programme. The names of the scholar officials who drafted the documents concerned are not recorded. There is no satisfactory record as to the effectiveness of these measures. Nor are they supplemented in this early period in the dynasty by information from unofficial sources that might supply a picture of life in the schools.

The earliest measures concerned the provision that official historians saw as central to the tradition, the cult of Confucius. In 619, an edict ordered the construction in what later became the state academy directorate of shrines for the duke of Chou and for Confucius, and ordered that offerings be made to them each season.[8] Thus from the founding of the dynasty, Confucius presided symbolically over the centre for official Confucian scholarship, education and preparation for entry into the civil bureaucracy. Further measures, designed to honour Confucius and other figures in the tradition, followed. In 623, Kao tsu visited the state academy directorate and observed, for the first recorded time in the dynasty, the *Shih-tien*, the ritual of homage to the duke of Chou and Confucius, or to Confucius and his favourite disciple Yen Hui. This rite was mentioned in the *Li chi* and had a more recent history of performance going back at least to the Wei (A.D. 220–64) and Chin (A.D. 265–420) dynasties. It was one of only two rituals that the dynasty prescribed for prefectural and county levels throughout the empire, the second being the twice yearly offering to the gods of the soil and grain.[9] Kao tsu repeated the ceremony in 624[10] and 625[11]. In 626[12], 631[13], 638[14] and 640[15], T'ai tsung is recorded as having attended the *Shih-tien*. At the 640 celebration, one of the most learned and productive official scholars of the first two reigns composed an offertory prayer, and after the performance gave a homily on the *Hsiao ching*.[16] This was K'ung Ying-ta (574–648, canonized *Hsien*), who claimed descent from Confucius and, by virtue of the fact that he lived at Ch'ang-an, was likened to the Later Han dynasty scholar Yang Chen (d. A.D. 124), 'the Confucius of Kuan-hsi'.[17] K'ung at this time held the scholarly post of secretary to the right of the crown prince's household (*t'ai tzu yu shu-tzu*), and therefore also symbolically represented the Confucian interest to the crown prince.

In the course of the first two reigns, high authority raised the status of the *Shih-tien*. In 647, the crown prince made one of the three offerings involved in it.[18] In 648, a prince from the Korean state of Silla attended, an indication of the prestige of the T'ang in East Asia.[19] After the celebration of 624, the court, following a practice that originated in the period of disunion, heard a debate between representatives of the three teachings, Confucianism, Buddhism and Taoism. At its close, Kao tsu, though he ranked Taoism first, judged that a Confucian, the canonical and lexical scholar Lu Te-ming (*c.* 560–630) (Ch. 3, p. 72), was the best individual contestant.[20] A debate was held in 638 under T'ai tsung, though this was in the Hung-wen kuan, the advisory college of the period, rather than in the state academy directorate. In this contest, it was K'ung Ying-ta who represented the Confucian side.[21]

In the course of the Chen-kuan period, the emperor made a first rearrangement of the relative standing of the main exemplars represented in the official Confucian temple. The changes that took place in the first instance appear slight; but over the longer term such adjustments began to reflect changes in the climate of Confucian thought itself. In 628, at the request of the scholar minister Fang Hsüan-ling (578–648, canonized *Wen-chao*) and of an erudit of the state academy directorate, the duke of Chou as the second figure in the temple was replaced by Yen Hui, Confucius's favourite disciple, and Confucius was given the title of Former Sage (*Hsien sheng*) rather than Former Teacher (*Hsien shih*).[22]

This decision was modified after T'ai tsung's death by a statute of the Yung-hui period (650–6), by which Confucius was again called Former Teacher; but thereafter the place of the duke of Chou in the official temple was increasingly questioned. It was held that, as a regent and member of the Chou dynastic house rather than a subject like the other figures represented in the temple, he was in a separate category from them. In 657 therefore, Confucius was returned to the status of Former Sage and the duke of Chou was removed from the temple and assigned to a separate cult for king Wen of the Chou, in which he was given offering as a correlative.[23] In this way, the dynasty used the cult to maintain a difference in status between the imperial house, symbolized by the duke of Chou, and the officials and scholars, whose symbol and ideal was Confucius. This was a distinction of which the T'ang scholar community, appraising the role of Confucius, was well aware.[24] At the same time, Yen Hui, who was considered an important moral exemplar from the start of the dynasty, and who in the late eighth century was to become a vehicle for the most spiritual ideals of the post-rebellion Confucian tradition, was given a permanent place as the second figure in the cult.[25]

As official scholars redefined the Confucian cult over the first two reigns, they deliberately divested the figure of Confucius of some of its more implausible or ahistorical accretions. In official literature, there is therefore no mention of the tradition that saw Confucius and Yen Hui as bodhisattvas (*p'u-sa*), a view that persisted unofficially almost certainly throughout the dynasty.[26] Similarly, the belief that women might aid conception by mounting the dais on which Confucius's statue stood, 'with their bodies exposed', found no echo in official sources, and was condemned in anecdotal literature later in the dynasty.[27] Nor, understandably, is there any hint in the sources for the official cult of the satire and ribaldry to which Confucius was subjected in such widely different contexts as a court entertainment in the mid-ninth century[28] and in popular ballads preserved at Tun-huang in modern Kansu.[29] Confucius was rather, in the phrase adapted from Mencius and used of him several times over the period, 'simply the greatest man since humanity began'.[30] The Confucian cult is likely to have been seen as primarily, if not exclusively, official. The question of whether it had been right to punish a teacher who had performed an unauthorized ritual to Confucius with his students, referring to an incident in the Han dynasty, was set as a 'judgement' (*p'an*) question later in the dynasty.[31] The importance the early T'ang official world accorded the *Shih-tien* is indicated by an edict of 648, which prescribed that the three offerings involved in each metropolitan celebration were to be made not by the low ranking officials hitherto involved but by the president, representing the emperor, the vice-president and the erudits of the state academy directorate. At prefectural level, the prefect, his assistant and an erudit were to celebrate, and at county level the magistrate, his assistant and the registrar were to perform the rites.[32]

In the course of T'ai tsung's reign, more measures were taken to increase the standing of the Confucian tradition. In 626, a descendant of Confucius, K'ung Te-lun, was honoured as marquis Pao-sheng, the first T'ang instance of a practice that was to last throughout the dynasty.[33] In the second half of the reign, the emperor carried out two measures affecting the status of pre-T'ang exegetical scholars of the Confucian canons. In 640, scholars from the Liang (A.D. 502–56), Northern Chou (A.D. 557–81) and Sui dynasties were posthumously honoured, and it was ordered that their writings be studied in the state academy directorate.[34] By commending the exponents of very different commentarial traditions, northern and southern, in this way, the state gave an early indication that it had an inclusive or pluralistic interest in the great range of exegetical and interpretative literature devoted to the Confucian canons. The measure also implied that such commentators, having lived recently, represented a period in the history of canonical scholarship subsequent to and distinct from that of their Han, Wei and Chin predecessors. Both this pluralistic attitude and this periodization, in turn, will be shown to have been an important feature of the early T'ang review of canonical scholarship itself (Ch. 3, p. 71 and pp. 77–9).

Recently deceased scholars like these did not qualify for representation in the Confucian temple. However, seven years after this measure, in 647, the first significant expansion of the arrangement of the temple took place. An edict ordered that twenty-two earlier commentators, from Tso Ch'iu-ming, to whom the *Tso chuan* and the non-canonical *Kuo yü* were ascribed, to Tu Yü (A.D. 222–84), who wrote a commentary on the *Tso chuan* and Fan Ning (339–401), a commentator on the *Ku-liang chuan*, be represented in the temple.[35]

The figures concerned in this expansion were commentators only; interpreters of the Confucian tradition like the philosophers Mencius, Hsün tzu (*c.* 315–236 B.C.) or Yang Hsiung (53 B.C.–A.D. 18) were not included. In this period, the doctrinal ideals of philosophers like these were by no means as highly esteemed as they were to become in the Neo-Confucian era, and the very fact that they were not technically commentators excluded them from representation in the temple. The later T'ang period, however, was to see the start of a radical change in this attitude. Scholars were increasingly to call in question the commentarial approach to the canons that had been basic to the official scholarship of the seventh century, and to appeal to ideas as much as to exegesis. Mencius and others were even, albeit unofficially, to find the places in the temple denied them officially in the seventh century.

The re-establishment of the official education system
The same edicts that under Kao tsu had established shrines to the duke of Chou and to Confucius started another development of great importance to T'ang official scholarship, the re-establishment of the official education system as an operation of the regular bureaucracy. Again the measures were piecemeal. In 618, three metropolitan schools, the Kuo-tzu hsüeh, T'ai hsüeh and Ssu-men hsüeh were re-founded on the site that in 627 or 628 became the state academy directorate, and their student quotas were prescribed.[36] Under T'ai tsung in 628, the orthography school was re-founded;[37] and in 632 that for law was also re-established.[38] With the school of mathematics,[39]

these made up the 'six schools' (*liu kuan*) to which T'ang institutional histories referred up to the middle of the eighth century.[40] T'ai tsung, commanding more wealth and stability than Kao tsu, also greatly expanded the Kuo-tzu hsüeh and increased the intake of the other constituent schools.

In the Chen-kuan period, as a result of this expansion, the total nominal enrolment of the schools at Ch'ang-an, at 3,260, was the highest in the dynasty.[41] In a policy likely to have been intended in part to ensure control of any exegetical teachers of major importance still active independently in the provinces, the emperor summoned scholars who had taught privately outside the metropolis and gave them academic office.[42] After this, influential independent teachers of the Confucian canons with the large followings and court connections typical of the period of disunion and the Sui are barely mentioned in T'ang sources. The Confucian scholarly world thus acquired the highly centralized character it was to retain for the following century.

The state, following Sui practice, also established official education beyond the capital. In the provinces at prefectural and county levels a system of schools was established, each containing humbler versions of the metropolitan shrine to Confucius and other figures in the tradition.[43] These were the 'branches and leaves' of the system of which the metropolitan directorate was the trunk.[44] In 628, medical schools were established at prefectural level.[45] Official historians cited the example of Wen weng, who under the Han had promoted Confucian learning in Szechuan, whose lectural hall at I-chou was identified in the early T'ang. Throughout the dynasty, Wen weng remained the often cited archetype of the local provincial official who raised the standard of education in his area.[46]

Surviving records attest to a few of the provincial schools or temples established in the early T'ang: a wall record at Tun-huang indicates that there was a 'commandery erudit' (*chün po-shih*) there at about this time;[47] at Chi-an county, on modern Hai-nan island, the assistant performed the *Shih-tien* and lectured on the canons to the students;[48] and in 637, an order was given to repair the Confucian shrine at Yen-chou, the prefectural town in Shantung associated with Confucius.[49] The education system empire-wide was now so extensive that its total enrolment, according to a later T'ang source, was as high as 60,000.[50] The position of the teachers employed in this system was given special recognition in the criminal code. Physical violence by a pupil on a teacher brought harsher penalties than that on a commoner, while the penalties were increased with the rank of the teacher.[51]

The formal purpose of the state academy directorate and its 'branches and leaves' was to provide preparation for the metropolitan examinations that led to civil office. In the first two reigns, these were also re-established. In 621, a decree required an annual 'tribute of qualified candidates' (*kung-chü*) from the provinces.[52] The first regular examinations, including the *chin shih* and the *ming ching*, were held the following year.[53] This year also saw the first imperial proclamation announcing a decree examination.[54]

The result of the growing stability of the dynasty and of successive calls for qualified personnel to enter its service was a stream of aspiring scholars towards the capital. The fervour that these prospective officials created exceeded even that caused by very similar measures in the period of disunion and the Sui.[55] It was recorded that, 'such a flourishing of Confucianism had never previously occurred'.[56] The numbers crowding into the directorate were estimated at eight thousand. A spirit of ambition seems to have spread among them and in the capital. When T'ai tsung sent an erudit from the state academy directorate to teach the Confucian canons to cavalry units at Ch'ang-an, and allowed any who had mastered a single canon to compete for civil office, he too symbolically expressed the hope that the civil values and skills to which they aspired would prevail over the militarism of the preceding age.[57]

From 650 to 755

The century following Kao tsung's accession in 650 saw the greatest expansion of the general administrative system in the dynasty. The institutional provisions in terms of which high authority, and the scholarly community, saw the prosperity of Confucianism all benefitted from the prevalent interest in innovation. Even during the Chou interregnum (690–705), despite unstable court politics and although the surviving records are strongly prejudiced against the regime of the empress Wu, the overall picture that survives is one of expansion for the state cult. But at the same time, the official records suggest that corrupution, inefficiency and the prevailing court fashion for euphuistic literary composition threatened the well-being of the Confucian school system. A few scholars, by urging sober Confucian priorities in reformist memorials, developed a tradition of protest against these trends. The T'ang restoration of 705 and the long reign of Hsüan tsung saw further expansion in the cult and the education system. But the picture, of unprecedented scale and yet of inefficiency or dereliction, retains an ambivalence that was to mark it until the An Lu-shan rebellion of 755, and the sharp deterioration in the system that followed.

By the end of Hsüan tsung's reign, as an indirect result of the 130-year period of internal peace, the learned world was both larger and less effectively centralized on the court than it had been at the start of the dynasty. Verse and some prose evidence survives from this time to attest in detail for the first time to Confucian-orientated scholarly life and educational attitudes independent of the metropolitan academic institutions. The emergence of this more independent intellectual and literary milieu marks the beginning of the long term trend toward the less court-centred Confucian tradition of the late eighth century. Some of the scholars involved in this development in the K'ai-yüan and T'ien-pao periods were to prove direct or indirect influences on the great intellectuals of the post-rebellion decades.

The metropolitan and provincial education system

Early in Kao tsung's reign, measures were taken that adjusted and further expanded the education system that Kao tsu and T'ai tsung had established. In 650, several vacant posts in the state academy directorate were filled, and erudits and assistant instructors were given honoraria.[58] In 662, as a result of the increasing interest in Lo-yang as a second capital, a duplicate directorate was established there.[59] Perhaps the specialist schools in law, orthography and mathematics had been allowed to run down, for this year all three were re-founded.[60] Over this period and under the empress Wu there were changes, mostly temporary and archaistic, in the names of most academic institutions.[61] These changes are to be seen as an aspect of the attempt by the empress Wu to create a separate identity for her own regime, rather than as involving substantial developments in the function of the bodies concerned.

Few details otherwise survive about the school system in the second half of the seventh century: drought or bad harvests in the capital region led to the dispersal by imperial order of the student body, as it did in the course of the Hsien-heng period (670–4),[62] and again later, in 709 and 710[63] and subsequently.[64] In 670, an edict ordered the prompt repair or construction of Confucian shrines and schools at provincial level.[65] Over this period the provincial system was, at least in name, generally established, and with it an empire-wide cult of Confucius. Shrines to Confucius with schools are attested at places as far apart as Ch'ang-chiang, and Hsin-tu counties in modern Szechuan[66] and at T'an-chou in modern Hopei.[67] At Shou-chou in modern

Anhui, the prefect personally tested the students' knowledge of the text and meaning of the canons and of contemporary government policy and local administration.[68]

In the course of Kao tsung's reign, however, new ministers gained control and the empress Wu began her ascent to power. The relatively open political milieu of T'ai tsung's reign, which had enabled scholar ministers and lower-placed official scholars to promote their ideals, without excessive risk, deteriorated. For the first time in the dynasty, the prestige and well-being of the capital educational institutions were checked. Official historians attributed the change partly to the increasing fashion for literary composition and to the climate in which composition skills flourished. The *Chiu T'ang shu* states that 'government and education gradually declined and Confucian techniques (*ju shu*) deteriorated, while special attention was given to literary officials (*wen li*)'. The admired spirit of the Chen-kuan era gave out, 'like the flame that burns up wax, while no one notices'.[69]

This growth in influence of composition skills was one of the most important trends affecting the scholarly community in the late seventh century (Ch. 6, pp. 225–32). Its effect on the official education system was complex and indirect. It worked against the continued effectiveness of the system in two ways. First, the schools themselves seem not to have provided instruction in the composition techniques that now acquired such great prestige in court and official circles. Inevitably, therefore, students acquired the training necessary for mastery of *belles lettres* fashion independently. Secondly, virtuosity in composition became more and more identified with the increasingly luxurious court itself and the lavish entertainments and verse competitions it held. Composition skills provided, in this milieu, a means of gaining quicker and irregular access to high official circles, and displaced mastery of the Confucian canons in this role.[70]

The scholars who spoke out against this development resented the rejection of austerity and restraint that accompanied it. Yet the trend they criticized was not as straightforwardly adverse to the interests of the scholarly element in the bureaucracy as they and official historians implied. In the course of the second half of the seventh century, the growing prestige of composition came to be reflected in the examination system. There, the ability to compose euphuistic texts on set themes worked in the longer term to the political advantage of the same scholars who condemned its more extreme expression. Over this period, the examination route to official status, and particularly the *chin shih*, which emphasized virtuosity in composition more than any other examination, steadily increased in prestige, and functioned more and more to identify the intellectual and scholarly elite within officialdom.[71]

At the formal administrative level, despite these developments, a continued enrolment of students in the state academy directorate was ensured, because, as in most periods in Chinese history, registration there brought practical career advantages. Regardless of the quality of instruction, membership of the directorate in itself made success at the regular examinations much more probable, while students, by virtue of their residence at Ch'ang-an, were in a position to establish contacts with metropolitan officials and so increase their chances of success.

Deterioration in the operating condition, as opposed to enrolment, of the directorate is, however, indicated by memorials submitted in 684,[72] 692[73] and 699.[74] The last of these, by Wei Ssu-li (d. 719, canonized *Hsiao*) stated that there had been a twenty year period of decline, that students had developed opportunistic attitudes rather than sound learning and that they were able to gain official status by bypassing the regular examinations. In the second, Hsüeh Teng (647–719) charged that dexterity in literary composition was being fostered at the expense of canonical scholarship. In another memorial, submitted in 695, he objected to the presence of barbarian students, 'trailing their robes in our schools and stepping high at the gates of our academies.'[75]

Continuity in appointments and a full establishment of directorate officials, however, is likely to have been maintained. Over this period K'ung Ying-ta's son and grandson both held office as vice-presidents of the directorate, a post K'ung himself had held. They provide an example of a family tradition of learning linked to a specific scholarly office, in a way instanced time and again, and greatly respected by the T'ang official community.[76] A rare vignette of directorate life, suggestive of the political ambition of the students, is provided by an episode of 691. A student of the T'ai hsüeh, perhaps to advertise his concern to care for his parents, memorialized directly to the empress Wu, asking for permission to return home to care for them. The great minister Ti Jen-chieh (630–700, canonized *Wen-hui*), however, told the empress that the sovereign should not be concerned with issuing orders for such low level cases. 'The student's request for leave is simply a matter for the directorate's assistant and registrar.'[77]

During the short reigns that followed the T'ang restoration of 705, the directorate reverted to its original name. In 706, an attempt was made to tighten up its internal rules. But, like the imperial library, the directorate at this time suffered from the appointment to it of heterodox religious figures.[78] Under Chung tsung (r. 705–710), there was the first example in the dynasty of an individual reformist academic administrator: Yang Ch'iao (d. c. 710, canonized *Ching*), as one of the vice-presidents, is said to have carried out repairs to the building, then later as president rigorously to have selected his own subordinates. At this time, student behaviour was sometimes very unruly. In trying to improve it, Yang Ch'iao was beaten up at night. Summary execution was prescribed for those responsible for the violence.[79]

Official historians viewed at least the first two decades of the long reign of Hsüan tsung more favourably than those of his two immediate predecessors, and for the K'ai-yüan period a series of measures intended to maintain and improve the official school system are recorded. Even as crown prince, Hsüan tsung tried to improve the standard of teaching and conduct in the schools.[80] Then in 714,[81] 717,[82] 733[83] and 738[84] he issued edicts, the purpose of which was to improve and expand the provincial school system. The edict of 733 gave permission for the running of private local schools, and allowed pupils from them to transfer to local official schools. That of 738 ordered the establishment of village schools, thus extending the official system to an even lower administrative level. In the capital, some of the most famous and productive official scholars, who made up the successful *ad hoc* academic commissions so characteristic of the reign, served in the directorate.[85] When in 725 Hsüan tsung founded his own advisory college, the celebrated Chi-hsien yüan, five of the scholars appointed to it were directorate officials.[86]

Again, however, despite these indications of prosperity, it is difficult to derive a consistent or detailed picture of official education at this time. The strict rules governing the state academy directorate incorporated in the *Liu tien* conflict with records of the unruliness of the students; edicts requiring reform seem to contradict statements that levels of education were very high. The elite within the official community, moreover, probably had an ambivalent attitude towards the general expansion the emperor brought about. In 729, Yang Ch'ang (c. 668–735, canonized *Chen*), the president of the state academy directorate, complained of the large numbers competing for official status by the various routes the dynasty provided. He indicated in effect that study in the schools for the regular examinations was becoming more and more uncertain as a means to gaining entry into officialdom. 'The three thousand students are wasting official revenue to no purpose; the erudits in the two directorates are superfluously consuming their celestial stipends.' His memorial ended with the request that the standard of the *chin shih* and *ming ching*, by far the most demanding examinations, be relaxed, and that their quotas of successful candidates be increased.[87]

Other evidence points to demoralization in the school system. The student community appears again to have been lively to the point of unruliness. Attitudes to curricula were dominated by the aim of passing the regular examinations, while vigorous political grafting was necessary for success.[88] The authoritarian Li Lin-fu, as a vice-president in the K'ai-yüan period, was said to have reformed conditions. When, from 736, he became chief minister, the mere threat of his anger was said to have brought fear to the students.[89] In 742, perhaps at his instigation, unruliness in the formal lectures that followed the *Shih-tien* was forbidden.[90]

In 750, Hsüan tsung founded another metropolitan school, the Kuang-wen kuan (College for the expansion of literature). In this, a small number of candidates preparing for the *chin shih*, were to be taught by two 'literary scholars'. It is ironical that this school, the one institution apparently designed to recognise the trend towards *belles lettres* that is so well documented for the preceding century, never operated as intended. Cheng Ch'ien (d. 762), the scholar appointed to head it, considered his posting an indication of failure. An anecdotal source indicates that the school's premises in the state academy directorate were still unbuilt at the outbreak of the An Lu-shan rebellion, and the timbers piled for its construction remained unused, to be pilfered by those in charge. The low prestige of the Kuang-wen kuan suggests that educational office involved removal from the mainstream of political life, and that ambitious officials tried to avoid appointment to the directorate.[91]

On the eve of the An Lu-shan rebellion, the provincial education system was nominally at its greatest extent. But the quota of students whose board was met by the state at the Ch'ang-an directorate was, according to the *Liu tien*, now only 2,210, a reduction of over one thousand on the figure for T'ai tsung's reign.[92] The harsh competition for success at the regular examinations and the very low quota of *chin shih* and *ming ching* passes continued to make problems for both metropolitan and provincial schools. There were also more indications from unofficial sources late in Hsüan tsung's reign that the senior posts in the directorate had lost standing,[93] and that enrolment there provided only practical advantages to the students. They therefore probably continued to prepare themselves independently of the official system for the examinations and for their official careers.

Expansion in the state cult of Confucius

The eve of the rebellion of 755 saw the state cult of Confucius on a much larger scale than ever before in Chinese history. It attained this position over the preceding century by the intermittent fiat of high authority. Again, it was Hsüan tsung who did more than any other sovereign to expand it. Its new grandeur reflected not only the unprecedented wealth of the dynasty, but also the indirect influence of the much richer iconography and temple art of the rival religions, and particularly that of Buddhism.

Many of the honours sovereigns bestowed on the cult took the form of ever higher posthumous titles for its exemplars. Posthumous office was one of the ways in which the dynasty honoured its own deceased servants, and these honours would therefore have been immediately appreciated by the official community. In 666, Kao tsung raised Confucius in rank, giving him the title of grand tutor, a post believed to have been held by the duke of Chou. The emperor honoured Confucius in this way when returning from mount T'ai, where he had successfully performed the greatest of the T'ang imperial rituals, the Feng and Shan rites (Ch. 4, p. 129). His journey took him to Ch'ü-fu county and the area associated with Confucius. In visiting Ch'ü-fu, he exploited a tradition established by Kao tsu of the Han in 195 B.C. His journey east therefore invited comparison with the great Han era, and celebrated the consolidation of T'ang rule.[94]

In 668, when the crown prince performed the *Shih-tien*, Yen Hui was given the title of minor tutor to the crown prince, and Tseng Shen, the disciple whom Confucius had commended for filial piety and to whom the *Hsiao ching* (*Canon of filial piety*) was ascribed, was made minor guardian.[95] In 681, the crown prince, the future Chung tsung, attended the *Shih-tien*,[96] and in 690 Confucius received the title of duke Lung-tao (Promoter of the way), while the duke of Chou was made prince Pao-te (Rewarder of virtue).[97] During the Chou interregnum, there is little other evidence relating to the Confucian cult. It is possible, however, that the imperial consort and favourite Shang-kuan Chao-jung (d. 710, canonized *Hui-wen*), promoting the female interest as the empress Wu herself had done, attended the *Shih-tien*.[98]

At the T'ang restoration of 705, the temple to Confucius at Yen-chou received attention, households in the vicinity of the ancient states of Lu and Tsou being required to supply offerings, and a new member of the K'ung line inherited a noble title.[99] In 712, an edict ordered that prefectural temples to Confucius be refurbished and the income from thirty neighbouring households be used to maintain each.[100] But over this period, Chung tsung and Jui tsung gave their interest and resources mainly to Buddhist and Taoist building projects. A succession of scholars, several of them connected with Ti Jen-chieh, opposed these projects in the name of Confucian reluctance to become involved with the supernatural world. But no resulting benefits for the Confucian cult are recorded.[101]

Just as he had promoted official education, so even before his accession Hsüan tsung paid attention to the Confucian cult. In 711[102] and 712,[103] as crown prince, he celebrated the *Shih-tien*. Perhaps he encouraged discussion of the observance, for in 711 Liu Chih-chi (661–721, canonized *Wen*), the great historian critic of the early eighth century, submitted a memorial critical of the archaistic dress used by participants.[104] In 712, Hsüan tsung raised the posthumous titles of Yen Hui and Tseng Shen, much as the crown prince had done in 668.[105]

After his accession, Hsüan tsung presided over further expansion of the Confucian cult. In 717 and 719, a ceremony was instituted whereby *ming ching* candidates arriving from the provinces made a formal visit to the temple of Confucius.[106] In 738, this ceremony became compulsory for all candidates taking the regular examinations.[107] The *Shih-tien* observance also underwent refinement: in 719, the emperor revived a closely related rite, the *Ch'ih-chou*, in which the crown prince was formally inducted as a student in the state academy directorate and presented the first of three offerings to Confucius. Later T'ang scholars who tried to ensure that the crown prince observed Confucian norms were to emphasize the importance of this ritual.[108]

In 723, slaughtered animal offerings in the *Shih-tien* as it was performed at county level were replaced by dried meat;[109] in 731, animal offerings were discontinued at prefectural level.[110] Later in the dynasty these measures, which were not permanent, were cited in an effort to economize on what had become a very expensive cult; but it is difficult to be certain about their motive in this period.[111] In 734, barbarian representatives were ordered to attend the directorate's rituals.[112] In 737, the music for the *Shih-tien* was prescribed.[113] In 740, it was ordered that the most senior officials, the three dukes (*san kung*), attend the metropolitan *Shih-tien*,[114] and at about the same time the vice-president of the state academy directorate proposed that both clerical and lay Buddhists should attend.[115]

The same theme of expansion applies to the figures represented in the temple. In a measure of 720, the ten close disciples whom Confucius had commended in a single *Analects* passage were provided with sitting statues and were to be given offerings with Confucius. Another statue, also sitting, was prescribed for Tseng Shen, whom Confucius had not mentioned with the ten. In imitation of the 'wall of Wen weng', the temple to Wen weng in Szechuan, likenesses of the seventy close Confucian disciples and of the twenty-two commentators introduced in 647 were drawn on the walls. The emperor himself composed a eulogy for Yen Hui.[116]

In 739, even greater honours were bestowed on Confucius. Raised by one rank in the noble hierarchy, he was now given the canonization title of prince Wen-hsüan. Instead of facing west, his figure was to face due south in temples throughout the empire. This was the position traditional for rulers since the Chou and once occupied by the duke of Chou in the temple he had shared with Confucius.[117] In a separate edict, Yen Hui, his favourite disciple, was made duke, while the other nine principal disciples were made marquisses. Earldoms were conferred on the remaining followers. Tseng Shen, however, lost the favoured position he had been given nineteen years before.[118] Confucius's lineal descendants, another of whom had been enfieffed in 717,[119] were now to be princes rather than marquisses, and renewed provision was made for Confucius's tomb at Ch'ü-fu.[120]

The arrangement of standard Confucian temples now resembled that of certain eighth-century Buddhist chapels surviving at Tun-huang, while the drawing on the walls was also parallel to both Taoist and Buddhist practice. Hsüan tsung himself promoted syncretic religious attitudes over this period, and his syncretism was expressed in ever grander debates between representatives of the three teachings. But there seems to have been no question of direct Buddhist or Taoist intrusion into the arrangements of the Confucian shrine.[121] The system still represented the state's interest in disseminating Confucian moral values and learning empire-wide. Confucian temples with schools attached are attested over the reign, for example, in Shan-chou in modern Shansi[122] and in Pien-chou in modern Honan.[123] On the eve of the rebellion, a text written out by the great calligrapher and scholar Yen Chen-ch'ing (709–84, canonized *Wen-chung*) was inscribed at the Confucian temple at Hsien-ning, Ch'ang-an.[124]

Late in 725, Hsüan tsung and the entire court travelled east to T'ai shan and performed the Feng and Shan rites there. On his return journey the emperor, like Kao tsung nearly sixty years before, visited Ch'ü-fu and honoured Confucius. This was the second and final occasion in the dynasty when the sovereign made this pilgrimage.[125]

Hsüan tsung's journey to mount T'ai, and the events associated with it, had the enthusiastic support of the great scholar minister Chang Yüeh (667–730, canonized *Wen-chen*) and the court, officials and prospective officials. They were later upheld as a climactic symbol of an era of great peace and a high point in the history of the dynasty.

In the final phase of Hsüan tsung's reign, the T'ien-pao period, there was an increase in the number of cults the dynasty established or endorsed with official approval. Some of these, as expressions of the emperor's commitment to Taoism, did not directly involve figures in the Confucian tradition. But in 742, Hsüan tsung honoured the Confucian scholars who had been buried alive in the Ch'in proscription of learning in 213 B.C., by building a new temple at the presumed site of their execution.[126] Shrines for a series of moral exemplars, of whom at least some already had state-approved temples, were established. They included some figures who were associated with Confucianism, for example, among several women, the mother of Mencius.[127]

One of the state-established cults that Hsüan tsung expanded over this period is of particular interest, in that it was designed to balance on the military (*wu*) side the civil (*wen*) cult to Confucius. The official scholarly community, which tended to resist the emperor's interest in military activity and to be hostile to the interests of the professional soldier class, resented the intended symmetry. The central figure of the military cult, corresponding to Confucius in the civil cult, was Lü Wang or Ch'i T'ai kung. T'ai kung, as he was referred to, was held to have started a career at the age of about eighty as teacher to king Wen of the Chou,[128] and to have written a military treatise, the *Liu t'ao* (*Six weapon cases*), and other works.[129] His name stood for wise counsel to the sovereign, for example in decree examination titles.[130] At least three of the foremost aristocratic clans of the T'ang, the Ts'ui clans of Ch'ing-ho and Po-ling, and the Lu clan of Fan-yang, besides lesser T'ang lineages and a total of forty-eight surnames, claimed descent from him.[131] His cult probably also, like that of Confucius, had a popular extension.[132]

T'ai kung had always been an official cult figure in the T'ang. Under T'ai tsung, as a military master, he had been given a temple at P'an-ch'i in Shansi.[133] Under Kao tsung, he was also accorded status as a correlative in the cult to king Wen of the Chou at Feng in Shensi.[134] He had been raised, probably by 699, to be grand tutor, just as Confucius had been in 666, and a famous general of the Former Han, Chang Liang, had been made minor tutor alongside him, to balance the position of Yen Hui in the Confucian cult.[135] In 706, temples to

T'ai kung in both capitals had been established; but in the early
K'ai-yüan period, these seem not to have been maintained.[136]
  Then in 731, shrines in the two capitals and in all prefectures were
ordered, with an arrangement parallel to that of the Confucian temple,
and a ceremony identical to the *Shih-tien*. Nine other generals besides
Chang Liang were probably chosen at this time, to balance the ten
close disciples of Confucius.[137] In 731, it was also directed that
provincial candidates participating in the military examinations that
had been introduced in 703 were to observe a departure ceremony
parallel to that prescribed for *chin shih* and *ming ching* candidates.[138]
From 747, military candidates were to make a visit of homage to T'ai
kung's metropolitan temple on arrival at the capital, and generals
leaving on campaign were to report there.[139]
  The T'ai kung cult, however, never completely corresponded to the
civil cult to Confucius. Articulate scholarly opposition to it survives
only from the post-rebellion period. But even under Hsüan tsung, in
the most prosperous period of the dynasty, its scale was limited. Under
T'ang rule, there was never an independent military directorate, the
cult being rather administered by the court of sacrifices. Nor was there
an empire-wide system of schools, to parallel the 'branches and leaves'
of the directorate, or the Taoist schools that Hsüan tsung had
established in 741. An anecdotal source shows that an appointment to
the staff of the metropolitan temple was made in the T'ien-pao
period.[140] But when a student in the state academy directorate
suggested that the T'ai kung cult have full directorate status and a
teaching operation, 'his memorial lapsed and was not replied to'.[141]

The development of private teaching
  The many biographies that survive from the seventh and eighth
centuries imply that the supreme aim of all men who had been
sufficiently educated was to gain entry to civil officialdom. Their
ambition was then for a career that would bring appointment to one of
the elite monitory or scholarly offices and access to the imperial
entourage. The official education system, though it was extensive,
governed by strict rules and sanctioned by an ever more elaborate cult
to Confucius, did not provide the training needed for the harsh
competition that these goals involved. The schools in all probability
operated poorly and encouraged less than scholarly attitudes in their
students. Their enrolment was greatly in excess of the sort of numbers
that the examiners admitted to the coveted *chin shih* and *ming ching*

degrees. The schools also probably failed to provide a training in precisely those composition skills that had come to be identified with the elite regular examination, the *chin shih*. The result was the rowdiness, political grafting and absenteeism at which both official and anecdotal sources hint.

In the long period of peace, these problems became more severe. Books in circulation increased in numbers and there were large private libraries.[142] Levels of literacy rose, and the numbers of prospective officials greatly increased.[143] But the quota for the *chin shih* remained static at the very low figure of about 25 successful candidates out of 1,000 or so a year. The number of posts available was also very much smaller than the numbers of those who, by the various means that the dynasty provided, attained official status and were qualified to start their official careers.[144]

As a result of these and other factors, two important, related developments began to be documented clearly in the private rather than official writing of the period. First, the best young prospective officials continued to derive their training in literary skills from sources outside the official education system, probably in most cases from private tuition provided by their families or their father's friends. Secondly, they came to rely also more and more on patrons or mentors within the bureaucracy for introduction to and advancement in their official careers. Sometimes these two roles, of teacher and political patron, combined, to produce what amounts to a sense of discipleship among the young scholars who benefitted from them.

A sense of loyalty to a particular senior scholar official may also have been promoted by the social and intellectual milieu at Ch'ang-an. Scholars visited one another in their private residences (*ssu ti*) and discussed history, religion and contemporary affairs. They might admit younger men as 'conversational clients' (*t'an k'o*) to contribute to their company, and such junior figures in turn looked to them for advancement.[145] The factional politics of the late K'ai-yüan period, and particularly the regime of the anti-scholarly and restrictive Li Lin-fu, with the political purges that accompanied it, must have heightened the sense of separate identity among the scholar elite and their dependants.[146] A sense of discipleship among the intellectual elite is also likely to have been encouraged by their social and religious experience of the Buddhist and Taoist churches. Some from provincial backgrounds owed their education in the Confucian canons to Buddhist or Taoist monastery schools.[147] Many of those appointed to the Confucian-orientated academic agencies kept the company of

prominent Buddhist or Taoist clerics or served alongside officials
whose ultimate loyalties in private life were to Buddhism or Taoism.
Some academic officials were themselves, in private, adherents of one
or the other of the two faiths. In one case, a prominent official scholar
was a recognized private teacher of the *San hsüan* (*Three mysteries*),
the Confucian-Taoist grouping of the *Chou i*, the *Lao tzu* and the
Chuang tzu.[148] Buddhism, even more than Taoism, as Confucians were
to concede in the ninth century, put much more effective emphasis on
personal discipleship than did the state Confucianism of the seventh
and early eighth centuries.[149] It is likely that the sense of loyalty
associated with Buddhist or Taoist teachers was transferred to the
more general social context of the scholarly bureaucracy.

Individual scholars had certainly played the role of political patrons
and literary mentors before the late K'ai-yüan and T'ien-pao
periods.[150] But in the unofficial prose writing of this period, freer and
more individual than before, this situation is much more clearly
recorded. The frustration that accompanied the quest for office,
especially under the regime of Li Lin-fu, was inevitably transmuted
into a sense of moral superiority, of forming what has been called 'the
Confucian opposition'.[151] This too coloured the letters, prose vignettes
and verse in which these attitudes were expressed. Most of those who
wrote in this way were examination candidates or graduates and their
sympathizers, and therefore members of the intellectual elite.

An influential and charismatic intellectual of the late K'ai-yüan and
T'ien-pao periods, Fang Kuan (697–763), exemplified some of the
attitudes this trend involved. He was well known as a beneficiary of the
great scholar minister and patron of literary officials Chang Yüeh. But
he also acknowledged a leading Taoist as his teacher and friend and
paid homage to a Buddhist prelate. It was natural that his own younger
followers should accord him the same sort of veneration and sense of
discipleship that he had accorded others, and he became in turn a
figure to whom 'the famous scholars of the time', as a historian later
put it, resorted. In 747, Fang Kuan was banished by Li Lin-fu to be
governor of I-ch'un in Szechuan. He was summoned back to the
capital only in 755, to be secretary of the left of the crown prince's
household. In the course of the An Lu-shan rebellion, he over-reached
himself politically and suffered a humiliating defeat. But later many
scholars saw him as a true mentor, and a man of great but frustrated
abilities. Even in the ninth century, his role as a patron was recalled.[152]

A less exalted example was Yüan Te-hsiu (696–754), a descendant of
the To-ba Wei imperial house and a *chin shih* of 733. Fang Kuan

admired him, so did Su Yüan-ming (d. 762), later a vice-president of the state academy directorate and a patron of Tu Fu (712–70) and Yüan Chieh (719–72), both writers of the T'ien-pao period who became politically alienated. Yüan Te-hsiu never attained high office, and retired to the warm-spring resort of Lu-hun near Lo-yang, a popular spot for scholar officials, where Fang Kuan himself had studied.[153] Several scholars acknowledged him as a teacher. When he died, Li Hua, a *chin shih* of 735 and his admirer, composed his epitaph and Yen Chen-ch'ing wrote it for inscription. One of his pupils was Yüan Chieh; another, Ma Yü, was a productive compilatory scholar, official historian and deputy director of the imperial library who died only in 816.[154]

Hsiao Ying-shih (706–58), descended from the Liang royal house and another *chin shih* of 735, provides another example. Though he had registered at one of the directorates, he was likely to have been an absentee student, preparing for the *chin shih* under an uncle surnamed Yüan, away from Ch'ang-an or Lo-yang.[155] He also later acknowledged Yüan Te-hsiu as his 'older brother' (*hsiung*).[156] He was the 'conversation client' of a group of official scholars, including the long serving official historian Wei Shu (d. 757). His career was unsuccessful, despite strong ambitions to become an official scholar and an attempt, during Li Lin-fu's chief ministership, to join the history office. In the late T'ien-pao period he moved from Ch'ang-an, and prepared followers for the *chin shih* at P'u-yang in modern Shantung. Several of them in turn became absentee students, leaving the state academy directorate and travelling east to receive his instruction. When he described his part in their success and cited the model of Confucius and Yen Hui, he expressed a sense of immediacy that is not to be found in earlier T'ang records concerned with education.[157] The roles of Yüan Te-hsiu and Hsiao Ying-shih were recognized by their disciples, for they honoured both with private canonization titles, that included the highly coveted designation of *wen*.[158]

It has often been pointed out that lines of transmission may be traced from Fang Kuan, Yüan Te-hsiu, Hsiao Ying-shih and others to some of the great intellectuals who were to extend the Confucian tradition two generations later, at the close of the eighth century.[159] These figures paid one another extravagant compliments. Those who were disciples, or friends of disciples, recalled their relationships long after their mentors were dead. Their expressions of indebtedness convey the sense of social cohesion in the eight-century scholar community. But what was passed down was primarily a commitment to literary and scholarly activities and a strong sense of sectional identity, that of the literary scholar in opposition to the social and political trends of his time. A philosophy for meeting political failure and a religious orientation was sometimes involved. But this was primarily discipleship with a view to public service, in an official community in which political connections were all important, rather than for reclusion or religious goals. A teacher or patron appears to have been considered successful to the extent that his disciples were successful in their examinations and in their official careers. Numbers of these elite circles were small, and in no way comparable to the hundreds who had flocked to hear teachers publicly expound canonical texts in the late period of disunion.

The post-rebellion period

In the period from the recapture of Ch'ang-an by loyalist forces in 757 to the end of the dynasty, the innovation and elaboration that had characterized the era of the dynasty's prosperity was no longer possible. The institutions that, to official historians, embodied the Confucian tradition functioned on a much smaller scale than in the pre-rebellion period. But many Confucian-orientated scholars retained both their political ambition and the commitment to public education that had always been central to their tradition. Over the second half of the eighth century and into the ninth, they submitted numbers of reform proposals. The relative straightforwardness of these indicates again that the educational institutions remained outside the mainstream of political life, their reform a meritorious but largely unrealistic cause. Here, the contrast is with the examination system, with the compilation of the dynastic history and with the directives for certain state ritual observances, all of which became vehicles for the political and factional struggles of the period. Nor do the many reform proposals for the schools give a reliable overall picture of how the education system operated.

The large unofficial literature that survives from the post-rebellion period, however, reveals much more clearly how some scholars privately viewed the school system and the Confucian cult. This literature indicates also that by the early ninth century the idea of private discipleship in the Confucian tradition had become a central preoccupation among a minority of the intellectual elite. The leader of this minority, the great revivalist Han Yü (768–824, canonized *Wen*), formulated most of his ideas on the teaching of Confucian truth without reference to the official schools. In emphasizing that instruction was not primarily an institutional matter, and in insisting that the

Confucianism he taught could not co-exist with Buddhism and Taoism, he brought to the tradition a sense of commitment that was new to it in T'ang times.

Deterioration in the official school system

In the course of the An Lu-shan rebellion, the students of the Ch'ang-an state academy directorate had fled, and the premises, used as troop billets, had deteriorated. When the court and metropolitan bureaucracy returned, there was no money with which to pay the academic officials. The pre-rebellion provision of board for the students was discontinued.[160] Under Su tsung, there seems to have been only one reform attempt, by the important institutional historian and associate of Fang Kuan Liu Chih (died *c.* 758).[161] The directorate probably remained neglected. Appointment to it was considered to involve removal from the political arena; even its senior post was one to which a jealous chief minister banished a scholarly rival.[162]

Not until the start of T'ai tsung's reign in 763 was enough stability regained to allow comprehensive attempts at restoration. From 763 to 766, a small number of official scholars tried to reform both the metropolitan directorate and the provincial school system and the examinations. Three scholars, themselves graduates and each later in charge of the examinations, brought forward concrete proposals that have survived. They included in their reform programme even the ceremonial aspects of the system, such as the visit of homage required of provincial examination candidates at the shrine of Confucius. The submission of one of these three scholars, Chia Chih (718—72, canonized *Wen*), provides one of the strongest mid-century indications that Confucian scholars considered examination-orientated education to fall far short of the kind of preparation and training in conduct that they envisaged as ideal.[163] Probably in response to these submissions, edicts were issued in 765 and 766 ordering the re-selection of students, the re-staffing of the directorate and the repair of its buildings.[164] A grandiose celebration was held in 766.[165] But evidence from some decades later indicates that from this period on the enrolment of state-supported students in the two capital directorates was about a quarter of that of the pre-rebellion period, and that it remained at about this level until well into the ninth century, when the system further deteriorated.[166]

Later in Tai tsung's reign, there were further intermittent efforts at reforming both the metropolitan and provincial schools. They follow the pattern of the first post-rebellion reform attempts, in that they also involved detailed proposals and were ineffective. Probably in 770, on the occasion of a *Ch'ih-chou* ceremony of induction for the crown prince, an official scholar, Kuei Ch'ung-ching (712–99, canonized *Hsüan*), included in a reform submission suggestions for the improvement of all aspects of the directorate's programme. In an attempt to raise the level of instruction in the canonical texts, he proposed specialist erudits for each of the five Confucian canons in combination with the *Analects* and the *Hsiao ching*. But 'because general custom had become long established' (*hsi su chi chiu*), no changes were accepted.[167] Under Tai tsung, the senior post in the directorate was again used for seconding a high-ranking official, in this case the official scholar and general service official Yang Wan (d. 777, canonized *Wen-chien*).[168] For some years too, despite the belief that it should be directed by a 'Confucian of renown', the directorate's affairs were managed by the eunuch imperial favourite and Buddhist Yü Ch'ao-en (d. 770).[169]

When Te tsung ascended the throne in 779, he was 'bent on searching for good administration'.[170] Until the end of the year, he was assisted by a chief minister, Ts'ui Yu-fu (721–80, canonized *Wen-chen*), who had wide connections in the scholarly bureaucracy.[171] For a while officials with scholarly ideals held power, and 'the world believed that it would be possible to restore the great peace of Chen-kuan and K'ai-yüan'. Reform suggestions followed: in 782, Kuei Ch'ung-ching, again vice-president of the state academy directorate, asked for the revival of court-attended lectures on the Confucian canons following the *Shih-tien*.[172] The veteran loyalist general service official and ritual scholar Yen Chen-ch'ing asked for the establishment of 'literary instructors' (*wen hsüeh*), to hold more power than the erudits they were to replace in prefectural and county schools.[173]

By 783, however, Te tsung's attempts to reimpose central authority on the semi-independent military governors of Hopei had failed, the capital was occupied by rebellious troops, and the court evacuated to Feng-t'ien in Shensi. This sequence of events left the state academy directorate unscathed; the students at least were not involved in the disorders.[174] But it set the terms of imperial rule for the remainder of the reign. After the return of the court, another 'restoration' (*chung hsing*), the third of the dynasty, was declared. But the spark of optimism of 779–80 was dimmed. The emperor became isolated and inaccessible to all but a succession of individual favourites, some of whom caused bitter resentment in the scholar community.[175] Mobility within the bureaucracy was reduced, and amnesties were no longer issued. Even under these conditions, however, there were calls for the reform of both metropolitan and provincial schools. In 787, there was a suggestion that local Buddhist monasteries in the metropolitan area might be converted into schools.[176] Decree examination questions, longer and more searching under Te tsung than before, demanded proposals for the revival of the dynasty's education programme.[177]

The general trend in the education system, however, was still towards deterioration.[178] Student behaviour was again often unruly and insulting; long periods of residence, up to twenty years, were tolerated,[179] and the social standing of students was criticized as low.[180] Junior officials with interest in and reputations for literary ability all tried to avoid appointment to the directorate;[181] its buildings leaked, and the academic officials had no funds with which to make improvements.[182]

The few records that suggest exceptions to the poor conditions need qualification, in that they are likely to reflect the factional or social ties of those who wrote them. Han Hui (732–94, canonized *Ch'eng*), a brother of the politically powerful commissioner for Huai-nan Han Huang (723–87, canonized *Chung-su*), was appointed president of the directorate late in 791. His biographer noted that, 'Since the outbreak of war, mostly undesirables (*mo liu*) had resorted there.' Han Hui appointed two scholars, one of whom was later a favourite of the emperor, to lecture on the *Tso chuan* and the *Ta Tai li chi* (*Record of ritual of the Greater Tai*). The quality of teaching and of the students dramatically improved, and 'the sound of their recitation and chanting was heard as between the Chu and the Ssu [rivers]'.[183] A number of writers also praised the tenure as directorate vice-president of Yang Ch'eng, who was banished to the post by P'ei Yen-ling (728–96, canonized *Miu*), the most detested of all Te tsung's favourites. In 798, Yang Ch'eng was dismissed for supporting a student under sentence of banishment, and over a hundred students demonstrated for his retention.[184] After his resulting banishment to Tao-chou in modern Hunan, Yang's case attracted much support from scholars, and came to be considered one of the most celebrated injustices of his age.[185] In another example, Han Yü, as an erudit in 802, praised a ceremony in the directorate and conditions in the capital.[186]

In early 805, the death of Te tsung released some of the pent-up reformist pressure that the emperor's restrictive rule had held back. A number of officials who had held posts in the metropolitan academic agencies, and some who had gone privately to hear a junior directorate official lecture on the Confucian canons, now became actively committed to a programme intended to redress some of the worst abuses of the time.[187] During the six-month period of this reform faction's power, however, there are no recorded initiatives relating to the official education system.

Hsien tsung, succeeding to the throne in late 805, tried in the first years of his reign to reclaim the sort of leadership of the official scholarly world that his great predecessors T'ai tsung and Hsüan tsung had had. Both at the start of his reign, and later as a result of military successes against the independent eastern provinces, there were real hopes of dynastic revival. For the school system, however, the pattern remained one of decline punctuated by reform initiatives.[188] In 806, the president of the directorate drew up stricter rules for students: slackness, gambling, rowdiness and insolence were forbidden and board was to be conditional on passing tests.[189] The same year, Yüan Chen (779–831) asked that the *Ch'ih-chou* be revived, and that the crown prince have a more effective training.[190] In 806, the directorate at Lo-yang was re-staffed and a quota of one hundred students prescribed.[191] In 807, a total of 550 students for the Ch'ang-an directorate and 100 for its Lo-yang counterpart was officially stipulated, with enrolments specified for each of the constituent schools.[192] In this way, the reduction of numbers to one quarter of their pre-rebellion strength which had obtained since Su tsung's reign was regularized. In 807, an attempt was made to revive the arrival ceremony for provincial examination candidates.[193] By 808, the directorate buildings had probably received some attention.[194] In that year there was also a proposal, echoing Kuei Ch'ung-ching's of nearly thirty years before, that a specialist erudit in the *Mao shih* be appointed.[195]

Despite these efforts, and the public praise they elicited,[196] further calls for reform show that no sustained revival can have taken place. One account, datable perhaps to 812, stated that the shrine to Confucius was in decay and the buildings of the constituent schools in a state of collapse.[197] The observance whereby examination candidates visited the shrine was modified or discontinued at this time.[198] Another scholar looked back to the prosperity of the Chen-kuan and K'ai-yüan eras, and beyond them to the Later Han, when the T'ai hsüeh had had 30,000 students and had played a role in political life.[199] Later in Hsien tsung's reign, another reformist official, Cheng Yü-ch'ing (746–820, canonized *Chen*), an associate of Han Yü, proposed twice that, 'because the T'ai hsüeh had long been derelict and the students in decline, civilian officials should deduct from their own incomes to reconstruct'.[200] Again, however, this evidence for deterioration conflicts with the numbers of officials with academic titles mentioned in both the official and the copious unofficial sources of this period.[201] Even if the directorate's premises were dilapidated and postings to it unpopular, therefore, its full establishment, at least on paper, was probably maintained.

In the provinces, from the rebellion of 755 on, it is impossible to derive a reliable overall picture of the state of the official school system. In the aftermath of the rebellion, at least in areas directly affected, the provincial system collapsed altogether.[202] Its restoration subsequently depended largely on the initiative of local administrators. In the Ta-li, Chen-yüan and Yüan-ho periods, individual prefects carried out reconstruction or reform, for example at Fu-feng county in modern Shensi, and at Yüan-chou in modern Kiangsi, both in 767.[203] In 769, Tu Fu, travelling in the far south, commended the local magistrate of Heng-shan in modern Hunan for his renovation of the Confucian temple and county school.[204] Reconstruction was carried out at Hao-chou in modern Anhui in 770; at Fang-chou in modern Shansi late in Te tsung's reign, and at a number of other places.[205] In the late summer of 773, Yen Chen-ch'ing used the prefectural school at Hu-chou, where he was governor, to discuss the final stages of a large phonological dictionary he compiled.[206]

Under Hsien tsung, the pattern is again of individual reports of renovation. Liu Tsung-yüan (773–819), banished to the far south for his part in the reform movement of 805, composed texts commemorating reconstruction of schools and temples to Confucius at Tao-chou in modern Hunan and at Lien-chou in modern Kwangsi.[207] Han Yü commended the reforming zeal of the prefect of Ch'ien-chou in modern Canton province. Exiled for his celebrated anti-Buddhist memorial to Hsien tsung in 819, he found the local school at Ch'ao-chou in modern Fukien long since abandoned, and ordered its re-establishment. He also recorded the reconstruction of the Confucian temple and school at Ch'u-chou in modern Chekiang. In his text commemorating this achievement, Han suggested that, 'although all commandery towns maintain their temples and schools to Confucius, these exist in name but not in reality, and fail in what they should be undertaking'.[208]

A few years later, Liu Yü-hsi (772–842), like Liu Tsung-yüan a former member of the reform party, also complained about the decline of the provincial school system.[209] A proportion of these reports of reform, however, were either by polemical Confucian revivalists like Han Yü, or by political exiles hoping for reappointment to Ch'ang-an.

In this as in later periods of Chinese history, there was some cynicism over the achievements of remote provincial administrators and over their motives for composing commemorative texts.[210]

For the reigns of Mu tsung (820–4) and Ching tsung (824–7), less information survives about the state school system. For the most part the record consists again of memorials proposing reform, while sardonic opinions were expressed on the quality of officials appointed to the directorate.[211] The scholarly and indecisive[212] Wen tsung (r. 827–840), inheriting a deteriorating situation,[213] had a strong commitment to Confucian canonical learning and to the reform of literary practice. In Cheng T'an (d. 842), who held high general service or scholarly office almost throughout his reign, he found a collaborator for a programme of restoration for the capital directorate.[214] In 833, in connection with the investiture of the crown prince and a planned *Ch'ih-chou* observance, the dynasty finally committed itself to searching for personnel to appoint as specialist erudits in the directorate. A post of erudit for each of the *Five canons*, also requiring expertise in the *Analects*, *Hsiao ching* and *Erh-ya* of each scholar selected, was established. Though the state found it difficult to finance these posts, they lasted, as titles at least, until very late in the dynasty.[215] Following Wen tsung's reforms, the operation of the directorate may have improved: the verse writer Li Shang-yin (813–58) claimed to have taught students in the T'ai hsüeh in the period 850–2.[216]

For the remainder of the dynasty, there is relatively little information to suggest that the directorate discharged its duty of teaching students the Confucian canons. Repair of buildings again appears to have depended on voluntary salary deductions. P'i Jih-hsiu (*c.* 834–*c.* 883), a literary official appointed an erudit of the Kuo-tzu hsüeh in 877 or 878 complained that, despite the scale of its establishment of posts and the wealth of its ritual, it failed in its responsibilities.[217] Perhaps his remarks mean that, even at this stage, the directorate's programme continued on paper and all posts were at least nominally filled.[218] A nominal enrolment of students may again have been ensured by the advantages registration gave in the continued competition for examination success and official status.

The metropolitan academic institutions suffered severe damage in the disorders of the final decades of the dynasty. During the Huang Ch'ao occupation and sack of Ch'ang-an in 880–3, the temple to Confucius in the directorate was burnt to the ground. Not long after this, K'ung Wei (d. 895), a lineal descendant of Confucius, whose clan had increased in influence since the start of the ninth century,[219] held the post of president of the directorate, just as his forbear K'ung Ying-ta had done at the start of the dynasty. In 890, K'ung Wei asked the emperor Chao tsung to permit salary deductions to reconstruct the temple.[220] After this, and up to the final years of the T'ang, appointments, even to low-ranking posts in the directorate, are recorded;[221] but the sources otherwise reveal nothing substantial about the directorate or the wider school system.

The cults of Confucius and T'ai kung in the post-rebellion period

Just as the destruction brought about by the An Lu-shan rebellion drastically affected the official school system, so it also brought to an end the T'ang expansion of the state cult to Confucius. In the three decades that followed, it was rather the parallel military cult that came to the fore. But although in the period as a whole there were very few edicts concerning the civil cult, comments by scholars in their unofficial writings pointed to the beginnings of a change in attitudes towards figures in the cult. This change parallelled evolution in scholarly attitudes generally. Eventually, in Sung times, it resulted in a significant reorganization of the temple.

The military cult, with T'ai kung as its central figure, came into prominence in the post-rebellion period because of a deliberate attempt by emperors and some civil officials to override the traditional hostility of scholars towards the soldier class and to recognize the necessity of military achievement in the restoration of the state. These officials tried to realize the balance between the civil and military cults that pre-rebellion measures for the T'ai kung cult had been intended to express. Other scholars, however, continued to resist the influence of the military in political life, and developed historical and ritual arguments in their opposition to the cult.

There was criticism of the cult not long after the re-capture of Ch'ang-an from the rebels in 757. The following year, Yü Hsiu-lieh (692–772, canonized *Yüan*), an official historian and ritual scholar, objected, on the grounds of historical incongruity, to having the Former Han general Chang Liang as the second figure in the T'ai kung cult.[222] Nonetheless, in 760, Su tsung significantly upgraded the cult: T'ai kung was canonized as prince Wu-ch'eng, to balance Confucius's designation as prince Wen-hsüan, and the imperial secretariat and chancellery were again ordered to amplify the iconography of the temple, with 'ten generals', as counterparts to the ten inner disciples of Confucius.[223] The *Shih-tien* ritual in the temple was to be conducted by the high-ranking Tai wei, as the ritual proxy of the emperor. Despite this imperial endorsement, however, under Tai tsung the cult was again allowed to lapse, and its buildings fell into disrepair.[224]

Two decades later, in 781, repair was again ordered.[225] In 782, Yen Chen-ch'ing submitted a request about the music to be used in the T'ai kung *Shih-tien*, and another expansion followed. The history office was ordered to draw up a long list of military figures for inclusion; sixty-four were named for drawing on the temple walls.[226] Some very recently deceased military figures were included. The most conspicuous of these was Kuo Tzu-i (697–781, canonized *Chung-wu*), the pre-eminent loyalist general of the post-rebellion decades. He had been compared by the emperor to T'ai kung himself, receiving the title Shang-fu, by which T'ai kung was also known, and he had died only in mid-781. This installation of very recent figures in the military temple had as yet no parallel in the more conservative civil cult of Confucius, and it may have added to scholars' resentment of the cult. The one corresponding attempt made in T'ang times to bring a T'ang figure into the Confucian shrine was to be unsuccessful.

The T'ai kung cult, therefore, still met with articulate opposition. In the course of a controversy about it that took place in 788 and involved some 80 officials, opponents of the cult compared T'ai kung unfavourably to Confucius, and objected to the synthetic or ahistorical character of the choice of his correlatives in the military temple.[227] As a result of these objections, the cult was down-graded, but allowed to continue. It was still operating in 790, when an edict ordered that music be supplied for it.[228] But it never enjoyed the prestige or resulted in the depth of documentation, official or unofficial, that the civil cult produced. The fact that appointments to the military temple are very seldom mentioned suggests that it may have lapsed in the ninth century.[229] Nonetheless, the ideal of a parallel military cult survived, and the last reference to it in T'ang sources shows that in 905 a request to rebuild the temple and revive the military *Shih-tien* was approved.[230]

The Confucian shrine itself received low priority in the piecemeal programme of restoration that followed the recapture of Ch'ang-an in 757. The first recorded post-rebellion performance of the *Shih-tien* was in 760.[231] In that year, there was an edict that middle and low ranking rituals be discontinued, and this has been interpreted as a ban on prefectural and county level *Shih-tien* rites.[232] But they are likely to have continued at the metropolis at least,[233] for the following year students were ordered to make one of the three presentations each celebration involved. In 766, two performances are recorded, the first followed by a debate between representatives of the three teachings, revived 'after a long lapse'.[234] Two more *Shih-tien* performances are recorded for 767, and two for 766.[235] Over this period they were attended by the politically powerful Buddhist eunuch Yü Ch'ao-en, who on one occasion lectured in person on the *Chou i*, in order, it was said, to 'mock the chief ministers'.[236]

For Te tsung's reign and subsequently, there are records of *Shih-tien* offerings at a number of places in the provinces. Like the school system itself, they are likely to have depended on the initiative of local administrators. Certainly the cult, with its twice-yearly offerings of slaughtered animals, the use of which was resumed in 766,[237] was expensive. Liu Yü-hsi, as prefect of Kuei-chou in modern Szechuan complained in about 823 of the cost, and suggested that it might be saved and used for education, and the *Shih-tien* offerings themselves be restricted to the metropolitan directorate.[238] This suggestion must have been ineffective, for in 836, as prefect of Hsü-chou in modern Honan, Liu himself recorded another *Shih-tien* observance.[239]

From Tai tsung's reign to the end of the dynasty, the official form of the *Shih-tien* and the official iconography of the Confucian temples appear not to have changed at all. The ritual scholar Kuei Ch'ung-ching proposed that the crown prince, as chief celebrant, instead of facing, in the position of ritual homage, due north towards the statue of Confucius, should face east. If, as his biography implied, his suggestion was accepted, it was probably later set aside. For the principle, as the ninth-century scholar Tu Mu (803–52) formulated it, was indeed that 'from the son of heaven to commoners all face north and acknowledge [Confucius] as their teacher'. By the Sung, moreover, Kuei Ch'ung-ching's proposal was condemned as sycophantic, a way of trying to gain favour with the imperial family by symbolically raising the crown prince above Confucian norms.[240]

In the provinces, the more decentralized political order of the ninth century may explain the fact that the iconography and ritual prescribed by the dynasty in the K'ai-yüan period was not always followed. Liu Tsung-yüan's note for the school and temple at Tao-chou in Hunan states that the prefect made offerings to Confucius and Yen Hui alone, thus deliberately excluding the 'ten wise men' and the long list of figures the T'ang had introduced over the seventh and eighth centuries.[241] In Fu-chien during Te tsung's reign, Ch'ang Kun (729–83), a reformer of the local school system and later a chief minister, was given posthumous offerings in the spring and autumn rituals.[242] More interestingly, at Ch'u-chou, Han Yü implied that the prefect had included drawings of Mencius, Hsün tzu and Yang Hsiung on the walls. These figures, as philosophers and interpreters of the Confucian tradition, rather than textual exegetes, had never been so honoured in the metropolitan temple. Han Yü, however, believed that they had been essential to the transmission of Confucian truth. In mentioning them, he indirectly commended the prefect for a view of the tradition that coincided with his own polemical re-appraisal of it.

In the post-rebellion period, intermittent debate about the relative status of Confucius' close disciples continued. Scholars still discussed the place of Tseng Shen, the disciple associated with filial piety, whose position had been controversial in the K'ai-yüan period. His status formed a theme in essays, and was mentioned in a court debate held between representatives of the three teachings in 827.[243] Another, late T'ang essayist argued that Confucius's inner disciple Chung-yu should not receive offering.[244] In the pre-rebellion period, such arguments, held before the emperor and the court, might have resulted in official readjustment of the arrangement of the temple. By now, however, the will to express re-assessment of historical figures in changes in official iconography seems no longer to have existed. These discussions rather resembled well rehearsed tests of casuistry, and they had no recorded effect on the official shrine.

The single attempt to introduce a T'ang Confucian into the temple, parallel to the introduction of such figures as Kuo Tzu-i into the military temple, was made in about 863, and concerned the Confucian revivalist Han Yü. P'i Jih-hsiu believed that Han was a proponent of true orthodoxy, when the age that had preceded him had seen only advocates of heterodox teachings. 'Supposing that he had been born in the age of Confucius, he might well have been among the [ten] disciples commended for mastery of the four categories of learning.' He was, P'i stated, adapting Mencius, 'the only [true] man since the [start of the] T'ang'.[245] In the event, however, Han Yü was not to be officially installed until 1084, in the same measure that brought Mencius, Hsün tzu and Yang Hsiung, the interpreters of the tradition who figured so importantly in his teaching, into the temple. But by this time, the scholarly world had come to accept the attitudes to Confucianism and its transmission that he had made central to his teaching.[246]

The development of an ideal of independent teaching

The ineffectiveness of their successive attempts at reform in the post-rebellion period only increased the disillusion of the scholarly elite with the official school system and with the Confucian temple.[247] The metropolitan schools remained important to students mainly for political and administrative reasons, for the advantages enrolment gave in the competition for office. Among the elite, private or unofficial scholarly or literary mentorship therefore became ever more important, and the attitudes of both mentors or patrons and disciples became more sophisticated. In some cases, the resulting relationships were recorded simply as expressions of indebtedness on the part of a junior to a senior official. Sometimes little more than scholarly or literary friendship linked with the vital element of political help was involved. But in the factionally divided and harshly competitive mid-T'ang bureaucracy, Confucian orientated scholars dignified such recognition and support as acts of profound insight.

The intellectual and literary figure Tu-ku Chi (725–77, canonized *Hsien*), for example, an erudit of the court of sacrifices under Tai tsung, himself indebted to Hsiao Ying-shih and Li Hua, 'delighted in assessing and bringing forward his juniors'.[248] The official historian and rescript writer Liang Su (753–93) said of Fang Kuan's nephew Fang Lin (*c.* 736–*c.* 793) that he was 'fitted to ascend a teacher's mat and to enlighten the uninstructed'.[249] The major intellectual figure Ch'üan Te-yü (759–818, canonized *Wen*) praised the ritual scholar Chung Tzu-ling (744–802) for exemplifying 'the way of the teacher' (*shih tao*).[250] Li Kuan (766–794), who graduated both as a *chin shih* and in a *po hsüeh hung tz'u* examination under Lu Hsüan kung (754–805, canonized *Hsüan*, and conventionally known as Hsüan kung) in 792, wrote to him reminding him that he was a disciple, and likening his position to that of the disciples of Confucius.[251]

Such relationships were again considered successful to the extent that they brought admission to official status or appointment to office. The reformer Liu Yü-hsi called himself the 'disciple' (*men sheng*) of the great institutional historian Tu Yu (735–812, canonized *An-chien*): he had written documents for Tu in Huai-nan, and came north to metropolitan office at about the time Tu returned to Ch'ang-an.[252] The chief minister of Hsien tsung's reign P'ei Tu (765–839, canonized *Wen*) called himself the disciple of the academic and general service official Liu T'ai-chen (725–792), a former pupil of Hsiao Ying-shih, under whom he had graduated in 789.[253] Both Liu Tsung-yüan and Lü Wen (*c.* 774–*c.* 813) wrote similarly of Ku Shao-lien (732–794, canonized *Ching*), the examiner who had admitted them to the *chin shih* degree in 793 and 798 respectively.[254] Ch'üan Te-yü, who was chief examiner in 802, 803 and 805, had his own 'Yen Hui' among his successful candidates.[255] Tu-ku Yü, a son of Tu-ku Chi and later Ch'üan Te-yü's son-in-law, when an examination candidate, wrote to Ch'üan of the sense of individual responsibility that Confucius and his disciples had shown.[256]

By the late eighth century, also, prospective officials emphasized the importance of such relationships by commending earlier T'ang examples of recognition and support. Li Ao (774–836, canonized *Wen*), for example, praised Chang Yüeh's recognition of Fang Kuan and Tu-ku Chi's of Liang Su, and the official scholar Wei Ch'u-hou (773–828) commended Chang Yüeh's recognition of the great K'ai-yüan scholar-minister Chang Chiu-ling (673–740, canonized *Wen-hsien*) and of Fang Kuan.[257] The scholars whom they praised in this way were all earlier members of the same remarkably cohesive, self-perpetuating intellectual elite to which they themselves belonged. Largely identified through the examination system that they themselves controlled, this elite dominated the Confucian-orientated scholarly world of the late eighth and early ninth centuries.

Several early ninth century intellectuals, however, took the issue of education outside the official arena and the examinations, and analyzed the problem of the failure of the official institutions and the transmission of Confucian truth at a much more general level than hitherto. The main figures involved here were Han Yü and Liu Tsung-yüan; but they treated these issues in greater detail probably because they were now of concern to the scholar community generally. Liu Tsung-yüan, commenting on Han Yü's role as a teacher, spoke of the absence of any tradition of teaching since the Han period, and of the very low esteem in which teachers were currently held. He also recorded that, as a young man, he had, 'intended to pass time in the T'ai hsüeh, and to receive a teacher's discourses'. But its poor reputation led him to abandon the idea.[258] Only in the case of Yang Ch'eng, demoted to the vice-presidency of the directorate by the detested P'ei Yen-ling in 795, did Liu locate an ideal in the school system of his time. Praising Yang Ch'eng, he emphasized that the true teacher never turned away a pupil, and likened his support of the students to the conduct of ancient exemplars like Tseng Shen, Mencius and Confucius himself. But Yang Ch'eng was already under sentence of banishment to the far south when Liu wrote, and Liu's commendation of him was also an implicit condemnation of the state of affairs in the directorate.[259]

It was, however, Han Yü more than any other scholar of his day who developed his position on instruction to a high level of generalization. In doing so, he drew the praise not only of followers in the decades after his death but also of the entire Neo-Confucian movement. Han's polemical statements on the role of the independent teacher are to be understood against the background of his own experience of academic office. He was given posts in the metropolitan school system no fewer than five times. An erudit of the Ssu-men hsüeh in 801–3, he became an erudit of the Kuo-tzu hsüeh in 806, first at Ch'ang-an and then at the duplicate directorate at Lo-yang. In 812, he was again an erudit at Ch'ang-an, and finally from late 820 or early 821, he was briefly president of the Ch'ang-an directorate.[260]

Han, however, left only scanty information about his experience in academic office. In 801–3, he complained of poverty, failure and deteriorating health; but he appears to have known his students, and claimed later with respect to one of them that 'an erudit and a student share the same *tao*'.[261] A general compliment by his follower Huang-fu Shih (*c.* 777– *c.* 835) suggests that he may have been conscientious as a lecturer.[262] When in 802 he recommended a number of candidates to the assistant examiner Lu San (d. 802), he wrote of them in terms of their conduct and literary abilities, and emphasized that, obedient to Confucius's injunction, he was 'promoting those whom he knew'. But he made no reference to the performance as students in the directorate of any of the ten.[263] In 806–9, he again complained of poverty and lack of recognition. Scholarly office required him to be 'sated with idleness and uselessness', and forced him to become 'used to eating pig-weed', that is subsisting on a small salary.[264] The leisure that tenure in the politically isolated Lo-yang directorate provided was no compensation for appointment to an institution that he clearly identified with the failure of his career, and he compared his lot with the similarly frustrated lives of Confucius and Mencius. His final appointment to the directorate, as its president, at the close of his career, was said to have been greeted with rejoicing by the students, who exclaimed that 'the directorate will no longer be lonely'. But Han himself, in a tenure that lasted for only six months or so, left no details as to his attitude to his post, apart from a single reform proposal involving the re-appointment of staff and an attempt to restore student numbers to the level prescribed by the *Liu tien*.[265]

Such lack of enthusiasm for the state academy directorate did not of course mean that Han Yü was indifferent to the canonical learning that, by statute, he was required to teach. On the contrary, he spoke at his most eloquent on precisely the issue of how the Confucian *tao* was to be transmitted. By 801, he had engaged in unofficial teaching, preparing and recommending candidates for the examinations, just as Hsiao Ying-shih had done five decades before. By this time too, he had already cited Confucius to justify his willingness to accept any student who asked for instruction.[266] Like Liu Tsung-yüan and their contemporaries and friends Li Ao and Lü Wen, he held that true teaching had long since died out.[267] For him, it was not dependent on official provisions for education or on the academic institutions in which he served so unwillingly. Rather, it concerned an individual relationship that, developed outside the official framework, took precedence over questions of official standing. A true teacher, he wrote, was qualified, not by age or formal seniority, but by learning and qualities of character.[268]

Han Yü expressed his concern for the independent Confucian teacher with an eloquence and boldness of style that have made his brief writings on the subject famous. In effect, he broke with the conventional outlook of the scholar community. Up to his time, scholars had been satisfied with piecemeal or local initiatives at reforming the official system, and with teaching and giving political help to their sons and the sons of their colleagues. Han can only have seen these activities as ineffective in the face of the political and social problems of his day. His pronouncements on teaching were therefore intended to dispel the notion that society could be regenerated by conventional reformist means. The freedom of his position from any specific bureaucratic context, its universalism, makes it one of the important statements of the T'ang phase of the Neo-Confucian movement. But again his views were not entirely isolated. Several scholars in this period paid tributes to Wang T'ung, the shadowy figure believed to have taught outside the official system just before the foundation of the T'ang.[269] Another insight, hinted at by Han Yü himself, took the form of the admission that artisans, musicians and others had been more effective than Confucian scholars because of the value they put on the teacher-disciple relationship.[270] A later generation of Han's admirers extended this observation to include the very Buddhism that Han had so vehemently attacked. Exponents of the Confucian tradition should, they implied, emulate the emphasis the Buddhists put on the teacher–pupil relationship.[271]

Han Yü therefore gave polemical and highly eloquent edge to views that were accepted by the relatively small numbers of scholars from which he drew his support. But his outlook on the official education system and on teaching is only one aspect of his perspective on the learned tradition of his day. It is to be related to the position he and others of his generation had towards other learned activities in which the T'ang state was involved. Of these, canonical scholarship and literary criticism differed from ritual and historical scholarship in registering most clearly the shift to less immediately state-centred or more independent perspectives.

3

CANONICAL SCHOLARSHIP

The Confucian canons occupied a central place in the intellectual life of T'ang China. They provided the basis of education for successive generations of the intellectual elite, and a part of the 'memorization corpus' that scholars took through their serving careers.[1] Mastery of the canons was assumed, to be mentioned in biographical accounts only if it was achieved very young, very quickly, or, just occasionally, very late.[2] There was no question of an alternative curriculum to any who aspired to official service.

The canons pointed those who studied them in the direction of an official career. They sanctioned almost all the important activities in which the state was involved. The very activity of governing was traced back to canonical sources, and the institutions that formed the T'ang state were likewise considered to have had canonical origins. T'ang scholars justified all the administrative operations with which this book is concerned by appeal to the canons: education, the ritual programme, the study and documentation of the past, both recent and remote, and the composition of literature in the service of the state.

The influence of the canons, however, like the political ambition of those who interpreted them, was greater even than this. Almost every policy or measure that the dynasty formulated might be introduced by, or might later elicit, relevant comment from them. They were quoted in the context of symbolically remote yet politically vital questions such as the management of the barbarians, and for issues central to the prestige of the dynastic house, like the maintenance of the imperial ancestral temple. They contained the principles of political morality, to which the conduct of all, from the sovereign to the individual serving official, should conform. The very comprehensiveness of the canonical corpus, the fact that it could provide guidance on almost the full range of issues that, in the political arena, scholars were confronted with, was one of the reasons for its unassailable position. There was a basic assumption among the intellectual elite that in any government context administrative competence was not enough. Their ideal was to 'embellish administration with Confucian [learning]' (*i ju shih li*).[3] To fail to do this would lead to an unacceptable lack of moral awareness, to a purely administrative mode of government that would degenerate into disorder and tyranny.

Confronted with the prestigious inheritance of the canons and their subsequent exegetical literature, the state undertook certain practical operations. The motive behind these was to ensure that the texts of the canons were widely disseminated, and that they were understood in ways compatible with the interests of the dynasty. The first of these operations was to determine, preserve and make widely available standard versions of the texts, and to provide, in the form of commentaries and sub-commentaries, a definitive understanding of them. High authority discharged this responsibility intermittently throughout the dynasty. When it was overlooked, individual scholar officials initiated attempts to attend to it. It resulted in a series of practical measures. The most important of these involved the display of the standard text of the canons at the state academy directorate, first written on wood and then, from the mid ninth century, engraved on stone. A single interpretation of the canonical texts, however, was never rigidly enforced, despite what appear to have been official initiatives in this direction. Successive emperors and ministers had a pluralistic attitude towards interpretation that was consistent with T'ang religious attitudes and with T'ang modes of thinking in other fields.

It was also the government's policy throughout the dynasty to make detailed knowledge of the canons and their commentaries a requisite of the examination system, through which the scholarly elite within the official hierarchy was recruited. The use of the canons in this way was never seriously questioned; but it proved difficult to administer meaningfully, The mechanical and unthinking approach to the texts and their commentaries that inevitably resulted among candidates provoked indignation among the minority of scholars for whom the canons provided authority for deeply held political and moral views.

For the great majority of serving officials, knowledge of the canons meant learning the texts sufficiently to acquire official status and to run successful careers. Their experience of intensive study did not extend much beyond the symbolic 'three winters' (*san tung*) in the much used phrase from the *Han shu*, deemed necessary to master them.[4] Their aims, like those that an official scholar enjoined on Hsüan tsung, the dynasty's greatest patron of scholarship, in 711 or 712, were practical, and their approach was sometimes even explicitly limited to what they called the 'general meaning' (*ta lüeh*) of the canonical texts, rather than their very detailed exegesis.[5] A minority within the scholarly elite, however, hoped that their special knowledge and skill in interpreting the canons would be of more specific benefit to the dynasty and use in their careers. They hoped to participate in the scholarly commissions set up by the dynasty to further its control over the canonical tradition or in debates about the value of commentaries and sub-commentaries. Such participation increased their own standing, and when successfully completed, brought promotion and substantial monetary reward. If they were not selected for commissions, individual scholars with expertise in specific canons sometimes submitted their own commentaries, and this in turn could bring them acknowledgement and reward. Whether undertaken on official commission or privately, canonical scholarship was understood to be a continuing process. Throughout the dynasty, there was a tacit assumption that a more accurate text and a better understanding were possible.

The pattern of the state's interest in the canons, combined with accidents of transmission, has resulted in an uneven picture of the tradition over the dynasty. Voluminous official sub-commentaries produced under T'ai tsung survive intact; but alongside them have to be set the laconic accounts of later attempts to re-establish the standard texts of the canons, or protests about their use in the examinations. Many unofficial works of commentary have been lost, so that an overview of the way in which attitudes to the canons evolved, though highly detailed at certain points, is indistinct at others. Nonetheless, over nearly three centuries, great changes are evident in the attitudes of scholars towards the canons. The early reigns saw the state's interest in controlling the tradition at its keenest and most successful. Official operations predominated. By the mid eighth century, however, the state's statutory provision of definitive texts, commentaries and sub-commentaries provoked a succession of scholarly controversies within the official community. As the examination system developed, the role of the canons in the examinations caused academic officials increasing dissatisfaction.

In the post-rebellion period, despite its lack of resources, the state continued to discharge its traditional responsibility of preserving and displaying definitive texts. But the scholarly world of the late eighth and early ninth centuries was much less effectively centralized on the court and no longer dominated by imperial commissions. State academic institutions no longer provided the main institutional framework in which the canons were reinterpreted, and the most important intellectual developments took place unofficially. Some scholars now reinterpreted the canons primarily to justify their own ideas on political reform and on questions of religious belief. Their writings were no longer necessarily intended for submission to high authority and use in the official education system. They represented the response of individual scholars to a more devolved and less court-centred political order.

This post-rebellion development within the scholar community towards an independent critical tradition in canonical learning may be seen as moving in two directions. These corresponded to the opposing extremes in the well-known Confucian polarity between governing the state on the one hand and the cultivation of the self on the other.[6] There was, first, a new interest in political theory, institutional history and technical administrative problems. This interest is to be linked with the utilitarian re-appraisal of the origins, institutions and functions of the dynastic state that took place among some scholars in the late eighth century. Secondly, at the opposite extreme, there took place the beginnings of the 'deep interiorization' of the tradition which was to culminate in the idealistic and introspective Confucian philosophy of the early T'ang phase of the Neo-Confucian movement.

The divergence of these two intellectual emphases did not threaten the social cohesion of the scholar community. Both represented aspects of the change in outlook away from immediate focus on the emperor and the court towards a more generalized concept of the state and the individual. Some scholars at the turn of the eighth century recognized the value of both approaches and even tried to promote both. Both claimed sanction from the full range of Confucian canonical texts. At the risk, however, of adopting an over-schematic approach, a group of texts or single text may be seen as especially important for each. Interest in institutions and in political theory often correlated with specialization in the *Ch'un-ch'iu* and its *Three traditions*, the *Tso chuan*, the *Kung-yang chuan* and the *Ku-liang chuan*. For the movement towards interiorization, it was the group later to be known as the *Ssu shu* (*Four books*), the *Analects*, the *Ta hsüeh* (*Great learning*), the *Chung yung* (*Doctrine of the mean*), and above all the *Mencius*, that registered particularly well the changing attitudes of T'ang scholars. The emergence of these two emphases indicate how radically, by the second half of the eighth century, the scholarly climate had changed. Their evolution forms a counterpoint to the main subject of this chapter, the interest of the state in canonical scholarship.

The reigns of Kao tsu and T'ai tsung

From the beginning of the T'ang, the Confucian canons were often quoted at court discussions and in a wide range of official contexts.[7] The dynasty also made knowledge of the canons central to the curricula of the schools and to the examinations. But they also inherited from the re-unifying Sui dynasty the more specific concern to impose order and unity on the great range of divergent commentarial literature to which by the early seventh century the scholarly community was heir. They supervised in this undertaking a relatively small but productive community of official scholars. The majority of these held office in the Ch'ang-an state academy directorate, the institution responsible for empire-wide education. These scholars produced a survey of the tradition of canonical learning, that, fully extant, is not only a major source for early T'ang scholarly attitudes, but also the most comprehensive account of the whole tradition from the medieval period.

The textual and exegetical traditions

In surveying existing canonical scholarship, early T'ang scholars were concerned with three distinct stages in the development of the tradition. The first was that of the texts themselves of the Confucian canons. Secondly, there were primary commentaries, usually written between the Han and the Chin dynasties, of which, in most cases, two or more existed for each canon.[8] Finally, there was a considerable body of exegetical or sub-commentarial literature that scholars had produced nearer T'ang times. The programme for canonical scholarship on which high authority embarked in the Chen-kuan period involved all these three stages. It demonstrates particularly well some of the features of early T'ang scholarship that recur in all the learned disciplines considered in this book. The emperor at first made use of the scholarship of individual scholars who had served under the Sui. Then, in the second half of the reign of T'ai tsung, a large *ad hoc* commission was appointed to produce the dynasty's own definitive exegesis. The work of this commission, like that in other disciplines in this period, again exploited material inherited from the Sui dynasty. It also expressed certain early T'ang political priorities, among which one that recurred in all fields of learning was the unification of the northern and southern traditions after the period of disunion. For all the ambition involved, the commission ran into short-term difficulties and failed to produce long-term solutions to the problems it set out to resolve.

In the early years of the dynasty, the T'ang almost incidentally managed to extend approval to the compilations of a major lexical and phonological scholar of the Sui. This was Lu Te-ming, a southerner by origin, who had represented the Confucian side in the three-teachings debate of 624 (Ch. 2, p. 33). Lu Te-ming had produced a series of phonological glossaries for a group of seven canons that included the Taoist texts *Lao tzu* and *Chuang tzu*, and in its Neo-Taoist emphasis was typical of the pre-T'ang southern dynasties. In this series, the *Ching tien shih wen* (*Explanations for canonical texts*), he drew in total from 230 works, in this breadth being characteristic of early seventh-century exegetes. He also supplied short surveys of both the primary commentaries and the sub-commentaries on each of the texts he glossed. Although he may have completed his compilations under Sui rule, he was honoured and given office by the T'ang. His Neo-Taoist outlook contrasts with the less speculative, more cautious attitudes of official canonical scholars of the second half of the Chen-kuan period.[9] T'ai tsung's approval of his compilations provides an early indication of the generally pluralistic outlook of the early T'ang state towards different interpretations of the canons. Lu Te-ming's glossaries enjoyed official favour until well into the eighth century, and circulated empire-wide.[10]

In 631, however, T'ang scholars took the first step in a programme intended to produce for the dynasty its own definitive text and exegesis of the canons. In that year, T'ai tsung commissioned Yen Shih-ku (581–645, canonized *Tai*), a member of a scholarly clan that claimed descent from Yen Hui, and one of the most prominent official scholars of the first two reigns, to 'determine' (*ting*) the text of the *Five canons*.[11] The choice of canons was significant, because it provides a first hint of the extent to which early T'ang official scholars followed their Sui predecessors in matters of scholarly policy. The group of five did not represent the complete range of Confucian texts, but rather those that had been particularly important under the Sui. They were: the *Chou i*; *Shang shu*; *Mao shih*; *Li chi*; and *Ch'un-ch'iu* with the *Tso chuan*. Yen Shih-ku therefore set aside the four texts that made up the long series of *Nine canons*, the *Chou li* and *I li*, and the *Kung-yang chuan* and *Ku-liang chuan*. The study of these last two was said to have been so neglected in the Sui period that 'they were almost without teachers to explain them'.[12]

The determining of a definitive text for the Confucian canons was not an undertaking that was original to the T'ang. In the period of disunion and the Sui, emperors had commissioned 'definitive versions' (*ting pen*), and these had therefore existed well before the T'ang.[13] Yen Shih-ku, pursuing the project in the imperial library, of which he became deputy director from 633, used versions of the canons dating from no earlier than the Chin (A.D. 265–420) and Liu Sung (420–79). In discussions arranged by T'ai tsung, he successfully defended his decisions. In 633, these 'definitive versions' were distributed throughout the empire. A list of standard-form characters that Yen Shih-ku compiled with these standard texts, the *Yen shih tzu yang* (*Mr Yen's model characters*), circulated widely.[14]

The fact that in several accounts Yen's project immediately precedes the second stage in the early T'ang programme for canonical scholarship has been taken to imply that his 'definitive versions' were used as its basis.[15] This was not, however, the case. This second stage began in 638, when T'ai tsung appointed a commission to compile sub-commentaries for the *Five canons*.[16] Its brief, differing considerably from that of Yen Shih-ku, was not only to provide exegesis of the texts of the canons, but also to explain the subsequent strata: the primary commentaries and the most recent, sub-commentarial layer. The commission was directed by the leading official scholar K'ung Ying-ta, the 'Confucius of Kuan-hsi', who was appointed president of the state academy directorate that year. It was made up of thirteen or more scholars, most of whom, appropriately, held basic office in one or other of the directorate's constituent schools.[17] It differed from the major historical and literary commissions of the period, therefore, in not being directed by a scholar minister of the seniority of Wei Cheng or Fang Hsüan-ling, and this is possibly an indication of its lower standing. This commission completed a version of the sub-commentary series four years later, in 642, when T'ai tsung gave it his approval.[18]

When this version was discussed in the state academy directorate, however, for reasons that are not recorded, it proved unacceptable. It is possible that at this stage T'ai tsung himself encouraged debate between members of the commission and other canonical scholars.[19] A new commission, of eleven, with basic posts similar to those of its predecessor, was appointed. In 643, K'ung Ying-ta left the commission, apparently because of his age, and over the final years of T'ai tsung's reign momentum was lost.[20] Then, a year after T'ai tsung's death, a new commission, to include among others K'ung Ying-ta's son, K'ung Chih-yüeh, was established. In 651 or 652, the project came under the direction of the senior scholar minister Chang-sun Wu-chi. In 653, Chang-sun Wu-chi, with a number of other high ranking ministers, submitted the series, which had taken fifteen years to complete, to Kao tsung. An edict the following year ordered the distribution of copies throughout the empire.[21] The series became known as the *Wu ching cheng i* (*The true meaning of the Five canons*).

The sub-commentary series, at a total length of 180 *chüan*,[22] was, like other seventh-century compilations, a cumulative work. Both in its basic features and in its detail, it was also the result of the need to compromise and to honour political priorities. Its editors sometimes sacrificed intellectual consistency to their loyalty to their chosen authorities, and had a compendious approach to the controversies that marked the pre-T'ang history of canonical scholarship.

Like all early T'ang official scholars, the compilers owed a considerable debt to their predecessors under the Sui. Two major features of the sub-commentary series, in particular, derived from Sui scholarship. The first was that, like Yen Shih-ku, the commission restricted themselves to the inner series of *Five canons*. Secondly, in selecting a single primary commentary for each of the *Five canons*, as seventh century practice demanded that they should, K'ung Ying-ta's commission adopted precisely those that had been in favour in the Sui.[23] For the *Chou i*, the commission selected the commentary by the Neo-Taoist philosopher Wang Pi (A.D. 226–49), and, for the *Hsi-tz'u* (*Appendices*) that of Han K'ang-po (fl. *c*. 385); for the *Shang shu*, the commentary attributed to K'ung An-kuo (fl. *c*. 156–74 B.C.); for the *Mao shih*, the commentaries first by Mao Heng of the Former Han, and then by the great eclectic Later Han commentator Cheng Hsüan (A.D. 127–200), whose approach to the canons was marked by the 'sense of factual enquiry' of the Old Text (Ku-wen) school. For the *Li chi*, the chosen commentary was also by Cheng Hsüan. Finally, for the *Ch'un-ch'iu* they selected the *Tso chuan* rather than either of its rivals, the *Kung-yang* or the *Ku-liang*, and for the *Tso*, the commentary by the scholar and soldier of the Three Kingdoms and early Chin Tu Yü (A.D. 222–84).[24] This range of primary commentaries, endorsing Sui decisions as it did, was said to have provided a balance between what was characterized as the northern commentarial tradition, more practical, less speculative and typified by Cheng Hsüan's acceptance in the north, and the southern, more philosophical and less concerned to gloss historical details, represented by the Neo-Taoist philosopher Wang Pi.[25]

K'ung Ying-ta's commission probably also owed much of the fabric of their sub-commentaries to their Sui predecessors. The exegesis of two Sui scholars, Liu Cho (544–610), who had actually taught K'ung Ying-ta, and Liu Hsüan (d. *c*. 606 aged 68 *sui*) was particularly important. Both were northerners and official scholars; both were recorded as unifying the northern and southern traditions, and both produced sub-commentaries for the canons in series.[26] It is possible that at least in the cases of the *Shang shu*, *Mao shih* and *Tso chuan*, K'ung's commission took much of their material from these scholars. K'ung's sub-commentary to the *Shang shu* sometimes used the term Great Sui (*Ta Sui*), implying that the Sui was the current dynasty.[27] In the sub-commentary to the *Tso*, the text attributes certain comments to Liu Hsüan; exactly the same comments appear, without attribution, in the *Mao shih* sub-commentary.[28] Though in neither case does this prove that more than the short passages concerned were of Sui origin, it is suggestive of a larger debt.

Whether as a direct result of the compilers' indebtedness to Sui predecessors or on their own initiative, the commission left in the sub-commentary series a work that clearly registers the intention to produce a single, standard interpretation of their texts. Each sub-commentary provides elaborate and comprehensive refutation of alternative viewpoints that its exclusive endorsement of a single primary commentary required it to reject.[29] In doing so, it analyzes the views of a wide range of authorities. The scale of its survey may be inferred by the number of sources that the series drew on. For example, Cheng Hsüan's primary commentary to the *Li chi* had cited 45 different sources by name. In K'ung's sub-commentary, this number was increased by nearly 200, the majority of the titles being of works from the period of disunion.[30] Wang Pi's philosophical commentary to the *Chou i* had not cited any authority by name, but K'ung's sub-commentary drew explicitly from 26 works of *Chou i* exegesis, besides other canons, apocrypha, lexical works, histories and philosophical texts.[31] Even these figures do not give an adequate impression of the compendious character of the series, or its capacity to record and sometimes to emphasize the controversies of the preceding period.[32]

This impressive breadth reflects another purpose underlying the series, that of refuting views that might carry political risks for the dynasty. Perhaps the theme in the exegetical tradition over which early T'ang scholars, and probably T'ai tsung himself, felt a special sense of threat concerned prognostication. They were not radical sceptics over divination as it was practised in the early seventh century, and they certainly did not deny that the future might be foretold. But they wanted to ensure that the activity should be controlled, and should not, as it had done in the pre-T'ang period, become a threat to dynastic power. In the late Former Han period, the later phase of the

New Text (Chin-wen) movement had developed a tradition of divination and prognostication to a level that was politically unacceptable
to the early T'ang. K'ung's sub-commentary series therefore often
attacked the texts that represented this tradition, dismissing them as
shallow and unreliable.[33]

K'ung probably again reflected the political priorities of the Chen-
kuan court when he countered some of the more mystical readings of
the Confucian canons that had been current in the period of disunion.
He indicated in the preface to the *Chou i* sub-commentary that he had
set aside Buddhist explanations of the text.[34] Inevitably, though, he
was influenced to some extent by Buddhism.[35] The Confucian–Neo-
Taoist synthesis that had developed in the south, as Lu Te-ming had
shown, remained an intellectual force in the early seventh century, and
its influence is to be seen in the sub-commentary series. K'ung
Ying-ta's exposition of certain *Chou i* passages indicates that he held
that the *tao* was 'without form' (*wu hsing*).[36] He defined both the *tao*
and the original 'oneness' of which the *Chou i*, the *Lao tzu* and the *Li
chi* spoke as 'void' (*k'ung*).[37] On the other hand, he also posited a
physical process whereby matter came into being, through the agency
of 'particles' (*chi*), which 'left the void and entered the realm of
being'.[38] This belief in a physical transition from being to non-being
has been seen as more indebted to Han cosmology than to the
Neo-Taoism of the period of disunion. K'ung's detailed formulations
of the shape of the universe may derive from a similar intention to
replace metaphysical speculation with a physically precise cosmology.[39]

Perhaps, however, the feature of the sub-commentary series that
best reflects the early T'ang scholarly milieu was its exhaustive
treatment of issues relating to the ritual. The dynasty's ritual programme (Chapter 4) was of enormous importance to the seventh- and
eighth-century scholar community. K'ung Y'ing-ta's commission
repeatedly testifies to this by the thoroughness of their examination of
the canonical origins of the ritual observances that made up the state
ritual programme. It was an irony that, despite the exhaustive
treatment K'ung accorded ritual issues, his position on many of these
issues was to be set aside by the authorities in the decades that
followed.

The policy of inclusiveness

K'ung's *Wu ching cheng i* series was an attempt, in part politically
motivated, to survey and delimit the vast canonical and exegetical
traditions. But the series did not treat the whole range of Confucian

canonical literature. Nor did its promulgation prevent further exegesis of the *Five canons* that it had glossed. In the Chen-kuan period, there were already indications that high authority adopted a more pluralistic attitude to the interpretation of the canonical corpus than that implicit in K'ung's series. T'ai tsung himself encouraged controversy among Confucian exegetical scholars. His early approval of Lu Te-ming's *Ching tien shih wen* series, with its southern commitment to classical Taoism, suggests the breadth of his interest. The list of sub-commentators of Liang, Northern Chou and Sui dynasties whom he honoured by edict in 640 (Ch. 2, p. 34) was more inclusive than might have been expected if a narrow concept of orthodoxy, based on K'ung's sub-commentaries, had dictated their selection. The same is true of the list of primary commentators represented in the temple by edict in 647 (Ch. 2, p. 35), for this included figures whose commentaries K'ung had expressly criticized.

Another incident of T'ai tsung's reign points even more clearly to a willingness to tolerate mutually exclusive interpretations of the canons. In 642, a collator in the imperial library submitted commentaries on the *Shang shu* and *Mao shih* which refuted the primary commentaries of K'ung An-kuo and Cheng Hsüan. In the context of seventh-century official scholarship, this was a particularly radical approach, first because it entailed rejecting the primary commentaries that two of K'ung's sub-commentaries had amplified. Secondly, it meant an exegetical approach that dismissed altogether the second, primary commentarial layer of the tradition and directly interpreted the text of the canons. Nonetheless, T'ai tsung ordered a discussion, and it was proposed that these new commentaries be taken into the imperial library, and that they be allowed to 'circulate together with' (*ping hsing*) the K'ung An-kuo and Cheng Hsüan commentaries. Only a detailed refutation, by an official from outside the academic establishment, holding financial office, ultimately brought about their rejection.[40]

The surviving evidence for the place of the canons in the education and examination system of the first two reigns also makes it plain that even at this early stage the system did not simply involve the *Five canons* 'determined' by Yen Shih-ku and glossed by K'ung's commission. Under T'ai tsung, examiners also used the *Chou li* and the *I li*,[41] and in 644 the crown prince demanded knowledge of the *Hsiao ching* as well as the *Li chi*.[42] More indirectly, a Japanese code that is held to have been based on the T'ang statutes of 651 listed in its official school curricula two commentaries for each of the canons. It also gave the long series of nine canons, not just the short series of five that Yen Shih-ku and K'ung Ying-ta had used.[43] It may have been, therefore, that by 651 the state had established two commentaries for each of the main series of canons, not one only, as K'ung Ying-ta's position implied it should have done.

In the course of the reigns of T'ai tsung and Kao tsung, moreover, official scholars compiled, probably on their own initiative, sub-commentaries to all the remaining canons in the long series of nine, with the possible exception only of the *Kung-yang chuan*. The most important scholar involved here was Chia Kung-yen, who compiled sub-commentaries for the *Chou li* and the *I li* that are extant. The fact that Chia also wrote sub-commentaries for the *Analects* and the *Hsiao ching*, and is recorded as having compiled a *Li chi* sub-commentary that must, in effect, have duplicated K'ung's own sub-commentary underlines the freedom of scholars to produce their own exegesis.[44] Chia's *Chou li* and *I li* sub-commentaries used the primary commentaries of the great Cheng Hsüan, and also relied on pre-T'ang exegesis. Though they were probably less detailed on philosophical questions, they were otherwise similar in perspective to K'ung's own *Li chi* and *Mao shih* sub-commentaries and may have been seen as complementing them.[45]

One at least of the other sub-commentaries official scholars compiled in this period, however, is likely to have related only uneasily to K'ung's series. This was the sub-commentary to the *Ku-liang chuan* compiled by Yang Shih-hsün, another academic official and a member of the commission that had worked under K'ung on the *Tso chuan* sub-commentary. Yang Shih-hsün used the primary commentary of Fan Ning (A.D. 339–401), a scholar in the same Ku-wen tradition as Tu Yü, the primary commentator to the *Tso chuan* whom K'ung had endorsed.[46] But in his sub-commentary to the *Tso*, K'ung had included emphatic attacks on the *Ku-liang* tradition. If the dynasty had envisaged enforcing, or even promoting, an intellectual orthodoxy, based on K'ung's series, it would hardly have accepted a sub-commentary that took the part of a canon that K'ung had tended to condemn.

The place in seventh-century exegesis of the remaining canon in the long series of nine, the *Kung-yang chuan*, is more difficult to determine. The *Kung-yang* was a particularly important vehicle for the New Text school of the Han and was the authority behind much of the Han tradition of prognostication that the early seventh-century scholars rejected. A sub-commentary to the *Kung-yang chuan* and the primary commentary of Ho Hsiu (A.D. 129–82) is extant; but its date is uncertain.[47]

Despite K'ung's efforts at producing a detailed and coherent survey of the canonical tradition, therefore, T'ang emperors, the educational agencies and examiners recognized a wider range of primary and commentarial literature than was consistent with his outlook. Some of them may also have retained a measure of traditional disdain for the detailed commentarial approach (*chang-chü hsüeh*) that K'ung Ying-ta's great project exemplified. In the context of political discussion and policy recommendation, so important to the T'ang official community, it was usual to cite the text of the canons direct, without reference to intervening exegesis. A relaxed sense of what was orthodox, and freedom to appeal directly to the canons, were to remain very important characteristics of the Confucian canonical tradition throughout the T'ang. In due course they led to major developments in attitude within the tradition.

Ch'un-ch'iu *scholarship in the early T'ang*

Of all the canons in the short or long series, the *Ch'un-ch'iu*, demonstrates particularly clearly the politically determined, state-centred outlook of the canonical scholars of the early T'ang. The early T'ang scholarly world believed that Confucius had edited a profound message into the text of the *Ch'un-ch'iu*, and they associated the canon particularly closely with his teaching. Scholar ministers under T'ai tsung cited the *Ch'un-ch'iu* in order to justify a range of policies. It was used to sanction the ideals invested in official history writing.[48] Officials quoted it to justify the attitude of radical separation that they consistently enjoined on successive emperors in managing the barbarians.[49] It also played a part in the maintenance of the imperial ancestral temple,[50] and in the interpretation of omens.[51]

In the scholarly community, preference for the *Tso chuan*, the least speculative of the *Three traditions* to the *Ch'un-ch'iu*, and by far the most copious in its concrete historical detail, was general. T'ai tsung himself had been taught the *Ch'un-ch'iu* and the *Tso*, and quoted from them in conversation.[52] The *Tso*, moreover, suited the T'ang temperament, with its love of action. It can be no accident that throughout the dynasty, when military men were commended for Confucian learning, this was the text that they were said to have known.[53] But the *Ch'un-ch'iu* and the *Tso* were also important for more philosophical reasons. The 'moderate scepticism' towards such activities as prognostication that K'ung Ying-ta's sub-commentary commission had urged is especially well exemplified in the outlook of early T'ang scholars on the *Ch'un-ch'iu* and its exegetical literature.

The main feature of K'ung's critique of the *Ch'un-ch'iu* and its *Three traditions* was its polemical advocacy of a cautious attitude to them.[54] An important reason for this caution lay in the pre-T'ang history of the *Ch'un-ch'iu* tradition, and the association it had come to have by the seventh century with the semi-popular tradition of prognostication and omen lore that derived ultimately from Han interpretations of the *Kung-yang chuan*. To scholars in the early T'ang, if it were not controlled, or if it were taken up by unwise emperors, this tradition might become a threat to the state. Scholarly exposition of the *Ch'un-ch'iu* provided a highly respected means for them to emphasize their views.

It was this cautious attitude to the *Ch'un-ch'iu* that led K'ung Ying-ta, obeying Sui precedent, not only to select the *Tso chuan*, the least speculative of the *Three traditions*, but also to use the primary commentary of the Ku-wen scholar Tu Yü. To K'ung, following Tu Yü, the canon, far from being a text-book for prophecy as the New Text tradition had had it, was simply a chronicle history. Compiled by 'more than one' archivist in the state of Lu, it had contained inconsistencies of style and format even before Confucius had edited it. Confucius had, by his use of select terminology, concealed moral judgements on events in the text. But he alone was not responsible for its profundity. There were also cases where later scholars had erroneously detected his hand in what were no more than accidental phrases in a composite text. For K'ung, the *Tso chuan*, compiled by Tso Ch'iu-ming, an archivist in Lu and a contemporary of Confucius, was a separate work. Tso Ch'iu-ming 'had not necessarily received instruction face to face from [Confucius]'. Moreover the *Tso*, composed much closer in time to the canon itself than the *Kung-yang* or *Ku-liang*, was much more reliable as a record of events.

K'ung also followed Tu Yü in refuting some of the beliefs that the New Text tradition had invested in the person of Confucius. It was not true, he argued, that Confucius had had an ambivalent attitude to the Chou dynasty, or that in editing the *Ch'un-ch'iu* he covertly 'demoted the Chou and made Lu the royal house'. K'ung argued rather, on the basis of *Analects* evidence and Confucius's use of the Chou calendar, that he was a loyal subject of the Chou. Nor was it acceptable to K'ung that Confucius should be known as the 'uncrowned king' (*su wang*).[55] Passages in the *Analects* in which he condemned usurpation again indicated that he was a loyal subject of the Chou. To call him the 'uncrowned king' was a calumny. 'Alas! Confucius has long been slandered. Only through Tu [Yü] is his innocence established.'

Elsewhere in the sub-commentary K'ung Ying-ta attempted to

discredit the *Kung-yang* and *Ku-liang* traditions, charging them, in an *Analects* phrase, with 'the scholarship of wayside hearsay and roadside gossip'.[56] In the sub-commentaries to other canons also, he criticized both these texts.[57] His purpose was to rid the *Ch'un-ch'iu* tradition as a whole of the superstitions that had become attached to it, and to divest Confucius of the royal and semi-divine status he had acquired. K'ung did not pursue this aim rigorously or consistently in the sub-commentary, for, when it suited his purpose to do so, he accepted evidence supplied by texts he elsewhere condemned as unreliable. But his basic position was fully consonant with the political priorities that, in court discussions, the Chen-kuan scholar ministers formulated for the emperor.

Early T'ang attitudes to the Mencius

The practical temper of early seventh-century canonical scholarship becomes particularly clear in the attitude of official scholars to the *Mencius*. The ancient philosopher who, from the ninth century on, was to provide one of the main sanctions for a revived, more introspective Confucianism, had a very different status in the early T'ang. Mencius himself had less standing than he had had in Han times, and a far lower position that he was to enjoy as the 'second sage' (*ya sheng*) of the Neo-Confucian era. Since he was not a commentator, he was not represented in the Confucian temple. There was no record of a local temple or cult to him, though his tomb may well have survived.[58] The pre-eminent Meng clan of the T'ang, from P'ing-ch'ang in modern Shantung, claimed descent from a related forbear who had been mentioned in the *Analects*, and references to Mencius as an ancestor are rare.[59] Mencius himself was not considered a canonical teacher, even though he was, in K'ung Ying-ta's words, 'a wise man of antiquity, in all the disciple of Tzu-ssu, not far distant from the sage Confucius'.[60] Official scholars entered the book that bore his name in the philosophical rather than the canonical division in the official bibliographical scheme, after books ascribed to two disciples of Confucius, Tseng Shen and Tzu-ssu.[61]

In their attitude to the content of the *Mencius*, however, seventh-century scholars provide an even greater contrast with their ninth-century successors. On the one hand, the *Mencius* contained much prescriptive information on such topics as ritual usage, taxation and land tenure, besides short, chance remarks on a wide range of practical subjects. On the other, it also had long comments on doctrinal questions, particularly on the interior emphasis within Confucianism, the emotions, fate and the moral quality of the nature (*hsing*). Early T'ang scholars found the *Mencius* important above all for the practical information the text contained. In the *Mao shih* sub-commentary, by far the greatest number of K'ung Ying-ta's citations of the *Mencius* concern remarks on ritual, social or administrative questions. Only one, on man's inner capacity to distinguish good and evil, bears on the interior life.[62] In the sub-commentary to the *Chou i*, the canon that of the inner series of five provided most detailed sanction for speculation on fate and the individual, K'ung did not draw once from the *Mencius*.[63] In Chia K'ung-yen's sub-commentaries for the *Chou li* and the *I li*,[64] and in the early T'ang encyclopaedias *Chün-shu chih yao* (*Essentials of good government from many books*), and *I wen lei chü* (*Literary material arranged by category*),[65] the pattern is similar; the citations are generally restricted to concrete matters, rather than to psychological or interior questions.

This neglect of the psychological theme in the *Mencius* does not mean that early T'ang scholars never considered interior ideas in Confucian terms. They certainly recognized as Confucian a process of self-cultivation, of, in the expression from the *Chou i*, 'making an exhaustive discrimination of truth and effecting the complete development of their natures' (*ch'iung li chin hsing*).[66] K'ung Ying-ta, defending Confucius from an implied charge that he was afraid of death, stated that he had 'effected the complete development of his nature' before dying,[67] and Yü Shih-nan (558–638, canonized *Wen-i*), in a commemorative text for the Confucian temple, stated that Confucius had no equal in the past, or the future, for self-cultivation as the *Chou i* defined it.[68]

When seventh-century Confucian exegetical scholars needed to cite Confucian formulations on interior questions, they probably relied on the commentaries on passages in the *Ta hsüeh*, *Chung yung*, *Li yün* (*Cycle of ritual*) and *Yüeh chi* (*Record of music*) chapters of the *Li chi*, and on the *Chou i* and *Analects*.[69] What may be inferred from their relative lack of interest in the *Mencius* is that, in this period, Confucian ideas on introspective doctrinal questions were not reviewed with the degree of precision or sense of enquiry that was focussed on problems of a political, institutional or ritual kind. The great majority of scholars and others in the China of Kao tsu and T'ai tsung turned to Buddhism or Taoism for answers to questions of ultimate value. Only from the late eighth century, in the more devolved intellectual milieu brought about by the political decline of the dynasty, did radical hostility to these religions develop among a minority of scholars, and a revival of interest in treating such problems in exclusively Confucian terms take place.

From 653 to 755

When compared to its history in the first two reigns, the official canonical exegesis that scholars produced over the century from the promulgation of K'ung Ying-ta's *Wu ching cheng i* until the outbreak of rebellion of 755 is sparsely documented. Probably few compilations of the length of the great sub-commentary series, or of the historical importance of late eighth- and early ninth-century re-interpretations of the canons were written, and none has survived. Although in other areas of learning, in state ritual for example and in official genealogy and in administrative fields such as statutory and criminal law, second or even third versions of early T'ang official compilations were commissioned, K'ung's sub-commentaries remained the only officially commissioned series in canonical exegesis.

Scholars in academic office over this century, nonetheless, continued on their own initiative to compile numbers of sub-commentaries or glossaries to the canons. In a succession of controversies that took place in the academic agencies, they also raised questions about the value of the officially established primary commentaries. Scepticism towards the established texts reached an extreme point when the historian Liu Chih-chi cast doubt on the value of certain features of the *Ch'un-ch'iu* and *Shang shu*. The problem of how his and other spirited opinions affected the standing of K'ung Ying-ta's official sub-commentaries is one that dominates an account of canonical scholarship for the hundred years from T'ai tsung's death.

In the school system and in the examinations, the authorities continued to use the established texts and approved commentaries. But, in the increasingly harsh competition for success, idealistic scholars considered the attitudes of candidates to the canons less than satisfactory. The tradition of complaint that grew up over candidates' outlook on their curricula was another feature of the canonical tradition in this century. Finally, towards the end of the period, under the changed conditions of the late K'ai-yüan (713–42) and T'ien-pao (742–56) periods, among the 'Confucian opposition' the more distanced attitude towards the court and the political centre was also expressed in the context of the study of the canons.

Criticism of officially established texts

Much evidence suggests that, from Kao tsung's reign on, K'ung Ying-ta's official sub-commentaries and the primary commentaries that they endorsed enjoyed general acceptance in the scholarly world and in the school system. Not only did high authority commission no second sub-commentary series, but no complete work of Confucian canonical scholarship survives from the second half of the seventh century, and relatively few from the first decades of the eighth. At Tun-huang, fragments of the primary commentaries endorsed by K'ung Ying-ta far outnumber those other commentaries, and fragments of K'ung's own sub-commentaries were preserved in some numbers there.[70] The impression is therefore given that the series, following its promulgation in 653, effectively displaced existing works, while new, unofficial exegesis posed no threat to its pre-eminence. In view of the immense prestige of official service and of the examinations in the canons as a means of gaining official status, it is not surprising to see the officially approved commentaries and sub-commentaries prevail in this way.

Despite the impression given by this lack of surviving material, however, over the century from 653 to 755, individual scholars initiated a series of attempts, supported in some cases by detailed scholarly argument, to add to or modify the existing range of commentaries. These attempts, coming from academic officials and resting more on scholarly grounds than those of administrative convenience, form a distinct body of material, peculiar to the second half of the seventh and the early eighth century.

In Kao tsung's reign, examples of compilations that might have threatened the place of the official exegesis are not well documented. But very brief accounts survive suggesting that the court considered the work of other canonical scholars. Early in the reign, the emperor ordered that the erudits and others should discuss the correctness of emendations and new glosses by Ts'ui I-hsüan, a commentarial and phonological scholar of this period.[71] Again, not long after the completion of K'ung's series and its extension, a certain Li Hsüan-chih, a disciple in ritual scholarship of the ritual exegete Chia Kung-yen and a representative on the Confucian side in three-teachings debates at court, wrote a dictionary for the three ritual canons that was said to have circulated widely. He was also an expert on the *Ch'un-ch'iu* with the *Tso chuan*, and on the *Mao shih*, Han histories and *Lao tzu* and *Chuang tzu*.[72] There is no evidence that the dynasty tried to suppress his activities; indeed, the fact that the titles of his compilations were recorded in his official biography indicates approval of them. But again there is not enough evidence to make detailed comment on his scholarship in relation to official exegesis possible.

Several decades later, in 703, Wang Yüan-kan (d. after 705), an erudit of the Ssu-men hsüeh and concurrently scholar of the Hung-wen kuan, submitted what were evidently controversial writings on the

Shang shu, Ch'un-ch'iu, Li chi, Hsiao ching and *Shih chi*. An edict ordered official scholars to discuss the advisability of his interpretations. Some senior scholars, who 'adhered exclusively to the commentaries (*chang-chü*) of earlier exegetes, deeply ridiculed him for tampering with former interpretations'. But others in more junior posts, among them the historian critic Liu Chih-chi and his colleague Hsü Chien (659–729, canonized *Wen*), came to his defence, and he was finally given an official commendation that praised his conduct and scholarship. Again, however, beyond the fact that they directly challenged established views, and that in one debate he advocated a mourning period of 36 rather than 25 months, nothing is known of his controversial opinions.[73]

In the long reign of Hsüan tsung, however, dissatisfaction among official scholars over the established commentaries is documented in some detail, very possibly because the strength of the emperor's own interest ensured the preservation of the records concerned. From the start of his reign, the emperor seems likely to have encouraged a climate in which discussion took place. Even before his accession, Chang Yüeh, later one of the great scholar ministers of his reign, proposed that Hsüan tsung convene a commission to re-establish the texts of the canons.[74] There then followed two episodes in which official scholars and former colleagues of Chang Yüeh tried to alter the statutory establishment of texts. The first of these started in 719, when an edict was issued ordering scholars to discuss the respective merits of primary commentaries for the *Shang shu* and the *Hsiao ching* by Cheng Hsüan and K'ung An-kuo, neither of which was established. In a second edict a few days later, the *Shang shu* was removed, and the discussion was limited to the *Hsiao ching* commentaries, to primary commentaries on the *Lao tzu* by Ho-shang Kung and Wang Pi and to a section of the *Chou i*. In this second edict, the possibility of a plurality of approved commentaries was made explicit: 'If more than one commentary is found to be about equal in doctrinal exposition, may they not all be made current?'

The debate that followed was narrowed in effect to argument over the value of one official and one unofficial commentary each for the *Lao tzu* and *Hsiao ching*. It is dominated in surviving accounts by the submissions of the great historian critic Liu Chih-chi. Liu, in advocating in both cases that the unofficial commentaries be adopted, was opposed by ten other official scholars led by Ssu-ma Chen, an erudit of the Kuo-tzu hsüeh and author of an important commentary on the *Shih chi* (Ch. 5, p. 174). Both sides argued over the transmission of the primary commentaries involved. They cited their occurrence as titles and their length in *chüan* as these were recorded in earlier sources, and discussed the evidence for their authorship and the value of their content. Liu Chih-chi, in arguing for flexibility and change, quoted the precedent of the *Tso chuan* and its establishment, after controversy, as late as the Han period.[75]

Invaluable as this debate is in showing the sophistication of early eighth-century views of textual transmission, its outcome itself was no less significant. The emperor ordered that the official commentaries remain the established ones, but that the study of the alternatives should be encouraged, so that their transmission would be ensured. Then, not long after the debate, in 722, Hsüan tsung produced his own commentary to the *Hsiao ching*.[76] Some years later, in 735, he wrote a *Lao tzu* commentary.[77] He also continued to be interested in the *Shang shu*, the other canon involved in the first stage of the debate.[78] By the completion of the *Liu tien* in 738, both his *Hsiao ching* and his *Lao tzu* commentaries had been officially established.[79] The emperor's compilation of these commentaries, against the background of his encouragement of discussion, confirmed his position as head of the scholar community. It placed him, as he surely intended, in the tradition of the scholar emperors of the pre-T'ang period, including even those of the scholarly Liang house in the south.

A second expression of dissatisfaction with officially established texts in the K'ai-yüan period was initiated by Yüan Hsing-ch'ung (653–729, canonized *Hsien*), another leading official scholar, a bibliophile, president of the state academy directorate and major figure in the Chi-hsien yüan, Hsüan tsung's own advisory college. The controversy he caused illustrates the other face authority might turn, when confronted with the demand for administratively inconvenient change. Yüan Hsing-ch'ung, who had compiled a sub-commentary to Hsüan tsung's commentary on the *Hsiao ching*, also undertook a sub-commentary for a reorganized version of the *Li chi* that Wei Cheng, the scholar minister of T'ai tsung's reign, had edited and that a descendant now promoted (Ch. 4, pp. 120–21). This reorganized version probably involved arranging the prescriptive parts of the text as a code for contemporary ritual practice. In 726, however, having presented the compilation, Yüan Hsing-ch'ung encountered the resistance of Chang Yüeh, who was now chief minister and president of the Chi-hsien yüan. Chang claimed that the *Li chi* was 'an inerasable authority' (*pu k'an chih tien*), and that it should not be changed. The outcome was that Yüan's sub-commentary, instead of being 'established in the schools, transmitted and taught', was 'stored in an inner depository and not in the end established in the schools'. Yüan consoled himself by writing a polemical essay, in which he bitterly condemned the exaggerated and inflexible respect paid to established primary commentaries. Like Liu Chih-chi, he cited the precedent of the *Tso chuan*, as a text whose history demonstrated the benefits of more flexible attitudes.[80]

The scholarly life of the second half of Hsüan tsung's reign was dominated by Li Lin-fu's autocratic control of administration, and by the emperor's growing commitment to Taoism. The freer atmosphere that had permitted controversies in the academic agencies, like those involving Liu Chih-chi and Yüan Hsing-ch'ung, was no longer possible. The two developments in official canonical scholarship of the T'ien-pao period were, rather, prescriptive. Both may be seen as expressing the interests of the emperor or of high authority. Neither is represented in surviving documentation by any record of debate in the community of official scholars.

The first concerned the *Yüeh ling* (*Monthly commands*). This was a chapter of the *Li chi* which had from pre-T'ang times been recognized as being distinct in its origins from the rest of the canon, and which contained a calendar of ritual and administrative prescriptions, given in terms of the *yin-yang* theory of the late pre-Ch'in period.[81] As one of the principal canonical sanctions for the cosmic dimension to the dynastic state, the *Yüeh ling* was of special importance to successive T'ang sovereigns.

Early in the dynasty, in 640, T'ai tsung had raised the question of how literally the *Yüeh ling* was to be followed.[82] The text had also played a prominent part in controversies about the Ming-t'ang.[83] A ritual that involved the reading out of the monthly or seasonal commands that it contained was associated with the building, and was the subject of debate in the late seventh and early eighth centuries (Ch. 4, p. 127).[84] Then, in about 725, Hsüan tsung appears to have had the text of the *Yüeh ling* separately re-determined.[85] From 738 for a brief period, he required the president of the court of sacrifices to introduce and lecture on one section of the text each month.[86] In 743, by imperial order, the *Yüeh ling* was placed at the head of the *Li chi*.[87] In 746, its name was changed by official edict to *Shih ling* (*Seasonal commands*).[88] At about this time, the chief minister Li Lin-fu directed a commission of eight, including the Taoist Ch'en Hsi-lieh (d. 757) and the prolific official scholar Lu Shan-ching, to compile a new commentary for it.[89] This commentary, which used the text re-determined earlier in the reign, survives. From this time on, the *Yüeh ling* was brought to the fore in the state ritual programme. Its portrayal of the emperor as ensuring the harmony of the cosmos by the quality of his government and by his ritual acts commended it not only to Hsüan tsung but also to post-rebellion rulers. But the *Yüeh ling* was also to register particularly clearly the difference between the public outlook of scholars, especially as this concerned the emperor, and their unofficial attitudes. It was to be the subject of incisive criticism by scholars writing unofficially about state ritual in the sceptical climate of the late eighth and ninth centuries (Ch. 4, pp. 155–57).

The second development in official canonical scholarship of the second half of Hsüan tsung's reign concerned the *Hsiao ching*. Much favoured for court lectures, and as a concise summary of Confucian teaching, the *Hsiao ching* was held to encapsulate Confucian teaching, just as the *Lao tzu* stood for Taoism and the *Chin-kang ching* (*Diamond sutra*) for Buddhism. In 743, Hsüan tsung ordered that a revised version of his own *Hsiao ching* commentary be distributed throughout the empire.[90] In an act of grace the following year, he required that all households have a copy.[91] In 745, the canon and his commentary were engraved in stone and set up in the state academy directorate. This, the first datable instance in the dynasty of the stone engraving of a Confucian canon, still stands at Sian. Alongside the text is an engraved list of the official scholars commissioned to prepare it.[92]

Complaints against the standards of canonical learning in the examinations

Hsüan tsung's promotion of his own commentaries on the *Lao tzu* and the *Hsiao ching* was ultimately addressed to the operation that played a large part in shaping T'ang attitudes to the canons, the examinations. Here in the K'ai-yüan and T'ien-pao periods the authorities ran into a number of practical problems. The increase in competition for office that took place over the K'ai-yüan period[93] affected for the worse the attitudes of candidates to examination curricula. Aiming for success, their approach was one of practical expediency, and they all opted for the shortest texts that the curriculum regulations allowed. The response of academic officials to this problem took the form of attempts to ensure that all the canons in the series of nine were studied by examination candidates, and that none was neglected. Scholars were also led to criticize more generally the place canonical learning had assumed in the examinations, and to condemn as particularly meaningless the rote learning of the canons that they involved.

The wish to see all nine of the canons figure in candidates' choice of text, and perhaps also to have more candidates from the state academy directorate successful in the competition for office, is evident from two mid K'ai-yüan memorials from the directorate's senior officials. In 720, a vice-president memorialized indicting that students were neglecting the *Chou li* and the *I li*, two medium canons, and the *Kung-yang chuan* and *Ku-liang chuan*, two minor canons, while, 'with their minds bent on passing, they all rushed to the *Li chi*, on the grounds that [for a major canon] its text was short'. He requested that lower pass standards for the context questions on the four neglected canons be approved.[94] In 728, Yang Ch'ang, the president, protested that the *Tso chuan* was also neglected, and asked that those who selected it or the other four should be given concessions in the competition for office.[95]

Dissatisfaction with the level of knowledge expected of candidates in the examinations was most eloquently expressed in this period by Liu Chih, a son of the great critic Liu Chih-chi, and later a reformer of the directorate (Ch. 2, p. 52). In a memorial submitted in about 735, Liu Chih criticized the basis of selection, especially the increasingly literary emphasis of the *chin shih* and the superficiality of the approach that required only rote learning of the canons.[96] Another way in which scholars expressed disapproval of the approach that examinations required was more indirect: they commended, in biographical tributes, those who did not study detailed exegesis of the canons (*chang chü*), but rather, in their concern for the world and its problems, sought for the deeper and more general meaning of the texts. Even those who went on to be successful in the *chin shih* might be praised in this way, in effect for an approach that transcended examination requirements.[97]

Perhaps in response to the complaints that Liu Chih and others submitted, there was some attempt in 737 to make both the *chin shih* and the *ming ching* a more substantial test.[98] In the T'ien-pao period, there were other, minor adjustments to the place of the canons in both the *chin shih* and the *ming ching* syllabuses. But, under the restrictive control of Li Lin-fu,[99] the basic problems remained unsolved. Nor did the brief three-year period from Li's death in 752 until the outbreak of the rebellion, during which *chin shih* quotas were relaxed, have any lasting effect on the system.[100]

Liu Chih-chi's views on the Ch'un-ch'iu and the Tso chuan

Despite the disdain that, on the grounds of its length, examination candidates showed the *Tso chuan*, this was still one of the canonical texts over which scholars of the canons expressed lively opinions. The *Ch'un-ch'iu*, the canon that was integrated with the *Tso*, moreover, retained its position as the cryptic but authoritative source for a wide range of principles, policies and ritual issues. It remained a much quoted authority in court and in the course of administration. Hsüan tsung cited it to encourage agriculture and to discourage the submission of omens. Individual scholars continued to refer to it in connection with history writing; it provided sanction for the management of the ancestral temple, for the problem of the length of the mourning period, and for the canonization system. In 731, Yü Hsiu-lieh, then a corrector at the imperial library, and later a major official scholar, even tried to prevent it from passing into Tibetan hands. His grounds were that it testified to a deteriorated political situation, in which the feudal lords were over-powerful in relation to the Chou emperor. It was not in the dynasty's interests, he argued, that the barbarians should know of such a development.[101]

For most of this century, official scholars continued to endorse the outlook on the *Ch'un-ch'iu* promoted in the first two reigns, namely that the *Tso chuan* was the most important of the *Three traditions* to the canon. Most of the works written over the period now exist only as titles. But the provocative critique of the whole tradition that Liu Chih-chi incorporated in his *Shih t'ung* (*Generalities on history*) of 710 does much to make good this loss. Liu's perspective on the *Ch'un-ch'iu* and the *Tso* represents an extreme point in the questioning of the authority of Confucius that is perhaps to be related indirectly to the success and confidence of seventh- and early eighth-century government. His great love for the *Tso* points again to the T'ang preference for detailed and vivid historical narrative.

Much of what Liu said about the *Ch'un-ch'iu* and the *Tso chuan* was not controversial in the context of seventh- and early eighth-century opinion. Just as K'ung Yung-ta had done, he argued that the *Ch'un-ch'iu* was one annal among many extant when Confucius, adhering strictly to the Chou calendar and paying particular attention to ritual and music, had edited the text.[102] Confucius's main aim, also, had been to show how retribution followed evil action and goodness brought success. What made Liu's critique original was that he characterized as shortcomings precisely those features of the *Ch'un-ch'iu* that others had accepted as essential to its sanctity as a canon. To Liu, the fact that Confucius, with copious material available to him, had limited the coverage of the *Ch'un-ch'iu* to the state of Lu was a demerit.[103] The way in which, by distorting the account, Confucius had edited his own judgements into the text was also unsatisfactory.[104] Liu's main attack on the *Ch'un-ch'iu* analyzed these grounds for dissatisfaction in twelve instances. His critique as a whole, despite formal deference to the canon, includes references to the 'straight brush', the 'clear mirror', the 'faithful echo'; also to clarity of structure, and 'making the good and evil plain'. In this way Liu indicated his impatience with the way in which Confucius was held to have concealed his judgements in the canon, and his own preference for a dispassionate and objective narrative.

A recurrent feature of Liu's criticism of the *Ch'un-ch'iu* was his appeal, sometimes explicit, sometimes implied, to other historical texts of the Chou period. Of those none was more important to him than the *Tso chuan*, the text he had loved since early youth.[105] Liu believed that the *Tso* had been edited into its final form by Tso Ch'iu-ming, who, as an archivist in Lu, had a status, he seems to imply, close to that of Confucius himself. Tso Ch'iu-ming had had access to a wide range of documents, and to the disciples of Confucius from all the states, thus greatly increasing the range of his evidence. The result was that the *Tso* was much more comprehensive than its two rival traditions, the *Kung-yang* and the *Ku-liang*.[106] Liu defended the *Tso* against the charge that it continued material not directly relevant to the *Ch'un-ch'iu*, for, '...supposing people down the ages had when studying the *Ch'un-ch'iu* merely drawn from the other two traditions, then our knowledge of the events of [the] 240 years [spanned by the canon] would be vague and imperfect, so that subsequent scholars would be like the blind and the deaf... '[107]

Liu's trenchant advocacy of the *Tso* as superior to the *Kung-yang* and *Ku-liang* represents a polemical formulation of the conventional seventh-century position. But his implication that the *Tso* was in some respects better than the *Ch'un-ch'iu* itself, and his attack on Confucius as editor of the canon exceeded the bounds of acceptable criticism. Later in the dynasty, it provoked indignant attempts to restore to the *Ch'un-ch'iu* and to Confucius himself the authority and solemnity that Liu had impugned. These attempts were an aspect of the general trend, from the middle of the eighth century, towards developing the comprehensiveness and independence from the rival religious systems of Confucian ideas and attitudes. Liu's criticism of Confucius, far from being followed up, was to be emphatically rejected.

The *Shih t'ung* is the only extant work of the pre-rebellion century to embody important opinions on the *Ch'un-ch'iu*. But in the reign of Hsüan tsung, academic interest in the canon continued. Probably in the mid K'ai-yüan period, official scholars planned, but never completed, a continuation of the canon, to cover the period from the Warring States to the Sui, for which Hsüan tsung was to write the 'canon', or main text, while a small commission appointed to the Hung-wen kuan composed the 'tradition' on the model of the *Tso*.[108] Soon after 735, also, a standard set of pronunciations and character readings was compiled for the *Ch'un-ch'iu* in the Chi-hsien yüan, by an otherwise unknown scholar, Lü Cheng.[109]

By the second half of the reign, there were signs of a shift away from exclusive endorsement of the *Tso* that had been conventional in the seventh and early eighth centuries. One of Liu Chih-chi's sons, Liu K'uang, himself an official historian, may possibly have tried to downgrade its status; he held that the use of full canonization titles in the *Chi chung Chou shu* (*Chou book from the tomb in Chi*), a Chou dynasty chronicle discovered in A.D. 281, and in the *Tso*, indicated that they 'were retrospectively prepared by later scholars and were not contemporary "orthodox form" histories'.[110] The prolific official scholar of the late K'ai-yüan and T'ien-pao periods Lu Shan-ching compiled a work in 30 *chüan* on the *Ch'un-ch'iu* and all the *Three traditions*, suggesting that he saw value in each.[111] But a more significant instance is provided again by Hsiao Ying-shih, the unofficial teacher whose students left the state academy directorate to receive his instruction. A disciple later described how, in compiling a work of history of his own, he adopted an eclectic approach to what were considered the traditional shortcomings of each of the *Three traditions*.[112] Hsiao taught away from the capital, in Shantung and possibly at Tan-yang, near modern Nanking. A member of the post-rebellion *Ch'un-ch'iu* school, Chao K'uang, was said to have been one of his followers.[113] An eclectic attitude to all three of the *Traditions* was one of the main features of this school. Hsiao Ying-shih therefore provides an important link between early T'ang attitudes to the canon, dominated by the outlook of historians and by preference for the *Tso chuan*, and the school that was in the late eighth century to express some of the most striking textual and philosophical insights of the Confucian tradition in T'ang times.

Disillusion with the study of the canons as a means to advancement

For the majority of T'ang scholars and aspiring officials down to the K'ai-yüan period, the study of the Confucian canons was identified above all with entry into bureaucratic service. The few with specifically scholarly ambitions aspired to enter the official scholarly agencies over which the emperor presided, and in which spirited scholars like Liu Chih-chi, Yüan Hsing-ch'ung and others served. Towards the end of Hsüan tsung's reign, however, the same complex political and social forces that had resulted in the evolution of a 'Confucian opposition', began also to bring about different attitudes to the study of the canons. This development took place mainly among relatively low-ranking, often provincial officials, aspirants to office and temporary or permanent recluses. Their attitudes were not of course new; but scholars now reasserted them in a new context and with stronger emphasis. By the T'ien-pao period, the largely provincial society which such writers addressed had developed its own values and literary styles.

In this milieu there was never any question of surrendering the ideal of official service under an enlightened ruler. Rather verse writers like Kao Shih (704–65, canonized *Chung*) and others complained about the unjust hardship involved in protracted study of the Confucian canons, necessary before a candidate could consider competing in the regular examinations.[114] Tu Fu, likewise, contrasted the suffering that study involved with the idle and luxurious lives of the sons of the highly placed.[115] Other scholars, like Sun Ti and Yen Chen-ch'ing, praised those who sought for deeper meaning in the canons and were not satisfied simply by detailed commentaries.[116] Some writers contrasted the opportunism of successful officials at court with the poverty and integrity they found in students and aspiring scholars in the provinces. They condoned failure, whether it was long-term or relatively brief, in highly traditional terms, as the justified and dignified refusal to serve except in acceptable conditions.[117] When the court was dominated by 'close ministers' (*chin ch'en*) who were morally unsuitable, the true scholar was right to withdraw and cultivate his own person until times changed.[118]

In this milieu, there was great respect for the religious recluse, the figure who in the words of one writer had, 'traced back his footsteps, taken leave of humanity, shut the door and maintained his solitude'.[119] As in the seventh century, for the majority of scholars the rival teachings of Buddhism and Taoism gave answers to the questions of ultimate value that their lives as contemplatives might raise. Interest in the supra-mundane faiths, moreover, in this period when Hsüan tsung was deeply committed to Taoism, did not conflict with attitudes at the apex of the official hierarchy. Some scholars and verse writers, however, drew on the Confucian learned tradition to justify their failure to gain access to high office. Individuals sometimes located a

philosophy of self-cultivation in the Confucian canons, or described
their withdrawal in terms drawn from the introspective strand within
classical Confucianism.[120] More typically, for numerous verse writers
of this period, the Confucian symbols of their situation were the 'old
fisherman of Ts'ang-lang', a figure representing composure in
retirement,[121] or the stronger image of Po I and Shu Ch'i, two
exemplars of the Shang dynasty who had starved to death on mount
Shou-yang rather than compromise their integrity by taking office
under the Chou. Confucius had cited both these figures in his teaching.
Mencius had referred to Po I alone, but had made him stand
emphatically for the idea that service to an emperor was conditional on
the emperor's moral acceptability.[122] To many of the politically
unsuccessful scholars of the later part of Hsüan tsung's reign, these
images, drawn from the canons, dignified their exclusion from the
political centre. In the post-rebellion period, it was to be the successors
to these alienated writers, as well as official scholars in metropolitan
posts, who would take up the Confucian canons with motives quite
different from those of their seventh century forbears, and make
existential demands of these same texts.

The post-rebellion period

In the first half of the T'ang, the dynasty had made two main
demands of the canonical tradition: that it express a range of political
values in the interests of the dynasty; and that it satisfy the practical,
administrative needs of the examination system. In the post-rebellion
period, despite the deterioration in political conditions, both the
problem of the definitive text of the canons and the question of their
function in the examinations remained important to the scholar
community. Until well into the ninth century, officials submitted a
succession of reformist initiatives aimed at restoring the health of the
dynasty through education and learning in the Confucian canons. They
also made a series of attempts at determining and preserving in
permanent form the texts of the canons.

From the late eighth century on, however, the most significant
reformist ideas derived not from the academic agencies, but from
scholars who formulated them in a society very different from the
court-centred community of the seventh and early eighth centuries,
and sometimes in places remote from Ch'ang-an. Most of the individual scholars concerned had some experience of academic office,
either in their own careers or through colleagues. But scholarly tenures
now very seldom involved participation in academic commissions like

those characteristic of the pre-rebellion period. In turn, the reformist ideas of both official scholars and of their colleagues in general service posts or on the periphery of official society reflected the more devolved character of scholarly life.

Efforts to reform canonical learning in the examinations

The government's evacuation of Ch'ang-an in 756 meant that for a year the regular examinations were conducted on an improvised basis away from the capitals. The examinations returned to Ch'ang-an in 758, and from 765, in order to reduce the burden on the capital's resources, were also established as a concurrent operation at Lo-yang.[123] From 758 on, the *chin shih* and *ming ching* were held, with very few exceptions, every year until the end of the dynasty. They also retained their importance as the main official operation with which scholars associated canonical scholarship. Like the school system itself, therefore, they became the focus for a long succession of reformist initiatives.

From Tai tsung's accession and the court's return late in 763 from its flight to Shan-chou, successive proposals for the reform of the schools and the examinations contained complaints at the ineffective role of canonical learning in both the *ming ching* and the *chin shih*. Typically, however, such memorials referred to the established texts by title only. They condemned mere rote learning, but did not go into more specific detail. Moreover, just as the dynasty's response to the deterioration of the school system had been intermittently to implement reform suggestions, so the characteristic response of authority to the ineffectiveness of the examinations was to welcome and discuss reformist ideas, while making no permanently effective changes.

In 763–4, a number of officials submitted the education system as a whole to radically critical review. The vice-president of the board of rites, Yang Wan, asked for the abolition of the regular Taoist examinations introduced on Hsüan tsung's order from 741, and suggested that the *ming ching* and *chin shih* be replaced by tests involving one of nine established canons or the *Hsiao ching*, *Analects* and *Mencius* combined as a single canon.[124] A discussion followed. In this, Chia Chih denounced the standards by which candidates were selected. Contemporary examinees, he claimed, were ignorant of the basic concepts of moral self-analysis, including even the attainments for which Confucius had praised Yen Hui. As a result of this discussion, in 764, certain relatively unimportant categories of 'annual tribute' were stopped. But an edict announced that, 'the *chin shih* and *ming ching* have been long established. Now suddenly to alter their curricula (*yeh*) would, we fear, cause difficulties to those [involved]'.[125]

Another, later detailed set of detailed proposals, from Chao K'uang, the pre-rebellion pupil of Hsiao Ying-shih and member of the *Ch'un-ch'iu* school, represents a first point of contact between a reform group whose ideas were developed in the provinces and the central academic system. Chao K'uang demonstrates the interest in institutional reform that often accompanied specialization in the *Ch'un-ch'iu*. He condemned rote learning of canons as 'childish', and advocated a series of new examinations, including one that would have involved collating the differences between the *Three traditions* to the *Ch'un-ch'iu*, and one on pre-Ch'in philosophers, including Mencius.[126]

Under Te tsung, intermittent and largely ineffectual attempts at reforming the role of official canonical scholarship continued. The issues involved were widely discussed in the official community and by prospective officials. Just as the state academy directorate officials had done under Hsüan tsung, reformers criticized the bias among candidates in favour of shorter or easier canons. Their criticisms led to the devising of several alternatives to the *ming ching* degree, intended to provide incentives for those selecting less popular canons. In 793, the emperor gave formal endorsement to a special examination on the three ritual canons that had been established in 789, and one on the dynasty's ritual code, to counteract what was described as the deterioration in the ritual scholarship.[127]

Towards the end of Te tsung's reign, some three or four of the chief examiners were literary scholars with reformist sympathies. These scholars had social contact with some of those who, in unofficial circles, developed new approaches to the canons. One of the main trends was an increased interest in Confucian analysis of questions of ultimate value, in the 'relation of heaven and man' (*t'ien jen chih chi*), and in interior questions, or 'nature and destiny' (*hsing ming*). This interest was perhaps partly a response to the decline of the dynasty, and to the political pessimism and frustration of the second half of Te tsung's reign. In the late Chen-yüan period, it became something of a vogue, not just for the alienated periphery of official society, but also among those who attained high office. The survival of a fuller record of questions and answers in this period, too, makes it clear that some examiners brought these ideas into the questions they set. Ku Shao-lien,[128] Kao Ying (740–811, canonized *Chen*)[129] and Ch'üan Te-yu[130] all set topics that reflected renewed interest in the interior pole or questions relating to traditional Confucian understanding of psychology. In one of the very few *ming ching* dissertation questions that survived from the dynasty, set on the *Li chi* in 805, Ch'üan Te-yü even foreshadowed the later Neo-Confucian grouping of the *Four books*, when he asked about the attitude to self-cultivation of the *Ta hsüeh* and the *Chung yung*.[131]

From the start of the ninth century on, there were further intermittent attempts at improving the standard of canonical learning required in the examinations. The reformist submissions these involved typically cited the canons by name only and complained of the poor state of candidates' knowledge of them.[132] Rote knowledge of commentaries, in particular, continued to be frequently condemned, often in tandem with criticism of the use of literary composition as a means of testing candidates (Ch. 6, pp. 241–44). In 823, an examination of the *Ch'un-ch'iu* and all of the *Three traditions* was proposed, to redress the unpopularity of these texts among candidates.[133] The establishment of this examination suggests that the eclectic approach that Chao K'uang and other members of the south-eastern *Ch'un-ch'iu* school had developed, and which was already reflected in examination questions in the late eighth and early ninth centuries,[134] was now officially accepted.

Later in the century, there were more attempts to reform the *ming ching* and *chin shih*, and these occasionally mentioned the place of canonical learning. The most radical proposal, operative for just one year after 833, involved abolishing *shih* and *fu* in its *tsa wen* section (Ch. 6, p. 244).[135] But the regular examinations ran on, much as before, until the very end of the dynasty; and it must be assumed that in the second half of the ninth century, in this area as in education more generally, the dynasty was no longer able to respond effectively to reformist suggestions.

The problem of the definitive text

Successive attempts to require more meaningful knowledge of the Confucian canons in the examination system concentrated on adjusting curricula or on promoting less literary and more practical demands of the learning the canons contained. But the need, at an administrative level, to provide candidates with a definitive version of the text of the canons remained central, and continued to cause difficulties. The dynasty also recognized a related ideal, that the imperial library should house the definitive version of the canons. In contrast to so many of the problems that confronted T'ang official scholars, this found its enduring solution late in the post-rebellion period.

Long before the T'ang, first in the Later Han and then under the San Kuo Wei, the text of the canons had been engraved in stone and

displayed in the precincts of the T'ai hsüeh.[136] The T'ang learned
world considered that these early engravings constituted a precedent,
and that their own dynasty should not only care for what remained of
them, but also, in due time, erect their own monumental stone
engravings of the texts of the canons. Under the Sui, in 586, the
authorities had tried to bring the remains of the early engravings from
Lo-yang to the capital. When T'ang scholars turned their attention to
them, they expressed abhorrence because, in the disorders at the end
of the Sui, parts of the engravings had been purloined for use as pillar
bases.[137] T'ai tsung's great scholar minister Wei Cheng, as director of
the imperial library, had collected what he could of the engraved
stones. Rubbings taken from them were preserved in the imperial
library. The dynasty also showed its reverence for the ideal of a stone
engraving by including the Han engraving in the curriculum of the
orthography school in the state academy directorate. The surviving
stone fragments were considered to contain the authentic forms of
characters for which variants had come to circulate.[138]

Early in the dynasty, T'ai tsung had attempted to solve the problem
of a definitive version of the canons by commissioning Yen Shih-ku,
whose 'established texts' had been completed in 633.[139] Despite Yen's
separate list of orthodox-form characters, which circulated widely, this
by no means ended the difficulties. Towards the end of the seventh
century, there was a new attempt to produce an authoritative text of
the canons, with the classical histories, the *Shih chi* and the *Han shu*
included. In 696, a commission of scholars, including the long-serving
official historian Wu Ching (*c.* 670–749), was convened in the imperial
library. No result, however, is recorded.[140] Then again, when Hsüan
tsung was crown prince, Chang Yüeh had submitted a proposal to him
asking that the text of the 'nine canons and three histories' be
re-determined; but again there was no public outcome.[141]

In the K'ai-yüan and T'ien-pao periods, the questions again came to
the fore. One official, an assistant instructor at the Kuo-tzu hsüeh and
finally a vice-president of the directorate, 'regretted that the errors in
the texts of the canons were so numerous and that successive generations had perpetuated them for so long'. He had been on the point of
determining the text of the *Three histories* and the *Five canons*, 'to
have them displayed at the gate of the school', when the death of his
father intervened and forced him to leave office.[142] Phonological
glossaries compiled in the Chi-hsien yüan in the late K'ai-yüan period
for the *Mao shih*, *Ch'un-ch'iu* and Taoist canon *Chuang tzu* may have
been the result of the demand for definitive readings of these texts.[143]

In the T'ien-pao period, the writer of an important collection of reminiscences, Feng Yen, himself a directorate student, raised the issue of a T'ang engraving of the canons with the directorate's erudits and students, again without success.[144] In the event, under Hsüan tsung, only the text of the *Hsiao ching* was given a stone engraving, as a part of Hsüan tsung's promotion of this concise summary of Confucian ethical norms.

After the rebellion, both the need for a definitive version and the ideal of a monumental engraving to reflect the greatness of the dynasty became more acute. The famous seal script calligrapher Li Yang-ping (fl. *c.* 765–80) described how he yearned 'to engrave stone in the seal script, to write out in full the *Six canons* and erect them in the Ming-t'ang, as an inerasable authority, to call them the T'ang canons in stone, so that a hundred ages hence no adjustments [in their texts] need be made'.[145]

At about this time, the text of the *Ch'un-ch'iu*, with exegesis by the military governor of Huai-nan, Han Huang, was engraved in stone and erected, probably at the Confucian temple at Jun-chou, modern Nanking. For reasons that are not clear, Han Huang's *Ch'un-ch'iu* scholarship was ridiculed in the T'ang. But for the far south-east to have anticipated the capital, even on the small scale that this short canon involved, was an indication of the favourable conditions that obtained there.[146] Han Huang was the political enemy of Chang Shen, a senior scholar at the Ch'ang-an state academy directorate. Perhaps because of this, his initiative in using stone at this time had no recorded parallel in the metropolis.

It was Chang Shen, this same enemy of Han Huang, who in 776 led a small commission of scholars charged with producing definitive texts of the *Five canons*. On this occasion, the texts were written on wooden panels and set in the walls of the corridors of the east and west sides of the Kuo-tzu hsüeh. Chang Shen and another scholar also compiled a supplement giving the correct orthography for disputed characters. This supplement, displayed separately as the *Wu ching wen tzu* (*Model characters of the Five canons*), was later engraved in stone and has been transmitted to modern times.[147]

Ten years later, in 786, another initiative, based on the imperial library and intended to produce a definitive text of the long series of nine canons was taken. But the director of the imperial library, Liu T'ai-chen (725–92), a former pupil of Hsiao Ying-shih, was unsuccessful in his request for a special commission to undertake the project.[148] Only a few years after this, Han Hui, a brother of Han Huang, as director of the imperial library, made yet another attempt to re-determine the canonical texts.[149] Under Hsien tsung, further efforts were made to arrive at definitive versions, and in the state academy directorate supplements giving correct orthography were produced, at least for the *Li chi* and the *Ch'un-ch'iu*.[150] In the course of the reign, the Confucian reformer Cheng Yü-ch'ing drew attention to the deteriorating condition of the version displayed in the directorate. Over this period, the texts were probably replaced or restored for display there.[151]

It was not until the reign of the scholarly emperor Wen tsung, between 829 and 831, however, that proposals resulted in the complete renovation of these texts in wood.[152] But the interest of the emperor and of Cheng T'an, his Confucian minister, went further than this. For it was in this period of relative weakness in T'ang power that the dynasty's ambition to complete a monumental stone engraving was finally achieved. Cheng T'an asked that 'the precedent of the Han be followed, and that stone be incised in the T'ai hsüeh, to display a model for ten thousand ages'. In 837, this stone engraving, of the long series of *Nine canons*, was completed and set up in the state academy directorate. The *K'ai-ch'eng shih ching* (*K'ai-ch'eng canons in stone*), as the engraving is known, are among the grandest examples of the highly developed art of stone engraving to have survived from the dynasty. But in some respects they caused disappointment. At the textual level, the drafting commission reverted to the choices made by K'ung Ying-ta at the start of the dynasty. The versions they chose were precisely those that, two centuries before, K'ung Ying-ta's sub-commentary commission and their contemporary sub-commentators Chia Kung-yen and Yang Shih-hsün had endorsed. The only exceptions were the *Hsiao ching*, for which the text that Hsüan tsung had used for his commentary was used, and the *Yüeh ling* for which the text that Li Lin-fu's commentary had glossed was adopted. Although in the stone engraving the names of these established commentaries were repeated at the head of each *chüan*, neither commentaries nor any other exegesis were included. Whether for this or for other reasons, the engraving was controversial, though few details of the ensuing debates survive. Yet this monumental achievement, as Wen tsung surely intended, preserved and displayed the texts of the canons for the state, until from the tenth century the widespread use of printing put the problems of circulation and transmission on a completely different footing.[153]

Post-rebellion Ch'un-ch'iu *scholarship*

These intermittent attempts at reform and renovation, however, took place in a scholarly climate very different from that of the early eighth century. Post-rebellion re-interpretation of the canons was distinguished by the fact that almost all of it was unofficial, by its dismissal of the compendious, commentarial approach to the text of the canons that had been officially in favour early in the dynasty, and by the keenness of the critical ideas that were now read out from the ancient Confucian texts. Post-rebellion *Ch'un-ch'iu* scholarship, particularly, contrasts with the official outlook of the early T'ang on the *Ch'un-ch'iu* and the *Three traditions*. In the central political arena, the *Ch'un-ch'iu* remained a sanction for the typical concerns of the T'ang scholar elite, for issues of ritual management, for a range of practical policy questions, and for principles of political morality. Emperors, ministers and officials continued to cite it with great frequency.[154] But the major intellectual movement associated with this text was promoted by academic officials at Ch'ang-an only at the start of the ninth century, in the middle of the three phases of its history. Its members, moreover, went far beyond the disdain for the commentarial and sub-commentarial approach to the canons that had become common in the eighth century. They saw the *Ch'un-ch'iu* not simply as an authority that would bring peace and stability to the world, but, in their metaphor, as a medicine that might effect an immediate cure on the body politic. They dismissed the official exegesis of the early T'ang, and rejected the traditional T'ang preference for the *Tso chuan*. They attempted to restore to Confucius the central authority that Liu Chih-chi's attacks on the *Ch'un-ch'iu* had threatened to take from him. The *Ch'un-ch'iu* had always provided T'ang scholars with justification for the principles of government they advocated; but members of the post-rebellion school used the text to a new extent, to sanction a range of reformist ideas.[155]

For thirty years after the An Lu-shan rebellion, the far south-east, preserved from the worst effects of militarism, provided the locale for the *Ch'un-ch'iu* school. Three scholars, Tan Chu (d. 770), Chao K'uang (fl. *c.* 770) and Lu Ch'un (d. 805), all of whom served or retired in this region, followed one another as the main figures of the school.[156] Tan Chu, originally a northerner who withdrew to Tan-yang near modern Nanking, compiled two works on the canon.[157] In these, he emphatically reasserted the belief that Confucius had edited the *Ch'un-ch'iu* with a far-reaching view of history and profound moral purpose. To

Tan Chu, the canon could 'remedy the decline of our age and reform the deterioration in ritual'.[158] Discarding early T'ang official reverence for primary commentaries and sub-commentaries, he charged that too much attention had been paid to the *Three traditions*. Though its detail was useful, the *Tso* particularly had been over-rated, and had been understood as a literary and historical rather than a canonical text. Scholars of the *Ch'un-ch'iu* should, in the *Analects* phrase, 'have no constant teacher' from among the *Three traditions*. Still less should they adhere to later exegesis.[159]

The second member of the school, Chao K'uang, served as a staff officer in the south-east and met Tan Chu in 770, to be influenced by his ideas, probably through Tan's son. Chao K'uang believed that Confucius, in editing the canon, had promoted 'constant laws', especially those to do with 'ceremonial offerings, court visits, hunts and marriages', and that these were true for all time.[160] He also held, adopting a theme from early *Kung-yang* exegesis, that Confucius in the *Ch'un-ch'iu* had illustrated issues of conduct for which unchanging norms did not apply, and for which understanding of 'expedient action' (*ch'üan*) was necessary. This was a doctrine that Confucius had described in the *Analects* as particularly difficult.[161] Expediency, however, like belief that institutions were always in a state of evolution, justified political toughness and interventionism. The reaffirmation of this idea may well be connected with the activist attitudes of some of the reformist scholars of Te tsung's reign, including even Tu Yu, with whom the *Ch'un-ch'iu* scholars were probably connected. Chao's insistence that certain rituals were specific to the son of heaven may be related to the reformers' emphasis on centralized authority, and to their insistence that 'power should come from one outlet'.[162] His belief also in the inevitability of institutional decline, justifying radical reform,[163] and his downplaying of the place of omens in the *Ch'un-ch'iu*[164] also coincided with the outlook of Tu Yu and the reformers.

Chao K'uang continued Tan Chu's efforts to demote the *Tso chuan*. He attacked as spurious the version of its transmission given by the Sui-T'ang exegete Lu Te-ming.[165] In his boldest textual conclusion, he criticized Tan Chu for 'following the old theory' and identifying Tso Ch'iu-ming as its author. The *Tso* was a superficial and inaccurate work, and Confucius in the *Analects* had reserved praise only for those who had lived before him in time. The Tso Ch'iu-ming of the *Analects* must therefore have been a different, much earlier figure than the man who had given his name to the *Tso chuan*.[166] Chao also argued that the

Tso chuan and *Kuo yü*, both traditionally and officially ascribed to Tso Ch'iu-ming, were actually by different hands.[167]

Lu Ch'un, the third member of the school, like other scholars with reformist sympathies, came north to the capital, probably late in Tai tsung's reign.[168] After in 781 Yang Yen fell from power, he was banished to the south-east, making the journey there with the official historian Shen Chi-chi, a friend of Tu Yu. But he soon returned to the capital, to hold a variety of metropolitan scholarly posts, and to take part in some of the state ritual controversies of the Chen-yüan period (Ch. 4, p. 153). Under Shun tsung, he was an elder scholar who combined commitment to reform with interest in the *Ch'un-ch'iu*.[169] A number of younger scholars, Han T'ai, Han Yeh, Ling Chun, Lü Wen and P'ei Chin were in the group of which he was now the senior figure. But the most important younger member was Liu Tsung-yüan, who took up with the school probably in 803.[170]

Despite the fact that some of these scholars held academic office, the canonical scholarship of the school in this its metropolitan phase remained unofficial. In contrast to the debates in which Liu Chih-chi and other K'ai-yüan scholars had taken part eight decades previously, the discussions of the school were not conducted at the emperor's request or in an official institutional framework. But at some point towards the end of Te tsung's reign, when Lu Ch'un had been demoted to be an erudit of the Kuo-tzu hsüeh, they presented his compilation of the school's scholarship to the throne, with a memorial describing its merits.[171] This point of contact between their unofficial scholarship and high authority, however, only underlines the differences between imperial direction of the learned world in the K'ai-yüan period and the early ninth century. Lü Wen, the author of the memorial of presentation, did not ask that the works of the group be established and taught in the schools; no discussion is recorded, and there is no record that the compilation was taken into the imperial library.

At about this time, the dramatic political events of Shun tsung's reign intervened. For six months in 805, members of the movement briefly enjoyed access to political power. But there is little indication, in the records for 805, that its tenets were prominent in the programme that the reformers implemented. By the ninth month of 805, the reform movement had been broken up. Its senior members or sympathizers, like Tu Yu and even Lu Ch'un, avoided recrimination; but many of its junior followers were exiled, among them the *Ch'un-ch'iu* scholars Han Yeh, Han T'ai and Liu Tsung-yüan.

The sequel to these reverses was that after 805 the *Ch'un-ch'iu* scholarship of the school was pursued among the exile group and their contacts, by letter and in the provinces. In the present picture too, it is Liu Tsung-yüan who was at the centre of this phase of the movement. Liu's response to the three earlier leaders of the movement, Tan Chu, Chao K'uang and Lu Ch'un, even in his exile, was one of excitement and almost unqualified approval.[172] Nearly a milennium and a half, he believed, had passed since Confucius had edited the canon, and 'hundreds and thousands' of scholars had wrangled over its meaning in essays, commentaries, sub-commentaries and treatises. But these three scholars had now at last realized its true meaning, so that 'common men and small children could understand it'.[173]

Liu Tsung-yüan traditionally has a position as one of the leading agnostic intellectuals of the T'ang. But in his response to the new *Ch'un-ch'iu* scholarship, he perpetuated precisely the school's paradoxical and basically conservative orientation. On the one hand, he adopted its critical approach, combining it with his own agnosticism in brief reviews of a number of early texts. On the other hand he held, no less than Tan, Chao and Lu had done, to the profundity and sanctity of the *Ch'un-ch'iu*. For all the critical boldness he showed, particularly in his extended analysis of the *Kuo yü*,[174] he held back from a systematic application of his ideas to canonical literature itself. Elsewhere in his writing too, Liu expressed an attitude of profound respect for Confucius and for the integrity of the teaching contained in those texts, the *Ch'un-ch'iu*[175] and *Analects*,[176] closely associated with him. Despite his reputation therefore, he was less direct as a critic than Liu Chih-chi, whose trenchantly expressed ideas of nearly a century before had been such a catalyst to the *Ch'un-ch'iu* school.

Liu Tsung-yüan, who died in the far south in 819, did not transmit the teaching of the *Ch'un-ch'iu* school to disciples of any importance.[177] But other adherents of the school, including one or two in academic office, continued the tradition.[178] Its eclectic approach now found general acceptance, to be endorsed by scholars such as the historian Liu K'o (d. *c.* 839),[179] by the monitory official Yin Yu, who in 823 successfully proposed the examination in the *Ch'un-ch'iu* and all the *Three traditions*,[180] and by the rescript writer Wei Piao-wei (*c.* 770–*c.* 829),[181] the decree examination candidate Liu Fen (fl. 828)[182] and others. Even late in the dynasty, scholars such as Ch'en Yüeh,[183] Ssu-k'ung T'u (837–908)[184] and Lu Kuei-meng (d. *c.* 881)[185] were in the same eclectic tradition. Yet another late T'ang scholar, P'i Jih-hsiu, a friend of Lu Kuei-meng and an ardent promoter of both Mencius and

Han Yü, was important in *Ch'un-ch'iu* scholarship in a different way: he compiled a short collection of comments on the text that constitutes nothing less than a point by point refutation of the attack that Liu Chih-chi had made one hundred and fifty years before.[186] It is no longer possible to relate the *Ch'un-ch'iu* scholarship of these late T'ang scholars to the political climate of their time. But they clearly promoted some of the same concerns that the post-rebellion school had formulated, an eclectic approach to the *Three traditions*, and a careful endorsement of the authority and sanctity of the canon and of Confucius as its editor.

The hsing ming *scholars*

The change that took place in the intellectual milieu of post-rebellion T'ang China is particularly well demonstrated by the successive stages in the evolution of Confucian interest in interior or psychological questions. Like the renewed interest in the *Ch'un-ch'iu*, this development again took place largely in unofficial society; but almost all its leading proponents were examination graduates, and most held academic office at some point in their careers.

The exponents of this *hsing ming* emphasis in its second, late eighth-century, stage held a number of attitudes in common with the *Ch'un-ch'iu* school. Like the *Ch'un-ch'iu* scholars, they dismissed inherited exegesis and were impatient of mechanical commentarial approaches to the canons. Like them too, they focussed on a small number of canonical texts. Their underlying motive was also to restore the authority of the Confucian tradition, in this case in the face of Buddhist and Taoist intrusion. Their greatest contribution was their attempt to redefine answers to questions of ultimate value in exclusively Confucian terms. They brought an area of experience that scholars had hitherto considered largely a private matter briefly into the centre of the scholarly arena, and gave it new priority for the political and social world of their time. Despite the fact that they were, like most T'ang officials, ambitious for high office, they took their ideas to some extent out of the state-centred, official context that had shaped so much of the early T'ang outlook on the canons, and made them universal statements about man. At the level of the individual text, they contributed substantially to the long process the end result of which was that the Confucian canon was reorganized, and the *Four books* and their authors were given the official recognition that in their own day were given to the series of *Nine canons*.

The early post-rebellion stage of this renewed interest among official scholars in the interior emphasis is not, however, as clearly documented as the corresponding stage in the *Ch'un-ch'iu* school. The background to the movement was the interest in seclusion, religious contemplation and the 'relationship between heaven and man' that had developed unofficially in the scholarly community before the rebellion. But again there was no sense in which this interest was restricted to those out of office or in low-level posts. Officials of any rank, whether in metropolitan or provincial posts, might pursue it, just as others, by involving traditional Confucian caution towards the supra-mundane, decline to do so.

Interest in contemplation or self-cultivation therefore is likely to have been common at most levels of educated society in the post-rebellion period. Even the emperor Tai tsung was said to have been concerned to 'effect the complete development of his nature'.[187] Such high ranking post-rebellion scholars as the official historian, reformer of the examination system and grand secretary Yang Wan and the vice-president of the state academy directorate Chang Shen showed a suggestive commitment to contemplative goals, or 'the complete development of their natures'. But again the private, unofficial character of their interest is indicated by the fact that it is recorded only incidentally, in a commemorative biography for a third official, Tu Ya (725–98, canonized *Su*).[188] Another senior official who may have had an interest in interior questions was Ts'ui Yu-fu, briefly a chief minister under Te tsung; the preface to his collected works, by Ch'üan Te-yü, describes him as having realized 'the sincerity and enlightenment of the *Chung yung*'.[189]

The south-eastern community of serving officials and refugee scholars, who provided the background for the first phase of the *Ch'un-ch'iu* school was also important in the development of the *hsing ming* emphasis. Chang I (d. 783),[190] Li Hua (*c.* 710–*c.* 767)[191] and Tu-ku Chi,[192] all of whom held academic office at some point in their careers, for example, all served in the far south-east, and each demonstrated an interest in interior questions. Some of these scholars also showed interest in the *Mencius*, much as Yang Wan had done. There is no suggestion, however, that their approach was exclusively Confucian; rather they were committed to Buddhism or Taoism, and analysed their experience mainly in Buddhist or Taoist terms.

In the Te tsung's reign, interest in the analysis of religious contemplation continued to be fashionable. Religious eclecticism and a sustained debt to the south-east is typified by two later figures who came north to serve in the ritual and scholarly agencies at Ch'ang-an. Both were important because they demonstrate the combination of personal political influence and private commitment to religious ideals that marked the first phase of the *hsing ming* movement. Liang Su (753–93), the first of these two, was from 770 until Tu-ku's death in 777, a follower of Tu-Ku Chi in the far south-east. Later, he was appointed a historian and Han-lin rescript writer, and was politically influential when in 792 Lu Hsüan kung directed the examinations. His interest in self-cultivation led him to write on meditation, from a lay Buddhist perspective.[193] He resisted appointment to Tu Yu's staff in the south-east, and condemned interventionist political figures in history like Kuan Chung (6th century B.C.) and Chu-ko Liang (A.D. 181–234), 'who concentrated on saving the ages [in which they lived] and called themselves beams and ridge-poles of the state'.[194] Liang Su played an important role in the examination career of Han Yü, and Li Ao also acknowledged him.[195]

Ch'üan Te-yü, the second of these figures, is especially important because of the great range of his connections in the scholar community. He maintained a friendship with Tu Yu until well into Hsien tsung's reign, when they were both elderly. He also knew the young reformer Liu Yü-hsi and had contact with Liu Tsung-yüan. His wide social circle suggests that neither interest in the *hsing ming* emphasis, nor indeed commitment to the sort of reform programme some of the *Ch'un-ch'iu* scholars supported, was an exclusively held position or a barrier to the kind of social activities that the T'ang scholar community valued.

Ch'üan Te-yü knew Liang Su and perhaps also the young Han Yü in the south-east,[196] and like Liang preferred capital tenures to service there. He held academic office, as an erudit of the court of sacrifices before 780, rescript writer for an exceptionally long period of nine years (Ch. 6, pp. 239–40), and a chief examiner in the period 802–5.[197] In his leisure, Ch'üan engaged in meditation in a Taoist monastic setting. In his account of this experience, he suggested that the Confucian ideal of 'sincerity and enlightenment' (*ch'eng ming*), which derived from the *Chung yung*, was the analogue to both Buddhist and Taoist meditation ideals.[198] He also used the term 'restoring the nature' (*fu hsing*), of the contemplative process as early as 787, over a decade before Li Ao wrote his treatise on this topic and gave the term detailed analysis.[199]

A final figure in this first phase of the movement, again important as a political sponsor, was Lu San, also a south-easterner. Liang Su knew him,[200] and Ch'üan Te-yü, who associated with him in the south-east,[201] recommended in 780 that he take his own metropolitan post as erudit of the court of sacrifices.[202] Lu San played a role in the early careers of the principal figures of the second stage of the *hsing ming* movement, Han Yü and Li Ao. Li Ao visited him in the south-east, and expounded his theory of the nature (*hsing*) to him. Lu San, Li Ao recorded, praised his insight in hyperbolic terms. In 802, Lu San assisted Ch'üan Te-yü, who was then chief examiner, and passed on to him the recommendations of Han Yü.[203]

When in 802 Lu San died, Ch'üan Te-yü wrote his epitaph,[204] and Li Ao composed a tribute in which he likened Lu to Yen Hui, Tzu-hsia and Mencius, all as much exemplars for the *hsing ming* scholars as Kuan Chung and Chu-ko Liang were to the political activists.[205] But although Li Ao described Lu San as 'effecting the complete development of his nature',[206] there is little detailed indication of his position over the Confucian doctrinal problems that were now to become so important.

The next phase of the *hsing ming* movement is marked by the survival of much more documentation, and by a sharp change in its orientation. Its outlook had been eclectic, accommodative and quietist. It had been an uncontroversial exploration of an area of human experience that did not conflict with, but rather complemented, the official career and the political arena, an indication of a scholar's seriousness as a human being but not much more. Now, however, it became more actively reformist, exclusively Confucian and strongly anti-Buddhist and anti-Taoist. This change not only caused dissension among its adherents; in a period when the emperor and the official community generally accepted eclectic attitudes to the three teachings,[207] it also cost the movement the respectability it had previously enjoyed. Its more political demands were now promoted by a small group of scholars. These men tended to be either in low-rank academic or general service posts, or else on the periphery of official life. Their strong commitment to anti-Buddhism marked them as a minority, distinct from their contemporaries in the scholar community.

The most important figures in this second phase of the movement, Han Yü and Li Ao, were, however, temperamentally very different. Though it can by no means have seemed to be the case at the time, the differences of position that developed between them on Confucian doctrinal questions were to have major historical importance. The issues were analyzed at an unofficial level; highly polished though their writings were, there is no indication that either intended them for high authority. Where for Li Ao the political aspect of their anti-Buddhism did not adversely affect his career, Han Yü at certain points in his career took major political risks in promoting his anti-Buddhist beliefs, even endangering his life for their sake.

Han Yü and Li Ao had probably formulated their different notions of an exclusively Confucian doctrine of the nature before 801.[208] Li Ao's long three-part essay 'On restoring the nature' (*Fu hsing shu*) shows a familiarity with psychological analysis and quietist ideas derived from the supra-mundane faiths. Three features of the position he described in it proved unacceptable to Han Yü: first his universalism, his belief that man's moral endowment did not vary with the individual;[209] secondly his apparently negative view of a central psychological component, the feelings, which he believed clouded or obscured the nature. Finally, Li posited a process of introspection or of 'effecting the complete development of the nature' that involved refining away the feelings through contemplation, and that led to the state of 'sincerity and enlightenment' (*ch'eng ming*) of which the *Chung yung* had spoken. This was in some respects a goal comparable to that of enlightenment in Buddhism. But Li formulated it in terms drawn from the Confucian canons, and saw the favourite disciple of Confucius, Yen Hui, as its main exemplar.[210]

Han Yü, who had been Li Ao's mentor in literary composition,[211] wrote a series of briefer and less profound statements on the same general subject. Showing much less concern for the existential values that Li Ao discussed, he adopted a position sanctioned by the *Analects* and by the pre-Buddhist Confucian tradition. Man was endowed at birth with nature and with feelings in one of three grades. Though those in the middle category might move in either direction, the upper and lower categories were not capable of change.[212] In contrast to Li Ao, therefore, Han Yü prescribed no process of self-cultivation by contemplation or of the refining away of the feelings. His perspective on the doctrinal questions Li Ao's analysis raised was rather that of a social reformer, albeit one who took his stand outside the official institutions in which he served. He believed in the interior value of sincerity (*ch'eng*); but the concept of quietness (*ching*), which had strong Buddhist and Taoist overtones, and which was important to Li Ao, did not apparently figure in his analysis.

The contrast in attitudes of Han Yü and Li Ao is highlighted by the different attitudes to the texts that, in the long term, they both did so much to promote. Both indicated their ultimate commitment to Confucian political and social ideals by citing the famous eightfold progression from the *Ta hsüeh*, from the well-ordered state to the cultivation of the individual self. For Li Ao, the starting point, the first of the eight steps, was the sentence, so celebrated in later, Neo-Confucian debate, 'the extension of knowledge lies in letting things come'. This he saw as applying to the state of liberated quiescence, of 'sincerity and enlightenment' in the *Chung yung* phase that he used, in which the feelings were refined away. Han Yü, using the same passage, stipulated, not a state of quiescence, but a simple process of self-correcting: 'What the ancients meant by rectifying the mind and making sincere the purpose was done by taking action'.[213]

Towards Mencius, however, their attitudes, while coinciding in some respects, contrasted even more in others. Li Ao's endorsement of Mencius was particularly significant at the doctrinal level. He adopted both the Mencian idea that the nature was good, and also Mencian universalism, that is the idea, voiced by Yen Hui in the *Mencius*, that any man might become a sage like the emperor Shun.[214] Han Yü's perspective on Mencius, on the other hand, was ambivalent and even inconsistent. He agreed with Li Ao in seeing Mencius as a transmitter of Confucius's own teaching, through Tseng Shen and Tzu-ssu, and he commended Mencius as 'the purest of the pure'.[215] He also made use of the Mencian idea that any man might, like Shun, become a sage. But he did so in the context of a tilt at what he saw as the prevalent custom of denigrating goodness in others, rather than in the context of a reformulation of contemplative values. He asked simply that men should improve themselves, and 'by thinking day and night, do away with those points at which they did not resemble Shun'. At the doctrinal level, however, he rejected the *Mencius* as an authority, saying that Mencius, in characterizing the nature as wholly good 'had found [one of the three categories] but missed the [other] two'. In his emphasis on 'wide love' (*po ai*), Han, ironically, showed more affinity for the ideas of Mo tzu, whom Mencius was generally praised for having attacked and refuted.[216]

It was a further irony therefore that Han Yü, Li Ao and others should have united in making Mencius a symbol for the anti-Buddhism of their movement. The view of Mencius here was, however, straightforward, unanalytical and commonplace. Mencius had promoted the teachings of Confucius, and resisted the heterodoxies of his own time, the philosophies of Yang Chu and Mo Ti.[217] His achievement 'was not less than that of [the sage emperor] Yü'.[218] But Han Yü's circle of followers took this conventional and widespread view of Mencius much further. Already in 795, Han Yü's follower Chang Chi (*c.* 765–*c.* 830) associated Han with the figure of Mencius. In the late Chen-yüan period, Li Ao and Lu San made the identification more directly. As much as a quarter of a century later, in a sacrificial graveside prayer for Han, Li Ao repeated the idea that Han was the Mencius of their time.[219]

Han Yü, Li Ao and others did not, however, continue to debate Confucian doctrinal ideas on interior questions with their initial intensity for so long a period. Rather it was anti-Buddhism at a more practical and political level that marked the movement in the Yüan-ho period and that continued to give life to the Mencian parallel. In this phase of the movement, it was the combative Han Yü,[220] rather than Li Ao, who took the bolder political action. In 819, particularly, he risked his life by submitting a memorial expressing sardonic contempt for the Buddhist religion and its attendant extravagances. Though this memorial did not present a profound or original case, it angered the emperor. While the Buddhist community 'set up a delighted clamour and tapping', Han Yü, saved from capital punishment only by the intercession of friends, was banished eight thousand *li*, to Ch'ao-chou in modern Fukien.[221]

After this, the Confucian inspired intellectual anti-Buddhism of the second stage of the *hsing ming* movement apparently very rarely resulted in political action. Only a small number of Han Yü's followers, themselves obscurely placed enough for their attitudes to be of little political consequence, remained actively anti-Buddhist. When, three decades later, harsh measures were taken against the Buddhist church, the pressure came from a much higher level in the official hierarchy, and was justified mainly in Taoist rather than in Confucian terms.[222] For the rest of the dynasty, Han Yü's influence proved greater in literary style than in doctrine,[223] and there was only fitful analysis by academic officials of the problem of the moral identity of the nature that he and Li Ao had raised.[224]

The increased level of interest in the *Mencius* was, however, sustained. Han Yü continued to be linked with Mencius, for example by Tu Mu, Sun Ch'iao and another admirer, Lin Chien-yen.[225] The late ninth-century scholar P'i Jih-hsiu combined respect for Mencius and Yen Hui, whom he saw as exemplars of self-cultivation, with fervent admiration for Han Yü.[226] P'i's friend Lu Kuei-meng also promoted Mencius, having studied the text, with the writings of Yang Hsiung and the canons, since boyhood.[227] At the very close of the dynasty, too, a certain Sun Ho, a *chin shih* of 897, 'loved the writings of Hsün tzu, Yang [Chu] and Mencius, and imitated Han [Yü] in his compositions'. He even styled himself Hsi-Han, to emphasize his dedication.[228]

These late T'ang acts of homage to Han Yü, however, were again socially and politically inconsequential. Han's attempt to restore the dynasty and to regenerate society by promoting a renewed Confucianism, purged of Buddhist and Taoist intrusion, had failed, like the comparable efforts of the *Ch'un-ch'iu* scholars to cure the illness of the state. Han's ideas had to wait for the re-assertion of strong dynastic power, under the Sung, to achieve official recognition.

4

STATE RITUAL

Confucian scholars of the T'ang period saw state ritual as one of the most important aspects of their learned tradition. A substantial proportion of what has survived of their writings, their official compilations, unofficial compendia and individual literary collections, concerned the dynasty's programme of ritual observances. This, consisting of about one hundred and fifty ceremonies, almost all of which were traced back to origins in the Confucian canons, was embodied in successive ritual codes commissioned by the emperor and compiled by scholars. Codification was itself the end result of a continuous process of scholarly controversy and drafting. The importance and prestige of this activity to the dynasty and to the scholar community was enormous. The distinctive character of the medieval Confucian outlook stemmed largely from it.[1]

State ritual scholarship derived much of its great prestige from the fact that it was closely associated with the imperial institution, and so with the source of political power. In the period of T'ang prosperity, it provided at the ideological, material and even logistical levels an immediately recognized and highly respected index of dynastic achievement. The great imperial rituals, for the many civil and military officials taking part, were at the same time solemn affirmations of the role of the dynastic house before heaven, and grandiose parades for a bureaucracy that commanded unchallenged prestige.

The observances that made up the dynasty's ritual programme were not all of equal standing. Those that concerned 'heaven' (*t'ien*) and the other unseen powers, in harmony with which the emperor ruled the world, formed a category of special importance. It was, however, an essential feature of the medieval state ritual tradition that these divinities were not transcendental, in the sense of existing in an altogether remote and separate realm. Nor did honouring them involve a radically world denying course. These deities functioned in and affected the real world, to the good government of which the emperor and his officials were committed. Their co-operation was essential to harmony in nature and in human society. The proper organization and scheduling of their rituals was, therefore, the function not of a priesthood or any group set apart, but of the court of sacrifices and the board of rites. Both these bodies were departments within the general administrative structure, and were staffed by officials drawn from the general service. 'Ritual officials' were drawn for the same community that supplied the other academic agencies. Ritual posts were subject to the same rules as other scholarly positions, as far as length of tenure, income and promotion were concerned. Problems concerning the rites were not considered radically different from other administrative issues. Many important ritual questions were debated by the central ministeries and academic agencies. Some, after discussion by a wide range of officials, were decided by the chief ministers, the highest executives in the administrative hierarchy.

The scholarly tradition that was brought to bear on the ritual programme was, like the Confucian canons in which it had its origins, accessible to all educated men. Within the scholar community, specialization in state ritual did occur. Some of the most eminent scholarly and aristocratic lineages had family traditions of specialization in state ritual. The subject also had its own dedicated exponents, who were occasionally allowed under the T'ang bureaucratic system to hold exceptionally long tenures in ritual office.[2] But for most ritual officials, service in ritual office alternated with tenures in other academic agencies, or with general service postings. This accessibility of the state ritual tradition to all scholars meant that it was possible for large numbers to participate in controversies about rites. Ritual therefore became a particularly vital aspect of the scholarly and political life of the learned community. Because it was largely recorded by historians who were themselves expert in the ritual tradition, it was also comparatively well documented.

In the T'ang period, the characteristic approach to state ritual was practical. Above all else, the erudits of the court of sacrifices and the many others who took part in controversies and in drafting, wished to have their submissions accepted and implemented, and to have the benefits of recognition. In keeping with this prescriptive mode, there was relatively little independent emphasis on the theoretical functions of state ritual observances. Nor was there much theoretical comment on the relation of the state ritual programme to the Buddhist and Taoist belief system or to the flux of beliefs and superstitions which co-existed with the official progamme, whether on an empire-wide or a local scale.[3]

Much of the writing about state ritual took the form either of drafting directives for state observances or of accounts of arguments about these directives. Throughout the dynasty, scholars who engaged in such debates required expertise in three areas: first, they needed a knowledge of and an ability to interpret the canonical sources that lay behind the rites; secondly, a command of historical ritual practice from Han times; and, finally, an ability to relate these elements to the wishes of individual sovereigns and to the resources of the T'ang, whether these were without precedent for their wealth, or much reduced, as in the post-rebellion period. There was a sense of competition associated with this activity of ritual drafting that parallelled the competitive spirit to be seen in court verse writing. In turn, the debates that resulted, often encouraged by the emperor, provided a medium for the political competition that was a permanent feature of T'ang bureaucratic life.

What few theoretical remarks scholars made about state ritual involved re-statement of traditional views on its theory and function, with emphasis on its importance to the state and to society. Their first justification for the ritual programme was cosmological. K'ung Ying-ta described ritual as integral to the universe from the beginning: 'Ritual has its roots in the great unity; this proves that before heaven and earth were divided ritual already existed.'[4] The great state rituals related to the elaborate system of 'cosmic reciprocity', in which events in the natural and human worlds were brought about by the moral action of the sovereign and by the moral condition of society. The ritual programme was also integrated with the calendar. Many of the divinities to which offerings were made had seasonal functions. The programme of rites bore a close relation to the prescriptions of the *Yüeh ling* chapter of the *Li chi*, which embodied the *yin–yang* cosmology of the late pre-Ch'in period at its most developed (Ch. 3, pp. 87–88). The *Yüeh ling* contained a ritual programme organized on a monthly basis, and in effect rivalled successive ritual codes as an authority for dynastic ritual.[5] Both the cosmological understanding of the rites and the *Yüeh ling* programme were especially important to the sovereign, since both posited a system that directly concerned the quality of imperial rule. The decision to perform rites might be conditional not simply on locating the ritually correct point on the calendar, but also on a physically and politically harmonious world. Droughts, floods, illnesses, invasions and even the weather conditions immediately prior to performances[6] were relevant to this view.

This cosmic view of state ritual dominated official documentation of the tradition, and was, publicly at least, supported by the overwhelming majority of serving officials. Their public writings indicate that throughout the dynasty they participated without obvious reluctance in reporting omens and forwarding other information that might reinforce for high authority the picture of a well governed world, maintained by correctly performed state ritual observances. But a distinction between public or official and private or unofficial attitudes, so germane to the fields of learning described in this book, is also relevant to scholars' attitudes to the state ritual tradition. There is little evidence to suggest that these cosmic divinities were meaningful in the unofficial intellectual or religious lives of scholars. Their remoteness, their identification with the apex of the official hierarchy, and the fact that only the emperor or his representatives might make offering to them, in turn meant that, when the dynasty suffered political decline, the major cosmic divinities also receded in importance. In the ninth century, when scholars in their unofficial writings re-appraised many aspects of the state and its functions, the cosmic dimension to the rites played little part in analysis of the function of ritual or in proposals for reform.

The state ritual programme, however, had another justification, that related more immediately to the well-being of the political and social hierarchy. Imperial rituals had a direct social function. They contributed to the stability and harmony of society. The emperor's rites were status specific, and their performance emphasized distinction of rank.[7] Scholars saw the major state observances as reinforcing the dignity and prestige of the imperial institution and the official hierarchy. At the same time, ritual was also seen as a form of restraint on the conduct of the emperor. Sometimes state rituals directly involved problems of political organization or issues of political principle. The provision for honouring the descendants of the dynasties that immediately preceded the T'ang, the Northern Chou and the Sui, embodied a major political concept, that of the voluntary cession of power by these dynasties to the T'ang.[8] The role of the military in the state ritual programme was clearly seen by T'ang scholars as an indication of their own position in official life, in relation to the powerful military element in the polity.[9] The rituals traditional to the crown prince were also understood to relate to the influence of the scholars. They gave the scholar community the means to promote their own ideals in his education and training.[10] Scholars could ensure the success of the great ritual undertakings by the authenticity of the directives they produced. But they also believed that they should curb extravagant or hubristic imperial initiatives, and ensure that the emperor and his ministers discharged his ritual responsiblities. The T'ang scholar community readily identified instances where individual ritual officials had betrayed their ideals and played sycophant to extravagant or illegitimate imperial or chief ministerial enterprise.[11] They also paid tribute to those ritual scholars whose efforts to argue an authentic case had been traduced, or who had otherwise been wronged.[12] Imperial rituals were, to the scholar community a 'public' concern. An official's duties in the state ritual programme had priority over his private ritual obligations, even when these concerned matters of taboo that might have grave implications for the individual.[13]

In their political and social role, state rituals expressed one of the main ideals of the medieval Confucian tradition. This saw the processes of governing and being governed as voluntary and free of coercion. Ritual government was therefore antithetical to government by punishments, by the administration of the criminal code, or, worse still, by the use of the military and the force of arms.[14] Rites, and the ritual tradition more generally, therefore expressed traditional Confucian optimism about the governmental process and about society. In a way that was distinctively medieval, T'ang scholars located their ideal of the perfectability of society in an activity that concerned primarily the emperor and the apex of the state. In this they contrasted with Neo-Confucians, for whom the individual and his psychological and moral constitution were the main locus for social ideals.

Finally, it was a central feature of scholars' attitudes to the tradition that ritual usage changed with time and would continue to do so. Confucius himself, in a much quoted observation from the *Analects*, had sanctioned this view.[15] Ritual, as emperors themselves urged, was based on the affective side of man's nature,[16] and his responses changed with time. T'ang scholars frequently justified this insistence on change. The ritual canons, they indicated, in much used phrases that echoed the *Han shu*, were often 'deficient and incomplete' as far as directives for specific rituals were concerned.[17] For numbers of the rites, there was 'no clear text' (*ming wen*), on which authentic directives might be based. Innovation and flexibility were therefore fully justified. This belief in a continuous process of change informed countless acts of grace (*ta she*), edicts and memorial submissions on ritual through the dynasty. It permitted emperors in the first half of the T'ang to expand the tradition, to celebrate the great dynastic rituals on an ever grander scale. It also allowed individual ritual scholars to anticipate imperial intentions, within the limits that their own ideals of political conduct imposed on them, to suggest change, and in so doing to advance their own careers.

Despite a central belief in historical evolution, state ritual as a learned discipline proved in some respects less adaptable to the political changes that took place over the dynasty than other disciplines. Undoubtedly, the fact that the great imperial rituals were specific to the emperor, and therefore involved the participation of most serving officials only at a distance, contributed to this lack of flexibility. State ritual contrasted in this remoteness with both canonical scholarship and *belles lettres*, disciplines that transcended status-specific functions and were of creative importance to the individual scholar, almost regardless of his position. In canonical learning and in *belles lettres*, the changed conditions that followed the rebellion of 755 resulted in a shift towards new, more introspective and self-analytical attitudes. Although changes in outlook did occur in state ritual, they were more limited. The clearest trend was towards conventional expressions of nostalgia and reformism, of which in the late eighth and early ninth century there were many. A more analytical approach towards the ritual tradition, parallel to those in canonical scholarship and literary criticism, was confined to the small number of reform minded and sceptically inclined intellectuals who questioned the cosmological function of the rites. Developments in these other disciplines suggest the trend in the late eighth and early ninth centuries towards a more devolved scholarly milieu, towards interest in re-defining the role of the individual in the polity and in society. But the much less pronounced evolution in attitudes to the state ritual tradition indicates rather the depth of the scholar community's commitment to the imperial Confucian tradition and to the T'ang dynastic state.

The reigns of Kao tsu and T'ai tsung

From the foundation of the dynasty, ritual scholars proved themselves indispensable to T'ang rule. It was they who, after a discussion ordered by Li Yüan, the future Kao tsu, provided him with directives for his formal accession, and who selected a propitious day for its rituals.[18] As T'ang power was consolidated, a number of factors added to the general interest in state ritual. First was the expectation that a newly founded dynasty should, after an appropriate lapse of time and with the help of ritual scholars, declare its own identity in terms of the state ritual tradition.[19] Secondly, there was a more specific wish to represent the preceding Sui dynasty as having violated the ideal of government by ritual.[20] Though in fact the interest in a state ritual programme that was already very evident in the Sui cannot have differed greatly from that of the early T'ang, the dynasty, for political purposes, tried to draw a sharp distinction. Early T'ang official scholars therefore identified the Sui with the 'punishments' that were antithetical to ritual, and claimed for the T'ang, in contrast, a special commitment to ritual. In the course of T'ai tsung's reign, they also exploited the ritual tradition as a means to celebrate the early political successes of the dynasty.

The intensity of the interest among early seventh-century scholars in state ritual scholarship is attested in a number of ways. In this period, scholars frequently specialized in the study of the three ritual canons, the *Li chi*, *I li* and *Chou li*. In the biographies of early T'ang Confucian scholars contained in the *Chiu T'ang shu*, this was a particularly often cited expertise,[21] and it was also mentioned in the epitaphs and other commemorative sources of the time.[22] Some of the best known official scholars of the period, like K'ung Ying-ta and Yen Shih-ku, are mentioned as being expert in the ritual canons.[23] Special attention to ritual scholarship is suggested by the fact that the group of scholars commissioned to compile the sub-commentary to the *Li chi* in K'ung Ying-ta's *Wu ching cheng i* series was the largest of those for any of the *Five canons*. It included one of the vice-presidents of the state academy directorate and two officials from outside institutions. To emphasize the connection between the sub-commentary and the dynasty's ritual programme, an erudit of the court of sacrifices was also included.[24]

Another indication of the importance of state ritual to the official scholarly community of the early T'ang is the place that K'ung's commission gave it in the series generally. In the *Mao shih* sub-commentary, the three ritual canons were quoted about half as often again as the historial canons, the *Shang shu*, *Ch'un-ch'iu* and its *Three traditions*.[25] This suggests that early T'ang scholars wished to locate and analyse ritual issues even in the ancient corpus of Chou dynasty song texts. This exegetical interest in state ritual questions was far from purely academic. There was sometimes a clear connection between scholarly exposition of the canons and the decisions early T'ang ritual scholars took over contemporary ritual issues. One example concerns the cult of Confucius himself. In the sub-commentary to the *Li chi*, K'ung supplied an argument, based on Cheng Hsüan's position, for expanding the iconography of the temple, to include figures other than Confucius and his favourite disciple Yen Hui. This provided nothing less than a justification for the expansion that the emperor ordered in 647 (Ch. 2, p. 35).[26] Another instance concerns the rituals extended to the descendants of the two preceding dynasties, the Northern Chou and the Sui. In the *Li chi*, it was recorded that king Wen of the Chou enfieffed descendants of Huang ti and of Yao and Shun, then, when he had more leisure, enfieffed the descendants of the Hsia and the Shang, the two dynasties that had immediately preceded the Chou. For the T'ang, two separate groups of descendants who should be enfieffed, one remote and one more recent, were therefore suggested, with the more recent group having greater status. But this division into two groups was apparently contradicted by a passage in the *Tso chuan*. K'ung Ying-ta's sub-commentary explained the apparent contradiction, maintained that the second group were more important and upheld the *Li chi*. It was, correspondingly, the descendants of the two most recent dynasties, the Sui and the Northern Chou, who were given prompt and generous ritual recognition by the T'ang, first by Kao tsu in 618, and then by T'ai tsung in 628.[27]

In the sub-commentary series as a whole, K'ung also gave particular space to the exegesis of passages that related to the great ritual enterprises which the Chen-kuan court was in the process of discussing, especially the construction of a Ming-t'ang or cosmic hall and the performance of the Feng and Shan rites on mount T'ai in modern Shantung. His own submission to the emperor, arguing extreme caution over the scale and plan of the Ming-t'ang, is to be related to his sub-commentary to a passage of the *Li chi* that describes the building.[28] Study of state rituals as they were documented in the canons therefore related to a tradition that had already acquired especial importance in T'ai tsung's court. The relevance of K'ung's sub-commentaries to living performances may also be indicated by the fact that, after the promulgation of the sub-commentaries in 653, scholars cited the *Li chi* sub-commentary, in non-commentarial contexts, much more often than any of the other four.[29]

The Chen-kuan ritual code

Against this background of intense interest, the official scholars of T'ai tsung's reign compiled a number of works relating to the dynasty's ritual programme. None of these survives;[30] but two resulted in discussion that was recorded. The first concerned the *Li chi*, the only one of the three ritual canons to be represented in the short series of *Five canons*. Since long before the T'ang period, scholars had recognized the *Li chi* as a collection of chapters of differing authorship and date, and early T'ang official scholars also saw it as having heterogeneous origins.[31] Long before the T'ang too, in the Chin, a scholar had rearranged the text of this canon under fifty systematic headings, probably with the intention of giving at least some of it prescriptive force in state rituals. In the early T'ang, this rearrangement commended itself to the scholar minister Wei Cheng, who provided a commentary for it. In 640, T'ai tsung expressed approval of Wei Cheng's compilation, and ordered that copies should be made for the crown prince and other princes, and that it should be accepted into the imperial library. This first of a succession of attempts to reorganize the *Li chi* then disappeared from the documentation. It was, however, to give rise to an important controversy in canonical scholarship eighty years later, in Hsüan tsung's reign, when another senior official scholar tried to give the *Li chi* prescriptive force (Ch 3, pp. 86–7).[32]

The second compilation was a much greater undertaking, and involved a large commission of scholars. The tradition of both northern and southern dynasties, inherited from the Han, had been for each dynasty to embody its own ritual directives in a ritual code.[33] The reunifying Sui dynasty had twice codified its state ritual programme. The second of the Sui codes, the *Chiang-tu hsin li* (*New rituals of Chiang-tu*) was in circulation under the T'ang at least into the ninth century.[34] Official sources record of the early T'ang that, in a classic and much used phrase from the *Shih chi*, it 'did not have the leisure' (*wei huang*)[35] to draft its own prescriptions, and that, despite demands that it declare its own identity in terms of the state ritual tradition, it followed Sui procedures.

In the stable middle years of the Chen-kuan period, however, the dynasty commissioned the first of its own codes. The supervision of the programme was given to the two great scholar ministers of the period, Wei Cheng and Fang Hsüan-ling, an indication of the importance of the project. The compilation itself was done by 'ritual officials'; but probably the term here denoted simply official scholars expert in state ritual. The long serving scholar Li Pai-yao (565–648, canonized *K'ang*), who had worked on the first of the two Sui codes, was included in the commission, as were the two most prominent official scholars of the first two reigns, K'ung Ying-ta and Yen Shih-ku. The completion of a preliminary stage was marked in 633, when Fang Hsüan-ling presented the emperor with a set of directives for twenty-nine observances.[36] These involved either modifying Sui practice or reviving rituals discarded by the Northern Chou and Sui, and they therefore provide some indication of the special character of the early T'ang state ritual programme. The motive behind them was probably to re-introduce certain rituals that had particular social or political value, and to purge the programme of the element of extravagance that the Sui was held to have introduced.

In the *cha*, therefore, the offering to the collective spirit world made at the end of the year, Fang Hsüan-ling proposed restricting offerings to the sun, moon, and stars, and excluded the five sky gods that had been included in the Sui version of this ceremony. This was consistent with the interpretation of the passage in the *Yüeh ling* that K'ung Ying-ta was to give in the *Li chi* sub-commentary.[37] Among the revived observances was one for the 'military rehearsal at the intermission in agriculture' (*nung-hsi chiang wu*). This ceremony, again mentioned in the *Yüeh ling*, expressed symbolically the ideal that three seasons of the year should be devoted to farming and one to training in combat. Like other rituals concerned with warfare, it seems to have met with little enthusiasm from civil scholars, who resisted the intrusion of the military into an area which they considered their own preserve. Emperors, rather than ritual scholars, appear to have promoted it, at least in the first half of the dynasty, when it was intermittently performed.[38] T'ai tsung himself, with his ambitious plans for campaigns beyond the frontiers, may well have been behind its revival.

Two other rituals which, in this interim stage in the preparation of the ritual code, the early T'ang scholars claimed to have revived, concerned the state academy directorate and its education programme. The first was a ceremony for 'nourishing the aged' (*yang lao*) that took place in the directorate, and the second a ritual entitled 'the crown prince enters the academy' (*huang t'ai tzu ju hsüeh*). Their revival correlates with early T'ang promotion of education and expansion of the official school system.[39]

The Chen-kuan ritual code, as it was known after it was finally approved in 637, probably incorporated the twenty-nine items contained in the interim submission of 633. In its broad outline, the code conformed to the model provided by the ritual codes of the period of disunion. The compilers used a traditional, five-fold division for the 150 or so rites involved.[40] The first division was for 'rituals of the auspicious' (*chi li*), observances that concerned cosmological and supernatural agents, or 'heaven' as in this context T'ang scholars elliptically referred to it. Secondly, there was a short division for 'rituals for guests' (*pin li*), ceremonies concerning the reception to be given envoys from outlying, non-Chinese states. The third division, also very short, was for 'army rituals' (*chün i*), rites for observance in connection with military activities. The fourth was for 'felicitation rituals' (*chia li*), which were mostly rites of passage and ceremonies relating to the imperial family and the official hierarchy. The final division was for 'rituals of ill omen' (*hsiung li*), rites for performance at times of bad harvests, sickness and other adversities.

The compilers of this first T'ang ritual code, however, departed from the traditional arrangements in certain significant respects. They appended a sixth section, concerning the deaths of emperors and other catastrophes, perhaps because they believed that the relatively open atmosphere of T'ai tsung's court would prevail as a norm, and that these unpropitious but politically momentous topics would always be discussed.[41] They also changed the order, making the rituals of ill omen the final section. The compiling commission also intended, for all the early T'ang emphasis on the role of ritual rather than punishments, that the code should express the ideals of frugality and restraint they so consistently urged on the emperor. Perhaps because of this emphasis on austerity, the code was thirty *chüan* shorter than its Sui predecessor.[42]

The Chen-kuan ritual code, like all early T'ang normative scholarly compilations, was intended to provide permanent provisions for the area of learning with which it was concerned. However, a combination of factors made it improbable that this compendium of ritual directives would remain in force for very long. The first was the increasing wealth and stability of the dynasty. With their greater resources, sovereigns after T'ai tsung developed their ambitions to undertake on an ever grander scale the major ritual enterprises suggested by the state ritual tradition. Secondly, the sense of competition among the scholar community was such that it was most unlikely to accept officially promulgated answers as final. Already under T'ai tsung, the court debated the grandest and most challenging of all the undertakings in the tradition, the Feng and Shan rites on the sacred peaks and the building of the Ming-t'ang as a central precinct for the dynasty's rites. These, often loosely linked in T'ang writing,[43] were not undertaken until the seond half of the century. But detailed directives had already been drafted for the Feng and Shan rites by 637, and, in 641, special commissioners were appointed.[44]

From 650 to 755

For the hundred years following T'ai tsung's death, the ritual programme of the dynasty remained of central importance to the sovereign and chief ministers. In the official scholarly community also and among prospective officials, a high level of interest in ritual continued. Despite sometimes violent court politics, the ritual tradition continued to provide, more than any other Confucian-orientated learned discipline, an index of the prosperity and confidence of the state and of the official community. The attitudes involved remained for the most part practical and outgoing. Despite the complexity and wealth of the belief system embodied in the first division of the state ritual code, little was added to the general theoretical position that had been restated under T'ai tsung.

Nonetheless, controversies that were significant for the scholar community took place. The most important concerned the place of the god of high heaven (*hao t'ien shang ti*). It involved rejecting a position that K'ung Ying-ta endorsed, and reflected the political centralization that the T'ang had achieved. As performances were held, scholars continuously reviewed the detailed directives for probably all the major rituals in the programme. This process resulted in the commissioning of two further codifications of the tradition, the second of which, completed under Hsüan tsung in 732, was later seen as embodying the highest achievements of T'ang ritual. In the hundred years from 650, the great non-recurrent ritual enterprises that the scholar community had discussed in the first two reigns were enacted. The immense prestige of the imperial rites, and the fact that the ritual tradition remained accessible to the entire scholarly community, meant that this was indeed the period in the dynasty when the tradition achieved its greatest recognition. Its influence was felt not least in recruitment procedures, for as the examination system expanded in this period, so the important state rituals became more firmly integrated into it.

The Ming-t'ang and the Feng and Shan rites

The involvement of scholars in this expansionist and prosperous phase in the history of T'ang state ritual, therefore, is indicated by their role in the two rather different undertakings that they recognized at the time as particularly momentous, and that dominate surviving documentation for state ritual in this century. The first of these was the Ming-t'ang, the Chou dynasty term for a building that was held, under various names, to have had a central place in the ritual and administration of the dynasties of high antiquity.[45]

The Ming-t'ang was planned at a time when there was imperial interest in the history of capital cities and palace buildings. In 658, Kao tsung commissioned a compilation on this topic from the senior official scholar and chief minister Hsü Ching-tsung and the scholars of the Hung-wen kuan.[46] The Ming-t'ang was, however, unique among the many buildings that the dynasty erected in the seventh century,[47] in the large volume of debate it generated. Its origins and history touched the central concerns of the scholar community far more deeply than those of any other building. Its plan related to the view of the cosmos and of the cosmic divinities that scholars defined. It was a central precinct for the rituals that it was their responsibility to draft. It concerned the traditional administrative ideals that they promoted, and therefore emphasized the shared role of the emperor and his officials in governing the empire. The building also embodied in physical form one of the most obsessive metaphors in the literature of the selection and promotion processes, in which almost all scholars were involved, that of choosing fine timbers for the great edifice of state.[48]

T'ang scholars recognized that the history of the Ming-t'ang had been long and controversial. The absence of precise directions in the canons permitted a range of interpretations, and encouraged competitive debate. As the dynasty's resources increased, the commitment to building a grandiose structure, remote in spirit from that suggested in the canons, became irreversible. But the building was also a symbolic expression of the stability and success of the dynasty. It could be undertaken only when 'the state in all four direction has no anxieties, the people are at peace and harvests abundant'.[49]

It was not finally until 688 under the empress Wu, therefore, that, after prolonged debate and hesitation, the order to demolish an existing palace, completed only twenty-three years before, and to build the Ming-t'ang on its site was finally given and implemented. The empress, however, set aside the cautious attitude that, under T'ai tsung, scholars like K'ung Ying-ta had advocated. Her building involved costly materials and was on a scale that far exceeded the modest construction that K'ung had urged. It was also sited within the imperial city at Lo-yang, not some distance to the south, as canonical authority had required. It was completed a year later, in 688, and the general populace allowed in to admire it.[50] Disaster followed a few years later; a newly built giant pagoda immediately adjoining it caught fire in 695, and the Ming-t'ang burnt to the ground.[51] An official of the period, the omissioner Liu Ch'eng-ch'ing, asked the empress to adjourn the court, while she considered what heaven intended by this catastrophe.[52] But the commitment to maintain a central ritual precinct of this kind over-rode more cautious interpretations of this disaster. A new building was ordered almost immediately and completed in 696.[53]

Renamed the T'ung t'ien kung (Palace linking with heaven), it was now used for a period, probably until a few months after the T'ang restoration of 705.[54]

If ritual scholars competed to make proposals for the construction of the building, they were involved in even more protracted discussion about the ritual programme which they believed should take place in it. In the course of arguments held from the start of the dynasty, well before it had been built,[55] some scholars, at one extreme, held that the Ming-t'ang should be used once a year for a single great ceremony only. Others, at the opposing extreme, proposed its use by the sovereign as many as eighteen times in the annual ritual calendar.[56] Several scholars compiled collections of directives for rituals specific to the Ming-t'ang, and the titles of five such works survive.[57]

Controversy focussed on three specific problems. The first to be raised concerned the question of which imperial ancestors were to be honoured by offerings in the Ming-t'ang, 'concurrently' (*p'ei hsiang*) with the heavenly powers. The building was not only a 'synapse for humanity', the symbolic and ritual point of contact between man, in the person of the sovereign, and heaven, but also following canonical authority and historical precedent, a dynastic shrine. The principle that was established in 656 and that was upheld, after irregularities under the empress Wu, probably until the end of the ninth century, was that the most recently deceased sovereign should be given offering.[58]

The second problem concerned the question of which deities should receive the main offerings in the principal Ming-t'ang rite, the 'great sacrifice' (*ta hsiang*). This debate, therefore, was about the position of the most important cosmological divinities in the official pantheon. In the Chen-kuan ritual code, on the authority of Cheng Hsüan and K'ung Ying-ta, the compilers had stipulated that at the great Ming-t'ang sacrifice the gods of the five directions (*wu fang ti*) should receive offerings. A few years after Kao tsung's accession, however, this position became controversial. By 657, when a large commission under Chang-sun Wu-chi codified the state ritual programme a second time, they had adopted the opposite position, which Cheng Hsüan's great opponent Wang Su (A.D. 195–256) had advocated. They removed the five direction gods from the directives and stipulated the god of high heaven alone. Following this, practice became confused, and it also became customary to include other deities in the Ming-t'ang rites. But in the following century, in the reign of Hsüan tsung, the position again changed. In the third and final codification of the dynasty, that of 732, the two earlier positions were in effect amalgamated. The five direction gods as well as the god of high heaven were included, and offering was also stipulated for the most recently deceased T'ang imperial ancestor.[59]

Chang-sun Wu-chi's rejection of Cheng Hsüan's five divinities and the preference of the ritual scholars of his time for the single supreme agent that Wang Su had advocated has been seen as an expression, in terms of state religion, of the political centralization the dynasty had achieved. It was implemented during the years 665–6, not just for the Ming-t'ang rites, but also for other important observances that involved the major cosmic divinities. The dynasty under Kao tsung certainly had the confidence to express political ideas through the ritual programme. But this reorganization of the cosmic pantheon points in addition to another, rather different feature of the climate in ritual and canonical scholarship. Rejection of the authority of Cheng Hsüan meant, inevitably, abandoning the authority of K'ung Ying-ta's sub-commentary to the *Li chi*, for this had in essence been an amplification of Cheng Hsüan's commentary. But the debate that took place under Kao tsung did not refer to K'ung or the implications for the status of his exegesis of the new position. Within a few years, moreover, Cheng Hsüan's five direction gods had regained a position in major state rituals which they were to retain in the following century. Just as in canonical scholarship the state tolerated different interpretations of the texts, so in state ritual as well, the authorities were able to reject, and then re-adopt, positions that they had only recently endorsed, and finally to arrive at a solution that, characteristically, included all options.

A third question, which arose in 698, concerned the frequency with which the sovereign should take part in a 'ritual announcement' (*kao shuo*), whether every month was correct or whether seasonal or even annual performances would be enough. In late 697, two erudits of the court of sacrifices argued against the authenticity of monthly ceremonies, while two other scholars tried to prove that in the Chou period monthly ceremonies had taken place. A total of seventeen canonical and ritual sources were cited or referred to by title in the controversy between these groups. Seasonal rituals were eventually ordered, even though the advocates of monthly performances were acknowledged to have had the stronger case. These seasonal performances were probably held in the Ming-t'ang, at least in the relatively brief period leading up to the court's return to Ch'ang-an in 706.[60]

The central and monumental character of the Ming-t'ang and its reputation in and beyond China enabled the empress Wu to use it for much more than the rituals sanctioned by the Confucian canons. In 690, a debate between representatives of the three teachings was held in the building. At the time of the empress Wu's usurpation, it was also mentioned in a commentary for the *Ta yün ching (Great cloud sutra)*, that was intended to provide elaborate support for her rule. In this commentary, the empress Wu was identified with the Maitreya, the Buddha of the future, and the Ming-t'ang was seen as the Magic City of which the Buddha had spoken. For a few years, therefore, the building provided the symbolic precinct for the aspirations of the Chou dynasty.[61]

At the T'ang restoration of 705, it was in the Ming-t'ang that Chung tsung formally succeeded to the imperial line. But his celebration of the great sacrifice there in the autumn of that year was probably the last time it provided a site for a major imperial ritual. After the T'ang restoration and the return to Ch'ang-an, political and scholarly reaction to the reign of the empress Wu, gaining momentum over the next few years, greatly reduced the enthusiasm of ritual scholars for the building. During his progress to Lo-yang in 717, Hsüan tsung intended to visit it; but ritual scholars dissuaded him from conducting an observance there.[62] In 722, 738 and 739, the Ming-t'ang underwent several modifications, reductions in use and changes in name.[63] It seems probable, too, that after 705 the great sacrifice and other rituals prescribed for it were conducted at an open-altar site or elsewhere at Ch'ang-an and not in the Lo-yang building. From the T'ien-pao period on, the history of Ming-t'ang rituals becomes even less clear; the compilers of the accounts of the building that survive in the *Chiu T'ang shu* break off at about his point. It is only an anecdotal historical source, therefore, that reveals that the Ming-t'ang was finally burnt down when, in the later stages of the An Lu-shan rebellion, the Shih Ssu-ming rebels fled from Lo-yang.[64]

The second great non-recurrent ritual enterprise in which scholars of this period, whether in ritual office or not, competed to participate was the celebration of the Feng and Shan rites on mount T'ai in Shantung. This observance was rare in the T'ang state ritual programme in not having explicit sanction in the Confucian canons. Nonetheless, performances had been recorded in the reign of the great Wu ti of the Han in 110 B.C., and under Kuang-wu ti in the Later Han.[65] Pre-T'ang scholars had treated the Feng and Shan rites prominently in the exegetical tradition, and K'ung Ying-ta had not doubted their authenticity as ancient rites. They were seen as a particularly solemn and prestigious announcement to the heavenly powers that the dynasty had become firmly established, and as an acknowledgement of the favour heaven had shown the ruling house. Again, therefore, they were closely identified with the political success of the dynasty. Even more than the Ming-t'ang, the Feng and Shan rites inspired erudition among scholars, grandiloquent hesitation from emperors, who wished to express ritually correct reluctance to perform them, and general enthusiasm.[66] Because the second of the two T'ang performances on mount T'ai was successfully conducted in a climate relatively free of ideological and political discord, it was particularly well documented.

From early in Kao tsung's reign the scholarly community continued to press for a performance of the rites on mount T'ai.[67] In 659, the senior official scholar Hsü Ching-tsung (592–672, canonized *Kung*) drafted directives. In 664, it was announced that the observance would be conducted at the winter solstice of 665–6. A great procession went east from Lo-yang, 'following on over several hundred *li*', its provisioning made easy by good harvests in the preceding years. Representatives of the Turks, Khotanese, Persian, Indian and central Asian states and from Korea and Japan attended. The emperor appointed four special commissioners for the rites, including the elderly Hsü Chung-tsung. Other scholars were engaged in revising directives until a late stage, and the ritual officials even accepted a recommendation from a relatively junior former military official.[68]

The ceremony consisted of three separate offerings, and each of these in turn, like many T'ang observances, involved three presentations. The first offering was held beneath the mountain and was made to the supreme deity, the god of high heaven (*hao t'ien shang ti*), with Kao tsu and T'ai tsung, the deceased grandfather and father of the reigning emperor, receiving concurrent offering. The Feng rites on mount T'ai itself followed. Finally the Shan rites, at which the god of earth (*huang ti ch'i*) was the principal deity and the empresses of Kao tsu and T'ai tsung received the concurrent sacrifice, were conducted on mount She-shou, five *li* away.[69]

Although mount T'ai had a special position as the principal of the five sacred peaks, and as the link between the human and spirit worlds, celebration of the Feng and Shan rites was not in theory limited to this mountain. T'ai tsung had suggested a performance on the central peak, mount Sung, while Kao tsung intended 'to go all round the sacred peaks [performing] the Feng [rites]'. In 682, after two postponements, he proclaimed his intention of celebrating on mount Sung, the central peak. A commission of six scholars, including the vice-president of the state academy directorate and three erudits of the court of sacrifices was appointed to draft directives. The emperor went as far as a shrine that had been erected to the south of the mountain, but then, because of natural disasters and a resurgence of Turkish power, and because he became ill, abandoned the observance.

The empress Wu attempted to legitimize her own rule by performing the great state rituals more lavishly than her predecessors. Long before her usurpation and declaration of the Chou dynasty, she had had an interest in the Feng and Shan rites. Late in 695, after petitions that she should do so, she proceeded to mount Sung, some four days' journey south of Lo-yang, and carried out an adapted version of the rites.[70] The official scholar who produced the necessary redrafting was Wang Yüan-kan, then a member of the Hung-wen kuan and one of several apologists for the empress in state ritual, whose new interpretations of the canons were to prove controversial in 703 (Ch. 3, pp. 84–85).[71] Other scholars produced eulogies or collections of directives for the performance.[72]

Such were the political and administrative achievements of the first decade of Hsüan tsung's reign that requests for another celebration of the Feng and Shan rites were made in great numbers, not only by ministers but also by junior officials and by those outside officialdom altogether. Over a thousand submissions were presented, by those ambitious to attract the emperor's attention.[73] Hsüan tsung, having duly hesitated, finally 'complied against his better wishes'. The journey east was planned for late 725.[74] The commissioner for the rites was the scholar minister Chang Yüeh, chief minister of the period 721 to 726. He, Liu Chih-chi's former colleague Hsü Chien, the deputy director of the imperial library, an erudit of the Kuo-tzu hsüeh and other ritual officials were ordered to draft directives in the Chi-hsien yüan, Hsüan tsung's own advisory college. Other scholars contributed on their own initiative, and even at a late stage modifications were discussed.[75]

The rites were similar in outline to the earlier performances, though all female participation and offering to deceased empresses was disallowed. Arriving at mount T'ai, Hsüan tsung met with severe cold and strong winds, which were taken as signs of heaven's displeasure. But he 'took no food and stood in the open before his tent, looking up to heaven and acknowledging his transgressions . . . ' Conditions improved miraculously, and the rites were duly enacted.[76] They were followed by a celebratory audience at the foot of the mountain of metropolitan and provincial officials, the lineal descendant of Confucius and an assembly of foreign representatives who greatly outnumbered those attending the celebrations under Kao tsu and the empress

Wu. The emperor himself composed a text for inscription, and the chief ministers Chang Yüeh, Yüan Ch'ien-yao (d. 731) and Su T'ing (670–727, canonized *Wen-hsien*) all contributed eulogies.

This celebration of the Feng and Shan rites, called even at the time 'an event in a thousand years',[77] was later conventionally considered one of the great achievements of the dynasty. Participation in it, even in a lowly capacity, was a signal source of price in an official's career. Some of the best known scholars of the era were able to claim a role in the event. Apart from those directly commissioned in the Chi-hsien yüan, others who had some part included the general service literary official Li Yung (678–747), who had wide connections in the scholar community; the *Wen hsüan* commentator of Hsüan tsung's reign Lü Hsiang; and the political patron and intellectual of the T'ien-pao period Fang Kuan. Ts'ui Mien (671–739, canonized *Hsiao*), a figure much respected by the scholars who lived through the An Lu-shan rebellion, presented a eulogy at the audience after the celebration, and was rewarded.[78] The long serving official historian Wei Shu compiled a narrative of the observance.[79]

This proved to be the last performance of the Feng and Shan rites under the T'ang. In 730 and 735, repeated requests for performances on mount Hua, for which Hsüan tsung had a special astrological affinity, and on mount Sung, were declined. In 751, a performance on mount Hua was planned but abandoned at a late stage, because of a disaster at a temple on the mountain and famine in the Kuan-chung hinterland of Ch'ang-an.[80]

In the post-rebellion period, the dynasty's ritual programme was much reduced, and the scholar community, at least in its unofficial life, put much less emphasis on the grand, cosmic role of the emperor in ritual. Nonetheless, admiration for successful ritual enterprises on the scale of those of the late seventh and early eighth centuries carried over into the very different conditions that now obtained. The Feng and Shan performance of 725, particularly, evoked nostalgia and provided a focus for expressions of loyalty to the ruling house. With time, its senior participants acquired heroic stature. Even as an organizational achievement, in the ninth century, the court's journey to the east inspired awe.[81] The other great state ritual enterprise of the late seventh and early eighth centuries, the Ming-t'ang, perhaps receded more abruptly in the experience of scholars. Like the 'ten thousand states' (*wan kuo*) that were to do homage in it, by the ninth century it had become little more than a rhetorical image. But the Ming-t'ang, despite its clouded history and identification with the empress Wu, as well as the Feng and Shan rites, retained a symbolic place in the outlook of the scholar community. When in 780 the scholar minister Ts'ui Yu-fu, a son of Ts'ui Mien, on his death-bed enumerated the three regrets of his career, one was that as chief minister he had not assisted in a performance of the Feng and Shan rites and a second that he had not built the Ming-t'ang.[82] His epigram expressed perfectly the prestige that both these undertakings commanded, and the nostalgia that scholars of the post-rebellion period felt for them. Both are to be seen as expressions of the energy and prosperity of the seventh- and early eighth-century state. They embodied the imperial ritual tradition at its grandest, and provided lavish public celebration of the cosmic role of the sovereign. The rites they involved, as expressions of dynastic success, caught the fervour and imagination of the scholar community as did no other dynastic enterprises.

The K'ai-yüan ritual code

The sustained interest in these great ritual undertakings already suggests why a lasting codification of the state ritual tradition should have proved so difficult. Even before T'ai tsung's death, it must have been apparent that the code of 637 would not be permanent. A comprehensive and updated state ritual code, moreover, was an ideal that neither the emperor nor the scholar community could set aside. By the early years of Kao tsung's reign, enough change had taken place to justify a second attempt at codification. The commission appointed to do this consisted of thirteen scholars and included the vice-president of the court of sacrifices, three of its four erudits, and an erudit of the T'ai hsüeh. The senior scholar minister Chang-sun Wu-chi, who dominates the surviving record of ritual debates in the first decade of Kao tsung's reign, was director. Hsü Ching-tsung and one of K'ung Yung-ta's sons, who held the office of secretary for the imperial tallies and seals (*fu-hsi lang*), were members. This second code, 130 *chüan* in length and comprising 229 *p'ien* as against 138 in the Chen-kuan code, was completed in 658, to become known as the Hsien-ch'ing code. Kao tsung himself wrote a preface for it, and it was distributed for use 'within and without'.[83]

Relatively few details of this codification survive, however, partly because it later suffered from identification with two of its compilers, Hsü Ching-tsung and the figure often associated with him, Li I-fu, both of whom became notorious for the political support they gave the empress Wu. For 'in their adjustments (*sun i*) they often went over into the sycophantic and scholars rushed to argue over [the directives

they drafted], holding that they were not as good as the Chen-kuan
rituals'.[84] But it is known that this code removed what had been the
sixth section in its Chen-kuan predecessor, the section for the deaths of
emperors, 'on the grounds that it involved anticipating untoward
events and that this was not an appropriate theme for discussion by
officials'. The Hsien-ch'ing code also formalized the adoption of the
single supreme cosmic agent, the god of high heaven (*hao t'ien shang
ti*), that had figured in discussions of the great sacrifice in the Ming-
t'ang and other major cosmic rituals. The code prescribed offerings to
this divinity at the round altar ceremony, at an observance to pray for
grain, at the summer sacrifice for rain, and at the great sacrifice in the
Ming-t'ang and at the suburban altars.[85]

The promulgation of the Hsien-ch'ing code, however, by no means
terminated argument over the dynastic ritual programme. The issue of
the place of Cheng Hsüan's five direction gods was soon brought back,
and by 667, they had been re-instated in major rituals.[86] Dissatisfaction
with the code led in 676 to its annulment and to the restoration of the
Chen-kuan code.[87] Then, the following year, the Hsien-ch'ing code
was formally described as 'not taking antiquity as its model' and the
Chou ritual was substituted for it.[88] 'From then on, the ritual officials
were still more without an authority and whenever there was a great
event, they collated the texts of rituals from ancient and modern times
and composed directives near the time concerned'.[89] The unsettled
court conditions and the special requirements of the empress Wu,
herself the compiler of two compendia on ritual,[90] caused further
changes. Under these circumstances, for individual scholars a
command of the state ritual tradition continued to be very advantageous in career terms.[91]

This confused situation seems likely to have continued even after the
restoration of the T'ang dynasty in 705. It is unclear, at least, what
authority was used for the directives for the important rituals under
Chung tsung and Jui tsung and in the first years of Hsüan tsung's
reign.[92] But in 717, the official historians were made responsible for
planning at least elements of the ritual programme, and this may have
meant that the principle of *ad hoc* management was still in force.[93] In
722, Wei T'ao (d. after 739), a vice-president of the state academy
directorate and son of a prominent ritual scholar and former directorate president Wei Shu-hsia (*c.* 637–707, canonized *Wen*), was made
ritual commissioner with responsibility for supervising the ritual programme.[94] Then in about 725, it seems probable that the emperor
ordered that the text of the *Yüeh ling*, the section of the *Li chi* that

prescribed ritual and administrative activities on a monthly basis, be re-established.[95]

The commissioning of the third and greatest T'ang ritual code was probably connected with these events, for the *Yüeh ling* posed in acute form the problems associated with literal implementation of canonical prescriptions. At least, it was the difficulty of reconciling the *Li chi* as a whole with contemporary state ritual practice that led to this third attempt to bring permanent stability to the tradition. In 726, a suggestion that the *Li chi* be reorganized and 'appended to the T'ang regulations' was passed to the Chi-hsien yüan. Here it met with the same resistance that the similarly conceived initiative by Yüan Hsing-ch'ung had done in the same year. (Ch. 3, pp. 86–87). Claiming that the *Li chi* was 'through successive ages an inerasable authority', Chang Yüeh, the college's director, proposed that instead of altering it, a new ritual code that would 'make a balanced adjudication' (*che chung*) between the Chen-kuan and Hsien-ch'ing codes should be compiled. A commission, headed by Chang Yüeh and based on the Chi-hsien yüan, was appointed. It included Liu Chih-chi's former colleague Hsü Chien and probably four other scholars.

This commission, however, failed to complete its project, and by the end of 730 both Chang Yüeh and Hsü Chien and another of its members were dead. At this point, Hsüan tsung appointed Hsiao Sung (*c*. 669–749), a senior official who had had general service rather than scholarly experience, to the Chi-hsien yüan to direct this and other scholarly projects. He enlisted several more scholars, one of whom was Lu Shan-ching, the productive commentator to the *Ch'un-ch'iu*, *Mencius* and *Wen hsüan*. In 732, the code was completed, approved and distributed.[96]

The K'ai-yüan ritual code, the earliest in Chinese history that is extant, had the same scope as the Chen-kuan and Hsien-ch'ing codes, its two lost T'ang predecessors. Like them, it grouped directives for the rituals in the state ritual programme under five traditional headings. The total number of rituals was just over 150. Some of them, like the Feng and Shan rites, had been the subject of prolonged and detailed discussion. The basic position the code's compilers adopted was pluralistic. They answered at least some of the ritual controversies of the preceding century by expanding individual rites and by incorporating recommendations that had previously been considered mutually exclusive. In the case of the Ming-t'ang, the code literally integrated the stipulations of the two previous codes, prescribing an annual total of eighteen ritual observances for the building. These were for the great sacrifice in the final month of autumn, twelve monthly readings of 'commands' (*ling*), and readings for the four seasons and the final month of summer.[97] In effect it combined the stipulations of the Chen-kuan and Hsien-ch'ing codes with regard to the god of high heaven and the direction gods, not only in the great Ming-t'ang sacrifice but in the southern suburban ritual and the summer prayer for rain.[98] It therefore exemplified the expansion that is to be seen in Hsüan tsung's reign in other learned activities and in education. Its inclusive, pluralistic policy also parallels the attitude of high authority towards canonical texts and commentaries in this period.

Besides incorporating ritual directives developed in the seventh century, the code embodied the ritual practice of the decades immediately prior to its production. The prescriptions it gave for the Feng and Shan rites accorded closely with those followed in the climactic performance of the winter of 725.[99] One or two other ceremonies contained in the code were relatively recent introductions, instituted barely in time, as it were, for inclusion. The military cult of T'ai kung, paralleling the ancient civil cult of Confucius, had been established on a significant scale only in 706, and then amplified in 731; but there are two sets of directives for it in the code.[100] Another cult, for the 'five dragons' (*wu lung*) which Hsüan tsung had developed in the course of his reign, was also included.[101]

For each of the rituals in the code, the compiling commission provided detailed directives. The principal participants, their placings, dress, movements and equipment, and the text of the prayers they were to use were prescribed. The timing of the various stages of the observance and the music and ancillary equipment used was stipulated. In the first division of the code, a ritual was normally treated in six sections. There was an initial paragraph describing the preliminary abstinences required of participants. The preparation and deployment of the equipment at the site of the observance were laid down. Then the directives for the principals, as they left the palace or other precinct and went to the site of the ritual; the order of procedure for the ritual itself; and finally the procedure for retiring were all prescribed. For twenty-five of the rituals concerned with 'heaven' in the first division, the compilers included directives for conducting the rituals by proxy, in the absence of the emperor.[102] When the directives of the code are set alongside the detailed regulations for the maintenance of ritual precincts and the supply of the ritual programme contained in the *Liu tien*, a remarkably detailed picture of the programme results. For example, the precise size of the silk offerings, and their colour, which varied according to the divinities to whom they were offered, was stipulated in the regulations for the imperial treasury and its staff.[103]

Later T'ang scholars considered the codification of 732 the most authoritative of the three the dynasty undertook. They came to regard it as a high point not only in ritual scholarship, but even, like the Feng and Shan rites on mount T'ai in 725, in the dynasty itself.[104] Yet in one sense it never came near fulfilling its formal purpose. It did not silence argument over individual rites any more than its predecessor codes had done. The climate remained one of expansion and innovation. In the fourth and fifth decades of the eighth century, there was no direct threat to the sense of wealth and security that had permitted state ritual to prosper so spectacularly. Revision of the directives for individual observances was resumed almost immediately after the emperor promulgated the code. The scholars of the Chi-hsien yüan, for example, redrafted the ploughing rite for a particularly important performance in 735.[105] The southern suburban ritual was revised for performance in 742.[106] In 745, certain rites were raised from minor to medium status.[107] Over this period, also, a number of cults to individual exemplar figures were established.[108] In 748, the provision of ritual status to the descendants of the two dynasties that had preceded the T'ang, the Northern Chou and the Sui, was expanded to include a descendant of the Northern Wei, enfieffed as duke of Han. In 750, as a result of a suggestion from a recluse and a discussion by senior officials, this provision was abolished altogether, only to be restored in 753.[109] It is also possible that the interest shown in the T'ien-pao period in the *Yüeh ling* section of the *Li chi* resulted in alterations in the state ritual programme.

The ritual tradition and the examination system

The importance of the state ritual programme to the dynasty and to the scholarly community was such that it greatly influenced the examination system. The role that state ritual came to have in the selection process in turn contributed substantially to the identity of the scholarly and intellectual elite within the official body. There were several distinct ways in which state ritual became a major theme in recruitment for office. The most straightforward was the use of the three ritual canons, the *Li chi*, *I li* and *Chou li*, as part of the established curriculum in the official school system and as examinable texts in the regular doctoral examinations. All three ritual canons were involved, probably from the start of the dynasty (Ch. 3, p. 77). Though its popularity among candidates appears to have derived from its relative brevity rather than because it contained important ritual material, in the K'ai-yüan period, the *Li chi* was particularly studied. Secondly, in the dissertation section of the *chin shih*, and in decree examinations, examiners used the more theoretical aspects of ritual as the topics for sub-questions. This theme in examination questions occurred early in the dynasty and lasted throughout it. In 646 and 688, the relationship between ritual and punishments was a topic;[110] in 719, there was a sub-question on the relationship between ritual and music.[111] The history of state ritual also provided questions: in 696, a knowledge of pre-T'ang discussion of the Ming-t'ang was demanded.[112]

From at least the early eighth century onwards, examiners set state ritual subjects in what had become the most prestigious section of the *chin shih*, the *tsa wen*, the test of composition skills. Candidates, in composing the *shih* and *fu* that the *tsa wen* section had come to comprise, wrote in a public, panegyric style in praise of the dynasty, emphasizing the cosmological role of the rites. They described perfectly executed observances performed by an august sovereign in a harmonious universe. They drew from the model compositions from the Han period or contained in the *Wen hsüan*. The first extant datable *fu* topic, set in 713, was on the ploughing rite.[113] The Ming-t'ang itself provided the *shih* topic for 718.[114] The record of topics and compositions for the reign of Hsüan tsung is fragmentary; but what survives shows that candidates brought the Ming-t'ang or Feng and Shan rites into their answers, even when the topics set might not require them to do so.[115] Although scholars from as early as the mid seventh century developed a tradition of criticizing the place of composition skills in the examinations (Ch. 6, p. 231), they never directly condemned the use of state ritual topics. On behalf of the dynasty, successive examiners in effect made mastery of the traditional language and imagery of state ritual an important, relatively non-technical requirement in recruiting the scholarly elite. In turn, candidates exploited the tradition of euphuistic and hyperbolic description, inherited from the period of disunion, to show their eagerness to serve the T'ang.

Even more significantly, as an indication of the importance of state ritual to high authority, ritual observances provided the theme for the voluntary submissions whereby individual scholars hoped to gain entry into or promotion within the official hierarchy. The Feng and Shan celebration of 725 resulted in large numbers of compositions, some certainly from outside officialdom, and these were examined by the emperor himself. Compositions on the great state observances were considered to add to a scholar's reputation and so help his career prospects. The *fu* on the Ming-t'ang that Li Po (701–762) composed was an exercise intended to express loyalty to the dynasty as well as powers of description.[116] A high flown account attributed to Hsiao Ying-shih of the offering to heaven at the round altar at the winter solstice also falls into this category.[117] In 751, the poet Tu Fu used state ritual observances as the theme for a submission that he hoped would secure him an official tenure. One of his topics concerned the celebration of Feng and Shan rites on mount Hua that scholars and others urged on Hsüan tsung at this period.[118]

Finally, from early in the dynasty, the great non-recurrent ritual observances provided occasions for special examinations. Through them, aspirants to office from outside the official school system, with its restrictive quotas, were able to compete for selection. Under T'ai tsung in 647, an examination was called in advance of the Feng and Shan rites then being planned.[119] Decree examinations were called in 664 in connection with the rites at mount T'ai in 666.[120] In a decree examination called for the celebration on mount Sung in 696, participants were 'numbered by the 10,000', according to Yen Chen-ch'ing. The candidate who came first was Ts'ui Mien, later a prominent court verse writer, official scholar and ritual specialist. Su T'ing, a scholar minister of Hsüan tsung's reign, was also successful.[121] In 725, candidates were again called to mount T'ai, and in 726 the emperor examined candidates at Lo-yang on the return journey.[122]

The Ming-t'ang also provided the occasion for special examinations: in 689 a decree examination was given the title of 'the great ritual in the Ming-t'ang' (*Ming-t'ang ta li k'o*): the name of a successful candidate is known from an epigraphical source.[123] In 695, after the loss of the first building, there was a request for frank admonition that was linked with a call for candidates in various categories of moral worth.[124] The southern suburban rites and the acts of grace that followed them also provided the sovereign with occasions for calling special examinations, for example in 696, 723 and 748.[125] A special examination followed the re-drafted ploughing rite of 735.[126] Changes in reign period were also accompanied by acts of grace and announcements of decree examinations.[127]

In making the state ritual programme integral to its recruitment process, the dynasty thus merged two central concerns of the scholarly community, the ritual programme and the selection system. But in doing this, high authority merely fused existing political energies. The state in effect exploited its own prestige and the eagerness of aspiring officials to serve it. How firmly state ritual had become a theme in the examinations is indicated by the fact that, even in the drastically changed conditions of the post-rebellion period, when great ritual enterprises were no longer possible, state rituals as topics for composition retained their place there.

The post-rebellion period
    The immediate and lasting effect of the An Lu-shan rebellion was drastically to reduce the wealth and the stability of the T'ang state. The post-rebellion ritual programme was therefore a much diminished operation. Not only were the great ritual enterprises of the expansionist phase of the dynasty no longer possible, but the recurrent programme also was subject both to short-term cuts and to long-term deterioration. Nonetheless, neither the imperial house nor the scholar community surrendered their interest in an activity that had acquired such importance in the previous reigns. Controversies about individual rites still occurred, and, in the increasingly factional bureaucratic milieu of the late eighth and ninth centuries, the tradition as a whole became more politicized. The prestige of the ritual achievements of Hsüan tsung's reign had the result that official scholars undertook no further complete codification to replace the K'ai-yüan code. Rather, they perpetuated their compilatory approach to the ritual programme by attempting a succession of supplements to it.

    In this period, the place of state rituals in the examinations benefitted from reformist initiatives, and some striking innovations in curricula resulted. But the theme that reflects better than any other the changed intellectual climate of the post-rebellion reigns is the critical outlook on the ritual programme that a small number of reformist intellectuals developed at the end of the eighth century and the start of the ninth. The principal scholars involved, Tu Yu and Liu Tsung-yüan, made state ritual a theme in a re-appraisal of the scholarly inheritance that affected all the disciplines considered in this book. Here for the first time was an indication of how some of the keenest Confucian-orientated thinkers analysed and justified this central element in their learned tradition.

The imperial ancestral cult
    The reduced scale of the state's ritual programme in the immediate post-rebellion period, and the emergency basis on which it was now often conducted, are shown most clearly by the fact that it was now the

imperial ancestral cult that came to the fore. Even in periods of peace, this cult represented, in a way that other official cults could not, the dynasty itself. It concerned primarily the deceased members of the T'ang imperial line. But the interest of the scholar community in the cult was probably increased by the fact that meritorious officials of successive reigns were also represented in it, through two of the posthumous status systems that the dynasty operated.

The imperial ancestral cult in the T'ang involved two separate operations: the maintaining of successive imperial mausolea, built on or into natural rock in hills some distance to the west of Ch'ang-an, and the proper upkeep of the imperial ancestral temples in the capital cities of Ch'ang-an and Lo-yang. At the time of the rebellion, five imperial mausolea had been completed, those of Hsien-ling, Chao-ling, Ch'ien-ling, Ting-ling and Ch'iao-ling. In 729, Hsüan tsung had chosen the site for his own burial, later the T'ai-ling.[128] The construction and maintenance of these mausolea, two of which, Chao-ling and Ch'ien-ling, were on a particularly grand scale, constituted a point of conflict between emperors, who wished for lavish and grandiose tomb complexes, and Confucian-orientated advisors, who asked for austerity.[129] But the mausolea also provided the sites for one of the important posthumous status systems in the gift of the sovereign. This was the provision for 'satellite' burials of meritorious officials and their immediate descendants, close to the tombs of the emperor they had served. Though this provision was operated on a large scale only in the case of T'ai tsung's mausoleum at Chao-ling, it provided a permanent monument to the ideal of dynastic service and of a close relationship with the sovereign.[130]

The imperial ancestral temple, maintenance of which constituted the second operation of the cult, was founded at Ch'ang-an in 618, with chapels (*shih*) for four deceased members of the imperial line.[131] From then on, it had given rise to numerous controversies. In 635, after debate, it was expanded to six chapels.[132] It was maintained at this number by the ritual 'displacement' (*ch'ien*) of the spirit tablet of an earlier member of the imperial line after a T'ang emperor died. Following the deaths of every seventh- and early eighth-century sovereign, from Kao tsu until Jui tsung, with the exception of Kao tsung,[133] there was argument about how and in what numbers deceased T'ang sovereigns and remoter, pre-T'ang members of the line should be represented in the temple. Some of these debates had a competitive aspect, and involved not only those in ritual office, but scholars from outside institutions as well. During the reign of the empress Wu, because of the empress's establishment of a separate Wu Chou ancestral temple, they acquired a highly political character.[134]

In 705, following the T'ang restoration, it had been decided, again after debate, to continue to maintain the Lo-yang temple, even though it duplicated that at Ch'ang-an.[135] In 716, however, after delay and a reversed decision, the empress Wu was deprived of the title of Sheng ti (Sage emperor), by which she had been represented in the temple.[136] In 717, a partial collapse of the Ch'ang-an building provoked wide discussion. Some scholars understood this as a highly portentous event, while others saw it simply as the inevitable result of the use of timbers dating from early in the period of disunion.[137]

Finally, the number of chapels in the temple had been maintained at six, when the tablets of Chung tsung and Jui tsung had been introduced, by the ritual 'displacement' of senior members of the line. A seventh place, facing east, had been kept empty. But in 723, at the suggestion of the Liu Chih-chi's fellow official historian Hsü Chien, Hsüan tsung further increased the number of chapels, so that they stood now at nine, a number less easily justified by the ritual tradition. This nine-chapel arrangement, defended in a decree that contains one of the best brief apologies for T'ang imperial love of expansion in state ritual,[138] was still in force in the post-rebellion period, and, moreover, was still controversial. It was followed in the late K'ai-yüan period by further attempts, initiated by Hsüan tsung, to elaborate the provisioning of offerings in the temple rites.[139]

The interest of the scholar community in the dynastic ancestral temple was also ensured by the fact that the spirit tablets of a highly selected few of their own number, on average about four a reign, were introduced into it. This great honour was granted to some of the foremost scholar ministers of the T'ang, but again it had highly political overtones. Not only were the numbers involved very small, but the honour, once given, was not necessarily permanent. In the first half of the dynasty, the spirit tablet of the scholar minister Fang Hsüan-ling was introduced into T'ai tsung's chapel by an edict of 649, but withdrawn in 653, because of his son's sedition. Hsü Ching-tsung's tablet was installed in 686, but withdrawn in 706 following the T'ang restoration.[140]

The rebellion of An Lu-shan put an end to the prosperity on which the imperial state ritual programme as a whole had depended; but the desecration of the sites associated with the imperial ancestral cult was a particular humiliation. During the warfare of 755–7, the Lo-yang ancestral temple was occupied by rebel troops, while that at Ch'ang-an

was destroyed, with all its equipment.[141] After the recapture of
Ch'ang-an, a sequence of scholar officials, holding either established
ritual posts or else the ritual commissionerships originally established
in the pre-rebellion period probably for imperial funerals, tried to
restore the state ritual programme and particularly the rituals associated with the imperial ancestral temple.[142] By the end of Su tsung's
reign, a range of imperial observances, including the southern suburban rites in 758 and 762, and, in a deliberately austere version, the
ploughing rite in 759, had been performed.[143] Under Tai tsung, the
southern suburban rites were performed again in the spring of 764.[144]
The post-rebellion official scholar and rescript writer Yang Wan was
said to have been effective in re-establishing the ritual programme.[145]

From the loss of Ch'ang-an in 756, however, it was the imperial
ancestral cult that most concerned the emperor, and provoked the
strongest response from the scholar community. Even before the court
returned to Ch'ang-an, Yü Hsiu-lieh, by this time a major official
scholar, was appointed to confront the problems caused by the
destruction of the temple.[146] On re-entering the capital, Su tsung
performed a rite of contrition that lasted for three days.[147] Later, an
observance involving offerings to newly made spirit tablets for the
deceased T'ang emperors was held.[148] Efforts to recover the temple
furnishings were abandoned in accordance with an edict in early
758,[149] and by the summer of that year a new nine-chapel temple was
complete, and the spirit tablets installed in it.[150]

The difficulties were, however, far from over. In 763, when the court
under Tai tsung returned from its evacuation in the face of Tibetan
incursions, and again in 766, the proper maintenance of the imperial
ancestral cult caused further controversy. On both occasions, the
initiator of criticisms of the way it was operated was the great loyalist
scholar and ritual specialist Yen Chen-ch'ing, and his opponent was
the politically powerful Yüan Tsai (d. 777, canonized *Ch'eng-tsung*), a
figure whom scholars particularly resented.[151]

Yen Chen-ch'ing, whose writings on state ritual were posthumously
edited by a disciple into a collection of ten *chüan*,[152] was particularly
significant in the post-rebellion history of the dynastic ancestral cult.
Even before the rebellion, as a junior officer at Li-ch'üan to the west
of Ch'ang-an, the county in which T'ai tsung's mausoleum stood, and
as an investigating censor, he had had experience of both the mausolea
and the ancestral temple at Ch'ang-an.[153] After the rebellion, he
considered that the maintenance not only of the imperial ancestral
temple but also of court protocol were important expressions of the

dynasty's will to recover its former stability.[154] As the ritual commissioner on the death of Tai tsung in 779, he took part in the two long running controversies about the ancestral temple that, from this point into the ninth century, dominate the record for state ritual. These were at one level issues of ritual management; but at another they reflected the instabilities and frustrations of the political situation at Ch'ang-an. Both issues were as characteristic of their period as concern for the Ming-t'ang and the Feng and Shan rites had been of the expansionist phase of the dynasty.

The first of these controversies, lasting for twenty-two years from late 781, involved the participation of several hundred scholars and is particularly well documented. It concerned the correct arrangement of the imperial spirit tablets in their chapels in the temple. Up to the deaths of Hsüan tsung and Su tsung, the ancestral temple, with nine chapels, had contained the spirit tablets of the five T'ang emperors from Kao tsu to Jui tsung, and the four pre-T'ang ancestors in the T'ang imperial line originally represented when the four-chapel temple was established in 618. One of these, Kao tsu's grandfather, moreover, though not the most senior in the line, had a special status, as T'ai tsu, the first T'ang ancestor to be enfieffed in the region corresponding to the ancient state of T'ang.

This nine-chapel arrangement meant, therefore, that the spirit tablets of emperors who had died after Jui tsung could only be introduced by 'displacing' remoter members of the T'ang imperial lineage. This happened in 763 or 764, after Hsüan tsung and Su tsung had been represented by spirit tablets in the temple. To make room for them, the tablets of the two remotest ancestors, Hsien tsu and I tsu, were taken out of the main temple and stored in a side room. Then the death of Tai tsung in 779 created the need for further 'displacement'. When, in 781, a collective offering (*hsia*) was planned for the temple, the question of whether these remote ancestors, displaced after the deaths of Hsüan tsung, Su tsung and Tai tsung, should be included in it became a matter of controversy.

To include the tablets of the two remote forbears Hsien tsu and I tsu, however, meant that T'ai tsu, Kao tsu's grandfather, who was junior to them but had special status, could not occupy the principal, east-facing position in the temple, as some ritual scholars now believed that he should. In the early T'ang, this east-facing position had been kept empty; but ritual scholars, confronted by the need to accommodate more deceased T'ang emperors, concluded that it should now be filled. The question was whether, as many believed, it should be T'ai tsu who should fill it, or whether, at *hsia* offerings, Hsien tsu as the most senior member of the line should hold it.[155]

The debate was started by Ch'en Ching (d. 805), a *chin shih*, former disciple of Tu-ku Chi, and an erudit of the court of sacrifices. When Ch'en Ching suggested that the two most remote T'ang ancestors might be excluded from the offering and T'ai tsu given the east-facing position, his proposal was 'put out to discussion'. Yen Chen-ch'ing, then at the height of his personal prestige, argued the opposite position and prevailed. The two remoter T'ang forebears were brought in, and T'ai tsu was given a position in one of the side rooms. The issue, however, remained controversial, and over the next two decades, as successive offerings were conducted, some of the most prominent scholars of the period submitted statements. These included Chang Chien (744–804, canonized *Hsien*), a scholar who had grown up in the south-east and known Yen Chen-ch'ing, and who was an erudit of the court of sacrifices in 784 and an official historian. The ritual scholar Liu Mien (d. after 803), the son of the important historian Liu Fang, who was related to Yen Chen-ch'ing and was said in his career to have attempted to realize Yen's concerns, was also among those who participated. There were major debates in 792, 795, 799 and 802. Ch'en Ching memorialized again in the course of this long running debate. Then, as it drew to a close, he submitted a statement adhering to his original position that the two displaced ancestors should be given separate premises and offerings. Finally, in 803, after prolonged indecision on Te tsung's part, Ch'en's position was accepted: the two remote ancestors concerned were hastily given separate precincts, T'ai tsu was granted the principal, east-facing position in the temple, and the emperor was congratulated on the resolution of the problem.

This long controversy, involving 112 participants in the year 803 alone, suggests the particular difficulties affecting the scholar community during Te tsung's reign. Though the emperor was said, on his accession, 'profoundly to esteem ritual and law', he became, after the humiliating reverses of his Hopei campaigns, suspicious, liable to take up with favourites and inaccessible. Perhaps because the general ritual programme, drastically affected by the An Lu-shan rebellion, had been further damaged by the occupation of Ch'ang-an in 784,[156] the emperor became especially meticulous over ritual directives, and cross-questioned scholars closely on their proposals.[157] He was particularly fastidious where the imperial ancestral cult was concerned.[158] There is some evidence that he tried to establish empire-wide dynastic temples, a measure none of his T'ang predecessors had attempted.[159]

Te tsung's attitude towards the imperial cult is made clearer by another ritual issue, involving the second site for the dynastic ancestral cult, the imperial mausolea, which was debated and resolved at its first discussion in 798. The outcome of this debate was that Te tsung, though usually miserly, approved lavish expenditure on large-scale new shrines for seven of the eight T'ang mausolea and repair of the eighth. He also inspected individually every item of furnishing made for these shrines.[160] Ch'en Ching, the scholar who had contributed three times to the debate on T'ai tsu's position in the ancestral temple, took part in discussion of this second issue too, managing in his submission to anticipate the emperor's own position. Te tsung came to hold him in great esteem, and believed that he might make a chief minister.[161] But instead, incapacitated by a sudden illness, he was appointed deputy-director of the imperial library. Ch'en Ching's role in both these debates, however, and the very large numbers of scholars who joined him in them, suggest that the imperial ancestral cult provided otherwise scarce opportunities of attracting the emperor's notice and gaining career advantages. It is probably not a coincidence that over this period several of the presidents of the court of sacrifices were appointed to chief ministerships.[162] The scholarly submissions that survive for these two issues for the most part show the traditional range for such discussions. But the history of the dynastic ancestral cult under Te tsung also suggests that the state ritual tradition had become further politicized.

Scholars saw the accession of Hsien tsung in 806 as a time of dynastic revival, and indeed there is some evidence of special attention being given to the state ritual programme. Like most T'ang emperors at the start of their reigns, Hsien tsung performed the southern suburban rites.[163] The system whereby the spirit tablets of meritorious officials were introduced into the imperial ancestral temple was brought up to date. Since the rebellion, those introduced had tended to be loyalist generals or general service officials who had been successful in military campaigns for the dynasty. The most straightforward case had been Kuo Tzu-i, introduced into Tai tsung's temple promptly after his death in 781, the only official to find a place there. In 809, P'ei Mien (703–69, canonized *Hsien-mu*) was introduced into · Su tsung's chapel, while three outstanding military figures, Tuan Hsiu-shih (d. 783, canonized *Chung-lieh*); Li Sheng (727–93, canonized *Chung-wu*); and, a month later, Hun Chen (736–99, canonized *Chung-wu*), were introduced into Te tsung's chapel.[164] A celebration of the ploughing rite was projected, after a long lapse in the performance of this ritual, for 811, though it was finally abandoned.[165] Towards the end of the reign, also, after the dynasty's military successes in Hopei, there were calls for the celebration of the Feng and Shan rites on mount T'ai.[166]

It was at the start of the following reign that the second of the particularly long-running controversies involving the imperial ancestral cult came briefly to the fore.[167] The issue, which was merely the most prominent of a number in the ninth century concerning the ancestral temple, was whether the dynasty was ritually correct in maintaining concurrently two imperial ancestral temples, at Ch'ang-an and Lo-yang. The Lo-yang temple, after its use as barracks by the rebels in the An Lu-shan rebellion, had been abandoned for some decades, though its spirit tablets had been retrieved and preserved. In 780, however, Yen Chen-ch'ing had proposed that the Lo-yang temple be re-established and maintained. Though no decision had been taken, the issue had been discussed intermittently in Te tsung's reign. The question was raised again in 820 by the administration at Lo-yang. Cheng Yin (752-829, canonized *Hsüan* or *Chao*), then governor of Lo-yang and a former president of the court of sacrifices, opposed maintaining a second temple.[168] The debate that followed included a major contribution by an erudit of the court of sacrifices, Wang Yen-wei (d. *c.* 845, canonized *Ching* or *Hsien*), later an important scholar and general service official.[169] But discussion without resolution followed until 845, when, probably for two reasons, the court renewed its interest in the issue. The authorities had abundant timber following the empire-wide suppression of Buddhism in 843.[170] It is also possible that the dynasty entertained contingency plans for evacuation to Lo-yang, and believed it prudent to maintain a second imperial ancestral temple in that connection.

At least fifty officials were now involved in the debate, which lasted into the next year. They reviewed the history of the Lo-yang temple, from its original establishment under the empress Wu and reconstitution in 705 as a T'ang shrine. Chou and Han precedents for a dynasty running more than one temple were quoted. The authority of the *Shang shu*, *Mao shih*, *Li chi*, *Ch'un-ch'iu* and *Tso* and *Ku-liang chuan* and the *Mencius* was cited. Though the more authoritative case was made by opponents of the second temple, this was set aside, and an edict ordered that the Lo-yang shrine be rebuilt and that the spirit tablets that had survived the An Lu-shan rebellion nearly a century before be reinstated there.

This was by no means the last of the ritual controversies in which official scholars engaged. In the second half of the ninth century, issues of ritual management still provided a medium for proving erudition and powers of arguments.[171] The ancestral temple and its proper rituals figure centrally in accounts of the disorders and emergencies that accompanied the final years of the dynasty. Following an earthquake, the Huang Ch'ao occupation of Ch'ang-an in 880–3 and the further evacuation of the city that took place in 885, the ancestral temple was again destroyed. By this stage, however, the government was too impoverished to undertake rebuilding the precinct that, above all others, stood for the dynasty. When, in 887, the emperor Hsi tsung had re-occupied the city, a precinct in the imperial workshops was used for the imperial ancestral cult. The ritual officials drafted an observance to express contrition that was based explicitly on the observances held in connection with the partial collapse of the temple structure at Ch'ang-an in 717 and its destruction by the An Lu-shan rebels in 757.[172]

Scholars participated in ritual drafting even after this, and the last information recorded for T'ang state ritual again concerned the arrangement of the imperial tablets in an improvised shrine. A president of the court of sacrifices was appointed as late as 904, and holders of scholarly office assisted in the rituals attendant on the abdication of T'ang power, in 907.[173]

Decline in the state ritual programme

The importance to the dynasty of the imperial ancestral temple meant that, even in the middle and late ninth century, the controversies involving its rituals were comparatively well recorded. From the middle decades of the ninth century, however, the rest of the dynasty's ritual programme is barely documented at all. The ritual monographs in the *Chiu* and *Hsin T'ang shu* cease to trace developments in most of the main rituals after the Yüan-ho period.[174] What little information has survived in other sources provides poor evidence for the extent to which the programme as a whole was implemented. As in other areas of administration also, the reform proposals that were submitted intermittently through the ninth century do not provide a good guide for what actually took place.

There was probably, however, deterioration throughout the period: in 828, the celebrated decree examination candidate Liu Fen stated that the southern suburban rites were neglected;[175] the reading of the seasonal orders was defunct before 834.[176] The *Ch'ih-chou* ceremony for the crown prince appears to have lapsed.[177] In 836, the scholarly emperor Wen tsung issued an edict attempting to restore decorum to rites held in the ancestral temple and at the suburban altars.[178] By 851, the southern suburban rites were again in difficulties and the Feng and Shan rites stated to be no longer possible. The archery ceremony in the state academy directorate was also defunct,[179] and a ritual whereby prefectural governors feasted departing metropolitan examination candidates was poorly performed.[180]

The last recorded southern suburban celebration was in 877.[181] After this, it was the ancestral temple that dominated accounts of T'ang state ritual. It can only be assumed that, in the successive emergencies that followed the Huang Ch'ao rebellion, the many other observances in the dynastic ritual code were at best fitfully performed.

The dynastic ritual code in post-rebellion times

The reduced scale of the post-rebellion ritual programme is particularly clear in the attitude of scholars towards the great ritual code of 732, the *K'ai-yüan li*. In practice, ritual specialists continued to depart from the code in re-drafting individual rites. As early as Tai tsung's reign, they may even have considered more systematic re-drafting of directives. But at the same time, both in debates and in compilations of ritual directives or surveys of the tradition, they cited the K'ai-yüan code with a frequency that shows that they considered it the major authority. Instead of attempting any further complete codification, they looked back at the K'ai-yüan code and promoted it as the expression of T'ang state ritual at its zenith.

In the post rebellion period, therefore, scholars compiled a number of supplements or revisions of the code. The first was in 780, when Yen Chen-ch'ing as ritual commissioner was ordered, with the erudits of the court of sacrifices and others, to condense the code's directives relating to the formal conduct of princesses of the imperial family.[182] Damage recorded as done to the ritual records in the disorders of 783 at Ch'ang-an may have added to the need for supplementary drafting. Chang Chien, as an erudit of the court of sacrifices from 784, was said to have played a role in making good the losses.[183] Another initiative came in 791 from Pao Chi (d. 792), a *chin shih* of 747, former financial official in the south-east and friend of Ch'üan Te-yü and of Hsiao Ying-shih's son Hsiao Ts'un. As director of the imperial library, Pao Chi took up a theme that had been of concern to high authority in the late pre-rebellion period. He asked that the points of conflict between the K'ai-yüan code and the prescriptive *Yüeh ling* chapter of the *Li chi* (Ch. 3, pp. 87–88) be reconciled. The request was approved; but Pao Chi died soon after, and the matter lapsed.[184]

In the court of sacrifices, re-drafting of directives for individual rites was apparently continual over this period. In 793, a rank of compiler (*hsiu chuan*) was instituted there.[185] In 801, the first supplement to the K'ai-yüan code was presented to the throne. This was likely to have been a collection of directives used in state rituals since the promulgation of the code, and particularly under Te tsung. But only the name of its chief compiler, Wei Chü-mou (749–801, canonized *Chung* or *Yin*), a verse writer from the south-east, friend of Yen Chen-ch'ing and Ch'üan Te-yü, advocate of a syncretic approach to the three teachings, and, from 796 a favourite of Te tsung, is known.[186]

The high status that the K'ai-yüan code enjoyed, even while scholars were willing to modify or vary its directives in the case of individual rites, is well illustrated by the major institutional compilation of the post-rebellion period, the *T'ung tien* of Tu Yu. In the *T'ung tien*, Tu in effect subjected the whole T'ang dynastic state to critical review (Ch. 5, pp. 203–05). He was also one of the few scholars of the period whose writing suggests a new and analytical attitude to the state ritual tradition. Yet he, no less than others, conceded the greatness of the codification of 732. In the *T'ung tien*, he included a condensation of the code that took up no less than two thirds of the total space he allocated to state ritual. But in a separate section, he traced the evolution that had taken place in a wider range of rituals before and since 732. In his entries for individual rites in this section, he indicated when the prescriptions of the code had not been binding, and when evolution in practice had continued.[187] This feature of his survey of state ritual shows that for the majority of rituals in the code, including, for example, the *Shih-tien* rituals to Confucius and to T'ai kung, the directives contained in K'ai-yüan code still held.[188] But for other observances, these directives had been displaced by revisions and by new prescriptions.[189]

The *T'ung tien* contains another, slighter indication of the willingness of late eighth-century state ritual scholars to go beyond the K'ai-yüan ritual code in the case of certain rites. This concerned the imperial funeral rituals that, in the seventh and early eighth centuries, had been judged 'not an appropriate theme for discussion by officials'. Tu Yu set aside the T'ang tradition that imperial funeral directives should be destroyed after use and be re-drafted after each emperor's death. He edited into the *T'ung tien* a set of directives, very possibly by the ritual commissioner of the time, Yen Chen-ch'ing, for the funeral of Tai tsung in 779.[190] This precedent was followed in 806, after the deaths of Te tsung and Shun tsung, when the ritual commissioner in charge of the funerals, the chief minister Tu Huang-shang

(738–808, canonized *Hsüan*), a relative of Tu Yu, appointed two ritual scholars to draft the directives needed. This time, the resulting texts were formally approved for permanent keeping in the court of sacrifices. They are not extant; but the sceptical intellectual Liu Tsung-yüan wrote a preface for them, praising them highly, and recording the contribution that the family of one of their compilers, his brother-in-law P'ei Chin, had made to state ritual from the seventh century, over no fewer than five generations.[191]

Official scholars made another attempt to revise the K'ai-yüan ritual code in 808, though no result is recorded.[192] In 816, another ritual scholar submitted a compilation in 30 *chüan* of ritual texts that post-dated the K'ai-yüan code.[193] In 818, another, similar initiative was taken. Cheng Yü-ch'ing, a chief minister and an associate of the Confucian revivalist Han Yü, was ordered to re-draft the court's 'ceremonial procedures' (*ch'ao i*). A commission, which included Han Yü, was appointed, and 'the ceremonial regulations of the court and the five [kinds of] ritual, auspicious and ill-omened, all underwent adjustment'. But again, no description, not even the title of a compilation, has survived.[194]

Another, better documented supplement to the K'ai-yüan code was also made in 818. Wang Yen-wei, the scholar who in 820 made a major contribution to the debate on the Lo-yang imperial ancestral temple, had started his career by working unofficially in the library of the court of sacrifices. There he compiled what was probably in part a register of ritual material from the start of the dynasty, and partly a compendium of imperial orders relating to rituals issued over the 'close-on ninety years' since the code's promulgation in 732. Wang Yen-wei's compilation led to his appointment as an erudit in the court of sacrifices. It was cited in ritual controversies; but again has not survived. Wang was also an expert on the canonization system, and may have compiled a separate treatise on it.[195]

Apart from these works, most of which bore an explicit relationship to the K'ai-yüan code, ritual scholars also compiled other compendia of directives. Most of these now exist as titles only: for example, a work entitled *Lei li* (*Rituals by category*), by the *Ch'un-ch'iu* scholar Lu Ch'un, is a particularly regrettable loss.[196] Chung Tzu-ling, the erudit of the court of sacrifices under Te tsung whom Ch'üan Te-yü had praised for exemplifying 'the way of the teacher', compiled a work on ritual dress in ten *chüan*, which he presented in 793.[197] In 795, the president of the court presented a work called *Ch'eng yü yüeh ling* (*Monthly regulations for carriages*), the title of which again suggests

the use of the *Yüeh ling* chapter of the *Li chi* as a framework for
dynastic ritual prescriptions.[198] Such compilations were produced
probably until very late in the dynasty. A ritual specialist of the late
ninth century and an expert in the K'ai-yüan code, Po Tsung-hui
(839–99) compiled a *Wang kung chia miao lu (Record of the family
temples of princes and dukes)* in five *chüan*.[199]

One such compendium does, however, survive: the *Ta T'ang chiao
ssu lu (Record of suburban and temple observances for the great T'ang)*,
in ten *chüan*, by Wang Ching, a compiler and then an erudit of the
court of sacrifices under Te tsung. This invaluable work provides
corroborative evidence independent of the official histories and the
T'ung tien and *Hui yao*, for the evolution and controversies surrounding a number of rituals, both those contained in the code and certain
Taoist observances outside its scope. Wang Ching probably held ritual
posts over twenty-five years, and was a true scholar of the T'ang ritual
tradition, critically aware of the historical development of state rituals.
His entry for the cult of T'ai kung includes an account of the
controversies the cult provoked among anti-military scholars after 788,
and is the only detailed source for its history at that stage.[200]

After the Yüan-ho period, scholars continued to re-draft individual
rituals. But partly because of the high esteem for the K'ai-yüan code,
which lasted through the Five Dynasties period, and partly because of
the deterioration in conditions, no further codification or supplementary compendia appear to have been produced.

The examination in state ritual

The importance to the dynasty of the state ritual programme
meant that, even after the rebellion, it provided a major theme in
examinations. In the *tsa wen* section of the *chin shih*, until the very end
of the dynasty, candidates continued to be required to describe in
hyperbolic imagery the idealized state ritual observance.[201] But in the
dissertation section of the *chin shih* and in decree examinations,
questions on state ritual became sometimes more searching and more
indicative of the changed conditions in which the state ritual
programme was conducted.

Two sub-questions set by the major Confucian scholar of Te tsung's
reign Lu Hsüan kung in 785, for example, indicated that there was
dissatisfaction with the attitudes of those involved in rituals: 'The ritual
officials deploy the equipment for the rites and music but do not know
the emotions [that they should have]; the students recite the text of the
ritual and music [canons], but do not investigate the observances [to

which they refer]'.[202] Another sub-question, set in a decree
examination of 788, asked what rituals might promote revival of
Confucian learning.[203] In 805, Ch'üan Te-yü required *chin shih*
candidates to comment on the long running debate about the position
of T'ai tsu's spirit tablet in the ancestral temple.[204] Po Chü-i's
collection of model dissertation questions and answers, the *Ts'e lin*
(*Forest of dissertations*) of 806, contained the question, 'How may the
collapse in ritual be remedied?' Another question in the *Ts'e lin*
required an explanation of the link between evolution in ritual practice
and social stability. Another concerned the proposition that attitudes
behind sacrifices had degenerated, and there was a further question on
extravagant burial. Po Chü-i's model answers took the position of the
moderate reformer: there had indeed been decline in state ritual, but
measures could be taken to prevent it getting worse.[205] The Chou
dynasty provided the model in rituals, but evolution was justified,
provided that basic intentions were honoured.[206] Lavish burials were
an evil that should be prevented.[207]

The most striking indication of the importance of ritual in the
examination system, however, is provided by the establishment of a
special curriculum in the state ritual programme.[208] In 786, it was
decreed that the K'ai-yüan code itself should be examinable in the *ming
ching*. Teaching was to be provided by the officials of the court of
sacrifices, and the examination took the form of one hundred questions
on the code and three dissertations. This examination probably
became operative only in 789, the year in which another syllabus,
requiring specialization in the three ritual canons, was also established
(Ch. 3, p. 96). In 793, these two examinations were made to run in
parallel. The names of a number of successful candidates from the
ninth century survive to indicate that these specialist *ming ching*
options were not as lacking in prestige as those in law, orthography or
mathematics. The use of the K'ai-yüan code as an examinable text ran
on through the Five Dynasties and until 993, when the Sung authorities
replaced the code with the first of their own codes.[209]

The K'ai-yüan code constitutes the only example of a T'ang normative institutional compendium providing a respected examination
syllabus. There were unsuccessful attempts by reformist scholars in the
second half of the eighth century and the first decade of the ninth to
have other T'ang compendia, including the *Liu tien* and the criminal
code, established as examination texts. Indeed had these attempts been
successful, the examination system might have developed a less literary
and classicist and more technical, administrative bias. The great ritual

code of 732, however, differed from the *Liu tien* and the criminal code in certain crucial respects. State ritual conventionally remained the vehicle for the highest ideals that the medieval Confucian tradition formulated about government, contrasting especially with the criminal code in that respect. Scholars of a range of different intellectual temperaments considered that the K'ai-yüan code symbolized the T'ang tradition of government at a moment of unprecedented success. When in 785, Liu Mien, the follower of Yen Chen-ch'ing, as an erudit of the court of sacrifices, referred to the code as 'an inerasable inheritance', he used a phrase that T'ang scholars normally applied to the Confucian canons themselves.[210]

Critical perspectives on the state ritual tradition
In the course of their serving careers, most of the major intellectual figures of the late eighth and early ninth centuries had experience of the state ritual programme. Ch'üan Te-yü, for example, held office three times in the court of sacrifices, once in 792 as an erudit and twice under Hsien tsung as the court's president.[211] Kao Ying, his fellow rescript writer and predecessor as chief examiner, was twice the court's president, in 801 and again in late 806.[212] Both Ch'üan Te-yü and Han Yü,[213] contributed to the long-running debate under Te tsung on the position of T'ai tsu's spirit tablet in the imperial ancestral temple. The official historian Chang Chien also held office as an erudit in the court and contributed to the debate.[214] Li Ao memorialized to Hsien tsung on the proper maintenance of the mausolea observances.[215] As a provincial official, he also participated in one of the sacrifices to 'mountains and great rivers' ordered in 810.[216] Under Hsien tsung, Han Yü was required to draft ceremonial directives.[217] The *Ch'un-ch'iu* scholar Lu Ch'un took part in the T'ai tsu debate in 795, and played a leading role in the controversy over the military cult of T'ai kung in 788.[218] As a very senior official, Tu Yu was required in 803 to report the conclusion of the T'ai tsu debate to the temple to Lao tzu.[219] In 803–5, Liu Tsung-yüan, like Yen Chen-ch'ing nearly fifty years before him, had experience of state ritual as part of his duties as an investigating censor.[220]

It is however their unofficial writings, rather than their official biographies or submissions made in an official context, that best reveal the attitudes of these scholars to state ritual. The differences in perspective between members of the scholar community, moreover, suggest the same polarity that may be seen in their outlook on other learned disciplines. Those scholars who were temperamentally drawn to the idea that the regeneration of society depended primarily on the individual and his moral and spiritual life appear to have had little critical perspective on state ritual. The most radical re-evaluation of the state's ritual programme came rather from scholars who, like Tu Yu and Liu Tsung-yüan, believed primarily in reform at the political and institutional level, and who in effect reserved spiritual questions to their private lives as Buddhists. These scholars not only had more incisive attitudes towards reform of dynastic government generally, they also wrote in political philosophical terms about the origins of the state and the function of its rituals.

Neither Han Yü nor Li Ao, therefore, subjected the state ritual programme in whole or in part to the analytical scrutiny they applied, in their different ways, to interior concepts, to man's nature and feelings. Indeed the state religious system, with its elaborate programme restricted to the emperor, seems to have been remote from their normal concerns. There is no mention, for example, in their unofficial writings, of the priorities within the Confucian pantheon that had so preoccupied ministers and official scholars in the seventh and early eighth centuries. The criticisms of ritual practice that have survived in their unofficial writings are not directed at the imperial ritual programme at all, but rather at observances at the individual or personal level. Both brought their anti-Buddhism to bear on private ritual practice. Both condemned the integration of Buddhist mourning practice with traditional Confucian prescriptions.[221] Li Ao criticized Confucian scholars for their insistence on 'solemnity of manner' (*wei i*), a term that sometimes concerned ritual.[222] He also promoted ritual at the personal and individual level as a means to attaining his goal of 'sincerity and enlightenment'.[223]

Those scholars who wrote unofficially about the state and its institutions, on the other hand, provided some incisive comments on the ritual tradition. They brought to bear on the state ritual programme not simply a sceptical intellectual temper, but also the experience that they derived from their careers as general service officials. They insisted that the ritual programme justify itself in an overall view of the polity, and that it have a social function. Less than two decades after the rebellion, the *Ch'un-ch'iu* scholars of the south-east already give some hint of this kind of approach. Chao K'uang, in his analysis of the triennial *ti* offering in the imperial ancestral temple as it was recorded in the *Ch'un-ch'iu*, emphasized that it was an imperial prerogative, despite the fact that the *Ch'un-ch'iu* entered it as conducted in the state of Lu. 'For the feudatories to perform the rituals of the son of heaven was not the duke of Chou's intention'.[224] This insistence on the status specific, exclusively imperial character of a ritual may be understood as an attempt to reassert imperial or central government authority at a time of growing provincial autonomy. For the reformist ideal was that authority should be centralized or that 'power should come from one outlet'.[225] Chao K'uang was also responsible for a particularly frank attack on the integrity of the *Li chi*. Since the *Li chi* incorporated the *Yüeh ling*, a major sanction for the cosmological aspect of the imperial ritual programme, his attack may also have been an indirect criticism of this element in imperial rites.[226]

The greatest scholarly monument to reformist interest in state ritual was, however, the *T'ung tien* of Tu Yu, the 200 *chüan* compendium that subjected almost the entire polity to critical review. Much of the *T'ung tien's* large ritual section is in the compilatory mode that was so basic to T'ang scholars. But both by editorial decisions and by inserted comments, Tu Yu indicated his own critical perspective on the dynasty's ritual programme. In the first place, he downgraded the importance of ritual by abandoning in the *T'ung tien* the order that had been traditional to monograph series in official histories since the start of the dynasty (Ch. 5, p. 167). This sequence would have put ritual at the head of the nine sections of his work, in effect making the dynastic ritual programme the most important of the state's functions. Instead, however, Tu Yu put it in fourth place, after 'food and goods' (*shih huo*), the selection system and posts. To justify this, Tu cited traditional formulations of the idea that observance of ritual could only be subsequent to economic well being. He quoted the *Kuan tzu*, 'When the granaries are full, people will know ritual', and adapted the *Analects*, making Confucius say, '[Only] when they have been made rich, instruct them'.[227]

Tu Yu certainly knew the state ritual tradition well, and he was among those who praised the K'ai-yüan code of 732 in hyperbolic terms. But he also implied an approach to the rites that played down their supernatural or cosmological dimension. He repeated that only the first of the five divisions of the code concerned 'heaven', or the cosmological. 'The remaining four', he state, 'all alike concern human matters'.[228] Tu criticized the view that the formal reading out of seasonal orders from the *Yüeh ling* was a ceremony of great antiquity.[229] He also implied a negative reappraisal of the great Feng and Shan rites of 725, for the *T'ung tien* includes a pre-T'ang essay arguing that these rites should be conducted once only in a dynasty and at its start.[230] He emphasized that man, rather than heaven, determined historical events.[231] As an administrator, he seems likely to have played down portentous events and occurrences that others might have seen as having cosmological or supernatural implications, for Ch'üan Te-yü said of him that 'irregularities in things (*wu kuai*), and flarings up of the ether (*ch'i yen*) did not impinge upon his mind'.[232] Thus, though he was probably not a radical sceptic, it is possible to read in his position disapproval of at least the extreme expressions of the tradition of correlative cosmology that were officially and publicly integral to the imperial ritual programme.

It was, however, Liu Tsung-yüan who expressed the strongest sceptical attitudes towards the cosmological element in state ritual, and who insisted most explicitly that the function of the rites was moral and social rather than supernatural.[233] Liu had developed his ideas, perhaps partly under Tu Yu's influence, before his banishment in 805. He expressed his views mainly in essays intended for circulation in the metropolitan world of the close of Te tsung's reign. Liu insisted that the supernatural element in state rituals was of minor importance, and that the main function of rites was to exemplify moral and social values. 'The sage in his attitude towards sacrifices does not insist that they be treated as supernatural'. Ritual offerings were 'an adjunct [only] of the true teaching'.[234] Liu believed that the mental attitude of 'reverence' (*ching*) mentioned in the *Li chi* was more important than the objective ritual directives, and emphasized that the purpose of ritual should be to exemplify reverence and love, and to reward virtue. The spirits in the *cha*, the collective offering to the supernatural world held at the winter solstice, were vague and elusive; the purpose of the sage must reside with man. Sacrifices were an ancient tradition, he conceded, but they may not have been the original intention of the sages.[235]

After his exile, Liu retained his sceptical and secular view of the state. An agnostic spirit and condemnation of superstition and omen lore pervade his *Fei Kuo yü* (*Condemnation of the Discourses of the states*), and in this he repeated that 'to offer sacrifices to the former kings is a means to assist the true teaching. It is not necessary to treat them as supernatural'.[236] In an essay believed to date from 814, he developed a radically critical position towards the belief system that lay behind the *Yüeh ling*. He held that the correlations it posited between the five elements, the five virtues and the calendar were baseless, and that the connection between failure to observe the prescriptions of the

Yüeh ling and plagues or catastrophes was 'merely the statement of purblind historians and did not originate with the sages'.[237]

For all his determined agnosticism, however, Liu Tsung-yüan, like Tu Yu, retained a place for the state ritual programme. Rituals were 'the inherited laws of antiquity; they should not be set aside'. Though, as Tu Yu seems to have done, he had strong reservations about the Feng and Shan rites,[238] he was glad when he heard that the ploughing rite was planned for 811, and expressed regret when it was cancelled.[239] He suggested, in a formal composition intended for high authority, that Hsien tsung's successes against the military governors of Hopei in 818 should be reported 'in temple and in suburb', that is through the rituals prescribed for the main imperial ritual precincts.[240] His praise, also, for the directives his brother-in-law P'ei Chin compiled for the funerals of Te tsung and Shun tsung show that he was by no means hostile to great dynastic ritual occasions.[241]

From Liu's death in 819 until the end of the dynasty, his ideas on ritual were relatively seldom referred to.[242] They are therefore to be seen as belonging to the period of the reform movement and its immediate aftermath, indeed the high point in the intellectual history of the second half of the T'ang. With justice, they are considered one of the most striking affirmations of the sceptical spirit to have survived from the dynasty. Yet even Liu Tsung-yüan's position contains a tension that points, ultimately, to the state-centred character of his basic position. Liu was more critical and expressed more scepticism about the state ritual programme than about any other topic in political philosophy on which he wrote. Yet at the same time, he adhered to the point of view of the serving official loyal to the dynasty, and hopeful for promotion in its service. He did not ask, therefore, that the ritual programme be abandoned. Rather, to ensure its preservation, he formulated a justification for it that emphasized its ethical and social function. He also believed that the offices of the imperial state, their insignia, ceremonial and administrative procedures were 'the means through which the *tao* is implemented'. To create a dichotomy between offices and the *tao* was therefore wrong.[243] Both his belief in the ultimate authority of the Confucian texts (Ch. 3, p. 104) and his endorsement of the state ritual tradition place his outlook within the mainstream of T'ang Confucianism.

Liu was also a characteristically T'ang figure in another respect: he was a committed lay Buddhist, especially during the period of his exile. His Buddhism was, moreover, a personal commitment that did not directly affect his outlook on the state. Rather it was his relegation of his religious life to the private side of his experience that freed him intellectually to survey the T'ang imperial state ritual programme in the agnostic spirit for which he is famous. The pluralism that is a recurrent feature of T'ang attitudes to questions of belief therefore was an essential background element in one of the most striking affirmations of the secular, sceptical spirit from the dynasty.

5

HISTORY

To medieval scholars, history involved mainly the narratives and other documentation of the post-canonical period, rather than the whole of the accessible past. As a discipline, therefore, it focussed on a delimited body of material, and was characteristically specific and concrete. Historical records, especially those of the Han period, were 'second to the canons', and were immediately familiar to educated men.[1] The detailed information they contained played an important role in the intellectual life of the dynasty. From the start of the T'ang, history had an importance to scholars that fully justified its position as the second of the four divisions by which, in the official bibliographical scheme, written sources were classified.

In formal bibliographical terms, the category of history writing was wider than the other disciplines under consideration. In the official bibliographical scheme, it was divided into thirteen sub-categories.[2] These were by no means of uniform importance; the classification of histories, like the classification of most categories of knowledge in the medieval world, implied a hierarchy of values. First came dynastic histories in the officially favoured composite form, which comprised annals (*pen chi*) and biographies (*lieh chuan*); then histories in the form sometimes advocated as superior to the composite, the chronicle (*pien nien*). Both these first and second sub-categories were seen, in the phrase that Mencius had used to describe the *Ch'un-ch'iu*, as making their central theme the 'affairs of the son of heaven', and therefore had priority.[3] They were followed by sub-categories of historical narrative that lacked their formality (*tsa shih*) or that treated rebel dynasties (*wei shih*).

The sub-categories listed next represented early stages in the compilation of histories, and were for court diaries (*ch'i-chü chu*) and veritable records (*shih lu*). Collections of biographies, which provided basic material for the completed composite form dynastic history, formed a category. There were also sub-categories for works on official posts, state ritual prescriptions, criminal law and administrative geography. These were all subjects that had been represented in the monograph series that the *Shih chi* and the *Han shu*, the classical dynastic histories, provided. Subject matter concerned less immediately with the state and its administrative hierarchy, namely genealogies and bibliographies, formed sub-categories at the end of the list. This thirteen-fold scheme remained virtually unaltered through the T'ang. Behind it, moreover, there was a sense of the unity of the discipline, and a belief that it was for historians to document changes that took place in all these fields.[4]

To the T'ang scholarly world, there were two main contexts in which accounts of the post-canonical past were important, and, corresponding with them, two different attitudes towards historical records. The first of these contexts comprised the higher levels of the political world. The classical histories, the *Shih chi* and the *Han shu*, contained the fullest and most concise account of the imperial dynastic state that the learned tradition supplied. They defined the state in all its roles, from the cosmological to the ritual, the institutional, the administrative and the military. Knowledge of these works was therefore an essential element of the learned tradition. It identified the intellectual elite within officialdom, and, for individual officials, when put to political use, could be highly advantageous in career terms. Secondly, there was a complex of attitudes centred on the specific operation of compiling an official record of the recent past, an activity that gave rise to much criticism and comment.

T'ang scholars' outlook on the remoter past was predominantly cautionary and practical. The *Shih chi*, *Han shu* and later compilations provided precedents and monitory examples, which, correctly understood, were considered to illustrate permanent truths about the emperor's conduct of affairs, the imperial state and political morality. Inherited histories constituted the material for what has been called the 'historical mode of argument'.[5] In this, scholars cited the historical precedent rather than the theoretical principle, the instance rather than the idea. In this approach, history was not of course a truly autonomous discipline, not an activity that meant sympathetically reconstructing the past. Narrative records of successive dynasties, rather, represented a corpus of more or less authoritative texts, from which scholars culled and manipulated information, usually quite specific, to bear on contemporary problems. Like canonical and ritual scholarship, therefore, history provided scholars with a means to promote their own skills and interests. The importance of the classical histories in this role is underlined by the large body of exegetical literature written for them in the first half of the dynasty.

History in its second role, the compilation of the definitive record of the recent past, centred on the history office, involved a small number of scholars, and was under the direction of chief ministers. In formal terms, it represented an extension of the commitment to study the past, and indeed official historians were expected to be learned in remote as well as recent history.[6] As the greatest scholarly monument to T'ang rule, however, the dynastic record touched emperors, chief ministers and the scholarly elite, more keenly than any other official scholarly enterprise. It had built into it the potential for a specific conflict of interest between the emperor or minister who supervised it and the official scholars who compiled the narrative and who tried to uphold the ideals they invested in it.

T'ang scholars believed that the dynastic record should conform to high principles. They expected it to be, in their own terms, both objective and definitive, and, in the much used phrase derived from the *Ch'un-ch'iu* tradition, to be incapable of improvement by the addition or substraction of a single character.[7] They defined it as the vehicle by which they could judge even the conduct of the sovereign himself. In this role it represented to them the measure of their moral and political influence. They repeatedly referred to two paragon archivists from the canonical era, Nan Shih and Tung Hu, for both of whom the *Ch'un-ch'iu* and the *Tso chuan* were the principal source. Both had risked execution by recording, or approving the recording of, murders of feudatories rather than betray the integrity of the accounts for which they were responsible. In citing their examples, official historians and others in the seventh and early eighth centuries indirectly emphasized their own ideal of independence from high political power, and pointed to the risks that this insistence on independence might entail.[8]

Despite the prestige of the dynastic history and of the ideals associated with it, the records concerning it over the three centuries of the T'ang show some bewilderingly conflicting tendencies. On the one hand, it is clear that the official record was often the focus for harshly competing political interests, involving not only the emperor but also, especially in the second half of the dynasty, rival bureaucratic factions; on the other, despite this apparently high level of interest, the process of compilation, even in the first half of the dynasty, sometimes ran down or stalled altogether. Many of the senior officials who were appointed to supervise the record appear to have done little or nothing in their tenures. The roles of numbers of the individual scholars appointed to the history office at the lower level of compiler are also often impossible to determine.

The vitality of T'ang scholars' interest in the post-canonical past, both remote and more recent, is, however, indicated by the way in which their outlook towards it evolved over the dynasty. The official operation was less affected than the increasingly important tradition of unofficial compilation, and of critical essays on historical topics. The most significant development took place in attitudes towards the institutions of the dynastic state, their justification and their history. Towards the end of the eighth century, in their comments on history, scholars expressed the insights gained by one and a half centuries of political and administrative experience in the greatest empire China had seen. The most striking of these insights came from the element in the scholar community that, in the late eighth century, believed in institutional and political means of restoring the T'ang to its former greatness. Their perspective on the past involved a shift away from the cosmological view of the state that had been so important to T'ang sovereigns in the period of the dynasty's political success. They introduced a new emphasis on the relative, perishable nature of the dynasty's institutions and used history to analyse basic issues of political principle.

The reigns of Kao tsu and T'ai tsung

The foundation and consolidation of T'ang rule provided the historians of the period with a sense of being at a vantage point in history. Their sense of being in control of events led them to formulate a view of the dynastic state that emphasized the grand cosmological framework of imperial rule, and to prescribe policy norms for the emperor and his successors that they justified by appealing in detail to the past. They extended their control not only over the records of the immediate pre-T'ang period, but also over the tradition of exegesis of the great Han histories, which by T'ang times had attracted a large commentarial literature. T'ai tsung's official historians also tried, without complete success, to define their own role before the emperor as guardians of an ideal of confidential and objective documentation of the events of the immediate past, by which even the emperor should be judged.

Informing their compilations was the same spirit that characterized other learned disciplines in the early T'ang. For in this period, scholars found the state-centred character of the tradition they inherited in no sense a restraint. Rather, in the relatively open atmosphere of T'ai tsung's court, they emphatically reaffirmed it. The 'affairs of the son of heaven', in the Mencian phrase, were indeed their first concern. Like the state-directed historical scholarship of other dynasties at their foundation, theirs was not an especially innovative programme. But the ambition of individual historians, rewarded usually by ennoblement and gifts of silk, combined with the stability and success of T'ai tsung's rule, to make this a productive period.

The study of Han history

In the seventh and early eighth centuries, more than at any other period in the dynasty, scholars expounded the works that stood at the head of the history division in the official bibliographical scheme, the *Shih chi* of Ssu-ma Ch'ien and, above all the *Han shu* of Pan Ku.[9] Outside the idealized Chou era, the Han represented the oldest and longest well-documented span of dynastic government that the T'ang learned world surveyed. T'ang scholars therefore considered that their own dynasty should emulate the scale of Han achievements and benefit from the lessons of Han history. T'ai tsung himself indicated this sense of competition, when he stated that he wanted to bequeath to posterity a record that would rival the two Han histories.[10] The parallelism of the Ch'in to the Sui and therefore of the Han to the T'ang added to the persuasiveness of this outlook.[11]

The Han histories also had a long reputation, dating back to the time when the illiterate sovereigns of the petty post-Han kingdoms had had them read and expounded, as works of practical statecraft.[12] Knowledge of Han history was general in the court by early T'ang times. T'ai tsung himself was complimented for statements that 'went beyond Pan Ku and Ssu-ma Ch'ien'.[13] Han precedents played a central role in Kao tsu's accession procedures.[14] Officials admonished T'ai tsung with Ch'in or Han examples of the danger of coveting foreign metals, silks and horses, the 'condensed wealth' of modern anthropology, and of the folly of extravagant palace buildings. The outlook of scholars on the non-Chinese world, sinocentric throughout the dynasty, was formulated in language drawn from the *Han shu*. Scholars echoed the *Han shu* in pointing to the risks of military adventurism beyond the borders of China. They persuaded the emperor of the merits and disadvantages of the Han system of administering the provinces, and of the need to control imperial princes.[15]

The text of the *Han shu* was intensively studied. The scholar minister

Wei Cheng included eight *chüan* of excerpts from it in his *Ch'ün-shu chih yao* (*Essentials of good administration from many books*), a compendium of writings on government intended for the emperor, making this much the largest source for the work.[16] A number of the official scholars of the period were expert in the *Han shu*, among them the southerners Yao Ssu-lien (d. 637, canonized *K'ang*) and Ou-yang Hsün (557–641). Another young student of this period, later an official historian, was described as 'just about able to recite it blind'. The *Han shu*, with the *Shih chi*, played a part in education; they were both included on the official school syllabus of the Hung-wen kuan, the advisory college of T'ai tsung's reign. They were probably also taught in the state academy directorate.[17]

The interest in Han history, however, went beyond this use in education and in the political arena. Early seventh-century scholars applied to it the full weight of the sixth-century commentarial tradition, brought from the south late in the period of disunion. Here the *Han shu* eclipsed other Han histories.[18] The most important representative of this intense interest in the *Han shu* was the ritual expert and philologist Yen Shih-ku (Ch. 3, pp. 72–73 and Ch. 4, p. 119), a member of one of the most eminent scholarly families of the first half of the T'ang and an heir to a family tradition of expertise in the *Han shu*. His *Han shu chu* (*Commentary to the Han shu*) was commissioned by the crown prince Li Ch'eng-ch'ien, who presented it to the throne in 641.[19]

Yen Shih-ku's commentary occupies a position in the history of *Han shu* scholarship as important as that of K'ung Ying-ta's sub-commentary series in the history of canonical exegesis. Like the sub-commentaries, it is a cumulative work, that owes most of its fabric to pre-T'ang scholarship. In his commentary, Yen Shih-ku distinguished between commentators on the text who wrote in the Later Han, Wei and Chin periods, and later exegetes. As K'ung Ying-ta had done in canonical exegesis, he maintained, albeit tacitly, a division between the northern and southern traditions of *Han shu* scholarship. His commentary is enlivened by citation of contemporary evidence, relating to monuments surviving from the Han to his own day, and artefacts, topographical details and even contemporary vernacular usage. But he also exemplified the 'moderate scepticism' that the scholarly world of the early T'ang urged on the emperor, by his caution towards the supernatural or miraculous. His scepticism over the claims of many genealogies, and his caution over historical place-name identifications are consonant with the same sceptical orientation.[20]

Histories of the five pre-T'ang dynasties

The recognized *Han shu* experts of the first reigns, such as Yen Shih-ku, Yao Ssu-lien and others, were among the scholars whom first Kao tsu and then T'ai tsung commissioned to compile histories of the more recent pre-T'ang past. They brought to bear on these the formal principles of organization and solemnity of purpose that they read out of the *Han shu*, and the scholarly and literary expertise that they acquired through intensive study of it. As well as being answerable to early T'ang imperial power, therefore, they wrote in the context of a long and highly developed tradition of historical compilation.[21]

Over the first two reigns, these same scholars completed a series of histories, based on the *Han shu* model, of the individual dynasties of the period of disunion. In editing the large amount of documentation that this involved, they also formulated for their own period a distinctive view of the dynastic state. This view emphasized two disparate features, each intended to reinforce the authority and permanence of the T'ang. First, scholars used both the narratives which they compiled and their editorial insertions to emphasize the crucial role imperial conduct might play in maintaining stable political control. Secondly, they gave prominence to the sanctions in remote antiquity and in cosmology for the principal activities of the state. In surveying the past, they also emphasized the idea of historical evolution, particularly in institutions, ritual and literary practice. In this way, they justified the interest that the emperor and his advisors had in institutional change, and in the expansion of state activities that T'ang stability had already made possible.[22]

The programme of compiling the histories of the pre-T'ang dynasties started soon after the foundation of the dynasty. Initially it involved a fairly small number of scholars. Like other early T'ang projects, it also entailed heavy reliance on pre-T'ang material and on expertise acquired before the foundation of the dynasty. It meant completing, to the satisfaction of high authority, processes that had begun, in some cases, decades before.[23] In 621, Ling-hu Te-fen (583–666, canonized *Hsien*), one of the longest-serving official scholars of the Sui and T'ang periods, advised Kao tsu that evidence for the history of recent dynasties would be lost after a decade or so. In early 623, the emperor commissioned histories of the Northern Wei (386–534); Northern Ch'i (550–77); Northern Chou (557–81) and Sui (581–618) in the north, and the Liang (502–57) and Ch'en (557–589) in the south. The total number of scholars appointed was seventeen, three for each dynasty, except for the Sui, for which Yen Shih-ku and one other scholar only were commissioned. At this early period of the dynasty, the compilation of histories was still, as it had been in the pre-T'ang period, done largely by individual scholars, often those who, like Yen Shih-ku, had a tradition of family specialization in the periods concerned. The bureau of compositions, nominally responsible, could not provide the expertise for an enterprise on this scale, and so the scholars selected held a wide range of offices. In this respect, the programme contrasted with practice later in the dynasty, when compilation of the dynastic history was almost always strictly confined to those holding concurrent tenure in the history office.

For reasons that are obscure, these scholars, having worked for a number of years, 'in the end could not complete [their project], and so stopped'. In 629, two years after his accession, T'ai tsung ensured that the ultimate credit for the pre-T'ang histories would be his by establishing a second commission. Only three members of the first were retained, and the work of compilation was now conducted in 'an inner department of the imperial library'. Five histories were now required; the Wei history being omitted. This second commission was directed by the two great scholar ministers of T'ai tsung's reign, Fang Hsüan-ling and Wei Cheng. Despite their involvement in other compilations, they played an active editorial role. Seven years later, in 636, T'ai tsung approved the work of this second commission, rewarded the compilers, and advanced their ranks in the noble hierarchy. He also used the occasion to condemn the writing of histories under the Sui dynasty, during which, he claimed, not a single history had been completed.[24]

The reliance of this programme both on inherited material and on relatively few scholars with pre-T'ang family traditions of expertise is illustrated particularly well in the case of the scholars selected for the two southern dynasties, the fifty-six year Liang and the thirty-three year Ch'en. Both histories involved the southerners Yao Ssu-lien and, at an earlier stage, his father Yao Ch'a (d. 602). The present Liang and Ch'en histories, mainly, though not exclusively by them both, still bear the marks of the southern, pre-T'ang stages in their compilation. In clear imitation of the *Han shu*, in which the name of Pan Ku's father Pan Piao, the originator of the work, was left in the text, in the *Liang shu* no fewer than twenty-six insertions were retained under Yao Ch'a's name, given with his Ch'en dynasty title. The *Ch'en shu* contains two similar references to Yao Ch'a.[25] The scholar ministers of T'ai tsung's reign held up the pleasure-loving court of the last Ch'en ruler as an extreme example of imperial irresponsibility. But the narratives of these two southern histories retain their pre-T'ang southern perspective, treating this same court milieu much less censoriously. Wei Cheng and Fang Hsüan-ling, rather, expressed the early T'ang abhorrence of southern court excesses in their editorial prefaces and assessments. These insertions were a recognized vehicle for precisely such independent perspectives, and were highly esteemed for that reason.[26]

T'ai tsung's commission of 629, therefore represented, at least in the case of these two southern histories, not much more than the finalization of a long process of editing and readjusting. Just as in the case of K'ung Ying-ta's sub-commentaries to the canons (Ch. 3, pp. 76–77), the completion of these histories did not put a stop to further, unofficial enterprise in the same field. Numbers of scholars throughout the Sui and early T'ang, some in academic office, compiled their own histories of the dynasties of the period of disunion. In a first surviving record of a discussion between T'ang scholars on privately undertaken history writing, the Neo-Taoist Wang Chi (d. 644) wrote to the southern scholar Ch'en Shu-ta (573–635, canonized first *Miu* then *Chung*), asking to borrow a Sui history that Ch'en had compiled, so that he might use it to complete his own version.[27] There is, again, no evidence that the authorities tried to prevent activity of this kind.[28]

All five of the histories completed in 636 consisted of basic annals (*pen chi*) and biographies (*lieh chuan*) only, and therefore lacked the treatise section included in the great classical histories. In 641, a commission of possibly as few as six was appointed to make good this deficiency. The ten monographs this small specialist commission compiled were completed in 656, and were for ritual (*li i*); music (*yin yüeh*); the calendar (*lü li*); astrology (*t'ien wen*); the five elements (*wu hsing*); economics (*shih huo*); law (*hsing fa*); offices and posts (*chih kuan*); geography (*ti li*) and bibliography (*ching chi*), all topics independently recognized as sub-categories of the history division in the official bibilographical scheme. Formally, they spanned all the five dynasties covered by the commission of 629–36. Almost immediately, however, they were appended to the *Sui shu*, and became conventionally known as the *Sui shu* monographs.[29]

The membership of this commission is again informative in the context of T'ang historical scholarship. As the historian critic of the early eighth century Liu Chih-chi pointed out, it contained only one scholar who had worked on the two previous T'ang historical commissions. This was Ling-hu Te-fen, recognized as one of the most industrious of the offical scholars of the early T'ang, selected probably because of his expertise, again a family tradition, in music and ritual.[30] Another member, Li Ch'un-feng (602–670), a rare example of an official historian with Taoist loyalties and a mathematician and astrologer, was chosen for his skill in astrology and the five elements. The whole monograph programme points to the idea, supported by evidence from the pre-T'ang centuries and from later in the dynasty, that the compilation of monographs was considered a specialist operation, separate from and probably secondary to, compilation of the basic annals and biographies. Being more technical and less immeditely politically fraught, the monographs did not involve the judgement so integral to the more political parts of the official narrative, and they therefore also provoked less critical comment.

The introductory passages of these monographs, however, were a vehicle for emphasizing both the antiquity and the cosmological framework of the dynastic state. The monographs on ritual,[31] law[32] and offices and posts,[33] areas that were to be significant in the evolution of attitudes in the scholarly community, all opened with references to, or used wording from, the *Chou i*, the canon that provided the sanction for much medieval cosmology. These opening passages adduced the idea that the rites, law and institutions of the dynastic state were integral to the cosmic process. This cosmological view of dynastic rule reflected the highly centralized seventh-century political order. It persisted as a convention in both official and some unofficial writings throughout the dynasty. In some unofficial writings on statecraft and history, however, scholars were to develop less cosmological perspectives on the state, while a small number were to reject altogether the idea that the polity had cosmological under-pinnings.

Histories compiled in the late Chen-kuan period
Official scholars of the early T'ang were involved in two more projects involving the history of the pre-T'ang period, resulting in three works that are extant, each in its own way significant in the longer-term context of T'ang historical writing. Two of these, the *Nan shih* (*History of the South*) and *Pei shih* (*History of the North*) were privately initiated and were completed only in 659. They were by Li Yen-shou, an official historian who served on three of the four official commissions of the first two reigns. Like so many T'ang historians, Li Yen-shou inherited a family tradition of historical scholarship. His father, Li Ta-shih, had provided him with chronicle-form drafts, which, however, Li converted to the composite form.

The *Nan shih* and *Pei shih* provide a first example of what were to amount to considerable numbers of privately initiated histories by official scholars or others, completed, or in many cases only planned, in the course of the dynasty. The two histories, like the examples that were to follow them, involved condensing and re-editing existing versions. Li Yen-shou reduced the material of the eight histories that formed the main sources by about a half. Many of his excisions were set pieces, edicts, memorials and literary compositions. But he made additions, including what has been characterized as valuable as well as less reliable material.[34] His completed surveys were 'histories that ran through successive dynasties' (*t'ung shih*), just as the *Shih chi* had done. They spanned the pre-T'ang period from the last dynasty that had controlled all China, the Chin (A.D. 265–420), to the Sui. They therefore served as an introduction to the reunification of China under the T'ang. On their submission, despite Li Yen-shou's low position, Kao tsung 'appreciated his histories and composed a preface for them himself'. They went on to enjoy a high reputation throughout the T'ang.[35]

The final historical project of the first two reigns to concern the pre-T'ang period was a new, officially commissioned, history of the Chin. Though it could not rival the Han, the Chin was important to the T'ang both as the last house to rule over a unified China and as the dynasty in which the imperial Li clan first rose to prominence.[36] The *Chin shu* (*Chin history*), initiated by an edict of 642, was approved probably only two years later.[37] It differed from other histories of the the pre-T'ang dynasties not only in the speed with which it was completed, but also because a large commission for a history, twenty-two scholars in all, was involved in compiling it. The director was again Fang Hsüan-ling, and the deputy director Hsü Ching-tsung. Three members of the commission were from the bureau of compilers, one from the imperial library, one was a court diarist. Li Ch'un-feng was again appointed, probably to undertake the monographs on the calendar, astrology and the five elements. T'ai tsung had a special interest in the *Chin shu* and composed four passages for it, brief but high-flown essays for the basic annals for two reigns and for two biographies. It was therefore designated 'imperially compiled'.[38]

As in the cases of the five histories completed in 636, the scholars compiling the new Chin history essentially adapted and integrated existing accounts into a single narrative. The commission under Fang Hsüan-ling also took to great lengths the monitory principle that all scholars invested in the histories of the period of disunion. They coloured certain passages of the *Chin shu* with their preoccupations to an extent that makes them scarcely less valuable as corroborative evidence for early T'ang political issues than as an accurate history of the Chin. They made especial use of the scantily documented history of the north in the period after 317, when it was lost to barbarian invasion,[39] to flatter the origins of the T'ang imperial line, the Lung-hsi Li clan.[40] They adapted their account to emphasize to the emperor one of their most deeply felt concerns, their anxiety over the dangers of imperial military adventurism.[41] In the *Chin shu* narrative, they also repeated warnings that they had given to T'ai tsung in court discussions in 637 of the dangers of devolving imperial authority by enfieffing imperial sons in separate, administratively independent kingdoms.[42] This issue, which concerned the advantages and disadvantages of rule through enfieffed relatives (*feng chien*) or through the centralized system of commanderies and counties (*chün hsien*), was later in the dynasty to become a major topic of political philosophy, and a touchstone for T'ang scholars' outlook on the dynastic state. Its introduction into the *Chin shu*, some five years after its discussion in T'ai tsung's court, is an indication that late in his reign it was still a potentially important issue between the emperor and his advisers.

Official accounts of the first two reigns

The *Chin shu* is therefore faulted as history, but valuable as an indication of the court-centred climate of historical scholarship under T'ai tsung. It suggests the extent to which official scholars were affected by the political context in which they served, and indicates that they were far from being, as they claimed, truly objective and without bias. The scholars who directed and compiled the record for the early T'ang itself, often the same men, were no less committed to their role of urging Confucian moral priorities on the sovereign.

In the course of the first two reigns, these official historians, under the direction of chief ministers, completed two *shih lu* (*veritable records*), one for the reign of Kao tsu and a second for T'ai tsung's reign to 640, each of twenty *chüan*.[43] At some time in the Chen-kuan period, the official scholar Yao Ssu-lien compiled a composite form *kuo shih*, probably of thirty *chüan*.[44] The two *shih lu*, however, were allowed to circulate, and the *Chen-kuan shih lu* in particular later in the dynasty circulated widely.[45] A second *shih lu* for T'ai tsung's reign, completed only in 654, was compiled during the years following 640.[46]

The compilation of these *shih lu*, however, was far from smooth. Differences arose, not from any wish for scholarly innovation or for underlying philosophical reasons, but because of a conflict of interest with T'ai tsung over the status of the *shih lu* before their completion. It was an essential feature of the court diaries and *shih lu* that scholars considered that the operation of compiling them was privileged and confidential. Only after they had been completed were *shih lu* to be made public and circulated. It was the historians' solemn duty, in compiling this confidential record, to apply ethical judgements with what they considered complete objectivity. As Wei Cheng indicated to T'ai tsung, they were to fulfil the ideal of 'perfect impartiality' (*chih kung*), if necessary by judging the sovereign himself.[47] The ideal, advocated throughout the dynasty, was that 'good and evil should always be recorded, in the hope that the ruler of men will not act wrongly'. This responsibility conferred great importance on the individual scholars involved in official history. It was a sticking point in the Confucian sanctioned system of political conduct in which the scholar community believed, and an obvious test of the influence of scholars at court.

Even under T'ai tsung's rule, however, official historians did not succeed in defending the ideals they so keenly advocated. Even more than the sovereigns who followed, T'ai tsung was concerned about how he was portrayed in the record. He wished particularly to justify his usurpation of the throne in 627, for this had involved the murder of two of his brothers and the deposition of Kao tsu, his father. The officials who were most exposed when he attempted to interfere were the chief ministers in charge of the record and the court diarists. Both groups took part in the policy discussions of the court that it was the function of the diarists to note down, and members of both were known individually to the emperor. Neither proved wholly able to resist T'ai tsung's interest in the record which they had in their charge. At least twice, in 635 and probably in 639, he tried to override the privileged status of the record and to discover in what terms his reign, and particularly his assumption of power was being recorded. In 640, he required one of the directors of the dynastic record, the scholar minister Fang Hsüan-ling, to hurry the completion of the *shih lu* of his father's and his own reign, so that he might inspect them.[48]

T'ai tsung was far from unique among T'ang emperors in his concern for his own place in history. But the accounts of his attempts at interference are fuller than those for any other sovereign. The reasons for this derived partly from the special atmosphere that obtained in the higher levels of the early T'ang bureaucracy. The court, though certainly a dangerous place for those who lacked judgement, was small and relatively open. It was possible for even middle-ranking scholar officials to discuss issues of political principle with the emperor. The

Chen-kuan court advisers, in redefining scholarly and political ideals for the dynasty, were able to locate them in the role and person of T'ai tsung himself. Later T'ang scholars were to idealize this freedom to discuss political conduct in the emperor's presence and to record their discussions. When this openness was lost, they frequently appealed to it as a standard, and made it a central theme in their discussions of official history writing.

Compilations on institutions

In the comment on the official dynastic history that survives from the first two reigns, there is a notable silence surrounding any monographs for the T'ang. There is no evidence that the scholar ministers or official compilers involved in the first two *shih lu* worked on this section of the dynastic history. The reasons for this may have been comparable to those that had led to the commissioning of specialist personnel for the *Sui shu* and *Chin shu* monographs. The topics the monographs covered were technical. In the case of the astrology monograph, the compilers dealt with a category of material that was mainly the responsibility of a single, specialist institution. Much of the material that the monographs on institutions were concerned with was consequent on and secondary to the political discussions and decisions of the court. Compiling it did not require the sort of judgement or command the great prestige that was attached to the more political parts of the record, the basic annals and biographies. The scholars who drafted the lofty introductions to the *Sui shu* monographs, so important as formulations of the early T'ang view of the dynastic state, may even have considered that these introductions were definitive descriptions of each of the areas concerned, and that as yet there was no need to produce new introductions for the T'ang.[49]

Nonetheless, in the Chen-kuan period, official scholars were engaged in major compilations on subjects that were represented in the monograph series. One example is the ritual code completed in 637, for this related to the monograph on state ritual usage.[50] Another is the *K'uo ti chih* (*Monograph on all the world*), presented to the throne in 642. This listed the administrative divisions of China according to a register of 639, and must have corresponded, at least notionally, to a treatise on administrative geography.[51] The new bibliography for the imperial library, in process of compilation in the Chen-kuan period, may similarly have been considered to have covered the topic of the bibliography monograph.[52] It had always been recognized that monographs might draw from the regulations and lists of the periods with which they were concerned.[53] It may well have been, therefore, that at this stage official scholars considered that the official codes, registers and catalogues in process of compilation were documentation enough. Surviving evidence shows that it was not to be until the second half of the seventh century that the monographs were started.

From 650 to 755

In the century following Kao tsung's accession, history maintained its great importance to the scholar community. The classical histories, the models for the official record of the T'ang, continued to be intensively studied. The dynastic record itself continued to provoke conflicts of interest, and its problems were described, in unique detail, by Liu Chih-chi, in his great work the *Shih t'ung*. Liu showed that, far from proceeding smoothly, the compilation of the record was attended by many irregularities and was increasingly politicized. But in this, the greatest period of sustained prosperity and stability that China had seen, the most important themes in historical scholarship were those that reflected the level of interest in the history of government. In the period since the foundation of the dynasty, the T'ang administrative hierarchy had maintained unrivalled prestige. Scholars of this period reflected the high status of the institutions in which they served by writing unofficial institutional compendia, accounts of individual institutions and essays on problems in statecraft. Towards the end of Hsüan tsung's reign, some of these writings already hint at the critical perspectives on the state that were to be developed in the late eighth century.

Exegesis of the classical histories

In the century following T'ai tsung's death, imperial patronage continued to confer prestige on the study and exegesis of the Han histories, mainly by commissioning or accepting commentaries, glossaries or abridgements. The numbers of works produced suggest that no single work of exegesis was endorsed as orthodox for the histories concerned. Most of these commentaries are now lost; but their titles remain to point to a high level of knowledge of the *Shih chi* and *Han shu* among the scholarly elite. In the political arena, officials continued to use the classical histories as the sanction for a wide range of policy recommendations or discussions. In scholarly society too, ignorance of these texts was treated with derision.[54]

At the commentarial level, perhaps because of the success of Yen Shih-ku's *Han shu* commentary, scholars worked more on the *Shih chi*. In the late seventh and early eighth centuries, the official scholars Wang Yüan-kan, Ch'u Wu-liang and Hsü Chien all compiled works of *Shih chi* exegesis.[55] Under Hsüan tsung, P'ei Chieh in 729, Lai Chen and Kao Ch'iao, all otherwise unknown, secured promotion or reward by submitting works on the *Shih chi*, *Han shu* or *Hou Han shu*.[56] Three major commentaries on Han histories from this century have survived to the present. The first was a commentary to the *Hou Han shu*, commissioned by Li Hsien, heir apparent under Kao tsung.[57] The other two works were on the *Shih chi*: the *Shih chi so yin* (*Search for the recondite in the Shih chi*), was by Ssu-ma Chen, the official scholar who had opposed Liu Chih-chi in the debate on canonical texts in 719 (Ch. 3, pp. 85–86),[58] and the *Shih chi cheng i* (*True meaning of the Shih chi*), was completed in 736 by Chang Shou-chieh.[59] Chang's commentary is of particular interest because it drew much of its geographical information from the *K'uo ti chih* of 642. It also contained as an appendix a list of the attributes required for each of a long list of canonization titles (Ch. 1, p. 11). This list was held to have been extracted from the *Chi chung Chou shu*, the Chou dynasty chronicle unearthed in A.D. 281.

The T'ang learned world was heir to a long tradition of criticism of the *Shih chi* and *Han shu*, and, despite their prestige, by no means all scholars expressed unqualified admiration for these texts. Liu Chih-chi saw the Han histories as, in different ways, essential to the whole tradition of historical scholarship. His *Shih t'ung* therefore subjected them to thorough review, and is likely to contain most of the criticisms that were brought against Ssu-ma Ch'ien and Pan Ku in this period. There was also a lively climate in criticism of *Han shu* exegesis.[60]

In the course of this century, scholars also applied the commentarial approach to the history of the Chin. The dynasty in which the T'ang royal house had originated continued to hold a special place in the T'ang official view. It marked the end of the period of post-canonical history that was believed to require and merit close scholarly study. An imperially sponsored compilation that condensed the span of history covered by the *Shih chi* and the histories that followed it up to the *Chin shu* exemplifies this periodization.[61] The *Chin shu* was the subject of exegesis by Hsü Chien and at least one other scholar.[62] In this period, the Yen clan to which the great early T'ang scholar Yen Shih-ku had belonged continued their tradition of expertise in the early histories. In the early eighth century, Yen Chiao-ch'ing was an expert in the *Chin shu*,[63] and his brother Yen Yu-yü (703–50) a *Han shu* specialist.[64] Their brother Yen Chen-ch'ing was intensely aware of the family tradition of historical scholarship. He also recorded other examples of commentarial work on the *Han shu*.[65]

Early eighth century interest in the *Chin shu*, however, marks the high tide of this commentarial approach to the post-canonical histories. Post-rebellion scholars certainly knew the Han and Chin histories in detail. Even some of the loyalist generals of the post-rebellion decades mastered the Han histories.[66] Some full length commentaries like those by Yen Shih-ku or Chang Shou-chieh were produced after 755.[67] But the great period in the T'ang for submitting exegesis of this kind to the throne appears to have passed with the wealth of the dynastic house and the disruption that followed the rebellion.

The dynastic record

A complete list survives of the *shih lu* that the history office produced for successive reigns in the century after 650. There are also references to successive, amplified versions of the *kuo shih* that integrated these *shih lu* into up-dated, comprehensive narrative records of the dynasty. A brief account of these compilations might suggest that the history office operated much as the regulations required, and that the only irregularities were those that sovereigns forced on the office. Thus in 656, Chang-sun Wu-chi, Yü Chih-ning (588–665, canonized *Ting*) and others submitted a version of the *kuo shih* that, adding 50 *chüan* to its length, brought it to 80 *chüan*.[68] In 659, the long-serving Hsü Ching-tsung was commissioned to compile a *shih lu* for the period from 649 to 658, and this work, 20 *chüan* in length, was added to the 80 *chüan* of the 656 version.[69] In 661–3, another record states, the chief minister Hsü Ching-tsung directed the history, further revision took place and the monographs, conventionally ten, were started.[70] The version in 100 *chüan*, however, displeased Kao tsung, and, after Hsü's death in 672, further work was ordered.[71] In 692–3, another version of the *kuo shih*, covering the period from the foundation to 683, was completed. This, it has been argued, adopted the political perspective of the empress Wu's Chou dynasty, founded in 690.[72] After its completion, the authorities, not for the last time in the dynasty, attempted to call in all copies of the preceding versions.

In 703, Liu Chih-chi, as a member of a commission that included a number of the outstanding official scholars of the period, worked on another version of the *kuo shih*, in 80 *chüan*. This was probably a revision of that of 693, and was again intended to embody a new imperial political perspective, in this case the impending restoration of the T'ang imperial line.[73] When, however, in 705 the empress Wu abdicated, this project lapsed. Slightly later, Liu Chih-chi, as a member of a commission of seven, worked on a *shih lu* for the empress Wu's reign. This was completed mid 706, nine days before the burial of the empress in the Ch'ien-ling mausoleum.[74] Revised versions of the *shih lu* for the empress Wu, Chung tsung and Jui tsung, on all of which Liu Chih-chi worked, were presented to Hsüan tsung in 716.[75]

Over this period, however, not only successive sovereigns, but also the ministers who directed the record interfered in their own interests. Linked with this trend, there is evidence for proliferation in the numbers of those involved in official history writing and for the inefficiency and dereliction at the history office that Liu Chih-chi was so vividly to describe.

Perhaps because of the prestige the operation had acquired under T'ai tsung, in the following reign the numbers of ministers involved in it, either in close succession or concurrently, increased. At one point when Chang-sun Wu-chi was the senior director, the total number of scholars involved, according to a vignette from the following century, was eighteen or nineteen.[76] Seven ministers are recorded as directors in 653,[77] three in an edict of 673.[78] At the middle level of the process also, the numbers of compilers increased, at least until Kao tsung, in an edict of early 671, ordered that they be cut down.[79] Political manipulation of the record by a minister is explicitly recorded for the first time in the case of Hsü Ching-tsung. Kao tsung himself asserted that Hsü had distorted the history of T'ai tsung's reign.[80] But a much more serious charge, brought against Hsü repeatedly in the eighth and ninth centuries, was that, with his fellow chief minister Li I-fu, he was responsible for a major attack on the principles that, under T'ai tsung, had ensured for the dynastic history a full record of court discussions. At some point when Hsü Ching-tsung and Li I-fu controlled the government, a period which lasted from 660 to 670, the court diarists were barred from attending confidential court deliberations and could therefore compile no account of politically sensitive and vital discussions. Later scholars saw this development as a betrayal of the ideal of openness that they believed had obtained under T'ai tsung.[81] But the chief ministers who followed, whether portrayed in official sources as good or evil, tacitly endorsed the step attributed to Hsü Ching-tsung and Li I-fu. They too controlled in their own favour the sources that made up the record. Only in the early phase of Hsüan tsung's reign was there a brief and limited recovery of early T'ang openness.

For the final decades of the seventh century, a number of names of the supervisors and compilers of the record survive.[82] In 693, a chief minister, Yao Shou (d. 705, canonized *Ch'eng*), tried to make good to some extent the loss of the full court record for which Hsü Ching-tsung and Li I-fu are said to have been responsible. He instituted a regular, quarterly-produced court record, the *shih cheng chi* (*Seasonal record of administration*), of, in the first instance, 40 *chüan*. Yet even this provision soon lapsed, and there was to be a succession of requests that it should be revived.[83]

Liu Chih-chi's criticisms of official history

Towards the end of the empress Wu's reign, there were further indications that the ideals which the scholar community associated with the compilation of the dynastic record had been subverted. In 703, several years before the completion of the *Shih t'ung*, Liu Chih-chi emphasized the solemn responsibility of the individual historian,[84] while two of his colleagues at the history office in this period showed their dissatisfaction at conditions there.[85] In 708, Liu tried to resign from the office, submitting a letter to one of the five senior officials who then directed the history. In this, he itemized the reasons for his indignation at the state of official history compilation.[86] More significantly, in the *Shih t'ung*, his great systematic review of the whole tradition of historical scholarship, he made the issue of the individual historian's relation to high authority second only to his major theme of the scope and formal organization of histories.

Liu expressed better than any other writer the difficulties inherent in the court-directed academic world of the late medieval empire. On the one hand, he implicitly endorsed the state-centred character of history writing and emphasized that historians depended on the state for the documentation they needed. On the other, he insisted that individual historians should be left free of excessive interference, to, as he put it, 'shut their doors and produce works of independent judgement'.[87] He stressed the antiquity of the historian's office, but condemned the supervision of the dynastic record by ministers, a practice he dated to the Northern Ch'i.[88]

Liu's acute awareness of the politically fraught character of official history is made clear by his abundant references to the paragon archivists of canonical antiquity, Nan Shih and Tung Hu, who had risked their lives rather than falsify the records they composed. He upheld, as Wei Cheng had done, the ideal of 'perfect impartiality' (*chih kung*) in the compilation of histories, and he condemned the 'crooked brush' (*ch'ü pi*), the distortion of the truth for political or personal reasons.[89] He censured even some of the great official historians of T'ai tsung's reign, among them Yen Shih-ku, for political bias. His criticism extended to some of the compilers of the T'ang record itself, and his condemnation of Hsü Ching-tsung was to be echoed by many later scholars.[90]

Liu's condemnation of the directors of the history office under whom he served was especially scathing. Those in the charge of the dynastic history were 'hatted apes', he wrote, high-ranking favourites, who combined indolence and weakness. The entire apparatus of official history suffered from their poor direction, and the history office was 'a den for time-servers', and a 'refuge for idlers'. Material, including the court diaries, was not available, confidentiality was farcical, and no single policy was upheld for the historian compilers to follow.[91]

With his letter of resignation, Liu Chih-chi in effect affirmed that it was middle-ranking official scholars who, in the face of corrupt direction, held ultimate responsibility for the ideals associated with the *kuo shih*. His boldness in demanding clarity and objectivity in history, even in the canonical *Ch'un-ch'iu* and the *Shang shu* (Ch. 3, pp. 90–91), later earned him notoriety. But a certain forthrightness, even before high political power, appears to have been an aspect of the style of middle-ranking or junior scholars in the first half of the eighth century. It is to be seen, for example, in Liu's fellow scholars Yüan Hsing-ch'ung and Wu Ching, or, a generation later, in the attitudes of Hsiao Ying-shih and Yüan Chieh. At least, Liu's condemnation of official history writing was contained within the official academic system. In the next decade he continued to serve as an official historian, working, as before, on the most sensitive records, the *shih lu* of recent sovereigns. The fact that two of his six sons followed him as official historians and that three of them enjoyed wide connections in the scholar community shows that there was no medium term animus against him. A few years after his death, moreover, Hsüan tsung ordered that a copy be made of the *Shih t'ung* and expressed approval of it.[92] Liu Chih-chi's biography, in the form of an epitaph text, was in circulation after the rebellion of 755.[93] Moreover, a succession of scholars in the eighth and ninth centuries, compiling histories of the pre-T'ang and T'ang dynasties, were to attempt the 'independent judgement' that he commended.

The dynastic record under Hsüan tsung

Just as he reformed the education system on his accession, so Hsüan tsung removed some of the abuses that had affected the history office under his predecessors. At the start of his reign, he appointed scholar ministers reputed for integrity as well as for learning and literary skill to direct the compilation of the record. Among them were Yao Ch'ung (651–721, canonized *Wen-hsien*) and Chang Yüeh from 713, and later Sung Ching (663–737, canonized *Wen-chen*) and Su T'ing, all examination graduates.[94] At the compiler rank, there was continuity with the previous reigns, for not only Liu Chih-chi but also Hsü Chien and Wu Ching remained official historians. They went on to prove themselves, in the judgement of the assessment writer in the *Chiu T'ang shu*, the most outstanding generation of official scholars of their age.[95]

The emperor himself reasserted the sort of interest in the process of compiling the record that T'ai tsung had shown. He was said to have had an especial interest in court diaries, housing them in separate and luxurious premises. He also allowed diarists long tenures.[96] He attempted to some extent to solve the problem of access to the political process for historians, by decreeing that those whose basic offices did not secure them a place at court should attend, taking positions below the court diarists.[97] Hsüan tsung also often mentioned the dynastic history, and required that the ritual, scholarly and administrative achievements of his reign be written into it. His scholar ministers followed him in recommending that specific events be included in the record. The success of the great advisory college of his reign, the Chi-hsien yüan; the climactic celebration of the Feng and Shan rites on mount T'ai in Shantung in the winter of 725; the debates in the court between representatives of the three teachings; the emperor's promotion of Taoism; his successes against the barbarians; even the copying out of the Buddhist *Tripitaka*; and many other undertakings, were referred, in elegant and oblique language, to the history office. So were natural phenomena and omens favourable to the emperor and the dynasty, like the ripening of grain following the ploughing rite of 735. These referrals of information to the history office by the emperor and by such scholars as Yao Ch'ung, P'ei Yao-ch'ing (681–743, canonized *Wen-hsien*), Chang Yüeh, Chang Chiu-ling and probably many others less favourably placed, demonstrated the cosmological view of the imperial role at its grandest and most successful. They were intended to reinforce a picture of harmonious government and prosperity.[98] The resulting record was to be, in the phrase that was normally applied to the Confucian canons and that Hsüan tsung applied to the dynastic history in 729, an 'inerasable authority' (*pu k'an chih tien*).[99]

In the history office, however, the operation of compiling a record for the dynasty proceeded no more smoothly or regularly in this period than in any other in the dynasty. What little information has survived about the editing and compiling of the dynastic record under Hsüan tsung points to the same conflict between individual enterprise and compilation by commission that had so preoccupied Liu Chih-chi. Towards the end of the reign, moreover, the compilation of the history and appointments to the history office were affected by the factional politics that accompanied Hsüan tsung's decline.

In the mid K'ai-yüan period, a measure of irregularity is suggested by the fact that two individual official historians are recorded as working on the dynastic record, not in the history office, but independently. Liu Chih-chi's colleague Wu Ching did so in the early K'ai-yüan period. In 715, and again in 726, he submitted his own versions for a T'ang dynastic history, which probably covered the T'ang up to the start of Hsüan tsung's reign.[100] The leading scholar minister of Hsüan tsung's reign, Chang Yüeh, first appointed to direct the history in 713, compiled a *shih lu* away from the capital, with imperial permission, in 720, and worked on the dynastic history independently at the capital up to 727.[101] In that year, however, a chief minister, Li Yüan-hung (d. 733, canonized *Wen-chung*), succeeded in having official history writing more strictly confined to the history office, and both Wu Ching's and Chang Yüeh's operations were transferred there.[102]

The compilation of the record proceeded, under Chang Yüeh's direction, at the history office until Chang's death in 729. That year, the general service official Hsiao Sung was appointed to the Chi-hsien yüan to expedite the *Liu tien*, the K'ai-yüan ritual code and other compilations. At the same time, he was given charge of the dynastic history.[103] This same year, Wu Ching was banished to provincial office.[104] The following year, Hsiao Sung established a new commission.[105] One of its members was Wei Shu, a member of a family famous for its scholarly attainments, a *chin shih* of 708, and a relative of the bibliophile official scholar Yüan Hsing-ch'ung and of the general service historian P'ei Yao-ch'ing. Wei Shu had 'won preferment through Confucian skills', had found favour with Chang Yüeh, and had been a court diarist. His service as an official historian lasted long after Hsiao Sung's demotion in 733, and he was destined to carry responsibility for the dynastic record over the following decades, much as Wu Ching had done up to 727.[106]

After Hsiao Sung's demotion, Wei Shu worked on the history under the direction of the scholar minister Chang Chiu-ling, until Chang's fall from power in 736.[107] In 737, Hsüan tsung appointed a Taoist favourite, Yin An, to a period of control that lasted until his death in about 740.[108] For eighteen years from 734, the authoritarian Li Lin-fu also held responsibility for the dynastic history. He probably selected official historians himself, for he was said to have exerted tight control on appointments generally, and to have prevented the return to the capital of the ageing Wu Ching. He had the history office moved, for security reasons, in 737, to premises north of the central secretariat that had originally housed a sub-department of the imperial medical service. He ended the provision whereby historian compilers not qualified by their basic office to do so attended court. He may also have tightened the prohibition against private compilation of T'ang history.[109]

Wei Shu's social and political connections in the bureaucracy were with such scholar ministers as Chang Yüeh and Chang Chiu-ling and with such official scholars as Sun Ti and Hsü Ching-hsien. It is unlikely, therefore, that he prospered under the Li Lin-fu. Nonetheless, his service lasted almost uninterrupted through Li Lin-fu's period of control and up until the eve of the An Lu-shan rebellion, while he compiled his own, unauthorized version of the T'ang dynastic history probably over the same period.[110] He was certainly not the only official historian serving over this period. The rescript writer and chief examiner Sun Ti was an official historian in the late K'ai-yüan period.[111] Among others whose appointment may be dated to the 730s was Liu K'uang, the eldest son of the Liu Chih-chi. Liu Chih-chi's second son, Liu Su is also likely to have received his appointment as an official historian in the late K'ai-yüan or early T'ien-pao period.[112] Another official historian of this period was Liu Fang, a *chin shih* of 735 under Sun Ti, the influential chief examiner and member of Wei Shu's circle. He was appointed in, or soon after, 738, his service was to span the rebellion period and he was later known as the scholar who completed Wei Shu's works.[113] Yet another was Kuei Ch'ung-ching, after the rebellion a controversial ritual scholar and proponent of the reform of the education system.[114] But Li Lin-fu seems likely to have blocked the entry to the office of Li Han (fl. c. 750–770), a *chin shih*, who was recommended by Fang Kuan and Wei Chih (696–760, canonized *Chung-hsiao*),[115] and of Hsiao Ying-shih, another *chin shih* of 735 under Sun Ti, whom Wei Shu sponsored for appointment as an official historian.[116] Partly because of Li Lin-fu, the pre-rebellion careers of these junior officials were largely unsuccessful, but they belonged to the group whose followers and disciples were to dominate the scholarly tradition after the rebellion.

It was Wei Shu's compilations that were destined, by chance, to survive the rebellion of 755. After the recovery of the capitals, the authorities tried, largely without success to make good the loss of the records for the K'ai-yüan and T'ien-pao periods destroyed in the sack of Ch'ang-an. It was then discovered that the only history of the reign to have survived was contained in the dynastic record that Wei had illegally compiled, probably in the period leading up to the rebellion. Wei failed to escape from Ch'ang-an in the crisis of 756, collaborated with the rebels and died in exile in Su tsung's reign. But any problems concerning the legality of his unofficial history, retrieved from the hills to the south of Ch'ang-an where he had hidden it, were now overlooked. Further updated, it was made the basis for a version of the *kuo shih* presented to Su tsung after 759.[117]

Official institutional histories

In the longer term, the most important development of the pre-rebellion century in historical compilation concerned not successive *shih lu* or the *kuo shih*, despite their problems, but histories of institutions and the attitudes associated with compiling them. For in this area, the pre-rebellion century was a time of significant change, when the success and prestige of the medieval state began to influence the outlook of both official and unofficial historians. Some scholars, surveying the history of the pre-T'ang and T'ang periods, emphasized that state institutions had been subject to continuous evolution. They showed their greatest adaptability and willingness to depart from the *Han shu* model in documenting changes that had taken place in administration.

Again it was Liu Chih-chi who, for all his loyalty to the model of the *Han shu* and the underlying conservatism of his outlook, advocated flexibility most clearly. He emphasized that the purpose of history was first and foremost to document change.[118] He recognized that the realities behind institutions changed, even when their names remained unaltered.[119] But it was above all in his comments on the monograph section of the composite-form history that he emphasized the historian's need to be flexible in documenting evolution. He showed that the topics of the monograph series had never been rigidly fixed. The conventional number was ten, but altogether, in those orthodox histories that had contained monograph series, sixteen topics had been covered. He asked for the inclusion of three new monograph topics, for genealogy, capital cities and tribute.[120]

Liu's remarks on the monograph series are the only ones of their kind from the early eighth century. Otherwise, as in the first T'ang reigns, the series provoked little or no comment that has survived. Nonetheless, in this period, not only were the monographs continued,[121] but the state also commissioned a number of normative institutional works that covered topics treated in monographs, and official historians even served on the commissions involved. Several of these works concerned topics central to the learned activities described in this book, namely institutions, ritual directives and bibliographies.

One major work of Hsüan tsung's reign that clearly related to the monograph tradition was the *Liu tien*. This was a normative compendium of permanently established T'ang offices and concerned the full range of the institutions of the T'ang state. Like the K'ai-yüan ritual code, its equal for the high standing it enjoyed in later T'ang times, the *Liu tien* was compiled in the Chi-hsien yüan. Though it was commissioned in 722, before the Chi-hsien yüan was formally established, it was finally completed only after years of delay and several changes of personnel, in 738 or 739. Its basic text listed the T'ang bureaucratic offices and prescribed their functions, usually reproducing administrative statutes promulgated in 719. The compilers' use of the same sequence as the *Sui shu* monograph on offices and posts, however, indicates their debt to seventh-century official history. After its completion, a commentary was written for it in the name of the chief minister Li Lin-fu. This entered the canonically sanctioned equivalent for each T'ang office, and, drawing on earlier sources, traced its evolution, to include changes made under T'ang rule and up to the late K'ai-yüan period. The *Liu tien* therefore provided detailed sanction from the past, recent and remote, for the contemporary state and its institutions, and bore witness to the great importance of the historical dimension in T'ang political thought. All the T'ang academic agencies were entered in it, and were given historical introductions in its commentary (Ch. 1, pp. 13–26).[122]

A second official compilation that clearly bore a relation to a monograph topic was the bibliography for the imperial collection completed in 721 in the Li-cheng tien, the institution that the Chi-hsien yüan replaced. In its organization and in its treatment of earlier T'ang official bibliographies, this work followed closely the model of the *Sui shu* bibliography (Ch. 6, pp. 221–22). Similarly, the ritual code of 732, commissioned in the Chi-hsien yüan to 'make a balanced adjudication' between the two earlier T'ang ritual codes, formed a major point in the history of the topic that provided the first monograph in the series

(Ch. 4, pp. 133–36). Other official compendia produced under Hsüan tsung may have been seen in the same way.[123]

Unofficial history writing

The *Liu tien*, the imperial catalogue of 721 and the ritual code of 732 were all normative official compilations, highly compartmentalized in their approach and intended, like the dynastic record itself, to be definitive. But, as the case of Liu Chih-chi had so clearly indicated, official projects like these were undertaken in a milieu in which individual scholars held lively and independent views on the past and on historical scholarship. On their own initiative over this pre-rebellion century, some of these official scholars and their colleagues outside academic office compiled histories that expressed the 'independent judgement' that Liu had commended. These works, the great majority of which survive as titles only, suggest a range of approaches to the past. At one extreme, scholars compiled revised, often condensed versions of recognized histories, usually with the ambition of achieving the word-perfect text of which the *Ch'un-ch'iu* tradition spoke. At the other, they assembled and edited a wide range of historical material to express views on contemporary policy issues. They reflected in these latter works especially the climate of this age of political expansion and prosperity.

A number of well known figures of this period favoured the more conservative approach, that of condensing and adjusting the political record. These scholars compiled or planned histories in the chronicle style, some of which were restricted to the pre-T'ang period, while others included the T'ang itself. In the seventh century Ch'en Tzu-ang (661–702), and in the early eighth Liu Chih-chi himself formulated plans to compile chronicle histories of this kind.[124] Towards the end of Hsüan tsung's reign, Ch'en Cheng-ch'ing, Hsiao Ying-shih and Li Han planned or were involved in similar enterprises.[125] Wu Ching condensed the histories of the period of disunion, on the grounds of their prolixity.[126] The unofficial versions of the T'ang dynastic record that both Wu Ching and Wei Shu produced were probably in the same tradition. Only a few of these works were completed and none survives as an original text. But the fact that the majority of them were to be compiled in the chronicle form suggests that their first purpose was the moralistic one of recasting the outline of political events, and of re-allocating the 'praise and blame' in it.

A more technical, less political and moralistic approach is apparent in accounts restricted to discrete aspects of the administrative system.

The intended readership of these accounts, in most cases, was probably the scholar community itself. Wei Shu wrote works on the censorate in ten *chüan*, on the Chi-hsien yüan in three *chüan*, and on official protocol; he also made an account of the two capitals in five *chüan*, which Hsiao Ying-shih, visiting Ch'ang-an from Ying-ch'uan in modern Honan, used.[127] These compilations were all later classified as works of history. On a smaller scale, several pre-rebellion scholars compiled 'wall records' (*t'ing pi chi*), texts for inscription on the walls of individual institutions that described their history from early times and their administrative functions. Some of these wall records concerned the academic and ritual agencies. The rescript writer and examiner Sun Ti wrote one for the Hung-lu court, the institution responsible for treating with barbarians. Li Hua, his graduate of 735, did the same for the bureau of compositions.[128] Liu K'uang, the eldest son of Liu Chih-chi, composed a wall record for the premises of the music office.[129]

By the end of the K'ai-yüan period, after a period of effective government, the emperor's grasp of administration had declined, and Li Lin-fu's control of the bureaucracy alienated the scholar community. Most of the writing from this period to the rebellion of 755 was lost, much of it probably in the course of the rebellion.[130] But there is some indication, in surviving titles, anecdotal literature and biographies, that, perhaps because of these background political factors, scholars in the period wrote more critically about the past and the political and administrative world in which they lived. Cheng Ch'ien, the scholar appointed unwillingly in 750 to the Kuang-wen kuan (Ch. 2, p. 42) and the patron of Tu Fu and Yüan Chieh, compiled a record of the T'ang that resulted in his banishment from the capital for about ten years. He also wrote on strategy and defence. Ch'u Kuang-hsi, called 'a man of great talent for the effective government of the empire' and a *chin shih* of 726 under the lay Buddhist Yen T'ing-chih (673–742), wrote a work entitled the *Cheng lun* (*True discussions*).[131]

Probably the greatest contribution to unofficial history writing in this period, however, was made by four of the sons of Liu Chih-chi. The compilations of these brothers, who belonged to the same circle as Li Hua and other Sun Ti graduates, ranged from collections of anecdotes to histories of individual institutions and even to a work on the principles of historical compilation. Liu Chih-chi's eldest son, the official historian Liu K'uang, wrote a long essay on frontier policy since Chou and Han times entitled *Wu chih* (*Military directives*). This drew extensively from the *Han shu* and, in effect, dismissed as wrongly

conceived pre-T'ang and T'ang policy towards the barbarians.[132] The
Wu chih was edited into the *T'ung tien* of Tu Yu, and is therefore
extant in complete form. It provides an important indication that mid
eighth-century official scholars, like their seventh- and early
eighth-century predecessors, advocated defensive, non-interventionist
policies towards the barbarian world. That the Liu brothers may
generally have written polemically is further suggested by a remark
that Li Hua made in a sacrificial graveside prayer for one of the
brothers: 'They were all ornaments to the state. Their writings
overturned the [histories of Ssu-ma] Ch'ien and [Pan] Ku. Their
reasoning defeated [the heterodox philosophies of Yang] Chu and
[Mo] Ti.'[133]

A certain amount is known about another important work by one of
the brothers, Liu Chih-chi's third son Liu Chih. This work, the *Cheng
tien* (*Compendium on administration*), resembled the *Liu tien*, in
containing a history of the institutions of government. It differed from
the *Liu tien*, however, because it included not only records of
institutional change drawn from the canons and from successive histories, but also theoretical or discursive writings. The one surviving
passage from the *Cheng tien* shows that, despite the depth of its
historical perspective, it was again a polemical work, intended to
persuade on current policy issues.[134] This passage, preserved in the
T'ang hui yao, concerns Liu Chih's position on the long-standing issue
of the respective merits of government through semi-independent fiefs
(*feng chien*) and the more centralized commandery and county (*chün
hsien*) system, administered through the bureaucracy. Liu Chih
opposed the views of the early T'ang advisers to T'ai tsung and of his
father's colleague Chu Ching-tse (635–709, canonized *Yüan*). He
endorsed the position of scholars of the Ch'in, Han and post-Han
period who had advocated enfieffment, attacked Li Pai-yao and others
for having dissuaded T'ai tsung from adopting the enfieffment system,
and charged that it had been their policy that had led to the usurpation
of the throne by the empress Wu.[135]

The importance of Liu Chih's approach derives from the way in
which he set a polemical policy recommendation in a lengthy historical
compilation. In emphasizing that policy factors, as much as the
conduct of individuals, played a role in historical change, he foreshadowed the more sophisticated approach of post-rebellion institutional historians to problems in history. Liu Chih shared his position
over decentralized government through enfieffment with the political

and scholarly patron of the T'ien-pao period Fang Kuan (Ch. 2, p. 49). In the crisis of the rebellion of 755, Hsüan tsung accepted their joint advice and implemented a limited plan for devolving military power to his sons as military commanders. Ironically, the results were disastrous for the scholar community. One of the princes, prince Lin, rebelled in the lower Yangtze region, and was defeated only after a disruptive campaign. Almost as important, the strained relations that developed between Hsüan tsung and Su tsung greatly damaged the post-rebellion standing of some of those scholars who had served Hsüan tsung in academic office in the K'ai-yüan and T'ien-pao periods.[136]

The post-rebellion period

The dramatic decline of T'ang power after the An Lu-shan rebellion had a complex effect on attitudes to the past. In the first place, it drastically altered the climate in which official history was written. The record under compilation continued to provoke a significant volume of comment; but behind persistent criticism was the deteriorating and increasingly factional milieu in which official scholarly life was conducted. Comment on the record indicates the continued importance of the official operation to the scholar community, and their refusal to surrender the ideals that they had inherited from the seventh century. But, as in most other official academic operations in the post-rebellion period, there appears to have been little that was radically new in the attitudes involved.

Post-rebellion decline, however, had a much greater effect on the unofficial scholarly world. The loss of the dynasty's wealth and power stimulated reform minded scholars to take further the critical approach to institutional and administrative problems that had been developed among Liu Chih-chi's sons and others towards the end of Hsüan tsung's reign. In the vigorous intellectual climate of the late eighth century, the same scholars who reappraised the canonical and state ritual inheritance also developed new perspectives on the past. Essays on historical topics, intended for private circulation, reached a high point in the medieval tradition of short critical analyses. The unofficial compilatory tradition also developed, and critical institutional compendia attained a peak of achievement in works addressed to a bureaucracy that was at the height of its sophistication and awareness of its past. In some of these works, scholars recorded views that were as radical and sceptical as any in the dynasty.

Successive shih lu *and T'ang ideals in official history*

From the recovery of Ch'ang-an in 757 until the middle of the ninth century, the official apparatus for compiling the dynastic record continued to run. Many of the chief ministers in this period are mentioned as directing the record. Official scholars, usually men whose careers were relatively well documented in both official and unofficial sources, compiled *shih lu* for the eight post-rebellion reigns from Su tsung until Wu tsung. Notes concerning the length of these *shih lu* and their compilers were preserved.[137] Although no completed version of the *kuo shih* subsequent to that presented to Su tsung after 759 is recorded, its compilation was still an immediate goal for historians, at least until Te tsung's reign.[138] Earlier versions of the T'ang *kuo shih* were widely read, and were quoted, by emperors, ministers, scholars and other officials.[139]

There were, however, many irregularities in the compilation of successive *shih lu*. These again usually involved politically and factionally motivated interference. But the crude political competition that lay behind much post-rebellion comment on *shih lu* was not usually described as such. Rather, scholars commented on the dynastic record in terms of the ideals that their predecessors had formulated for official history writing at the start of the dynasty. In the second half of the dynasty, these early T'ang principles retained both their prestige and their relevance to official history.

One of the ideals that had been central to the compilation of history in the Chen-kuan court was that the emperor should not interfere with the court diaries or *shih lu* under compilation. It was for successive official historians to resist the emperor's curiosity about the terms in which his reign was recorded. Only then would the record, factual and in their terms objective, be of value to posterity. Only then, also, would scholars fulfil their duty to uphold Confucian priorities in both history writing and government. In the post-rebellion period, emperors continued to involve themselves in the compilation of the T'ang record, much as T'ai tsung had done, and official scholars faithfully recorded episodes that echoed T'ai tsung's dialogues with his advisers.

One episode that implied a double parallel to the Chen-kuan era, took place in 757.[140] Su tsung had by this time, as T'ai tsung had in 627, secured his father's abdication in his own favour. But his usurpation divided the scholarly bureaucracy, and seriously affected the perspectives from which the official historians loyal to Hsüan tsung and those whom he had himself appointed considered recent events.[141] When the emperor asked how this rule was being recorded, Yü

Hsiu-lieh, then an official historian and his loyal supporter, merely took refuge in a bland reformulation of the early T'ang ideal. The ruler's activities, he affirmed, were all being written down.

There is no explicit record of Tai tsung's attitude to the record being compiled for his own reign, though he, like most T'ang sovereigns, referred specific events to the history office.[142] The autocratic Te tsung was very restrictive over appointments to the office, and required a special interview of one scholar.[143] He also suspended, for a period after the tenure of Li Mi (722–89), the provision whereby chief ministers supervised the history.[144] Probably in about 785, Chang Chien, an official historian and ritual scholar with a south-eastern background, 'submitted a memorial in which he expounded the advantages and weaknesses of the historian's office, pointing them out and clarifying them very incisively, [so as to] make good the royal regulations'. But regrettably, no details of the arguments Chang used or of any response from Te tsung are preserved.[145] Hsien tsung discussed the dynastic record several times with his ministers. In 812, he criticized the *shih lu* for Su tsung's reign, because it 'gave false praise to great ministers', and he gave instructions that compilers were not 'fictitiously to embellish' their account of his own reign.[146] In the mid ninth century, the scholarly Wen tsung, in an episode the record of which was clearly intended to echo those in the Chen-kuan court two centuries before, attempted to gain access to *shih lu* under compilation.[147]

In real terms, however, the influence of successive post-rebellion emperors on the compilation of the record is likely to have been less important than the related problem of control of the history by competing interests within the bureaucracy, mainly by those chief ministers who were active in their role as directors. The record of discussion and complaint to which this problem gave rise, however, is again likely to be imperfect. In some cases, as so often in the T'ang, documentation has been preserved for political reasons, to reflect credit or discredit on those involved. Probably even moderate chief ministers were committed to maintaining their own control of the records sent to the history office. But in the century following the rebellion, official historians, or other agencies in the central bureaucracy, memorialized intermittently to protest against the restrictions that affected diarists and historians. They characterized the institution of the *shih cheng chi* by the chief minister Yao Shou in 693 as a regrettable compromise, a step back from the ideal of open participation the diarists had enjoyed under T'ai tsung. They also recorded

certain political acts that violated the court diarists' ideal of access to
the political process.

In 796, for example, the *T'ang hui yao* records that the greatly
resented imperial favourite P'ei Yen-ling secured the removal of two
official historians, one of them Chang Chien and the second Chiang I
(747–821, canonized *I*), from monitory offices in which they would
have been able to attend court discussions.[148] In 808, under Hsien
tsung, an examination candidate made a very rare reference to
official history in an examination script, when he implied that
historians were relegated to the sidelines of political life.[149] Hsien
tsung discussed the *shih cheng chi* with Li Chi-fu (758–814,
canonized *Chung-i*), a chief minister and an assiduous supervisor of
the dynastic record, in 813.[150] In 817, he ordered the revival of a
quarterly record of court discussions, compiled by the diarists and
forwarded to the history office.[151] His successor Mu tsung instituted
an annual, rather than a quarterly, record of court discussions, in
response to a request from the central secretariat and chancellery.[152]
Wen tsung attempted to re-instate a quarterly record by measures of
831 and 835.[153] But by 838, complaints were again made,[154] there
were further measures in 841,[155] and the issue was raised again
perhaps as late as 852.[156] Finally, in 905, there was another reference
to the problem. Historians at the rank of compiler were characterized
as of low standing, and not 'privy to the confidential and important
matters of the inner court'.[157]

The problems behind this succession of references to the early T'ang
ideal of access to court information for historians were beyond
practical solution. The compilation of almost all of the six *shih lu* for
the reigns of emperors from Su tsung to Hsien tsung was affected by
political or factional interests.[158] Those involved ranged from the
eunuch faction at the court, who particularly resented the way in which
they were portrayed in the *shih lu* for Te tsung and Shun tsung, to
those chief ministers who were active in the roles as directors. The
factional political climate affected the attitudes especially of the middle
ranking compilers on whom the burden for maintaining the ideal of the
'perfect impartiality' of the record fell. By the early ninth century, the
indignation that had run through Liu Chih-chi's account of conditions
at the history office a century before was replaced in some cases by
resignation and by unwillingness to take part in the compilation of *shih
lu*.

It was Han Yü who expressed this attitude of reluctance most clearly.
In 813, Han was commissioned to compile a second version of the *shih*

lu for the brief reign of Shun tsung. At this time, the dynastic record was directed, for a second period, by Li Chi-fu, a chief minister who exerted tight control over it. The rescript appointing Han, by Po Chü-i (772–846, canonized *Wen*), commended him for 'having no contact with power or influence, and bringing about his reputation by his own [efforts]'.[159] But Han Yü's reaction to the commission was far from enthusiastic. His reservations, given in correspondence with the *Ch'un-ch'iu* scholar Liu K'o, show that he believed that the political self-interest of its directors vitiated the material of official history to an extent that made it almost worthless. 'In extreme cases', he wrote, 'the fondnesses or hatreds of the factions adhered to will be so different that good and evil deeds may be constructed out of nothing'.[160] Liu Tsung-yüan, commenting to Han on this correspondence, urged him to set aside ill-founded timidity and fulfil the commission. He asked Han to concede that a post in the censorate or as a chief minister was much more dangerous than a tenure in the history office. He pointed out that editing the *Ch'un-ch'iu*, for all its politically fraught character, had not caused Confucius's death.[161] Han's eventual acceptance of Li Chi-fu's commission resulted, after Li's death, in the brief *shih lu* for Shun tsung's reign. But the troubled sequence of factionally motivated revisions that this text underwent, lasting until years after Han's death, only underscored the difficulty of the idealistic compiler's task.

The circumstances for the *shih lu* of later ninth-century reigns, those of Mu tsung, presented in 833, of Ching tsung, presented in 845, of Wen tsung, presented in 854, and of Wu tsung, presented between 870 and 874, are less well documented;[162] but it is most unlikely that conditions for official historians improved during this period. Ministers were appointed as supervisors of the history until the final years of the dynasty; a director was named as late as 904. But the drastic deterioration in political conditions meant that, after the record for Wu tsung's reign, no *shih lu* was completed.[163]

Criticism of the biographies

The political or factional interest that lay behind this troubled history of irregularities, revisions and delays to *shih lu* also informed the individual biographies that were attached to them and that went on to form the largest section of the *kuo shih*. Biographies not only constituted the eighth of the thirteen sub-categories of history in the official biographical scheme; they were also a particularly widely practised form in T'ang China. As laudatory commemorative tributes, they ensured for many officials of all ranks the perpetuation of their names and therefore a form of immortality that had the full sanction of the Confucian tradition.[164] Laudatory biographies were self-evidently open to exaggeration or falsification. In society at large, there was cynicism over such commemorative texts, and this cynicism was also expressed in connection with biographies intended for the history office.[165]

In the T'ang period, official scholars compiled numerous collections of biographies, many restricted to discrete categories of scholar or exemplar. Again, almost all these collections are lost. But it is reasonable to infer that the individual biographies they contained were similar in perspective to those that survive in the dynastic histories and in other sources. In the seventh century, Li I-fu[166] and Hsü Ching-tsung[167] both compiled collections. The ritual specialist, director of the dynastic record and owner of a large library, Wang Fang-ch'ing (d. 702, canonized *Chen*) compiled a collection of biographies of exemplars of filial and fraternal devotion in fifteen *chüan*.[168] The empress Wu herself made a collection of women's biographies in 100 *chüan*.[169] In Hsüan tsung's reign, Hsü Chien compiled biographies of recluses in three *chüan*.[170] The official scholar Yin Yin wrote a work that documented the achievements of some of the most prominent surnames, while Liu Fang compiled a work that may have given an account of scholars' achievements. Yen Chen-ch'ing, who was related to both these men, cited these works in demonstrating the scholarly pre-eminence of the Yen clan.[171] Longer biographies of politically important individual officials were also composed. A biography of Ti Jen-chieh in three *chüan* by Li Yung that may have emphasized his role in the restoration of the T'ang line in 698 is a pre-rebellion example.[172] After the rebellion such biographies were written for great loyalist general service officials and military commanders, like Yen Chen-ch'ing's brother Yen Kao-ch'ing (d. 756, canonized *Chung-chieh*),[173] the loyalist commander Chang Hsün (709–57),[174] or the loyalist generals Kuo Tzu-i,[175] and Tuan Hsiu-shih,[176] whose campaigns had enabled the dynasty to survive. There are indications that the writing of biographies of heroic figures, even of humble origin, became something of a vogue in the post-rebellion period.[177]

Official historians themselves were frequently involved in compiling collections of biographies. Two of the most important in the reigns of Te tsung and Hsien tsung, Chang Chien and Chiang I, compiled collections of biographies of chief ministers.[178] Another example is the official historian Ma Yü, the pupil of the pre-rebellion teacher Yüan Te-hsiu, who compiled a work entitled *Ch'ing hsiang chuan* (*Biographies of ministers and chancellors*).[179] Many more titles of

collections of biographies survive, and the T'ang scholar community
had access to a large literature of this kind, a proportion of which had
official or semi-official standing.

Throughout the T'ang, however, the most coveted eventual
destination for a biographical text was not the grave of its subject, or a
collection of biographies, but the dynastic history itself. Inclusion of an
ancestor's biography in a history, even if the history was of a pre-T'ang
dynasty, was, like an ancestor's canonization title, a source of great
pride.[180] But the very prestige of inclusion resulted in charges of
manipulation and cynicism. The unreliability of reports of conduct
(*hsing chuang*), in the form in which they reached the history office,
provoked criticism. There were also controversies over the inclusion or
rejection of individual biographies in successive *shih lu*, and over the
way in which their subjects were portrayed and categorised. Already in
the early eighth century, Liu Chih-chi criticized the Chen-kuan scholar
ministers and official scholars for including unmerited entries for their
fathers or grandfathers in the histories of the pre-T'ang dynasties. He
also censured the version of the *kuo shih* completed in 693 for
over-reliance on reports of conduct.[181] The classification of individual
biographies caused disagreement under Hsüan tsung. Wei Shu, for
reasons that are not clear, in his own version of the dynastic history,
abolished the category reserved for 'cruel officials'.[182]

The problem of unreliable reports of conduct and of political
manipulation of biographies or of biographical information in *shih lu*
and in the *kuo shih* appears to have worsened after the rebellion.
Individual officials were represented by biased or distorted accounts.
Some major, controversial figures were left out; in the *shih lu* for Tai
tsung's reign, Yen Chen-ch'ing's outspoken memorials against Yüan
Tsai were not included,[183] while Fang Kuan, the unsuccessful chief
minister who inspired loyalty from so many scholars, was given no
biography at all.[184] The authorities also received intermittent complaints that reports of conduct were too laudatory and lacking in
objectivity. In 763 and again in 791, it was stipulated that reports of
conduct should be composed by assistant staff of the deceased officials
concerned, and not by their more partisan allies or family members. In
810, this policy was reaffirmed.[185] In 806, Po Chü-i referred indirectly
to the problem of unreliable accounts.[186] The clearest charges,
however, came in 819, from Li Ao, then an official historian, and
probably hopeful of a commission to compile the *shih lu* for Hsien
tsung's reign. Li argued that reports of conduct had become far too
laudatory and lacking in straightforward narration. The events of a

man's career, objectively related, should speak for themselves. The purpose of the dynastic record was, in the much used phrase that Li repeated, 'to encourage goodness and reprove evil', by a dispassionate record of events.[187]

The scholar community promoted their ideal of a complete and objective historical record for the dynasty and their belief in the exemplary function of official biographies in another series of comments relating to them. Several scholars, in compiling unofficial biographies of meritorious figures, closed them with the remark that they should be included in the dynastic history. Sometimes the subjects of these biographies were celebrated loyalist officials of the post-rebellion period, sometimes obscure figures. Some scholars contacted colleagues in the history office over such cases, or submitted their texts to the emperor. Ch'üan Te-yü reported in 796 on the filial conduct of a great grandson of Liu Chih-chi, which had been reported to the history office ten years before.[188] Both Liu Tsung-yüan[189] and Yüan Chen[190] approached Han Yü as an official historian with detailed accounts in this way. Li Ao composed the biography of a loyalist woman and commended it to the history office. The chief minister P'ei Tu admired his text.[191] Han Yü himself, before his appointment to the history office in 813, wrote a comment on Li Han's biography for Chang Hsün, which Li had presented to the emperor with a fervent plea that it be included in the dynastic history.[192]

The increase in numbers of these approaches to individual official historians after the rebellion was as characteristic of their own time as the directives of Hsüan tsung that his achievements be referred to the history office had been of the K'ai-yüan era. Hsüan tsung had related his military and administrative successes to the grand cosmological framework of dynastic rule. In promoting their biographical accounts, scholars of the post-rebellion period shifted emphasis away from great dynastic enterprises towards the political and military problems of the dynasty and the achievement of individuals in trying to restore the T'ang to its former greatness.

Unofficial histories

The same dissatisfaction with the reliability of the biographies intended for the history office that Li Ao had expressed led a number of scholars in the post-rebellion period to continue the pre-rebellion tradition of compiling their own versions of the history of the dynasty. Liu Fang, whose career as an official scholar ran on into Te tsung's reign, compiled an important record of the history of the dynasty up to

778 called the *T'ang li* (*Calendar of the T'ang*), which gave his own assessment of events and may also have included more discursive essays.[193] Lu Ch'ang-yüan, a friend both of Li Ao and Han Yü, compiled a T'ang history.[194] Han Yü,[195] and Li Ao himself[196] were among those who either undertook or merely planned such works. The *Ch'un-ch'iu* scholar Ling Chun compiled a chronicle history covering an unspecified period after the Han.[197] Po Chü-i encouraged a friend to undertake a similar work for the T'ang.[198] Later, Wang Yen-wei, the ritual scholar and expert on the canonization system, wrote a chronicle style history of the dynasty in 70 *chüan*.[199] Sun Ch'iao, the great admirer of Han Yü, modified and rewrote the work by Lu Ch'ang-yüan.[200] Another late T'ang writer in the same tradition was Ch'en Yüeh, whose *T'ang t'ung chi* (*Comprehensive record for the T'ang*), Ssu-ma Kuang cited.[201]

Almost all of these works that were completed are now lost, and it is possible at best to infer the attitudes of their compilers. But most were in the chronicle form that was still upheld, in this period, as providing the best vehicle for moral judgement of events. Some of them are also likely to have embodied precisely the moralistic concern for the role of individuals, and the desire to adjust 'praise and blame' in the political record that underlay Li Ao's concern for truth in biographical accounts and that lay behind the suggestions scholars forwarded to the history office. Han Yü called it 'punishing evil and flattery in those already dead, and letting the secluded light of hidden virtue shine out'. Li Ao spoke of using the 'praise and blame' technique of the *Ch'un-ch'iu* so that, 'the rich and noble who were not also illustrious for their merit and virtue would not necessarily have fame in later generations, nor would the poor and base whose virtue was perfect necessarily be prevented from shining forth for all time'. These and other scholars[202] underlined the view that a historical compilation was above all an instrument that would vindicate the Confucian system of ethical priorities and produce a record that would sort out for all time the good and the evil.

Historical criticism in short essays

As well as compiling or planning compiling long unofficial histories, scholars of the T'ang also reviewed the past in short essays, notes, commemorative texts or even poems. In the post-rebellion period, this tradition of writing greatly expanded. Scholars treated a copious range of topics in this way; but certain themes tended to recur. In invoking the past, they usually addressed, either directly or obliquely, the problems of their own time. Though a writer might adopt a range of approaches, there was a polarity between interest in the performance of individuals and their political conduct on the one hand and impersonal, often institutional issues on the other.

The great men of the past, therefore, provided topics, especially when there was a tradition of controversy surrounding them. Kuan Chung, the adviser to duke Huan of Ch'i, the first of the five hegemons, and Chu-ko Liang, the strategist of the Later Han came into this category. To idealistic scholars like Yüan Chieh, Li Han and Liang Su, Kuan Chung in effect represented 'expedient means' rather than morally correct conduct, and was therefore unacceptable as a model. To the reformers of the latter part of the Te tsung's reign, including Tu Yu, however, he was the archetype of the talented and effective administrator.[203] Chu-ko Liang was extolled as an able leader, of a kind the contemporary world greatly needed. In the immediate aftermath of the rebellion, Hsiao Ying-shih praised his powers of strategy; and the young reformers of Shun tsung's reign compared themselves to him. For the idealistic Liang Su, on the other hand, he stood for an unacceptable degree of political intervention.[204]

Scholars also used traditional analytical categories in impersonal analyses of history. The sequence of values *chung*, loyalty, *ching*, reverence, and *wen*, refinement, were believed to have correlated with the Hsia, Shang and Chou dynasties. The change that had taken place in these ancient dynasties was seen in turn as justifying change in the recent past. Tu-ku Chi was said to have discussed this subject with Fang Kuan before the rebellion. It figured in the thought of the *Ch'un-ch'iu* scholar Tan Chu, and Li Ao and Han Yü also referred to it.[205]

The discussion that has a claim to represent the keenest in post-rebellion analysis of the history of government concerned the problem of enfieffment (*feng chien*). By the late eighth century this issue had, as a policy option, twice divided the T'ang scholarly community, first under T'ai tsung and then during the An-lu-shan rebellion itself. Integral to this problem, in the second half of the eighth century were several contemporary issues. One was what attitude was appropriate to the decentralized political order and semi-independent provincial war-lords of the period. A second was whether the ideal of the impartial interest (*kung*) should prevail over the private interest of the ruling house, and whether succession to any office should be determined by blood or by merit. The enfieffment issue was also compounded with the question of whether recruitment to office should be devolved from the capital and conducted locally or remain centralized at Ch'ang-an.

The problem therefore offered post-rebellion scholars a chance to comment on how the central government should relate to the provinces and how the imperial line should relate to the bureaucracy, which they represented and which was now more developed than ever before.

It was, above all, the scholars who believed in institutional change who commented on the history of the enfieffment issue. Chao K'uang followed Liu Chih-chi in emphasizing that the Han dynasty version of enfieffment had been different from that of high antiquity. He also followed Liu Chih in seeing in the devolved Han system of administering the provinces a model for the decentralized system of appointment to office that he advocated.[206] Both Tu Yu, in frequent brief editorial insertions in the *T'ung tien*,[207] and Liu Tsung-yüan, in a longer essay,[208] argued against enfieffment. Both did so in terms of the ideal of the centralized bureaucratic state, and implicit in their positions was an interest in delimiting the power of the emperor. Tu Yu, like Liu Chih and Chao K'uang, believed in decentralized recruitment and appointment to office. Nonetheless, he argued emphatically that a system of government that devolved political power in other respects was wrong.

Liu's essay argued that the enfieffment principle had never been 'the intention of the sages' of high antiquity, but represented a compromise that circumstances had forced on them. He pointed out, using evidence from history, as Li Pai-yao had done at the start of the dynasty, that administration through the enfieffment of imperial relatives had never coincided with long-term stability. The enfieffment idea, he suggested, should therefore be detached from the question of the duration of dynasties, a spurious association advocated by its proponents. Li Pai-yao's submission, characteristic for the seventh century, had been a successful attempt to persuade the emperor against a course of action. Liu Tsung-yüan's essay, on the other hand, much more detached and philosophical in its tone, was, like so much of the creative prose writing in this period, intended for a private readership. It was followed in the late ninth century by another analysis of the enfieffment issue, by the rescript writer and book collector Li Ch'i (d. 895, canonized *Wen*). Li took as his theme the essays written by post-Han advocates of enfieffment, and refuted them in detail.[209]

The histories in the examinations
The importance of the post-canonical past to the scholarly elite was such that, both formally at the level of curricula, and in more general terms, it played a major part in examinations. The two great

histories, the *Shih chi* and *Han shu* had been examinable texts in the
seventh and early eighth centuries, though no examples of questions or
answers survive.[210] Han histories provided a proportion of the case
lore that was used to provide material for 'judgements' in higher
doctoral and selection examinations.[211] As part of the 'memorization
corpus', detailed knowledge of the classical histories was assumed in
candidates for the *chin shih* degree.

In the post-rebellion period, critics of the literary emphasis that the
chin shih had acquired advocated the use of Han and post-Han
histories for curricula. The *Ch'un-ch'iu* scholar Chao K'uang proposed
the use of the *Hou Han shu*, with the monographs of Ssu-ma Piao,
annotated by Liu Chao. He also suggested making examinable the
San-kuo chih, the *Chin shu*, histories of the northern and southern
dynasties, the *Chen-kuan cheng yao* (*Essentials of the government of
the Chen-kuan period*), and T'ang *shih lu* up to that for Jui tsung's
reign.[212] Under Hsien tsung, in 806, Yüan Chen suggested in a decree
examination answer that the *Liu tien*, the criminal code and T'ang civil
ordinances (*ling*) be used as curricula.[213] If these suggestions had been
followed, the interest in contemporary institutions and in the history of
government that was so prevalent in the intellectual community would
have become central to the recruitment and selection processes. But,
despite its openness towards the past, T'ang authority apparently
preferred that the main formal curricula should concern politically
remoter and potentially less controversial periods, and these demands
were never taken up.

There was, however, some response among examiners to successive
demands for the use of histories. Under Te tsung, the three Han
histories provided the curriculum for a decree examination.[214] In 822,
a regular examination in the *Shih chi*, *Han shu* and *Hou Han shu* was
instituted, its three texts balancing the *Three traditions* to the *Ch'un-
ch'iu* and the three ritual canons, which were also now examined in
special examinations.[215] This examination ran on till the end of the
dynasty; but, like the others, it lacked the prestige of the *chin shih*,
and no questions or answers have survived. In decree examinations
and in the dissertation section of the *chin shih*, sub-questions relating
to the history of the T'ang itself recurred in large numbers. They
usually cited the Chen-kuan and K'ai-yüan periods as offering ideals to
be recovered, or the great officials of the reigns of T'ai tsung and
Hsüan tsung as exemplars. The condition of official education
(Chapter 2) and of the state ritual programme (Chapter 3) provided
questions; but the history office, and the compilation of the official
dynastic record, never figured in the examination record.

Questions on episodes in remoter history that suggested contemporary issues were also set: for example, land policy in the Chou and Han dynasties or the Han emperor Yüan ti's promotion of Confucianism.[216] There were also questions on issues of political philosophy: selection policy itself from Han times on featured recurrently.[217] So did the change in balance between *wen* and *chih*, and the correlation of *chung, ching* and *wen* with the Hsia, Shang and Chou.[218] The enfieffment issue was also used: the rebellion of the Wu and Ch'u princes in 154 B.C. was seen as resulting from Han Kao tsu's enfieffments at the start of the Former Han; it was set as a sub-question in a decree examination of 806.[219] Po Chü-i's *Ts'e lin*, containing a dissertation on the enfieffment issue, also indicates that it was in the repertory of examination questions.[220]

Some of Po Chü-i's collection of model dissertation questions and answers, and other examination questions set at this period, echoed the phrasing of questions set as long as forty years before.[221] This repetition might suggest that T'ang examinations were largely a matter of routine. Topics, even those that involved recent history, recurred or were expected to recur. Nonetheless, there was a marked correlation between many of the examination questions that have survived and discussions in the scholar community that resulted in letters and essays intended for private circulation. Historical topics like the enfieffment issue, the role of *chung, ching* and *wen* in history, the comparative merits of past examplars like Kuan Chung and Chu-ko Liang and the history of selection policy were all treated at length and by numbers of writers in unofficial literature as well as raised in examinations. Examiners thus reflected the character of contemporary interest in the past, much as they had brought contemporary interest in *hsing ming* and psychological analysis (Ch. 3, pp. 96–7) into the examinations. As representatives of the intellectual elite, they recruited to their own community by requiring knowledge of issues that were its own live concern.

Attitudes to the monographs
Scholars such as Han Yü and Li Ao idealized the dynastic history as a document that would sort out for all time, by its allocation of 'praise and blame', the demoralizing political and factional struggles through which they lived. Their outlook on the past suggests little interest in radical institutional reform or in the history of institutions. Their moralistic interest in history was, however, counterbalanced by the approach that, instead of emphasizing the political conduct of the individual, focussed on institutional evolution, impersonal forces and long term trends.

In the post-rebellion period, this second, more technical approach, involving institutions and policies, became widespread. Increasingly in official and unofficial biographical sources, knowledge of institutional precedent, often in T'ang government, is mentioned.[222] Many literary officials were asked to compile or up-date the 'wall records' for particular official premises that had become common in the eighth century. These compositions described, often in political philosophical terms, the function of the institutions involved, traced the evolution that had taken place in them and listed personnel appointed to them.[223] They point to the high level of awareness of institutional history that prevailed in the official community.

It seems surprising, therefore, that the amount of comment on the institutional monographs for the dynastic history, in theory the definitive record of the dynasty's institutional evolution, is negligible. There was no parallel, for this section of the *kuo shih*, to the deeply felt comments on the solemn role of the official historian that Han Yü, Liu K'o or Sun Ch'iao gave in letters, or Li Ao expressed in his memorial of 819.[224] Starting in 764, the greatly resented chief minister of T'ai tsung's reign Yüan Tsai directed the Chi-hsien scholars in compiling a series of monographs that ran through successive dynasties (*t'ung chih*).[225] The topics of this series may have corresponded to monographs in orthodox form histories. The ritual and academic scholar Kuei Ch'ung-ching was selected to compile a treatise on ritual that may have belonged to Yüan Tsai's series.[226] A catalogue that Ch'en Ching compiled for the imperial book collection may have been envisaged as a supplement to the official bibliography monographs.[227] Official sources record also that the official historian K'ung Shu-jui revised a geography monograph, and that scholarly opinion approved of it.[228] These scattered references cannot be confidently accepted as referring to ongoing official monographs for the *kuo shih*. But apart from them, there is no direct information on how the institutional and ritual monographs proceeded in post-rebellion times.

The reason for this paradox, of poverty of documentation for the monographs on the one hand, and of widespread post-rebellion interest in the history of government on the other, may have been that, as in the seventh and early eighth centuries, the monographs continued to lack the special prestige attached to the *shih lu* and the biographies. Especially after the promulgation of the *Liu tien* and the K'ai-yüan ritual code, the updating of monographs on officials and posts and on state ritual may have been seen, even by official historians, as a relatively mechanical exercise, to be undertaken by specialists, but again much less important than the political record.

Nonetheless, official historians, supervisors of the dynastic record and many others, continued on their own initiative to compile works that covered the same topics as individual monographs. Chia Tan (730–805, canonized *Yüan-ching*), a chief minister under Te tsung recognized for his knowledge of institutions, was one of the leading scholars of the administrative geography of the dynasty.[229] Li Chi-fu, also known for his command of T'ang institutional history and especially assiduous as a supervisor of the dynastic record, compiled a household, taxation and military compendium. He actually made use of the resources of the history office to do so. He also condensed the *Liu tien* into a work of one *chüan*.[230] The succession of supplements to the K'ai-yüan ritual code that official scholars produced (Ch. 4, pp. 147–50) likewise notionally related to the monograph on ritual. An official historian of Te tsung's reign, Shen Chi-chi, compiled a *Hsüan chü chih* (*Treatise on selection*) in ten *chüan*, and it is by no means impossible that he intended material from this treatise for eventual inclusion as a new monograph topic in the dynastic history. Shen was a historian with keen views,[231] and a friend of the great institutional historian Tu Yu. It is again possible that he and Tu Yu developed a common view of the importance of documenting the recruitment and selection systems. For Tu Yu not only reserved the second of the sections of the *T'ung tien* for selection; he also included in this section an eloquent and highly critical policy memorial by Shen on the reform of the examination system and another equally incisive criticism by him of the place of *belles lettres* in it.[232]

Institutional compendia

Late eighth-century interest in institutional change also led to the compilation of numbers of comprehensive compendia on the institutions of the dynasty. Some of the best known scholars of the period produced such works, including Lu Hsüan kung[233] and Yüan Chen.[234] Their compilations now exist as titles only; but interest in the history of the T'ang bureaucracy is fully illustrated by the two long unofficial compilations that have survived. The *Hui yao* of Su Mien and the *T'ung tien* of Tu Yu represent two very different outlooks on the history of the T'ang, both prevalent among the intellectual elite in the period. The first was largely conservative and conventional, the second offered a radical and sceptical reappraisal of the origins and purpose of the dynastic state. Only the *T'ung tien* was submitted to the emperor, but both works became well known in the ninth century.

Su Mien's *Hui yao* was originally completed probably towards the end of the first decade of the ninth century, in 40 *chüan*. Little is known about its author; but his brother Su Pien was said to have improved conditions in the revenue department after the death of P'ei Yen-ling, and to have had a library exceeded in size only by the imperial and Chi-hsien libraries. In 853 on imperial order, the *Hui yao* was expanded, and late in the Five Dynasties a third stratum was added, updating the work to the close of the T'ang. The original *Hui yao* assembled excerpted documents, usually decrees, but also memorials and discussions, and used them to trace changes in the T'ang governmental structure. The documentation that it provides for the scholarly agencies; the school system; the canonization system; for scholarly controversies and the titles of books presented to the emperor makes this a particularly valuable source for the history of T'ang Confucian attitudes. But it is also a selective work, intended to promote a moralistic reading of T'ang institutional history. The lists of officials that it includes in its sections on canonizations and on decree examinations, for example, are incomplete and biased in favour of the civil scholarly tradition in the bureaucracy to which the work was addressed.[235]

Su Mien and the compilers of the *Hsü hui yao* of 853 inserted their own critical comments in the documentation they selected. Some of these comments concerned questions of accuracy; others provided assessment of the conduct of individuals or of trends in the bureaucracy. Usually these amounted simply to endorsements of conventional evaluations of central figures in T'ang political history. Su Mien believed that the institutions of the regular bureaucracy provided sufficient means of government, and condemned Yü-wen Jung (d. 730 or 731) and other financial officials of the late K'ai-yüan and T'ien-pao periods for introducing commissionerships.[236] Like many other post-rebellion writers, he indicated respect for Fang Kuan.[237] Other insertions concern condemnation of extravagance and of superstition, attitudes well within the boundaries of T'ang scholarly convention.[238] Su Mien also condemned Hsü Ching-tsung and Li I-fu, the chief ministers of Kao tsung's reign who had terminated the arrangement whereby the court diarists had had access to inner court discussions.[239]

In one of his insertions, Su Mien claimed of the *Hui yao* that it was 'a branch of the dynastic history' and that it aspired to the principles of history writing embodied in the *Ch'un-ch'iu*.[240] Su Mien certainly read the T'ang official dynastic record.[241] But the impression the *Hui yao* gives is rather of a wide ranging repository of information, edited without great critical originality, and intended for officials and prospective officials, to supply them with a political orientation and to meet

their need for factual knowledge of the history of all aspects of the
T'ang state.

The *T'ung tien* of Tu Yu, like the *Hui yao*, was a monument to
T'ang interest in institutions; but the outlook of its compiler is of much
greater interest than that of Su Mien. Like almost all longer T'ang
compilations, the *T'ung tien* was a cumulative work. Like the *Hui yao*,
it was probably based on a large private library. Its principal source
was the *Cheng tien* by Liu Chih, though Tu Yu did not agree with all
the policy recommendations that the *Cheng tien* contained.[242] But Tu
Yu also drew from other compilations, written from a variety of
viewpoints. Despite the inconsistencies that this sometimes made
inevitable, the *T'ung tien* sustains a polemical outlook. Tu Yu argued a
radical perspective on dynastic government and a series of specific
policies. He divided the work into nine sub-sections. Though these
vary in length, its plan invites comparison with the monograph series
of official histories. Tu Yu's wish to focus on 'man' rather than on
'heaven' led him to omit as topics the five elements, astrology and the
calendar. His provincial general service background and distaste for
belles lettres made the bibliography of the dynastic book collections
remote from his interests. But he included, possibly under the influence of his friend the official historian Shen Chi-chi, a section on the
examination system. Border defence, traditionally covered by the
section of official histories devoted to foreign tribes, was also allocated
a section. Tu Yu, however, made a point of changing the order
conventional since the start of the dynasty for monograph series. He
put food and goods first, examinations next, then offices and posts,
ritual and music, followed by war and punishments, administrative
geography and border defence. This new sequence, which he outlined
in his preface, was intended to emphasize that economic conditions
and sound recruitment policies for the bureaucracy were prerequisite
to the stability of China.[243]

Tu Yu divided each of the subject sections of the *T'ung tien* into
sub-sections, recording on the one hand administrative changes affecting the subject concerned, and on the other memorials, discussions and
critical views. The latter category of material, especially if it concerned
the post-rebellion period, he selected in order to support his own
views. In his section on the examinations, he included memorial
submissions by Liu Chih, Shen Chi-chi and Chao K'uang, all of which
were highly critical of T'ang emphasis on composition skills. To these
he added his own short preface and comments that argued the case
against composition skills emphatically and from a historical perspec-

tive.[244] In contrast to Su Mien, when Tu Yu lists the names of individuals, he supplies a few only, and his criteria are those of political or military achievement in a long historical perspective, rather than general prestige in the T'ang official community.[245]

The view of the state that the *T'ung tien* contains is marked by this same critical, sceptical and impersonal outlook. Tu Yu believed that China's superiority to other states derived from favourable geographical and climatic factors.[246] History had been a progression; in ancient times the Chinese had lived much as the barbarians of the present. The bureaucratic state, as embodied in the centralized prefecture and county system of administration, had been achieved by the Ch'in only after a succession of dynasties spanning 1,900 years.[247] Tu's forceful advocacy of the superiority of the prefecture and county system of administration that the Ch'in had introduced, showing that historically it had resulted in greater stability for the population, is a recurrent theme, emphasized by editorial insertions throughout the book. He also upheld the primacy of agriculture, emphasized the need to avoid overstraining the people by harsh criminal laws or taxes, and condemned the numerical growth of the non-essential commercial and clerical professions. He attributed the general loyalty of the T'ang population after the An Lu-shan rebellion to the dynasty's original, compassionate legal code and taxation demands.[248]

Tu Yu's principal theme, however, was that the institutions and administrative provisions of the dynastic state were perishable, that long term decline was inevitable and adaptation essential. Emphasis on evolution had, of course, been a consistent strand in submissions to the throne and in official scholarly compilations since the start of the dynasty. But Tu Yu argued for compromise, adaptation and change in the context of a massively documented account of how the Chinese state had evolved since early times. He no longer considered the state in terms of its cosmological underpinnings; nor was imperial conduct for him any longer in the fore as a determinant of good order and the locus for his political ideals. He rather promoted the well being of the entire polity as more important than the interests of the imperial clan.

The views of the state and its history that the *T'ung tien* contains were echoed by other scholars of the early ninth century. Some like Liu Tsung-yüan, were close to him in intellectual and religious outlook. Others who seem to refer to his views had very different perspectives on the problems that he treated. Han Yü, for example had little of Tu Yu's faith in institutional evolution. Nonetheless he reiterated Tu's picture of the competitive conditions in remote antiquity and his emphasis on the achievements of the Ch'in. Indeed it is quite clear that Tu's views, though polemical, were not considered extreme in the scholar community. As a senior official at Ch'ang-an, in the period from 801 until his death in 812, he enjoyed the respect and company of many scholars. His *T'ung tien* was enthusiastically acclaimed by contemporaries, and his views were referred to until the end of the dynasty. Ch'üan Te-yü, for example commended the compendium in two of the four commemorative texts he composed for Tu. Cheng Yü-ch'ing praised it in a sacrificial graveside prayer to Tu. Liu Yü-hsi, Tu Yu's disciple, mentioned it in 836. At the end of the dynasty, Ssu-k'ung T'u praised Tu's administrative policies.[249]

Ch'üan Te-yü was also among those who testified to another, very different aspect of Tu Yu's career, the interest he took in Buddhism, probably especially during his retirement.[250] The compassion and moderation for which Ch'üan and others praised Tu as an administrator may have derived from his Buddhist beliefs. But more important, just as private commitment to Buddhist religious goals freed Liu Tsung-yüan[251] to review the Confucian-sanctioned T'ang state ritual programme in agnostic terms, so the sceptical and secular tenor of Tu Yu's reappraisal of the history of the Chinese polity derived from the fact that his religious experience was confined to a separate, private compartment of his life. Han Yü attempted to revive Confucianism by redefining Confucian values and rejecting the religious pluralism that was a basic feature of most T'ang scholars' attitudes to questions of belief. But Tu Yu's striking reappraisal of the Confucian-sanctioned medieval polity was made possible by just such religious pluralism.

6

ATTITUDES TO LITERARY COMPOSITION

Of all the Confucian-sanctioned activities that the T'ang state endorsed and its scholarly elite practised, literary composition had the widest following. The emperor, the chief ministers, official scholars and general service officials, and beyond them literate society at large, all respected it. Over the dynasty, moreover, attitudes towards Confucian-orientated *belles lettres* evolved more than attitudes to any other learned discipline, and more scholars took part in this evolution than in any other scholarly activity. Skill in composition was distinct from the ability to compile that was required of official scholars. It meant the ability to compose prose and verse, usually in pieces of no great length, in a range of some fifteen or so genres.[1] It involved demonstrating command of a tacitly acknowledged 'memorization corpus' of canons, histories and *belles lettres*, facility and even speed in composition. It required an aesthetic sense and an ability to innovate, within certain limits, which themselves changed over the dynasty.

Composition as a scholarly activity shared common features with and yet differed significantly from official history and state ritual. Like history and ritual, it concerned the apex of the state. Dexterous composition was an essential element in the process of formulating the public communications of the government. Unless they were expressed in language that demonstrated control of the long heritage of official literature and of the canonical sources that lay behind it, these communications could not hope to command the respect of officials. The great formal pronouncements by the emperor, the acts of grace, edicts of investiture, or decree examination announcements that were issued in his name, were all introduced by high flown and erudite phrases adapted from the canons and the histories. Their composition involved, in a phrase formulated by Confucius himself and much repeated in the T'ang, 'giving [due] elegance and finish to royal commands'.[2] The association of composition skills with, above all, the politically vital function of rescript writing reinforced their importance and made them of enormous interest to an intellectual elite obsessed with status in the official hierarchy. The post of grand secretary, of controller of rescripts, or, in the post-rebellion period, of rescript writer in the Han-lin academy were therefore among the most coveted of all tenures.

There was, however, a second context in which literary composition was important, and which made it different from official history writing and state ritual. The emperor and the court were also heirs to a tradition in which *belles lettres* provided a medium for relaxation and for competitive recreation. Verse composition, particularly, played an important part in court excursions, feasts and other celebrations, some of which might take place on the premises of the advisory colleges themselves. To lead in stylistic innovation in this milieu, or even to be a member of the court literary circle, was to have a place in the most prestigious society in the civilized world.

The ability to compose, however, was by no means restricted to the few who held prestige appointments in the central secretariat or the drafting agencies, or to the court on its more relaxed occasions. Skill in composition was not restricted, in the way that the compilation of the official history and the organization of imperial rituals were, to specific agencies or operations of government, or even to admission to court social circles. Rather, it provided what even canonical scholarship could hardly supply, a challenge to the creative and affective experience of the individual, however he was placed. In this role, verse composition especially became an activity open to all, from the sovereign to society at large. Prodigious quantities were written in the course of the dynasty. In the hands of the relatively small number of true masters, verse may be seen as one of the great monuments of T'ang civilization. During the dynasty, conditions were to change in the court and beyond it; but literature retained a place as a greatly enjoyed, respected and much practised means of expression.

Throughout the T'ang, scholars reflected the rather different functions that literature had in their careers by the ambivalence of their attitude towards what they called 'the arena of letters' (*wen ch'ang*). They sometimes emphasized the solemn role of literature in the service of the state, and justified it in lofty, canonically sanctioned terms. At other times, they downgraded its recreational aspect, finding that in this role it lacked the sense of responsibility that they advocated. According to the context they addressed, they might endorse or condemn the literary world in which they lived. In the course of the dynasty, however, the same trend towards a less court-centred outlook that is apparent in other disciplines asserted itself in attitudes towards literary composition. Comment on literary practice became more and more an individual matter, as, in the second half of the dynasty, scholars wrote more about their own experience of literature.

T'ang scholars at all periods, whether writing officially or unofficially, commented on the literary scene by citing ancient ideals. High Confucian theory provided striking ideas about the nature and function of literature. Just as they integrated other learned disciplines with their view of the cosmos, so writers throughout the T'ang gave literature its cosmological dimension. As *wen*, the patterning of the feelings expressed in words, it was correlated with the patterns of the sky and of the terrestrial world.[3] The instinct to compose verse was held to be part of the natural order, to be, as K'ung Ying-ta put it in the preface to his sub-commentary to the *Mao shih*, 'coeval with the creation of the world'.[4] T'ang scholars frequently repeated these lofty claims for literature, and reiterated their canonical sanction from the *Chou i*. Their cosmological view of literature was not, however, located exclusively in the role of the emperor and in dynastic rule. In this respect it differed from their cosmological view of state ritual and their public endorsement of the cosmic role of the emperor as it was to be recorded in the dynastic history. The cosmic emphasis in literary theory, is, rather, to be seen as a constant reminder of the importance that scholars accorded their own role, and their own claim, by virtue of their mastery of 'human pattern' (*jen wen*) to participate in the cosmic process. Behind this position was the realization that literature was politically important, as a medium which the scholarly elite alone fully mastered. Through it, they could gain access to the emperor, and further their own political interests and those of the scholar community.

T'ang scholars also re-interpreted traditional Confucian observations on the function of literature in ways that expressly concerned the political world in which they lived. They re-stated ideas on the verse tradition that derived from the *Mao shih*: verse was a natural phenomenon and reflected the condition of the society that produced it. It 'made known the feelings of those below'.[5] The idea that verse particularly should reflect the moral condition of the people and the attitude towards high authority of the governed remained important through the dynasty. This concept justified the idea that literary practice was always changing in response to evolving conditions. In turn, this awareness of change informed the keen interest that many Confucian-orientated commentators showed in the history of litera-

ture, and especially in changes in verse styles both during the
pre-T'ang period and in the T'ang itself.

A belief that *belles lettres* could go astray and cease to express
Confucian priorities lay behind the strand of disapproval in scholars'
attitudes to literary practice. They saw canonical grounds for ranking
the *belles lettres* of their own time as a 'mere skill' (*i i*). Literature
(*wen hsüeh*) was the last of the four divisions in Confucius's teaching.[6]
The very independence of literary composition from other learned
activities, and its development as a separate activity, indicated, in this
view, that an ideal had lapsed. For ideally, administration, moral
conduct and literary practice were all integrated activities that should
testify to a harmoniously governed society. It was only with the *Ch'u
tz'u* (*Songs of Ch'u*), the late Warring States anthology that stood at
the head of the literary division in the fourfold official bibliographical
scheme, that *belles lettres* and Confucian learning had become 'different streams'. Literature, in this outlook, was good only to the extent
that it exemplified either good government or concern for good
government. The literature of the period of disunion, especially that of
the late southern courts, was an expression of a sybaritic and irrespons-
ible milieu. Throughout the T'ang, scholars used it as a negative
standard, by which to admonish the current world.[7]

The ambivalence of the interest high authority had in *belles lettres*,
combining fascination for it with a tendency to disapprove of the more
extreme forms it had taken, is clear in the practical steps it took to
commission compilations in this field. It monitored the tradition by
compiling very large anthologies of *belles lettres*. Such compilations,
made by large commissions of official scholars, were selective, and
involved the rejection of unsuitable material. Like compilations in
other learned fields, they were more numerous in the seventh century
and fell away in the post-rebellion period. Emperors also commissioned shorter encyclopaedias as aids for practitioners of *belles lettres*,
and their production followed the same pattern. The compilation of
up-to-date catalogues for the dynasty's collection of literature, though
clearly not concerned with *belles lettres* alone, had similar principles.
In the pre-rebellion period, several of these catalogues were produced,
but again after 755 there was only one recorded catalogue title for the
imperial collection.

At a lower level in the hierarchy, composition skills proved of
immense importance in another way. Their great prestige in the court
and in the official community led to their taking an increasingly
important place in the examination process. This resulted, from the

late seventh century, in the ascent to pre-eminence of the *chin shih*, the examination that, more than any other, tested composition skills. Study of the 'memorization corpus' and practice in the styles of verse and prose composition currently in fashion, therefore, became obligatory for ambitious prospective officials, displacing in importance, though not excluding, knowledge of canonical texts. This development did much to shape the criteria by which the intellectual elite identified themselves and perpetuated their own power within the civil bureaucracy. From the eighth century onwards, especially, many successful scholar officials owed the start of their careers to their ability to compose fluently in prose and verse as the *chin shih* tested it. But for some Confucian-orientated reformist scholars, particularly in the post-rebellion period, this development turned ambivalent attitudes to composition skills into open criticism. The succession of protest memorials on the role of *belles lettres* in recruitment that these scholars submitted forms a major theme in their outlook on the literary tradition.

The main shift that took place in attitudes to literary composition, however, was brought about first by the expansion in the numbers of the educated, and secondly by the political breakdown and decentralization that followed the An Lu-shan rebellion. Even before the rebellion, a sophisticated and vigorous literary society beyond the court had developed. In the post-rebellion period, the values of this society evolved further away from those prevalent in the court-centred society of the seventh century. Literary ability in the service of the state retained its importance. But, in the more devolved intellectual community of the late eight and early ninth centuries, scholars developed a tradition of detailed comment on their own experience with literature that has no counterpart in the records that survive from the first reigns of the dynasty.

This much more personal and analytical note in many letters, prefaces, introductions and essays from the mid eighth century on, provides a parallel to the concern for Confucian self-cultivation based on reinterpretation of the canons (Ch. 3, pp. 105–112). Both represent the trend away from the official scholarship of the seventh century, towards a less court-centred outlook. Both may also be seen as registering fundamentally conservative attitudes towards the responsibilities of the Confucian scholar in society. But it was the practice of literature, more than any other activity in which T'ang scholars engaged, that was central to the self-image of their community, their outlook on the world, and their efforts to cure the ills they saw around them.

The reigns of Kao tsu and T'ai tsung

From the start of the dynasty, court and scholarly circles greatly esteemed skill in literary composition. Both Kao tsu and T'ai tsung built up the imperial collections of literature, and commissioned compilations based on them that were intended to promote knowledge of and skill in *belles lettres*. T'ai tsung was, despite his claims of lack of erudition, a skilled composer of verse. But the attitude of his Confucian advisers was marked by the tone of disapproval that was to be a strand in the Confucian outlook on *belles lettres* throughout the T'ang. It is consonant with the climate of this early period that scholar ministers should have defined their perspective on literature in an almost exclusively public context, that is in discussions with the emperor, or in prefaces, essays and normative collections intended for the emperor and the court to read.

Early T'ang literary collections

The art of literary composition that so fascinated the early T'ang court was a learned activity. It set value on an effortless command of the inherited tradition and on dexterity in composing. In the period of disunion, this mastery had been facilitated by short reference works and by larger reference collections.[8] The early T'ang court extended its control over this tradition, by commissioning works in both categories. The first was a relatively short encyclopaedia, the *I wen lei chü* (*Literary material arranged by category*). Commissioned in 622, it was finished two years later, in 624, and was thus one of the few scholarly projects to have been completed while Kao tsu was on the throne. More than ten scholars worked on it, among them Ling-hu Te-fen, then deputy director of the imperial library. Four were concurrently members of Kao tsu's commission for the histories of the pre-T'ang dynasties.[9]

The *I wen lei chü* gathered *belles lettres* material under 46 sections and 727 sub-sections. Its section headings include those for celestial phenomena, earth, topography, man, emperors, officials, sages and worthies, and for established themes in the verse tradition: travel, landscape viewing and resentment of maladministration. These were followed by sections for ritual, music, bureaucratic offices, war, weapons, clothing, food, games and for the objects of the natural world that recurred in verse: plants, stones, cereals, fruit, trees, birds, beasts, fish and insects. The *I wen lei chü* thus in effect presented the prospective writer with a concise account of the cosmos, assembled through quotation of those pre-T'ang writings of which its compilers approved.

T'ang court scholars, in surveying and editing inherited literature, compiled a second work that was on a much larger scale and fulfilled a slightly different purpose. The *Wen ssu po yao* (*The wide ranging and the essential in literary thought*), of which the preface and some fragments are all that now survive, was in 1,200 *chüan*. A commission of fifteen of the leading court scholars of the Chen-kuan period took part in its compilation. Wei Cheng was its director. Its dependence on the imperial library for material is suggested by the appointment to the commission of Fang Hsüan-ling, then the library's deputy director. The calendrical and *yin-yang* expert Lü Ts'ai, then an erudit in the court of sacrifices, was also a compiler.[10] The size of the *Wen ssu po yao* was such that it was later ranked with the largest of the pre-T'ang anthologies, the *Yü lan* (*Imperial reading*) of the Northern Ch'i.[11] Like other works in this tradition also, it was claimed to be comprehensive, for 'the way of heaven and earth was complete in it; the relation of man to the spirits was there'.[12] It was thus planned to represent the best in composition on a wide range of subjects, and was more of a reference anthology than, like the *I wen lei chü*, a prompt book designed for quick consultation.

The imperial library

These selective reference compendia were in part the products of an intention to monitor the whole of the literary tradition, not simply that of *belles lettres*. They drew their subject matter from all four of the divisions by which the imperial collection of books was classified. From the start of the T'ang, this collection was maintained and held in the imperial library. In the pre-T'ang period, the library had come to command great prestige. In the south, in the first half of the sixth century, it had benefitted particularly from the patronage of the Liang royal house. In the early seventh century, the Sui emperor Yang ti's addiction to literature had also added to its prestige.[13]

Much of the Sui imperial collection was lost in 622, while it was being transferred by boat from Lo-yang to Ch'ang-an.[14] But, following the Sui and pre-Sui precedents that they themselves documented,[15] the T'ang authorities conducted empire-wide searches for books. In 622, Ling-hu Te-fen, as deputy director of the library, took the first initiative.[16] This was followed by measures by T'ai tsung and by Wei Cheng as director, starting in 628. A staff of twenty collators and over one hundred copyists was set up, and 'after a few years the imperial library was gloriously and wholly complete'.[17] But collecting continued, first under the southerner Yü Shih-nan (558–638, canonized

Wen-i), whom T'ai tsung called a 'walking library', as director in 633, and then under others, including Yen Shih-ku, deputy director from 633 and director from 641.[18] Copying went on, uncompleted, into Kao tsung's reign.[19] A separate collection of books was made for the Hung-wen kuan, the main advisory college under T'ai tsung.[20] A catalogue for the imperial collection, presumably in preparation at this time, was not completed until the Yung-hui period.[21]

The programme of searches for books that the dynasty started in this way had the concealed, altogether non-literary, motive of destroying or proscribing material judged treasonable or subversive. The pre-T'ang dynasties had done this for works concerned with prognostication and augury. There is evidence that in early T'ang certain categories of writing were suppressed. But, perhaps because those in power wanted to avoid any suggestion of the Legalist harshness they projected on the Sui, the official records do not mention destruction of any written works.[22]

Again following a pre-T'ang tradition, high authority used the imperial library to take in copies of both officially and privately compiled works in all the divisions of literature, when these were submitted to the throne. Already in 619, a scholar whose name is not known presented a privately compiled work and was rewarded by an appointment to office. The enormous literary anthology in 1,200 *chüan*, the *Wen ssu po yao*; Wei Cheng's commentary to the re-ordered version of the *Li chi*, the *Lei li* (Ch. 4, p. 121); Yen Shih-ku's collected commentaries to the *Han shu* (Ch. 5, p. 164); the administrative geographical compendium of 642, the *K'uo ti chih* (Ch. 5, p. 172), are all recorded as being taken into the imperial library.[23] Submission and acceptance of a work was an implementation of the policy of 'the road of presenting books' (*hsien shu chih lu*), that had first been formulated under the Former Han.[24] It helped high authority to extend control over unofficial literature, and secured substantial financial reward for the authors or compilers involved.

Court attitudes to belles lettres

T'ai tsung's scholarly advisers expressed more openly the selective approach to inherited literature that they invested in anthologies like the *I wen lei chü* or the *Wen ssu po yao* when they discussed the role of *belles lettres* with the emperor. Wei Cheng, Fang Hsüan-ling and others considered obsession with composition skills to be a potential threat to the austere principles of conduct that they urged on the emperor. They insisted that he should reject the sybaritic excesses of the Liang and Ch'en courts in the south, and that the *belles lettres* of their own time should embody the austere values of the Confucian system of political conduct.

They had good reason, in their own terms, to be concerned. Kao tsu had already appointed scholars with pre-Sui southern backgrounds to literary posts. Among them was the rescript writer and historian Ch'en Shu-ta, whom Hsü Ling (507–83), the compiler of the *Yü-tai hsin yung* (*New songs from jade terraces*), the definitive anthology of southern palace verse, had greatly admired. Ch'en Shu-ta, in turn, had recommended for T'ang appointments southern scholars who had hitherto disdained coming north. T'ai tsung himself betrayed his fascination for southern *belles lettres* in a number of ways. He particularly esteemed Yü Shih-nan, an elderly southerner who had come north when the Sui conquered the Ch'en, and who had known Hsü Ling. He also commissioned Ch'u Liang (558–645, canonized *Wen-k'ang*), another southerner and acquaintance of Hsü Ling, to compile an anthology of fine lines from early verse.[25] The emperor also composed in the 'palace style' (*kung t'i*), with which Hsü Ling was identified and which represented the southern court style at its most unrestrained. Towards the end of his reign, T'ai tsung indicated his interest in *belles lettres* more generally by composing a strikingly high-flown tribute to the Chin critic Lu Chi, for inclusion at the end of Lu's *Chin shu* biography.[26] At his wish, the Chen-kuan court held verse competitions at excursions and feasts, in the southern manner, probably more than official sources admit.[27]

Confronted with what they saw as the emperor's dangerous interest in the southern court milieu, therefore, the Chen-kuan scholar ministers provided T'ai tsung with emphatic warnings of the risks it entailed. In the preface to his *Ch'ün-shu chih yao*, Wei Cheng tried to turn the emperor away from interest in the sort of *belles lettres* anthologies that 'recent emperors have compiled', for these, he said, had been marked by frivolity and irresponsibility.[28] Wei Cheng and Fang Hsüan-ling condemned southern court literature, and singled out Hsü Ling and his fellow writer in the 'palace style', Yü Hsin (513–81), as particularly subversive of good order.[29] Yü Shih-nan admonished T'ai tsung against composing superficial or erotic verse, and reminded him of the example that he should set.[30]

In answer to these warnings, T'ai tsung made a number of statements that suggest that he was aware of the dangers that caused his scholar ministers such concern. He ranked Yü Shih-nan's skill in literary composition, together with his calligraphy, as the last of Yü's accomplishments.[31] He remarked of Tzu-yu and Tzu-hsia, the two disciples whom Confucius had commended for their literary ability and learning, that 'their virtuous [conduct] was not up to their [literature and] learning'.[32] In 637, he stopped the bureau of compositions from compiling an anthology of his own *belles lettres*. He also criticized the histories of the Former and Later Han for including in the texts of *fu* by Yang Hsiung, Ssu-ma Hsiang-ju and Pan Ku, ordering that the history of his own reign should contain the texts only of incisive and politically constructive memorials.[33]

The official scholars of the Chen-kuan court duly recorded these and similar statements, and used them to formulate the austere approach to *belles lettres* that they hoped would prevail in the T'ang court. Their admonition, however, is unlikely to have had much effect on the prevailing climate. In his policy memorial of 637 advocating the prefecture and county system of administration (Ch. 5, p. 170, p. 197), the official scholar Li Pai-yao praised T'ai tsung for giving priority to the discussion of government, and for relegating *belles lettres* and metaphysical speculation to the end of the day. But he also characterized the state as not yet wholly reformed or free from extravagance. 'This is because custom has been of long standing, and it is difficult conclusively to change it. We request that [the emperor] be ready to remove the ornamental and to practise the austere, to change *wen* for *chih*.' Nearly a century and a half later, critics of a climate in which *belles lettres* had consolidated a position of great importance in official life were to refer to his position. They saw in the relatively open and politically powerful Chen-kuan court a lost opportunity to establish more austere values.[34]

Belles lettres *in the early T'ang bureaucracy and selection system*
The court did not, however, function in isolation. Throughout the official hierarchy and in the selection system, composition skills commanded great prestige. The role of composing official texts for the emperor, particularly, was already one of high status. The period of the foundation provided in this, as in other fields of learning, scholars who were later upheld as models: Yen Shih-ku and Ch'en Shu-ta under Kao tsu, and Ts'en Wen-pen (595–645, canonized *Hsien*) under T'ai tsung were to be praised into the late ninth century. Some of their compositions, like the military communications, acts of grace and abdication edicts that Ch'en Shu-ta composed in the course of the transition between the Sui and the T'ang, were especially momentous for the dynasty.[35] Li Pai-yao also composed rescripts, as his father had done under the Sui and his son and great-grandson were later to do.[36] The office of grand

secretary already had great prestige. In the early Chen-kuan period, T'ai tsung offered it to the *Ch'un-ch'iu* and *Tso chuan* specialist Chu Tzu-she, provided that he successfully discharged a mission to Korea. Having judged on his return, however, that Chu Tzu-she had failed, the emperor appointed him to the state academy directorate instead.[37] The composition of solemn religious and ritual texts on behalf of the dynasty was also highly respected. The bureau of compositions, the institution mainly involved, probably enjoyed its highest status at this point in the dynasty. Some of the best known scholars of the early T'ang, among them Yü Shih-nan, held office there. Hsü Ching-tsung, appointed to the bureau in 634, considered that service there was prerequisite to true fame.[38]

Both the cautious attitude of the scholar ministers to the southern literary heritage, and the state's demand for scholars qualified in the literary tradition, found expression in comment on the place of literary skill in the early T'ang examination system. During the first two reigns, none of the regular examinations formally required the ability in verse or rhymeprose writing that from the early eighth century was to dominate the *chin shih* examination. Nonetheless in T'ai tsung's reign, composition skills already had a place in the examinations. The extent to which dexterity in composition should provide a criterion for selection, an issue that was to preoccupy critics throughout the dynasty, was also raised at this early stage.

In 627, for example, Tu Ju-hui (585–630, canonized *Ch'eng*) emphasized to the emperor that in selection examinations true abilities and conduct, as assessed by a man's own local community, were being neglected and attention was being paid to speech and literary ability.[39] In 639, according to several accounts, the chief examiner failed two candidates with reputations for outstanding literary ability. When T'ai tsung showed surprise, he was told that literary skill alone was insufficient and that 'a man of superficially alluring literary skill will not become a good vessel (*ch'i*)'. The emperor then approved the examiner's decision to reject the candidates.[40] Another official of the period, Tai Chou (d. 633, canonized *Chung*), recommended by Tu Ju-hui on his death-bed, managed the promotion examinations in 630, and is said to have suppressed those with literary accomplishment (*wen ya*). In 631, another president of the board of civil office, Yang Ch'üan, did the same. Both are recorded as having brought about the disapproval of public opinion (*wu i* or *shih lun*).[41]

By adopting this position, a few officials at least promoted the principle that administrative competence should be the determining factor in recruitment and selection, and insisted that relatively little weight should be given to composition skills. Later in the dynasty, a succession of critics were to adopt similar positions and to demand reform. Nonetheless, there was to be an inexorable trend for the great prestige accorded to composition in court and in official society to be expressed more and more in the examination process. In the course of time, this trend was to have important and complex implications for the identity of the T'ang scholar community.

From 650 to 755

During the century after T'ai tsung's death, skill in composition grew in importance to the dynasty, both in the public operation of government and as a much more relaxed means for social recreation. From the second half of the seventh century, however, official sources suggest that the sovereign and the court set aside the cautious attitude towards literary entertainment that T'ai tsung's scholar ministers had tried to promote as the norm. The resulting attitudes, these sources state, greatly affected for the worse both the regular academic institutions and the selection system. A few Confucian-orientated scholars tried, by submitting memorials of protest, to uphold the ideals prescribed by the scholar ministers of the early T'ang. Under Hsüan tsung, there was at first a reaction towards more austere attitudes; but not much suggests that it was effective. Rather, the posts associated with composition increased in prestige, while from the K'ai-yüan and T'ien-pao periods on, those appointed to them tended more and more to be holders of the *chin shih* degree, the qualification above all associated with literary skill.

During this century, the authorities again commissioned encyclopaedias and large anthologies. The imperial library continued to search for and to accept, copy and catalogue written works. Another theme in the history of literary attitudes in this century was the court's recognition of the *Wen hsüan*, the famous Liang dynasty anthology of prose and verse. Historically the most important development for the Confucian tradition, however, concerned not literary attitudes centred on the court, but rather the evolution of literary practice in society beyond it. Especially towards the end of Hsüan tsung's reign, verse writing became more widely practised than ever before. The themes and attitudes expressed in this verse, now no longer exclusively court-centred, but freer and more individual, foreshadowed the shift in perspective that was to take place within the Confucian tradition as a whole in the post-rebellion period.

Official literary compilations

Both Kao tsung and the empress Wu continued the early T'ang tradition of imperial interest in large anthologies and encyclopaedias. They also showed the same commitment to survey and select from the entire field of *belles lettres*, and to provide books for use in composition. Their reigns saw a succession of literary anthologies. The *Wen kuan tz'u lin* (*Forest of words from literary halls*), in 1,000 *chüan* was submitted in 658 by Hsü Ching-tsung.[42] It was followed by numbers of other works, some perhaps restricted to specific genres: the *Lei pi* (*Heaped discs of jade*), in 30 *chüan*, of 661;[43] the *Ku wen yüan* (*Garden of ancient writings*), of uncertain date;[44] the officially commissioned *Yao shan yü t'sai* (*Bright colours of jade from precious hills*) in 500 *chüan*, completed in 663, in which Hsü Ching-tsung was involved;[45] the *Li-cheng wen yüan* (*Garden of letters of beauty and truth*), in 20 *chüan*, again involving Hsü Ching-tsung;[46] the *Lei lin* (*Forest of writings in categories*), by Yü Li-cheng, a vice-president of the state academy directorate and son of the prominent southern court scholar of T'ai tsung's reign Yü Chih-ning.[47] If some of these collections were made on private initiative, their compilers were members of court literary society, their titles were recorded in official sources, and in most cases they were accepted into the imperial library.

The best documented of these works was the *San chiao chu ying* (*Pearls and blossoms of the three teachings*). Commissioned by the empress Wu, probably at the request of the crown prince and his academic advisers, in 699, it was presented to the throne in 702.[48] Its purpose was to provide a comprehensive anthology to replace the *Wen ssu po yao* and its principal pre-T'ang models. The compilation was started in the literary college founded by the empress Wu in 699, the scantily documented K'ung ho fu, later, in 700, renamed the Feng ch'en fu; but the work may have been completed in the Hung-wen kuan. The directors were the imperial favourite Chang Ch'ang-tsung and the prominent official scholar, supervisor of the dynastic record and president of the state academy directorate Li Ch'iao (644–713). The commission numbered at least twenty-five, a proportion of whom held general service rather than academic office. It included the great scholar minister of Hsüan tsung's reign Chang Yüeh; the long serving official scholar Hsü Chien, a colleague and admirer of Liu Chih-chi; and Liu Chih-chi himself. Like so many T'ang scholarly commissions, however, this group found it difficult to complete their project. Its members 'conversed day and night, gathering in meetings to compose verse; but over several years had not set brush [to paper]'. The conviviality of their proceedings is suggested by the reminiscence of

Chang Yüeh, that they disregarded seniority in arranging where they sat. Verse written by the compilers during these meetings was itself made into an anthology of five *chüan*. This enjoyed such celebrity that it circulated far and wide; parts of it, including three poems by Liu Chih-chi, survived at Tun-huang.[49]

The completed *San chiao chu ying* contained significant innovations. Separate sections for Buddhist and Taoist material were introduced. There were also sections for kinship (*ch'in shu*); genealogy (*hsing ming*) and remote regions (*fang yü*).[50] These topics invite comparison with Liu Chih-chi's suggestions for new monographs for the dynastic history (Ch. 5, p. 182), and indeed derive from the same court scholarly milieu. The *San chiao chu ying* had a high reputation in the eighth century; in 719 Hsüan tsung ordered that it be supplemented.[51] An early post-rebellion writer, however, criticized it because it 'only anthologized [the compositions of] court scholars'. This comment, though laconic, is to be set alongside similar statements that confirm the extent to which in the seventh and early eighth centuries literary life was court-centred. It also provides an indication of how much this situation was to change after the rebellion.[52]

The long reign of Hsüan tsung was a productive period for anthologies like the *San chiao chu ying*. First the Hung-wen kuan and then the Chi-hsien yüan provided the premises in which most of the works concerned were compiled. It seems possible that official scholars started a fourth large anthology, perhaps a further expansion of the *Wen ssu po yao* or *San chiao chu ying*. But if this was the case, it was probably never finished, despite an edict urging completion. A collection of only 20 *chüan* restricted to verse and rhymeprose was all that was achieved.[53] But there were other large anthologies or encyclopaedias, including a work attributed to Chang Yüeh, the *Hsüan tsung shih lei* (*Material by categories [composed for] Hsüan tsung*) in 130 *chüan*.[54]

The Chi-hsien scholars also completed a much shorter literary encyclopaedia, designed as a basic reference source for the training in *belles lettres* of the imperial princes. This was the *Ch'u hsüeh chi* (*Record for early learning*) of 726. In some respects this was little more than an abridgment and rearrangement of the early T'ang *I wen lei chü*. The compilers, under the direction of Hsü Chien, also assumed that literary composition required command of a comprehensive and concise description of the world, drawn from existing *belles lettres* sources, and they organized their compilation under headings similar to those of the *I wen lei chü*. They included material that post-dated it, often on the theme of T'ang dynastic greatness. If a composition by

T'ai tsung was included under any heading, it was placed at the opening of the relevant part of its entry.[55]

In the late K'ai-yüan and T'ien-pao periods, however, very few official encyclopaedias or anthologies appear in the record.[56] Their absence may be due partly to the fact that much of the documentation for the reign of Hsüan tsung was lost in the An Lu-shan rebellion. But the emperor's growing commitment to Taoism certainly diverted the academic agencies from the sort of activity that they might otherwise have undertaken. The control of the scholarly institutions by the anti-literary Li Lin-fu may also have restricted activities. Interest in composition skills in court circles, in the official community and in literate society did not for a moment diminish. These developments, rather, helped to promote among certain mid eighth-century writers the sense of alienation from high authority that became one of the important trends of the period.

Catalogues of the imperial collection

The compilation of large anthologies like the *San chiao chu ying* and its smaller late seventh-century forerunners was recognized as possible only on the basis of a comprehensive collection of literature. This and more general reasons motivated a number of initiatives to build up the imperial collections in this period. Already in the Yung-hui period, five decades before the *San chiao chu ying*, a catalogue of all books extant in the preceding Chen-kuan era had been completed.[57] In 666, a commission had been appointed to edit, correct and recopy the dynasty's collection.[58] In 676–7, the collection at the Hung-wen kuan had been re-organized.[59] Another initiative came in the final years of the seventh century, for the compiling of the *San chiao chu ying* coincided with the appointment of its directors as commissioners to reorganize and build up the imperial collection.[60]

In the years 705–6, although the library was said at this time to have suffered from inappropriate appointments at senior level, another catalogue was produced, probably for books written in the years from 650 to the accession of Chung tsung in 705.[61] Then again in 709, 'because there were many gaps in the book [collection], metropolitan officials with learning were ordered to divide up the empire and go through it collecting picture-diagrams (*t'u*) and books'.[62] The library had a reputation for comprehensiveness at about this period: one young scholar, Li Yung, a son of the *Wen hsüan* commentator Li Shan (d. 689), was secured admission there, to enable him to see its 'tens of thousands of scrolls'.[63] A writer was not automatically accorded the honour of having his works accepted into the library; but numbers of compilations, officially and unofficially initiated, are recorded as entering the library in this period.[64] The imperial library was not, however, the only collection of great size in the early decades of the eighth century. Two private collections, both belonging to official scholars from aristocratic families famous for their scholarship, were said to rival it. The fact that the owner of one of these, the historian Wei Shu, increased his family's holdings of books from 2,000 to 20,000 *chüan* suggests that there was a flourishing trade in books in the Ch'ang-an of this period. Other large libraries are also mentioned.[65]

During the reign of Hsüan tsung, even more attention was given the imperial book collections. Official commissions and individuals also continued to present works to high authority. Hsü Chien, for example, had no fewer than seven of the compilations in which he was a collaborator accepted.[66] From early in the K'ai-yüan period, a programme for reselecting, augmenting and cataloguing the collection, which was said to have been neglected in the previous reigns, was started. To manage this programme, the emperor commissioned two scholars who had served on his staff when he was crown prince. One, Ma Huai-su (*c.* 659–*c.* 718, canonized *Wen*), a southerner and former disciple of the *Wen hsüan* scholar Li Shan, was concurrently director of the library, while the second, Ch'u Wu-liang (646–720, canonized *Wen*) was a grand counsellor and reader to the crown prince.[67] Commissioners for editing and repair of books (*pien-hsiu shih*) were also appointed.[68] At this time, the imperial collection was still at Lo-yang, the capital under the empress Wu. At least during its preliminary reorganization, it was housed in the eastern corridor of the Ch'ien-yüan tien, the former Ming-t'ang (Ch. 4, pp. 124–28). A commission of twenty or so scholars, including junior general service officials from counties near Lo-yang, was involved. Rare editions were 'borrowed from among the people' for copying. When in 717 Hsüan tsung visited Lo-yang, all officials were permitted to view the collection 'without restriction' (*tsung*).[69] The following year, an order was given that it be moved to Ch'ang-an. But copying by scholars from the academic institutions continued at both Ch'ang-an and Lo-yang. The court of the imperial treasury (*t'ai fu ssu*) presented high quality paper from I-chou in Szechuan on a monthly basis, ink from Shang-ku chün in modern Hopei every quarter and 1,500 rabbit skins for brushes annually from the commanderies of Ho-chien, Ching-ch'eng, Ch'ing-ho and Po-p'ing, again in modern Hopei.[70]

In 719 or 720, the prominent official scholar Yüan Hsing-ch'ung, himself the owner of a very large library, succeeded Ch'u Wu-liang as director of the project. He drafted in new scholars, including Wei Shu, who was related to him by marriage and was then the junior officer of Li-yang, to the east of Ch'ang-an. In 721, Yüan submitted a catalogue for the collection of 200 *chüan*.[71] This catalogue, the *Ch'ün-shu ssu pu lu (Record of all books in four divisions)* was a normative compilation that excluded works deemed unsuitable. It probably incorporated both the Yung-hui and Shen-lung catalogues, supplementing them and providing annotation for them. As a result of successive searches for books, the number of works it listed, 2,655 in 48,169 *chüan*, was increased by over six thousand *chüan* when compared to the catalogue of 705–6.[72] The new catalogue conformed to the classification scheme that early T'ang scholars had used in the *Sui shu* bibliography monograph.[73] Like the latter work, it also contained brief historical and critical prefaces for each division and sub-division, and these were very similar to those composed by Wei Cheng nearly ninety years before. According to an entry in the *T'ang hui yao*, they were by the young scholar Wei Shu.[74]

A condensed and revised version of this catalogue, in 40 *chüan*, the *Ku-chin shu lu (Record of books ancient and modern)*, compiled shortly after Yüan Hsing-ch'ung's catalogue, listed 3,060 books and a correspondingly larger number of scrolls, 51,852.[75] The Chi-hsien yüan now housed the fine imperial copies of all officially approved books. Other official libraries, the imperial library itself and those at the Hung-wen kuan, the history office, the Ssu-ching chü and the Ch'ung-wen kuan had what may have been in some cases the originals of the imperial copies.[76]

Following the death of Yüan Hsing-ch'ung in 729, both the imperial library and the Chi-hsien yüan came under the direction of Ch'en Hsi-lieh, a Taoist imperial favourite, appointed in 731.[77] The same year, a total number of scrolls in the Chi-hsien library was 89,000.[78] But the authorities continued to conduct general searches for books as well as to look for and accept the specifically Taoist items that the emperor demanded.[79] The standing of the library in the bureaucracy remained high in this period; junior posts there were customarily given to intellectually able examination graduates, and commanded great respect. Nine of the twenty-seven scholars who graduated as *chin shih* under the rescript writer and Chi-hsien scholar Sun Ti in 734 were appointed to collatorships there.[80] Even late in his reign, Hsüan tsung was keenly interested in the library, 'regarding the offices of director and deputy-director like those of assistant or secretary in the department of affairs of state'.[81]

Searches for books continued into the T'ien-pao period. In 742, the prospective official historian Hsiao Ying-shih, who had graduated as *chin shih* under Sun Ti in 735 and then been a corrector in the library, was ordered to 'take in lost books in Chao and Wei; but he did not report for a long while, and was impeached by the authorities'.[82] In 745, the contents of the Chi-hsien library were again quantified.[83] In 752, there was an order that the Chi-hsien and imperial libraries should supplement each other's holdings.[84] Early in 754, the Taoist Ch'en Hsi-lieh, by then no longer in favour with the emperor, was appointed commissioner for picture-diagrams and books.[85] In the Chi-hsien yüan, there was a continuous copying operation until 755, resulting in a substantial increase in holdings over those of 721.[86] On the eve of the rebellion, the holdings in the Chi-hsien and imperial libraries were likely to have been the fullest that China had seen.

Wen hsüan *studies*

The imperial libraries thus appear to have functioned effectively in this period as the prestigious destination for many literary works, and as the central resource for the compilation of large official anthologies and catalogues. The emperor, the court and the academic institutions also provided the centre in which fashions in *belles lettres* continuously developed. The tendency in the seventh and early eighth centuries for literary activity to be drawn into the court and central academic agencies is exemplified by the history in the early T'ang of what were called at the time *Wen hsüan* studies. In this period, the prestige of the anthology compiled by the scholarly Liang crown prince Hsiao T'ung (501–31) in sixty *chüan* to include most genres of *belles lettres* reached its peak. Successive T'ang emperors enthusiastically promoted the *Wen hsüan*, and this led a number of provincial and metropolitan scholars to present their *Wen hsüan* commentaries to the throne. By the early eighth century, *Wen hsüan* scholarship, which at the start of the dynasty had been based in the south-east, the homeland of the southern dynasties, was a part of the court literary culture at Ch'ang-an.[87]

The first recorded commentary to the *Wen hsüan*, appropriately, was by a descendant of the Liang royal house, Hsiao Kai, also a *Han shu* scholar and a Sui academic official.[88] There are both direct and indirect indications that by early T'ang times, the *Wen hsüan* was studied and esteemed. The editors of the officially commissioned literary encyclopaedia of Kao tsu's reign, the *I wen lei chü*, included a high proportion of the anthology in their compilation.[89] The *Liang shu* incorporated a long and highly eulogistic biography of Hsiao T'ung.[90] Several other scholars were mentioned as specializing in the anthology; one was Ts'ao Hsien (*c.* 527–630), another southerner and former Sui academic official. Though, on account of his age, Ts'ao Hsien did not accept T'ang office, T'ai tsung himself was said greatly to have esteemed him. He had several hundred disciples, to whom he taught the anthology, so that 'at this the study of it greatly flourished'.[91]

One of these disciples was Li Shan, also a southerner and a *Han shu* scholar. Li presented his own commentary to the *Wen hsüan* in 658, and it was accepted into the imperial library. It drew from a total of some 1,700 sources, including both the Confucian canons and Buddhist works. It did not however satisfy his son, Li Yung, who produced his own work. After a period of banishment, Li Shan taught the *Wen hsüan* unofficially in the area of modern Honan, and 'from all directions students came over great distances'.[92] Records of such unofficial teaching away from the capitals, relatively common for canonical scholarship in the pre-T'ang period, are rare for Confucian-orientated subjects for the century following the foundation of the T'ang. But the *Wen hsüan* was never, like the Confucian canons, an 'established' text, no statutory provision existed for teaching it officially, and, essential though mastery of it was for composition skills, its status was guaranteed by the great prestige of the *belles lettres* it incorporated rather than by official provision.[93]

Imperial interest in the *Wen hsüan* continued in the late seventh and early eighth centuries. The emperor Kao tsung esteemed it so much that he had P'ei Hsing-chien (619–82, canonized *Hsien*), a scholarly general service official whose cursive calligraphic style (*ts'ao-shu*) was admired, copy the text on silk.[94] The emperor rewarded P'ei with an honorarium of 500 bolts of silk. Under Hsüan tsung, its influence may be seen in the choice of topics for composition in the *tsa wen* section of the *chin shih* examination, now gaining prestige.[95] The emperor himself took a lead in promoting the study of the *Wen hsüan*. In 718, he enthusiastically accepted the collected commentaries of five scholars. The best known of this group, Lü Hsiang, perhaps as a result of these commentaries, became a Han-lin attendant in 722, then a successful court diarist and finally a grand secretary, all tenures involving composition skills.[96]

These collected commentaries, which are extant, did not mark the end of interest in the *Wen hsüan*. In 731, Hsiao Sung, director of the Chi-hsien yüan and another Liang descendant, who had been 'over-joyed at its continued reputation', requested to produce both a sequel anthology and another commentary, to be compiled by a commission of scholars under his direction.[97] The commentary, however, appears not to have been completed. But the prolific official historian and canonical commentator Lu Shan-ching, himself a member of Hsiao Sung's commission and a Chi-hsien scholar, compiled his own commentary, fragments of which have survived in Japan.[98] By T'ien-pao times, there were over ten anthologies that claimed to be sequels to the *Wen hsüan*.[99] The compiler of one at least of these compilations was rewarded with a junior officership. The prestige of the anthology within China had the result that it was highly esteemed among the Tibetans and in Japan and Korea.[100]

In the changed climate of the post-rebellion period, however, the *Wen hsüan* was to lose some of this great prestige. Though it remained important in education and for composition skills, the anthology came to be identified with a superficial approach to learning.[101] As was often the case with the changed attitudes of the post-rebellion period, there was an indication of this shift before 755. Significantly, this came in connection with the place of *belles lettres* in the examination system. Liu Chih, the son of Liu Chih-chi and compiler of the *Cheng tien*, in his review of examination curricula (Ch. 3, p. 89), sardonically condemned the emphasis put, from the late southern dynasties, on the *Ch'u tz'u* and the *Wen hsüan*, and the use of encyclopaedias and composition skills. They provided, he implied, no test for administrative competence in high office.[102]

Court literary entertainments

The high standing of the *Wen hsüan* and the rewards given to its commentators are to be related to a court milieu in which interest in *belles lettres*, far from being restrained as the early T'ang scholar ministers wished, became more and more a fashionable element in increasingly lavish entertainments. In the most prestigious society in the civilized world, successive sovereigns and members of the imperial family favoured official scholars and holders of literary offices for participation in court gatherings, feasts and excursions. Anecdotes from the late seventh and early eighth centuries show how quick or felicitous composition on these occasions brought these scholars both recognition and material reward. Sung Chih-wen (d. *c.* 713), a *chin shih* of 675, was recognized as an innovator in the tonal rules for the five-word line in verse. At an excursion at Lung-men outside Lo-yang, the empress Wu conferred on him a brocade robe for a poem that, though not the first to be completed, was judged the best turned by any of those present.[103] Another verse writer, Shen Ch'üan-ch'i (d. *c.* 713), also a *chin shih* of 675, and an innovator in the tonal pattern for the seven-word line, was rewarded for composing felicitously at a court dance display.[104] In the period when women dominated the court, the consort Shang-kuan Chao-jung also promoted literary feasts and competitions.[105]

In this period, a court occasion might result in a hundred or so poems, which were then collected into an anthology. In 691, when the court sent off commissioners to the ten provinces, the resulting collection was ten *chüan* in length.[106] In 711, a hundred poems were written for the Taoist prelate Ssu-ma Ch'eng-chen on his departure for mount T'ien-t'ai in modern Chekiang.[107] Feasts and competitions were very frequent; in 709, thirteen are recorded, and in the first four months of 710, seventeen. They particularly involved the twenty-four scholars of the Hsiu-wen kuan, as the expanded Hung-wen kuan had been renamed. The fact that one of its scholars compiled an account of their activities is an indication of the prestige of participation. Many of the outstanding official scholars of the period, like Li Ch'iao, Ts'ui Jung (653–706, canonized *Wen*), Liu Chih-chi and Hsü Chien, as well as renowned verse writers like Shen Ch'üan-ch'i, Sung Chih-wen and Hsü Yen-po (d. 714) were members.[108] Chang Yüeh later recorded of this period, '[Holders of] high office considered detailed erudition to be a priority; great ministers held lack of literary [ability a cause for] shame'.[109]

Court verse competitions were later particularly identified with what was characterized as the lax court milieu of Chung tsung. Hsüan tsung's reign started with measures aimed at austerity and the reassertion of classical priorities, but little suggests that the climate changed.[110] Later in the reign, verse competitions and feasts were held every ten days, and numbers of scholar ministers and officials took part. The official scholar Ts'ui Mien, for example, on at least two occasions received rewards for verse compositions at feasts held in the court in the course of the K'ai-yüan period.[111] The famous loyalist scholar Yen Chen-ch'ing recalled how in the T'ien-pao period his older brother Yün-nan's (694–762) verse style was especially appreciated. 'Whenever there were compositions on set topics (*ying chih*) and court verses to set rhymes (*ch'ang ho*), he would always provide fine and startling couplets (*tui*), and every one commended them and took pleasure in them.' In 750, Yen Chen-ch'ing was a serving censor within the palace, and 'at court audiences and feasts we would always be in the same row'.[112] When in 753 Yen, having incurred the displeasure of Yang Kuo-chung, was posted to P'ing-yüan in modern Hopei, the emperor 'feasted him and others and composed poems and presented him with silk, to demonstrate esteem for his conduct'.[113] Just as Chung tsung had done, Hsüan tsung often repaired to the warm spring palace complex at Li-shan to the east of the capital. Here, informal sources suggest, the court enjoyed a very full life of entertainment, probably until the eve of the An Lu-shan rebellion, and verse competitions certainly played a part in this.[114]

Rescript writers and the advisory colleges

The central place of composition skills in the highly competitive milieu of the court both reflected and reinforced their importance in the official community at large. In the administration, the high prestige of literary ability was indicated by its association with politically powerful offices, especially those involving proximity to the sovereign. The main administrative role concerned continued to be that of rescript writing. In the century following T'ai tsung's death, the increase in importance of rescript writing, precisely because it was politically fraught, was not, in institutional terms, a smooth process. Successive sovereigns divided their delegation of it between the grand secretaries and scholars whom they selected and appointed to advisory colleges, and with whom they enjoyed a more confidential relation-ship. Throughout the period, there was a correlation between appointment to draft rescripts and participation in court verse competitions.

Kao tsung and the empress Wu, by-passing the regular offices, gave the task of composing edicts to 'scholars of the northern gate' (*pei men hsüeh shih*). The informality of the title by which this group was known indicates that they were outside the regular bureaucracy; but they came to wield considerable influence in decision-making.[115] Because of the instability of court political life, the positions of such scholars were far from secure.[116] Some underwent banishment when their patrons fell from power. Yüan Wan-ch'ing (d. *c.* 689) was initially commi-sioned as a 'literary scholar' (*wen shih*) with others to work on a number of the empress Wu's compilations. As a 'scholar of the northern gate', he so gained the confidence of the empress that 'it was ordered that he should sort through and decide on all inconclusive court deliberations and memorials from the officials, thus sharing power with the chief ministers'. Later, he formally held the post of grand secretary, only, in 689, to be traduced and to die in banishment in Ling-nan.[117]

The court verse writer Sung Chih-wen appears to have asked to be a 'scholar of the northern gate', but to have been rejected on the grounds of his lack of discretion. Under Jui tsung, his reputation again prevented him from becoming a grand secretary.[118] Shen Ch'üan-ch'i, conventionally associated with him from the mid eighth century on, however, succeeded where he failed.[119] The historian critic Liu Chih-chi was briefly a grand scretary in 704;[120] his colleague in the history office, Chang Yüeh, held the same post just before him.[121] Other major official scholars and court verse writers, who directed rescripts under the empress Wu were Li Ch'iao and Ts'ui Jung.[122] The consort Shang-kuan Chao-jung was also reponsible for edicts.[123]

During the K'ai-yüan period, the political power of grand secretaries was reduced, and the office became more concerned with composition skills. The prestige of composing imperial documents was, however, undiminished, and the careers of some of the official scholars who wrote rescripts are particularly well documented. The emperor himself keenly appreciated the quality of rescripts. Early in his reign, he ordered a scholar minister, Su T'ing, to present a collection of his own rescripts for his perusal.[124] The literary biography section of the *Chiu T'ang shu* lists some eleven scholars who were acclaimed in his reign as rescript writers, whether as grand secretaries or holding some other basic office. Four of these later rose so high that their general reputations as scholar ministers eclipsed their fame as rescript writers; but in each case the role literary skill played in their careers was later recognized. In each case, their canonizations included or consisted of the most coveted designation of all, that of *wen*.[125] Of this list of eleven, ten were recorded as *chin shih* or decree examination graduates, and thus registered the increasing role of the examination system as a selector of scholars with composition skills.[126]

Over this period, several officials held in succession both the post of grand secretary and that of vice-president of the board of civil office, which at this time controlled the recruitment and the promotion examinations. In this way the influence of literary men in selection was significantly increased. The careers of two grand secretaries, Wang Ch'iu (d. 743, canonized *Wen*) and Hsi Yü (680–748, canonized *Wen*) followed this pattern.[127] The *chin shih* and decree examination graduate Sun Ti, also canonized *Wen*, a pupil of Chang Yüeh, was appointed a rescript writer in 736 and again in 741, serving for a total of eight years. He was a chief examiner in 734 and 735, and admitted to the *chin shih* degree some of the important scholars of the middle decades of the eighth century. Yen Chen-ch'ing, one of his most famous graduates, recorded that his service as a rescript writer was recognized by an edict of commendation.[128] Sun Ti paid three of his successful candidates of 735, Hsiao Ying-shih, Li Hua and Chao Hua (d. 783) a high compliment when he described them as 'capable of directing the composition of edicts'.[129] Wei Chih, a rescript writer alongside Sun Ti and later a vice-president of the board of rites, was an assiduous chief examiner in 742. In making his selection, he gave prominence to the verse the candidates had composed before their examination.[130]

After 736, an institutional change was effected that was to make all but permanent this connection between grand secretaries, with their association with composition skills, and the politically rewarding role of chief examiner. In that year, the board of rites replaced the bureau of merit assessments in the board of civil office as the institution responsible for administering the regular annual examinations. One of the grand secretaries, after relinquishing his post, now conventionally became a vice-president of the board of rites. In this way, the criterion of composition skills for which the grand secretaries themselves stood became more firmly built into the selection process.[131]

Under Hsüan tsung, the tendency was again to give writing of imperial documents semi-formally to attendant officials of proven literary skill. These officials were the successors to the 'scholars of the northern gate', and, like them, enjoyed a confidential relationship with the emperor. Over the reign, their position became to some extent formalized by their appointment to two of the most successful of the dynasty's advisory colleges. These were the Chi-hsien yüan, the functions of which initially included responsibility for drafting documents, and the Han-lin yüan, which took this function over from the former body (Ch. 1, pp. 15–16). The Han-lin yüan, formally founded only in 738, was in pre-rebellion times more than simply an institution for drafting imperial documents. It exemplifies the tendency for an advisory college to reflect its founding emperor's own enthusiasms, for it also provided Hsüan tsung with a range of entertainment. But it was its involvement with drafting documents, and the political role inseparable from this activity, that led to the Han-lin's ascendancy to great political influence in the post-rebellion period.[132]

Belles lettres *and the examination system*

The great value the court and civil bureaucracy put on composition skills, and the increasing tendency for rescript writers to become chief examiners, inevitably affected the place of *belles lettres* in the most significant route of entry into the official hierarchy, the examinations. Over this century, *belles lettres* came increasingly to play a determining role in the most prestigious examination of all, the *chin shih*. Despite the qualities of learning and quick wittedness it required, however, some scholars protested that dexterity in composition did not correlate well with administrative competence. By the end of Hsüan tsung's reign, composition skills had become essential to the *chin shih*; but a tradition of polemic against their place in it had also developed.

A post-rebellion critic of the examination system dated the start of what he held to be the subversion of the examinations by *belles lettres* to the point when, in 680–1, the requirement for composition (*tsa wen*) was introduced into the *chin shih* as one of its three sections.[133] At this early stage, the genres required were relatively practical ones: admonitions, inscriptions, essays and memorials. But from this time on, the increasing monopoly of the *tsa wen* section of the *chin shih* by *shih* and *fu*, the most literary and least practical of all genres, was an inevitable consequence of their high standing in court society and in the metropolitan literary world.

The prevailing literary fashion, particularly of the court, directly influenced the style of candidates' compositions. Hsü Yen-po, a decree examination graduate, academic official and leading court verse writer, in his search for novelty of diction, preferred to use obscure terms for current ones, 'even when referring to institutions like the imperial library'. *Chin shih* candidates, ambitious to follow the fashion he set, were said to have imitated him.[134] Two other celebrated composers of court verse, Shen Ch'üan-ch'i and Sung Chih-wen, both themselves *chin shih* of 675, were appointed chief examiners, Shen in 702 and Sung in 708. Like Hsü Yen-po, Sung Chih-wen was known for his abstruse diction; but both are likely to have elicited from their candidates precisely the technical dexterity that they so glamorously exemplified at court.[135] The fashion for technical virtuosity was also felt in decree examinations, the category of recruitment test that proved, over the dynasty, particularly responsive to changes in the literary and intellectual climate. From 676, special decree examinations were called for those whose 'diction fulfilled literary rules', or even for speed in composition. They are frequently recorded until Chung tsung's reign, but less often thereafter. They were not in practice restricted to the literary genres, like *shih* and *fu*; but their titles point to the prevailing fashion.[136]

In the first years of his reign, Hsüan tsung required austerity in the style of examination answers as in the life of the court.[137] Nonetheless, it was precisely in the K'ai-yüan and T'ien-pao periods that the *tsa wen* section of the *chin shih* came to be wholly monopolized by *fu* and *shih*.

From 754, moreover, these genres also figured in decree examinations, while the *po hsüeh hung tz'u* examination, established in 731, also included them.[138] This period also saw the firm establishment of the custom whereby candidates, in the harsh competition for examination success, promoted their own compositions informally to examiners or to senior officials in the bureaucracy at the capital.[139]

In the late seventh and early eighth centuries, individual scholars protested against this inexorable trend away from the austere norms that Confucian-orientated scholar ministers had formulated under T'ai tsung. High authority also tried corrective measures from time to time. In 674, a sardonic submission by a memorialist whose post is not recorded reasserted the traditional priority of morality (*te hsing*) over literary ability (*wen hsüeh*), of the first over the fourth of Confucius's four categories of instruction, in selection examinations.[140] In 685, a similar memorial condemned the use of 'judgements' as 'not giving priority to virtuous conduct and not putting speech and conversation last'.[141] In 692, Hsüeh Teng, an omissioner of the right and friend of Liu Chih-chi, submitted the role of *belles lettres* in recruitment examinations to sardonic criticism.[142] Under Hsüan tsung, criticism continued. In a memorial of 715, Chang Chiu-ling, then an omissioner, condemned the use of poems and 'judgements' in examinations.[143] In about 735, Liu Chih-chi's son the institutional historian Liu Chih submitted a review of the principles behind recruitment to office from Han times that echoed Hsüeh Teng's memorial of 692, and asked that the system of recruitment be devolved to the provinces. Literature did indeed have a function, he conceded, but it was to provide a means of communication between the ruler above and the people below. To use literary skill as the criterion for selection for the entire civil service was 'to entrust administration to Tzu-yu and Tzu-hsia [the disciples whom Confucius had commended for skill in literature], while charging [Jan]-yu and [Chi]-lu [the disciples whom he praised for administrative ability] with literature. How absurd!'[144]

Liu Chih's criticisms are unlikely to have been the only ones in this period. From a few years later, there is also a record of a discussion, held at P'ing-yang commandery, on the difficulty, in recruitment to office, of combining the demand for the Confucian categories of good conduct and composition skills.[145] In a long letter to the official historian Wei Shu written in about 740, Hsiao Ying-shih, citing his own experience of the examinations, also characterized the inadequacy of composition tests.[146] In 753, a former *chin shih* complained bitterly to Sung Yü who directed the selection examinations, about the superficiality of the tests that they involved. He sardonically pointed out that the duke of Chou and Confucius, 'if the elaborateness of their diction were examined, would not have been up to Hsü [Ling] and Yü [Hsin] (writers in the palace style)'.[147]

Indictments of the role of dexterous composition by scholars like Liu Chih and Hsiao Ying-shih and their seventh century predecessors meant that in the post-rebellion period reformers, confronted by a much deteriorated political situation, were to have a long tradition of polemic to draw on. But in the second half of Hsüan tsung's reign, despite these protests, the literary art continued to increase its importance in examinations. The interest in literature as a means to an official career was so much a feature of the society of this time that numbers of scholars later recalled it. For, 'at that time, the world was at peace, and not to find preferment through literary skill would be a cause of shame for students', or, 'from K'ai-yüan times, the world was at peace, and scholars, whether worthy or not, were ashamed not to succeed through literature'. 'In the T'ien-pao period, those who throughout the world sought for preferment directed their purpose to letters.'[148]

Independent literature in the K'ai-yüan and T'ien-pao periods

The celebration of composition skills in a secure and prosperous court, however, took place against a background of literary practice that, in the first half of the eighth century, began to change profoundly. At the root of the change was the effect of the long period of internal peace and the increased numbers of the literate.[149] For, despite the magnetism of the court, verse practice continued to be, as Confucian theory had always implicitly recognized it was, an independent phenomenon beyond the control of high authority. The amount of verse writing, far from contracting as a few austere minded Confucian critics might have wished, on the contrary greatly increased.

It was, however, the attitudes expressed in this verse that were of particular significance. They show that the monopoly that the court and advisory colleges had enjoyed as the centre of the literary world was now much less complete. The scholars with empire-wide literary reputations at the close of the seventh century and the early years of the eighth, like the examination graduates Shen Ch'üan-ch'i, Sung Chih-wen, Hsü Yen-po or Li Ch'iao, had all been court figures and practitioners of the sort of technical innovation that an exclusive milieu appreciated.[150] Many of the verse writers whose works survive from the second half of Hsüan tsung's reign, however, never participated in the court literary entertainments that had been essential to the success of these men. Rather, they conveyed a sense of remoteness from, or even hostility to, the court and those they termed the 'close ministers' (*chin ch'en*).[151] The themes they introduced were seldom wholly new; composition remained largely a learned activity, and precedents for most of the topics on which they wrote may be found in pre-T'ang writing, often in the famous *Wen hsüan* itself. But their writing was often much freer, less mannered and much closer to their own experience than the compositions of the court.

A number of features in this verse were historically important. One is the alienated, often provincial perspective from which at least some of it was written. Some scholars saw the government at Ch'ang-an as closed off, highly privileged and competititve, and they complained about the frustration of decades of study, and the over-abundance of able men that made appointment to office so difficult.[152] Tu Fu's command of the whole literary tradition, the fact that he had 'worn out ten thousand scrolls in reading', and his self-analytical temperament made his the verse that most fully conveys the disillusioned atmosphere of this pre-rebellion world. As he expressed it in late 755, using the familiar timber metaphor, 'No new wood is needed for the edifice of government'.[153] Other writers described the merits of a calm and bucolic life, removed, even if by a short distance only, from the dust and contamination of the capital. They promoted, sometimes clearly by way of compensation for their own lack of success in the official career, the one alternative goal to official service acceptable to scholars, that of seclusion and contemplation.[154]

The verse of this period was not, however, always a vehicle for direct or indirect complaint or for expressions of commitment to quietism. The experience of travelling through a relatively peaceful continent resulted in verse of great exuberance. Li Po, briefly appointed to the Han-lin yüan in 744, is considered to exemplify this energetic temper. His disdain for restraint and convention led him openly to deride Confucian scholars and their attitudes. Some of his longer poems, for example his 'Exile's letter', describing journeys of hundreds of miles and friendships that spanned several decades, were among the best literary monuments to the peace of Hsüan tsung's reign.[155] The verse style that Ts'en Shen (d. 770) created in connection with his prolonged official service in Central Asia, conveying excitement at the exotic people, desert landscape and harsh extremes of climate of the far west, is also unique to this period.[156]

Outgoing attitudes and experience of society beyond the court combined in another and more pointed theme that began to be important in the T'ien-pao period. Alienated writers focussed on the contrast between the extravagance of the court and of the wealthy, and the hardships endured by the people beyond. To emphasize this contrast was fully consonant with the traditional Confucian belief that literature should communicate 'the feelings of those below'. In the writing of Tu Fu and of Yüan Chieh (719–72), a *chin shih* of 754 who had 'hoped for a leisurely office to do with letters', this theme was particularly conspicuous.[157] Their poems were intended for sympathetic middle- or high-ranking officials at the capital. Men like Cheng Ch'ien,[158] appointed unwillingly to the newly founded Kuang-wen kuan in 750, or Su Yüan-ming, a vice-president of the state academy directorate on the eve of the rebellion and a long term associate of both Tu Fu and Yüan Chieh,[159] had not surrendered ambition and were committed to the service of the dynasty. But they had suffered in career terms at the hands of ministers like Li Lin-fu and Yang Kuo-chung who dominated the court, and were likely to have been receptive to new perspectives on the world beyond the capital. It was to be among scholars in similar positions that, in the changed conditions of the post-rebellion period, more analytical attitudes to the theory and function of literature would develop.

The post-rebellion period

The An Lu-shan rebellion extinguished the prosperity and confidence that had been essential to the brilliance of Hsüan tsung's court. Thereafter, the T'ang court still engaged in traditional literary pursuits, and individual emperors showed keen discrimination in their appreciation of verse.[160] But, just as its wealth and political power was small in comparison with the prosperity of the pre-rebellion period, so the court's domination of literary practice was greatly reduced. This did not mean, however, that, beyond the court, *belles lettres* were any less important to the civil bureaucracy or the scholar community. In this period, examination graduates, who had themselves been selected on the basis of their skills in composition, exerted almost complete control over the recruitment system. Former *chin shih* graduates expanded their influence in the elite posts within the central bureaucracy, and consolidated their monopoly of offices associated with composition skills. The political power of former examination graduates was such that in the examination system itself, despite persistent reform attempts, the dexterity in composition for which they stood retained its place.

The major change in outlook that took place in the late eighth and early ninth centuries is to be related not to literature produced in a court of official context, but to the great volume of unofficial writing in which academic officials as well as others engaged and which has survived to the present. The trend towards a wider literary world, already apparent in the K'ai-yüan and T'ien-pao periods, was now greatly expanded. Prose compositions of great originality and sophistication circulated privately, to be commented on and appreciated by colleagues and friends. Unofficial correspondence contained discussions not only of current political concerns and historical topics, but also of all aspects of literature. Verse achieved a greater psychological range: whimsicality, cynicism over political ambition, private symbolism and self analysis are all distinguishing features of ninth-century writers. The tenor of much of this literature, when compared with that of the K'ai-yüan era, was more reflective and less outgoing. With justice it has been said that 'from about 800 poetry began to move indoors'.[161]

In this more decentralized literary milieu, there was great emphasis on individuality of style. Confucian literary theory, moreover, despite its ideal of literature as a state-centred activity, proved remarkably congruent with the new attitudes. It could not, any more than in the pre-rebellion period, extend its approval to all that was written. But individual scholars used traditional Confucian ideas to comment on and often to justify their own, more adventurous, attitudes and values. In doing so, writers like Han Yü, Po Chü-i and others indicated how far their outlook had evolved away from that of their predecessors in the early T'ang.

Decline in the role of the imperial libraries

Throughout the post-rebellion period, however, official literary institutions continued, at least in principle, to be the centre of the literary world. The imperial library still held the definitive collection of the dynasty's written works. It still also intermittently discharged its traditional function of searching for, copying and cataloguing books. But the evidence for how it operated is much reduced, and its relationship with the other official libraries, those in the Chi-hsien yüan, the Hung-wen kuan, Ch'ung-wen kuan, Ssu ching chü and history office, is not clear. On the other hand, more large private collections were recorded than before. One, probably used by Su Mien, the compiler of the *Hui yao*, was even said, like some of the great private libraries before the rebellion, to have compared in size to the imperial and Chi-hsien libraries.[162]

During the An Lu-shan rebellion, the imperial library, in contrast to that of the Chi-hsien yüan, had suffered badly.[163] In late 757, Yü Hsiu-lieh, then vice-president of the court of sacrifices, made efforts to recover lost historical works.[164] In 764, Yüan Tsai, an admirer of Yü Hsiu-lieh, despatched commissioners to the south to search more generally for pictures and diagrams (*t'u*) and books.[165] Similar initiatives were probably taken under Te tsung.[166] Works were still presented to the throne in the second half of the eighth century; but it is only infrequently recorded that they were retained for the imperial or Chi-hsien libraries.[167] An important example is Yen Chen-ch'ing's phonological dictionary in 360 *chüan*, presented in 777. An imperial order required that copies be consigned to both the imperial and Chi-hsien libraries, and Yen Chen-ch'ing was given an honorarium of 500 bolts of silk.[168] There is a slight indication that during Te tsung's reign the crown prince's library may have been reorganized and improved.[169] The new entries in the dynastic collection were catalogued under Te tsung, by the ritual scholar Ch'en Ching. But this was the last catalogue for the dynasty's collection for which a title was recorded.[170]

In the second half of the eighth century a number of well known scholars held the senior posts in the library. Among them were the pre-rebellion patron of Tu Fu and Yüan Chieh, Su Yüan-ming; the former south-eastern financial official, Pao Chi; and the reformer of the school and examination systems, Hsiao Hsin (702–91, canonized *I*). Liu T'ai-chen, a former pupil of the pre-rebellion teacher Hsiao Ying-shih, grand secretary and chief examiner, was an active director early in Te tsung's reign.[171] So was Han Hui, the brother of the south-eastern official Han Huang.[172] In 796, Chang Chien, the official historian, was transferred to the deputy directorship of the library by P'ei Yen-ling, and was then promoted to be its director.[173] The ritual scholar Ch'en Ching was assigned the deputy directorship during his terminal illness.[174] It was probably because of its association with elderly, infirm, formerly high-ranking officials that the library, removed as it was from the main political arena, came to be called the 'sick ward (*ping fang*) for chief ministers'.[175] But appointment to its junior posts held no such connotation of political defeat: it continued to be customary and very common for young and intellectually able examination graduates to be given collatorships there. There are innumerable instances of this, among them three of the 'ten talents of the Ta-li period', the best known verse writers of Tai tsung's reign. Po Chü-i and Yüan Chen both started their careers in this way.[176] The Chi-hsien library offered similar opportunities at junior level, and the young Liu Tsung-yüan held office there from 798 until 802.[177]

The imperial library in the ninth century retained a full establishment. It probably also retained some association with *belles lettres*,
for it was still an institution to which a verse writer might appropriately
be appointed.[178] Its staff were engaged in copying books in 823, when
the library successfully petitioned for a bronze seal to replace that lost
in the An Lu-shan rebellion.[179] In 830, the library buildings were
reported to be in a seriously dilapidated condition.[180] But in 836,
perhaps as part of Wen tsung's campaign to revive official scholarship,
it was again ordered to search for books. The collection, now standing
at 54,476 *chüan*, was said to have been 'restored to completeness'.[181]
For the later reigns, however, though appointments to the library at
both senior and junior levels were made until the end of the dynasty,
there are no further records of catalogues or copying activity.

In the post-rebellion period as a whole, there were no imperially
commissioned sequels to the very large official anthologies or literary
encyclopaedias of the seventh and early eighth centuries. This tradition
was, rather, continued on private initiative. Scholars made numerous
unofficial compilations, spanning a wide range of approaches and
subject matter. By no means all were confined to *belles lettres*; but one
at least was promoted as yet another sequel to the *Wen hsüan*, despite
the decline in standing of the Liang anthology. In extant sources,
however, acceptance of such compilations into the imperial library was
very rarely recorded.[182]

In the disorders of the final decades of the dynasty, the imperial
collection was destroyed, first in the course of the Huang Ch'ao
occupation of the capital, and then again, after further attempts at
recovery, under the last T'ang emperor, Chao tsung. In 909, the Liang
dynasty moved the capital from Ch'ang-an to Lo-yang, and managed
to preserve only a proportion of the holdings that had survived at the
very end of the dynasty. The imperial collection in the early Five
Dynasties period was said to have reached barely 10,000 *chüan*. When
in the late tenth century, the Sung dynasty started to re-form a
dynastic collection, major additions came from Szechuan and the
Yangtze area, remote from the ravaged homeland of the T'ang.[183]

Rescript writing and political power

The imperial library was an 'outer repository' (*wai fu*), associated
with literary men, but removed from the politically vital functions of
the central government.[184] The decline in its condition and
effectiveness contrasts ironically with the continued prestige of those
essential offices in the central bureaucracy that continued to require
literary skills. In the post-rebellion period, when many of the offices in

the ministries came to function only nominally,[185] rescript writing preserved both its political importance and its high reputation. When discharged by members of the Han-lin yüan, it very frequently led on to the highest political offices. It therefore retained its role as one of the main vehicles by which the scholarly and literary elite in the bureaucracy maintained their political influence.

A post-rebellion writer suggested that at the time of the rebellion, 'the works of literary men were broken off in mid course'.[186] But even at the height of the crisis, composition skills proved essential to the dynasty. In 757, Hsüan tsung appointed as grand secretary, Li K'uei (711–89, canonized *Kung*), later an unconventional chief examiner. He also had the services of Chia Chih, whose father had been a rescript writer at the beginning of his reign. When Su tsung became emperor, a celebrated calligrapher, Hsü Hao (703–82, canonized *Ting*), composed rescripts as his grand secretary, and also wrote the edicts in which Hsüan tsung relinquished the throne, an admired double achievement.[187] Other rescript writers under Su Tsung included Su Yüan-ming, the pre-rebellion patron of Tu Fu and Yüan Chieh; Wang Wei (699–759), the celebrated verse writer; and Chia Chih and Yang Wan, both later chief examiners and proponents of the reform of the selection system (Ch. 2, p. 52 and Ch. 3, pp. 95–6).[188] Under Tai tsung, Ch'ang Kun (729–83), an anti-Buddhist and anti-Taoist, was first a court diarist, Han-lin scholar and grand secretary, and later a chief examiner. As chief minister from 777, Ch'ang Kun was said to have cleared the corruption caused by Yüan Tsai's venal control of government, and to have followed 'public opinion' (*kung i*), probably the views current among the officials at the capital, in making his own appointments. During his tenure as chief minister, literary skill apparently became an even more important criterion for office. Ch'ang Kun's renown as a rescript writer under Tai tsung was balanced by that of the turbulent Yang Yen (727–81, canonized *P'ing-li*), later a chief minister, an associate of Tu Yu and the major figure in the financial reforms of the start of Te tsung's reign.[189]

Te tsung's first appointment as chief minister, the scholarly Ts'ui Yu-fu, had been a grand secretary late in Tai tsung's reign, a post that 'the world had long hoped he would hold'. As a member of one of the elite aristocratic families of the T'ang and the son of Ts'ui Mien, the official scholar and court verse writer of the K'ai-yüan period, he had extensive connections with the pre-rebellion scholarly world. On the basis of these connections, he made large numbers of appointments, up to 800, according to later accounts. His death in 780 was viewed as a severe loss for the reformist cause.[190] The most celebrated composer of rescripts in Te tsung's reign was, however, Lu Chih (754–805, canonized *Hsüan*, conventionally known as Lu Hsüan kung). A *chin shih* of 773, appointed a Han-lin scholar in 779, his abilities not only as a deft composer of imperial documents but also as a formulator of policy were such that his career prospered during the crises of the first five years of the reign. Lu Hsüan kung was thus able to enter a period of very close relations with Te tsung, which lasted until, in 795, he lost the bitter struggle with P'ei Yen-ling. His success in arguing and presenting idealistic Confucian policies, and perhaps even his condemnation of 'expediency' (*ch'üan*) in administration, are likely to have influenced the political orientation of the *hsing ming* scholars. His influence on the official and unofficial scholarly community was greatly increased by his role as chief examiner in 792. Many of those whom he selected became prominent in official and private scholarship over the next two decades, while their role in the history office was especially important.[191]

The prestige of rescript writing under Te tsung is also indicated by less well known cases. P'eng Yen (d. 784), like Ch'ang Kun an anti-Buddhist and anti-Taoist, was frustrated in his ambition to manage rescripts. 'Because he sought it so intemperately, he was demoted in contemporary estimation' (*shih i*). He ended by accepting the post in the rebel regime of Chu Tzu, for which he was later executed.[192] Te tsung himself, like Hsüan tsung before him, especially appreciated the quality of the public documents that were issued in his name. He promoted a verse writer Lu Lun (d. after 796, canonized *Kung*) 'out of seniority, and was about to entrust him with the supervision of rescripts; but almost immediately [Lu] died'. Lu Lun illustrates again the connection between fame as a verse writer and appointment to compose rescripts. He had been one of the 'ten talents of the Ta-li period', the most celebrated verse writers of Tai tsung's reign, of whom three others, members of the Han-lin yüan, were involved with rescripts.[193] Te tsung also relied on two brothers, sons of a Taoist priest, with whom he had grown up in the eastern palace, whom he appointed to the Han-lin, and whose official style he greatly admired.[194]

Two more rescript writers under Te tsung were major figures in the scholar community. Both were unusual for the exceptional length of their tenures. Kao Ying wrote rescripts for nine years, and Ch'üan Te-yü, an admirer of Lu Hsüan kung's official compositions, for eight. Both were political enemies of P'ei Yen-ling. Both must have owed their long tenures to their ability to adapt to Te tsung's difficult approach to administration. Ch'üan Te-yü produced a collection of rescripts in fifty *chüan*, but Kao's caution made him burn his copies of the documents he had composed. When asked why he did not, as his predecessors did, retain a collection, he replied that 'royal statements should not be kept in private houses'.[195] Both Ch'üan Te-yü and Kao Ying were sympathetic to *hsing ming* ideas, and their literary skill and the apparent lack in their surviving writings of an active interest in institutional reform correlate well with the profile of many of those connected with the movement. Like Lu Hsüan kung, both went on to be influential chief examiners.[196]

Under Hsien tsung, tenure in the Han-lin, combined with directing rescripts, proved time and again to be rewarding in career terms. From early in his reign, Hsien tsung consulted Han-lin scholars, calling them 'well selected'. He instituted a senior rank within the college, that of scholar-in-attendance (*hsüeh shih ch'eng chih*). There followed numerous instances of men entering the Han-lin, directing rescripts, becoming scholars-in-attendance, and at a later stage being appointed chief ministers. As a mid-ninth-century commentator implied, literary officials had an extraordinary success rate in achieving high court posts.[197] Li Chiang (764–830, canonized *Chen*); Ts'ui Ch'ün (772–832); and Wang Yai (d. 835), all of whom had been admitted to the *chin shih* by Lu Hsüan kung, followed this route.[198]

Composition skills were acknowledged as insufficient in themselves to ensure this level of success.[199] But it is striking that numbers of early ninth-century Han-lin scholars and rescript writers also had far-reaching reputations as prose or verse writers. Po Chü-i and Yüan Chen were especially well known for their verse.[200] Han Yü, though never a Han-lin scholar, was widely acknowledged in the scholar community for his literary ability. He was a rescript writer from 814 and a grand secretary for a period in 816. Other rescript writers also were specifically commended for the quality of their *belles lettres*.[201] The effect of this combination of great political power and recognized literary ability was that the Han-lin posts acquired enormous prestige. This prestige was reflected in the commemorative texts that a succession of scholars composed for the college's premises.

Under Mu tsung, Ching tsung and the emperors who followed, the same career pattern held. In Mu tsung's reign, three Han-lin scholars, Li Te-yü (787–849), Yüan Chen and Li Shen (d. 846), each of whom wrote rescripts, were held to have been particularly able; they all went on to be chief ministers.[202] Another, the official historian Shen

Ch'uan-shih (769–827), a son of Shen Chi-chi, was a Han-lin scholar and grand secretary, but declined to become a scholar-in-attendance in the Han-lin. His reason for this underlines the political power of the senior rank in the college. He believed that his appointment would lead to a chief ministership, a post for which he did not consider himself qualified. Later, one of his sons also held office in the Han-lin.[203] Li Ao was another who had a reputation for composition; he 'prided himself on his literary skill and considered that he should manage rescripts. Because for a long time his wish was not fulfilled, he was depressed and unhappy.' Eventually, under Wen tsung, he was both a director of rescripts and a grand secretary.[204]

In later reigns, rescript writing maintained its prestige, and appointment to direct rescripts was recorded in the careers of many scholars. Some are mentioned for their ability to keep confidence, others for the extent to which the emperor depended on them and others again for the skill that had brought them appointment, the quality of their writing. Appointments to compose rescripts also indicate that, in this as in earlier periods of the dynasty, there was remarkable continuity within families in tenure of scholarly office. Tu Mu (803–52), a grandson of the institutional historian and chief minister Tu Yu; Liu Ching, a grandson of the official historian of the rebellion period Liu Fang; and Sun Chien, whose grandfather Sun Ti and uncle Sun Su had been rescript writers, were all appointed to direct rescripts.[205] In the careers of late ninth century writers, a provincial dimension became more common, as men with literary ability willing to brave the risks 'served with their brushes on the staffs of the feudal lords'.[206] But the T'ang itself appointed rescript writers until very near the dynasty's final demise, and composition skills, and the posts in the bureaucracy reserved for them, remained important as long as T'ang administration lasted.[207]

Criticism of composition skills in the examinations

The high reputation and political success of the major rescript writers, even in a period when the dynasty was in decline, underscores the continued prestige of composition skills in the service of the dynasty. It may seem paradoxical then that throughout this period a strong tradition of criticism of the role of *belles lettres* in official life persisted, and that some of it came from the very scholars whose successful careers included tenures as rescript writers. This apparent paradox is partly to be explained by the context in which this criticism was voiced. As a function of high political power, rescript writing was self-evidently necessary, and it was also dignified by the Confucian tradition. Probably for these reasons, and because so many of the high-ranking members of their own community were engaged in it, scholars usually refrained from direct criticism of the role of rescript writing in political life. Protest over the role of composition skills in official life was therefore either very general, or else focussed on a lower stage in the official hierarchy, on the examination system and the recruitment and selection processes.

In attacking the role of literary skill in the examinations, critics identified one of several obvious and persistent ills. By the reign of Te tsung, their position had already been dignified by over a century of comment by T'ang scholars. The continued demand for dexterity in manipulating vocabulary and composing on sententious topics was obviously irrelevant to the dynasty's problems. The priority given to *shih* and *fu* seemed a particular incongruity. It was seen as a relatively recent development in history, and it could be attacked in terms of the ancient Confucian priority of 'virtuous conduct' over 'literary skill'.[208]

Critics of the place of *belles lettres* in the examinations varied from those who simply demanded a more serious and socially committed tone to those, much fewer, who advocated the abolition of composition tests altogether. Bitter complaints against composition skills in the examinations and the values they encouraged among candidates were voiced early in Tai tsung's reign. Reform proposals for the official education system and examinations submitted in 763 by Chia Chih, Yang Wan and others contained sardonic denunciations of obsession with *belles lettres*. But the radical proposals affecting the *chin shih* degree submitted at this time were resisted by the Han-lin scholars, whom Tai tsung consulted.[209] Later, the *Ch'un-ch'iu* scholar Chao K'uang listed the use of *shih* and *fu* as the salient weakness of the examinations, and proposed to substitute for it a wide-ranging and much more practical syllabus.[210] In 778, the official scholar Shen Chi-chi, reviewing the role of composition skills in selection since the reign of the empress Wu, adopted a similar position.[211] In 781, Chao Tsan, then a grand secretary, proposed dropping *shih* and *fu* from the *chin shih* and reverting to more practical genres. But custom, vested interest and the prevailing climate of esteem for *belles lettres* prevented so radical a solution, and by 785, or soon after, *shih* and *fu* were restored.[212]

A moderate reforming position, however, became conventional in the scholar community in the second half of Te tsung's reign. The proper role for composition skills was discussed in letters, prefaces and memorials, and by candidates as well as senior officials.[213] Influential examiners like Lu Hsüan kung and Ch'üan Te-yü entertained reformist ideas. In the *chin shih* examination of 802, Ch'üan Te-yü set a dissertation question on the appropriate role for composition skills in the examinations. In correspondence with the ritual scholar Liu Mien, he allowed that skill in *shih* and *fu* was not a qualification for high office, and implied that as an examiner he had therefore reduced its importance.[214] Kao Ying, the chief examiner from 799 to 801, was complimented for the canonical emphasis of the topics he set for composition.[215] But, even more than their outlook on the reform of the official education system, the attitude of the majority of the scholar community to this problem shows the limits to their interest in reform. None of these influential examiners seriously considered doing away with a provision that so confirmed their identity and advanced the political cause of 'literary men'.

The views of some of those general service officials of the second half of Te tsung's reign who in their surviving writings reveal a commitment to institutional reform were, however, sometimes more radical. Tu Yu, the compiler of the *T'ung tien*, was their most trenchant advocate. Like Ch'üan Te-yü, his acquaintance over three decades, he had entered the bureaucracy not through the examination system but through the *yin* privilege provided by the rank of his father. But unlike Ch'üan, and most unusually among the scholars of his period, he refrained from even considering that *belles lettres* should have a role in selection. He condemned without reservation the literary component in the examinations. He held, endorsing Confucius's own remark, that the majority of men were of medium talent and had 'natures that could be changed', and that there was no difference between the amount of talent present in utopian antiquity and his own time. What had gone wrong, rather, was the basis of selection, not only the use of 'words' rather than 'deeds', but the emphasis on 'frivolous words'. In terms of the polarity between *wen* and *chih*, he suggested, the dynasty in the Chen-kuan period had lost its opportunity to correct an imbalance towards *wen*.[216] Tu Yu, who corresponded on this question with the ritual scholar Liu Mien, not only reserved a separate section of the *T'ung tien* for the history of the selection system, but also chose for inclusion in this section a succession of T'ang memorials critical of the role of *belles lettres* in the examinations, including submissions by Liu Chih, Chao K'uang and his own friend the official historian Shen Chi-chi.[217]

The failure of the reform movement in 805 may have had the result that radical ideas like these were identified with political defeat. But

under Hsien tsung a less drastic reforming position was often promoted, again even in the course of the examination process itself. In a
decree examination answer of 806, Yüan Chen criticized the scope of
the *chin shih* and its use of *belles lettres*, and in one of 808, Huang-fu
Shih did the same.[218] Candidates also continued to complain bitterly
about their own experience of *shih* and *fu* in the examinations. Shu
Yüan-yü (d. 835) adapted a traditional term of reproach for them
when he said that they amounted to no more than 'the petty skill of
carving worms' (*tiao ch'ung wei i*), that is a pedantic and unimaginative
exercise. Disciples or admirers of Han Yü, like Shen Ya-chih, Sun
Ch'iao and Niu Hsi-chi, expressed similar views.[219]

There was yet another short-lived reform in the reign of Wen tsung,
when the court, in imitation of the Chen-kuan ministers two hundred
years before, discussed high Confucian priorities. In 834, *shih* and *fu*
were again withdrawn from the *chin shih*. But a year later, they were
back, and the system remained essentially unmodified. From this time
until the last recorded, datable *shih* and *fu* topics were set, in 901, the
dynasty's most prestigious examination remained formally a test of
composition skills rather than of practical administrative competence.[220]

Literature as the scholar's 'own charge'

This extraordinary persistence of a feature of the examinations
that many scholars conceded was an abuse cannot be explained simply
by what T'ang scholars termed 'long standing custom'. The deeper
cause lay in the scholarly community itself. Writing generally, and
verse in particular, was an almost universal interest and integral to
social life. Reform-minded, Confucian-orientated official scholars
might express reservations about literary practice in the selection
system; but they were often themselves examination graduates and
members of the same society as examination candidates and prospective officials. They looked to the examination system, and
especially to the *chin shih* examination, as a means to perpetuate their
own political influence. They also benefitted, in terms of their own
standing in the scholar community and in the official hierarchy, from
their mastery of the literary tradition. Instead of dismissing *belles
lettres*, therefore, they attempted to restore their respectability. They
justified their participation in the literary world of their day by
referring to Confucian ideals about literature, and condemning current
practice for failing to approach these ideals.

In the post-rebellion period, however, the reform of literature that

many scholars advocated meant not just simply maintaining the tone of
rescripts, to make them, in the phrase from the *Han shu* much used of
imperial pronouncements, 'of a spirit with the three ages [of high
antiquity]'.[221] It also meant the exploration and definition of appropriate values for the unofficial, private or independent writing that was
now so important to them. For the indirect result of the much larger
and less court-centred scholarly world of the period was that Confucian
critical ideals, in the early T'ang the virtual monopoly of a few scholar
ministers and official scholars, were now brought to bear by larger
numbers of writers on private as well as on official writing. But critics
in this period retained the central ambivalence towards *belles lettres*
that had marked early T'ang attitudes, and the seriousness of the
ancient Confucian ideals that they promoted sometimes coexisted
uneasily with their enjoyment of composition itself. The result was a
lively climate of polemic, in which ideas on literary composition,
literary history and the role of letters in society were exchanged in
correspondence and recorded in essays and prefaces. Each scholar
found a different solution to the problem of combining an acceptable
seriousness with the adventurousness in style and subject-matter that
he and the society around him valued. Even minor figures, or those
with little reputation for letters, reviewed literary history or promoted
their own critical concerns.[222] The unofficial writing on literary practice
that resulted exceeds in quantity private writing on any other learned
topic. The 'arena of letters' therefore provided the most broadly based
intellectual indication of the shift that had taken place since the early
T'ang period in the outlook of the Confucian-orientated scholar
community.

Already the generation of literary figures that lived through the
rebellion showed a change in their outlook on literature. Writers like
the Sun Ti graduates of 734 and 735, Hsiao Ying-shih, Li Hua and Yen
Chen-ch'ing, no longer praised the court literary figures of the late
seventh and early eighth centuries. Instead they demanded that writing
be committed to the cause of political and social reform, and judged
past writers by this standard. They condemned compositions that were
simply descriptive or were dominated by technical prosodic requirements. They reformulated traditional definitions of verse and literature
and emphasized that an individual's writing was the expression of his
moral nature, as well as the reflection of the spirit of the age that had
produced it.[223]

These writers united in singling out one figure from the late seventh
century who expressed for them the values that they required. This

was Ch'en Tzu-ang, whom a contemporary described as reviving literature after a five hundred year period of decline. The sense of community that post-rebellion writers felt with Ch'en was probably social as well as literary and political. Ch'en had had a role in the examination success in 696 of Ts'ui Mien, the court scholar of the K'ai-yüan period, for whom Li Hua and Yen Chen-ch'ing wrote tributes. Ts'ui Mien was the father of Ts'ui Yu-fu, chief minister at the start of Te tsung's reign, and a figure who commanded particularly wide loyalties in the scholar community. But Ch'en Tzu-ang had written verse protesting against extravagant policies under the empress Wu, and the reasons for the admiration he received lay also with the politically committed tenor of his writings. Homage to Ch'en Tzu-ang was paid not only by Sun Ti graduates and mid eighth-century scholars, but also by the major writers of the early ninth century, such as Han Yü, Liu Tsung-yüan, Po Chü-i and Yüan Chen.[224]

The generation that succeeded Li Hua and Hsiao Ying-shih also commented on the literary tradition. They followed T'ang practice in using the laudatory prefaces that they composed for the collected works of fellow officials to give short reviews of literary history, usually incorporating a sequence of names of writers of whom they approved. In these prefaces, they emphasized the moral function of literature and its connection with the spirit of its age, and indicated their commitment to the idea of change in history. Liang Su, for example, combined both emphasis on evolution in literary practice and expression of loyalty to his mentors in the scholar community when he wrote that the T'ang dynasty had lasted for 'nearly two hundred years', and that its literature had undergone, in a phrase drawn from the *Analects*, 'three changes' (*san pien*). The first of these changes he attributed, as others had done, to Ch'en Tzu-ang himself, for by his 'refinement and elegance' (*feng ya*) Ch'en had 'reformed superficiality and excess'. Next, Liang stated, Chang Yüeh, the great scholar minister of Hsüan tsung's reign, and then, nearer his own time, Li Hua, Hsiao Ying-shih and Tu-ku Chi and brought about further reform.

The concept of 'three changes' was also used by Liu Mien, perhaps the most rigorous advocate of traditional Confucian literary ideals of the post-rebellion period. Liu Mien saw the literary tradition as in decline since the age of the Confucian canons. He characterized three changes in literary practice from the time of Confucius to the nadir provided by the southern Ch'i and Liang dynasties. He expressed the hope that the T'ang would see a revival, and regretted his own inability to bring it about.[225] He held, as Li Hua had done, that the literature of an age took its character from the age itself, and that the literature of remote antiquity had been not a discrete skill but integrated with government and society. But in his writing he also implied belief in the contrasting position, that literature was the expression of an individual's character, and that an individual might use it to transcend the decadence of his time. Literature was thus the vehicle for a scholar's highest ideals. '[The present state of the literary art] is not the fault of literature, but of those who practise it', he wrote. 'Literature has no limit, only man's talents are limited'.[226]

This belief that literature, though it reflected the age in which it was produced, was, in the much employed phrase that Tseng Shen had used in the *Analects*, an individual's 'own charge' (*chi jen*) ran through the comments of the well-known scholars who came after Liu Mien. Han Yü made his views on literary composition and practice the central theme of his teaching. It was a basic feature of his position that composition skills involved profound commitment and should be very much more than a means to office. He rebuked those students who undertook the study of composition simply as a means to advance their official careers, implying that theirs was a very superficial approach. Rather, literature should be the vehicle through which the individual declared his identity and furthered his duty of reforming society. It was a long term commitment, which would bear fruit only after intensive and dedicated study.

Han Yü, following Liu Mien, and true to his own anti-Buddhism, held that the feelings, which the Buddhists believed in refining away, played an essential part in any art.[227] He also stressed that moral training and mastery of the canons were necessary to sound writing, for they would nurture the 'breath' (*ch'i*), the spirit energy that would ensure acceptable style.[228] He suggested that the kind of deprivation and failure of which, referring to his own and others' careers, he often spoke lay behind much good literary composition. He implied that literature other than that produced in an official context might be a true expression of an individual's worth. He also gave play to the idea that exotic vocabulary and imagery might ensure the success of a composition. His interest in the bizarre, shared with his friend Meng Chiao (751–814), earned him the censure of those of his colleagues who tried to promote him as the exemplar of all that was serious and committed in their campaign to revive Confucian values.[229] But both his critical remarks on the function in composition of the unusual and the style of his works influenced the terms of discussion well into the ninth century.

Li Ao was an early disciple of Han Yü in literature.[230] His commitment to composition was to span a much longer period than the interest in Confucian interior questions that he also shared with Han. His critical position appears to have been more moralistic than that of his mentor. Like Liu Mien, he opposed the ideal that literature was 'a mere skill' (*i i*).[231] He seems to have tried to integrate his ideas on the nature (*hsing*) with the practice of literature, for he suggested that goodness in the nature of an individual would always find expression in writing, and that, conversely, practice (*hsi*) of literature would lead to goodness.[232] More than any other writer of his eneration, he justified adventurousness in writing by promoting the ideal of 'ancient literature' (*ku wen*). He attributed this aim to Han Yü, but claimed that it was his own as well, since he was 'not in concert with the present age'.[233]

Liu Tsung-yüan's general critical position was close to that of Han Yü and Li Ao, but there were again differences of emphasis that reflected his career and intellectual temper. In the early, metropolitan phase of his career, he had relatively little to say about literary practice, perhaps because he was influenced by Tu Yu's hostility to *belles lettres*. His critique of writing, and of his own experience with it, started with his exile, and his great interest in the subject was, as Han Yü pointed out, a result of the failure of his career. Liu advocated strict adherence to Confucian canonical models, and to the *Mencius*, the *Ch'u tz'u* and the *Shih chi*. At least when approached by students, he was fully as moralistic as any writer of his period. Like Han Yü, he treated literature as far more than a means of access to the official career. Like Han, also, he despised plagiarism, believed that a writer should be independent and insisted on a concise diction and absence of verbiage.[234]

A different approach to literary practice was justified in this period by appeal to the ancient Confucian ideal that writing should 'express the feelings of those below'. In this ancient idea, moderate reformers found a principle that perfectly justified both their more distanced involvement with high political power and their literary inventiveness. Even in the early eighth century, the period when the T'ang court provided the centre of the literary world, scholars had referred to the idea that verse was a spontaneous phenomenon and an indication of the condition of the populace.[235] Both Tu Fu and Yüan Chieh, in their verse of the T'ien-pao period, had focussed on injustices among the people. But after the An Lu-shan rebellion, descriptions of popular conditions and administrative injustices became a fashion which broke new ground in terms of style and subject matter. The credit for reviving the idea of 'poetry collecting officers' (*ts'ai shih kuan*) and of creating a style of protest verse that treated current social injustices or political wrongs belongs to Po Chü-i and Yüan Chen. Already by 806, Po had developed the critical position behind this idea and had evolved a direct, balladic style to treat its subject matter. His most detailed apology for his 'new *yüeh fu*' verse followed a few years later in a celebrated letter that he wrote to Yüan Chen in late 815.[236]

The deteriorating political conditions that the generations following Han Yü and Po Chü-i experienced took their views on literary practice further in the direction of the unofficial and experimental. The main features of their outlook on literature are therefore partly explicable in terms of their reduced involvement in the sort of writing associated with a successful career at the time of the dynasty's prosperity.[237] Middle and late ninth-century writers were even more interested in analysing the psychology of composition and in emphasizing originality, innovation and individual style. Shen Ya-chih, a follower of Han Yü, used a horticultural metaphor that Han Yü had already hinted at: 'A man who is skilled at cultivation will have the plants tamped firmly with fine soil and will water according to season. The tips of branches and shoots will be sharp. Now the canons, histories and the learning of the hundred philosophers are to the mind irrigation and no more'.[238] Sun Ch'iao, another fervent admirer of Han Yü, stressed originality even more: a writer should 'say what others do not say, reach where others do not reach. He should hasten to the exotic and rush to the strange'.[239] The famous verse writer Li Shang-yin took this emphasis on independence beyond the borders of Confucian acceptability, when he expressly attacked the idea that Confucius supplied the only values for literature, and demanded complete freedom from the tyranny of past exemplars. 'To wield the brush should not mean plundering the canons or histories, or honouring taboos over certain times and ages.'[240]

Still a generation later, the main prose collections were by men who saw little or no official service. The generation of P'i Jih-hsiu and Lu Kuei-meng certainly knew literary history and commented on T'ang literature; but they appear to have introduced few new critical ideas. Their greatest achievement was in the field of practice itself. They developed still further the tradition of unofficial writing to which the generation of Han Yü had given so much.[241] Their collected works provide a measure of how greatly the T'ang scholar's world had changed since the period in the eighth century when the great ambition of the man of letters had been to 'give [due] elegance and finish to royal commands'.

7

CONCLUSION

Over the three centuries of the T'ang dynasty, scholars showed the commitment to the preservation and study of the Confucian canons and to official service on Confucian terms that have defined the Confucian tradition throughout the history of imperial China. Through service on successive official scholarly commissions in the first half of the dynasty, they reviewed the entire Confucian learned tradition, and compiled large numbers of works for which they claimed the sanction of the canons and histories. In the course of the second half of the dynasty, they re-evaluated unofficially both the Confucian commentarial tradition and the conventional Confucian-sanctioned view of the origins and function of the state they served.

The dynasties that followed the T'ang also at their outset reviewed the tradition of learning that they inherited. Just as the T'ang had done, the Sung, Ming and Ch'ing dynasties commissioned a range of official compilations in most important areas of scholarship. Though wider in scope than the seventh-century systematization of learning, their scholarly programmes had essentially the same purpose. Like the T'ang also, later periods in Chinese history witnessed radical reappraisals of the Confucian inheritance that derived from society beyond the learned institutions at the capital. But the preceding chapters have suggested that several features gave T'ang Confucianism, whether official or unofficial, a distinctively medieval identity: when compared with Neo-Confucians, T'ang scholars had a pluralistic approach to beliefs and were not preoccupied with a sense of orthodoxy; a great deal of their scholarly output, when compared to that of later Confucians, was invested in the practicalities of the state ritual programme, in ritual directives or debates on rites; a very high proportion of their writings, whether official or not, tended to be compilatory; but at the same time they had a keen recognition of an interest in change, not only in the institutions of government but in history, literature and culture more generally. These features, it was argued, derived from the social and political milieu in which official scholars served. It remains, in conclusion, to resume the factors that gave the medieval scholarly milieu its special character, and briefly to suggest the nature of the legacy of T'ang Confucianism to the tradition of the pre-modern era.

The main feature of the milieu in which T'ang scholars lived was the intense competition to gain entry to the bureaucracy at Ch'ang-an and to rise high in the hierarchy. Competition for political influence and ambition for the rewards of high office lay behind many T'ang attitudes. These motivations combined with the idealism inherent in the Confucian canonical tradition to determine much that was distinctive about late medieval Confucian-orientated scholarship. T'ang Confucian scholars served the dynasty with expectations both of a material and an idealistic kind. The political system of the T'ang both sanctioned acquisition of status and provided the locus for the ideals of successive generations of scholars. The standing of the imperial entourage of which successful official scholars formed, or hoped to form, a part was indeed such that they appeared to have 'ascended among the immortals'.[1] The prestige of official service at the highest levels of the hierarchy dominated all non-clerical literate society. The substantial rewards for a successful official career were both formal and informal. Senior posts, especially those for officials of the fifth degree and above in the three ministries, carried enormous standing. The official hierarchy as a whole was systematically organized to demonstrate the prestige of ascending rank. It provided elaborate sumptuary, sartorial and emblematic scales of seniority. It offered a system of ennoblement and honorary titles. The obsession with status systems even extended to provision for deceased officials. All posthumous honours, canonization, posthumous office, or the much more rarely implemented burial near the emperor's tomb and representation in the imperial ancestral temple, were highly coveted, and carefully recorded in the official and unofficial accounts of individual careers. For the clans and families that made up the T'ang scholarly elite, a relatively small and cohesive community when compared to the devolved educated community of later periods, these indications of status provided powerful incentives for continued loyal service to the dynasty.

Besides these formal status systems, official service might bring private wealth and spectacularly increased living standards. Individual scholar officials embarked on their careers in widely different economic circumstances. But numbers of the scholars whose names have recurred in this book, even those from elite lineages, started their lives in relative poverty, often in the provinces. In their private writing, they often contrasted the lives of the rich and highly placed with the poor and unrecognized, and identified their own early experiences as times of deprivation. In the early eighth century, Fang Kuan's father had been a chief minister and was disgraced at the end of the empress Wu's reign. Fang Kuan claimed that his own upbringing had been 'indistinguishable from [that of] a peasant'.[2] Hsiao Ying-shih, a descendant of the Liang imperial house, described the collapse of his family estate in the seventh and early eighth centuries, and the poverty of his own upbringing.[3] His disciple Liu T'ai-chen, who later held some of the highest academic tenures, was forced to break off his early instruction under Hsiao because of poverty.[4] The great loyalist scholar and calligrapher Yen Chen-ch'ing recorded having experienced such poverty in early youth that he was unable to afford paper on which to practise writing.[5] At least one of the scholars whom Han Yü recommended to the assistant examiner Lu San in 802 came from a background of deprivation in which 'his land was inadequate and taxes many, and he had insufficient [means] to care for his parents. In his leisure from ploughing, he read and composed'.[6]

If their careers were successful, however, many officials at all periods of the dynasty acquired wealth and property on a large scale. Frugality or restraint was, in the T'ang tradition, considered a powerful factor that ensured the durability and success of individual families. It was also one of the values that idealistic scholars tried most consistently to promote in the political arena. Excessive displays of wealth were considered a betrayal of the Confucian ideal of austerity, and socially unacceptable in a scholar or 'book-man' (*shu sheng*). Innumerable biographies of both high-ranking and less successful officials therefore commended an austere life style in their subjects.[7] Nonetheless, many successful scholar officials, at all periods of the dynasty, ended their careers with estates and large households. Under T'ai tsung, Yen Shih-ku had an estate and collected antiques,[8] while Li Pai-yao retired to an estate that he landscaped himself.[9] In the K'ai-yüan period, the rescript writer and examiner Wei Chih had a spectacularly grand and well-staffed residence.[10] Hsiao Fu, grandson of Hsiao Sung, the chief minister of Hsüan tsung's reign, differed from his brothers because, while they lived ostentatiously, he 'dressed in clean clothes and lived alone in a single room, keeping the company only of men of letters and Confucians'. He had, however, an estate at Chao-ying, which a chief minister of the time, Wang Chin, the brother of the poet Wang Wei, coveted.[11] In the early ninth century, Ch'üan Te-yü described Tu Yu's estate as large and especially fine.[12] The *chin shih* under Liu T'ai-chen, chièf minister and associate of Li Ao and Han Yü, P'ei Tu had a particularly well-appointed garden at Lo-yang which, like Li Pai-yao, he landscaped himself.[13] Po Chü-i's estate at Lo-yang was well staffed and quite large.[14]

An official's reputation during his life time and after his death also, in practice, constituted a form of status sanction. It was of great importance to his family, his disciples and followers and his fellow scholars. It was measured not only by the dynasty's formal status provisions, but also in unofficial commemorative tributes composed for him and circulated in the scholar community. A scholar's place in the bureaucratic lore of the dynasty, in the lively, vengeful and very retentive memory of the official community, was also of vital concern. 'Public discussion' or 'the opinion of the time' (*kung i* or *shih lun*) is an often mentioned factor, at all levels of documentation, in the assessment of an individual scholar's or of a family's performance. Many of the informal, anecdotal compilations by scholar officials that have survived from the T'ang are no less dominated by the values of the official hierarchy. These works indicate that the scholar community passed informal judgement on their peers often with great deference, but condemned mercilessly those whom they believed to have failed or to have betrayed their interests. A scholar's achievements, and indeed his failures, implicated his descendants. His commitment to achieve imperishability, to 'establish merit, establish virtue, or establish words',[15] in the often repeated dictum from the *Tso chuan*, was monitored by a community that was extremely aware of its own social and political history.

The great prestige of the successful official career and the enormous rewards and standing that it brought to individuals and to their families dominated the lives of medieval scholar officials. Their dependence on the official hierarchy for their status and their material prosperity served to increase their loyalty to it. The continuity in official life that T'ang stability provided and that, in some cases, enabled individual families to maintain an association with individual scholarly posts in the bureaucracy over three generations or more, also increased their sense of commitment. The result of this was the great ambition to serve, the large numbers of prospective officials and the harsh competition for office that are frequently mentioned in the official, unofficial and anecdotal sources for the late medieval state.

It is true that, within the official hierarchy, the scholarly tenures that have figured in the preceding pages occupied an ambivalent place. Most of the tenures in the academic agencies, even the senior ones, were not considered 'strategic positions'. But the learning and mastery of the literary tradition that were associated with them carried very great prestige in the court and in official society. Many of the men who dominate the record of T'ang state scholarship remained in scholarly posts at the capital for most of their careers. Men like Li Pai-yao, Ling-hu Te-fen, Yen Shih-ku and K'ung Ying-ta under T'ai tsung, or Wang Yüan-kan, Hsü Chien, Yüan Hsing-ch'ung, Liu Chih-chi and Wei Shu in the first decades of the eighth century, were life-long, in effect professional, scholars, whose great private libraries, in some cases, testify to the stability of their lives and their dedication to learning. This career pattern was less common after the rebellion of An Lu-shan; but there were still official scholars whose careers in academic posts spanned several decades, and who did not alternate their academic tenures with general service provincial posts or tenures in the three ministries.

Nonetheless, the medieval community of official scholars was small enough and the prestige of learning great enough to ensure that official scholars who spent their careers in the academic agencies were not politically isolated or far removed from the apex of the administrative hierarchy. Many were given concurrent tenures in the consultative colleges, and this brought them into proximity with the court in both administrative and social contexts. The use of *ad hoc* scholarly commissions, which drew a high proportion of their personnel from the academic agencies, meant that official scholars had direct contact with the emperor or senior scholar ministers. Many of the scholars who served for long periods in the learned institutions involved themselves in the political and administrative issues that were of major concern to the emperor and the court. Most official scholars were not simple 'book-men', in the pejorative sense in which the term was sometimes applied in the T'ang. Throughout the dynasty, numbers of them submitted keen comments on contemporary problems. The submission by Li Pai-yao opposing the enfieffment principle in the context of a court discussion of 637, provides an early example of a learned policy submission of a kind that many official scholars delivered in the course of their careers.[16] Their concerns ranged from ritual issues to matters of defence and strategy against the barbarians and to economic and financial management. The very range of their comments underlines the comprehensiveness of their view of the polity.

In the post-rebellion period, the emergency conditions under which the central government functioned meant that fewer scholars had life-long service in the academic agencies. But officials with scholarly backgrounds and experience of academic or ritual office became even more deeply involved in contemporary issues than before the rebellion. Under Su tsung soon after the recovery of the capitals, Su Yüan-ming, the patron of Tu Fu and Yüan Chieh, a scholar who held office in the state academy directorate as a rescript writer and in the imperial library, 'several times expounded the successes and short-comings of the administration'.[17] A high proportion of the post-rebellion official scholars mentioned in the preceding pages, like him, memorialized on general administrative topics. Under Tai tsung in 765, Tu-ku Chi as an omissioner of the left, submitted a keen memorial that opened with a plea that the emperor should be accessible to his advisers.[18] The following year, Yen Chen-ch'ing, as president of the board of justice, memorialized on the principle that the emperor should keep channels of communication with officials open.[19] The deep and lasting hostility that the scholar community showed to those who, like Hsü Ching-tsung, Li Lin-fu, or the Te tsung favourite P'ei Yen-ling, blocked channels of access to the emperor indicate the value that T'ang scholars put on this involvement in the political centre and their concern that it should not be denied them. This involvement of scholars in contemporary affairs in turn affected their outlook on the academic operations that they conducted. It meant that much of their scholarly outlook on the past and on the literary tradition derived its priorities from their experience of the changing political realities of their own day. Despite the fact that their scholarship was often compendious and followed inherited models, it had a practicality and an element of contemporary reference that was again characteristically medieval.

Equally important for T'ang scholarship, even the learned issues that were the first concern of official scholars were brought into the centre of the political arena and, like questions of administrative policy, discussed in the presence of the emperor. In this way, dissention and competitive debate were made integral to many of the scholarly operations of the dynasty. In canonical scholarship, these issues concerned the text itself of the canons, as debates from the time of Yen Shih-ku's commission of 633 until the K'ai-ch'eng stone engraving indicate. They also involved the secondary level, that of the primary commentaries, which prompted the controversies in which Liu Chih-chi, Yüan Hsing-ch'ung and others participated. It is true that administrative convenience, which necessitated providing an authoritative, standard version of canonical and commentarial texts for examin-ation candidates, resulted in the rejection of some suggestions for alternative syllabuses. 'Long standing custom', or bureaucratic inflex-ibility also killed off some proposals for change. When Hsüan tsung, the greatest imperial patron of scholarship of the dynasty, wrote a commentary, this in effect ruled out commissioning further official exegesis for the canon concerned. But even the promulgation of an imperial commentary did not mean that at unofficial levels further exegesis of the canon concerned was proscribed.

The dynasty's state ritual programme, particularly, provided a focus for controversies. Some of the many debates that were held were even formally conducted, with the adherents of two opposing viewpoints drawn up on opposing sides. Putting a ritual problem out for discussion (*ch'u i*) was a regular procedure that might involve a large number of officials. Sometimes, issues of considerable political or theoretical importance were given public discussion. After an initial controversy between the court of sacrifices and his grandson, discussion of the canonization appropriate for the chief minister of Kao tsung's reign Hsü Ching-tsung was thrown open on imperial command to 'officials of the fifth grade and above in the department of affairs of state'.[20] The principle of whether an official's private obligations had precedence over his official ritual duties was formally discussed probably early in Te tsung's reign, in connection with the case of a ritual official who had claimed that he could not observe abstinence because of a personal taboo.[21] Of the four fields of learning described, only official history lacked this element of open participation. In this case, rather, the competition that was universal in T'ang bureaucratic life expressed itself in efforts by emperors, chief ministers and factional interests to control the content of the record. But even here, diversity and disagreement were in fact expressed in the many unofficial chronicle form histories that members of the scholar community compiled or planned. They undertook these essentially to reallocate the 'praise and blame' that they believed to have been wrongly distributed in the official record. Verse composition, as an activity that was not of itself political, was in a different category from the other disciplines con-sidered. Yet the 'arena of letters' of the seventh and early eighth centuries was also centred on the court, and was a medium for the same sense of competition and ambition that pervaded other learned activities.

The political and learned issues that concerned the scholar commu-nity and their great interest in literary composition were used in the examination system, through which members of the intellectual and official elite were selected. Here the T'ang academic system showed perhaps its greatest flexibility. The examinations were constantly criticized for the impractical and superficial approach that they encouraged among candidates. But they were, by the standards of the examinations of the late imperial period, remarkable for the way in which they expressed the contemporary political and intellectual milieu and the changes that took place in it.

This involvement of scholars in the political arena and relatively open attitude towards dissent over learned issues within the Confucian tradition had considerable advantages for the dynastic house. To have well qualified scholars willing to speak their minds to the emperor and his court was in itself a sign of achievement, an indication that the dynasty was politically successful. The imperial house itself gained prestige from its association with the descendants of the families that had a close historical link with the Confucian tradition. K'ung Ying-ta, the descendant of Confucius, particularly, was one of the pre-eminent canonical and ritual scholars of T'ai tsung's reign, who submitted advice on the ritual issues that then preoccupied the court. In the course of his career, T'ai tsung honoured him successively with honoraria of 200 bolts of silk, 100 bolts, a catty of gold and 300 bolts, quite apart from promotions, with accompanying increases in income, and ennoblement.[22] The K'ung line went on to supply a succession of official scholars in the seventh century. A thirty-fifth generation descendant of Confucius, Han Yü's associate K'ung K'uei, was president of the state academy directorate briefly up to 817.[23] The line re-emerged to attain high office and influence at the end of the dynasty. Formal commendations for members of the scholarly Yen clan by T'ai tsung[24] and by Hsüan tsung, and Hsüan tsung's endorsement of their claim of descent from Yen Hui, Confucius's favourite disciple[25] again enabled the dynasty to affirm that it valued continuity and dedication to scholarly ideals. Numbers of the Yen clan served in academic and tutorial posts in the seventh and early eighth centuries.[26] In turn, imperial recognition of their scholarly achievements was repeated in the aftermath of the rebellion, at a time of acute crisis for the dynasty, when, in appreciation of Yen Chen-ch'ing's loyal service to him, Su tsung acknowledged his memorial submissions with further high flown tributes to the Yens. Tai tsung repeated these tributes,[27] and as late as 777, when Yen submitted his phonological dictionary, he received a large honorarium, 500 bolts of silk, and doubtless a citation as well.[28]

T'ai tsung particularly, and perhaps also Hsüan tsung at the start of his reign, seem also to have enjoyed seeing Confucian scholars in competitive debate on learned issues. Their interest in this extended beyond the formal debates between representatives of the three teachings that were a T'ang court tradition. Permitting Confucian scholars to argue among themselves was also a way of ensuring their continued loyalty and support. Encouragement of debate constituted a form of approval for scholars, a recognition that their activities were dignified and worthwhile. It also meant that, at least on issues over which the dynasty had an open mind, the emperor secured the most authentic answers that he could from the learned community, members of which were required to test their recommendations in the process of argument against their fellow scholars.

This relative openness of the T'ang official scholarly milieu, it need hardly be said, extended to the less formal or private context. The same scholars who monitored the social and political history of their own society so closely were also deeply committed to unofficial discussion of the contemporary political world and about religion, history and literature. There are frequent references to the love of debate among the intellectual elite, to individuals who were skilled in argument, or to groups who established reputations for the quality of their conversation. The late K'ai-yüan and T'ien-pao periods, the era of Fang Kuan, Wei Shu, Liu Fang and Hsiao Ying-shih, particularly seem to have been a time when far ranging discussions took place among scholars at Ch'ang-an.[29] After the rebellion, there are references to groups with reformist interests reviewing history, analyzing political problems and discussing religious issues both in the far south-east, the Yangtze valley and the capital.[30]

Intellectual openness towards the Confucian tradition both in the official and the unofficial contexts had as an important concomitant the relaxed attitude to questions of orthodoxy in doctrine that has been a recurrent theme in the preceding pages. Assured as emperors were of the loyalty of a scholar community eager for official service, they had little need to demarcate limits beyond which their suggestions became inadmissible. There was relatively seldom any need either for them to define or reassert acceptable boundaries for the Confucian-orientated learned tradition. Only in the case of prognostication did the dynasty attempt harshly to enforce limits on unofficial activity. The Confucian canons were a deeply trusted and respected authority, which had first been selected and promoted by the Han, an era of imperial government that T'ang scholars believed merited emulation. The canons were certainly vague and not easily interpreted on many issues, but this vagueness, particularly over the many ritual questions that were the special concern of medieval scholars, provided the basis for the competitive debates in which scholars invested their erudition and ambition. Because the canons lacked a 'clear text' on many specific rituals, they did not stand in the way of the changes and the expansion in which, at least in the first half of the dynasty, T'ang sovereigns were keenly interested.

The freedom to continue to review the Confucian exegetical tradition, therefore, was based on the coincidence of the interests of the sovereign and the scholar community. The emperor and the scholars who administered the academic agencies and the examination system had primarily an administrative concern for a standard text of the Confucian canons or an officially delimited range of commentaries and sub-commentaries for them. The state had no other interest in enforcing a narrow Confucian orthodoxy, nor was the scholar community committed to defining one.

When the dynasty did endorse a particular interpretation of the canonical or ritual tradition, it tended not to sustain its exclusive position for very long. Rather, it avoided the problem of having to reject alternative positions by including all options in a pluralistic approach. This process was seen in the attitude to K'ung Ying-ta's sub-commentary series, which, though officially commissioned, never supplied an exclusive orthodoxy for the dynasty. It was also seen, in the reign of Kao tsung, in the adoption of Wang Su's sky divinity as the supreme cosmic agent, the temporary exclusion of Cheng Hsüan's five direction gods as recipients of sacrifice in major state rituals, and their readmission to these rites soon afterwards. This relaxed attitude towards the interpretation of the Confucian learned tradition is to be related to the religious pluralism that was the norm throughout the medieval period. An account of non-Confucian religious attitudes lies outside the scope of this book; suffice it to say that when emperors might be actively committed simultaneously to such very different belief systems as Buddhism and Taoism, the fact that there were divergencies within the Confucian exegetical tradition cannot have seemed of itself important.

The lack of any sense of rigid orthodoxy among T'ang scholars is made particularly clear by their use of the terminology that, in later periods, came to designate the heterodox and politically and legally unacceptable. Individual scholars often invoked the *Analects* term 'strange doctrines' (*i tuan*), which meant heterodox or unacceptable

ideas. They applied it in discussion concerning canonical texts and
their interpretation,[31] in exegesis of the classical histories,[32] in debates
about ritual directives,[33] and even in commenting on prevalent values
in verse writing.[34] The term usually denoted an opinion or a position
that was unacceptable to the writer concerned, for reasons often of
incompatibility with the standards of sobriety or austerity that were
one of T'ang scholars' most insistent concerns. It was sometimes
applied to the tradition of superstition and interest in prognostication
which T'ang official scholars frequently condemned. But it did not
generally carry any suggestion of failure to conform to a statutory or
legally defined body of doctrine.

The term 'pure Confucian' (*ch'un ju*) was also used in the T'ang. It
had positive connotations, but was not a term of very strong
commendation. Feng Yen, the late eighth-century writer of a
collection of reminiscences, for example, applied it to the sort of
scholar to be appointed to the prefectural or county school system, a
posting that more ambitious scholars certainly avoided.[35] Liu Chih-chi
was called a 'pure Confucian'.[36] Tu Fu complimented Su Yüan-ming,
the vice-president of the state academy directorate on the eve of the
rebellion and rescript writer of Su tsung's reign, in the same way.[37] But
there is nothing in Liu Chih-chi's writings or in the scanty
documentation that survives for Su Yüan-ming to suggest that they
were puristically or exclusively Confucian in their religious allegiances.
The term 'pure Confucian', rather, seems to have suggested scholarly
attitudes, particularly towards administration, not rigorous or exclusive
dedication to a particularly clearly defined set of beliefs.

This tolerance of the scholar community towards diversity, combined with their involvement in a changing political situation, were
features that encouraged change in the tradition. The evolution in the
outlook of scholars that took place over the dynasty, moreover,
reflected precisely the changes in the political and social position of the
scholar community. This evolution may again be summarized in terms
of the classic polarity within the Confucian tradition suggested by the
Ta hsüeh (Ch. 3, p. 70). There was a shift towards an increased
recognition in scholarship of administrative experience, of the great
success of T'ang government institutions and of the importance of the
bureaucratic state in relation to imperial power. This trend culminated
in the long unofficial compendia of the early ninth century, of which
the *T'ung tien* by Tu Yu is the most important surviving example. At
the other extreme of the polarity, in response to the highly developed
religious values of the supra-mundane faiths of Buddhism and Taoism,

among a minority of scholars, a revival took place of Confucian-defined idealistic and introspective values for the individual.

Tu Yu's reappraisal of the origins and function of the state and repeated insistence that adaptation to present circumstances was essential was a particularly clear expression of T'ang belief in institutional evolution. Tu Yu's outlook on the state was utilitarian, and he adopted ideas on political management mainly on the grounds of what he believed to be their effectiveness in solving the political problems of his time. Similarly, he had an eclectic attitude to the pre-Ch'in corpus of writing on statecraft and by no means confined his sources to the Confucian canons. Liu Tsung-yüan's eloquent account of the emergence of the ideal of the 'public weal' in Chinese history also represents T'ang scholars' commitment to the bureaucratic state. But the faith in history as a progression and in institutional change as a key to stability that both these scholars demonstrate was characteristic of the T'ang in another respect. Both Tu Yu and Liu Tsung-yüan believed in the irreducible set of Confucian moral priorities and in moral self-improvement. Indeed Tu Yu's entry in the *T'ung tien* for the official school system even cited in its commentary the eight-fold progression from the *Ta hsüeh* and the *Chung yung* doctrine of the nature, both basic texts for the interior emphasis within Confucianism.[38] But their reformist outlook on the polity did not involve their promoting introspective values as a priority in their programme. They followed the great majority of Confucian scholars in the dynasty not in denying the importance of spiritual values, but in reserving these questions to their private lives, and in seeing them in terms largely of the supra-mundane faiths.

Han Yü, on the other hand, appealed for the regeneration of the dynasty through the moral reform of the individual, and rejected the religious pluralism and the demarcation between private religious loyalties and public office that had been the norm in official society. For him, Confucian ideas were no longer to be 'bound to occasions' or to institutions or academic programmes, but were to provide the basis for an existential revival of the Confucian view of man in the service of the state. But his was a minority position, and was characterized as such by his friends and contemporaries. His efforts were largely ignored by a bureaucracy most of whose members had conventionalized their approach to the dynasty's problems and to the acute need for effective reform. Behind both Han Yü's position and that of Tu Yu, however, lay the same endorsement of the two defining characteristics of Confucianism, commitment to the ethical priorities that the

Confucian canons defined and to the ideals of official service under the dynasty. Here, in the unofficial writings of scholars of very different intellectual temperaments, was proof that T'ang emperors were justified in tolerating controversy and encouraging debate among their Confucian advisers. The scholarly elite, much more articulate and freer of imperial direction in the late eighth century than before, reasserted its ultimate loyalty to the ideals of dynastic rule, and to the only ideology that prescribed in detail for the conduct of the individual in the service of the state.

The contribution of the T'ang dynasty to the Confucian tradition, therefore, is to be seen at several levels. In the first half of the dynasty a loyal, vigorous and politically ambitious scholar community expanded the scheme of state-directed learning that it inherited from the Sui. T'ang official scholarship was, in some respects, mechanical, but it involved a thorough review of the entire learned tradition. Reflecting the compartmentalization that was basic both to the academic agencies at Ch'ang-an and to the medieval scholarly tradition, Confucian-orientated official scholarship remained largely free of intrusion from the rival religious systems. But because the scholars who were responsible for it were also involved in the political world of their day, it also adapted and kept pace with institutionally the most sophisticated dynasty that China had seen. The successful completion of many academic projects under T'ang rule meant that the tradition of official scholarship that the dynasty bequeathed to the dynasties of the later imperial period was greatly strengthened. But the very tolerance of the state towards diversity of opinion combined with the continued prestige of official service, even in the period of the dynasty's decline, to ensure a second major development. The insights concerning the nature of the T'ang state and the place of the individual in it that scholars writing unofficially developed in the late eighth and early ninth centuries, were also a major legacy to the later tradition. In the course of time, they too were taken into the official tradition, to become a strand in the amplified Confucianism of the pre-modern empires.

NOTES

List of abbreviations

CKCY	*Chen-kuan cheng yao*
CTCC	*Ch'ien T'ang Chih Chai*
CTS	*Chiu T'ang shu*
CTShih	*Ch'üan T'ang shih*
HJAS	*Harvard Journal of Asiatic Studies*
Ho chih	*T'ang shu ching chi i wen ho chih*
HTS	*Hsin T'ang shu*
HYISIS	*Harvard – Yenching Institute Sinological Index Series*
KFSPWK	*K'ai-feng Shih Po-wu-kuan*
SS	*Sui shu*
STTS	*Shih t'ung t'ung shih*
TFYK	*Ts'e fu yüan kuei*
TKCK	*Teng k'o chi k'ao*
THY	*T'ang hui yao*
TLT	*Ta T'ang liu tien*
TT	*T'ung tien*
TTCLC	*T'ang ta chao ling chi*
TTKYL	*Ta T'ang K'ai-yüan li*
TWT	*T'ang wen ts'ui*
WYYH	*Wen yüan ying hua*

1 Introduction

1 The subject of the T'ang antecedents of Neo-Confucianism and its secondary literature has been thoroughly reviewed and enormously elucidated by Barrett (1978).

2 Amy Auerbacher Wilson, Sidney Leonard Greenblatt and Richard W. Wilson eds., *Methodological issues in Chinese Studies*, New York: Praeger Publishers, 1983, p. 18.

3 Especially during the T'ai-ho period (A.D. 477–500); see Hsiao Kung-ch'üan (1953) p. 404 and n. 1 on p. 415.

4 Ebrey (1978), esp. chs. 2–4, pp. 15–86.

5 Twitchett (1973), esp. pp. 76–83.

6 For introductory remarks on T'ang scholars attitudes to the military, see Pulleyblank (1976), pp. 33–9, and McMullen (1987b).

7 The term *che chung* is used, for example, of the compilation of the ritual code of 732 (*THY* 37/670); of the compilation of the bibliography to the

imperial book collection in 721 (*Yen Lu kung wen chi* 10/5a, 'The classification into categories, assessment and putting in sequence were all evaluated and decided by Yin Chien-yu'); of the criminal laws of the dynasty (*CTS* 85/2812, biog. of T'ang Lin, Kao tsung, requiring that appropriate adjustments be made to their severity or laxity). Also, of unofficial works, *HTS* 47/1441, *Ho-chih* p. 43, Ch'en Yüeh's *Che chung Ch'un-ch'iu (Judging appropriately between [the Three traditions to] the Ch'un-ch'iu)* in 30 *chüan*; *Ch'üan Tsai-chih wen chi* 11/4a-b, of Tu Yu's *T'ung tien; Ch'üan Tsai-chih wen chi* 14/12a and 36/7a, of the ritual directives of the ritual scholar Chung Tzu-ling; *CTS* 148/3992, of Li Chi-fu's mastery of institutional history; *THY* 12/298, Hsü Chien, reviewing the history of the imperial ancestral temple.

8 Jack Goody, *The domestication of the savage mind*, Cambridge: Cambridge University Press, 1977, p. 41.

9 *STTS* 6/1b; *CTS* 21/816; *Li chi chu shu*, preface 1b; cf. *HTS* 199/5679, biog. of Liu Ch'ung.

10 *CTS* 151/4061, of Wang O, 760–815, canonized *Wei*; cf. *CTS* 99/3105, biog. of Yen T'ing-chih; Kao I comp., *Ch'ün chü chieh i (Humourous stories for living in a crowd)*, p. 59; also Ch. 5, note 54.

11 T'ang official and unofficial sources often mention 'Confucian dress' (*ju i* or *ju fu*); the emperor in rescripts of appointment to scholarly office was made to refer to those who served him in Confucian dress, e.g. *Yüan shih Ch'ang-ch'ing chi* 47/2a; *Po Hsiang-shan chi* 5/32/67. Cf. also *Feng shih wen chien chi* 5/26. Prospective officials or those out of office wore Confucian dress, eg. *WYYH* 232/8b, Cheng Ch'ang; *T'ang Huang-fu Tseng shih chi pu-i* 1/6a; *Ch'üan Tsai-chih wen chi* 23/1b, 23/8a, 29/4a, 39/11b; *Han Ch'ang-li chi* 7/ *Wai chi* 2/65 and Owen (1975), p. 35. Dress was often mentioned when a scholar was involved in military activity, to emphasize his civil identity; e.g. *Ho yüeh ying ling chi* 1/69, T'ao Han; *CTS* 157/4158, historian's comment on Wang Hung and Hsi Shih-mei; *CTS* 137/3766, biog. of Yü Shao. The phrase *ju fu* was canonical; see *Li chi chu shu* 59/1a, and it is possible that its use in T'ang times was metaphorical as much as literal.

12 The term *shu sheng* was used of e.g. Wei Cheng, the great scholar of T'ai tsung's reign, see *CKCY* 1/23; of Ch'en Tzu-ang, *Ch'en Tzu-ang chi* p. 254, separate biography by Lu Ts'ang-yung; of Chang Chiu-ling, the scholar minister of Hsüan tsung's reign, see *TCTC* 214/6822, 736.16 (probably a quotation from the *T'ang li* of Liu Fang); of Yüan Tsai, the chief minister under Tai tsung, see *CTS* 118/3412, biog.; of the great loyalist general service official and scholar Yen Chen-ch'ing, *CTS* 128/3590, biog.; of the official scholar of the K'ai-yüan period Yüan Hsing-ch'ung, *CTS* 102/3177; of the general service official and scholar Liu Chih (though probably with Sung wording), *TCTC* 219/7003, 765.5; of the official scholar and rescript writer Li Chien, contemptuously, by a military governor in 820, *CTS* 25/958; of the general service official Tu Ya, condemning his extreme extravagance as unbefitting a *shu sheng*, *CTS* 146/3963; of the *chin shih* Li Jih-chih, who had attained what he considered to be too high an office for a scholar, *CTS* 188/4927; of the

chin shih Liu Hun, by the emperor Te tsung, in disbelief at his knowledge of border strategy, *CTS* 125/3555; of the official scholar Wang Yen-wei, *CTS* 157/4154. With the exception of Wei Cheng, who had started his career in the disorders before the foundation of the dynasty, and of Liu Chih, about whose examination career there is no record, all were examination graduates. For a late T'ang example of the term, see *TCTC* 259/8431, 892.25.

13 For references to Han Kao tsu's celebrated exchange with Lu Chia, see *SS* 75/1705; *TCTC* 195/6134,637.12, T'ang Chien to T'ai tsung; *CTS* 189A/4940; *WYYH* 617/5b, memorial of Chu Ching-tse; *Ch'ü-chiang Chang hsien-sheng wen chi* 16/2a–b.

14 For examples of the phrase *ch'u chiang ju hsiang*, see *TCTC* 193/6084, 630.32, of Li Ching; *P'i-ling chi* 6/6a, of Niu Hsien-k'o; *Po Hsiang-shan chi* 6/37/28, of Li Chi-fu; *Po Hsiang-shan chi* 9/61/59, of Yüan Chen. The canonical sanction for combining *wen* and *wu* derived from *Shang shu chu shu* 4/2a, and *Mao shih chu shu* 10B/4b. Yin Chi-fu, the subject of the *Mao shih* ode, supplied a given name in the T'ang, e.g. *Yüan-ho hsing tsuan* 2/12a, Wei Chi-fu, and 7/11a, Ma Chi-fu; and *CTS* 148/3992, Li Chi-fu. In T'ang biographies and other commemorative sources, there are very many examples of general service officials being praised for combining *wen* and *wu*; e.g. *Ch'ü-chiang Chang hsien-sheng wen chi* 18/1a, Chang Chiu-ling of Chang Yüeh; *Yen Lu kung wen chi* 14/13b, Ling-hu Huan of Yen Chen-ch'ing; *Ch'üan Tsai-chih wen chi* 22/4b, Ch'üan Te-yü of Tu Yu.

15 Max Weber, *The religion of China*, translated and edited by Hans Gerth, with an introduction by C.K. Yang, New York: The Macmillan Company, 1964, p. 111.

16 *WYYH* 696/9a, Hsiao Chih-chung; *CTS* 99/3098, biog. of Chang Chiu-ling; *Lu Hsüan kung han-yüan chi* 14/13a–b. (Cf. the different phrasing in *TCTC* 230/7417, 784.11).

17 *CTS* 165/4313 and 179/4669 Liu Kung-ch'i; *CTS* 190B–5045, Sun Kung-ch'i; *HTS* 75A/3297, Cheng Kung-ch'i.

18 Officials frequently mentioned the term *chih kung* in praising the performance of examiners, often those under whom they had themselves been successful; e.g. *WYYH* 678/4a and 6b, Hsiao Ying-shih, of Sun Ti, under whom in 735 he graduated *chin shih*, and Miao Chin-ch'ing, 689–765, canonized *Wen-chen*, director of selection examinations from 739 until 743; *P'i-ling chi* 6/3a, Tu-ku Chi, of Miao Chin-ch'ing; *Ch'üan T'ang wen* 538/14b, P'ei Tu, of Liu T'ai-chen, Hsiao Ying-shih's pupil and the chief examiner who failed Han Yü, 'He held fast to an impartial mind and set aside the discussion of the multitude. He trod the path of righteousness and blocked up the door to private [favours].'

19 Wechsler (1985), p. x, pp. 103–4, p. 139; McMullen (1987) at notes 42–9.

20 For the canonization system, see *TLT* 2/50b; *TLT* 14/16b; *TT* 104/550.3–552.3; *THY* 79/1455–80/1489; *Feng shih wen chien chi* 4/23-5; *TTKYL* 142/18a-b, containing directives for announcing posthumous office and canonization 'standing at the south-east of the coffin and facing north'; McMullen (1987b), at notes 44–58. The *THY* list of scholars canonized

wen is incomplete. It omits, for example, the names of Liu Chih-chi, *CTS* 102/3174; and of the *chin shih* and father of Chang Yüeh's wife Yüan Huai-ching (or possibly Huai-shen); see *HTS* 58/1457, *Chang Yüeh-chih wen chi* 20/8a–9b and *Ch'ü-chiang Chang hsien-sheng wen chi* 18/3a.

21 Twitchett (1976), pp. 98–197; Pulleyblank (1976), pp. 43–60; Peterson (1979), pp. 464–560.

22 This hyperbole is quoted from a discussion by the official scholar of Te tsung's reign Shen Chi-chi. The passage reads 'To succeed in becoming an official is like ascending [to be] among the immortals; not to be an official is like sinking to the bottom of an abyss (*ch'üan*). The delights and pleasures of the one and the grief and bitterness of the other are as far apart as heaven and earth', see *TT* 18/101.1. For 'mounting the blue sky', see *Ch'üan Tsai-chih wen chi, pu k'o* 4b; cf. *Ch'üan Tsai-chih wen chi* 17/14a, for the same phrase.

23 For the *T'ang liu tien*, des Rotours (1932), pp. 99–102; Yen Keng-wang (1953), pp. 69–76; and des Rotours (1975), pp. 183–201. For some late eighth- and ninth-century references to it, see *THY* 64/1120, in 788; *THY* 18/365, in 806; *Ch'üan Tsai-chih wen chi* 31/3a, wall record dated 800, and 31/5a, wall record dated 807; *CTS* 148/3990, biog. of Pei Chi; *Po Hsiang-shan chi* 6/41/85; *Han Ch'ang-li chi* 7/37/19.

24 For the *T'ung tien* of Tu Yu, see des Rotours (1932), pp. 84-5. For a more critical assessment of this compendium, see Pulleyblank (1960), pp. 98–102. See also below, Ch. 5 at notes 242–9; also McMullen (1987).

25 For the *T'ang hui yao*, see des Rotours (1932), pp. 92–3, and Pulleyblank (1960), p. 98, and below, Ch. 5 at notes 235-41.

26 *CTS* 42–44/1783-1928.

27 *HTS* 46–49B/1181–1322.

28 For rescripts of appointment and their various categories, see *TLT* 9/7a–8b; *Han-lin chih* 2a–b, Bischoff (1963), pp. 46–7; and Tonami (1975), pp. 348–69, esp. pp. 349–55.

29 See principally *WYYH* 797/5a–10a; 799/1b–6b.

30 This central ideal for the T'ang scholar community is often referred to: e.g. in the context of advisory colleges generally, *HTS* 46/1183; and as a principle of government that had been realized in the Han, *WYYH* 741/15b, Niu Hsi-chi; of the Chi-hsien scholars, *TLT* 9/27b; of a group of 13 Chi-hsien scholars appointed in 765, *P'i-ling chi* 4/5b and *TCTC* 223/7172–73, 765.5; of a proposal in 779 for officials to wait in atten- dance, *TCTC* 225/7262, 779.20; of the proposed advisory college of 781, *CTS* 149/4036–37, biog. of Shen Chi-chi; of the Han-lin scholars, *WYYH* 797/9a, Tu Yüan-ying, *Liu Yü-hsi chi* 19/164. It was also used of individual scholars in the offices that involved close attendance on the sovereign or the crown prince; e.g. of the consort Shang-kuan Chao- jung, *WYYH* 700/5b, Chang Yüeh; of Hsü Chien in the Chi-hsien yüan, *Ch'ü-chiang Chang hsien-sheng wen chi* 19/10b; *CTS* 98/3080, of P'ei Yao-ch'ing attending Jui tsung as crown prince; *Po Hsiang-shan chi* 5/31/63, rescript appointing K'ung K'uei a grand counsellor; *WYYH* 918/5b, of Ku Shao-lien.

31 That a succession was recognized in pre-T'ang and T'ang times is indicated by the list in *TLT* 8/41a–b and 9/22a–b. Cf. *CTS* 43/1847, commentary and 43/1851, commentary; also *WYYH* 797/6a–b, wall record for the Han-lin yüan by Wei Ch'u-hou. See also Ikeda (1971), p. 48.

32 The number 18 (*shih pa*), with the addition of *tzu*, 'master', provided a graphic pun on Li, the surname of the T'ang imperial house. For examples of 18, see *TLT* 9/22a; *THY* 64/1117; *CTS* 72/2582, biog. of Ch'u Liang, of the Wen-hsüeh kuan under T'ai tsung. For the Hung-wen kuan under T'ai tsung, see *THY* 57/977; *CTS* 90/2915, biog. of Chu Ching-tse, who refused to be included in a group of 18 in about 704. In the K'ai-yüan period there was also a group of 18; see *HTS* 59/1560. The Chi-hsien scholars were initially 18, a director, deputy director and 16 scholars; see Ikeda (1971), p. 86 and pp. 91–2, quoting *Chi-hsien chu chi* and *Chih kuan fen chi*. 18 poems, including one by Hsüan tsung himself, (with a preface by Chang Chiu-ling) were recorded at a later feast in the Chi-hsien yüan; see below note 36.

33 For the Hung-wen kuan, see *TLT* 8/41a–44b; *THY* 64/1114–17 and 77/1402–03; *TT* 21/124.3; *CTS* 43/1847–48; *HTS* 47/1209–10; des Rotours (1947), pp. 169–73; also the wall record by Ch'üan Te-yü, *Ch'üan Tsai-chih wen chi* 31/4b–6a; Owen (1977), pp. 231–3.

34 For the Ch'ung-wen kuan, see *TLT* 26/22b–23a; *THY* 64/1117–18; *TT* 30/173.2–3; *CTS* 44/1908; *HTS* 49A/1294; des Rotours (1947), pp. 584–5; Guisso (1978), p. 28. Also *Yang Ying-ch'uan chi* 3/8a–9a; *WYYH* 699/5b, Ku Shao-lien.

35 For the K'ung ho fu, see *CTS* 78/2706, biog. of Chang I-chih; *CTS* 190B/5015, biog. of Yüan Pan-ch'ien; Guisso (1978), p. 147. Mention of this institution has been all but eliminated from official documentation by historians hostile to the empress. E.g., *CTS* 173/2591, biog. of Hsüeh Chi, a well known calligrapher and verse writer and a grand secretary, makes no mention of his membership of it. But the *CTCC* epitaph that Hsüeh composed for Wang Te-piao indicates that soon after Wang's death in 699 Hsüeh was a confidential attendant (*nei kung feng*) of the K'ung-ho kuan.

36 For the Chi-hsien yüan, see *TLT* 9/22a–28a; *THY* 64/1118–21 and 77/1402–03; *TT* 21/126.3; *CTS* 43/1851–52; *CTS* 97/3054, biog. of Chang Yüeh; *HTS* 47/1212–13; *TCTC* 212/6764, 725.7. *WYYH* 168/2b–6a records a series of 18 poems, including one by Hsüan tsung himself, composed at a feast in the Chi-hsien yüan probably between 729 and 733, which forms one of the most high-flown tributes to the official scholarly world from the entire dynasty. For the preface to this series, see *WYYH* 709/12b–13b, Chang Chiu-ling. Wei Shu, one of the most important of the official scholars of the K'ai-yüan and T'ien-pao periods, wrote his own account of the Chi-hsien yüan, the *Chi-hsien chu chi*, prefacing it in the 2nd month of 756. Passages of this text survive in the Sung encyclopaedia *Yü hai* by Wang Ying-lin, and in the Sung institutional history *Chih kuan fen chi* by Sun Feng-chi. For these and for an exhaustive collection of primary material relating to all aspects of the Chi-hsien yüan in the first half of the eighth century, see the article by Ikeda On (1971).

37 For the Han-lin yüan, see *THY* 57/977-84; *CTS* 43/1843–54; *HTS* 46/1183–84; also the ninth century wall records for the premises of the Han lin: by Wei Ch'u-hou; Yüan Chen; Ting Chü-hui and Tu Yüan-ying, at *WYYH* 797 6a-10a, and Bischoff (1963). Professor Bischoff provides a translation and annotation of the *Han-lin chih* by Li Chao, composed in 819, in the edition of *Pai ch'uan hsüeh hai*, with note of variants for other editions. It is conspicuous that *TT* has no entry for the Han-lin yüan, though students attached to it are mentioned, at *TT* 15/85.1, double column entry.

38 *CTS* 149/4036–37, biog. of Shen Chi-chi. Cf. *THY* 26/508; *TCTC* 225/7262, 779.20, proposal of Ts'ui Yu-fu.

39 For grand secretaries, see *TLT* 9/13a-16a; *THY* 55/943–48; *TT* 21/125.3; *CTS* 43/1850; *HTS* 47/1211. Some rescripts appointing grand secretaries are at *WYYH* 382/1a–7b. For an important study of the place of grand secretaries in the central government and of promotion patterns involving the post, see Sun Kuo-tung (1980), pp. 37–39, and esp. pp. 41–52.

40 Sun Kuo-tung (1980), p. 45 and n. 52 on p. 74; see also below, Ch. 6 at note 131.

41 For the state academy directorate, see *TLT* 21/1a–18; *THY* 35/633–43; *TT* 27/160.3–62.2; *CTS* 44/1890–92; *HTS* 48/1265–68. Some rescripts of appointment to the directorate are at *WYYH* 400/8a–10b. For a brief description of the premises in the early ninth century, see *WYYH* 816/1b, Shu Yüan-yü. Liu Tsung-yüan, *Liu Ho-tung chi* 26/434–36, has a wall record for the premises of the assistant instructors' office in the Ssu-men hsüeh. Among the best modern accounts of the T'ang education system are Taga Akigorō (1953), summarized in English by P.A. Herbert (1985); Kao Ming-shih (1970). For a clear instance of T'ai hsüeh referring to the directorate, see *CTS* 189B/4978, biog. of Feng K'ang.

42 For the Kuang-wen kuan, see below, Ch. 2 at note 91.

43 *TLT* 2/47a.

44 For the court of sacrifices, see *TLT* 14/1a–66b; *THY* 65/1134–37; *TT* 25/147.2–48.3; *CTS* 44/1872–77; *HTS* 48/1241–47. Some rescripts of appointment to the court are at *WYYH* 396/1a–2b. Tu-ku Chi, *P'i-ling chi* 17/6b–7b, has a wall record for the premises of the vice-presidents of the court. *THY* 65/1137 has an example, dated 858, of the demotion of a president of the court of sacrifices to the presidency of the state academy directorate. Wechsler (1985), in his account of the institutional framework of the T'ang state ritual programme, does not mention the court. For a very brief introduction to the court and its functions, see McMullen (1987a). For the library or records department of the court, see *WYYH* 699/5a, preface to *Wen ssu po yao; CTS* 149/4024, biog. of Chang Chien; *Liu Ho-tung chi* 21/368; *CTS* 157/4154, biog. of Wang Yen-wei.

45 *CTS* 62/2379–80 and *CTS* 194A/5155, Cheng Yüan-shou; *THY* 95/1711, Chang Wen-shou in 650; *CTS* 196B/5245, Wei Lun, promoted president in the course of his embassy.

46 The high prestige of the erudits of the court of sacrifices is suggested by *THY* 65/1136; *TT* 25/148.1; *TLT* 14/16b and *TLT* 2/23a, listing them as *ch'ang ts'an kuan*; also rescripts of appointment to the post, e.g. *WYYH*

400/5a–6a; *Po Hsiang-shan chi* 6/38/35; *Yüan shih Ch'ang-ch'ing chi* 47/3b; *Ch'üan T'ang wen* 725/5b–6a, Ch'en Shang.

47 *TLT* 2/46b.
48 For the canonization system, see the references given above at note 20.
49 For the system of approval for private canonizations, for those whose rank did not qualify them, see *TLT* 14/17a; *TT* 104/551.1; *THY* 80/1488–89, and, for some examples, Ch. 2, at note 158. Perhaps the most celebrated example of the dynasty was Tu Fu, canonized as *Wen hsien-sheng*; see *Yüan shih Ch'ang-ch'ing chi* 56/4b. *Pei shih* 56/2039 provides an example of this practice in the pre-T'ang period.
50 *TT* 15/85.1, double column entry, lists the total no. of acolytes at 862; *TLT* 2/54b. For their examinations (*chien shih*), see *TLT* 4/7a; *CTS* 43/1829. For girl acolytes, see *CTS* 51/2173; *HTS* 13/337; *TCTC* 209/ 6636–37, 709.14. A 42nd generation descendant of Confucius was an acolyte at the end of the T'ang; see *K'ung tzu shih chia p'u* 3/35a. A member of the Yen clan, who claimed descent from Yen Hui, also served as an acolyte; see *Yen Lu kung wen chi* 9/13b. In *Ch'üan Tsai-chih wen chi* 37/9a, Ch'üan Te-yü justifies the system in terms of transmitting merited good fortune (*ch'ing*) from one to the next generation.
51 *TLT* 14/51b–52b; *TT* 25/148.2–3; *CTS* 2/37; *CTS* 44/1876; *HTS* 48/1245. Cf. Ch. 2, note 45.
52 For the history office, see *STTS* 11/1a–17a; *TLT* 9/28a–30a; *THY* 63/1089–64/1114; *THY* 30/553 (for the Ta ming kung); *TT* 21/126.3– 127.1; *CTS* 43/1852–53; *HTS* 47/1214. For its identity as an inner office (*chin shu*), see *Po Hsiang-shan chi* 7/43/17. Some rescripts of appointment to the history office at compiler level are at *WYYH* 400/1a–2b. Li Hua's wall record for the premises of the compilers' office in the bureau of compositions, *WYYH* 799/2b–4b, provides a very brief outline of the early T'ang association between the bureau of compositions and the writing of history, and this is amplified by Hung (1960), pp. 93–107. Cf. the more considered judgement of Twitchett (1985), pp. 20–1, note 44, pp. 23–7, notes 53–7. An association between the bureau of compositions and the history office, nominal after 629, continued into the early eighth century; see *STTS* 11/11a–b and *TT* 26/155.3–56.1, which states, 'Early on, the secretaries of the bureau of compositions had supervised the preparation of the dynastic history and texts like steles, eulogies and so on, and had separately managed the business of the [? history] bureau, and the assistant secretaries had been their deputies. [But now] the bureau [of compositions] simply had the name for compiling histories, being in fact without the responsibility. The responsibility was wholly with the history office.' A continued association between the bureau of compositions and history writing is suggested by the way in which appointment to the post of court diarist or historian compiler and to secretary of the bureau might follow each other or be held concurrently; see e.g. *CTS* 186A/4955, biog. of Liu Chih-hung; *CTS* 94/2996, biog. of Ts'ui Jung; *CTS* 188/4928, biog. of Ts'ui Mien. Cf. also the later remark of Liu Yü-hsi that 'the bureau of compositions is territory where compiling is done, and only [scholars with] historians'

talents should reside there'; *WYYH* 591/5b, adopting the reading *shih*,
historian, for the *li*, official, in *Liu Yü-hsi chi* 12/113.

53 *THY* 63/1102, entry dated 832.

54 For a full account of these two offices see Twitchett (1985), pp. 5–15;
TLT 8/23a–25a; 9/19a–20a; *THY* 56/961–65; *TT* 21/123.3–24.1; *CTS*
43/18/1845; 43/1850–51; *HTS* 47/1208; 47/1212. Some rescripts of
appointment are at *WYYH* 383/1a–3b. See also *CTS* 4/77, and Guisso
(1978), p. 19 and note 89 on p. 214.

55 *TLT* 2/23a; *TT* 15/84.2, double column entry; cf. *Yen Lu kung wen chi*
4/2b, letter to Kuo Ying-i.

56 Li Hua's wall record, *WYYH* 799/3a, emphasized the traditional court
monitory function of the diarists. Kao tsung, in appointing Hsing
Wen-wei as a court diarist (*yu shih*), did so on the grounds of his ability
to admonish; see *CTS* 198B/4960.

57 For the forwarding of information under a range of categories to the
history office from both central and provincial administrations, see
principally *THY* 63/1089–90. Twitchett (1985), pp. 35–6, translates this
important passage. For the function of the bureau of astrology (*t'ai shih
chü*), see *TLT* 10/26a; for the involvement of the bureau of merit
assessments (*k'ao kung ssu*) in verifying reports of conduct (*hsing
chuang*), see *TLT* 2/50b-51a; *THY* 80/1488; and Twitchett (1961), pp.
103–5. For the role of the erudits of the court of sacrifices, see above,
note 46.

58 Solomon (1955); Pulleyblank (1957), pp. 336–44; Dull (1964), pp. 71–9;
Twitchett (1985), pp. 109–19.

59 For the imperial library, see *TLT* 10/1a–35b; *THY* 65/1123–25; *TT*
26/155.1–157.1; *CTS* 43/1854–56; *HTS* 47/1214–17. These accounts
include descriptions of the subordinate agencies, the bureau of compositions (*chu tso chü*) and the bureau of astrology (*t'ai shih chü* or *ssu
t'ien t'ai*). Some rescripts of appointment to the imperial library are at
WYYH 399/1a–3b and 400/6a–8a. See also the wall record for the
secretaries' premises in *Ch'üan Tsai-chih wen chi* 31/2a–3a; and *Yang
Ying-ch'uan chi* 2/7a–8a. For the term *san ko*, referring to the library,
see e.g. *WYYH* 701/5b, Li Hua; for its name *yün ko*, e.g. *CTS* 102/3171,
biog. of Liu Chih-chi; *THY* 36/660; *Yüan Tz'u-shan chi* 3/38; for *yen ko*,
e.g. *TLT* 10/4b; and for its vaguer appellation *nei fu*, e.g. *THY* 36/658,
CTS 102/3178, biog. of Yüan Hsing-ch'ung. For its 'inner department',
and 'outer department', *CTS* 189A/4940 and *SS* 32/908; Twitchett
(1985), pp. 23–7 gives a full discussion.

60 *TT* 26/155.1–2.

61 *TT* 26/155.3.

62 For the prestige, in career terms, of the bureau, in the early T'ang, see
Po K'ung liu t'ieh 74/17b–18a, remark by Hsü Ching-tsung.

63 *TLT* 10/23a–33b; *THY* 42/749–56 *TT* 15/85.2–3, double column entry;
CTS 43/1855-56.

64 *Feng shih wen chien chi* 3/1; *TT* 15/83.2; *THY* 58/1009; *THY* 59/1024–25.

65 *TT* 15/84.1; *TWT* 26A/11b–13b, Shu Yüan-yü; *Feng shih wen chien chi*
3/1–2.

66 For the *chin shih*, see *TLT* 2/20a, 2/52b–53a, 4/4b–5b; *TT* 15/83.1–84.2 gives a general account of the T'ang regular examinations; *CTS* 43/1829; *HTS* 44/1166–69; *Feng shih wen chien chi* 3/1–2; des Rotours (1932), pp. 31–2 and *passim*; Twitchett (1976a), pp. 14–5. Herbert (1986a), provides further background. *Fan-ch'uan wen chi* 12/181, Tu Mu, lists some of the most celebrated *chin shih* ministers of the dynasty.

67 For the *ming ching*, see *TLT* 2/20a, 2/51b–52b, 4/4b–5b; *THY* 75/1373–77; *CTS* 43/1829; *HTS* 44/1161–62; *Feng shih wen chien chi* 3/1–2; des Rotours (1932), pp. 32–3 and *passim*; Twitchett (1976a), pp. 14–5.

68 For the very few extant *ming ching* examination questions, see *Ch'üan Tsai-chih wen chi* 40/5a–7b; 11a–13b; 16a–19a, and below, Ch. 3 at note 131.

69 For the specialist examinations in law, orthography and mathematics, see *TLT* 2/53a, 4-5b–6a; *THY* 76/1399; *HTS* 44/1162; des Rotours (1932), pp. 34–5 and *passim*. Very occasionally, a decree examination might call for those with skill in one of these categories; see e.g. *TTCLC* 102/520–21, decree examination edict of late 710.

70 For decree examinations, see: *Feng shih wen chien chi* 3/11–12; *THY* 76/1386–95; *TT* 15/84.1; des Rotours (1932), pp. 41–2 and *passim*; Twitchett (1976a), p. 14. *Fan-ch'uan wen chi* 12/181, Tu Mu, lists Yao Yüan-ch'ung, Liu Yu-ch'iu and Chang Yüeh as the most meritorious decree examination graduates of the dynasty. *Liu Yü-hsi chi* 19/163 also has a list. The enormous numbers participating in some decree examinations are suggested by, e.g. *Yen Lu kung wen chi* 5/16a; *CTS* 91/2963, biog. of Chang Chien-chih.

71 For the conflict between the relative ease of certain decree examination syllabuses when compared to those of the regular doctoral examinations, see *TFYK* 639/22b-23a, memorial of Yang Ch'ang and Ch. 2, note 87.

72 For the higher doctoral examinations, see des Rotours (1932), pp. 47–8 and n. 1 on pp. 220–21; Twitchett (1976a), p. 15.

73 For selection and promotion examinations, see *TLT* 2/5a–b; *TLT* 2/44a–49a; *THY* 74/1333–47; *THY* 75/1373; *TT* 15/87.2; des Rotours (1976a), pp. 42–55; Twitchett (1976a), pp. 17–8; and Herbert (1986).

74 Ichihara Kōkichi (1963), p. 119; Nunome Chōfū and Ōno Hitoshi (1980), p. 21.

75 Hsü Sung in *TKCK* quotes the *Teng k'o chi*, which enters scholars appointed to office after submitting written works; the first example in the dynasty is in the year 618 (*TKCK* 1/1b); the last in 854 (*TKCK* 22/28a). Perhaps the most celebrated instance in the dynasty was the poet Tu Fu; see *WYYH* 54/3b–4a, *TKCK* 9/30b–31a, and Hung (1952), pp. 67–8; also *WYYH* 610/7b–8b; Hung pp. 79–80. The practice was apparently considerably more common before the rebellion of 755 than after it.

76 T'ang official sources themselves hint at this sort of distinction between technical and non-technical activities. E.g. *TLT* 2/7a, which gives different regulations for the technical posts in the imperial library, the palace department, and the court of imperial accoutrements (*t'ai p'u*

ssu); cf. also *THY* 67/1183, and *TT* 15/85.2–3, double column entry, decree of 697.
77   *TLT* 10/13a–19a.
78   *SS* 33/969–72 and *CTS* 46/2006–09.
79   See *CTS* chs. 102 and 149 for historians; *CTS* ch. 189 for canonical scholars; *CTS* ch. 190 for literary men.
80   See below Ch. 6 at note 178.
81   For accounts of successive official genealogies, see Twitchett (1973) and Johnson (1977), pp. 45–88.
82   For the calendar, see *THY* 42/749–52; *CTS* 32–34/1151–1291; *HTS* 25–30B/533–804; Needham, Vol. III, *passim*.
83   For the criminal code, see Wallace Johnson (1979).
84   For some examples of long tenure in the same or similar scholarly office, see Wang Ching and Wei Kung-su, Ch. 4, notes 200 and 193; Shih Shih-kai, Ch. 2, note 187 and *HTS* 200/5707; Kuei Ch'ung-ching, Ch. 2, note 167 and *TFYK* 561/5b. These career patterns contrast sharply with the very varied careers of certain general service scholar ministers or scholarly general service officials: Chang Yüeh, for example, held 41 posts in the course of his career; see *WYYH* 936/5b, epitaph by Chang Chiu-ling; Mu Ning, 716–94, held 25; see *WYYH* 943/9a. Miao Chin-ch'ing, 24; see *TWT* 68/4b, epitaph by Li Hua; Chou Li-chen, 656–719, a *ming ching* graduate, also 28; see *CTCC* epitaph and cf. *CTS* 186B/4852–53, biog.; Ts'ui Hung-li, 767–831, a *chin shih* graduate also 28; see *CTCC* epitaph and cf. *CTS* 163/4265–66, biog. In this, they were comparable with general service military officials. Hun Chen, 737–800, for example, held 28 posts; see *Ch'üan Tsai-chih wen chi* 13/3b. Official historians, by contrast, often had very long associations with the history office; for the example of Wu Ching, see Ch. 5, note 100; for Wei Shu, Ch. 5, note 106 and Ch. 6, note 74; for K'ung Shu-jui, Ch. 5, note 228; for Chang Chien, who served as an official historian for 'close on 12 years', see *Ch'üan Tsai-chih wen chi* 36/3b; cf. *CTS* 149/4025, which suggests 20 years; for Chiang I, see *CTS* 149/4028. In this, they were helped by the fact that appointments to the history office were concurrent tenures.

2 The school system and the cult of Confucius
1   *Shen chien* 2/13b.
2   *CKCY* 2/18; *TTCLC* 105/537; *TFYK* 50/1b–3a; cf. *CTS* 189A/4939–40.
3   *TFYK* 50/2a.
4   *CKCY* 6/185; *TCTC* 192/6054, 628.17.
5   *CTS* 189A/4952–53, biog. of Hsiao Te-yen. This set phrase, deriving from *Shang shu chu shu* 11/11a, represents an ideal often cited by T'ang writers, for example, *I wen lei chü*, preface p. 27; *CTS* 71/2558, biog. of Wei Cheng; *TCTC* 193/6085, 630.33, Wei Cheng; *THY* 26/503, edict of 720; *Chiu chia chi chu Tu shih* 28/427; *WYYH* 742/2a–3a, Li Su; *CTS* 149/4028, biog. of Chiang I; *Ta T'ang chiao ssu lu* 3/16a, explaining how the Han dynasty had introduced tablets (*hu*), rather than swords for those attending court.

6 *CKCY* 2/18.
7 *SS* 75/1705. For a comprehensive study of Wei Cheng, see Wechsler
   (1974); p. 112 describes Wei Cheng's contribution to the *Sui shu*.
8 *TT* 53/304.2; *THY* 35/635; *CTS* 1/9; *TTCLC* 105/537; *TFYK* 50/1a–b.
   This edict was remembered by the ninth century reformer and scholar
   Liu Yü-hsi; see *Liu Yü-hsi chi* 20/183.
9 For canonical references to the *Shih-tien*, see *Li chi chi shu* 12/2b–3b and
   20/5a–6a. A brief conspectus of the *Shih-tien* before and during the T'ang
   is in *TT* 53/303.3–306.3. The other main sources for this observance in
   the T'ang are *TLT* 4/36b–38a; *Ta T'ang chiao ssu lu* 10/5b–9b; *THY*
   35/640–43; *CTS* 24/916–23; *HTS* 15/372–77. Until the Five Dynasties, the
   Shih-tien was classified as a middle grade ritual; see *TLT* 4/33a; *CTS*
   21/835; *CTS* 24/918; *Ch'üan T'ang wen* 874/1a–2a, Ch'en Chih-yung.
   CTS 189A/4944, biog. of Hsü Wen-yüan, attests a performance in 623.
   Hsü lectured on the *Ch'un-ch'iu* after the observance. For the prefectural and county levels, see *TLT* 4–39b–40a; *Han Ch'ang-li chi* 6/31/58;
   quoted in *Fan-ch'uan wen-chi* 6/106 and *HTS* 164/5058; cf. *Ta T'ang
   chiao ssu lu* 1/16b.
10 *THY* 35/640; *TT* 53/304.2; *TFYK* 50/1b–3a.
11 A *Shih-tien* performance in 625 is suggested by a Buddhist source, *Chi
   ku-chin Fo Tao lun heng* 3/381.1; Lo Hsiang-lin (1954), p. 86, however,
   points out that this is likely to be an error for 624.
12 *T'ang chih yen* 1/5.
13 A performance in 631 is implicit in the *THY* statement that 'from 631,
   T'ai tsung frequently went to the Kuo-tzu hsüeh and T'ai hsüeh...';
   THY 35/633; also, *T'ang chih yen* 1/5.
14 *TFYK* 50/3a–b.
15 *TT* 53/304.2; *THY* 35/640; *CTS* 24/916; *HTS* 15/373; *CTS* 73/2602, biog.
   of K'ung Ying-ta. This performance is also attested by the *CTCC*
   epitaph for Wang Te-piao, d. 698, aged 80 *sui*.
16 *CTS* 73/2602, biog. of K'ung Ying-ta. The practice of lectures on the
   Confucian canons preceded the T'ang; see *I wen lei chü* 55/986–90, citing
   Analects 7/3 as a sanction.
17 In *Shang shu chu shu*, preface 1a, K'ung Ying-ta called Confucius, 'my
   forebear born at the end of the Chou', a phrase that he took from the
   preface ascribed to K'ung An-kuo, *Shang shu chu shu* 1/4b. In *Mao shih
   chu shu*, preface 1a, he again called Confucius his forebear. The original
   'Confucius of Kuan-hsi' had been Yang Chen; see *Hou Han shu* 54/1759;
   also *CTCC* epitaph for Yang Ssu-li, d. 876, who claimed descent from
   him; also *Kuo shih pu* 1/21.Yü Chih-ning, in the stele for K'ung's tomb
   at T'ai tsung's mausoleum at Chao-ling applied the title to K'ung; see Lo
   Chen-yü (1909) 1/17a. T'ai tsung mentioned the title to another official,
   Hsiao Te-yen; see *CTS* 189A/4953; cf. *CTS* 24/922, edict by T'ai tsung.
   In verse and less formal writing, T'ang scholars sometimes referred to
   the remote provenance of members of the K'ung clan; see *Huang-fu Jan
   shih chi* 3/19a; *Han Ch'ang-li chi* 6/33/79; *Chin shih ts'ui pien* 117/20b.
   Cf. also *TCTC* 228/7351, 783.22, referring to K'ung Ch'ao-fu as a 37th
   generation descendant of Confucius. Much material relating to the

K'ung clan is collected in K'ung Shang-jen comp., *K'ung tzu shih chia p'u*, see 3/26a–35b, for the 32nd to 42nd generations, spanning the T'ang period.

18 *CTS* 1/59; *TFYK* 260/19a–b; *THY* 35/640 dates this to 646.
19 *CTS* 199A/5335–36; cf. *CTS* 1/62.
20 For the pre-T'ang background to the three-teachings debates, see Lo Hsiang-lin (1954), p. 85 and note 5 on p. 96. For the debate of 624, see note 9 above and *CTS* 189A/4945, biog. of Lu Te-ming.
21 For the debate of 638 in the Hung-wen kuan, see *Chi ku-chin Fo Tao lung heng* 3/383.1; Lo Hsiang-lin (1954), pp. 87–8.
22 *CKCY* 7/212–13; *TFYK* 604/1a–b; Hayashi (1916), p. 137. The distinction between a sage (*sheng*) and a worthy man (*hsien*) was a precise one, made in classificatory schemes, for example that of the *I wen lei chü* 20/358–62 and 20/362–65.
23 *THY* 35/636–37, memorial by Chang-sun Wu-chi and Hsü Ching-tsung, dated 657, referring to 'the text of the Yung-hui statute'; *WYYH* 764/1a–3a; *CTS* 24/918; *TFYK* 604/2b–3b.
24 *Chou i chu shu* 1/3b; *TWT* 84/400, Liu Mien; *Ch'üan Tsai-chih wen chi* 14/3a–b; *Han Ch'ang-li chi* 3/11/63; *WYYH* 742/10a, Niu Hsi-chi.
25 *I wen lei chü* 20/362–65, entry for *hsien*, much of which refers to Yen Hui.
26 *Kuang hung ming chi* 8/17a; *Wan shan t'ung kuei lu*, by Chih-chüeh Ch'an shih, preface by Shen Chen dated 1072, 3/988a. I am grateful to Professor Glen Dudbridge for this reference.
27 *Pei shih* 3/88; *Feng shih wen chien chi* 1/7. Cf. Shyrock, (1932), p. 120 and note 34 on p. 128. In 774, prayers were offered in the Confucian temple; but this is recorded as an irregularity; see *TCTC* 225/7227, 774.15.
28 *TFYK* 50/15a.
29 Waley (1960), pp. 89–96.
30 *Mencius* 2A/2; this phrase was alluded to or adapted in an edict of 627, 12th month, *Chin shih ts'ui pien* 55/11b; in a commemorative inscription of 666, *Chin shih ts'ui pien* 55/12a; by Chang-sun Wu-chi and Hsü Ching-tsung in their memorial on the Confucian temple; see above note 23 and *WYYH* 764/2b; in an edict expanding the iconography of the Confucian temple in 739, *TFYK* 50/8a, *CTS* 24/290. The same phrase is quoted later in the dynasty, in a memorial of 788 by Li Hsü, attempting to prove the superiority of Confucius over his counterpart in the military cult, *THY* 23/437 and *Ta T'ang chiao ssu lu* 10/12b–13a; by Li Ao, *Li wen kung chi* 8/56b; by Tu Mu, *Fan-ch'uan wen chi* 6/106, quoting Han Yü.
31 *WYYH* 509/2b–3b, for the question and two answers extant. Both answers cite the precedent of Liu K'un, from whose biography the language of the question is drawn. Liu K'un taught 500 disciples and observed his own version of Confucian rituals. He came under suspicion from Wang Mang for intention to usurp; see *Hou Han shu* 79A/2550. The relation of this *p'an* to T'ang practice is a question for further research.
32 *THY* 35/640–41; *TFYK* 604/1b–2b. Liu Yü-hsi, *Liu Yü-hsi chi* 20/183,

refers to the memorial by Hsü Ching-tsung that brought about this change, but dates it to 646; *CTS* 4/917–18; *HTS* 15/374.

33 For the pre-T'ang origins of the practice of honouring the descendants of Confucius, see Shyrock (1932), p. 98. For the edict of 626, see *Chin shih ts'ui pien* 55/11b. The edict was referred to in an inscription for the Confucian temple by Yü Shih-nan, *Chin shih ts'ui pien* 41/19a. *TFYK* 50/3a dates this to 636; but Hsü Sung in *TKCK* 1/7a argues that the epigraphical evidence is to be accepted. *TFYK* 50/4b–15b enters subsequent ennoblements of K'ung descendants under the T'ang. There is also a summary account of the practice in *TT* 53/305.3.1. As marquis Pao-sheng, the descendant of Confucius, at least on the authority of the K'ai-yüan code of 732, was allocated a special place in certain state rituals; see e.g. *TTKYL* 18/2b.

34 *CKCY* 7/214; *CTS* 3/51; *CTS* 189A/4941–42.

35 *CKCY* 7/214; *TT* 53/304.2; *THY* 35/636; *CTS* 3/59, 24/917; 189A/4942; *TFYK* 50/3b, 604/1b. This measure was referred to by Chang-sun Wu-chi and Hsü Ching-tsung in 657; see *THY* 35/636. See also the comment of Hsü Ching-tsung, *THY* 35/639.

36 *CTS* 189A/4940; *HTS* 44/1163; *TCTC* 185/5792, 618.28. The total quota was initially 342. Hsü Sung, *TKCK* 1/1a, believed that a quota of students may have been determined even before Kao tsu ascended the throne. See also Kao Ming-shih (1970), p. 3. In the Sui, up to 601, the state academy court (*kuo-tzu ssu*) had been under the court of sacrifices. From 601 to 607, it was an independent court, and in 607, it was reclassified as a directorate (*chien*). The T'ang at first placed the state academy under the court of sacrifices, but in 627 or 628 made it an independent directorate. *TT* 27/161.2; *THY* 66/1157; *CTS* 44/1890–91; *HTS* 48/1265–66. *CTS* 149/4017, biog. of Kuei Ch'ung-ching, suggests a date of 617 for the reclassification of the *kuo-tzu ssu* as a directorate under the Sui.

37 *THY* 66/1163; *TLT* 21/51a–16a.

38 *CTS* 3/42; *TLT* 21/14a–17a.

39 *THY* 66/1163; *TLT* 21/16a–17a.

40 *CTS* 44/1891.

41 *CKCY*, ed. of Shanghai: Ku-chi Ch'u-pan-she, 1978, 7/215–16, is in error in including the Kuang-wen kuan in this expansion; the ed. prepared by Harada Tanishige, 7/213, notes the Kuang-wen kuan as a variant. For the Kuang-wen kuan, see below at note 91. *THY* 35/633 gives the figure 3,260; *CTS* 189A/4941; *T'ang chih yen* 1/56. Later in the dynasty, Li Kuan gave the round number of 3,000, with reference to the early part of the dynasty; see *TWT* 26A/7a. *HTS* 198/5636 says 3,200. *TT* 15/85.1 says 2,610.

42 *CKCY* 7/213; *CTS* 189A/4941; *HTS* 198/5636. Examples of teachers with large followings in the pre-T'ang period are Li Hsüan, biog. in *P'ei shih* 81/2726; Pao Chi-hsiang, biog. in *Pei shih* 81/2728; Ma Ching-te, *Pei shih* 81/2730; Fang Hui-yüan, *Sui shu* 75/1716; and Pao K'ai, *Sui shu* 75/1716. In the early T'ang, Ma Chia-yün had had a large following and was given an official post; see *TFYK* 768/12a–b. So were Ch'in Ching-t'ung, *CTS*

189A/4955–56 and *TFYK* 768/15a–b, and Wang Kung, *CTS* 72/2603. See also Kao Ming-shih (1971), pp. 213, 219–20.

43 *CTS* 189A/4940.

44 *TWT* 26A/8a, memorial by Li Kuan.

45 *CTS* 2/37; cf. *CTS* 44/ 1876.

46 For Wen weng, see *Han shu* 89/5181–83, and commentary by Yen Shih-ku, noting that his school hall was still in existence within the city wall at I-chou. Wen weng was cited, for example, in the early T'ang in *Sui shu* 73/1673; in the late seventh century in the *CTCC* epitaph for Wang Chieh, d. 711, whose father Wang Shan-hui had been a successful administrator in the southwest; in *WYYH* 885/1a, by Wang Po, in an inscription for the Confucian temple at I-chou in modern Szechuan; Ts'en Shen, *Ts'en Chia-chou shih* 1/27a, and Tu Fu, *Chiu chia chi chu Tu shih* 60/249, both mentioned him. Later in the dynasty, he was referred to, for example, by Liang Su, *WYYH* 972/12b; by Lü Wen, *Lü Ho-shu wen chi* 9/8a; by Liu Tsung-yüan, *Liu Ho-tung chi* 5/76.

47 Tun-huang Wen-wu Yen-chiu-so (1978), pp. 43–4; confirmed by the author's own observation, Feb. 1981. *Feng shih wen chien chi* 1/7 suggests that local teaching posts had low status.

48 *CTS* 187A/4874, biog. of Wang I-fang.

49 *CTS* 3/48; *HTS* 15/373. For comment on Confucius's tomb, see K'ung Ying-ta's gloss at *Li chi chu shu* 8/9b–10a. The passage includes the observation that the tomb did not accord with ancient rules for burial and had probably been added to in later times.

50 *TT* 15/85.1 says 60,710 for the provincial system; *HTS* 44/1180 gives the total number as 63,070.

51 *T'ang lü shu i* 23/510; Kao Ming-shih (1971), pp. 220–1.

52 *T'ang chih yen* 1/1; *TKCK* 1/2b.

53 *T'ang chih yen* 1/1; *TKCK* 1/3b.

54 *TFYK* 67/20a–b; *TTCLC* 102/518; *TKCK* 1/3a–b and comment by Hsü Sung.

55 *Liang shu* 48/661–62; *Sui shu* 75/1706.

56 *CTS* 189/4941; *THY* 35/633; also *CKCY* 7/213, which puts the number at 'little short of 10,000' at the directorate itself.

57 *THY* 35/633; *CTS* 189/4941; *HTS* 198/5636.

58 *TFYK* 50/3b–4a.

59 *TT* 27/161.2, double column entry; *THY* 66/1157; *CTS* 4/82, and 24/918.

60 *THY* 66/1163; *CTS* 24/918; *HTS* 48/1268.

61 *TT* 27/161.2; *CTS* 44/1890–91, commentary; *HTS* 48/1266.

62 *CTCC* epitaph for Ts'ui Shao, a student at the T'ai hsüeh from 669, and later a *ming ching* graduate. He died aged only 25 *sui*, and was likened to Yen Hui on that account; *Ta T'ang hsin yü* 11/169.

63 *TTCLC* 105/537–38.

64 For example, *TFYK* 50/7b, drought of 734; *TFYK* 50/12a, great heat in 755; in 804, *Ch'üan Tsai-chih wen chi* 23/8a–b; *Han Ch'ang-li chi* 7/37/17–18 and commentary and *THY* 76/1385; in 834, *CTS* 17B/554.

65 *TFYK* 50/4b, referred to by Wang Po, in his text for the Hsin-tu Confucian temple; see *Wang Tzu-an chi* 13/6b–7a.

66 For the school and temple at Hsin-tu and at Chiu-lung county, I-chou, modern Szechuan, see *Wang Tzu-an chi* 13/1a and *Yang Ying-ch'uan chi* 4/1a. For that at Ch'ang-chiang county, Sui-chou, Szechuan, see *Yang Ying-ch'uan chi* 4/8b. The text by Wang Po for Chiu-lung county was commended by Yang Chiung; see *Yang Ying-ch'uan chi* 3/2b. Later in the dynasty, Sun Ch'iao referred to it; see *TWT* 84/10b.

67 For the temple at T'an-chou, modern Hopei, which had, here recorded for the first time in the dynasty, drawings and written eulogies for the 72 disciples of Confucius, see *CTS* 185A/4795–96, and *HTS* 100/3944, biog. of Wei Hung-chi [Wei Chi].

68 *CTS* 185A/4792, biog. of Kao Chih-chou.

69 *CTS* 189A/4942. This simile for an imperceptible trend occurs in *Han shu* 56/2517. The contemporary scholar official Ti Jen-chieh used the term *wen li*, pejoratively, of the chief ministers and literary scholars Li Ch'iao and Su Wei-tao; see *CTS* 89/2894. A different construction was put on the events of Kao tsung's reign by Lu Chao-lin, *c.* 641–*c.* 680, the contemporary and friend of Wang Po and Yang Chiung. Lu Chao-lin saw Kao tsung's court as concerned with *li*, officials, while he himself was concerned with *ju* and *Mo*, and the empress Wu's court as concerned with laws, *fa* (cf. *CTS* 50/2143), while he himself was concerned with the philosophy of classical Taoism; see *Yu yu tzu chi* 5/3a. Cf. also *CTS* 88/2866, biog. of Wei Ssu-li.

70 See *T'ang chih yen* 1/112, and below, Ch. 6 at notes 133–6, for this development.

71 The increase in prestige of the *chin shih* is particularly well characterized by the scholar of Te tsung's reign Shen Chi-chi; see *TT* 15/84a and *WYYH* 759/1a.

72 *Ch'en Tzu-ang chi* 9/213.

73 The 693 memorial, by Hsüeh Teng (Ch'ien-kuang), was premised on the ineffectiveness of the school system, as its preamble in *TT* indicates; see *TT* 17/94.3, *WYYH* 696/5a, *TWT* 28/3b.

74 *CTS* 88/2866, biog. of Wei Ssu-li; *TWT* 28/2b. For this memorial, see also Guisso (1978), pp. 149–50, who notes that Wei was made rector of the university. *TCTC* 206/6542–43, 699.26 states that students from the Hung-wen kuan and the Kuo-tzu hsüeh were able to act as acolytes in great state ceremonies, and so find a route into the bureaucracy. Cf. *Han Ch'ang-li chi* 4/14/28–29. For disparaging remarks on state education at about this time, see *Wang Tzu-an chi* 7/16a–b; *THY* 66/1157.

75 *TT* 200/1085.3.

76 *Yüan-ho hsing tsuan* 6/2b and *HTS* 198/5644–45, biog. of K'ung Ying-ta. The son, K'ung Chih-yüan, was brother of K'ung Chih-yüeh, who worked on the Hsien-ch'ing ritual code; see below, Ch. 4 at note 83. The grandson's given name was Hui-yüan or Yüan-hui. For some examples of T'ang emphasis on the transmission of scholarly traditions within families, see Kao Ming-shih (1971), pp. 245–8 and 251–3. K'ung Ying-ta, K'ung Chih-yüan and K'ung Hui-yüan were all buried at Chao-ling, T'ai tsung's mausoleum; see *THY* 21/413.

77 *TCTC* 204/6476, 691.30; *HTS* 115/4209, biog. of Ti Jen-chieh.

78 For the reform edict of 706, see 35/635. For the appointment of Yeh

Ching-neng to the directorate, see *THY* 67/1182; *CTS* 91/2930, biog. of Huan Yen-fan; *CTS* 51/2174, biog. of Shang-kuan Chao-jung. *TCTC* 208/6589, 705.18. Huan Yen-fan compared the magician unfavourably to K'ung Ying-ta. *TCTC* 208/6598, 706.7 states that a Taoist priest was appointed president of the state academy directorate in a supernumerary capacity. There are also indications that appointment to the senior posts in the directorate meant removal from the main political arena provided by the three ministeries. See *CTS* 190B/5009–10, biog. of Kuo Cheng-i; *HTS* 115/4220, biog. of the official scholar Chu Ching-tse; cf. *CTS* 90/2915; *CTS* 7/145, of Yü Wei-ch'ien. *CTS* 6/132, referring to Li Ch'iao, gives an example of the opposite.

79 *CTS* 185B/4813–14; *HTS* 130/4493, biogs. of Yang Ch'iao. The rescript appointing Yang to the directorate, by Su T'ing, is at *WYYH* 400/18a.

80 *TFYK* 260/19b–20a, 25b. Cf. *WYYH* 652/2a, Chang Yüeh; Chang was reader in attendance on Hsüan tsung as crown prince, sharing his duty with Ch'u Wu-liang, later a vice-president of the state academy directorate; *CTS* 97/3051, biog. of Chang Yüeh, and *CTS* 102/3166, biog. of Ch'u Wu-liang.

81 *TFYK* 50/5a–b.

82 *TFYK* 50/6a–b; *T'ang chih yen* 1/10.

83 *T'ang chih yen* 1/6, double column entry.

84 *TTCLC* 73/407–08; *CTS* 9/209; *TCTC* 214/6832, 738.4; *TFYK* 85/27b–28a.

85 E.g. Yüan Hsing-ch'ung, biog. in *CTS* 102/3177 and Hsü Chien, epitaph by Chang Chiu-ling, *Ch'ü-chiang Chang hsien-sheng wen chi* 19/7b.

86 For members of the Chi-hsien yüan whose basic offices were in the directorate, see Ikeda (1971), p. 92, quoting *Chi-hsien chu chi*.

87 *TFYK* 639/22b–23a; *THY* 75/1376; *HTS* 130/4496, memorial by Yang Ch'ang.

88 *Feng shih wen chien chi* 3/1.

89 *Feng shih wen chien chi* 5/11. A sycophantic commemorative stone, set up by the students, met with a tough response from Li Lin-fu. In a panic, they erased the inscription and moved the stone by night. *CTS* 123/3518 makes the Pan Ching-ch'ien mentioned here a director of the imperial library; but a tenure in the state academy directorate is confirmed by *Ta T'ang chiao ssu lu* 8/12b and *HTS* 149/4802. For another example of students setting up a stele for a president of the directorate, after reforms to the curricula in 728, see *CTS* 185B/4820, biog. of Yang Ch'ang. A commemorative stone was also erected for a popular teacher at the Lo-yang directorate in Hsüan tsung's reign; see *CTS* 189B/4975, biog. of Yin Chih-chang.

90 *TFYK* 50/10b–11a.

91 For the Kuang-wen kuan, see *TT* 27/161.2; *THY* 66/1163; *Kuo shih pu* 2/35, giving a date of 746; *CTS* 24/921 and 44/1892; *HTS* 48/1267 and 202/5766, biog. of Cheng Ch'ien; also *Kuo shih pu* 3/53. Appointments to the Kuang-wen kuan were made well into the ninth century; see *CTS* 24/932, giving a date of 842; also *CTCC* epitaph for Lu Chiu, d. 851, aged 58 *sui*.

92 *TLT* 21/2a–3a.

93 *WYYH* 678/5a, Hsiao Ying-shih.

94 *TT* 20/114.2, double column entry; *THY* 35/637; *CTS* 24/918; *CTS* 86/2829; *CTS* 5/90; *TFYK* 50/4a. A text was composed by Ts'ui Hsing-kung, d. 674; see *Chin shih ts'ui pien* 55/5a and *Shih-mo chien hua* 3/41. For an incident on this occasion, see *Ta T'ang hsin yü* 8/133.

95 *THY* 35/637; *CTS* 24/918; *TFYK* 50/4a.

96 *TT* 53/304.2 records a *Shih-tien* attended by the crown prince both in the second year of Yung-lung, second month and the first year of K'ai-yao, second month. *THY* 35/641 does the same. *CTS* 5/107, has only Yung-lung 2. Since the K'ai-yao period started only in the 9th month of 681, and its first year therefore ended three months later, these references are likely to be to one and the same performance.

97 *THY* 35/637; *CTS* 24/918.

98 *Chang Yüeh-chih wen-chi* 21/13b.

99 *TFYK* 50/4b.

100 *CTS* 7/158; *CTS* 24/919; *TFYK* 50/5a.

101 For warnings against Buddhism and Taoism or their clerics, over this period before Hsüan tsung's reign, see *CTS* 89/2893, biog. of Ti Jen-chieh (cf. *THY* 30/552–53); *TCTC* 208/6589, 705.18 and *CTS* 91/2929, biog. of Huan Yen-fan; *CTS* 88/2870, memorial of Wei Ssu-li; *TT* 21/124.1–124.2, memorial of Hsin T'i-p'i; *THY* 47/836–37, memorial of Yao Ch'ung.

102 *TTCLC* 29/108; *TFYK* 260/19b; *CTS* 7/158; *CTS* 24/919.

103 See below at note 104.

104 *WYYH* 706/5a; *TWT* 40/6a; *THY* 35/641–42; *CTS* 102/3171–73, biog. of Liu Chih-chi; Fu Chen-lun (1963), pp. 122–3. A summary of this memorial is also in *TT* 53/304.2. *TT* was based on the *Cheng tien* by Liu Chih-chi's son Liu Chih, and it is possible that this memorial by his father was part of Liu Chih's original compilation.

105 *TFYK* 50/50a; *THY* 35/637; *CTS* 7/158; *TFYK* 260/19b–20a.

106 For the measure of 717, see *TTCLC* 105/538; *TFYK* 50/6a–b. For 719, see *THY* 35/642.

107 *CTS* 24/919.

108 *TTCLC* 29/108; *THY* 35/642; *CTS* 8/180; *CTS* 24/919; *CTS* 107/3258, biog. of Li Ssu-ch'ien, d. after 737; *TFYK* 260/20b; (This ritual had, however, been performed before; see *TFYK* 257/9b, and cf. *CTS* 102/3173, memorial of Liu Chih-chi). Des Rotours (1947), p. 443, n. (3), notes that he is unable to find a reference to the *Ch'ih-chou* in the K'ai-yüan ritual code. This may have been because it was simply a variant of the *Shih-tien* itself. Cf. the remark implying this by the post-rebellion ritual scholar Kuei Ch'ung-ching, *THY* 4/45–46. For later indications of the value that Confucian-orientated advisors put on the *Ch'ih-chou*, see e.g. *TWT* 27/5b, memorial of Li Chiang; *WYYH* 721/13b, essay by Niu Hsi-chi; *CTS* 166/4330, memorial by Yüan Chen. For canonical sanction for this observance, see *Li chi chu shu* 20/9a–b. *THY* 26/496–97 describes another set of rituals the purpose of which was to

train the crown prince. That the crown prince's education was a vehicle for the ideals and political ambitions of the scholar community is also suggested by *CKCY* 4/101–02; *CKCY* 4/104–8; *CKCY* 10/102–3; *TFYK* 260/25a–b; *THY* 4/47; *CTS* 75/2641–2, biog. of Chang Ta-su; *CTS* 166/4327–31, biog. of Yüan Chen.

109 *TT* 53/304.3 states county level; *THY* 35/642 says prefectural. *Liu Yü-hsi chi* 20/919 has prefectures only.
110 *CTS* 24/919; *Sui T'ang chia hua* 2/29.
111 *Liu Yü-hsi chi* 20/184.
112 *TTCLC* 128/689.
113 *TT* 53/304.3.
114 *TT* 53/304.3; *TFYK* 50/10b.
115 *TT* 53/304.3; *THY* 35/642.
116 *Analects* 11/3. For Wen weng, see note 46 above; *CTS* 24/919–20; *THY* 35/639. The reason for Hsüan tsung's choice of Yen Hui for his eulogy rather than Confucius was probably that his father Jui tsung had composed for Confucius, and filial piety required Hsüan tsung to undertake a lesser role. At about this time there was a request that both texts be engraved, and that the model of the metropolitan temple be followed throughout the empire; see *Ch'üan T'ang wen* 405/12a. *CTS* 46/2003 enters a work entitled *I-chou Wen weng hsüeh t'ang t'u (Picture of the school of Wen weng at I-chou)* in one *chüan* that, since it was present in the imperial collection by 721, (see Ch. 6, notes 71–5), may have played a role in this expansion.
117 *THY* 35/638. *THY* 25/638, final column, edict of 705, indicates that Confucius had officially been given the south facing position before.
118 *THY* 35/637–38; *CTS* 9/211; *CTS* 24/920–21. This expansion was admired later in the dynasty; see *P'i tzu wen sou* 9/93–95.
119 *TFYK* 50/6a.
120 Repair of the temple at Ch'ü-fu was commemorated by a text composed by Li Yung; see *WYYH* 846/1a; *TWT* 51/4b. Ku Yen-wu, in *Chin shih wen tzu chi* 3/20b, dates this 719.
121 For a three-teachings debate in which 100 represented each side, see Lo Hsiang-lin, p. 90; for another debate, omitted by Lo, held in 728, *HTS* 139/4631–32, biog. of Li Mi. For the syncretic approach that was in favour towards the end of the reign, *TFYK* 37/17a–b, debate of 735 and memorial of Chang Chiu-ling.
122 *Pa chiung shih chin shih pu cheng* 50/23a–30a; *Wei shu* 79/1758; *CTS* 185B/4816, biog. of Chiang Shih-tu.
123 *CTS* 185B/4811, biog. of Ni Jo-shui.
124 *Yen Lu kung wen chi* 22/6a, text by Ch'eng Hao with date of 4th month of 755. The editor Huang Pen-chi (*chü jen* 1821), however, expresses doubt about the authenticity of this.
125 *CTS* 8/189; *TFYK* 50/7b; *TCTC* 212/6767, 725.14. See also below, Ch. 4, notes 73–79.
126 *CTS* 24/926; *TFYK* 50/11a; *WYYH* 847/1a; *TWT* 22/1a, Chia Chih.
127 *THY* 22/430–32. The mother of Mencius was frequently cited in epitaphs for women; e.g. *CTCC* for a sister of Tu-ku Chi, who died aged 52 or 53

sui in 776 or 777; *KFSPWC* epitaph for a wife surnamed Lei, who died in 804 aged 94 *sui*.

128 *CKCY* 4/128, memorial by Yü Chih-ning; *Wang Tzu-an chi* 7/12a; *Huang-fu Ch'ih-cheng wen chi* 4/7b–8a; *Shih chi* 32/1477–80. T'ao Hsi-sheng (1972c), pp. 231A–232B gives some account of the T'ang cult of T'ai kung. For a general account of the T'ai kung cult, see McMullen (1987b).

129 Works attributed to T'ai kung in the T'ang included *T'ai kung chia chiao (Family instruction of T'ai kung)*, for which see the edition collated and annotated from Tun-huang MSS by Iriya Yoshitaka (1960), pp. 31–60; *T'ai kung liu t'ao (Six weapons cases of T'ai kung)*, quoted in *I wen lei chü* 71/1230, 84/1439 etc.; *T'ai kung ping fa (Military models of T'ai kung)*, also quoted in *I wen lei chü*, 60/1082, 1088, 1090 etc. For the former, see *CTS* 47/2039; *HTS* 59/1549; *Ho chih* p. 240; and three other works entered in the *T'ang shu* bibliographies, *T'ai kung yin mou (Secret strategies of T'ai kung)* and *T'ai kung chin kuei (Metal box of T'ai kung)*, for both of which see *CTS* 47/2039; *HTS* 59/1549; *Ho chih*, p. 240; and *Chi chu yin-fu ching (Collected commentaries to the canon of secret tallies)*, for which see *HTS* 59/1520 and *Ho chih* p. 191. The *Shih chi* commentator and compiler of the *Shih chi cheng i* of 736, Chang Shou-chieh, even attributed the creation of the canonization system jointly to the duke of Chou and T'ai kung; see *Shih chi*, appended material by Chang Shou-chieh, p. 18. But cf. the claim of Li Hsü in 788 that T'ai kung was responsible for one work only, the *Liu t'ao*, *Ta T'ang chiao ssu lu* 10/13a and *HTS* 15/379, and the slighting opinion of the *T'ai kung chia chiao* held by Li Ao, *Li Wen kung chi* 6/42a.

130 *TKCK* 5/3b–4a; *TKCK* 5/17b.

131 *Feng shih wen chien chi* 4/30. For an example of the Ts'ui clan of Ch'ing-ho claiming descent from T'ai kung, see *CTCC* epitaph for Ts'ui Ch'ien-li, d. 796, aged 62 *sui*. For the Po-ling Ts'ui clan, see *Yen Lu kung wen chi* 5/15b and Ebrey (1978), p. 34. For the Lu clan of Fan-yang, *CTCC* epitaph for Lu Ming-yüan, d. 746, aged 58 *sui*. For the Kao clan of Po-hai, see *WYYH* 892/6b, spirit path stele for Kao Ch'ung-wen, 746–809, canonized *Wei-wu*.

132 This may be inferred from the existence of the Tun-huang MSS referred to in note 129 and from Li Ao's remark.

133 *CTS* 24/910; *WYYH* 764/1a, memorial by Chang-sun Wu-chi. Cf. *Ta T'ang chiao ssu lu* 10/14a and *HTS* 15/379, memorial of Yen Yüeh, stating that a temple for T'ai kung had been set up at P'an-ch'i in the Chen-kuan period, confirmed by Wang Ching himself, *Ta T'ang chiao ssu lu* 10/9b. The prominent Ch'un-ch'iu scholar Lu Ch'un, criticising the cult in 788, proposed that it be restricted to the local operation at P'an-ch'i; see *Ta T'ang chiao ssu lu* 10/14b–16b.

134 *CTS* 24/910; *CTS* 24/915; also *TTKYL* 50/7a, giving a prayer text for T'ai kung as a correlative.

135 *WYYH* 605/5a, memorial of Ts'ui Jung; cf. Fu Chen-lun (1963), referring to his memorial. This measure may have coincided with the empress Wu's initiative of 699 to hold military rehearsals (*chiang wu*), which was

delayed by the officials; see *CTS* 89/2900, biog. of Wang Fang-ch'ing and
THY 26/502–3. For Chang Liang, see *Shih chi* 55/2033–49, esp. p. 2048,
where Chang Shou-chieh quotes the *K'uo ti chih* of 642 identifying the
site of his tomb. At least two military texts were associated with Chang
Liang; see *CTS* 47/2039–40 and *HTS* 59/1549–50, *Ho chih*, p. 241, and
cf. *SKCSTMTY* pp. 2038–9. For a claim of descent from Chang Liang,
see *KFSPWK* epitaph for the recluse Yang Wu-sheng, 734–98, whose wife
was of the Chang clan of Nan-yang.

136 *THY* 65/1134; *HTS* 15/1246–7, commentary.

137 *THY* 23/435; *Ta T'ang chiao ssu lu* 2/12b; 10/9b; *TT* 53/306.3; *CTS*
24/935; *HTS* 15/377; *TCTC* 213/6795, 731.5; *TCTC* 221/7091, 760.3,
commentary of Hu San-hsing. It is possible that the 10 listed by Hu in
the context of the redrafting of the temple arrangement in 760 were in
fact the original ones honoured in 731, or else the cult may have been
expanded to include a larger number of generals than ten. At least the
760 list as the sources give it is either inaccurate or incomplete. An
independent contemporary source states that one of the generals selected in 760 was the T'ang commander Kuo Chih-yün, whose biogs. are at
CTS 103/3189 and *HTS* 133/3544; see *P'i-ling chi* 6/5b–6a, canonization
discussion. Indication that in 731 ten generals, not merely Chang Liang,
were included in the cult is given in *THY* 23/435–6; *HTS* 15/377; *TT*
53/306.3 and the directives for the *Shih-tien* to T'ai kung in *TTKYL* 55.
Other sources, however, *TTKYL* 88/4a–b, *Ta T'ang chiao ssu lu* 10/9b,
and *Sui T'ang chia hua* p. 29, mention only offering to T'ai kung and
Chang Liang in 731, and therefore suggest that the cult did not include
ten generals at this stage.

138 *TT* 53/306.3; *THY* 23/435. For the start of the military examinations, see
TT 15/83.2; *CTS* 24/935; Guisso (1976), p. 102.

139 The date of 747 is supplied by *TT* 15/83.2, *TFYK* 33/19b and by *Ta T'ang
chiao ssu lu* 10/9b, and adopted by *CTS* 24/935.

140 For the appointment to the military temple in the T'ien-pao period, see
Feng shih wen chien chi 10/12. Cf. also *TT* 25/148.3.

141 *Feng shih wen chieh chi* 4/30. Feng was a student of the state academy
directorate at about this time; see *Feng shih wen chien chi* 2/19.

142 *Ta T'ang hsin yü* 3/73, of Li Hsi-yü; 7/115–6 and *CTS* 89/2899 and 2901,
biog. of Wang Fang-ch'ing; *CTS* 102/3182, biog. of Wu Ching; *CTS*
102/3184, biog. of Wei Shu.

143 *Yüan Tz'u-shan chi* 5/74; cf. *TT* 15/84.1, double column entry, and
WYYH 759/1a–2a, Shen Chi-chi; *TT* 18/104.1, Tu Yu.

144 *TT* 17/96.2, memorial by Liu Chih; Herbert (1986a), pp. 95–8.

145 *CTS* 102/3185, biog. of Wei Shu; *WYYH* 678/7a–b, Hsiao Ying-shih; cf.
CTS 111/3321, biog. of Fang Kuan; *Yen Lu kung wen chi* 9/1b, spirit
path stele for Kuo K'uei, 727–50.

146 Li Lin-fu's particular dislike of literary scholars is indicated at *TCTC*
215/6853, 742.2; his accession to power, contempt for the mere
'book-man' Chang Chiu-ling and blocking of channels for admonition, at
TCTC 14/6822–5, 736.16. He was indirectly responsible for the beating
to death of the celebrated writer Li Yung (*CTS* 190B/5043 and *TCTC*

215/6874, 746.13–747.1). See also Pulleyblank (1955), pp. 86–92 and
Hung (1952), pp. 47–50 and pp. 52–3. For later T'ang condemnations of
Li's autocratic control of government, see *Yen Lu kung wen chi* 1/1b;
Sun Ch'iao chi 2/1b; or, in more general terms, *Li Wen kung chi* 10/76a;
CTS 17B/573, court discussion under Wen tsung in 838.

147   Yen Keng-wang (1959), gives over 200 examples of scholars undertaking
study in provincial mountain and monastic retreats, dating them
whenever possible. Cf. the *CTCC* epitaph for Chang Hung, d. 778 aged
70 *sui*, whose first attempt to gain entry into officialdom from being an
acolyte was unsuccessful, who then prepared himself in the Yü-ch'uan
monastery at Hou shan, to obtain the *ming ching* aged 22, and whose
literature was admired by the rescript writer Hsi Ang.

148   *CTS* 189A/4974–5, biog. of Yin Chih-chang. The interest of members of
the scholar community in Buddhism in the late K'ai-yüan period is well
described by Li Hua, *WYYH* 701/7a–8b, preface to collected works of
Yang Chi. Cf. also *WYYH* 678/7a–b, Hsiao Ying-shih.

149   *P'i tzu wen sou* 9/96–7 and *Shen Hsia-hsien wen chi* 9/96b.

150   *CTS* 189B/4974–5, biog. of Yin Chih-chang; *HTS* 200/5703, of
Wang Tao-kuei. See also Kao Ming-shih (1971), pp. 225–6.

151   I am indebted to Professor Stephen Owen for this phrase.

152   For Fang Kuan at this stage, see *TCTC* 215/6875, 747.1. Also *TWT*
87/1a–2a; *CTS* 111/3320–4, biog. and Pulleyblank (1960), pp. 87 and
98–9. For his Taoist mentor, Ching Fei, see *THY* 50/876; and his interest
in Buddhism, *Ch'üan T'ang wen* 332/15a. For later expressions of respect
for Fang Kuan, see *WYYH* 744/3a–6b and *WYYH* 785/1, Li Hua; *WYYH*
946/6a–b, Liang Su, quoting Li Hua; *WYYH* 840/14a, Yen Ying; *WYYH*
792/10a, Liang Su, report of conduct for Tu-ku Chi; *WYYH* 703/7b,
double column insertion, Liang Su; *Ch'üan Tsai-chih wen chi* 13/10b; *Liu
Ho-tung chi* 9/127–8; *WYYH* 800/2b, Cheng Ch'u-hui; *WYYH* 742/12a,
Niu Hsi-chi. *Kuo shih pu* 1/18 and 3/49; *Tzu chih t'ung chien k'ao i*, at
TCTC 217/7003, 765.5, quoting the *T'ang li* of Liu Fang.

153   The popularity of Lu-hun is suggested by e.g. *Ts'en Chia-chou shih*
2/8a–b; 3/18a and 21a; *CTS* 202/5758, biog. of Lü Hsiang; *TWT* 16B/2a,
poem by Sung Chih-wen. A relative of Wang Wei also retired there to
work the field in the image of T'ao Yüan-ming; see *Wang Mo-chieh
ch'üan chi chien chu* 3/37. For Fang Kuan at Lu-hun, see *CTS* 111/3320.
Cf. also Yen Keng-wang (1959), p. 700. For its warm springs, see *Feng
shih wen chien chi* 7/13. Fang Kuan was buried there; see *Chiu chia chi
chu Tu shih* 27/418.

154   For Yüan Te-hsiu, see *WYYH* 744/3a–b, Li Hua; *WYYH* 946/2b, Li Ao,
epitaph for Ma Yü; *T'ang chih yen* 4/48; *CTS* 158/4163, biog. of Cheng
Yü-ch'ing, of his father Cheng Tzu, a pupil of Yüan Te-hsiu; *CTS*
190B/5050–1, biog. of Yüan Te-hsiu; also the references given by Sun
Wang (1957), pp. 11–3 and 28–30.

155   *WYYH* 130/2b.

156   *T'ang shih chi shih* 21/306; *CTShih* 154/1595, which reads *hsiung* for
Yüan; *HTS* 202/5769.

157   *CTShih* 154/1593–4, confirmed in the epitaph for Hsiao's pupil Tai

Shu-lun, by Ch'üan Te-yü, *Ch'üan Tsai-chih wen chi* 24/6a; *Yin hua lu* 3/89; *T'ang shih chi shih* 21/207 and *HTS* 200/5769 speak of Hsiao as 'making the recommendation of his juniors "his own charge"'. See also note 253 below.

158 For Hsiao's private canonization, see *Yin hua lu* 3/89; *Fo tsu t'ung chi* 8/189.3; for Yüan Te-hsiu's, see *CTS* 190C/5051, biog. Yüan Te-hsiu's uncle, the father of Yüan Chieh, had had a similar private canonization; see *Fo tsu t'ung chi* 8/189.3.

159 See e.g. Ch'ien Mu (1957), pp. 123–7; Ch'ien Tung-fu (1962), pp. 7–16; Pulleyblank (1960), pp. 85–8, 92–7; Lo Lien-t'ien (1977), p. 220. Some of the important statements tracing the connections between these scholars are at *Ch'üan Tsai-chih wen chi* 48/1, sacrificial prayer for Pao Chi; *WYYH* 702/8b–9a, Li Chou; *WYYH* 703/6b–8a, Liang Su; *Yin hua lu* 3/89.

160 *CTS* 24/924.

161 *WYYH* 930/3a, sacrificial prayer for Liu Chih by Li Hua, refers to him as 'greatly enlightening the students'. *CTS* 102/3174 mentions Liu Chih's reform initiative for the directorate; *Chüan Tsai-chih wen chi* 41/2b–3a, letter to Liu Mien, appears to refer to it; but the details of any measures that Liu took have since disappeared. Ch'üan indicates that Liu's appointment to the directorate involved removal from the main political arena; cf. Ch. 5, notes 135 and 136. Yen Chen-ch'ing's brother Yen Yün-nan, 694–762, held the vice-presidency of the directorate under Su tsung as his last tenure; see *Yen Lu kung wen chi* 8/7a.

162 *CTS* 149/4008, biog. of Yü Hsiu-lieh.

163 For Yang Wan, see *CTS* 24/921–2; *TWT* 28/6b; *CTS* 119/3430–32, biog. *HTS* 198/5637 listed Yang Wan as one of the three leading post-rebellion ministers and advocates of reform of the official school system. For Hsiao Hsin's reformist memorial of 765, *TT* 53/303.2; *THY* 36/668; *CTS* 24/922–23; *CTS* 146/3961–62, biog. For Chia Chih, *CTS* 24/921–22; *WYYH* 765/3b; *TWT* 28/7b; *CTS* 190B/5029–31, biog.; *CTS* 119/3432–34, biog. of Yang Wan. Herbert (1986), pp. 98–105 contains an account of this debate.

164 *TT* 53/303.2; *THY* 36/668; *TFYK* 50/12a–13b.

165 *CTS* 24/924; *CTS* 184/4763–65, biog. of Yü Ch'ao-en. *Kuo shih pu* 1/23. This was stage-managed to meet the wishes of Yü Ch'ao-en, who was then politically the most powerful eunuch at court and who administered the directorate from 766 until 768.

166 *CTS* 24/924.

167 Conflicting dates are given for this submission: *THY* 66/1157 and *TFYK* 604/14a state 770. *CTS* 149/4016 and *HTS* 164/5036, biogs. of Kuei, both imply, though less precisely, that it was early in the Ta-li period. Hayashi (1916), p. 162, following this, suggests 766. Hsü Sung, *TKCK* 11/19b–21b, however, has the date of 780. The long-serving Kuei appears to have held the post of vice-president of the state academy directorate twice, in the early years of Ta-li (*CTS* 149/4016) and again from 780 (*CTS* 149/4016 and 4019; *THY* 4/45; *THY* 35/642). But all sources agree that this reforming memorial was submitted in connection with a

Ch'ih-chou ceremony for the crown prince in the directorate. It would seem natural for such a ceremony to follow soon after the crown prince's induction. Te tsung was inducted as crown prince in 764; see HTS 7/182; TCTC 223/7160, 764.5 and TFYK 257/10b–12a. CTS 13/401, moreover mentions his 'Ch'ih-chou years'. This might imply a Ch'ih-chou ceremony in 764, or not long after, or 'early Ta-li', as Kuei's biogs. imply. Shun tsung was inducted as crown prince in 779–80; see Solomon (1955), p. 1 and note 5 on p. 10, and CTS 12/324; CTS 14/405; HTS 7/205; TCTC 226/7273/779.13; TFYK 257/12a–13a. Since Kuei actually proposed a reform of the Ch'ih-chou in 780 (THY 4/45–6), and was active in seeking reform of state academy procedures as late as 782 (THY 35/642), during his second tenure as vice-president, Hsü Sung's late date of 780 cannot be ruled out.

168 CTS 119/3434–5, biog. of Yang Wan.

169 CTS 184/4763–5, biog. of Yü Ch'ao-en; CTS 24/923–4; Kuo shih pu 1/23. For Yü Ch'ao-en's Buddhism, see Yen Lu kung wen chi 4/2b.

170 See CTS 130/3622–3, biog. of Li Mi and TCTC 226/7272, 779.9, for Te tsung's intention to resist the heterodox superstitions and prognostication that had so influenced Su tsung and Tai tsung. Cf. also WYYH 167/7b, poem by Li I, written in 780, mentioning the Feng and Shan rites.

171 CTS 1219/3440–1, biog. of Ts'ui Yu-fu. Praise for or favourable mention of Ts'ui Yu-fu came from a number of scholar officials; e.g. WYYH 946/6a, Liang Su, epitaph for Fang Lin; Ch'üan Tsai-chih wen chi 33/1a; Han Ch'ang-li chi 5/19/21–2; HTS 152/4842, biog. of Li Chiang. Cf. TCTC 27/7329, 782.16; Yen Lu kung wen chi 14/8a. Ch'üan Tsai-chih wen chi 23/8a, epitaph for Chou Wei, 746–805, implies that Ts'ui Yu-fu had a particular interest in the imperial book collections and made informed appointments to collatorships.

172 See above, note 167.

173 Feng shih wen chien chi 1/7; THY 69/1216. This proposal seems to have had no permanent effect; see e.g. Han Ch'ang-li chi 6/31/58, where erudits are referred to. Feng Yen had great respect for Yen Chen-ch'ing, mentioning him at a number of points in the Feng shih wen chien chi. He was, moreover, known to Yen, who mentions him as a governor of Hsing-chou in 777; see Yen Lu kung wen chi 5/19b.

174 Han Ch'ang-li chi 4/14/35–6.

175 CTS154/4102, biog. of Hsü Meng-jung; cf. Po Hsiang-shan chi 7/47/59–60, Ts'e lin 36, on blocking of access since Chen-yüan times; also CTS 136/3755–56, biog. of Ts'ui Sun and CTS 135/3729, biog. of Wei Chü-mou; T'ang yü lin 6/201.

176 THY 35/635.

177 TTCLC 106/542–4; cf. TTCLC 69/387, act of grace of 785, by Lu Hsüan kung, stating that, 'Since Wei and Chin corrupt customs have not been reformed. The state academy and district schools merely put value on superficiality and ornament. The board of selection and the bureau of rites do not investigate true conduct.'

178 Liu Ho-tung chi 25/417; 34/539.

179 *Han Ch'ang-li chi* 4/14/35; *Liu Ho-tung chi* 9/130; and *HTS* 194/5572,
     biog. of Yang Ch'eng, confirming that Ho Fan was still a student in 798.
     In the pre-rebellion period, the maximum time of residence was appar-
     ently nine years; see *THY* 35/634; Herbert (1985), p. 81.
180 *Kuo shih pu* 2/35.
181 *Liu Ho-tung chi* 26/435–6; cf. *CTS* 173/4497, biog. of Li Shen, referring
     to the start of Hsien tsung's reign.
182 *TWT* 26A/7a, Li Kuan. For the problem of identifying Li Kuan, see
     Ts'en Chung-mien (1961b), pp. 375–9.
183 *CTS* 129/3606; *HTS* 126/4440, biogs. of Han Hui; Ts'en Chung-mien
     (1962), pp. 180–81; *Ch'üan Tsai-chih wen chi* 20/7a and 48/2a–3a.
     Another Han, Han Ch'ün, was also appointed to the directorate under
     Te tsung; see *HTS* 126/4438. *THY* 79/1458 enters Han Hui as canonized
     Ch'eng, but with a variant spelling of his given name.
184 *Liu Ho-tung chi* 9/130 says 160 students, with the commentary noting a
     variant of 270; *Liu Ho-tung chi* 34/539, commentary, says 200. Cf. *TCTC*
     235/7581, 798.9 and *CTS* 192/5133, biog. of Yang Ch'eng. But Liu's own
     statement in *Liu Ho-tung chi* 34/539, of 'one hundred and several tens' is
     likely to be a fair approximation. Waley (1949), p. 66 says 'nearly 300'.
185 Yang Ch'eng biogs. are in *CTS* 192/5132 and *HTS* 194/5569. See also
     TCTC 233/7514; 235/7566–8, 795.2; 235/7569, 795.9; 235/7581, 798.9;
     WYYH 703/3b, Liang Su; *Liu Ho-tung chi* 9/129–32; 34/538–40; *Han
     Ch'ang-li chi* 4/14/35–6; 6/30/48; 5/19/20–21. *Po Hsiang-shan chi* 2/2/26–7;
     2/3/42. Yang Ch'eng was remembered until the end of the dynasty; see
     Yüan shih Ch'ang-ch'ing chi 2/2a–3a; cf. *Ssu-k'ung Piao-sheng wen chi*
     4/3a, referring to *Han Ch'ang-li chi* 4/14/24–6.
186 *Han Ch'ang-li chi* 5/19/10–11; Hanabusa (1964), p. 67, dating the
     composition to 802. *Han Ch'ang-li chi* 5/23/61, identifying Wu Shao-i,
     rather than the Wu Ju-heng for whom Liu Tsung-yüan composed a text
     for the Ssu-men hsüeh, for which see *Liu Ho-tung chi* 26/434. For
     another instance in which Han praised a directorate official, see *Han
     Ch'ang-li chi* 6/33/78 epitaph for Tou Mou, 749–822.
187 Liu Yü-hsi, Liu Tsung-yüan and Han T'ai all went to listen to Shih
     Shih-kai, assistant instructor of the Ssu-men hsüeh on the *Mao shih*, the
     Ch'un-ch'iu and the *Tso*. See *Han Ch'ang-li chi* 5/24/71-72 and commen-
     tary; and Pien Hsiao-hsüan (1963), pp. 28–9; also *HTS* 200/5707, biog. of
     Shih Shih-kai. The *Ch'un-ch'iu* scholar and reformer Lu Ch'un was
     briefly demoted to be an erudit of the Kuo-tzu hsüeh at the start of Te
     tsung's reign; see below, Ch. 3, note 169.
188 *Po Hsiang-shan chi* 7/48/77–8, *Ts'e lin* 60.
189 *THY* 66/1159.
190 *CTS* 166/4327–31. At the start of the memorial, Yüan Chen referred to
     an edict ordering the repair of schools.
191 *TFYK* 50/14b.
192 *THY* 66/1160; *T'ang chih yen* 1/6–7.
193 *THY* 66/1159.
194 This seems to be the implication of the decree examination question of 808;
     see *TTCLC* 106/545; and *Huang-fu Ch'ih-cheng wen chi* 3/7a for the answer.

195 *TWT* 26A/8b.
196 *Han Ch'ang-li chi* 2/5/44.
197 *WYYH* 816/1b–3a, Shu Yüan-yü, d. 835.
198 *THY* 35/643; *HTS* 15/376.
199 *TWT* 27/5b, Li Chiang. Cf. *TT* 13/75.3 for a mid-T'ang summary of the Han situation; also *Liu Ho-tung chi* 34/539, for recollection of past numbers and political power of the T'ai hsüeh students. Li Te-yü, on the other hand, disapproved of this Later Han student involvement in politics; see *Li Wen-jao wen chi* 10/10b.
200 *THY* 66/1160; *CTS* 158/4166, biog. of Cheng Yü-ch'ing. Cf. the act of grace of 819 ordering repair of buildings of the state academy directorate in both capitals, by implication at state expense; *WYYH* 422/12b. The text of this act of grace in *TTCLC* 10/59–60 differs considerably from that in *WYYH*. Both versions, however, mention honouring the descendants of Confucius and of the 'two kings and three honoured states' (*erh wang san k'o*), for whom see Ch. 4, notes 27 and 109.
201 Kao Ming-shih (1970), pp. 38–45 provides names of officials appointed to the directorate in the post-rebellion period, though his list is not exhaustive.
202 There is the example of Hsü-chou in modern Honan, which had to wait until 836 for restoration; see *Liu Yü-hsi chi* 3/27. For the temple at Yen-chou, given a new gate in 773, see *Chin shih ts'ui pien* 99/2b, text by P'ei Hsiao-chih.
203 For Fu-feng county in modern Shensi, *WYYH* 814/1b–3a, text dated 767; for Yüan-chou in modern Kiangsi, text also dated 767, see *WYYH* 814/3a–4b.
204 *Chiu chia chi chu Tu shih* 60/249; Hung (1952), pp. 263–4.
205 For Hao-chou in modern Anhui, see *CTS* 125/3545–6, biog. of Chang I; for Ch'ang-chou in modern Chiangsu, see *WYYH* 737/8a; for Fang-chou in modern Shansi, *Han Ch'ang-li chi* 6/30/46; for Cho-chou in modern Chihli, *Ch'üan T'ang wen* 480/7b-9b, Wei Nien; for Fu-chien, *HTS* 150/4810, biog. of Ch'ang Kun and *HTS* 203/5786, biog. of Ou-yang Chan; for Fu-chou, *WYYH* 703/5b, Liang Su and *P'i-ling chi* 9/4a; for Ch'en-liu in modern Honan, *WYYH* 703/5b and 846/3b–5a, Liang Su, and Tsen Chung-mien (1962b), pp. 389–90. The Confucian temple at Hung-chou in modern Kiangsi may also have been restored, since *Ch'üan Tsai-chih wen chi* 14/4a records the title of a commemorative stele for it by Ch'i K'ang. Lo Hsiang, d. 809, canonized *I*, revived local education at Lu-chou in modern Anhui; see *Ch'üan Tsai-chih wen chi* 23/6a–b and *HTS* 197/5628, biog.
206 *Yen Lu kung wen chi* 7/8b.
207 *Liu Ho-tung chi* 5/74 and 77.
208 *Han Ch'ang-li chi* 6/30/42; 7/5/84; 6/31/58–9. For an important sequel to Han's Ch'u-chou text, see *Fan-ch'uan wen chi* 6/105–06. See also *Kuang-ch'uan shu po* 9/111–112 for a note by the Sung author Tung Yu (fl. *c.* 1130) on the later history of this stele.
209 *Liu Yü-hsi chi* 20/183; cf. 3/27, and note 202 above.
210 *Feng shih wen chien chi* 5/11–14; also *Po Hsiang-shan chi* 7/48/83–4, *Ts'e-lin* 68. Cf. Ch. 5 at note 165.

211 Liu K'o, in *Niu Yang jih li*, cited by Pulleyblank (1959), p. 157.
212 For Wen tsung's indecisiveness, see *TCTC* 243/7854, 827.3; 246/7933-4, 838.7.
213 This is evident from the celebrated decree examination answer of Liu Fen in 828; see *CTS* 190C/5064; *HTS* 178/5295; *TCTC* 243/7858, 828.4.
214 *TTCLC* 29/106; *CTS* 176/4571–72, biog. of Chou Ch'ih; *CTS* 171/4573–4, biog. of Cheng Su; *CTS* 173/4489–92, biog. of Cheng T'an.
215 *THY* 66/1162; *CTS* 17B/551 and 555; *TFYK* 50/15b. *CTS* 173/4491-2, biog. of Cheng T'an, implies a date of 835 or after. *THY* 92/1672, dates to 837; *CTS* 17B/565, to 836. However, des Rotours (1947), p. 450, is wrong to infer from Cheng T'an's biogs. and *CTS* 17B/565 that these posts were established in 836; it was the source for their financing, in all probability, that needed reclassifying then. The appointment of an erudit for the *Chou i* is mentioned in 834; see *CTS* 17B/555. For some subsequent appointments to these specialist posts, see e.g. *Teng k'o chi k'ao pu*, p. 122, Chao ?-chih, erudit of the *Li chi*; *CTCC* epitaph for a Sun who died in 850 aged 61 *sui*, whose epitaph was composed by his nephew Hsü, an erudit of the *Ch'un-ch'iu* (his existence is confirmed by *HTS* 73B/2955); *CTS* 18B/640, Li Hsin, erudit of the *Li chi*; *HTS* 183/5385 and *TCTC* 260/8491, 896.29, Chu P'u, erudit of the *Mao shih*.
216 *Li I-shan wen chi* 4/20a. The dating is derived from *Fan-nan wen chi hsiang chu* 7/26a. Cf. *CTS* 190C/5078, biog. of Li Shang-yin.
217 *P'i tzu wen sou* 9/96–7.
218 Cf. note 201 above. One genuine scholar at least was Li Fou, president of the directorate in the late T'ang; see introduction to *K'an wu yin-te*, (1934), p. (i).
219 *CTS* 179/4652. Another K'ung in this period was K'ung Wen-yü, who claimed descent from Confucius, and who petitioned in 869 to repair the Confucian temple at Ch'ü-fu, which was not under his administration; see *Chin shih ts'ui pien* 117/22a. This renovation was commemorated in 870; see *Chin shih ts'ui pien* 117/20b, Chia Fang. *Shih-mo chien hua* 3/41, gives an account of the connection between these two compositions.
220 *THY* 35/1640; *TFYK* 50/16a; *CTS* 20A/740; *CTS* 179/4651, biog. of K'ung Wei.
221 *P'u-yang Huang yü-shih chi, pieh lu*, p. 355. Huang T'ao was an erudit of the Ssu-men hsüeh in the period 898–900. *CTS* 20A/768, Chang Ch'eng-feng, appointed acting president of the directorate in 900; *CTS* 20A/780, Ou-yang T'e, appointed erudit in the Kuo-tzu hsüeh in 904. See also Kao Ming-shih (1970), pp. 44–5.
222 *TT* 53/306.3–307.1; *THY* 23/435.
223 *TT* 53/307.1; *THY* 23/435; *Ta T'ang chiao ssu lu* 2/12b and 10/9b; *CTS* 24/935 (*CTS* traces no developments after this); *HTS* 15/377; *TCTC* 221/7091, 706.13. *HTS* 60/1617, *Ho chih*, p. 365, enters a work entitled *Wu-ch'eng wang miao shih che tsan (Eulogies for the ten wise men in the temple of prince Wu-ch'eng)* by Lu T'ing, an erudit in the Kuo-tzu hsüeh. Lu T'ing is listed in *HTS* 73A/2934 as the son of Lu T'ung-tsai. The Sung compilation *Yen-chou t'u ching* enters Lu T'ung-tsai as being appointed to the governorship of Yen-chou on the 28th day of the 6th

month of 742. His son's career is therefore likely to have spanned the middle decades of the century, and his eulogies may well have been composed in connection with the expansion of 760.

224 *Ta T'ang chiao ssu lu* 10/12a; *HTS* 15/377.

225 *Ta T'ang chiao ssu lu* 10/12a.

226 *THY* 23/435–6 implies a date of 782 for this expansion. *Ta T'ang chiao ssu lu* 10/12a, however, states that in 781 'here was an edict that the authorities should effect repair, and revise the matter of the sacrifice . . .' Moreover, Wang Ching in his own commentary, 10/9b, dates the major iconographical expansion involving the history office to 783. But perhaps this simply marks the completion of the process of re-establishment. *THY* 23/436, and *CTS* 137/3766, biog. of Yü Shao and *HTS* 203/5783 following *THY*, disagree with Wang Ching again in stating that redrafting of the music for the cult was given to Yü Shao in 786; Wang Ching, *Ta T'ang chiao ssu lu* 10/10b, has this at 790. For Kuo Tzu-i, see *CTS* 120/3449–66, biog.

227 From Kuan Po, in the second month of 786; see *THY* 23/436; *HTS* 15/378–9 (not in Wang Ching's account, and possibly misdated by *THY*); from Li Hsü and 46 others, the most articulate being the *Ch'un-ch'iu* scholar Lu Ch'un, in the eighth month of 788. Support for the cult was given by 24 military officials, led by Ling-hu Chien, the son of a prominent soldier of the An Lu-shan rebellion period. The result of the debate was a compromise, in which the cult was to be managed by the court of sacrifices, and the offerings made by military officials; see *Ta T'ang chiao ssu lu* 10/14b–16a; *TT* 53/307.1–307.2; *THY* 23/436–38; *HTS* 15/380.

228 See above, note 226.

229 *Ch'üan Tsai-chih wen chi* 25/9a–b mentions an assistant (*cheng*) at the T'ai kung temple. Other references to T'ai kung occur: in *Po Hsiang-shan chi* 2/2/21, he is made to balance Confucius in a couplet of a poem describing a commemorative stele. *TWT* 66/6a, Liang Su, has an inscription at P'an-ch'i; its theme is that T'ai kung was fortunate to have coincided with the early Chou. Only a single phrase 'military dress' (*jung i*) points to T'ai kung in his military role.

230 *THY* 23/439.

231 *HTS* 15/376.

232 *TCTC* 221/7091, 760.13; *HTS* 15/376–7.

233 *TFYK* 50/13b, double column entry.

234 *CTS* 24/923; *HTS* 15/376.

235 *TFYK* 50/13b–14a.

236 *CTS* 24/923–24; *CTS* 184/4763–64, biog. of Yü Ch'ao-en; *Kuo shih pu* 1/23.

237 *TFYK* 50/13b.

238 *Liu Yü-hsi chi* 20/183–84; Pien Hsiao-hsüan (1963), p. 123, dates Liu's tenure of this governorship from 822 to 824.

239 *Liu Yü-hsi chi* 3/27.

240 *THY* 35/643 dates this 799, the year of Kuei's death according to his biog. in *CTS* 149/4019. *CTS* 149/4015 mentions Kuei as holding the same

titles as the *THY* account, but implies that the submission was soon after the start of the Tai tsung's reign; *HTS* 164/5036, biog., implies a similarly early date. For Tu Mu's remark, see *Fan-ch'uan wen chi* 6/106. The Sung assessment is given at *HTS* 164/5058.

241 *Liu Ho-tung chi* 5/75–76; condemned by the Sung compiler of *HTS*, *HTS* 164/5058.

242 *HTS* 150/4810, biog. of Ch'ang Kun.

243 *TWT* 5/2a, Li Kuan; *Po Hsiang-shan chi* 9/59/39; Waley (1949), pp. 169–70; Lo Hsiang-lin (1954), pp. 93–4. For other debates after the reign of Hsüan tsung, see Lo, pp. 94–5.

244 *WYYH* 360/10a–11a, Lai Ku, a *chin shih* of the period 860–73.

245 *P'i tzu wen sou* 9/93–95.

246 T'ao Hsi-sheng (1972b), p. 85b.

247 *Li Wen kung chi* 8/57a–b.

248 *HTS* 162/4993; Liang Su said of Tu-ku that 'he looked on me as a friend, and I looked on him as a teacher'; see *WYYH* 703/6a.

249 *WYYH* 946/5b–6b. Fang had been praised by Li Hua and appointed 'Confucian office' (*ju chih*) under the chief ministerships of Ch'ang Kun and Ts'ui Yu-fu.

250 *Ch'üan Tsai-chih wen chi* 31/3a–b. For Chung Tzu-ling, see also Ch. 4, note 197.

251 *Li Yüan-pin wen chi* 3/19.

252 *Liu Yü-hsi chi* 3/28. Liu elsewhere expressed respect for Tu Yu for his family; see 39/393. Later he himself became a teacher; see Pien Hsiao-hsüan (1963), p. 107.

253 For P'ei Tu and Liu T'ai-chen, see *Ch'üan T'ang wen* 538/15b and *TKCK* 12/24b–26b, where P'ei lists over 20 of Liu's disciples. Liu T'ai-chen had himself been a disciple of Hsiao Ying-shih; see *T'ang shih chi shih* 27/422, 28/436; *TWT* 85/10a; *WYYH* 702/10b, Ku K'uang; *CTS* 137/3762, biog. of Liu T'ai-chen.

254 *Liu Ho-tung chi* 30/496–97; *WYYH* 988/4b–6b; Lü Wen; Ts'en Chung-mien (1962b), pp. 403–5; *WYYH* 918/3b–7a.

255 *Fan-ch'uan wen chi* 14/212, report of conduct for Shen Ch'uan-shih.

256 *Ch'üan Tsai-chih wen chi* 42/6a–8b.

257 *Li Wen kung chi* 7/49b; *TWT* 86/1a–b, Wei Ch'u-hou.

258 *Liu Ho-tung chi* 19/341–42; 34/539–43.

259 *Liu Ho-tung chi* 34/538–40; the references here are, for Confucius himself, *Analects* 5/22; for Hsün tzu, *Hsün tzu* 30/13/106; for Tseng tzu, *Mencius* 4B/31/33; for Mencius, *Mencius* 7B/30/67.

260 Hanabusa (1964), pp. 378–81.

261 *Han Ch'ang-li chi* 4/17/68–70; 5/19/20–21.

262 *Huang-fu Ch'ih-cheng wen chi* 6/6a.

263 *Han Ch'ang-li chi* 4/17/75–7; *Analects* 13/2.

264 *Han Ch'ang-li chi* 2/4/18. For remarks on his tenures of academic office from 806 to 809, see *Han Ch'ang-li chi* 3/8/9–11; 2/4/29–30; 2/4/31.

265 Li Ao, *Li Wen kung chi* 11/80b–81a, recorded that Han's action on taking up the post of president of the state academy directorate was to take food with an academic official 'of coarse demeanour', who was 'able to

expound ritual', but with whom the other officials had refused to eat. This was perhaps a practical demonstration of his ideal that knowledge was to be respected regardless of standing. For Han's proposal to increase student numbers to those prescribed by the *Liu tien*, see *Han Ch'ang-li chi* 7/37/19–20 and Hartman (1986), p. 101.

266   *Han Ch'ang-li chi* 4/16/59–60; *Analects* 7/29; Hanabusa (1964), p. 67.
267   *Lü Ho-shu wen chi* 3/1a–3a; *Li Wen kung chi* 7/50b; *Han Ch'ang-li chi* 4/14/23; 3/12/75–77; 4/14/34. For some indication of how sympathetic these ideas were to the Neo-Confucian era, see Dardess (1983), pp. 32–4.
268   *Han Ch'ang-li chi* 3/12/77–79. There was even a late tradition that Han had premises specially for teaching; see *T'ai-p'ing kuang chi* 54/331 and 409/3315. See Kao Ming-shih (1971), p. 230 and, for the term here used, *hsüeh yüan*, pp. 242–4.
269   Wechsler (1977), pp. 240–55 cites ninth-century mentions of Wang T'ung. Li Ao, in *Li Wen kung chi* 6/42a, gives a negative view of Wang T'ung, but nonetheless an indication that he was under discussion; *Han Ch'ang-li chi* 2/5/41, commentary; *Fan-ch'uan wen chi*, preface by P'ei Yen-han, p. 3; *P'i tzu wen sou* 4/36–39; *Ssu-k'ung Piao-sheng wen chi* 5/1a–b; 9/1a–b.
270   *Han Ch'ang-li chi* 3/12/76; *HTS* 177/5275, biog. of Wei Piao-wei; *TWT* 86/6b, Lin Chien-yen.
271   See above, note 149.

3 Canonical scholarship

1   Hartman (1986), p. 236.
2   References to early mastery of the canons are very numerous in biog. accounts at all levels of documentation. For the cases of some well known scholars, see *STTS* 10/11a, specifying the *Tso chuan*, quoted by Pulleyblank (1961), p. 137; *WYYH* 924/5b–6a, Ts'ui Yu-fu, of Tu-ku Chi, specifying the *Hsiao ching*; *WYYH* 678/5a–7a, Hsiao Ying-shih, specifying the *Analects* and *Shang shu*; *WYYH* 690/11b, Lu Kuei-meng, specifying the *Six canons*, with *Mencius* and Yang Hsiung. For some examples of late, but successful acquisition of learning, *Yüan Tz'u-shan chi*, Appendix p. 166, Yüan Chieh at 17 *sui*; *Ch'en Tzu-ang chi*, Appendix p. 252, Ch'en Tzu-ang at 17 or 18 *sui*; *Yen Lu kung wen chi* 9/10a–b, of Hsien-yü Hsiang, 693–752, who learnt to read only at twenty, and succeeded at the *chin shih* at 'close on forty'. For an instance of notably rapid learning, see *Yen Lu kung wen chi* 9/5a, spirit path stele for Yen Yüan-sun, who mastered the *Shang shu* 'in six days, including the commentary'.
3   For the term *li* or *li tao* in this negative sense, see *WYYH* 884/9a, Chang Chiu-ling, spirit path stele for P'ei Kuang-t'ing; *T'ang Lu Hsüan kung han-yüan chi* 6/8a and *TTCLC* 106/542, Lu Hsüan kung, decree examination question of 785; *WYYH* 689/1b, Liu Mien, letter to Ch'üan Te-yü, attributing *li tao* to the Sui; also *Yüan Tz'u-shan chi* 9/135. For *li tao* in the careers of officials, see e.g. *CTS* 77/2673, biog. of Yang Tsuan, d. *c.* 652; *CTS* 113/3353, biog. of P'ei Mien, d. late 769 or early 770; *CTS* 129/3599, biog. of Han Huang; *CTS* 146/3965, biog. of Li Jo-ch'u, d.

799. Confucian (*ju*) values were also opposed to administrative ones (*li*) in e.g. *CTS* 102/3164, biog. of Ma Huai-su; *CTS* 157/4156, biog. of Wang Yen-wei. Cf. also *Yu yu chi* 5/3a, Lu Chao-lin, characterizing Kao tsung's reign as esteeming *li* against *ju* and Mo. The term was not, however, necessarily negative, when the official concerned also had learning and integrity; see e.g. *P'i-ling chi* 6/9a canonization discussion for Lü Yin; *CTS* 96/3025, biog. of Yao Ch'ung. For the phrase *shih li i ju*, see *P'i-ling chi* 20/3a–b, sacrificial graveside prayer for Wei Yüan-fu and cf. *P'i-ling chi* 6/9a, canonization discussion for Lü Yin.

4 *Han shu* 65/2841, biog. of Tung-fang Shuo. For T'ang use of this phrase, see e.g. *CTCC* epitaph of Ts'ui Chih-tao, d. 682, aged 72 *sui*, an examination graduate; *CTCC* epitaph for Ts'ui Kuang-ssu, d. 732 aged 71, a decree examination graduate in the three teachings.

5 *CTS* 190B/5016–7, biog. of Liu Hsien; see also below, note 97.

6 Schwartz (1959), pp. 52–3; *Li chi chu shu* 60/1a.

7 A rough indication of how often, in the surviving record of court discussions, the canons were quoted is provided by Harada Tanishige's index to *CKCY*; see p. 69 for the *Mao shih* and p. 80 for the *Ch'un-ch'iu*. See also below, notes 48–51.

8 For the period of primary commentaries, see Honda (1935), pp. 156–206; P'ei P'u-hsien (1969), p. 237–40. For sub-commentaries, see Mou Jun-sun (1960), pp. 356–9.

9 The juxtaposition of Confucian (*ju*) and classical Taoist (*hsüan*) was common in the period of disunion, as the numbers of scholars commended for mastery of both traditions suggests; e.g. *Nan Ch'i shu* 54/929, biog. of Ku Huan; *Ch'en shu* 33/447, biog. of Shen Pu-hai; *Liang shu* 3/96, of the emperor Liang Wu ti himself. *KFSPWK* epitaph for the Sui official Chang Po, *tzu* Fang-chin, shows that this juxtaposition still occurred late in the period of disunion or in the Sui. *TT* 27/161.1 indicates that in the Liu Sung dynasty (420–79) *ju* and *hsüan* with literature (*wen*) and history (*shih*), constituted the four categories of learning, and were therefore the antecedents of the four categories (*ssu pu*) of the T'ang.

10 Lu Te-ming, biog. *CTS* 189A/4944–45. For the *Ching tien shih wen*, see preface by Lu Te-ming; *CTS* 46/1983; *HTS* 57/1446 and *Ho chih* p. 51. Thompson (1979), pp. 56–61 and notes, reviews in detail the evidence concerning the chronology of Lu Te-ming's life. Evidence for the wide circulation of the *Ching tien shih wen* derives from the survival of fragments at Tun-huang and at Nara, for which see Thompson, p. 58, note 31. That this work remained highly respected by official scholars in the T'ang may be seen by the remarks of Chang Shen, who was required to re-determine the text of the *Five canons* in 776. Chang Shen called the work 'uniquely thorough', and used it in the version of the canons he erected in the state academy directorate. See below, note 147. Lu Te-ming's account of the transmission of the *Tso chuan* also figured in the writings of the *Ch'un-ch'iu* school in the post-rebellion period; see below note 165, and *Ch'un-ch'iu tsuan li* 1/12b, Chao K'uang. For the three-teachings debate of 624, see Lo Hsiang-lin (1954), pp. 85–7.

11 For Yen Shih-ku's commission, see *CKCY* 7/215–16, dating 630; *CTS* 73/2594, biog. of Yen Shih-ku; *CTS* 189A/4941; *CTS* 3/43, dating promulgation to 633.

12 *SS* 32/933.

13 For pre-T'ang 'definitive versions' (*ting pen*), see *Tso chuan chiu shu k'ao cheng*, by Liu Wen-ch'i (1789–1856), preface 3a–4b. Liu Wen-ch'i shows that K'ung Ying-ta's sub-commentary cited 'definitive versions' in its exegesis for the *Chou i* appendices, the *Shang shu*, and the *Li chi*, while in the *Mao shih* and *Tso chuan* sub-commentaries 'definitive version' citations were particularly numerous. In some cases, e.g. *Tso chuan chu shu* 49/3b, the sub-commentary rejected 'definitive version' readings. For references in pre-T'ang histories to determining the text of the canons, see *SS* 66/1554, biog. of Lang Mao, under the Northern Ch'i; *SS* 75/1715, biog. of Hsiao Kai.

14 For the *Yen shih tzu yang*, see *Yen Lu kung wen chi* (*SPTK* ed.), *Pu i* 2a–3a. Yen Chen-ch'ing also mentions, critically, a later work in the same tradition, by Tu Yen-yeh.

15 P'ei P'u-hsien (1969), p. 242.

16 *THY* 77/1404 implies that the work was submitted in 638; but this is the earliest date at which the project is mentioned, and is therefore likely to be the date of its commission. For other accounts of the project, see *CKCY* 7/216; *CTS* 189A/4971; *CTS* 73/2602–3, biog. of K'ung Ying-ta; *TFYK* 606/14b; *CTS* 4/71.

17 See the lists of names given in the prefaces to each of the sub-commentaries, before the mention of imperially ordered revision. Su Ying-hui (1968), pp. 182–4 notes discrepancies between the Tun-huang version and transmitted versions over the names of co-compilers.

18 *Chin shih ts'ui pien* 47/9a and *CTS* 73/2603, biog. of K'ung Ying-ta mention that K'ung's reward for completing the commission was 300 bolts of silk, about standard for a senior academic official for a large project.

19 The objections came from Ma Chia-yün; see *CTS* 73/2602–3, biog. of K'ung Ying-ta and *CTS* 73/2603, biog. of Ma Chia-yün. It is conspicuous that 642 was the year in which T'ai tsung ordered a discussion in connection with another, more radical submission concerning canonical exegesis; see *CTS* 74/2620, biog. of Ts'ui Jen-shih and *TFYK* 606/14a–b. The new director of the project, Chao Hung-chih, 572–653, canonized *Hsüan*, had been a member of the *I wen lei chü* commission (see below, Ch. 6 at note 9) and had lectured on the *Hsiao ching*; see *CTS* 188/4921–22, biog., which does not, however, mention his service on the sub-commentary commission.

20 *CTS* 73/2602, biog. of K'ung Ying-ta. Yü Chih-ning's stele text for K'ung's grave at Chao-ling does not mention the project following K'ung's submission in 642; see *Chin shih ts'ui pien* 47/9a–b and Lo chen-yü (1909) 1/17b.

21 *TKCK* 2/2b–4b, citing a Northern Sung edition of the sub-commentary. A fragment preserved at Tun-huang gives a list of the names of scholars responsible for the final revision, with names of collators, in one case of a student of the Ssu-men hsüeh; see Su Ying-hui (1968), pp. 192–3. Su,

pp. 186–7, refutes the suggestion of Ts'en Chung-mien that this belongs to a copy of the *Shang shu cheng i*. There is some discrepancy among the sources that mention the dates of the revision that took place after T'ai tsung's death. K'ung Ying-ta's *HTS* biog., 198/5645, states that the revision was ordered in 651, but makes no mention of Chang-sun Wu-chi. *THY* 77/1405 states that a revision was ordered in 651, but under Chang-sun Wu-chi. A date of 652, rather than 651, for Chang-sun Wu-chi's direction is put forward by Su, p. 185, on the basis of a citation of the *Hui yao* in *Yü hai* 42/32a–b. This leads Su to suggest that a revision in 651 under Yü Chih-ning was followed by the appointment of Chang-sun Wu-chi as director in 652. All sources except *Chung-hsing kuan ko shu mu*, quoted in *Yü hai* 37/10a, Su, p. 184, agree that the final completion was in 653. Cf. Thompson (1979), pp. 69–71 and notes.

22 Lo Chen-yü (1909), 1/18b, stele by Yü Chih-ning, referring to the first submission of the work, reads 170 *chüan*, *CTS* 73/2602, biog. of K'ung has 180 *chüan*, *CTS* 46/1968, 1970, 1971, 1974, 1978, and *Ho chih*, pp. 13, 18, 21, 16 and 38 have a total of 180 *chüan*. By the Sung, the series is entered with a larger number: see *HTS* 57/1426, 1428, 1430, 1433, 1440, and *Ho chih*, pp. 13, 18, 21, 26, and 38; also Yang Hsiang-k'uei (1958), p. 8, note 1.

23 For indication that the same primary commentators were in favour under the Sui, see the short accounts of the history of the exegesis of each canon: *SS* 32/912–13 for the *Chou i*; *SS* 32/914–15 for the *Shang shu*; *SS* 32/918 for the *Mao shih*; *SS* 32/924–26 for the *Li chi*; *SS* 32/932–33 for the *Ch'un-ch'iu*. The fact that K'ung Ying-ta participated in the compilation of both *SS* and the sub-commentary helps explain this consistency.

24 For Wang Pi, see A.F. Wright (1947), pp. 124–61. An invaluable concise history of the *Shang shu* and K'ung An-kuo's commentary is given by Hung (1957), note 5 on pp. 99–100 and p. 79 and note 103 on pp. 124–5. For Tu Yü's commentary, see Yeh Cheng-hsin (1966).

25 For the relationship between northern and southern traditions, see Mou (1960), p. 393; also *Liang shu* 48/678, biog. of Lu Kuang; *Pei shih* 81/2709; *SS* 75/1705–06.

26 Liu Cho's biogs. are at *SS* 75/1718–19 and *Pei shih* 82/2762-63. Liu Hsüan's at *SS* 75/1719–23 and *Pei shih* 82/2763–67. See also *SS* 75/1726–27 and *SS* 75/1707. For K'ung Ying-ta's debt to both, see *TFYK* 768/13b. For the debt of other early T'ang official scholars to Liu Cho, see *TFYK* 768/13b and *CTS* 198A/4951, biog. of Kai Wen-ta, and *TFYK* 768/14b and *CTS* 198A/4949, biog. of Chang Shih-heng.

27 For instances of *Ta Sui* occurring in the text of the sub-commentaries, see *Shang shu chu shu* 3/9b and 19/17a. The latter reference supplies a date of 'early K'ai-huang' for the abolition of castration as a punishment.

28 See Chien Po-hsien (1970), quoting the Ch'ing scholar Liu Wen-ch'i. In *Tso chuan chu shu* 39/8b and *Mao shih chu shu* 1/10a, the two sub-commentaries have almost identical texts, except that the *Tso chuan* passage includes four additional words, 'Liu Hsüan also says', before the phrase, 'When shield and spear have been put down', which both passages contain. The passages then continue to run almost exactly

parallel for several columns. The omission of the phrase 'Liu Hsüan also says' from the *Mao shih* sub-commentary justifies the speculation that much of the sub-commentary series may have originally contained attributions of this kind, which were removed in the course of editing.

29   K'ung's method was to follow the primary commentary wherever possible. This led him, however, to refute Liu Hsüan at certain points. Liu Hsüan had written two treatises identifying and refuting errors in the primary commentary to the *Tso chuan* by Tu Yü, which K'ung Ying-ta endorsed. For these works, the *Ch'un-ch'iu kuei kuo (Reproving the errors in [Tu Yü's] Ch'un-ch'iu commentary)* and *Ch'un-ch'iu kung mei (Attacking the blind spots in [Tu Yü's] Ch'un-ch'iu commentary)* see the recensions by Ma Kuo-han (1794–1857), in *Yü-han shan fang chi i shu.* K'ung therefore attacked Liu for faulting the primary commentary he otherwise endorsed, for 'giving exposition to Tu and yet attacking Tu'. For instances of K'ung refuting Liu Hsüan's attack on Tu Yü, see e.g. *Tso chuan chu shu* 49/4b; 49/10b.

30   Yeh Ch'eng-i (1970), pp. 313–322, at p. 314; Ho Hsi-ch'un (1966), pp.1–2.

31   Wang Chung-lin (1959), pp. 1–111.

32   For example, in the preface to the *Chou i* sub-commentary, 2a–7a.

33   For the background to New Text (Chin wen) prognosticatory books (*ch'an shu*), see Fung Yu-lan tr. Derke Bodde (1953), pp. 88–132; also Tjan Tjoe Som (1949), pp. 100–20. For another condemnation of the apocryphal and prognosticatory texts of the late Former Han period by K'ung Ying-ta and others, see *SS* 32/940–41. Bodde (1953), p. 89, translates part of this important passage. See also *SS* 32/948. *SS* 78/1743–64 constitutes the early T'ang official world's cautious endorsement of the idea of prognostication. For criticism of apocryphal and divinatory texts in the sub-commentary series, see *Shang shu chu shu* preface 2a; 8/14b; *Chou i chu shu* preface 7a; Yang Hsiang-k'uei (1958), p. 11. Early T'ang attitudes to divination were also embodied in the revision of the *Yin-yang shu (Book on yin and yang)* undertaken on imperial commission by the polymath Lü Ts'ai, for which see *THY* 36/651–56; *TT* 105/558.2–559.3; *CTS* 79/2719–27, biog.; *CTS* 47/2044; *HTS* 59/1557 and *Ho chih* p. 252. Also, Hou Wai-lu and Chao Chi-pin (1959), pp. 1–21; Needham (1956), p. 387. For later T'ang references to Lü Ts'ai's *Yin-yang shu*, see *Feng shih wen chien chi* 5/21; this and the inclusion of excerpts in *TT* and Su Mien's comment on the passage of work he excerpted for the *Hui yao* (*THY* 36/656) suggest that its pre-suppositions were supported by the scholar community in the eighth and early ninth centuries.

34   *Chou i chu shu* pref. 1a.

35   Honda (1935), pp. 232–3; Mou Jun-sun (1960).

36   *Chou i chu shu* 7/18b–19a; Yang Hsiang-k'uei p. 9.

37   *Chou i chu shu* 7/7a; 3/11b; Yang Hsiang-k'uei pp. 8–9.

38   *Chou i chu shu* 1/8b; cf. also *Chou i chu shu* 7/15b for further exposition of *chi*.

39   *Shang shu chu shu* 3/3b and *SS* 19/505 ff. See also Cullen (1976), pp. 107–9.

40 *CTS* 74/2620, biog. of Ts'ui Jen-shih. T'ai tsung's encouragement of debate among canonical scholars is also suggested by *CTS* 73/2602–03, biog. of K'ung Ying-ta; *CTS* 73/2603, biog. of Ma Chia-yün.

41 For the place of the *Chou li* and the *I li*, see the decree of 635, *THY* 75/1375; *TFYK* 639/19a; *TKCK* 1/15a.

42 For the place of the *Hsiao ching* in early T'ang promotion of education, see *TKCK* 1/5b-6a, edict of seventh month of 624; *CTS* 73/2602, biog. of K'ung Ying-ta, indicating that he lectured on the canon at the state academy directorate in 640. K'ung also compiled a sub-commentary to the *Hsiao ching* for the crown prince, often the focus for educational ideals; see *CTS* 73/2602; *HTS* 57/1443; *Ho chih* p. 45. See also *THY* 35/640, showing that Chao Hung-chih lectured on this canon again in 648, after a *Shih-tien* observance at the directorate; Chao's biog., *CTS* 188/4922, indicates that he lectured again on the canon, to Kao tsung, with scholars, academic officials and the students of the Hung-wen kuan attending. For later examples, see *CTS* 22/864, Hsing Wen-wei in 690 in the Ming-t'ang; *THY* 35/642, Ch'u Wu-liang in 719. For such lectures, see *TLT* 21/6a.

43 Kao Ming-shih (1977), p. 11B.

44 Chia Kung-yen had worked on the revision of the *Wu ching cheng i* directed by Chang-sun Wu-chi; see *TKCK* 2/4a, memorial of submission. He has a very brief biog. notice at *CTS* 1289A/4949–50, which enters both these sub-commentaries. For these works, see also *CTS* 46/1972; *HTS* 57/1433; cf. *Ho chih*, p. 22, p. 24; also *SKCSTMTY*, p. 364–5 and p. 387–8. *HTS* 57/1433 also enters a *Li chi cheng i* in 80 *chüan* by Chia Kung-yen; cf. *Ho chih* p. 26. In addition, the bibliographies list a *Hsiao ching* sub-commentary, *CTS* 46/1981; *HTS* 57/1442; *Ho chih*, p. 45; and an *Analects* sub-commentary, *CTS* 46/1982; *HTS* 57/1444; *Ho chih*, p. 48.

45 Chien Po-hsien (1975), p. 75 cites *Wen hsien t'ung k'ao* 181/1a–b quoting a remark by Tung Yu, fl. *c.* 1130, that Chia Kung-yen's *Chou li* sub-commentary owed to the exegesis of Ch'en Shao, biog. *Chin shu* 91/2348, and Shen Chung, biogs. *Chou shu* 45/808–11 and *Pei shih* 82/2741–2. *SKCSTMTY*, p. 387, quoting Chia's own preface to the *I li*, indicates his debt to the sub-commentaries of Huang Ch'ing of the Ch'i and Li Meng-che of the Sui. Yang Hsiang-k'uei (1958), pp. 12–13, suggests that his ritual scholarship was much stronger than his cosmology, and notes his reliance on apocryphal works. Cf. the remark of Chu Hsi, quoted in *SKCSTMTY*, p. 365, that the *Chou li* sub-commentary was the best of all the canonical sub-commentaries.

46 For Yang Shih-hsün, see *Tso chuan chu shu*, pref. 2a by K'ung Ying-ta, mentioning him as an erudit of the Ssu-men hsüeh. Cf. also the remark of the *SKCSTMTY* editors, p. 519, on him and on the integrity of the present text of the *Ku-liang* sub-commentary. *CTS* 46/1979 and *HTS* 57/1440, *Ho chih* p. 40 enter this sub-commentary. Yang Hsiang-k'uei, pp. 13–4, shows that Fan Ning quoted Tu Yü to refute *Kung-yang* concepts. Yang Shih-hsün in turn refuted Ho Hsiu's primary commentary to the *Kung-yang*, in order to endorse Fan Ning's use of Tu Yü. The

sub-commentary was therefore broadly in the same Old Text (Ku-wen) tradition as K'ung Ying-ta's sub-commentary to the *Tso chuan*.

47 Neither *CTS* nor *HTS* bibliography enter this sub-commentary. See *Ch'ung-wen tsung mu* 1/24–5; *Chih chai shu lu chieh t'i* 3/4a. The *SKC-STMTY* editors, pp. 517–8, cite Tung Yu in identifying Hsü Yen as of late T'ang date. Yang Hsiang-k'uei, p. 14, accepts a ninth-century origin. However P'an Chung-kuei (1955), p. 11, believes it to be of Northern Ch'i date and probably by Kao Yün, whose biogs. are at *Pei shih* 31/1117–32 and *Wei shu* 48/1067–96.

48 For the role of the *Ch'un-ch'iu* and the *Tso chuan* in the seventh-century outlook on history compilation, see *Tso chuan chu shu* 10/1b quoted in *SS* 33/966, to sanction court diaries. Wei Cheng's admonition to T'ai tsung in 640, for which see *CKCY* 7/220 and Ch. 5, note 47, is an adaptation of this passage. The *Ch'un-ch'iu* and the *Tso chuan* were the primary sources for both Tung Hu and Nan Shih, much cited archetypes for the upright historian; see below, Ch. 5, note 8. Cf. also *THY* 46/815, Ch'u Sui-liang, discussion of 652.

49 *CKCY* 9/285.

50 *CKCY* 8/263.

51 *CKCY* 10/297 and *CTS* 72/2566–67, Yü Shih-nan, interpreting a mountainslide, the appearance of snakes and of floods, to T'ai tsung. *THY* 36/651–56, *passim*, Lü Ts'ai, *Yin-yang shu*, used evidence from the *Ch'un-ch'iu* to refute contemporary superstition relating to life expectancy and auspicious dates for burial.

52 For a clear statement that the *Tso* predominated, see *SS* 32/933; cf. *Pei shih* 81/2709. See also Hung (1957), p. 79, p. 124 note 101. For examples of early T'ang specialization in the *Tso chuan*, see *CTS* 189A/4944, biog. of Hsü Wen-yüan; p. 4948, biog. of Chu Tzu-she; p. 4950, biog. of Li Hsüan-chih; p. 4950, biog. of Chang Hou-yin; p. 4952, biog. of Hsiao Te-yen. A more eclectic approach had, however, been current in the period of disunion, and was even encouraged by the Liang royal house; see *Liang shu* 40/574, biog. of Liu Chih-lien; also *Pei shih* 81/2726, biog. of Li Hsüan; *Pei shih* 82/2760, biog. of Fang Hui-yüan. Cf. also the *Ch'un-ch'iu* exegetical titles that include the *San chuan* in *SS* 32/932. For T'ai tsung's own instruction in the *Tso chuan*, see *CTS* 189A/4950, biog. of Chang Hou-yin. In *CKCY* 7/221, he cited the *Ch'un-ch'iu*, duke Chuang 16th year, in discussing the tabooing of his own given name; see *Tso chuan chu shu* 47/7b.

53 For examples of generals who knew the *Tso chuan*, see *CTS* 104/3212, biog. of Ko-shu Han, d. 756; *CTS* 141/3850, biog. of T'ien Hung-cheng, d. 821; *CTS* 151/4061, biog. of Wang O, 760–815; *Yen Lu kung wen chi* 8/12a, Li Kuang-pi, 708–64; *Ch'üan Tsai-chih wen chi* 19/1b, Ma Sui, 726–95; *Ch'üan Tsai-chih wen chi* 13/4, Hun Chen, 737–800.

54 This summary of K'ung Ying-ta's view of the *Ch'un-ch'iu* and the *Tso chuan* is drawn from *Tso chuan chu shu*, preface by Tu Yü with sub-commentary by K'ung Ying-ta, *passim*.

55 Despite K'ung's condemnation of the title *su wang*, it remained current throughout the T'ang; see e.g. *Ch'üan T'ang wen* 175/5b, Ts'ui Hsing-

kung, commemorative text of 666; *STTS* 20/14a–b and Hung (1969), p. 6 and note 19 on p. 15; *Ta T'ang chiao ssu lu* 10/13a, Li Hsü in 788, attempting to prove the superiority of Confucius over T'ai kung; *TWT* 26A/7a, Li Kuan, asking for repair of the T'ai hsüeh; *Ch'üan Tsai-chih wen chi* 23/1b, of Wei Chü-mou's commitment to Confucianism.

56   *Analects* 17/12.

57   For K'ung's criticism of the *Kung-yang* and *Ku-liang* commentaries, see e.g. *Shang shu chu shu* 4/7b–8a, quoted by Chang Hsi-t'ang (1935), p. 8; *Li chi chu shu* 53/29a; *Tso chuan chu shu* 1/16a.

58   A tomb to Mencius is mentioned in *T'ai-p'ing huan yü chi* 21/8b. The *Yü-ti kuang chi* of *c.* 1111–7, 7/73, also mentions a tomb. A local temple to Mencius was established in 1083, when Mencius was enfieffed as duke of the state of Tsou. Mencius's official introduction as a recipient of offerings in the Confucian temple followed in 1088; see *Shan-tung t'ung chih*, p. 13; T'ao Hsi-sheng (1972b), p. 85.

59   *Yüan-ho hsing tsuan* 9/15b. The Meng clan of P'ing-ch'ang in modern Shantung claimed descent from duke Huan of Lu, whose second son Ch'ing-fu had adopted the surname Chung-sun, later changed to Meng-sun. In the T'ang period, the Meng clan of P'ing-ch'ang claimed descent from Meng Ching-tzu, a member of this family who figured in the *Analects*, 8/4. See the *CTCC* epitaphs for Meng Chun, d. 714 aged 56 *sui* and for Meng Hui, d. 733 aged 65 *sui*. Mencius himself was a great grandson of Meng Ching-tzu. The *KFSPWK* epitaph for Meng Shih, d. 704 aged 70 *sui*, would seem uncommon in claiming for him direct descent from Mencius. Meng Ching-su, prioress of a Taoist monastery, for whom Ts'en Wen-pen wrote a stele in 638, was traced, in imprecise terms, by descent from the circle of Confucius and Mencius; see *Chin shih hsü pien* 4/5a. I am grateful to Professor van der Loon for this reference.

60   *Li chi chu shu* 16E/13a.

61   *SS* 34/997; see also *SS* 34/999 for description of Mencius, Tzu-ssu and Hsün tzu as true disciples of Confucius in the Chan-kuo period. *CTS* 47/2024, *Ho chih*, pp. 168–9. Mencius's association with Hsün tzu, deriving in part from the juxtaposition of their biogs. in *Shih chi* ch. 74, was as characteristic of the medieval period as the juxtaposition of K'ung and Mo. For examples of the former, see *TKCK* 2/3a , memorial of 653 by Chang-sun Wu-chi; *Yang Ying-ch'uan chi* 3/2a; *STTS* 3/14a; *TWT* 84/2a, Liu Mien; *WYYH* 680/10a, P'ei Tu. The Sung *pi-chi* writer Hung Mai (1123–1202) commented critically on the latter juxtaposition; see *Jung chai hsü pi* 14/135–6.

62   *Li chi chu shu yin shu yin-te*, Peking: Harvard-Yenching, 1937, p. 8; *Mao shih chu shu yin shu yin-te*, p. 12. For the one exception, see *Li chi chu shu* 2/6a. The passage quoted here is the same passage that the scholar minister Wei Cheng anthologized in the *Ch'ün-shu chih yao*, 37/2b–3a. K'ung Ying-ta simply followed Cheng Hsüan in citing the *Mencius*, and did not use the passage to amplify a view of the nature.

63   For the *Chou i* sub-commentary, see Wang Chung-lin (1959), pp. 1–111.

64 For Chia Kung-yen's citations from the *Mencius*, see *Chou li yin-te fu chu shu yin shu yin-te*, p. 161, and *I li yin-te fu Cheng chu Chia shu yin shu yin-te*, p. 61.

65 See especially *I wen lei chü* 21/384–87, entry for *hsing ming*. Though the views of Hsün tzu are represented, in a *fu* by Chung Chang-ao of the Chin, no mention is made of the *Mencius* in the entry.

66 *Chou i chu shu* 9/2a.

67 *Tso chuan chu shu* 1/16a–b, referring to *Li chi chu shu* 7/9b–10a. In his gloss on the term *meng tien*, K'ung Ying-ta argues that Confucius had feelings like ordinary men and dreamt like ordinary men.

68 *Yü Pi-chien chi* 1/14a; cf. also 15b.

69 For formulations of the nature of the sub-commentary series, see *Chou i chi shu* 1/4a–b; *Li chi chu shu* 52/1b (*Chung yung*); *Mao shih chu shu* 18C/7b; *Li chi chu shu* 27/6a–b (*Yüeh chi*). See also Yang Hsiang-k'uei (1958), pp. 8–11.

70 Ch'en T'ieh-fan (1969), pp. 149–81, reviewing the *Chou i*; *Shang shu*; and *Mao shih*; Su Ying-hui (1968b).

71 *CTS* 77/2689, biog. of Ts'ui I-hsüan; *TFYK* 606/14a–b, undated edict, probably in Kao tsung's reign. The biog. states that 'in the end the matter did not proceed'.

72 *CTS* 189A/4950, biog. of Li Hsüan-chih. His glossary, the *San li yin i* (*Sounds and meanings in the Three ritual canons*), is mentioned in the biog., but not in the *CTS* bibliography.

73 For Wang Yüan-kan, see *THY* 77/1405; *CTS* 189B/4963, biog. His compilations are not entered in the *CTS* bibliography; but see *HTS* 57/1428, 1434, 1441, 1443, 1457, 1500, and *Ho chih*, pp. 19, 29, 42, 45, 68, and 152. Wang Yüan-kan's *HTS* biog., 199/5666–68, includes an argument by Chang Chien-chih, *c.* 625-after 705, canonized *Wen-chen* in 808 (*THY* 80/1488), refuting his contention that the mourning period should last for 36 months.

74 *Chang Yen kung chi* 13/1a; *WYYH* 652/2a–b.

75 For Liu Chih-chi's debate, see *THY* 77/1405–10; *TTCLC* 81/467–68; *TFYK* 50/6b–7a; *TKCK* 6/1a–8a; *Ta T'ang hsin yü* 9/143–44; Hung (1957), pp. 74–134.

76 *THY* 36/658; *CTS* 102/3178, biog. of Yüan Hsing-ch'ung; *CTS* 8/183. For Hsüan tsung's preface and its date, see *TKCK* 7/13b, note by Hsü Sung; for a rubbing of the text, see *Tō Gensō Sekidai Kōkyō*.

77 For the *Lao tzu* commentary, see *THY* 36/658; *TFYK* 53/16a; also *THY* 77/1410–11.

78 For the *Shang shu*, see *THY* 77/1410–11; *TFYK* 50/11a–b; *TKCK* 9/6a; *HTS* 57/1428.

79 *TLT* 21/6b.

80 For Yüan Hsing-ch'ung's argument, see *CTS* 102/3178–81, biog. of Yüan Hsing-ch'ung; *THY* 77/1410; *Ta T'ang hsin yü* 2/117; Kramers (1955).

81 For seventh-century views of the origin of the *Yüeh ling*, see K'ung Ying-ta, *Li chi chu shu* 14/1a; *SS* 32/925; Lu Te-ming, *Ching tien shih wen* 1/22a.

82 *CKCY* 2/29–30.

83 For the place of the *Yüeh ling* in Ming-t'ang controversies, see e.g. *THY* 11/272; 11/277; *CTS* 22/857; 22/869 etc. Cf. also the role of the *Yüeh ling* under the empress Wu in 699, in determining the scheduling of a military rehearsal ceremony; *THY* 26/502–03 and *CTS* 89/2900, biog. of Wang Fang-ch'ing. Also the memorials on the scheduling of executions, which according to *Yüeh ling* theory had to be in the autumn; *CTS* 102/3175 and *WYYH* 617/6b–8a, Hsü Chien; *Ch'ü-chiang Chang hsien-sheng wen chi* 7/8b.

84 For the ceremony of reading out seasonal commands, an observance that was associated with the text, see *THY* 26/491–92; *TT* 70/385. 1–386.1, with disapproving comment by Tu Yu.

85 For arguments that the text of the *Yüeh ling* was separately determined in about 725, see 'T'ang Yüeh ling chu po', by the Ch'ing scholar Ch'eng Jung-ching, in *T'ang Yüeh ling hsü k'ao*.

86 *THY* 26/491–2; *STTS* 24/914.

87 *THY* 75/1374.

88 *THY* 77/1410; *CTS* 9/219; *TFYK* 50/11b.

89 For the commentary, see *T'ang Yüeh ling chu*. This version of the text displaced earlier officially determined versions; see Chang Shen, *Wu ching wen tzu hsü (Preface to model characters of the Five canons)*, quoted in *TKCK* 11/5b, double column entry); see also below at note 153.

90 *THY* 77/1411; *THY* 36/658. For the *Hsiao ching* as a text representing Confucianism, see Lo Hsiang-lin (1954), pp. 91–2, showing that Hsüan tsung produced commentaries to all three. Before this, Wang Te-piao, d. 699 aged 80 *sui*, had done the same; see his *CTCC* epitaph. Later, the south-eastern scholar and Te tsung favourite Wei Chü-mou, 749–801, canonized *Chung*, did likewise; see *Ch'üan Tsai-chih wen chi* 23/2b–3a.

91 For the order to distribute empire wide, see *TTCLC* 74/417, act of grace of 12th month of 744 (corresponding to 1st day of 2nd month of 745 on the Julian calendar); *CTS* 9/218; *TKCK* 9/6a–b, noting variant date.

92 For the *Shih t'ai Hsiao ching*, see above, note 76.

93 For the increase in the numbers of candidates, see Yang Ch'ang, memorial of 729, *THY* 75/1376; *TT* 17/96.1; *TFYK* 639/22b–23a; also the memorial of Liu Chih, *TT* 17/98.3 on the increase in the numbers of those with official status. See also Guisso (1978), pp. 87–106 and Herbert (1986a), pp. 205–8, for the seventh-century background.

94 *TT* 15/83.2; *THY* 75/1376; *TFYK* 639/22a–b.

95 *THY* 75/1376; *TFYK* 639/22b–23a; *CTS* 185B/4820 and *HTS* 130/4496, biogs. of Yang Ch'ang; Herbert (1986), p. 208.

96 *TT* 17/96.1–97.1; Herbert (1986a), pp. 95–8.

97 For some commendations of scholars who were educated in the reign of Hsüan tsung, and whose attitude to the canons transcended the limitations of mere exegesis, see *WYYH* 955/7b, Sun Ti, epitaph for his father; *Yen Lu kung wen chi* 9/10a, of Hsien-yü Hsiang; *Yen Lu kung wen chi* 8/1b, of Kuo K'uei; *Ch'üan Tsai-chih wen chi* 19/1b, of Ma Sui; *Ch'üan Tsai-chih wen chi* 23/3b, of Wei Yü; *Liu Ho-tung chi* 8/114–5, of Liu Hun; *WYYH* 972/9b, Liang Su, of Tu-ku Chi.

98   *TLT* 4/5a–b; *THY* 75/1377; *TFYK* 639/24a–25a; Herbert (1985), p. 86.
      TKCK 8/16b, note by Hsü Sung, cites a comment in *TFYK* stating that
      this reform was in response to a memorial by Yao I. *THY* 76/1379
      mentions a reform proposal by Yao I in 736.

99   In 740, only 15 *chin shih* were passed; in 741, only 13; see *TKCK* 8/27a;
      8/30a; 9/25a; 9/27b. Li Lin-fu also affected decree examinations, as the
      unusually direct indictment by Yüan Chieh indicates; see *Yüan
      Tz'u-shan chi* 4/52, and Sun Wang (1957), pp. 16–7. See also *Feng shih
      wen chien chi* 3/2.

100   *Feng shih wen chien chi* 3/2; *T'ang chih yen* 14/154; *TFYK* 640/2b; des
      Rotours (1932), p. 141, note 2.

101   For Hsüan tsung's mentions of the *Ch'un-ch'iu*, see *THY* 28/534, in 725;
      CTS 8/201, in 734. For Yü Hsiu-lieh's request of 731, see *THY* 36/667;
      WYYH 694/12a; *CTS* 196A/5232. After a discussion, his proposal was
      rejected. The influence of the canon in history writing is to be seen for
      example in the projected extension of the *Ch'un-ch'iu* and the *Tso chuan*
      by P'ei Kuang-t'ing and others; see below, note 108. For a more modest
      extension of the *Ch'un-ch'iu*, see *CTS* 190B/5013, biog. of Liu Yün-chi.
      For the *Ch'un-ch'iu* in the management of the ancestral temple, see
      THY 17/353; 17/355 etc.; in policy towards the barbarians, *Ch'ü-chiang
      Chang hsien-sheng wen chi* 16/3b; in argument over the length of the
      mourning period, *HTS* 199/5666–68, memorial by Chang Chien-chih.

102   *STTS* 1/5b; 3/3b; *Tso chuan chu shu* 1/5a, both quoting *Mencius* 4B/21.
      Liu Chih-chi also quoted *Mo tzu*, who suggested the figure of 100, which
      in turn was supported by the *Kung-yang* tradition; see *Kung-yang chu
      shu* 1/1a–b and *STTS* 1/5b and commentary at 1/7a. Cf. also *SS* 42/1197,
      biog. of Li Te-lin, for the same *Mo tzu* citation.

103   *STTS* 14/8b–9a.

104   *STTS* 14/7b-8a.

105   *STTS* 10/11a, quoted by Pulleyblank (1961), p. 137.

106   *STTS* 14/14a–20a.

107   *STTS* 14/18a–b.

108   *WYYH* 884/10b, epitaph for P'ei Kuang-t'ing by Chang Chiu-ling; *CTS*
      84/2807, biog. of P'ei.

109   See note 143 below.

110   Liu K'uang's opinion is preserved in Lu Ch'un, *Ch'un-chiu Tan Chao chi
      chieh tsuan li (A compilation of the principles of the collected commenta-
      ries to the Ch'un-ch'iu by Tan [Chu] and Chao [K'uang])*, 1/11b. Liu
      K'uang's statement is also quoted by James Legge in Prolegomena to
      The Chinese Classics, Volume V, The Ch'un Ts'ew, with The Tso Chuen,
      Hong Kong: Lane Crawford and Co., and London: Trübner and Co.,
      1873, p. 31.

111   For Lu Shan-ching's compilation, see *Nihonkoku genzaisho mokuroku*
      p. 4; Niimi Hiroshi (1937), p. 135. Lu was known posthumously as a vice-
      president of the state academy directorate, which suggests that this
      academic tenure was his highest substantive post; see *CTS* 118/3415,
      biog. of Yüan Tsai.

112   *T'ang shih chi shih* 27/422; 28/426; *CTShih* 209/2174, Chia Yung. Hsiao's

remark was an adaptation of Fan Ning's in his preface to the commentary on the *Ku-liang chuan*, see *Ch'un-chiu Ku-liang chuan chu shu*, pref. 5b–6a. This remark was also quoted by Chang Chiu-ling, though without reference to the *Kung-yang chuan*; see *Ch'ü-chiang Chang hsien-sheng wen chi* 16/4b. Later in the dynasty, it became a tenet of the eclectic *Ch'un-ch'iu* scholars; see *TWT* 95/3b, Liu K'o; *Ch'un-ch'iu shih li*, pref. by Liu Fen.

113 *HTS* 202/5768, biog. of Hsiao Ying-shih.

114 *Ho yüeh ying ling chi* 1/80, Kao Shih; 1/60, Wang Wei.

115 *Chiu chia chi chu Tu shih* 1/1, Hung (1952), pp. 56–7.

116 See above, note 97.

117 See above, Ch. 2, note 146.

118 For the term *chin ch'en* in this period, see Ch. 6, note 151.

119 *Yen Lu kung wen chi* 12/5a; *Ho yüeh ying ling chi* 3/114, Yen Fang; Yen Keng-wang (1959), p. 696; cf. *Ts'en Chia-chou shih* 1/171–18a and *Yüan Tz'u-shan chi* 8/116–17 for post-rebellion examples.

120 *CTCC* epitaph for the *ming ching* graduate Cheng Shen, prefect of Ch'ing-chou, d. 734 aged 83 *sui*; he maintained that his nature was united with the *tao*, and that 'in all his actions, he did not violate goodness' (*Analects* 6/7).

121 For the 'old fisherman of Ts'ang-lang' (Ts'ang-lang weng), see *Mencius* 4A/9, in which Confucius commends the fisherman, here referred to as a boy; also David Hawkes (1985), pp. 206–7. For examples of the Ts'ang-lang image in the verse of the K'ai-yüan and T'ien-pao periods, see *Ho yüeh ying ling chi* 1/52, Ch'ang Chien; 1/73 and 74, Li Hsin; 2/82, Ts'en Shen; 2/99, Wang Ch'ang-ling.

122 For Po I and Shu Ch'i, see *Analects* 18/8; 7/15; 16/12. For Mencius's references to Po I, see *Mencius* 2A/2; 2A/9; 5B/1; 6B/6. A temple to Po I and Shu Ch'i stood in this period; see *Ch'üan T'ang wen* 357/1b, text by Liang Sheng-ch'ing. This is to be dated to 725, according to Ku Yen-wu, *Chin shih wen-tzu chi* 3/25a. See also *Ho yüeh ying ling chi* 1/73, Li Hsin. For the image of 'gathering ferns' (*ts'ai wei*) associated with them, see *Shih chi* 61/3123, biogs. of Po I and Shu Ch'i; *Ho yüeh ying ling chi* 1/61, Wang Wei; 1/73, Li Hsin; 2/95–6, Ch'u Kuang-hsi. For later comment on or commemoration of Po I and Shu Ch'i, see *Huang-fu Ch'ih-cheng wen chi* 2/1a–2a; *Han Ch'ang-li chi* 3/12/97–8.

123 *TKCK* 10/2b. For the unconventional performance as chief examiner of Li K'uei, in 759, see *THY* 76/1379 and *CTS* 126/3559, biog. For the examinations at Lo-yang, see *TFYK* 640/11a and *TKCK* 10/18a–19a. Probably the first Lo-yang examiner was Yang Wan (*CTS* 11/276), while Chia Chih, holding the basic office of president of the right of the department of affairs of state (*shang shu yu ch'eng*) was chief examiner at Ch'ang-an. That Hsü Sung is probably correct in this emendation is indicated by the later accounts of a *chin shih* success in 765, that of Hsü Shen. Hsü was passed by Chia Chih (*Ch'üan Tsai-chih wen chi* 24/1a–b), and Li Ao specifically recorded of him that he was 'entered on the register at Ching-ch'ao fu (i.e. Ch'ang-an) and was offered as a *chin shih* candidate' (*Li Wen kung chi* 11/91a). Cf. Fu Hsüan-ts'ung (1980), p. 190, note 1.

124 *THY* 76/1395–96; *TT* 15/84.1; *CTS* 119/3430–34, biog. of Yang Wan; *CTS* 190B/5029–31, biog. of Chia Chih; *TFYK* 640/4b–10b; *TKCK* 10/7a–13b.

125 *THY* 76/1399; *CTS* 11/275; *TCTC* 223/7165, 764.19; *TFYK* 640/10b–11a; *TKCK* 10/17a–18a. In this year, the annual tribute of candidates in the categories of child prodigies and 'the filial and fraternal who give their strength to the fields' was stopped.

126 For Chao K'uang's submission, see *TT* 17/97.1–99.1; also *WYYH* 765/6a–8a, for the first part. The post of prefect of Yang-chou, by which he is referred, was probably his highest tenure. In *Lü Ho-shu wen chi* 4/5a, he is called 'the late prefect of Yang-chou'; in *Ch'üan Tsai-chih wen chi* 41/6a, he is also referred to as 'Chao of Yang-chou'. For his proposals, see also Herbert (1986a), pp. 108–11.

127 For the *San li* examination in 789–93, see *TT* 15/84.1–84.2; *THY* 76/1396–97; *TFYK* 640/13b–14b; *CTS* 44/1892, commentary; *HTS* 44/1159; des Rotours (1932), p. 130 and n. 1. For the names of successful candidates, see *TKCK* 27/38a (Five Dynasties period); *CTCC* epitaph for Fan Yin, died 870 aged 42 *sui*, mentioning a relative, Wang Hsiu-fu, as a successful candidate.

128 Ku Shao-lien, himself a *chin shih* of 770 and a former grand secretary, was examiner in 793, 794, and 798. In 793, in the *po hsüeh hung tz'u* examination, he set the topic 'Yen tzu does not repeat his faults' (*Analects* 6/7; 6/11). Han Yü's answer, *Han Ch'ang-li chi* 4/14/32–33, contained references to concepts of 'sincerity and enlightenment' drawn from the *Chung yung*. Tu Huang-shang said of Ku that he was 'thoroughly versed in [the relations between] heaven and man, and exhausted fully the beginnings of nature and destiny'; see *WYYH* 918/3b–7b. For another important tribute to Ku as an examiner, see *WYYH* 988/4b–6b, Lü Wen.

129 Kao Ying, himself also a *chin shih* of 763, and a former grand secretary, was chief examiner in 799 and 800. In 800, Kao set the line 'By nature men are close; by practice they grow apart', from *Analects* 17/2. For a translation of Po Chü-i's answer, see des Rotours (1932), pp. 335–42. In his preface for Po's collected works, Yüan Chen named this *fu* as being celebrated among new *chin shih* candidates at the capital; see *Yüan shih Ch'ang-ch'ing chi* 51/1a.

130 Ch'üan Te-yü was recognized as an exception in not having taken a regular examination, a fact of which he seems to have been proud; see *Kuo shih pu* 2/33 and *Yin hua lu* 2/77. He was, however, more conventional as an examiner in having been a grand secretary; see Ch. 6, note 195. In his second *chin shih* dissertation question of 802, *Ch'üan Tsai-chih wen chi* 40/3a–b, he asked for comment on the *Analects* 6/7 statement that 'for three months Yen Hui did not contravene goodness', and the *Mencius* 2A/2 remark that 'at forty my mind was no longer moved'. Cf. *Ch'üan Tsai-chih wen chi* 37/10b–11a, in which he attributed importance to the latter phrase. It also figured in *Li Wen kung chi* 2/7b.

131 In 805, Ch'üan Te-yü's *ming ching Li chi* dissertation question opened with the sentence, 'The *Ta hsüeh* contains the way of illuminating virtue;

the *Chung yung* has the techniques for exhausting fully the nature'; see *Ch'üan Tsai-chih wen chi* 40/17a. Ch'üan expected candidates to be 'thoroughly versed in the principles of nature and destiny'; see 40/10a–b; but cf. his own understanding of *hsing ming* primarily as destiny, 30/8a–b.

132 *Yüan shih Ch'ang-ch'ing chi* 28/5a–b, decree examination answer of 806, containing one of the strongest denunciations of the knowledge of the canons required in the examinations.

133 *THY* 76/1398; *TFYK* 640/17b–18b; *CTS* 44/1892; *CTS* 16/502; *HTS* 44/1159 and 1161; des Rotours (1932), p. 29, p. 34, pp. 149–50, dates 822 or 823; *TKCK* 19/28a–29a and note by Hsü Sung on p. 29a dates 823.

134 *Lu Hsüan kung han-yüan chi* 6/10a; *WYYH* 473/6b; *TTCLC* 106/543; *TKCK* 12/3b–4a. Ch'üan Te-yü's extant *ming ching* dissertation questions on the *Ch'un-ch'iu* and the *Three traditions*, (for 802, see *Ch'üan Tsai-chih wen chi* 40/5a and 6b–7a; for 803, 40/11a and 13a; for 805, 40/16b and 18a–b), were for the *Tso chuan* and the *Ku-liang chuan*; the *Kung-yang chuan* is not represented. Ch'üan mentioned his own addiction to the *Ch'un-ch'iu* in *Ch'üan Tsai-chih wen chi* 30/1a–3a.

135 *TKCK* 21/5a–b and note by Hsü Sung; *CTS* 17B/551; cf. *TFYK* 641/4a–b; *TTCLC* 29/106.

136 For the two early engravings, see Tsien Tsuen-hsuin (1962), pp. 73–9.

137 *SS* 75/1718, biog. of Liu Cho; *SS* 32/947; *Feng shih wen chien chi* 2/18–19. Sections of Ts'ai Yung's engraving, however, remained buried at Lo-yang, and some were discovered later in the dynasty, to find their way into private possession; see *Liu Pin-k'o chia hua lu*, p. 9.

138 *Feng shih wen chien chi* 2/18–9. For the place of the 'canons in stone' in the syllabus of the orthography school, see *TLT* 21/16a; also *TKCK* 11/5a, Chang Shen. The entries in *SS* 32/945–6 and *CTS* 46/1986–87 also indicate the importance the scholarly world attached to these engraved texts.

139 For Yen Shih-ku's established versions', see above at note 11. The language used to describe his commission deliberately echoes that of Ts'ai Yung's biog. in *Hou Han shu* 60B/1990.

140 *CTS* 183/4728, biog. of Wu Min-chih; *CTS* 191/5099, biog. of Li Ssu-chen confirms the dating.

141 *Chang Yen kung chi* 13/1a; *WYYH* 652/2a–b.

142 *CTCC* epitaph for K'ai Hsiu-yüan, died 733 aged 55 *sui*; *Teng k'o chi k'ao pu* p. 98 indicates that he was a *ming ching* of the year 700.

143 *THY* 36/658; *Ch'ü-chiang Chang hsien-sheng wen chi* 15/1a–b; *Yü hai* 42/34a–b and 45/18b–19a; Ikeda (1971), p. 67.

144 *Feng shih wen chien chi* 2/19; the account ends with a lament that an engraving in stone would have to wait 'until the [Yellow] river flowed clear'.

145 For Li Yang-ping's proposal, see *TWT* 81/7a–b. This letter may be dated to the reign of Tai tsung, by Li Yang-ping's reference to 'eight generations'. Cf. *WYYH* 703/2b, Liang Su, referring to Te tsung as the ninth, and *Liu Ho-tung chi* 1/22, Liu Tsung-yüan referring to Shun tsung as the tenth emperor of the dynasty. In 780, Li Yang-ping was an

assistant in the state academy directorate, see des Rotours (1975a), p. 92.
146 *CTS* 129/3602, biog. of Han Huang; *WYYH* 973/4b, report of conduct by
     Ku K'uang; *WYYH* 769/6a–b, Lu Kuei-meng; cf. *T'ang yü lin* 2/49. For
     the hostility between Han Huang and Chang Shen as a vice-president of
     the directorate, see *CTS* 69/3445, biog. of Ch'ang Kun. For the
     suggestion that a work of *Ku-liang* exegesis be engraved in the south-
     east, see *Ch'üan Tsai-chih wen chi* 20/2b–3a.
147 *TKCK* 11/1a and 11/4b–6b, quoting a rubbing of the stone engraving of
     837. This text praised Ts'ai Yung's stone engraving version, and claimed
     to have used it in determining certain variants. The assistant was Yen
     Ch'uan-ching, a *hsiao lien* graduate, and possibly a member of the same
     clan as Yen Shih-ku and Yen Chen-ch'ing, both noted philologists. The
     list of standard characters that Chang Shen and he compiled was cited by
     Wang Ching in *Ta T'ang chiao ssu lu* 1/7a. An account of its transmission
     is given in *SKCSTMTY* pp. 855–6. A *fu* on the theme of the version of
     the canons on the roofed wall in the state academy directorate is at *WYYH*
     61/2b–3b, and would seem to describe the version done by Chang Shen's
     commission. Another, *WYYH* 61/3b–4b, seems to refer to the K'ai-
     ch'eng engraving in stone. For Chang Shen, see also *Kuo shih pu* 3/54.
148 *THY* 65/11246. Liu T'ai-chen's spirit path stele by P'ei Tu, *Ch'üan T'ang
     wen* 538/14b, refers very briefly to this incident. It also shows that Liu
     held tenures typical of a post-rebellion academic official, in the court of
     sacrifices, as a court diarist, rescript writer and grand secretary and chief
     examiner, besides this tenure as director of the imperial library.
149 *Ch'üan Tsai-chih wen chi* 20/3a.
150 Two titles entered in the *HTS* bibliography suggest an attempt to
     re-determine the text of the canons in 818; *HTS* 57/1434, *Ho chih* p. 30,
     has a *Li chi tzu li i-t'ung (Variants in the character standards in the Li
     chi)*, in one *chüan*, with an additional note, 'determined on imperial
     order in 818'. *HTS* 57/1441, *Ho chih* p. 43, enters a *Ch'un-ch'iu chia
     chien (Additions and excisions from the Ch'un-ch'iu)*, again in one
     chüan, with the note, 'prepared and determined by the state academy
     directorate in 818'. *Chih chai shu lu chieh t'i* 3/55 states that this was 'in a
     similar category to the *Wu ching wen tzu*'.
151 *THY* 66/1160, dated 12th month of 819.
152 For the 831 renovation, see *Liu Yü-hsi chi* 8/73–74. Pien Hsiao-hsüan
     (1963), p. 70, dates this record to between 828 and 831. For the Wei
     Kung-su mentioned, see Ch. 4, note 193.
153 For the K'ai-ch'eng engraving in stone, see *THY* 66/1162; *THY* 77/1411;
     CTS 17B/571; *CTS* 173/4490–91, biog. of Cheng T'an, implying a date of
     830 for the commission; *TCTC* 245/7930, 837.12; *CTCC* epitaph for
     Chao ?-chih, d. early 835 aged 59 *sui*, states that as an erudit of the *Li
     chi*, he 'concurrently directed the matter of the canons in stone'. *Shih
     ching k'ao* 2/1a–8a; *SKCSTMTY*, pp. 856–7, describing the *Chiu ching
     tzu-yang*, by T'ang Yüan-tu, and its relation to the *Wu ching wen-tzu* of
     776. Taga (1953), p. 263, called the K'ai-ch'eng engraving 'an epitaph for
     the T'ang school system'.
154 For post-rebellion emperors citing the *Ch'un-ch'iu*, see *CTS* 10/262, Su

tsung; *TTCLC* 1/2 and *THY* 66/1156, Te tsung; *THY* 29/537 and *TCTC* 236/7620, 805.28, Hsien tsung. Wen tsung had a scholarly interest in the *Ch'un-ch'iu*; see *HTS* 200/5707, biog. of Shih Shih-kai; *TFYK* 40/28b, describing Wen tsung's compilation *Yü chi Ch'un-ch'iu Tso shih lieh kuo ching chuan (Imperially compiled canon and commentary for the various states [drawn from] the Ch'un-ch'iu and the Tso chuan)*. This work was referred to the history office in 835.

155 For the post-rebellion *Ch'un-ch'iu* school, see Pulleyblank (1960), pp. 88–91; and (1959), p. 147; Chang Ch'ün (1974), pp. 149–59; Yoshihara (1974), pp. 67–104; and (1976), pp. 633–53; Inaba Ichirō (1970), pp. 389–96.

156 For references to all three scholars, see *CTS* 189B/4977, biog. of Lu Ch'un; *Kuo shih pu* 3/54; *HTS* 168/5127–8; *HTS* 200/5705–07. For some characterizations of the far south-east as an area of stability where, after the rebellion, scholars gathered, see *TWT* 73/6b, Li Han; *WYYH* 988/5a–b, Lü Wen; *Liu Yü-hsi chi* 2/15.

157 For Lu Ch'un's account of Tan Chu and Tan's relationship with Chao K'uang and with himself, see *Ch'un-ch'iu tsuan li* 1/18a-19a. Tan Chu compiled two works, the *Ch'un-ch'iu t'ung li (General principles of the Ch'un-ch'iu)* in 3 *chüan*, and the *Ch'un-ch'iu chi chuan (Collected commentaries to the Ch'un-ch'iu)*. According to *Ch'un-ch'iu tsuan li* 1/18b, his work was completed in 770.

158 *Ch'un-ch'iu tsuan li* 1/1b.

159 *Ch'un-ch'iu tsuan li* 1/5b–6a; for the idea of 'no constant teacher', *Ch'un-ch'iu tsuan li* 1/6a, see *Analects* 19/22.

160 *Ch'un-ch'iu tsuan li* 1/7a-b.

161 *Ch'un-ch'iu tsuan li* 1/7b; *Analects* 9/30. D.C. Lau, *Confucius: the Analects*, Harmondsworth, Middlesex: Penguin Books, 1979, p. 100, translates, 'the exercise of moral discretion'.

162 See the two essays on the *ti* sacrifice by Chao K'uang, *Ch'un-ch'iu tsuan li* 2/13a–19a; also 2/12a.

163 *Ch'un-ch'iu tsuan li* 6/10b.

164 For the small space the *Ch'un-ch'iu* scholars gave to analysis of omens, see *Ch'un-ch'iu tsuan li* 6/10b–11a, 9/7a.

165 *Ch'un-ch'iu tsuan li* 1/12b, quoting *Ching tien shih wen*.

166 *Ch'un-ch'iu tsuan li* 1/10a–b.

167 Chao's argument that the *Tso chuan* and the *Kuo yü* were by different hands was not new; see *Tso chuan chu shu* 59/5a and 37/9a, where it is given as the opinion of Fu Hsüan and of the Sui exegete Liu Hsüan. See Hung (1937), p. xlv. *HTS* 200/5706, biog. of Tan Chu implies that it was Tan who argued that the *Tso* and the *Kuo yü* were by different authors; this is likely to be an error, in view of the above.

168 Lu Ch'un had an 11-year discipleship under Tan Chu; see *Ch'un-ch'iu tsuan li* 1/16b. Following Tan's death, and with the help of his son, and in consultation with Chao K'uang, he copied out Tan's work, completing an account of the school's writings in 775. Lu Ch'un compiled three works relating to the *Ch'un-ch'iu*. The *Ch'un-ch'iu chi chuan tsuan li (Compilation of the principles from collected commentaries to the Ch'un-*

ch'iu) in 10 *chüan*; see *HTS* 57/1441, *Ho chih* p. 42; *SKCSTMTY* p. 522; and *Ku ching chieh hui han* 18; the *Ch'un-ch'iu wei chih (Concealed import of the Ch'un-ch'iu)* in 3 *chüan*; cf. *HTS* 57/1441, *Ho chih* p. 42, both of which read 2 *chüan*, and do not attribute the title to an author; *SKCSTMTY* p. 523; and *Ku ching chieh hui han* 19; and *Ch'un-ch'iu chi-chuan pien i (Resolution of doubts from collected commentaries to the Ch'un-ch'iu)* in 10 *chüan*; see *SKCSTMTY* p. 524 and *Ku ching chieh hui han* 20. *HTS* 57/1441 and *Ho chih* p. 42 enter an unattributed *Ch'un-ch'iu pien i* in 7 *chüan*, and also a *Lu Chih chi chu Ch'un-ch'iu* in 20 *chüan*, which may derive from *THY* 36/660.

169   The main sources for Lu Ch'un's career are *Liu Ho-tung chi* 9/132–33 and 31/504–05; *CTS* 189B/4977, *HTS* 168/5127–28, biogs.; *HTS* 200/ 5705–07. From these, from successive contributions he made to ritual controversies, and from other evidence, it appears he was recommended to the court and appointed to a junior post in the court of sacrifices probably between 775 and about 778 (*Ch'un-ch'iu tsuan li* 1/19a); then became an omissioner of the left (*CTS* 189B/4977) in the period of Yang Yen's financial reforms. He was banished to the south following Yang Yen's downfall, making the journey with the official scholar Shen Chi-chi in 781 (*T'ai-p'ing kuang chi* 352/3697 and Dudbridge (1983), p. 61 and note 9). Later he became an erudit of the court of sacrifices, in 785 (*Ta T'ang chiao ssu lu* 4/8a, cf. *CTS* 21/844); a supernumerary secretary to the board of punishments in 788 (*Ta T'ang chiao ssu lu* and *HTS* 15/379); a secretary to the board of granaries, with concurrent ritual responsibilities in late 790 (*CTS* 149/4032, biog. of Liu Mien); and a secretary of the left of the central department of the ministry of affairs of state (*tso ssu lang chung*) in 795 (*THY* 13/313; *TT* 50/290.3). He was demoted to be an erudit of the Kuo tzu hsüeh and held this post in 803 (see *Liu Ho-tung chi* 9/133, *CTS* 189B/4977, *Lü Ho-shu wen chi* 4/4b–5b and *THY* 36/660 and note 171 below; also *TCTC* 236/7603, 803.13). He then served as prefect in Hsin-chou, modern Kiangsi, and T'ai-chou, modern Chekiang (*CTS* 189B/4977 and *Liu Ho-tung chi* 9/133). When the reform movement gained power, he was recalled as grand secretary in the chancellery, and finally reader to the crown prince (*Liu Ho-tung chi* 9/133 and *CTS* 189B/4977–8). Probably some time during the period 802–3, he may have corresponded with Ch'üan Te-yü on selection policy; see Ch. 6, note 213.

170   *Liu Ho-tung chi* 31/504–06; see also *Liu Ho-tung chi* 11/172–3, a slightly different grouping; *CTS* 135/3736; *TCTC* 236/7603, 803.13; *TCTC* 231/7609–10, 805.6; also Pien Hsiao-hsüan, *Liu Yü-hsi nien-p'u* pp. 28–9. For Ling Shih-hsieh, see *Liu Ho-tung chi* 25/413; cf. 43/720–21 and *CTS* 135/3736 for the reformer Ling Chun, who later wrote a *Hou Han Ch'un-ch'iu*. For Lü Wen as a pupil of Lu Ch'un, see *Lü Ho-shu wen chi*, preface by Liu Yü-hsi, 1b; Lü also wrote on the importance of the *Ch'un-ch'iu* to a relative; see *Lü Ho-shu wen chi* 3/1a–3a. For some other *Ch'un-ch'iu* specialists in this period, see *CTS* 160/4209, biog. of Yü-wen Chi; *CTS* 189B/4978, biog. of Feng K'ang and *THY* 36/660; *HTS* 200/5708, biog. of Shih Shih-kai; *Huang-fu Ch'ih-cheng wen chi* 2/9a.

171 For the memorial of presentation, see *Lü Ho-shu wen chi* 4/4b–5b. This enters Lu Ch'un's post as erudit of the Kuo-tzu hsüeh. *THY* 36/660, however, enters the work as by Lu Chih, secretary of the chancellery, probably a double error in that the character printed is the given name of Lu Hsüan kung and because Lu Ch'un was not yet promoted. For Lü Wen's career, focussing on his T'u-fan mission of 804–5, on which he accompanied the official historian Chang Chien until Chang's death, see *CTS* 137/3769 and *HTS* 160/4967, biogs. and Ogawa (1964), pp. 70–84. On this mission, Lü was nearly joined by another second generation disciple of Tan Chu, Tou Ch'ün; see *CTS* 155/4120, biog. of Tou.

172 Liu quoted Lu Ch'un in his exile period: in *Liu Ho-tung chi* 31/505, commenting on Lu Ch'un's gloss on the 11th year of duke Hsüan (*Tso chuan chu shu* 22/8a and 9b–10a), Liu remarked, 'We see here the sage's praising and blaming, bestowing and taking away, and wherein its appropriateness resides. This is what is called "defects and good points not being concealed".' Lu Ch'un, *Ch'un-ch'iu wei chih* 2/30b–32a, concludes with the same phrase. For the problem of identifying Yüan of Jao-chou, the recipient of Liu's letter, see Ts'en Chung-mien (1962b), pp. 409–10.

173 *Liu Ho-tung chi* 9/132.

174 For the *Fei Kuo yü*, see *Liu Ho-tung chi* 44–45/746–88; see also particularly Gentzler (1966) esp. pp. 184–6. At the close of the *Fei Kuo yü*, *Liu Ho-tung chi* 45/788, and in a letter to Lü Wen, *Liu Ho-tung chi* 31/506–7, Liu condemned the attitude that considered the *Kuo yü* close to the canons. Ironically, it was later classified as a work of *Ch'un-ch'iu* scholarship; see *HTS* 57/1441 and *Ho chih* p. 43.

175 *Liu Ho-tung chi* 31/305; 44/767–68; *Tso chuan chu shu* 13/5a–8a (9th–10th year of duke Hsi). Hsün Hsi, adviser to duke Hsien of Chin, had allowed the duke to kill his heir apparent and set up another son, the child of his favourite concubine, in his place. Hsün Hsi had sworn to instruct his son and to remain true to him till death. After the duke's death, however, this son was killed, and Hsün Hsi, far from dying with him, instituted yet another son as heir. Only when this son in turn was killed did Hsün Hsi die. In the *Ch'un-ch'iu*, the style used in narrating the death of Hsün Hsi was traditionally interpreted as meaning that he was a good man, rather than a bad one, for it conformed with the style used in two other episodes in which good advisers were murdered (*Tso chuan chu shu* 5/2a–b, 2nd year of duke Huan; *Tso chuan chu shu* 9/3a, 12th year of duke Chuang). To Liu Tsung-yüan, however, it was beyond doubt that Hsün Hsi was culpable. Confucius's purpose in the *Ch'un-ch'iu*, in using a form of words that implied he was good, was rather 'to stir up those who might be unable to die [in comparable circumstances]'. Confucius therefore drew attention, in isolation from the earlier facts of his career, to Hsün Hsi's eventual death. In this, Confucius, in Liu's view, was fulfilling the principle he had announced in *Analects* 7/29, that he 'should not enquire into a man's past'. Liu further suggested that Confucius used a similar pedagogic technique when in the *Ch'un-ch'iu* he charged that Chih, heir apparent of Hsü, had murdered his father, when

all Chih had done was to fail to taste his father's medicine before him or prepared it badly (*Tso chuan chu shu* 48/12a–b, 19th year of duke Chao).

176 *Liu Ho-tung chi* 4/68–70. In the first part of a two section note on the *Analects*, Liu conceded that the text was written down finally probably only by Confucius's disciples' disciples. In the second part, he held that the anomalous opening to the final chapter (*Analects* 20/1), which gives the words of the emperor Yao, represented statements that Confucius constantly recited in his teachings and that his disciples, only partially understanding, had transmitted and reproduced when they compiled the text. Both parts of the note imply that the text of the *Analects* contained Confucius's own teaching. For respect for the profundity of Confucius's thought, see also *Liu Ho-tung chi* 16/297–98, and Ch. 4, note 243.

177 Even in the far south, however, Liu had met a *Ch'un-ch'iu* specialist; see *Liu Ho-tung chi* 5/76.

178 The most interesting instance is that of Tou Ch'ün, who was taught the *Ch'un-ch'iu* in the south-east by a disciple of Tan Chu. He compiled a work in 30 *chüan* which was twice presented on his behalf to Te tsung but not acknowledged. Liu Yü-hsi and Liu Tsung-yüan were said to have despised him (but cf. *Liu Ho-tung chi* 38/606–07), and he later avoided accompanying the official historian Chang Chien and the *Ch'un-ch'iu* scholar and Lu Ch'un disciple Lü Wen on their mission to the Tibetans; see *CTS* 155/4120–1, biog. and *Tou shih lien-chü chi* p. 15a. For *Ch'un-ch'iu* scholarship in the middle and late Yüan-ho period, see also *Han Ch'ang-li chi* 6/34/85–86, Fan Shao-shu; *Han Ch'ang-li chi* 4/18/81–82, Yin Yu; *Han Ch'ang-li chi* 2/5/38–40, Lu T'ung. Inaba (1970), p. 383, notes that Lu T'ung was the author of a work called the *Ch'un-ch'iu che wei* (*Selecting the subtle in the Ch'un-ch'iu*) in 4 *chüan*. This is entered in *Chün chai tu shu chih* 1B/4a.

179 *TWT* 95/2b–3a, Pulleyblank (1959), pp. 147–9.

180 See above, note 133.

181 Wei Piao-wei was author of a work entitled *Ch'un-ch'iu san chuan tsung li* (*Gathering of the principles of the Three traditions to the Ch'un-ch'iu*); see *HTS* 57/1441 and *Ho chih* p. 42.

182 For Liu Fen, see *CTS* 190B/5064. A preface to Tu Yü's *Ch'un-ch'iu shih li* is identified as by him in *SKCSTMTY* pp. 520–2.

183 Ch'en Yüeh was the author of a work entitled *Che chung Ch'un-ch'iu* (*Judging appropriately between [the Three traditions to] the Ch'un-ch'iu*), in 30 *chüan*, pref. in *Ch'üan T'ang wen* 829/3b–4b; see also *HTS* 57/1441 and *Ho chih* p. 43 and *Ssu-k'ung Piao-sheng wen chi* 3/2b.

184 *Ssu-k'ung Piao-sheng wen-chi* 3/1a–2a.

185 *WYYH* 796/6a–b, endorsing a remark attributed to Wen-chung tzu, and attacking the *Ch'un-ch'iu* scholarship of Han Huang (*CTS* 129/3603, biog. and *HTS* 57/1441 and *Ho chih* p. 42) as it was preserved in a stone inscription at Jun-chou, probably in the Confucian temple there. Lu Kuei-meng and another late T'ang scholar, Ch'en Shang, discussed the idea of Liu Chih-chi that the *Ch'un-ch'iu* was an historical rather than a canonical text; see *WYYH* 690/10b–11b, and cf. *T'ang yü lin* 2/56–7.

186 *P'i tzu wen sou* 3/35; *STTS* 14/2b–11a; Inaba (1970), pp. 389–90.

187 *TT* 105/549.2.

188 *Ch'üan Tsai-chih wen chi* 13/10b, spirit path stele for Tu Ya, who had been appreciated by Fang Kuan before the rebellion, and for whom cf. also *CTS* 146/3962–64, biog. Another example of a high-ranking official with this interest is Ch'i K'ang; see *Ch'üan Tsai-chih wen chi* 14/1a.

189 *Ch'üan Tsai-chih wen chi* 33/2a, preface to Ts'ui Yu-fu's collected works. Ts'ui Yu-fu had a south-eastern background, in common with other scholars who developed an interest in self-cultivation; see Ebrey (1978), pp. 96–8.

190 For Chang I and his commentary on the *Mencius*, see *CTS* 125/3545–6, biog.; *THY* 36/659; cf. also *Ch'üan Tsai-chih wen chi* 14/1b.

191 *WYYH* 820/4a–5a; *WYYH* 860/1a–10b, Li Hua; *Fo tsu t'ung chi* 7/189.1; *P'i-ling chi* 9/2b. Liang Su, in a sacrificial graveside prayer written on behalf of Tu-ku Chi for Li Hua, *WYYH* 982/2a, described him as 'taking a leisured journey (*yu yu, Mao shih chu shu* 17D/1b) in the realm of *hsing ming*'. For Li Hua's interest in Mencius, among other pre-Ch'in texts, see *WYYH* 742/4b.

192 *P'i-ling chi* 3/3a; 17/7b–8a; 9/1a–4a; also *P'i-ling chi* 20/6a for Tu-ku discussing 'life and death'. Tu-ku was, however, aware of the *Analects* statement that Confucius was reluctant to discuss *ming*; see *P'i-ling chi* 20/5a and *Analects* 9/1. Cf. also *Liu Ho-tung chi* 8/115, report of conduct for Liu Hun, for the example of another scholar who declined to discuss such questions.

193 For Liang Su's debt to Tu-ku Chi, see *WYYH* 737/8a–b; *WYYH* 703/4b–6b; *WYYH* 972/9b–13a; *WYYH* 982/3a–4b. For Liang's interest in 'effecting the complete development of his nature' and his identification of this as a Buddhist process, see *TWT* 61/5b–8a. Cf. *Fo tsu t'ung chi* 7/189.2. His disciple Lü Wen, an adherent of the *Ch'un-ch'iu* school, also spoke of a process of 'effecting the complete development of the nature', as, by implication, a non-Confucian process; see *Lü Ho-shu wen chi* 1/7a–b. Liu Yü-hsi, in commenting on the early intellectual life of Wei Ch'u-hou, an official scholar, said that he 'exhausted the source of *hsing* and *ming*', and linked this with his interest in Buddhism; see *Liu Yü-hsi chi* 19/164.

194 *TWT* 92/11a–b, pref. by Ts'ui Kung.

195 For Liang Su's role in Han Yü's examination career, see *Han Ch'ang-li chi* 4/17/76–77.

196 For Ch'üan Te-yü's connection with Liang Su, see *WYYH* 966/2b–3b, epitaph for Ch'üan's mother by Liang; also *WYYH* 983/3a–b, sacrificial graveside prayer by Ch'üan. For Ch'üan's connection with the young Han Yü, see *Ch'üan Tsai-chih wen chi, pu k'o* 5a–b. The Chung-ling referred to is in Kiangsi, where Ch'üan held office in 'early Chen-yüan', that is in about 785, when Han Yü was 18 *sui*. For Ch'üan's south-eastern background, see also e.g. *Ch'üan Tsai-chih wen chi* 39/3b–4b.

197 *CTS* 148/4002 biog.

198 *Ch'üan Tsai-chih wen chi* 1/11b–12a; cf. 45/8b, memorial of 797, for comparable vocabulary.

199 *Ch'üan Tsai-chih wen chi* 32/8b, dated 781; and 32/6b, dated 787.

200 *Ch'üan Tsai-chih wen chi* 24/11a. When Han approached Lu San with recommendations for the *chin shih*, he stressed the precedent of Liang Su's recommendations to Lu Hsüan kung, a point that was the more telling to Lu San because he had known Liang Su; see note 195.

201 *Ch'üan Tsai-chih wen chi* 36/8a–9a.

202 *Ch'üan Tsai-chih wen chi* 46/5b; cf. also *Ch'üan Tsai-chih wen chi* 36/8a–9a, written probably in 802, on the same or a similar occasion as that described in *Han Ch'ang-li chi* 5/19/6–7.

203 *Li Wen kung chi* 2/7b; also *Li Wen kung chi* 17/140b, and cf. *Li Wen kung chi* 13/110b–111b. For Han Yü's connection with Lu San, see *Han Ch'ang-li chi* 4/17/75; cf. 3/11/68–69; 5/19/6–7.

204 *Ch'üan Tsai-chih wen chi* 24/10a–11b.

205 *Li Wen kung chi* 13/110b–111b. For Li Ao's high estimate of Yen Hui, as the disciple of Confucius who attained most and who best understood his doctrines, see below note 210. For Han Yü's emphasis on Yen, *Han Ch'ang-li chi* 5/19/21–22; also Chang Chi, letter to Han, in *Han Ch'ang-li chi* 4/14/38. References to Yen Hui and his inner life are frequent over this period; e.g. *Ch'üan Tsai-chih wen chi* 42/9b; 1/12a; also Ch. 2, note 255.

206 *Li Wen kung chi* 17/140b. Li used the same phrase in *Li Wen kung chi* 2/8a.

207 Eclecticism was the imperial attitude in the final years of Te tsung's reign; see *Ch'üan Tsai-chih wen chi* 23/2b–3a and *CTS* 135/3728–29, biog. of Wei Chü-mou. *Ch'üan Tsai-chih wen chi* 45/8b, memorial of 797, is likely to refer to the same event.

208 I am grateful to Professor T.H. Barrett for letting me see his detailed argument dating the composition of the *Fu hsing shu* to before 800 or 801. Neither Hanabusa (1964), p. 69, nor Hartman (1986), pp. 204–6, dates Han Yü's *Yüan hsing*; but cf. Rideout (1948), pp. 406–7.

209 *Li Wen kung chi* 2/5a; 4/27a–b.

210 For Li's focus on Yen Hui, see *Li Wen kung chi* 1/2b–3a; 2/7a, quoting *Analects* 6/7 and 11/18 and *Chou i chu shu* 8/8a–b.

211 *Liu Yü-hsi chi* 19/166.

212 *Han Ch'ang-li chi* 3/11/59–67; *Analects* 17/2. This statement had general currency in T'ang: e.g. *Han shu* 63/2869 and commentary by Yen Shih-ku; *THY* 40/729, Liu Chih-chi; *TT* 13/73.1, Tu Yu; *Liu Ho-tung chi* 33/527–28; *Han Ch'ang-li chi* 2/4/23. It was even used with reference to the barbarians, who might, 'with practice', draw closer to the Chinese; see *TTCLC* 128/689, edict of late 738, ordering them to 'observe the ritual in the state academy directorate'. See also *Po Hsiang-shan chi* 7/45/30, *Tse-lin* 2; 7/46/57, *Ts'e-lin* 34.

213 *Li Wen kung chi* 2/9a–b; *Han Ch'ang-li chi* 3/11/62.

214 *Li Wen kung chi* 2/11a; 2/7b.

215 *Han Chang-li chi* 3/11/63; 3/11/72–73.

216 *Han Ch'ang-li chi* 3/11/63–64. For this inconsistency, see the remark by Shao Po (fl. *c.* 1120) quoted in *Ching i k'ao* 232/1a–b.

217 E.g. *WYYH* 980/12b, Li Hua; *Huang-fu Ch'ih-cheng wen chi* 2/8a, of Ku K'uang. Even the Buddhists laid claim to this idea, see *Fo tsu t'ung-chi*

7/189.1, quoted by Hou Wai-lu (1959), p. 334. See also *TWT* 86/1b, Wei Ch'u-hou. For further evidence of an interest in Mencius in this period, see *Huang-fu Ch'ih-cheng wen chi* 2/1a–2a.

218 *Han Ch'ang-li chi* 4/18/85, dated 820, Hanabusa (1964), p. 69.

219 For Li Ao's identification of Han Yü as a Mencius figure, see *Li Wen kung chi* 7/50a–b; and after Han's death, 16/120a–b. For Lu San, *Han Ch'ang-li chi* 3/11/68–69, dated 802, Hanabusa (1964), p. 67. For Chang Chi's promotion of Han Yü as a Mencius figure in 795, see *Han Ch'ang-li chi* 4/14/36. See also Ch'en Yin-k'o (1936), pp. 39–43.

220 *CTS* 171/4454, biog. of Li Han, describes Han Yü as 'unyielding and censorious; *CTS* 160/4207 describes Li Ao in much the same terms. For a provincial anti-Buddhist initiative by Li Ao, see *Li Wen kung chi* 10/80b–82a.

221 *Huang-fu Ch'ih-cheng wen chi* 2/6a–b and 6/5a–b.

222 Kenneth Ch'en (1956), pp. 67–105. For Li Te-yü's role, see T'ang Ch'eng-yeh (1973), pp. 535–62.

223 For brief accounts of Han Yü's disciples and followers, see Ch'ien Chi-po (1958), 5/77–113; Lo Lien-t'ien (1977), pp. 212–20.

224 *Huang-fu Ch'ih-cheng wen chi* 2/46–56; Hartman (1986), p. 206; *Fan-ch'uan wen chi* 6/106–7, favouring Hsün tzu's view. Huang-fu Yung, a *chin shih* who held senior academic office, wrote a work entitled *Hsing yen (Statements on the nature)* in 14 sections. Po Chü-i, his friend for 24 years, wrote of him, in Mencian language, that 'his mind was not disturbed'; see *Po Hsiang-shan chi* 9/61/68.

225 *Fan-ch'uan wen chi* 6/9a–10b; *Sun Ch'iao chi* 2/7b; *TWT* 86/6b–7a, Lin Chien-yen.

226 *P'i tzu wen sou* 9/95–6; 9/99–100; 3/23–4.

227 *WYYH* 690/10b, Lu Kuei-meng.

228 For Sun Ho, see *T'ang shih chi shih* 61/928; *TKCK* 24/19a.

4 State ritual

1 For an analysis of the role of ritual in the T'ang state, with special focus on the first two reigns, see Wechsler (1985); for an introductory account of the scope and organization of T'ang dynastic ritual codes, see McMullen (1987a).

2 For the careers in ritual office of some particularly long-serving ritual scholars, see below, note 94, for Wei T'ao; note 193 for Wei Kung-su; note 200 for Wang Ching; for the record of the P'ei family, over five generations, see below, note 191.

3 For the attitude of some administrators to popular local cults, especially those in the south-east, see *THY* 77/1414 and *CTS* 89/2887, biog. of Ti Jen-chieh; *CTS* 156/4129, biog. of Yü Ti; *Ch'üan Tsai-chih wen chi* 23/6a–b, epitaph, and *HTS* 197/5628, biog. of Lo Hsiang, d. 809; *CTS* 16/503, memorial of Li Te-yü, *Li Wen-jao wen chi, wai-chi* 4/5b–6a and *WYYH* 740/13a–b, essay by Li Te-yü; *HTS* 200/5719, biog. of Lin P'i. Also *Yin hua lu* 5/108–9; *Kuo shih pu* 3/65. For particular incidents, *Yüan Tz'u-shan chi* 7/105–06, Sun Wang (1957), p. 50 and *TCTC* 220/7054, 758.15 and 7058, 758.17; *HTS* 202/5772–3, biog. of Su Yüan-ming.

4 *Li chi chu shu* pref. 1a, quoting *Li chi chu shu* 22/10b.

5 For the *Yüeh ling*, see Ch. 3, notes 81–89; also below, notes 198, 229 and 237.

6 *CTS* 23/899–90, Feng and Shan rites of 725; *CTS* 14/420, suburban sacrifice of 807.

7 For background to the social function of ritual, see Wechsler (1985), pp. 26–30; Ch'ü T'ung-tsu (1961), pp. 226–41; also *Li chi chu shu* pref. 1a.

8 *THY* 24/461–63; Wechsler (1985), pp. 135–41, and below at notes 27 and 109.

9 The antithesis between ritual and military activity was expressed by Wei Cheng in a poem commending the Han ritual official Shu-sun T'ung, who by his ritual directives made Kao tsu 'aware how exalted it was to be an emperor' (*Shih chi* 99/2723, biog.). Wei Cheng composed the poem 'because he was afraid that the emperor would take pleasure in military achievements'. T'ai tsung replied by wryly adapting *Analects* 9/11, saying, 'You are binding me with your rituals'; see *T'ang shih chi shih* 4/45–6; cf. Wechsler (1985), p. 30. Shu-sun T'ung remained an often cited archetype for the ritual official; see *SS* 33/972; *TFYK* 565/19a; Lo Chen-yü (1909), 1/19b, stele text for K'ung Ying-ta by Yü Chih-ning; *WYYH* 617/5b, Chu Ching-tse; *Ch'üan Tsai-chih wen chi* 46/21a–b.

10 *TT* 47/272.3–273.1, memorial of 715, and *HTS* 200/5693–94, biog. of Ch'en Chen-chieh; also Ch. 2, note 108.

11 *THY* 37/670, double column entry, of Hsü Ching-tsung and Li I-fu; *CTS* 21/830; *CTS* 25/944; *CTS* 102/3165 and *CTS* 85/2814, of Chu Ch'in-ming and Kuo Shan-yün; *CTS* 84/2807, of the canonization proposed for P'ei Kuang-t'ing.

12 For T'ang Shao, see *CTS* 85/2814; for Sun P'ing-tzu, see *CTS* 25/952–53.

13 *CTS* 136/3753–54, biog. of Lu Mai, 739–798. Lu Mai justified his position by stating that, 'The meaning of the *Ch'un-ch'iu* is that one should not refuse royal business because of domestic business.'

14 McMullen (1987a), note 80.

15 *Analects* 2/23; for T'ang citations of this remark, see e.g. *Li chi chu shu* preface 1a; *SS* 6/105; *WYYH* 482/3b, decree examination answer by Chang Chien-chih; *CTS* 25/953, edict of 722; cf. *Po Hsiang-shan chi* 7/45/38–9, *Ts'e-lin* no. 15; *Li I-shan wen chi* 5/2a, sacrificial graveside prayer for the ritual scholar Wang Yen-wei.

16 *CTS* 24/912, T'ai tsung in 629; *TTCLC* 74/416, Hsüan tsung in 735; *CTS* 25/953, Hsüan tsung in 722.

17 *Han shu (i-wen chih)* 10/3087 and 10-3115; *SS* 32/924–6; *SS* 33/971–72; *THY* 11/272, Yen Shih-ku; *CTS* 21/826, edict of late 677; *CTS* 22/874, memorial of 717; *WYYH* 652/2a, Chang Yüeh; *THY* 80/1478, canonization discussion; *Han Ch'ang-li chi* 4/14/34; *TT*, quoted by *Yü hai* 39/21b.

18 *Ta T'ang ch'uang yeh ch'i-chü chu* 3/38–39. Cf. *T'ang chien* 1/3. Wechsler (1985), pp. 91–101, gives a detailed account of Kao tsu's accession.

19 *HTS* 107/4059–60, biog. of Fu I. The memorial here paraphrases *Shih chi* 84/2492, biog. of Chia I. Cf. *TTCLC* 2/6; *CTS* 7/136 and *TCTC* 208/6583, 705.2 listing the ritual and emblematic changes made on the restoration of the T'ang in 705.

20 *HTS* 107/4050, biog. of Fu I; cf. *CTS* 50/2133–4, characterizing the
    severity of Sui laws; *SS* 74/1691.
21 E.g. *CTS* 189A/4949, biog. of Chang Shih-heng; p. 4953, biog. of Hsü
    Shu-ya; p. 4950, biog. of Chia Kung-yen; p. 4950, biog. of Li
    Hsüan-chih; *CTS* 73/2603, biog. of Wang Kung; *CTS* 189B/4970, biog. of
    Kuo Shan-yün; p. 4964, biog. of Wei Shu-hsia.
22 *KFSPWK* epitaph for Tu Ch'ing, d. 667 aged 45 *sui*; *KFSPWK* epitaph
    for Tuan Wen-hui, d. 663 aged 25 *sui*.
23 For Yen Shih-ku's expertise, see *CTS* 73/2595 biog. For K'ung Ying-ta's
    special knowledge of the *Li chi*, *CTS* 73/2601 biog. For characterization
    of the practical nature of T'ang interest in the ritual canons, see *Nien-erh
    shih cha chi* 20/399–400.
24 *Li chi chu shu* pref. 1a.
25 *Mao shih chu shu yin shu yin-te*, pp. 19–21, 28; 5–8; 14–15; 17–18; 11;
    26.
26 *Li chi chu shu* 20/5a–b.
27 *THY* 24/461; *TLT* 4/39b and 55b; *CTS* 43/1832. *Li chi chu shu* 39/6b–8a
    and *Li chi chu shu* 25/10a–b; *Tso chuan chu shu* 36/6b–7a. K'ung Ying-ta
    stipulated that the enfieffment of the descendants of the two most recent
    dynasties was the 'greater ritual'. He also amplified the rationale behind
    the cult, 'The son of heaven through successive generations establishes
    their descendants. Though they were destroyed because of their evil, and
    though their present descendants are again without achievements or
    virtue, he must still preserve them. The reason for his preserving the
    descendants of the two ages is that he still respects and venerates what
    their past sages can provide as models and symbols.' *Ta T'ang chiao ssu
    lu* 10/20a locates a temple to the Sui royal house in the T'ung-kuei ward
    and to the Northern Chou ruling house in the Huai-chen ward. See also
    Wechsler (1985), pp. 137–8 and notes.
28 K'ung's submission on the Ming-t'ang is at *THY* 11/271 and *CTS*
    22/849–50. His biog., *CTS* 73/2602, states that scholars followed his
    theories, though in the longer term that was untrue. He included
    discussion of the Ming-t'ang, its plan and function in e.g. *Li chi chu shu*
    16/19a–b and 29/1b–3a, and in *Mao shih chu shu* 16E/1b–3a. *SS*
    6/119–23, of which he was a compiler, contains an account of the Ming-
    t'ang from Liang to Sui. Wechsler (1985), pp. 195–211, gives a full
    account. For K'ung's discussion of the Feng and Shan rites, see *Li chi
    chu shu* 24/5a; also *Li chi chu shu* 11/19b; also *Shang shu chu shu* 3/6b
    and 8a. Professor Wechsler's account, pp. 170–94, indicates that these
    rites were not mentioned in the Confucian canons themselves. For K'ung
    Ying-ta, however, the *Li chi chu shu* 24/5a passage provided the main
    canonical sanction, while the non-canonical *Kuan tzu* and *Po hu t'ung*
    supplied more detail. In *SS* 7/139, K'ung and his fellow editors made
    similar citations from all three texts.
29 *THY* 13/303, *TT* 50/188.1 and *CTS* 26/996, in 676; *Ta T'ang chiao ssu lu*
    1/2b, 2/16b, 3/4a, 4/5b etc.; also *THY* 12/288, referring only to 'the
    sub-commentary'. For some instances of citation of K'ung's other
    sub-commentaries, see *Liu Ho-tung chi* 31/501–03, referring to *Chou i*

cheng i, and *CTS* 25/960, citing the sub-commentary to the *Ch'un-ch'iu* and *Tso chuan*.

30 For the titles of some early T'ang ritual compilations, see below note 44.

31 *Li chi chu shu*, preface 1b, and *SS* 32/924–6. Besides this, it was common for T'ang scholars to describe the canonical ritual tradition as severely deteriorated by Han times; see above, note 17.

32 *THY* 36/651; *CTS* 71/2559, biog. of Wei Cheng; *CTS* 102/3178, biog. of Yüan Hsing-ch'ung; *TFYK* 607/12a; Kramers (1955), pp. 121–2, p. 124.

33 *TT* 433.2; cf. also *Liang shu* 3/96, *SS* 33/969–70; *Ch'en shu* 33/448, *SS* 33/970.

34 For both Sui codifications, see *CTS* 21/816. For the first, the *Wu li* in 130 *chüan*, see also *CTS* 72/2571, biog. of Li Pai-yao, showing that he was involved in both this and the first T'ang codification; *TT* 41/233.3. Liu Cho, the canonical sub-commentator, who was a major influence on K'ung Ying-ta, was also involved; see *SS* 75/1719. For the second, the *Chiang-tu hsin li (New rituals of Chiang-tu)* or *Chiang-tu chi li (Collected rituals of Chiang tu)* in 120 *chüan*, see *SS* 32/939; *CTS* 46/1975 and *Ho chih* p. 29. The Chiang-tu code was cited throughout the T'ang; e.g. *THY* 12/286 and 291; *CTS* 26/981; *CTS* 25/958; *CTS* 89/2898–99, biog. of Wang Fang-ch'ing. The measuring of codes' length in *p'ien* may be a deliberate archaism; see *Han shu* 30/1710 and *CTS* 22/816, referring to Han ritual.

35 *Nan shih* 71/1730; *THY* 37/669; cf. *TT* 41/233.3 for *wei hsia*, *CTS* 21/816; *TFYK* 654/1a. The *locus classicus* for these terms was *Shih chi* 121/3117, *ju-lin chuan*.

36 *THY* 37/669 and *TT* 41/233.3 implies that the *Chen-kuan li* was completed and promulgated in 633; but this date probably refers to the preliminary revision consisting of 29 items. *CTS* 21/816–17 and *HTS* 11/308 give no date, nor does *CTS* 46/1975, *Ho chih* p. 29. The following passages imply 637 for the final completion of the code: *CTS* 3/46; *CTS* 70/2529, biog. of Wang Kuei; *CTS* 72/2577, biog. of Li Pai-yao; *CTS* 73/2595, biog. of Yen Shih-ku; *CTS* 73/2602, biog. of K'ung Ying-ta; *HTS* 58/1491; *TCTC* 194/6127, 637.10. K'ung Ying-ta's engraved stele text by Yü Chih-ning indirectly supports 637; see Lo Chen-yü (1909), 1/15b–16a and 18b. The confusion may have arisen because the new code was first referred to as *Hsin li*, or even *Wu li*, and only later by the reign period in which it was produced, thus leading later scholars to believe in two codifications. The date of 637 for the completion of the code is not inconsistent with *CTS* 23/882, since, according to *CTS* 3/46, the code was submitted in the first month. Ikeda (1972), p. 822, has 637.

37 *THY* 37/669; *Li chi chu shu* 17/8a–b; cf. *SS* 7/147–9 and *CTS* 24/911. The *Yüeh ling* mentions only the 'honoured ones of heaven' (*t'ien tsung*). These are identified in K'ung's sub-commentary as the sun, moon and stars, and distinguished from Cheng Hsüan's 'six honoured ones' (*liu tsung*). Cf. *TTKYL* 22/1a–23/13a, showing the large number of divinities given offering in the K'ai-yüan version of this ritual.

38 *Li chi chu shu* 17/9a; Bodde (1975), pp. 349–59. For some pre-T'ang instances of this ritual, see *TCTC* 140/4400, 496.16; *TCTC* 141/4411,

497.21; *TT* 76/414.1–415.3. For the importance of this ceremony to
T'ang emperors, see *CKCY* 34/266; *THY* 26/503–04; *TT* 76/415.3–16.1;
CTS 89/2900, biog. of Wang Fang-ch'ing; *CTS* 85/2814, biog. of T'ang
Shao; also *TTKYL* 85/1a–6b.

39   For the *yang-lao* rite, see principally *Li chi chu shu* 13/9a–12a, and
28/3a–4a (the same passage); *Li chi chu shu* 20/15b–16a; also Bodde
(1975), pp. 361–80. The directives are given in *TTKYL* 104/1a–7b.

40   K'ung Ying-ta provided explanation of the term *Wu li* at several points,
e.g. *Li chi chu shu* 1/1b and 14/18a–b; *Shang shu chu shu* 3/7a and 3/15a.
Also *Chou li chu shu* 17/1a–b; 18/1a and 19/1b–2a. *SS* 6/105 cites the
second *Shang shu* passage, stating that the *chi li* division of the code
had to do with 'the ghosts and spirits'. See also *I wen lei chü* 38/673. Tu
Yu, *TT* 41/233.1, develops this idea, making the *chi li* division correlate
with 'heaven' and the remaining four divisions with 'man'; see below
note 228.

41   *THY* 37/669–70. Cf. *CTS* 3/46–7; *CKCY* 4/99–100, where T'ai tsung
referred to his own decline, in the context of his anxiety over the crown
prince and his many other sons.

42   *CTS* 21/817. One group of rituals that was absent from the first
codification was that of offerings to certain pre-T'ang emperors, revived
early in Kao tsung's reign; see *CTS* 24/915, and *TTKYL* 50/1a–8a, and
Wechsler (1985), pp. 139–140.

43   See e.g. *CTS* 21/816, referring to the Former Han and using archaic
terminology; *T'ang shih chi shih* 1/10, Tsung Chin-ch'ing; *I wen lei chü*
38/698 and *Ch'u hsüeh chi*, quoting Ts'ai Yung; *TWT* 1/5b, Li Po; *Li
Wen-jao wen chi*, pref. by Cheng Ya, 5a; also note 82 below.

44   For discussion and planning of the Feng and Shan rites under T'ai tsung,
see *CTS* 21/817, Fang Hsüan-ling's submission of 633, and, principally,
CTS 23/881–4 and *TTCLC* 66/367–69. *THY* 7/95 has a convenient
summary. Wechsler (1985), pp. 176–83 gives a full account. Cf. also the
two compilations of directives on the Feng and Shan rites, *CTS* 73/2595,
biog. of Yen Shih-ku, referring to the *Feng Shan i-chu shu (Book of
directives for the Feng and Shan rites)*, submitted in 637, and *HTS*
58/1490, *Ho chih* p. 135, listing a similar work, the *Huang ti Feng Shan i
(Directives for the imperial Feng and Shan)* in 6 *chüan* by Ling-hu
Te-fen, who was appointed commissioner for the Feng and Shan rites in
641. *HTS* 201/5731, biog. of Hsieh Yen, also enters a work entitled *Yü
tieh chen chi*. For mention of the Feng and Shan rites in the verse of the
Chen-kuan period, see e.g. *WYYH* 209/9a, Yüan Lang; *WYYH* 190/3a,
Ts'en Wen-pen; *WYYH* 167/3a, Hsü Ching-tsung. In the following
century the *Ch'u hsüeh chi* anthologized the submissions of Li Pai-yao,
Chu Tzu-she, Ts'en Wen-pen and Kao Jo-ssu requesting T'ai tsung to
perform the rites; see *Ch'u hsüeh chi* 13/333–37.

45   For the names by which the Ming-t'ang had been known, see *THY*
11/273, Yen Shih-ku; *THY* 11/276, Ch'en Tzu-ang; *THY* 12/288–89,
Wang Fang-ch'ing. Kao tsung, in an edict of 651, was made to summarize
the history of the building: 'Though the regulations for it have varied,
yet in that it was set under the centre of heaven and has provided a

synapse for humanity (*jen chi*), spread forth good government and bestowed instruction, they have been one and the same'; see *THY* 11/274; *TTCLC* 73/409 and the very similar wording in *TTCLC* 73/409–10. See also *I wen lei chü* 38/689 and *Ch'u hsüeh chi* 6/328.

46   *CTS* 82/2763, biog. of Hsü Ching-tsung. Cf. *TCTC* 194/6103, 733.12 for a later instance where an identified Han palace site was used for wine taking. *I wen lei chü* 62/111–27 and *Ch'u hsüeh chi* 24/568–72 indicate that palaces, especially of the Han period, were a topic for *belles lettres* composition.

47   For brief mention of construction of palace buildings, see e.g. *CTS* 3/46, 3/51 (cf. 3/52), 3/59, 4/80, 4/83–84, 5/98, 5/104, 5/110; *CTS* 89/2886, biog. of Ti Jen-chieh. The Ch'ien-yüan tien, on the site of which the Ming-t'ang was built, was completed in 665; see *CTS* 4/86 and *TCTC* 201/6344, 665.8. *THY* 30/552–3, statement by Li Jen-kuei to Ti Jen-chieh in 679, suggests the very different attitude of scholars to other palace buildings: 'The slopes and ponds, towers and pavilions of antiquity were all inside the deep palaces and concentric walls, because it was not desired that outside people should see them, through fear of harming the attitudes of the people...'

48   For the timber metaphor, see *SS* 66/1567; *WYYH* 695/2b–3a, Wei Cheng; *WYYH* 462/8a–b and *TKCK* 3/17a–b, decree of 689 by the empress Wu; *WYYH* 479-1a–b and *TKCK* 3/29a, decree examination question of 694; *WYYH* 52/7b–8a, *fu*, probably for an examination, by Hao Ming-yüan ('A great sea is formed by the homing of a hundred rivers; the Ming-t'ang is constructed by the combining of many timbers'); *TT* 17/97.1, Liu Chih; Hung (1952), p. 88; *Ho yüeh ying ling chi* 2/88, Hsüeh Chü; *Shen Hsia-hsien wen chi* 8/80a–b.

49   Under Kao tsung, the plan of the Ming-t'ang was discussed for two years following Kao tsung's edict of 651; see *THY* 11/274–6; *CTS* 22/853–5. In 667, Kao tsung again raised the question; see *THY* 11/276; *CTS* 22/855–6. In 684, Ch'en Tzu-ang proposed construction; see *THY* 11/276 and *Ch'en Tzu-ang chi* 9/207–14. For the order to build, see *THY* 11/277; *Feng shih wen chien chi* 4/27; *CTS* 22/862; *CTS* 6/118; *TT* 44/253.3–54.1; *TFYK* 564/7a; *CTS* 190B/5013, biog. of Liu Yün-chi; *TCTC* 204/6447, 688.15. Forte (1976), pp. 189–91, n. 47, contains a bibliography and critical account of the construction of the building.

50   *THY* 11/277; *CTS* 22/862; *TCTC* 204/6447, 688.15. For conflicting remarks on the siting, see *THY* 11/273, Yen Shih-ku; *THY* 11/276, Ch'en Tzu-ang; also K'ung Ying-ta, *Li chi chu shu* 29/2a–b. For a convenient diagrammatic representation of the direction of the territory in the *ping-ssu* angle (*ping ssu chih ti*), see Fung Yu-lan (1953), p. 15.

51   *THY* 11/278; *TT* 44/254.1; *Feng shih wen chien chi* 4/27; *CTS* 22/865–67; *CTS* 6/124; *TCTC* 205/6498–6501, 695.3.

52   *THY* 11/278; *CTS* 22/865–7; *TCTC* 205/6499, 695.3.

53   *THY* 11/279; *Feng shih wen chien chi* 4/27; *CTS* 6/125; *CTS* 22/867; *TT* 44/254.1.

54   *TFYK* 564/7a; *CTS* 22/873; *TT* 44/254.1. *CTS* 6/119ff. implies that the Ming-t'ang was used fairly regularly until Chung tsung's reign. For

Chung tsung's succession in the T'ung t'ien kung, see *CTS* 7/136 and *TTCLC* 2/6–7 for the act of grace that followed. The last performance in the Ming-t'ang seems to have been Chung tsung's in the ninth month of 705; see *TT* 44/254.1 and *TTCLC* 73/410–11 for the act of grace that followed. *TT* adds, '(After?) the great sacrifice in the last month of autumn, they resorted to the round altar to conduct performances until the time of Jui tsung.'

55 *THY* 12/286, submission by erudits of the court of sacrifices, makes this point explicit.

56 *CTS* 89/2899, biog. of Wang Fang-ch'ing.

57 The *Ming-t'ang hsin li (New rituals for the Ming-t'ang)*, in 3 *chüan*, by Yüan Pan-ch'ien, see *HTS* 58/1492 and *Ho chih* p. 137. Yüan's biog., *CTS* 190B/5015, indicates that he also composed a monumental text for the Feng and Shan rites on mount Sung; the *Ta hsiang Ming-t'ang i chu (Directives for the great sacrifice in the Ming-t'ang)*, in 2 *chüan*, by Kuo Shan-yün, *CTS* 46/2009; *HTS* 58/1491, and *Ho chih* p. 133; the *Ming-t'ang hsin li (New rituals for the Ming-t'ang)* in 10 *chüan* by Li Ssu-chen, d. 696, *CTS* 191/5099, biog. and *HTS* 58/1492 and *Ho chih* p. 137; the *Ming-t'ang i chu (Ritual directives for the Ming-t'ang)* in 7 *chüan*, by Yao Fan and others, *CTS* 46/2009, *HTS* 58/1490 and *Ho chih* p. 133; the *Ming-t'ang i (Directives for the Ming-t'ang)* in 1 *chüan*, by Chang Ta-tsan (or -i), *CTS* 46/2009, *HTS* 58/1490 and *Ho chih* p. 133. The last two titles cannot be dated with complete certainty, but are likely to be seventh century. Cf. *CTS* 189B/4964, indicating that other scholars too compiled directives.

58 For this long running and highly complex controversy, see Wechsler (1985), pp. 207–11; *THY* 12/283–85; *TT* 44/252.2–54.1; *CTS* 21/821–30; *TTCLC* 73/410. For practice and debate under the empress Wu, see *CTS* 22/864–65; *THY* 12/285; *TT* 44/253.2–254.1. For later examples of the most recently deceased T'ang sovereign being given offering in the great Ming-t'ang sacrifice, see *CTS* 22/873, *THY* 12/291; *TCTC* 208/6595, 705.39, *TT* 44/254.1, showing Chung tsung giving offering to Kao tsung; *TTKYL* 10/10b, prescribing Jui tsung as recipient of offering by Hsüan tsung; *THY* 12/291–2 and *TCTC* 223/7160, 764.4, memorial by the ritual commissioner Tu Hung-chien, prescribing that Tai tsung should give offering to Su tsung. *THY* 12/292 indicates that Shun tsung was to be given offering at the grand Ming-t'ang sacrifice in 806 and Hsien tsung in 820.

59 For this complex controversy, see Wechsler (1985), pp. 208–11. A brief but concise summary of the position of these cosmic agents in the great sacrifice in the Ming-t'ang as prescribed by the two codes was given by Wei An-shih in a memorial of 677; see *THY* 12/284 and *CTS* 21/827. The memorial of Wang Chung-ch'iu, in late 732, also resumes the differences between the two codes for the great sacrifice in the Ming-t'ang; see *CTS* 21/835–6 and *HTS* 200/5700, biog.

60 *THY* 12/285–91; *CTS* 22/868–73; *TT* 44/253–54 omits this controversy.

61 *CTS* 22/864; Guisso (1978), p. 38 and notes 98 and 101 on p. 223 and note 107 on p. 224; p. 46 and notes 163–6 on p. 226; Forte (1976), pp. 163–4.

62 *TT* 44/254.1; *THY* 11/280–81; *CTS* 22/873–76; *TCTC* 211/6728, 717.10.

63 *TT* 254.1–54.2; *THY* 11/281; *TTCLC* 108/561; *CTS* 22/876; *CTS* 9/212; *TCTC* 212/6753, 722.18; *TCTC* 214/6839, 739.11.

64 *CTS* 22/876; *HTS* 13/338; *Feng shih wen chien chi* 4/27.

65 For a summary of the pre-T'ang history of the Feng and Shan rites, see Wechsler (1985), pp. 170–6 and notes. For Han Wu ti's performance, *Shih chi* 28/1397–99. The subject has been given a classic account in the monograph of Chavannes (1910).

66 *CTS* 23/884.

67 *TCTC* 200/6316, 659.8; cf. the wording in *THY* 9/95–6; also the memorial on the rites entered, out of sequence, in *CTS* 23/893–4.

68 *CTS* 4/87; *CTS* 67/2487, biog. of Li Chi. *CTS* 23/884 and *CTS* 82/2763, biog. of Hsü Ching-tsung do not mention Hsü's part; but the anti-Hsü anecdote in *HTS* 223A/6337 and *TCTC* 201/6345–46, 665.11 indicate that he accompanied the emperor east. For other scholars involved, *CTS* 23/886–88, the memorial by a former relatively junior military official, Li Ching-chen, the recommendation of which was accepted by the ritual authorities, is particularly striking. The productive scholar Meng Li-chen compiled a *Feng Shan lu (Record of Feng and Shan rites)* in 10 *chüan*; see *HTS* 58/1490 and *Ho chih* p. 135.

69 For the organization of the rites, see *CTS* 23/888; *TTCLC* 66/369–70 edict of Lin-te 2/10th month) Wechsler (1985), esp. pp. 185–8 and notes.

70 See *TCTC* 204/6471, 691.5 for petitions. For T'ai tsung's proposal to celebrate on mount Sung, see *Wei Cheng kung chien lu* 4/45; *THY* 7/81; *TFYK* 36/5a–b. The postponements were in 676; see *TFYK* 33/6b; and 679; see *CTS* 5/104–05; *TFYK* 36/5a. Cf. also *CTS* 5/110, for building of a palace on mount Sung, and *THY* 30/556–57 for a memorial warning that political and economic conditions did not justify this. *CTS* 5/111 and *CTS* 23/889–90; *TCTC* 207/6563, 696.1. Also the poem by Sung Chih-wen, *WYYH* 167/5a. P'ei Shou-chen's *Shen yüeh Feng Shan chu (Directives for the Feng and Shan on the sacred peak)*, 10 *chüan*, was probably compiled for this occasion; see *CTS* 46/2009; *HTS* 58/1491 and *Ho chih* p. 133.

71 *CTS* 189B/4963, biog. of Wang Yüan-kan.

72 *CTS* 190B/5015, biog. of Yüan Pan-ch'ien; *CTS* 94/2996, biog. of Ts'ui Jung.

73 For the number of submissions, see *CTS* 23/891; *THY* 8/106, quoting *TFYK* mentions, more impressionistically, *ch'ien pai.*

74 For Hsüan tsung's performance of the rites, see *THY* 8/105–23, which reproduces the accounts of the main official sources, including *CTS* 23/891–904; *TFYK* etc. See also *CTS* 194A/5175–77, account of the T'u-chüeh.

75 For the commission in the Chi-hsien yüan, see *CTS* 23/892; for other scholars involved, see *CTS* 23/895–6; for late modifications, see the emperor's consultation of Ho Chih-chang, *CTS* 23/898–900.

76 *CTS* 23/899–900.

77 *CTS* 99/3098, biog. of Chang Chiu-ling.

78 For some participating officials, see e.g. *CTS* 194/5176–77, account of

the T'u-chüeh and *HTS* 202/5758, biog. of Lü Hsiang; *CTS* 100/3124, biog. of Lu Ts'ung-yüan; *CTS* 111/3320, biog. of Fang Kuan; *CTS* 190B/5041, biog. of Li Yung; *CTS* 98/3080, biog. of P'ei Yao-ch'ing, and cf. *Wang Mo-chieh ch'üan chi chien chu* 21/299, commemorative stele for P'ei. Also *Wang Mo-chieh ch'üan chi chien chu* 19/275; *WYYH* 169/11a, Chang Chiu-ling; *Yen Lu kung wen chi* 5/16b, and *WYYH* 701/5a, Li Hua, of the official scholar and general service official Ts'ui Mien; *WYYH* 462/5a; *WYYH* 775/7b, Sun Ti; *CTS* 99/3088, biog. of Ts'ui Jih-yung; *HTS* 200/5704, biog. of Lu Chien, d. aged 71 *sui* after 726.

79 *HTS* 58/1492 and *Ho chih* p. 137.

80 For the history of requests for Feng and Shan rites on mount Hua or mount Sung late in Hsüan tsung's reign, see McMullen (1984), pp. 37–40. Also *WYYH* 610/7b and Hung (1952), pp. 79–80; and *THY* 50/877 for another mention of the establishment of a Hua-feng kuan, in 748. Hsüan tsung's affinity for mount Hua was based on the time of his birth; see *CTS* 23/904.

81 *Sun Ch'iao chi* 6/4b and 10/1b. Also below, note 166.

82 Des Rotours (1975), p. 108. In the light of Ts'ui Yu-fu's career, as a member of the Po-ling Ts'ui clan, a *chin shih* and a supervisor of the dynastic record, this remark seems intended to cap the celebrated three regrets of the seventh-century scholar Hsüeh Yüan-ch'ao; see Ch. 5, note 78.

83 For the Hsien-ch'ing code, see *TT* 41/233.3; *THY* 37/670; *THY* 36/656; *CTS* 21/817–18; *HTS* 58/1491 and *Ho chih* p. 136. This second code was not apparently entered in the imperial catalogue of 721, at *CTS* 46/1975 or 2009.

84 *THY* 37/670 double column entry; *CTS* 21/818. Cf. *CTS* 189/4964, biog. of Wei Shu-hsia and *CTS* 188/4925, biog. of P'ei Shou-chen, stating that at Kao tsung's death the directions for obsequies were mostly lapsed or deficient.

85 Fukunaga (1976), p. 12; *CTS* 21/835–6, memorial by Wang Chung-ch'iu; Wechsler (1985), p. 116.

86 Wechsler (1985), pp. 116–7; *THY* 9A/148–9; *TT* 43/247.3; *TTCLC* 67/376.

87 *TT* 41/233.1; *THY* 37/670; *CTS* 21/818; Wechsler (1985), pp. 116–7.

88 *THY* 37/670; *TT* 41/133.3; *CTS* 21/818; cf. also *THY* 12/285, memorial of 677, citing this measure. *TT* 41/233.3 and *CTS* 21/818, however, make it clear that both codes were still used.

89 *TT* 41/233.3; *THY* 37/670 double column entry; *CTS* 21/818. *KFSPWK* epitaph for the son of Ho Chi, junior officer of Yü-ch'ien county in Hang-chou confirms Ho Chi's participation in drafting the directives necessitated by this fluid situation

90 For the empress Wu's ritual compilations, see the *Wu hou Tzu-ch'en li yao (Essentials of the Tzu-ch'en palace rituals of the empress Wu)* in 10 *chüan*, *CTS* 46/1975, *Ho chih* p. 29 and *HTS* 58/149, *Ho chih* p. 136; also *Yüeh shu yao lu (Record of the essentials of books on music)* in 10 *chüan*, *CTS* 6/133, *CTS* 46/1975, *HTS* 57/1436 and *Ho chih* p. 31. *Ssu-k'u wei shou shu mu t'i yao* 2/27 indicates that the latter work had a ritual theme.

91 *TFYK* 564/19b; *TT* 41/233.3 mentioning T'ang Shao, for whom see *CTS* 85/2813–14, biog. and Wei Shu-hsia, for whom see *CTS* 189B/4964, biog. At about this period, Wei Shu-hsia was compiler of a work entitled *Wu li yao chi (Record of the essentials of the five categories of ritual)* in 30 *chüan*; see *HTS* 58/1491 and *Ho chih* p. 136; while another ritual expert, Tou Wei-hsien compiled a *Chi-hsiung li yao (Essentials of rituals auspicious and ill-omened)* in 20 *chüan*, see *CTS* 183/4726, biog., *HTS* 58/1491 and *Ho chih* p. 135. Again, neither work is mentioned in the *CTS* bibliog.

92 The compilations by Wei Shu-hsia and Tou Wei-hsien mentioned above might possibly have had prescriptive force over this period.

93 *THY* 64/1107–8.

94 *CTS* 21/818. Wei T'ao has no *CTS* biog., though *CTS* 189B/4965 mentions that he was the son of the ritual scholar Wei Shu-hsia and that he became president of the court of sacrifices. His biog. in *HTS* 122/4355–60 describes his role in the ritual controversies of the K'ai-yüan period.

95 See Ch. 3, note 85.

96 The date given in *THY* 37/671, 29th year of K'ai-yüan, 9th month, is likely to be a corruption for 20th year and 9th month, for which see *TT* 41/233.3; also *CTS* 21/818–19; *CTS* 27/1031; *TFYK* 6564/8b. For membership of the commission, see *TTKYL*, prefatory section; also Ikeda On (1972), p. 822, which lists members of the first and second commissions, citing Wei Shu's *Chi-hsien chu chi* as evidence in the case of two members of the second. Chang Yüeh, Hsü Chien, Li Jui and Shih Ching-pen were on the first; Hsiao Sung, Wang Chung-ch'iu, Chia Teng, Chang Hsüan, Lu Shan-ching and Hung Hsiao-ch'ang on the second.

97 *TTKYL* Chs. 10–11; Chs. 99–103.

98 *CTS* 21/835–36, memorial of Wang Chung-ch'iu.

99 At least three members of the first commission for the K'ai-yüan code, Chang Yüeh, Hsü Chien and Shih Ching-pen, had also been involved in drafting for the 725 performance on mount T'ai.

100 For the T'ai kung cult, *TTKYL* 55, and Ch. 2, note 137.

101 For the cult of the five dragons, see *TTKYL* 51/5b–8a; *THY* 22/433–34; des Rotours (1966).

102 McMullen (1987a), note 26.

103 *TLT* 20/8a–b.

104 See below at notes 182–95.

105 *THY* 36/658; *Yen Lu kung wen chi* 5/16b, inscription for the former house of Ts'ui Mien, composed in 776.

106 *TTCLC* 67/177, edict of 742; *THY* 9B/184, citing *HTS* 13/337.

107 For the alteration in grade of certain rites in 745, those to Feng po and Yü shih, see *TT* 44/257.1; *Ch'üan Tsai-chih wen chi* 29/8a. In *TLT* 4/33a, these were classified as minor observances; but in 745, they were raised to medium.

108 *THY* 22/431–2.

109 *THY* 24/462–63; *CTS* 9/224 and 227; *TCTC* 216/6899, 750.11 and 6918, 753.3.

110 For the *chin shih* question of 646, the second datable *chin shih* question to survive from the dynasty, and the answers of Chang Ch'ang-ling and Hao Lien-fan, see *WYYH* 497/9a–11a; *TKCK* 1/22b and 1/25b–26a and 26b–27b. For the decree examination question of 688 and answers by Chang Yüeh, see *WYYH* 477/1a–6a and *TKCK* 2/11a–12b and 13b–16b. *WYYH* 497/7a–498/13a gives a sequence of examination questions and answers on the theme of punishments or punishments and ritual, concluding with five specimen questions and answers by Po Chü-i, for which see also *Po Hsiang-shan chi* 7/47/71–7/48/75, *Ts'e lin* nos. 53–7.

111 For the sub-question on ritual and music and ritual set in 719, see *WYYH* 484/1a–485/9b and *TKCK* 6/8b–9a and 6/10b–28b, giving answers by six candidates. *WYYH* 497/1a–7a comprises specimen questions and answers by Po Chü-i on this theme, for which see also *Po Hsiang-shan chi* 7/48/78–81, *Ts'e lin* nos. 62–64 and 7/45/38–9, *Ts'e lin* no. 15.

112 *WYYH* 481/4a–b and *TKCK* 4/8b–9a and 4/13a–b, answer of Ts'ui Mien. See also below, at note 121.

113 *WYYH* 70/1a–3a and *TKCK* 5/12b–14b. It is possible that a very similar topic was set in 843, since Shih Kuan, a successful *chin shih* candidate of that year (see *TKCK* 22/7b, quoting *T'ang chih yen*) is represented by an examination style *fu* on this theme.

114 *T'ang shih chi shih* 20/300, Ts'ui Shu; *TKCK* 8/24b–25a.

115 *WYYH* 477/6a, Chang Yüeh, mentioning the Ming-t'ang, in a decree examination answer of 688; *WYYH* 497/10a, Chang Ch'ang-ling, mentioning a Feng on the central sacred peak in a *chin shih* dissertation answer of 646.

116 *Li T'ai-po wen chi* 1/1/12–27; Waley (1950), pp. 1–4.

117 *WYYH* 55/1a–2a, Hsiao Ying-shih; cf. also *CTS* 94/3006, biog. of Hsü Yen-po.

118 For Tu Fu's *fu* on the Feng and Shan rites on mount Hua, see Ch. 1, note 75.

119 *TTCLC* 66/369; *TFYK* 35/31b-33b, 35/33b–34b; *TKCK* 1/27b–28a and 1/28b. The edict cancelling the projected Feng and Shan celebration ordered those recommended to go to the capital as candidates in normal years.

120 For special decree examinations of 664 held in connection with the planned Feng and Shan rites of 666, see *TFYK* 36/1b and *TKCK* 2/13b.

121 For examinations in connection with the 696 celebration on mount Sung, see *WYYH* 481/1a–7b and *TKCK* 4/8a–b. *Teng k'o chi k'ao pu* p. 98, epitaph for Ni Jo-shui, indicates that he was successful in this examination. His *CTS* 185B/4811 biog. does not mention this. For Ts'ui Mien and the large numbers of candidates, see *Yen Lu kung wen chi* 5/16a; for Su T'ing, *HTS* 125/4399, biog.

122 *CTS* 8/188; *TKCK* 7/17a; *TFYK* 643/12a and *TKCK* 7/17a.

123 *TKCK* 3/19a, quoting an epigraphical source.

124 *TTCLC* 73/410; *CTS* 6/124; *TKCK* 4/1a–b.

125 *TKCK* 4/10a entry for 696, note by Hsü Sung; *CTS* 100/3116, biog. of Su Chin. For the 723 performance, see *TTCLC* 68/380–81; *TFYK* 85/8a–11a

and *TKCK* 7/14b. For that of 748, *TFYK* 86/10a–186 and *TKCK* 9/12a, *Yüan Tz'u-shan chi* 4/51–53.

126 *CTS* 8/202; *TTCLC* 74/415–16; *TKCK* 8/11a–b.

127 E.g. T'ien-pao 1; see *CTS* 9/214; *TTCLC* 4/21–22; *TKCK* 9/1a.

128 For a particularly full account of the first three T'ang imperial mausolea, see Wechsler (1985), pp. 142–60. For mention of the five, see *CTS* 25/973; cf. *TLT* 14/27, which lists six. Hsüan tsung chose the site for his own burial in 729; see *THY* 20/397.

129 For admonition against extravagant burial in the context of Kao tsu's tomb, see especially *CTS* 72/2568–69, biog. of Yü Shih-nan; *WYYH* 623/1a–2b; *THY* 20/393–94, memorial dated 635. Also Fang Hsüan-ling and others; see *THY* 20/39–95 and *TCTC* 194/6114–15, 635.11; Wechsler (1985), pp. 149–50. For Wei Cheng's criticism in the context of T'ai tsung's tomb, see *HTS* 97/3871; *TCTC* 194/6122–23, 636.10 and Wechsler (1985), p. 156. Warning against extravagant burial lasted as a theme in admonition into the ninth century; see *CTS* 89/2886, biog. of Ti Jen-chieh; *CTS* 149/4011–13, biog. of Ling-hu Huan, memorial to Te tsung; *Po hsiang-shan chi* 7/48/82, *Ts'e lin* no. 66.

130 *THY* 21/412–17.

131 For Kao tsu's four-chapel temple, see *THY* 12/292; *TT* 47/269.3; *CTS* 1/5; *CTS* 25/941; *TCTC* 185/5794, 618.34. Wechsler (1985), pp. 126–7, discusses the canonical sanction and historical precedent for a four-chapel temple.

132 For the expansion to six chapels, after controversy, see *THY* 12/292–33; *TT* 47/269.3–70.1; *CTS* 3/45; *CTS* 25/941–4; *TCTC* 194/6115, 635.12; Wechsler (1985), pp. 128–9.

133 For the maintenance of the six-chapel arrangement on the deaths of T'ai tsung in 649 and Kao tsung in 683 see *THY* 12/293–94; *TT* 47/270.1; *CTS* 25/944; *TCTC* 199/6269, 649.17.

134 For the empress Wu's establishment of a separate temple for the three T'ang emperors in 688, see *TT* 47/270.1 and *CTS* 25/944. She had taken an earlier step in this general direction in 684, when she had established a five-generation temple for the Wu clan at Wen-shui, Ping-chou, modern Shansi; see *TCTC* 203/6422, 684.25. For the measure of 690, see *TT* 47/270.1; *CTS* 25/945; *TCTC* 204/6467–68, 690.15. This involved the virtual closing down, but not the destruction of, the T'ang imperial ancestral temple at Ch'ang-an. Cf. Guisso (1978), p. 128 and note 11 on p. 278. For further measures by the empress Wu relating to the ancestral temple, see *CTS* 25/944–5.

135 *THY* 12/294–97; *TT* 47/270.1; *CTS* 25/945–49; *TCTC* 208/6590, 705.23 and 24.

136 *THY* 12/294–97; *TT* 47/270.1–70.3; *CTS* 25/949–52; *TCTC* 210/6656, 710.10; *TCTC* 211/6719–20, 716.16. Also for the contribution of the commoner Sun P'ing-tzu in late 717, related to the partial collapse of the temple earlier that year, which was suppressed by the chief minister Su T'ing in favour of the position of his cousin Su Hsien, an erudit of the court of sacrifices, see *THY* 17/353–55; *TT* 47/217.1, giving cross-reference to *TT* 51/294.3–95.2; *CTS* 25/952–53; *TCTC* 211/6729–30, 717.13.

137 *THY* 17/352–53; *CTS* 8/177 and 8/178; *CTS* 25/952–53; *TCTC* 211/6725–26, 717.1 and 201/6730, 717.14.

138 *THY* 12/298; *TT* 47/270.3; *TTCLC* 75/424 and 75/426–27; *CTS* 25/953–54; *CTS* 8/183 and 8/185; *TCTC* 212/6750, 722.10. There is a useful summary in the commentary to *TCTC* 227/7309–10, 781.7. See also des Rotours (1947), p. 321, note 1.

139 For the provisioning controversy of 735–36, see *TTCLC* 74/415–16, act of grace following the ploughing rite of 735; *THY* 17/349; *TT* 47/271.1–71.2; *CTS* 25/969–72; *TCTC* 214/6818–20, 736.10.

140 *THY* 18/370–2; *TLT* 4/35b–36b; cf. *TT* 50/290.3–291.2.

141 *THY* 17/355–56. *CTS* 9/235 refers to the temple having been fired, but the tablets being temporarily housed in the Ch'ang-an palace. These must, however, have been the newly made spirit tablets: cf. *CTS* 10/248, *CTS* 10/252, and a later T'ang recollection *THY* 17/357. For the occupation of the Lo-yang temple by rebel troops, see the later T'ang recollection, *THY* 16/336.

142 An incomplete list of post-rebellion ritual commissioners is given in *THY* 37/672. For Ts'ui Ch'i, see also *THY* 17/355–56 and *CTS* 115/3374, biog.

143 For Su tsung's performance of the *nan chiao* rites in 758, see *TTCLC* 69/383–85. For the *nan chiao* rites of 762, see *TCTC* 222/7119, 762.6 and the text of the act of grace at *TTCLC* 69/384–85. For the ploughing rite, see *CTS* 10/254; *CTS* 24/913–14; *TTCLC* 74/414–15; *TCTC* 221/7067, 759.2.

144 *CTS* 119/3435, biog. of Yang Wan.

145 For the *nan chiao* performance in 764, see *TTCLC* 69/385–86, and *Yen Lu kung wen chi* 9/2a.

146 *CTS* 149/4007, biog. of Yü Hsiu-lieh. *WYYH* 972/10a–b, Liang Su, report of conduct for Tu-ku Chi, an erudit of the court of sacrifices under Tai tsung, also spoke of severe damage to the ritual records (*t'ai ch'ang tien ku*).

147 *THY* 17/355–56; *CTS* 10/248; cf. also *CTS* 128/3592, biog. of Yen Chen-ch'ing.

148 *CTS* 10/248; Hsüan tsung, as retired emperor, followed in visiting the spirit tablets, *CTS* 10/249.

149 *TCTC* 220/7052, 758.1.

150 *CTS* 10/252; *TCTC* 220/7053, 758.11.

151 For Yen's quarrel with Yüan Tsai in 763, see *Yen Lu kung wen chi* 14/6b–7a, report of conduct by Yin Liang and 14/11b, spirit path stele by Ling-hu Huan; *THY* 17/356; *CTS* 128/3592, biog. of Yen Chen-ch'ing; *TCTC* 223/7157, 763.11. For his disagreement in 766, see *Yen Lu kung wen chi* 14/7a, report of conduct by Yin Liang; 14/12b, spirit path stele by Ling-hu Huan; *CTS* 128/3595, biog. of Yen Chen-ch'ing.

152 *Yen Lu kung wen chi* 14/8a, report of conduct by Yin Liang, enters this work, compiled on Yen's instructions by his disciple Tso Fu-yüan, as *Li i (Rituals)*, in 10 *chüan*. The title occurs, with minor variations, in Yen's epitaph by the official historian Ling-hu Huan, *Yen Lu kung wen chi* 14/14b and in *HTS* 58/1491, *Ho chih* p. 137. Tso Fu-yüan came from

Fu-chou in modern Kiangsi, where Yen Chen-ch'ing had been governor; see *Yen Lu kung wen chi* 7/8b.

153 *Yen Lu kung wen chi* 12/5a, preface to poem written in 778.

154 *Yen Lu kung wen chi* 4/2a–3a, letter to Kuo Ying-i.

155 For this long debate, see principally *TT* 50/288.3–290.3 and *THY* 13/306–14/317. The *TT* account (and that part of the *THY* account contained in *THY* 13) ends with the memorial of the *Ch'un-ch'iu* scholar Lu Ch'un. This is dated in *THY* 13/313 to 795. As a very senior official, Tu Yu was himself ordered to report the outcome of the long debate to the T'ai ch'ing kung, temple to Lao tzu; see *THY* 14/316 and *CTS* 26/1010. See also *TCTC* 227/7309–10, 781.17; *TCTC* 236/7600, 803.4; *HTS* 200/5710–16, biog. of Ch'en Ching, emphasizing Ch'en's role throughout the long debate; *Han Ch'ang-li chi* 4/14/29–30; *Liu Ho-tung chi* 8/124; *P'i-ling chi* 6/1a–2b, memorial of 766, on T'ai tsu; *Ch'üan Tsai-chih wen chi* 29/8a–10b. Wechsler (1985), pp. 126–35, provides invaluable background information.

156 *Ch'üan Tsai-chih wen chi* 22/7a–b, epitaph for Chang Chien; *CTS* 149/4024, biog. of Chang Chien. For the escape from destruction of the imperial ancestral cult precincts, see *TCTC* 231/7436, 784.9.

157 For Te tsung's fastidiousness over ritual matters, see *CTS* 149/4032, biog. of Liu Mien. The scholars questioned with Liu Mien were all ritual experts; see *CTS* 180B/4975, biog. of Hsü Tai; *CTS* 189B/4977–78, biog. of the *Ch'un-ch'iu* scholar Lu Ch'un; *CTS* 149/4023–25, biog. of Chang Chien.

158 *CTS* 139/3799, biog. of Lu Hsüan kung; cf. also *CTS* 135/3721 and 3726, biog. of P'ei Yen-ling, in which both P'ei and Lu Hsüan kung appear to play on Te tsung's interest in the ancestral temple.

159 *Ch'üan T'ang wen* 480/7b, text by Wei Nien. *Li chi chu shu* 16E/2a indicates that *ch'ing miao* was a term that might apply to the imperial ancestral temple; *THY* 65/1134 has it referring to the dynastic ancestral temple in the T'ang. Cf. *TTCLC* 75/423–24; *THY* 15/325; *TFYK* 585/7b–8a, and Wechsler (1985), pp. 129–30 for Yen Shih-ku's successful opposition to T'ai tsung's proposal to establish a dynastic temple at T'ai-yüan in modern Shansi. This was quoted later in the dynasty; *CTS* 26/993; *THY* 16/344.

160 *Liu Ho-tung chi* 8/124; *CTS* 136/3755; *HTS* 200/5716, biog. of Ch'en Ching. Ch'üan Te-yü also contributed to this debate; see *Ch'üan Tsai-chih wen chi* 29/5a; also 44/6b–7a, memorial congratulating Te tsung on completing the restoration. Cf. Te tsung's early intention to be lavish in provisioning the Yüan-ling, mausoleum of Tai tsung, and the memorial of Ling-hu Huan, *CTS* 149/4011–12 biog.

161 *Liu Ho-tung chi* 8/124 and 12/188 and *HTS* 200/5716, biog. of Ch'en Ching.

162 For examples of scholars being transferred from the presidency of the court of sacrifices to a chief ministership, see *CTS* 136/3756 and *TCTC* 235/7592, 800.20, Ch'i K'ang; *Liu Ho-tung chi* 12/192, *CTS* 147/3976 and *TCTC* 236/7604, 803.17, Kao Ying. Cf. also *CTS* 145/3935 and *TCTC* 233/7518, 789.3, Tung Chin; also, a few years later, *CTS* 147/3973 and

Liu Ho-tung chi 12/186, commentary, Tu Huang-shang; *CTS* 148/4003 and 4004, biog. of Ch'üan Te-yü.

163 *CTS* 14/420; *TTCLC* 70/391–92, act of grace.

164 *THY* 18/371–72.

165 For the planned ploughing rite, see *Liu Ho-tung chi* 43/736; *HTS* 14/359–60; *HTS* 200/5721, biog. of Wei Kung-su; for the edict cancelling the performance, see *TTCLC* 74/415; also *Liu Ho-tung chi* 33/533.

166 *Liu Yü-hsi chi* 17/148, memorial written for P'ei Tu(?) presenting a picture of the 725 performance, with a strong hint that the ritual be done again. This is dated 830 in *Liu Yü-hsi nien-p'u* p. 156. Also *Han Ch'ang-li chi* 7/39/38; dated 819, by Hanabusa (1964), p. 69.

167 *THY* 15/327–46; *CTS* 26/979–95; *TCTC* 248/8017, 845.16 and commentary. *HTS* 13/342 gives a brief, one paragraph summary.

168 *CTS* 159/4180–81, biog. of Cheng Yin; *CTS* 26/980.

169 *CTS* 157/4154–57, biog. of Wang Yen-wei; *CTS* 26/980–82.

170 *TCTC* 248/8017, 845.16; cf. also *Li Wen-jao wen chi* 10/6a–b, proposal by Li Te-yü to use timbers from a Buddhist monastery to build a temple to the T'ang ancestor Chao-wu.

171 For other controversies, see *TCTC* 248/8025, 846.8, discussion on expansion to 11 chapels; *TCTC* 248, 846.18, discussion on the prayer texts for Mu tsung and Ching tsung in the temple; *TCTC* 249/8061, 856.9, discussion of the place of the spirit tablets of Mu tsung, Ching tsung and Wen tsung in the temple.

172 *CTS* 25/962–64.

173 *CTS* 20A/781; *CTS* 20B/810.

174 E.g. for the ploughing rite, *CTS* 24/913–14 gives no information after 759; *HTS* 14/359–60 gives none after 810–11. *TTCLC* 74/415 also enters nothing after 810–11. For the T'ai kung military cult, *CTS* 24/936 enters nothing after 760; *HTS* 15/380 nothing after 788. *THY* 23/438 has nothing in the final century of T'ang rule except for the request of 905 that the cult be revived. For the cult to Confucius and its *Shih-tien* ritual, *CTS* 24/924 enters nothing after 766; *HTS* 15/377 nothing after 814. *THY* 35/639–40 and 35/643 contains very little after 814, apart from the final entry describing the firing of the temple in 890.

175 For this remark, see *WYYH* 493/5a, and *CTS* 190B/5096, biog. *TTCLC* 106/548 also contains the question.

176 *THY* 26/492.

177 For Wen tsung's claim that he was about to revive the *Ch'ih-chou*, see *CTS* 17B/551; *TTCLC* 29/107; *TKCK* 21/5a; the same decree established the erudits of the *Five canons*, for which see Ch. 2, note 215.

178 *Ch'üan T'ang wen* 72/13a–b, decree by Wen tsung.

179 *Sun Ch'iao chi* 10/1a and *TWT* 49/2b–3a, Sun Ch'iao.

180 For the deterioration of the *hsiang yin chiu* ceremony, see *WYYH* 690/8b, Liu Ch'iu. However claims that this ritual had lapsed were made before, even at the height of the dynasty's prosperity: see *THY* 26/498, edict for the year 710; and in the post-rebellion decades, *WYYH* 737/8a–b, Liang Su.

181 Later *nan chiao* observances are conveniently listed in the supplemen-

tary *THY* 10A/203–04. The last listed occurred under Hsi tsung in 877.
TTCLC 72/400–06 contains the act of grace for this performance.

182 *THY* 83/1529–30; *THY* 6/69–70; *Feng shih wen chien chi* 5/21; *CTS*
150/4046, biog. of Hsien, prince of Chen.

183 *Ch'üan Tsai-chih wen chi* 22/7a–8a; *CTS* 149/4023, biog. of Chang Chien.

184 *THY* 77/1411. Pao Chi's death occurred after this and before the 5th
month of 792; see *Ch'üan Tsai-chih wen chi* 48/1a. *T'ang Yüeh ling k'ao*
in *T'ang Yüeh ling chu, pu i* states only K'ai-yüan, not *K'ai-yüan li*.
Another initiative may have been taken in 786: Kuan Po, who
memorialized in connection with the debate on T'ai kung and the
military temple, was then described as 'administering the drafting of
ritual directives'. See *THY* 23/436; *CTS* 130/3628, biog.

185 *THY* 65/1136. The post was later held, sometimes as a concurrent
tenure, by some of the productive ritual scholars of the reigns of Te
tsung and Hsien tsung: e.g. Wang Ching, as compiler of the *Ta T'ang
chiao ssu lu*; see *HTS* 58/1492; Chiang I (Wu), see *CTS* 149/4028, biog.;
Wei Kung-su, compiler of new directives for the ploughing rite in 810;
see *HTS* 200/5721. Compilers were sometimes specially rewarded in acts
of grace; see e.g. *TTCLC* 10/62, act of grace of 820.

186 *Ch'üan Tsai-chih wen chi* 23/2b; *THY* 36/659; *CTS* 135/3729, biog. of Wei
Chü-mou; *HTS* 58/1491, *Ho chih* p. 137. For Wei's south-eastern
background, see *Yen Lu kung wen chi* 7/7b and *Ch'üan Tsai-chih wen chi*
35/1a–2b.

187 The *TT* ritual section is divided into two sub-sections: *TT* 41–105 traces
the evolution (*yen ko*) of rituals from early times until, in some cases,
the middle Chen-yüan period. *TT* 106–40 contains Tu Yu's abridgement
of the K'ai-yüan ritual code. For Tu Yu's praise of the K'ai-yüan code,
see *TT* 41/233.3; for his account of the division of the *TT* ritual section in
two, see *TT* 41/234.1, double column entry; *TT* 106/561.1, double
column entry. For criticism of Tu Yu's abridgement of the code, see
SKCSTMTY p. 1714.

188 For entries for the ritual to Confucius in the 'evolution' (*yen ko*) section,
see *TT* 53/304.3; to T'ai kung, *TT* 55/307.2. The ploughing rite, despite
the re-drafting in the Chi-hsien yüan in 735, still apparently retained the
form prescribed in *TTKYL* ; see *TT* 46/264.3.

189 For rituals where the *TT* enters significant changes after the K'ai-yüan
code, and does not endorse the code as the authority, see e.g. the *she
chi* rite, *TT* 45/262.3, double column entry, entering changes made in
late 771 and in 789; or the ancestral temple rites; see *TT* 47/271.3,
entering an imperial order of 793 forbidding the use of mats in ancestral
temple or *nan chiao* rites.

190 *Yen Lu kung chi* 3/1a–15b, and editorial comment, 15b–16a; also *TT*
80/432.2, 433.3; 83/448.1; 84/451.2–3, etc.

191 *Liu Ho-tung chi* 9/146; 21/367–9; 40/653; *HTS* 58/1492. For P'ei's great
great grandfather, P'ei Hsing-chien, see Ch. 6, note 94; for his great
grandfather, P'ei Kuang-t'ing, see Ch. 3, note 108. For his grandfather
P'ei Chen and his father P'ei Ching see *Chin shih ts'ui pien* 84/1a; *WYYH*
792/6b–9b, report of conduct by Tu-ku Chi; *HTS* 108/4091. A contemp-

tuous remark by Su Mien on the removal of the *kuo hsü* section of the ritual code of 658, *THY* 37/670, was about contemporary with Liu's preface.

192 *Lü Ho-shu wen chi* 5/10b–12a.

193 The *Li ko hsin i (New directives for the ritual hall)* by the long-serving ritual scholar Wei Kung-su entered only material subsequent to the K'ai-yüan code; see *HTS* 11/309 and *HTS* 58/1491. For Wei Kung-su, see his brief *HTS* 200/5721 notice; *CTS* 171/4455, biog. of Li Han. He was a compiler in the imperial library in 826; see *THY* 36/662; and an erudit in the court of sacrifices in 829–30; see *Liu Yü-hsi chi* 8/73 and Ch. 3, note 152.

194 *CTS* 158/4165, biog. of Chen Yü-ch'ing; *TFYK* 564/20a; *CTS* 155/4118, biog. of Ts'ui Yen; Hanabusa (1964), p. 380.

195 For Wang Yen-wei's unofficially initiated *Ch'ü-t'ai hsin li (New rituals of Ch'ü-t'ai)*, in 30 *chüan* sometimes referred to as the *Yüan-ho hsin li (New rituals of the Yüan-ho period)*, see *THY* 37/671; *THY* 36/661; *CTS* 157/4154, biog. of Wang Yen-wei; *TFYK* 564/10b; *HTS* 11/309; *HTS* 58/1492. There was also a continuation, also in 30 *chüan*, which is briefly described in *HTS* 11/309. *Liu Yü-hsi chi* 39/396 implies that Wang Yen-wei was successful in an examination on the *Five canons*. Hsü Sung, *TKCK* 27/32a understands this as success in the *ming ching*. For later citation of the *Ch'ü-t'ai hsin li*, see e.g. *THY* 14/318; *THY* 19/391; *CTS* 25/964–65. For Wang Yen-wei's canonization compendium, see *SKC-STMTY* p. 1714, entry for the canonization compendium of Su Hsün of the Sung. *Liu Yü-hsi chi* 39/396 also indicates that Wang's father was a compiler of ritual directives.

196 *CTS* 189B/4978, biog. of Lu Ch'un; *HTS* 57/1434, entered under the name of Lu Chih.

197 For Chung Tzu-ling, see *Ch'üan Tsai-chih wen chi* 24/11a–13a, 31/3a–b; 36/6b–7a; *CTS* 26/1008; *Kuo shih pu* 3/54. *HTS* 200/5707, biog. of Chung Tzu-ling; *HTS* 58/1493.

198 *THY* 36/659; *HTS* 59/1538, Ho chih p. 222; cf. *TFYK* 607/18b, Wang Yai's *Yüeh ling t'u*.

199 *WYYH* 946/4a–b, epitaph by Lo Kun.

200 For Wang Ching as a ritual official in 793, see *HTS* 58/1492; in 812, see *CTS* 17/4455, biog. of Li Han; in 819, *CTS* 160/4206, biog. of Li Ao.

201 In 901, the final year for which datable *tsa wen* topics survive, the title set for *shih* composition was 'On withdrawing from court at the Wu-te palace and looking towards the spring scene over the nine thoroughfares'; see *TKCK* 24/25b. The chief examiner, Tu Te-hsiang, was a son of Tu Mu and therefore a great grandson of Tu Yu; see *TKCK* 24/26b quoting *T'ang yü lin*.

202 For the first in 785, see *WYYH* 486/1b, *Lu Hsüan kung han-yüan chi* 6/7a and *TTCLC* 106/542. For the second in 785, *WYYH* 473/5b, *TTCLC* 106/543, and *Lu Hsüan kung han-yüan chi* 6/9a–b. *Po Hsiang-shan chi* 7/48/77, *Ts'e lin* no. 60, draws very closely on the wording in this question.

203 In 788, candidates were told that T'ai tsung had dispensed with punish-

ments and executed only 29 criminals in 630 (*TCTC* 193/6084–85, 630.33). A sub-question asked 'For reviving learning and venerating Confucianism, what rituals are most telling?' See *TTCLC* 106/544; *TKCK* 12/19a–b. Cf. also *Po Hsiang-shan chi* 7/47/73–74.

204 *Ch'üan Tsai-chih wen chi* 40/9b–10a; *TKCK* 15/7a.
205 *Po Hsiang-shan chi* 7/47/78–79, *Ts'e lin* no. 62.
206 *Po Hsiang-shan chi* 7/47/79–80, *Ts'e lin* no. 63.
207 *Po Hsiang-shan chi* 7/47/81–82, *Ts'e lin* no. 65.
208 *THY* 76/1396–97; *TT* 15/84.2; *CTS* 44/1892 commentary; *HTS* 44/1165; *TFYK* 640/13b–14b; des Rotours (1932), p. 133, p. 148, p. 177.
209 For some successful candidates' names, see *TKCK* 27/37b–38a. Also, for soon after the institution of the examination, *CTS* 135/3737, biog. of Ch'eng I, after he had taken the *ming ching*; *CTS* 157/4150–51, biog. of Hsin Mi, also as a second examination; *CTS* 188/4936, biog. of Ting Kung-chu, also as a second examination; *Yüan shih Ch'ang-ch'ing chi* 55/1b, P'ei I (Hsü Sung *TKCK* 27/37b–38a, does not supply his given name; but *HTS* 182/5375 confirms his identification). For mid ninth century examples, see *TKCK* 22/24b for Lin Hsü, in 851. For late T'ang examples, *TKCK* 27/38a, Tu Nien; Lo Hsiu-ku; see biog. of Lo Yin, 833–909, in *Wu Yüeh pei shih*, reprinted in *Lo Yin chi*, appendix, p. 325.
210 For the phrase *pu k'an chih tien* or variants of it applied to individual Confucian canons or to the canons in series, see *TT* 52/300.1, memorial by P'eng Ching-chih, of the three ritual canons; *STTS* 1/5b; *CTS* 21/843–44; *CTS* 8/180 and 27/1031, edict of 719; *CTS* 21/818, Chang Yüeh in 726; *CTCC* epitaph for Chang Chi-shu, d. 851, aged 62 *sui*; *TWT* 81/7b, Li Yang-ping; *Ta T'ang chiao ssu lu* 10/15b. It was also applied to the *kuo shih*, by Hsüan tsung in the edict appointing Hsiao Sung as its director, *TTCLC* 51/263; and by the late T'ang rescript writer Hsüeh T'ing-kuei, *WYYH* 400/1b. Cf. also *Li Wen kung chi* 6/39b, of Li Ao's ambition to improve on the *kuo shih*.
211 *Ch'üan Tsai-chih wen chi* 29/8a–12b, 46/18a–b; *CTS* 148/4002–05, biog. of Ch'üan Te-yü.
212 *CTS* 147/3976, biog. of Kao Ying; *THY* 18/365, memorial dated 12th month of 806.
213 *Han Ch'ang-li chi* 4/14/29–32 and commentary; Hanabusa (1964), p. 378.
214 *Ch'üan Tsai-chih wen chi* 22/7a–8a, epitaph for Chang Chien and *CTS* 149/4024, biog.
215 *Li Wen kung chi* 10/77b–79b; *THY* 18/362–63.
216 *Li Wen kung chi* 4/24a–b.
217 See above, note 194. Cf. *Han Ch'ang-li chi* 7/ *Wai chi* 1/64 and commentary. This enters a memorial on the organization of the ancestral temple following the death of Mu tsung. A similar memorial is contained in *CTS* 25/958–59, as submitted by the 'ritual commissioner', and there is serious doubt about its attribution to Han Yü.
218 *Ch'üan Tsai-chih wen chi* 29/10a; *TT* 50/290.2; *THY* 13/313–14. For Lu's contribution to the T'ai kung debate, in 788, see *Ta T'ang chiao ssu lu* 10/14b–15b.
219 *CTS* 26/1010.

220 *Liu Ho-tung chi* 26/432; *Yen Lu kung chi* 12/5a.
221 *Han Ch'ang-li chi* 5/23/61–62; also *Huang-fu Ch'ih-cheng wen chi* 6/4a; *Li Wen kung chi* 4/2b–24a.
222 *Li Wen kung chi* 2/3b.
223 *Li Wen kung chi* 2/2b.
224 *Ch'un-ch'iu tsuan li* 2/11b–12a.
225 *TT* 8/45.1; 12/67.2–3, Tu Yu; 18/101.1, Shen Chi-chi; 17/96.2, Liu Chih; *Kuan tzu* 3/66; *Shang tzu* 5/4a.
226 *Ch'un-ch'iu tsuan li* 2/16a; 2/18a; 2/14b, double column entry.
227 *TT* 1/9.1, pref. by Tu Yu, citing *Chou i chu shu* 8/2b; *Shang shu chu shu* 12/5b; *Kuan tzu* 1/1 (cf. 3/64; 3/98); *Analects* 13/9. Cf. K'ung Ying-ta, *Tso chuan chu shu* 26/7a–b, for citation of the same *Kuan tzu* and *Analects* passages.
228 *TT* 41/233.1; cf. *SS* 6/105; also K'ung Ying-ta, *Shang shu chu shu* 3/15a, for a similar account of the 'three rituals' in relation to the 'five rituals'.
229 *TT* 70/385.1–386.1. There is evidence from a Sung source that Tu Yu held that the *Yüeh ling* originated not in the *Lü shih ch'un-ch'iu*, as K'ung Ying-ta believed, but in the *Kuan tzu*, a text in which he had a special interest, and that Lü Pu-wei had merely edited it. See the preface dated 1174 by Lo Mi entitled *Shu T'ang Yüeh ling*, in *T'ang Yüeh ling chu pu i*, p. 1; and *Yü hai* 12/11a, quoting a *TT* note. In this Tu differed from Liu Tsung-yüan; see *Liu Ho-tung chi* 3/38.
230 *TT* 54/312.1, quoting *Hou Han chi* 8/13b–14b. For another statement by Tu indicating belief in functional rituals, see *TT* 74/403.1.
231 *TT* 12/71.2; *TT* 31/177.2.
232 *Ch'üan Tsai-chih wen chi* 22/5a. For the expression *ch'i yen*, see also *Tso chuan chu shu* 9/5a. I am grateful to Professor Dudbridge for a discussion of this term.
233 For a detailed account of Liu Tsung-yüan's attitude to 'heaven' see Lamont (1973) and (1974).
234 *Liu Ho-tung chi* 26/432.
235 *Liu Ho-tung chi* 16/296–97.
236 *Liu Ho-tung chi* 45/787.
237 *Liu Ho-tung chi* 3/54–55. For the term 'purblind historians' (*ku shih*), see also *Ch'üan Tsai-chih wen chi* 11/5a.
238 *Liu Ho-tung chi* 1/18; cf. *T'ang chien* 4/29. This view of the Feng and Shan rites was echoed in an essay by the mid ninth century writer Lin Chien-yen; see *TWT* 34/5b–6b.
239 *Liu Ho-tung chi* 43/736; 33/533; cf. *THY* 10B/255; *TTCLC* 74/415; *HTS* 14/359–60; *HTS* 200/5721, biog. of Wei Kung-su.
240 *Liu Ho-tung chi* 1/5 and 6.
241 *Liu Ho-tung chi* 21/367–69.
242 Cf. Lamont (1973), pp. 197–9; *WYYH* 740/10a–11b, Niu Seng-ju; *Li Wen-jao wen chi, wai chi* 4/5b–6a and *WYYH* 740/13a–b, Li Te-yü.
243 *Liu Ho-tung chi* 3/51–2; *Tso chuan chu shu* 49/7b. Liu Tsung-yüan argued that the saying attributed to Confucius, 'Preserving the *tao* is not as good as preserving the office', was 'definitely not the statement of the sage, but an error by those transmitting it'. Again, therefore, in this

essay, he preserved the authority of Confucius, while, in the manner of the *Ch'un-ch'iu* scholars and of his own *Fei Kuo yü*, faulting the transmission of an early text.

5 History

1 *THY* 76/1398, memorial of 822; cf. *SS* 33/992–3 and *STTS* 6/11b, 10/4a–b; and the great frequency with which the canons and histories were mentioned together, e.g. *CTS* 189A/4962, biog. of Hsiao Te-yen; *CTS* 187A/4876, Yüan Pan-ch'ien; *WYYH* 652/2a–b; *CTCC* epitaph for K'ai Yüan-hsiu.

2 *SS* 33/953–96; *CTS* 46/1963, 1987–2022, esp. p. 1987. Cf. the tenfold scheme of minor historical genres offered by Liu Chih-chi, *STTS* 10/1a.

3 For the respective merits of the two forms, see *STTS* 2/1a–5a; *WYYH* 678/8a–9a, Hsiao Ying-shih; *Huang-fu Ch'ih-cheng wen chi* 2/2a–3b. The praise T'ai tsung gave to the *Han chi* of Hsün Yüeh, echoed by Liu Chih-chi, probably contributed to the high status of the chronicle form; see *CKCY* 5/64; *CTS* 62/2388, biog. of Li Ta-liang; *SS* 33/959; *STTS* 2/2b; cf. also *Ch'en shu* 34/467–68.

4 *SS* 33/992–93.

5 I owe this phrase to the late Professor A.F. Wright. Cf. Hartwell (1976), pp. 690–96.

6 *SS* 33/992–93; *THY* 23/435; *Li Wen kung chi* 9/66a.

7 *Shih chi* 47/1944; *Tso chuan chu shu* pref. 1a–b. With the related idea of 'praise and blame' (*pao-pien*) through a single character (*i tzu*), this idea was very frequently applied to contemporary literary practice and to the canonization system as well as to official history; *STTS* 3/1a, 14/10b; *CTS* 98/3074, biog. of Li Yüan-hung; *WYYH* 678/4b, Hsiao Ying-shih (understanding *ts'u* for the text's *chieh*); *CTS* 190B/5030, biog. of Chia Chih; *WYYH* 400/2b, Ch'ang Kun; *WYYH* 742/12a, Niu Hsi-chi; *WYYH* 400/1b, Hsüeh T'ing-kuei; *Ch'un-ch'iu tsuan li* 1/7b; *WYYH* 367/4b, Tu-ku Yü; *WYYH* 690/11b, Lu Kuei-meng; *Ch'üan Tsai-chih wen chi* 40/7a and 48/1b.

8 Hung (1969), p. 22 and notes 38 and 39, and *Tso chuan chu shu* 21/6b for Tung Hu and 36/3b–4a for Nan Shih. For some T'ang references to Tung Hu and Nan Shih, see *SS* 33/992; *Chin shu* 113/2904; *THY* 63/1102, Chu Tzu-she; Lo Chen-yü (1909), 1/1b, Chao-ling stele for K'ung Ying-ta by Yü Chih-ning; *THY* 64/1106, of Wu Ching; *STTS* 10/7a, 20/14b, 15a–b; *WYYH* 678/4b; Hsiao Ying-shih of Wei Shu; *CTS* 149/4038, historian's assessment; *WYYH* 383/1b, Chia (Chih); *WYYH* 400/2a, Ch'ang Kun; *P'i tzu wen sou* 1/5; *WYYH* 690/11b, Lu Kuei-meng. Nan Shih even supplied a given name; e.g. *Chung-hsing hsien ch'i chi* 2/301, Chang Nan-shih; *Kuo shih pu* 3/56, Ts'ai Nan-shih; *CTS* 137/3761, Lu Nan-shih.

9 For the high prestige of *Han shu* studies in the seventh century, see *SS* 33/95–97; also *Nien-erh shih cha chi* 20/399–401; Masui Tsuneo (1976), p. 20. In the T'ang, the *Shih chi* and the *Han shu* were grouped with a third work covering the Han and called the *San shih* (*Three histories*), to balance the *San chuan* and the *San li*. In early T'ang, this third work was

the *Tung kuan Han chi*, a history of the Later Han compiled by a
number of scholars over several reigns. Probably by the statutes of 651,
however, the *Tung kuan Han chi* was replaced by the *Hou Han shu* of
Fan Yeh, 398–445, though this situation was later changed. See Kao
Ming-shih (1977), pp. 7–16, and Yoshikawa Tadao (1979), p. 309, n.3.

10   *WYYH* 610/11a, Hsiao Ying-shih, quoting the *Chen-kuan shih lu*; cf.
CKCY 10/304 for a comparable remark, dated 635; and Wu Ching's
claim in the pref. to *CKCY* that T'ai tsung's rule exceeded even that of
kings Wen and Wu of the Chou and Wen and Ching of the Han. Nearly
two centuries later, the Confucian scholar and official historian Li Ao
was to judge that the T'ang history did not measure up to the works of
the Chou or Han; see *Li Wen kung chi* 6/39a, letter to Huang-fu Shih.

11   *CKCY* 5/61; 7/218; 10/299; *SS* 74/1691. Cf. *WYYH* 610/10a, Hsiao
Ying-shih.

12   *San kuo chih, Shu shu* 43/1050; *Wei shu* 24/621; cf. also Liang Wu ti,
Nan shih 50/1252 and Hsiao Chao ti of the Northern Ch'i, *Pei Ch'i shu*
6/79 and 36/475.

13   *CTS* 66/2465, biog. of Fang Hsüan-ling. For T'ai tsung's mention of
episodes in Ch'in or Han history, see e.g. *CKCY* 5/175; 6/178; 9/289. In
CKCY 7/217, he mentioned 'recently seeing the histories of the Former
and Later Han'.

14   Wechsler (1985), pp. 95–9; for a reference by Kao tsu to Han legal
policy, see *CTS* 50/2134.

15   For metals, silks and horses, see *CKCY* 2/65–66; *CKCY* 10/307–08; *CTS*
71/2559–60, biog. of Wei Cheng; *CTS* 74/2616, biog. of Ma Chou. For
palaces and mausolea, see *CKCY* 5/59–62. For military adventurism,
CKCY 9/27; 9/283; 9/286; *CTS* 80/2736, biog. of Ch'u Sui-liang. For
enfieffment, *CKCY* 3/91, and 4/100–01; *CTS* 72/2575, biog. of Li
Pai-yao; *CTS* 74/2617–18; biog. of Ma Chou; *CTS* 80/2730–31, biog. of
Ch'u Sui-liang. For imperial princes, *CKCY* 4/118–19; cf. *CKCY* 7/215.

16   *Ch'ün-shu chih yao*, table of contents and chs. 13–20. For the submission
of this work in 631, see *THY* 36/651.

17   *CTS* 73/2592, biog. of Yao Ssu-lien and *SS* 33/954 listing 3 works of *Han
shu* exegesis by Yao's father Yao Ch'a; *CTS* 189A/4947, biog. of
Ou-yang Hsün; *CTS* 73/2600, biog. of Ku Yin; p. 4955–56, biogs. of Liu
Na-yen, Liu Po-chuang, Ch'in Ching-t'ung and his brother Ch'in Wei;
CTS 188/4932, biog. of Lu Nan-chin; *CTS* 84/2797, biog. of Hao
Ch'u-chün. *CTS* 46/1988, *HTS* 58/1456 and *Ho chih* p. 62 enter a work
entitled *Yü ch'üan ting Han shu* (*Han shu imperially evaluated and
determined*) in 81 *chüan*; *HTS* describes this as a work of collaboration
between Hao Ch'u-chün and Kao tsung. For the place of the *Shih chi*
and *Han shu* in the teaching of the Hung-wen kuan, and possibly also
the state academy directorate, see *THY* 64/1115, of Hsü Ching-tsung and
THY 76/1398, memorial of 822; also *Shih chi so yin*, postface p. 9, of Liu
Po-chuang.

18   *SS* 33/957; cf. *Shih chi so yin*, postface pp. 9–10.

19   *CTS* 73/2595–96 biog. of Yen Shih-ku. Also *CTS* 189A/4954 biog. of
Ching Po. Yoshikawa, pp. 264–71, discusses the common ground

between Yen Shih-ku's commentary and relevant material first in the *Yen shih chia hsün* (*Family instructions of the Yen clan*) of Yen Chih-t'ui, and, secondly in the *Han shu chüeh i* (*Resolution of dubious points in the Han shu*), 12 *chüan*, by Yen's uncle Yen Yu-ch'in, as this work is preserved in citations in the *Shih chi so yin* of the following century. Yen Shih-ku's nephew Yen Chao-fu was also involved in the preparation of the commentary, see Yoshikawa, p. 271.

20 Yoshikawa, pp. 234–42. Of Yen Shih-ku's list of 23 *Han shu* exegetes, only Ts'ui Hao post-dated the end of the Chin. Ts'ui Hao, however, glossed not the *Han shu* itself, but Hsün Yüeh's chronicle-form abridgement of it, the *Han chi*. Yen may have included Ts'ui Hao not only as the only northerner to produce a work of Han historical exegesis but also, though Yoshikawa does not suggest this, because T'ai tsung so esteemed the work (note 3, above). Yoshikawa, pp. 278–91, argues that Yen Shih-ku's opinions differed from those of the late southern exegete Yao Ch'a, as these are preserved in a number of citations in the *Shih chi so yin* of the following century. For place names, see Yoshikawa p. 287. For scepticism towards the exotic or supernatural, see Yen's commentary at *Han shu* 65/2874, biog. of Tung-fang Shuo. For scepticism over genealogies, see Yoshikawa pp. 288–9. The everyday appeal of some of Yen's glosses is suggested by his note on football, cited in *Feng shih wen chien chi* 6/5.

21 The sanction of the *Han shu*, coinciding with early T'ang promotion of Confucian scholarship, has been seen in the reintroduction of a section of biographies for Confucian scholars (*ju lin chuan*) in two of the histories of the pre-T'ang dynasties completed under T'ai tsung, the *Liang shu* and *Sui shu*; see Masui Tsuneo (1976), p. 120.

22 *SS* 26/719, preface to monograph on offices and posts, gives particular emphasis on change in high antiquity, using no fewer than three key terms for this idea: *sun i*; *yen ko*; and *wen chih*.

23 *THY* 63/1090–91; cf. *THY* 35/643; *CTS* 73/2597–98, biog. of Ling-hu Te-fen; *TFYK* 554/15a–16a; *TTCLC* 81/466–67; Kanai (1940), pp. 10ff.; Hung (1960–1), p. 94; Twitchett (1985), p. 24, notes 54–5.

24 *CTS* 71/2549–50, biog. of Wei Cheng; *CTS* 73/2598, biog. of Ling-hu Te-fen; *CTS* 70/2536, biog. of Ts'en Wen-pen; *CTS* 73/2592–93, biog. of Yao Ssu-lien; *CKCY* 7/218; *THY* 63/1091; *STTS* 12/29a, 'original note', states that Yao Ssu-lien's commission was from 628 and not from 629, as were those of other members of T'ai tsung's commission. This contradicts Yao's *CTS* biog., 73/2593, but if true suggests that T'ai tsung's reconstruction of Kao tsu's commission was more piecemeal and less concerted than the main sources imply. A family tradition of historical scholarship, on the model of Ssu-ma T'an and Ssu-ma Ch'ien or Pan Piao and Pan Ku, was admired throughout the T'ang. As well as Yao Ch'a and Yao Ssu-lien, Li Te-lin and Li Pai-yao, working on the *Ch'i shu*, provide an example of father–son continuity in history compilation; see *SS* 42/1209, biog. of Li Te-lin; *CTS* 72/2577, biog. of Li Pai-yao; and *STTS* 12/27a–b. For commendation of later T'ang examples, see *WYYH* 944/7a, Liang Su, of Liu Chih-chi and two of his sons, Liu K'uang and

Liu Su; also *Po Hsiang-shan chi* 6/37/30, Po Chü-i, of Shen Chi-chi and his son Shen Ch'uan-shih; *TFYK* 561/5a–6a, of Kuei Ch'ung-ching and Kuei Teng.

25 *CTS* 73/2592–93, biog. of Yao Ssu-lien. Yao Ch'a's rank under the Ch'en is confirmed by *SS* 33/954 and *TFYK* 607/5b. A work by him entitled *Liang shu ti chi* in 10 *chüan* is entered in *SS* 33/956. *STTS* 4/8a records a work entitled *Liang lüeh* by Yao Ch'a and charges that it was misnamed an 'abridgement' (*lüeh*). For Yao Ch'a's *Han shu* scholarship, see Yoshikawa, p. 250, pp. 278–283, pp. 286–87; some 50 citations are preserved in the *Shih chi so yin*; see p. 279 and n. 72 on p. 316. *STTS* 12/19a–20a gives accounts of the compilation of the Liang and Ch'en histories. See also Kanai (1940), pp. 12–31; Wang Shu-min (1981), pp. 67–70; and Mou (1968), for the differences in perspective between Yao Ssu-lien and Wei Cheng.

26 *CTS* 73/2592, biog. of Yao Ssu-lien; *CTS* 71/2550, biog. of Wei Cheng; *CTS* 70/2536, biog. of Ts'en Wen-pen. Such insertions had also been anthologized, as discrete compositions, in the *Wen hsüan*, chs. 49–50.

27 *TWT* 82/6b.

28 *CTS* 79/2727, biog. of Lü Ts'ai, recording a *Sui chi* in 20 *chüan*; *CTS* 190A/4988, biog. of Ts'ai Yün-kung, recording a *Hou Liang ch'un-ch'iu* in 10 *chüan*; *CTS* 187A/4876, a *San kuo ch'un-ch'iu*, by Yüan Pan-ch'ien in 20 *chüan*; *CTS* 68/2507, a *Hou Wei shu* in 100 *chüan* and a *Sui shu* in 30 *chüan*, by Chang Ta-su.

29 *CTS* 79/2718, biog. of Li Ch'un-feng; *STTS* 12/29b, mentioning only four scholars; *THY* 63/1093, reading '*Wu tai shih* . . .', where '*Wu tai shih chih* . . .' is required, and giving the presentation date, 656, only. *CTS* 78/2700, biog. of Yü Chih-ning does not mention the commission by name; *CTS* 73/2600, biog. of Li Yen-shou mentions in addition the prominent official historian Ching Po, and this is confirmed in *HTS* 58/1457, but is not mentioned in Ching Po's *CTS* biog., 189A/4954–55. Li Yen-shou's account of the *Pei shih* has Ch'u Sui-liang as a compiler of 'the ten Sui monographs'; see *Pei shih* 100/3343; but again this is not mentioned in Ch'u Sui-liang's *CTS* biog. For references to these as *Sui shu* monographs, see *Pei shih* 100/3343 and 3354; *STTS* 12/29b; *CTS* 46/1964; *CTS* 102/3164, biog. of Ma Huai-su; *Feng shih wen chien chi* 2/11; *Ta T'ang chiao ssu lu* 3/3b.

30 *STTS* 12/29a–b, *CTS* 73/2598, biog. of Ling-hu Te-fen; *CTS* 79/2718, biog. of Li Ch'un-feng. For Li's expertise in astrology, the calendar and the five elements, see Needham Vol. 3 (1959), *passim* (romanized as Li Shun-feng).

31 *SS* 6/105, opening of the monograph on ritual, states, '[Rituals] are the means to make complete (*mi lun*; see *Chou i chu shu* 7/5b for this phrase) heaven and earth; they provide the warp and woof of *yin* and *yang*; they discriminate the subtle and mysterious and penetrate the minute and profound. They link with the hundred divinities and regulate the ten thousand events.'

32 *SS* 25/695, opening of the monograph on punishments, 'The sage kings looked up and drew their model from the stars; they looked round and

observed dangers and pitfalls (*hsi k'an*; see *Chou i chu shu* 3/20a). They made good the five vapours and derived their rules from the four seasons."

33 *SS* 26/719, opening of the monograph on offices and posts, 'The [*Chou*] *i* states, 'Heaven is lofty and earth is low, and [their hexagrams] *ch'ien* and *k'un* are accordingly fixed (*Chou i chu shu* 7/1b). The low and high are set forth and the noble and base have their positions.' Hence the sages took *ch'ien* and *k'un* as their model and created their rules. They handed down their instruction according to the low and the high; they established posts and divided out offices. They granted jade tablets and conferred territory.'

34 *Pei shih* 100/3343–44, and for the memorial of presentation, 3344–45. See also *CTS* 73/2600–01, biog. of Li Yen-shou; *STTS* 1/13a. For the scope of these two histories, see Yang Chia-lo (n.d.), pp. 1–15; Wang Shu-min (1981), pp. 84–8.

35 *TT* 17/98.1, Chao K'uang. Cf. also the praise for Li Yen-shou's other compilation, the *T'ai tsung cheng tien* (*Compendium of the government of T'ai tsung*), in 30 *chüan*, *THY* 36/657; *CTS* 5/105; *CTS* 73/2601, biog. of Li Yen-shou.

36 For early T'ang respect for the Chin, see *THY* 36/651; note 16 above and notes 61–63 below; also Ch. 2, note 35.

37 For the edict commissioning the new Chin history, see *TTCLC* 81/467; this required that the work should be done 'at the place where the dynastic history is compiled', and that the model of the five pre-T'ang histories should be followed. See also *THY* 63/1091; *CTS* 66/2462–63, biog. of Fang Hsüan-ling, which singled out Li Ch'un-feng's treatises for commendation and otherwise included an incomplete list of members of the commission; *CTS* 79/2718, biog. of Li Ch'un-feng; *CTS* 73/2598, biog. of Ling-hu Te-fen, dated 646. Liu Chih-chi's comments on the *Chin shu* are at *STTS* 4/2a, 3a and 8b–9a; also at *STTS* 15/1b–12b; his account of its compilation is at *STTS* 12/14b–15a. See also Jan Chao-te (1957), pp. 71–78.

38 *THY* 63/1091; cf. *CTS* 199A/5335–36. The first two passages were essays for the basic annals of Hsüan ti; see *Chin shu* 1/20–22, and Wu ti; see *Chin shu* 3/81–82. The assessments were for the calligrapher Wang Hsi-chih, *Chin shu* 80/2107–08, whose calligraphy T'ai tsung bought from a descendant; see *CTS* 89/2899, biog. of Wang Fang-ch'ing; and for the verse writer and historian Lu Chi, *Chin shu* 54/1487–88, with whose *Wen fu* (*Rhymeprose on literature*) T'ai tsung showed familiarity by silent quotation; see *THY* 7/94 and *TTCLC* 66/369 and Fang p. 534.

39 *STTS* 12/21a–2a; Rogers (1968), esp. pp. 40–51 and p. 69.

40 *Chin shu* chs. 86–7, pp. 2221–2271.

41 Rogers (1968), p. 50 indicates that T'ai tsung recognized the folly of Fu Chien's military adventurism and compared it to that of Sui Yang ti; see *CKCY* 9/268. This remark of T'ai tsung is dated to 630, long before the compilation of the *Chin shu*. Both Fang Hsüan-ling and Ch'u Sui-liang, compilers of the *Chin shu*, were also fervent opponents of T'ai tsung's plan to invade Korea in person, and submitted memorials against it. For

Ch'u Sui-liang, see *CTS* 80/2735–35, biog. and *CKCY* 9/271–72; for Fang
Hsüan-ling, *CTS* 66/2464–66, biog.; *CKCY* 9/273–77 and 270–71 and *TT*
186/992.3–993.1.

42 Rogers, pp. 45–6 and n. 255 on p. 100; p. 148 and n. 472 on p. 255; also
Chin shu 113/2903. The force of Professor Roger's argument is,
however, reduced by the fact that the *Chin shu* editors included the long
memorial by Liu Sung, d. *c*. 301, that advocated enfieffment; see note
135 below.

43 *CKCY* 7/220; *STTS* 12/30b; *THY* 63/1092; cf. *THY* 63/1103; *CTS*
189A/4954, biog. of Ching Po; *TCTC* 197/6203, 643.12. Cf. also *Nien-erh
shih cha chi* 16/339; Hung (1960–61), p. 98 and note 23 on p. 105;
Pulleyblank (1950), p. 450; Twitchett (1985), pp. 74–8 and notes gives a
full account.

44 This 40 *chüan* version is not mentioned in Yao Ssu-lien's *CTS* biog.,
73/2592–93; but see *STTS* 12/30b; also Pulleyblank (1950), p. 450 and
Twitchett, (1985), pp. 137–8.

45 For later citation of the *Chen-kuan shih lu*, see e.g. *THY* 36/660, by the
emperor Hsien tsung; *THY* 13/304, by the court of sacrifices in 739; *CTS*
149/4031, by the ritual scholar Liu Mien in 786; *WYYH* 610/11a, by the
prospective official scholar Hsiao Ying-shih. Cf. also *THY* 63/1097,
which speaks of '*shih lu* that are already compiled, submitted and
announced to those below'. Cf. also *STTS* 10/11b. Chao K'uang, the
Ch'un-ch'iu scholar and reformer, suggested that T'ang *shih lu* from the
reigns of Kao tsu to Jui tsung be examinable texts; see *TT* 17/98.1.

46 *CTS* 73/2599, biog. of Ling-hu Te-fen; *CTS* 73/2600, biog. of Ku Yin;
CTS 81/2758, biog. of Sun Ch'u-yüeh, mentioning a reward of 700 bolts;
CTS 189A/4955, biog. of Ching Po, giving date of 'early Yung-hui' for its
completion. See *Nien-erh shih cha chi* 16/339; Pulleyblank (1950), p. 450;
Twitchett, (1985), pp. 78–80.

47 *THY* 56/961–62, remark by the court diarist Tu Cheng-lun in 627; *CKCY*
7/219, Ch'u Sui-liang in 639 and Fang Hsüan-ling in 640; *SS* 33/966;
CKCY 7/220, Wei Cheng in 640, specifying the ideal of 'perfect
impartiality' (*chih kung*).

48 *THY* 63/1102; *WYYH* 623/11b–12a; and *HTS* 198/5648, biog. of Chu
Tzu-she, memorial of 635; *CKCY* 7/218–19, Ch'u Sui-liang and Liu Chi,
dated 639; *CKCY* 7/219–20, Fang Hsüan-ling and Wei Cheng, dated 640.
THY 63/1102–03, however, dates these incidents 642, fourth month, and
includes another, involving Ch'u Sui-liang, occurring in the seventh
month. (Cf. *CTS* 73/2642, biog. of Chang Hsüan-su, in which Ch'u
Sui-liang again mentioned the historian's role). Another incident took
place in 648, when T'ai tsung expressed concern over the record; see
THY 63/1103. Several scholars have pointed to the effect T'ai tsung's
domination of the process of compilation, even though it was indirect,
has had on *CTS*, which was based on the *shih lu* for Kao tsu and T'ai
tsung. The editors of the *SKCSTMTY*, pp. 1027–8, were among the
earliest; but see also Bingham (1937), pp. 368–74; Somers (1971), cited
by Twitchett (1985), p. 52, note 11. Another indication, hitherto
unnoticed, that *CTS* exaggerates T'ai tsung's role in the foundation of

the dynasty at the expense of Kao tsung's is provided by the four
meritorious officials introduced into Kao tsu's chapel by edict of 640
(*THY* 18/370 and *CTS* 26/1011). Wang Shen-t'ung and Wang
Hsiao-kung have no *CTS* biographies at all, while the other two, Yin
K'ai-shan and Liu Cheng-hui, who have biographies (*CTS* 58/2311 and
CTS 58/2312), saw service under T'ai tsung. All the meritorious officials
introduced into the dynastic shrine in the seventh and eighth centuries,
on the other hand, have *CTS* biogs.

49 Cf. note 29 above, for the failure of *CTS* biogs. to record their subjects'
membership of the *Sui shu* monograph commission. The *CTS* compiler,
reviewing the prefaces contained in Wu Chiung's catalogue of 721, found
them so similar to the corresponding passages in the *SS* bibliography
monograph, that he omitted them; see *CTS* 46/1964, *Ho chih* p. 6.

50 Ch. 4 at notes 40–42.

51 *THY* 36/651, dating 641; *CTS* 76/2653–54, biog. of Li T'ai; *TFYK*
560/28b, and the preface to the edition of 1980, by Ho Tz'u-chün, pp.
1–6. The enormous honorarium for this compilation, 10,000 bolts of silk,
was in line with honoraria for imperial princes submitting scholarly
works; cf. note 57 below.

52 Ch. 6, note 21.

53 *Hou Han shu*, appendix, preface to the commentary for the supplemented monographs, by Liu Chao, fl. *c.* 510, p. 1.

54 *Ta T'ang hsin yü* 11/173.

55 *CTS* 189A/4963, biog. of Wang Yüan-kan; *HTS* 200/5689–90, biog. of
Ch'u Wu-liang; *WYYH* 893/9b, Chang Chiu-ling, epitaph for Hsü Chien.
See also *Yen Lu kung wen chi* 12/4a–b, mentioning a work of *Han shu*
commentary based on that of Yen Shih-ku and Yen Yu-ch'in that was
never copied and circulated, and *Yen Lu kung wen chi* 9/5b, for a *Hou
Han shu* commentary that was lost.

56 *Feng shih wen chien chi* 3/12.

57 *CTS* 5/102; 86/2832, biog. of Li Hsien; *TFYK* 258/14b. The reward of
30,000 bolts of silk was one of the largest for the completion of an
academic project. See also *SKCSTMTY* pp. 983–4; Kao Ming-shih
(1977), p. 9; Wang Shu-min (1981), pp. 41–8. For Li Hsien's induction as
crown prince in 675, demotion in 680 and suicide in 684, see Guisso
(1978), pp. 23–4. In the Liang period Liu Chao (biogs. *Liang shu* 49/692
and *Nan shih* 72/1777) had written a commentary to Fan Yeh's *Hou Han
shu* and to a series of Later Han monographs drawn from another Later
Han history, the *Hsü Han shu* of Ssu-ma Piao (biog. *Chin shu*
82/2141–42). In the early T'ang, Ssu-ma Piao's monographs were not
automatically attached to Fan Yeh's history, and Li Hsien's commentary did not cover the Ssu-ma Piao monographs. By the post-rebellion
period, this situation had changed. When Chao K'uang proposed a
syllabus that included dynastic histories, he recommended that 'the *Hou
Han shu* with the monographs that Liu Chao provided with commentary
should form a single history'; see *TT* 17/98.1. Kao Ming-shih (1977), p. 9,
suggests that Li Hsien's commentary was given full recognition only after
his rehabilitation in 710; for which see *TCTC* 209/6650, 710.10.

58 *HTS* 58/1957; *Ho chih* p. 69; *SKCSTMTY* pp. 975–6. For Ssu-ma Chen, see Hung (1957), p. 80 and note 111 on p. 120 and above, Ch. 3 at note 75. For Ssu-ma Chen's debt to the *Han shu* commentaries of Yao Ch'a, Yen Shih-ku and Yen Shih-ku's uncle Yen Yu-ch'in, see Yoshikawa Tadao (1979), pp. 278–91.

59 *HTS* 58/1457; *Ho chih* p. 69; *SKCSTMTY* p. 976. For Chang Shou-chieh and the date of completion of the *Shih chi cheng i*, see appendix to *Shih chi*, p. 11, preface by Chang Shou-chieh. The geographical glosses of this sub-commentary, which were one of its strengths, owed to the *K'uo ti chih* of 642; see also Ho Tz'u-chün in preface to *K'uo ti chih chiao chi* (1980), pp. 3–6. For other evidence that the *Chi chung Chou shu* contained *Shih fa* definitions, see *TLT* 14/17b, accepting the emendation of the commentary.

60 For the critical climate in *Han shu* studies, see e.g. *Wang Tzu-an chi*, pref. by Yang Chiung, recording that Wang Po wrote a work entitled *[Han shu] chih hsia* (*Pointing out the errors in [Han shu scholarship]*), at the age of nine *sui*, and that this related to Yen Shih-ku's commentary. Also *CTS* 189A/4946, biog. of Li Shan. The *Han shu cheng i* by Seng Wu-ching, by virtue of its entry in *CTS* 46/1988 and *HTS* 58/1454, *Ho chih* p. 64, should also be a work of this period. Liu Chih-chi, *STTS* 5/11b–13a gave a review of early and later commentaries to the histories.

61 For this work, the *Tung tien hsin shu* (*New book from the eastern palace*), see *CTS* 46/1994; *HTS* 59/1563; *Ho chih* p. 80, p. 267; *TFYK* 607/12b.

62 *HTS* 58/1457–58, *Ho chih* pp. 69–70. The second work was presented in 732, by Kao Hsi-ch'iao.

63 *Yen Lu kung wen chi* 7/4a.

64 *Yen Lu kung wen chi* 9/13b, spirit path stele for Yen Yu-yü.

65 *Yen Lu kung wen chi* 5/3b–4a, 11/4b–5a.

66 *CTS* 104/3212, biog. of Ko-shu Han; *Yen Lu kung wen chi* 8/12a, Li Kuang-pi; *Ch'üan Tsai-chih wen chi* 13/4a, epitaph for Hun Chen.

67 E.g. *HTS* 58/1457, *Ho chih* p. 69, commentary presented by Ch'en Po-hsüan, in the Chen-yüan period.

68 See *THY* 63/1093, and the parallel statement by Liu Chih-chi, *STTS* 12/30b, and Twitchett (1985), pp. 138–40.

69 Hsü's 659 commission, with four scholars under his direction, is recorded in *THY* 64/1093, and no date for the completion and presentation of this *shih lu* is given. *CTS* 82/2763, biog. of Hsü Ching-tsung dates his first appointment to direct the *kuo shih* to 656 and states that in 663, on promotion to be minor tutor to the crown prince 'as before he directed the preparation of the *kuo shih*'. Li I-fu, often linked with Hsü as a chief minister of equal opprobrium, was confirmed as a director of the *kuo shih* in 657, and so may have held the 659 commission jointly with Hsü; see *CTS* 82/2767.

70 This second account of Hsü's updating of the *kuo shih* is given by Liu Chih-chi in *STTS* 12/30b. Though in dating Hsu's direction of the history to the Lung-shuo period (661–3) it differs from the *THY* account, it agrees broadly with Hsü's *CTS* biog. Liu's is the only account to mention

the constituent parts of the history, including the unfinished monographs; but in concluding with the statement that 'in aggregate it formed
100 *chüan*', Liu agrees with the *THY* account, which gives the same
total. It seems likely that the new elements in Hsü's version of the
Lung-shuo period were first the 20 *chüan shih lu* for Kao tsung's reign to
658 which he had completed earlier. This would have had attached to it
the biogs. of the deceased ministers of the Yung-hui period (and possibly
accounts of foreign tribes, since these also came technically under the
heading of biogs.), and so fitted Liu's description. Secondly, it would
have embodied the politically inspired alterations Hsü carried out to the
80 *chüan* version of 656. In making the total 100 *chüan*, therefore, Liu
may have discounted the monographs, which had merely been 'begun'
(*ch'i ts'ao*).

71   *THY* 63/1093 is here remarkably consistent with the *CTS* 84/2795, biog.
     of Li Jen-kuei; *CTS* 81/2755, biog. of Li Ching-hsüan; *CTS* 84/2799,
     biog. of Hao Ch'u-chün. The fourth scholar listed, Kao Chih-chou, was
     at the junior level of compiler; his *CTS* biog., 185A/4792, dates his
     appointment to 671. Three at least of this commission were still in office
     in 675; see *CTS* 5/100–01. See also *STTS* 12/30b–31a; Pulleyblank
     (1950), p. 451; Twitchett (1985), pp. 141–42.

72   *STTS* 12/31a; Pulleyblank (1950), pp. 451–2; Twitchett (1985), pp.
     142–4; for Liu's condemnation of Niu Feng-chi as being 'devious and
     deluded', see *STTS* 11/11b; see also Wei Shu in *Chi-hsien chu chi*,
     quoted by *Yü hai* 46/42a. In the ninth century, Liu K'o, commenting on
     T'ang historians, found Niu Feng-chi worthy of inclusion in his list; see
     TWT 82/4b. Tu Mu also mentioned his version of the *kuo shih*; see
     Fan-ch'uan wen chi 7/114, epitaph for his great grandson Niu Seng-ju,
     780–848, canonized *Wen-chen*, also an official historian.

73   *STTS* 12/31a; *THY* 63/1094. Pulleyblank (1950), p. 452; Twitchett
     (1985), p. 144–5; Fu Chen-lun (1963), pp. 59–60. Liu Chih-chi's list is a
     short one, presumably including only names he approved of. *THY*
     supplies five more names, including that of the director, the notorious
     Wu San-ssu, who according to his biog., *CTS* 183/4734–35, had already
     directed the history in the period 694–9. The basic offices and appoint-
     ments to the history office of those in the *THY* list are usually borne out
     by their *CTS* biogs., e.g. *CTS* 94/2994, Li Ch'iao; *CTS* 90/2914, Chu
     Ching-tse; *CTS* 98/3061, Wei Chih-ku; *CTS* 94/2996, Ts'ui Jung.

74   *THY* 63/1094; *CTS* 102/3173, biog. of Liu Chih-chi and *CTS* 92/2953,
     biog. of Wei Yüan-chung make no mention of Liu's participation in this
     first version of the *shih lu*; but Liu himself does, *STTS* 12/31a–b; and
     CTS 102/3182, biog. of Wu Ching includes Liu in its list. See also Fu
     Chen-lun (1963), pp. 68–9; Hung (1969), note 8 on pp. 15–16;
     Pulleyblank (19650), p. 452; Twitchett (1985), pp. 88–92. *CTS* 6/132–3;
     TCTC 208/6603, 706.18; *CTS* 102/3182, biog. of Wu Ching. I am grateful
     to Professor Twitchett for mentioning the close correlation of dates.

75   *THY* 63/1094–95; Twitchett (1985), pp. 92–8.

76   *Ta T'ang hsin yü* 7/118; *HTS* 125/4410; Ikeda On (1971), p. 78.

77   Two memorials of 653 enter a total of seven names: the first, dated the

24th day of the 2nd month, by Chang-sun Wu-chi presented the *Wu ching cheng i*; see *TKCK* 2/2b–4b. The second, nearly nine months later, on the 19th day of the 11th month, again by Chang-sun Wu-chi, presented the *T'ang lü shu i*; see *T'ang lü shu i* memorial of presentation, pp. 15–17. The lists coincide but for the inclusion in the first of Chang Hsing-ch'eng and Kao Chi-fu, neither of whom participated in the criminal code discussions, and for the inclusion of Lai Chi, who took no part in the sub-commentary, in the second. The appointment of all seven to direct the history is, however confirmed in each case by their *CTS* biogs. Of the seven, only one, Kao Chi-fu, had been appointed in the preceding reign, and then shortly before T'ai tsung's death. Cf. *Nan pu hsin shu* p. 38, stating that Lai Chi had been 'ashamed not to have prepared the history'.

78 See above note 71. The great prestige of directing the *kuo shih* is indicated by the well-known remark of Hsüeh Yüan-ch'ao, d. 683; see *Sui T'ang chia hua* 2/17; *T'ang yü-lin* 4/140–41. Guisso (1978), note 59 on p. 248, notes on the basis of *CTS* 73/2590 that Hsüeh had in fact been a compiler of the history. But there is a distinction between merely compiling the record and directing it, and it was presumably the latter role that Hsüeh coveted.

79 *THY* 63/1100; *TTCLC* 81/467; *STTS* 11/11a.

80 *THY* 63/1093–94.

81 *STTS* 12/30b. By the time Liu Chih-chi condemned Hsü, opinion had already gone against him. In 706 his spirit tablet had been removed from Kao tsung's shrine in the ancestral temple (*THY* 18/371). The clearest statement that Hsü Ching-tsung and Li I-fu were responsible for the banning of the diarists from the inner court is Su Mien's much later comment in *THY* 56/961. *TCTC* 211/2728–29, 717.12, describing how the paragon scholar minister Sung Ching tried to restore the system that had operated under T'ai tsung, also blames Hsü and Li. For later references to the exclusion of the diarists, see *THY* 56/962, memorial of 796 by Chao Ching; *THY* 56/963, edict of 817, dating the event to 150 years before, that is to 667; *THY* 63/1104, entry dated 693 describing the *shih cheng chi*; *THY* 64/1109 speech in 813 by Li Chi-fu, in garbled form; *THY* 64/1111, memorial of 821 by the secretariat and the chancellery; *THY* 64/1112 memorial of 843 by the secretariat and the chancellery.

82 *CTS* 183/4729, biog. of Wu Ch'eng-su; *CTS* 183/4734–35, biog. of Wu San-ssu; *WYYH* 884/1b, epitaph for Yao Ch'ung by Chang Yüeh; *CTS* 96/3021 does not mention this appointment, but supplies evidence for its dating. *CTS* 94/2994 states that in 698 Li Ch'iao 'concurrently compiled the dynastic history', rather than that he directed it (*chien hsiu*). But his basic offices were the same as Yao Ch'ung's, and it is not conceivable that as a fellow chief minister he acted in a capacity junior to Yao's.

83 *THY* 63/1104; *THY* 64/1109; *Nan pu hsin shu* p. 23, implying that it recorded the business of the secretariat and chancellery alone; *THY* 6/122 confirms Yao Shou's appointment as a chief minister in 692; *CTS* 89/2902. For later references to the *shih cheng chi*, see note 81 above. See also Twitchett (1985), pp. 55–7.

84 *THY* 63/1101; *CTS* 102/3173, biog. of Liu Chih-chi; Fu Chen-lun (1963), pp. 62–3.

85 *THY* 63/1100, memorial of Chu Ching-tse dated 703; also *THY* 63/1100, statement of Liu Yün-chi dated 702. Other scholars promoted the ideals associated with the dynastic record at about this time; see *CTS* 102/3175, biog. of Hsü Chien; *CTS* 98/3061–62, biog. of Wei Chih-ku; *THY* 64/110–86, of Wu Ching.

86 Fu Chen-lun (1963), pp. 71–72; Hung (1969); Pulleyblank (1961), pp. 135–66.

87 *STTS* 10/8b–9a.

88 *STTS* 11/2a–4a; cf. the exhaustive gloss on historians in canonical antiquity given by K'ung Ying-ta in *Tso chuan chu shu*, pref. 2a, (giving ref. to *Li chi chu shu* 29/3a–4a). In *STTS* 11/10a–b, Liu suggested the Northern Ch'i for the start of chief ministerial direction of the dynastic history; but in *STTS* 10/7a–b, Liu implies the reign of K'ang ti in the Chin (reigned A.D. 343–44).

89 *STTS* 11/15b; cf. *STTS* 20/8b–9a, *STTS* 6/21a.

90 *STTS* 10/7b–a; *STTS* 7/10a–b.

91 *STTS* 10/9a.

92 For Liu K'uang and Liu Su, see *WYYH* 944/7a–b, Liang Su; *CTS* 102/3174; Fu Chen-lun (1963), pp. 13–15.

93 *Yen Lu kung wen chi* 8/3a.

94 For the appointments of Chang Yüeh and Yao Ch'ung in 713, see *TTCLC* 51/263 and *CTS* 97/3051, biog. of Chang Yüeh; for the appointment of Sung Ching in 717, see *Yen Lu kung wen chi* 4/9a. *TTCLC* 51/263 contains the edict appointing both Sung Ching and Su T'ing, but supplies no date. All four were examination graduates; all had double character canonizations that included the designation *wen*. It is conspicuous that Chang Yüeh's is the only appointment mentioned in the *CTS* biogs. of all four scholars. There may have been factional reasons for this, deriving from the later stages in the completion of the *kuo shih* of Wei Shu and Liu Fang. Chang Yüeh himself directed the dynastic record in the K'ai-yüan period; moreover, Wei Shu benefitted from the patronage of Chang Yüeh (*CTS* 102/3183–84, and *Yen Lu kung wen chi* 5/2b), and may have wished to give extra prominence to his role.

95 *CTS* 102/3185–86.

96 *T'ang yü lin* 2/46; *Nan pu hsin shu* 1/3; cf. *Chin shih ts'ui pien* 84/2b, epitaph for P'ei Chen, court diarist in the K'ai-yüan period, which mentions 400 *chüan* of ?diaries since the start of the dynasty as having been missing or deficient. Another example is Ch'ang Wu-ming, 689–744, who was a court diarist in the K'ai-yüan period and composed *K'ai-yüan chu chi* (*K'ai-yüan records*) in 30 *chüan*; see *WYYH* 942/10b, epitaph by Ch'ang Kun. (*Chu chi* is a collective term suggesting notes or records before their preparation as *shih lu*; see e.g. *CKCY* 7/219; *WYYH* 383/3a; *Li Wen kung chi* 10/75a.)

97 *HTS* 47/1208; cf. *TCTC* 211/6728–29, 717.12; Twitchett (1985), pp. 18–19.

98 For the Chi-hsien yüan, see *WYYH* 168/2b and *T'ang shi chi shih* 2/14; for the Feng and Shan rites, *TWT* 198/7b, Su T'ing; for the *San chiao*

debate, *TFYK* 37/17a–b; for the emperor's *Lao tzu* commentary, *TFYK* 53/15a; for Hsüan tsung's promotion of Taoism, *Ch'üan T'ang wen* 299/5b–6b; for successes against the barbarians, *Ch'ü-chiang Chang hsien-sheng wen chi* 14/4b–5b; for the copying of the *Tripitaka*, 13/4b; for the success of the ploughing rite, 14/4b. For other incidents, *TFYK* 840/19a, Chang Yüeh; *CTS* 22/873, Yao Ch'ung; *CTS* 96/73034, biog. of Sung Ching; also the anecdote in *Ta T'ang hsin yü* 5/93. Hsüan tsung also ordered that the meritorious deeds of the officials of his own reign should be recorded, possibly for his own inspection; see *TTCLC* 81/468. See also *TFYK* 258/15a.

99 *TTCLC* 51/263; see also Ch. 4, note 210.

100 *CTS* 102/3182; *HTS* 132/4529, biogs. of Wu Ching. *THY* 63/1098–99, biog. of Li Yüan-hung. Pulleyblank (1950), pp. 453–6; Twitchett (1985), pp. 148–54. Wu Ching's career as an official scholar may have started as early as 696; see *CTS* 183/4718, biog. of Wu Min-chih and *CTS* 191/5099, biog. of Li Ssu-chen. *THY* 63/1095 and *Han Ch'ang-li chi* 7/ *Wai chi* 2/70 suggest that in the post-rebellion period a T'ang history in Wu Ching's name circulated. A proposal that Wu Ching be retrospectively canonized is contained in *Ch'üan T'ang wen* 432/2b.

101 *CTS* 97/3052–53, biog. of Chang Yüeh; *THY* 63/1098–99.

102 *CTS* 98/3074, biog. of Li Yüan-hung; *THY* 63/1099.

103 *TTCLC* 51/263; *CTS* 99/3095, biog. of Hsiao Sung.

104 *CTS* 102/3182, biog. of Wu Ching.

105 *CTS* 102/3184; *HTS* 132/4530, biogs. of Wei Shu; *Yü hai* 46/42a. The commission included the productive official scholar Lu Shan-ching; Niimi (1937), pp. 135–7; Twitchett (1985), pp. 155–6.

106 For Wei Shu, see *CTS* 102/3183–85 biog.; for his role as a court diarist, *THY* 56/962. Wei Shu's most eminent scholarly relatives are listed in his *CTS* biog. They include Wei Shu-hsia, c. 637–707, canonized *Wen*. The Wei clan maintained its extraordinary ascendancy over scholarly and literary office until late in Hsüan tsung's reign; see *CTS* 92/2962, biog. of Wei Pin.

107 *CTS* 99/3099 biog. of Chang Chiu-ling, dating his direction of the history office to 734. Yang Ch'eng-tsu (1964), p. 70, dates the appointment to late 733, with a further edict in 734 (p. 75).

108 *THY* 63/1089; *HTS* 200/5703, biog.; *Wang Mo-chieh ch'üan chi chien-chu* 7/91 and commentary.

109 *CTS* 106/3237, biog. of Li Lin-fu; *CTS* 102/3182, biog. of Wu Ching; *THY* 63/1089; *HTS* 47/1208; also, confirming that in 746 he held this appointment, *TKCK* 9/10b, quoting an epigraphical source. *Feng shih wen chien chi* 10/7; *HTS* 202/5766, biog. of Cheng Ch'ien; *T'ang yü lin* 2/47. For Li Lin-fu's eventual replacement by Yang Kuo-chung, see *HTS* 206/5848, biog. of Yang Kuo-chung; *TCTC* 216/6914, 752.14.

110 *CTS* 102/3184; Twitchett (1985), p. 158. Wei Shu's connections with Chang Yüeh, Chang Chiu-ling, Sun Ti, and Hsü Ching-hsien are specified in *Yen Lu kung wen chi* 5/1b, preface to the collected works of Sun Ti; *Yen Lu kung wen chi* 11/5a, epitaph for Yin Chien-yu; *CTS* 102/3184, biog. of Wei.

111 *WYYH* 775/5b, commemorative text by Sun Ti for P'ei Kuang-t'ing.

112 *WYYH* 383/3a. Liu K'uang was already a historian compiler and concurrently an erudit of the court of sacrifices when he was appointed a court diarist; the rescript of appointment was by Sun Ti, who was a rescript writer from 736, and again from 741 until 745 or later; see *CTS* 190B/5044, biog. of Sun Ti and *Tō Gensō sekidai Kokyō*, vol III, p. 111. Liu Su, Liu K'uang's next brother, is inherently likely to have been appointed not more than ten years after his older brother; see *WYYH* 944/7a–7b, epitaph by Liang Su; also Fu Chen-lun (1963), p. 13. Cf. also *WYYH* 980/2b, sacrificial graveside prayer by Li Hua.

113 The date of Liu Fang's appointment may be inferred from an epigraphical text by Yen Chen-ch'ing for a woman member of the Yen clan who died in 737 aged 84 *sui* and was buried in 738. In this, Yen refers to Liu Fang, who was a son-in law to the woman's eldest son, as 'a good historian of the present time'; see *Yen Lu kung wen chi* 11/1b. 'Good historian' (*liang shih*) was the term originally applied by Confucius to Tung Hu (see note 8 above) and used conventionally in the T'ang to commend official historians. Liu Fang's brief biog. in *CTS* 149/4030 is misleading in calling him an historian scholar of Su tsung's reign, since his service under Hsüan tsung is likely to have been much longer, while in the post-rebellion period he was an official historian in 766 (*THY* 36/666), and, on the evidence of *THY* 36/666, double column entry, was still active in scholarship after 785. Liu Fang's father in law, Yin Chia-shao, mentioned in Yen's text, is independently attested in *Yüan ho hsing tsuan* 4/1a. Liu was a *chin shih* of 735 under Sun Ti (*WYYH* 701/7b, preface to the collected works of Yang Chi by Li Hua), and 738 would not be too early in his career for a junior level tenure in the history office.

114 *TFYK* 561/5b. In 745, the history office was administered by the decree examination graduate and grand secretary Li Hsüan-ch'eng; see *Tō Gensō sekidai Kokyō*, vol III, p. 111.

115 *WYYH* 703/7b, preface by Liang Su, stating that 'those in position in the state took no heed and it lapsed'.

116 *WYYH* 678/2b–10a, Hsiao Ying-shih; *WYYH* 744/5b, Li Hua; cf. *HTS* 202/5768, biog. of Hsiao.

117 *THY* 63/1095; *CTS* 149/4008, biog. of Yü Hsiu-lieh; *CTS* 102/3184–85, biog. of Wei Shu; Pulleyblank (1950), p. 456; Twitchett (1985), pp. 154–8. *CTS* 84/2807–08 contains a brief essay by Wei Shu on the canonization title for P'ei Kuang-t'ing. An erudit of the court of sacrifices had proposed that it be *K'o*; but Hsüan tsung had ordered that it be the highly complimentary designation *Chung-hsien*. Wei Shu's essay argued that posthumous titles and canonizations had become too laudatory, and that the original suggestion should be adopted. The original context of this essay is not clear; but its 'praise and blame' approach, reference to the *Ch'un-ch'iu* and introduction in the *CTS* text as, 'The historian official Wei Shu says', suggest that it may have been taken from one of Wei Shu's own histories.

118 *STTS* 8/8a.

119 For example his remark on the *feng chien* system under the Han as compared with the Chou system; see *STTS* 2/11a–b; cf. *STTS* 6/20b.

120 *STTS* 3/14a–16a.

121 Ch'ung-wen tsung mu 2/46–47; Pulleyblank (1950), p. 449 and pp. 464–5, referring to Wei Shu's version of the dynastic history.

122 For the T'ang liu tien, see Ch. 1 at note 23.

123 For the bibliography of 721, see below, Ch. 6 at notes 71–74. The fact that Wei Shu, later an official historian, had special responsibility for the history division and wrote the general prefaces (THY 36/658) emphasizes the connection between this bibliography and the compilation of the dynastic history. For the ritual code of 732, see Ch. 4 at notes 96–103.

124 Ch'en Tzu-ang's planned work was to be called the Hou Shih chi (Later Shih chi); see Ch'en Tzu-ang chi, appendix, p. 254, separate biog. by Lu Ts'ang-yung. For Liu Chih-chi's projected work, see STTS 10/12b and Pulleyblank (1961), p. 138.

125 For Ch'en Cheng-ch'ing, see WYYH 610/8b–11a, Hsiao Ying-shih. For Hsiao Ying-shih's own work, see WYYH 678/8b. For Li Han's planned history, see TT 3.2, preface. Its date, however, remains conjectural.

126 CTS 102/3183, biog. of Wu Ching; HTS 58/1458, Ho chih p. 70. HTS 58/1461; cf. also the work entitled T'ang shu pei ch'üeh (Omissions in the history of the T'ang made good), by Wu Ching, entered in HTS 58/1467, Ho chih p. 87.

127 For Wei Shu's compilations, see CTS 102/3185 biog.; HTS 58/1507, Ho chih p. 165; HTS 58/1477, Ho chih p. 105; also Hsiao Ying-shih, WYYH 678/3a and, for the Chi-hsien chu chi, see Ikeda (1971), passim. Another example of a work on the censorate was the Yü shih t'ai tsa chu (Various notes on the censorate), in 5 chüan, by Tu I-chien; see CTS 190A/4999, biog.; HTS 58/1477, Ho chih p. 105. This was later referred to by Su Mien; THY 60/1055.

128 For the growing fashion for pi chi, see Feng shih wen chien chi 5/13 and T'ang yü lin 8/262, quoting the Liang ching chi of Wei Shu. Sun Ti's wall record for the Hung lu court is at WYYH 799/1b–2b; Li Hua's for the bureau of compositions at WYYH 799/2b–4b.

129 CTS 102/3174, partially preserved in Yü hai 105/7a, 11b etc.; see also HTS 57/1436, Ho chih p. 33. I am grateful to Mr Stephen Jones for drawing my attention to this. Liu K'uang also compiled a work entitled T'ien kuan chiu shih (Former events relating to heavenly offices); see HTS 58/1478 and Ho chih p. 105.

130 For example Sun Ti's writings, Yen Lu kung wen chi 5/2a; Ts'ui Mien's, WYYH 701/5a, Li Hua; Hsiao Ying-shih's, WYYH 701/6b–7a, Li Hua.

131 For Cheng Ch'ien's T'ien-pao chün fang lu (Record of military defence for the T'ien-pao period), see HTS 59/1551, Ho chih p. 245. For Ch'u Kuang-hsi's Cheng lun, see Ho yüeh ying ling chi 2/95; HTS 59/1513, Ho chih p. 176; also a work entitled Chiu ching wai i-shu (Unofficial sub-commentaries for the Nine canons) in 20 chüan mentioned by Ho yüeh ying ling chi alone. HTS 60/1603, Ho chih p. 341, enters a particularly large collected works, 70 chüan.

132 TT 200/1086. 1087.2; L. S. Yang (1968), p. 23, pp. 29–30.

133 WYYH 980/2b.

134 For Liu Chih's Cheng tien, see CTS 147/3982 and HTS 166/5085, biogs. of Tu Yu; Kanai (1939), and Pulleyblank (1960), pp. 98–9.

135 For Liu Chih's view on enfieffment, see *THY* 47/830. Liu accused the early T'ang of rejecting the arguments of Shun-yü Yüeh of the Ch'in (*Shih chi* 6/254); Chia I (201–169 B.C., *Han shu* 48/2230–60; *TT* 148/773.2 also gives a very condensed account of his position on enfieffment); of Ts'ao Chiung (c. A.D. 207–264, *Wen hsüan* 52/10–21a); Liu Sung (d. c. 301, *Chin shu* 46/1294–1307); and Lu Chi (261–303, *Wen hsüan* 54/1a–13b). In a memorial of the late K'ai-yüan period contained in *TT* 17/96.1, Liu argued in favour of enfieffment in the context of his demand for decentralization of the selection process. For Chu Ching-tse's important essay on the enfieffment issue, see *TWT* 34/9a–10a. For a possible citation from the *Cheng tien*, see *CTS* 166/4336, biog. of Yüan Chen; cf. *Ch'üan Tsai-chih wen chi* 41/2b–3.

136 *TCTC* 218/6983, 756.10; *WYYH* 980/2b, sacrificial graveside prayer by Li Hua, appears to allude to this episode involving Fang Kuan and Liu Chih; *HTS* 147/4793, biog. of Liu Yen, who argued by letter with Fang Kuan against enfieffment, on the grounds that the princes had no experience of administration. Chao Ping-wen (1159–1231) recorded that, 'In discussing the disorders of the T'ien-pao, Fang Kuan requested to share out the prefectures and commanderies, in order to enfieff the imperial sons. When An Lu-shan heard this, he remarked, "The empire will never be mine." But afterwards the crown prince obstructed the proposal, and discussion was discontinued'; quoted by Chang Shih-chao (1971), pp. 99–100.

137 For very full details of post rebellion *shih lu* and their compilation, see Twitchett (1985), pp. 102–28.

138 *WYYH* 703/3a–b, preface by Liang Su, describing Li Mi as compiling a *T'ang shu*.

139 For some examples of post-rebellion scholars reading the *kuo shih* or individual *shih lu*, see *Yen Lu kung chi* 8/2b; *THY* 53/916, Hsien tsung in 807; *THY* 80/1488, officials of the chancellery and secretariat in a memorial of 808; *THY* 52/899, Li Fan, memorial of 810; *THY* 74/1335, Su Mien; *Ch'üan Tsai-chih wen chi*, preface by Yang Ssu-fu, 1a–b; *WYYH* 490/3b, decree examination answer by Shu Yüan-pao in 825; *Liu Yü-hsi chi* 15/136; *Yin hua lu* 5/106, Chao Lin. In *Fan-ch'uan wen chi* 9/143, Tu Mu stated that P'ei Mien, d. 769, had a biography in the *kuo shih*.

140 *THY* 64/1108; *CTS* 149/4007–08, biog. of Yü Hsiu-lieh. *THY* supplies a precise date, the 23rd day of the 6th month. This precision, repeated when Yü memorialized about the *kuo shih* and *shih lu* later that year (*THY* 63/1095; *TFYK* 560/19a–b), indicates that as an official historian he kept a detailed narrative record. This in turn, with the evidence of *Ch'ung-wen tsung mu* 4/46–47, reinforces the argument that he, rather than Liu Fang, may have written the post-rebellion section of the basic annals of the *kuo shih* presented to Su tsung after 759; see following note.

141 This construction differs slightly from that of Pulleyblank (1950), p. 449 and 456, and rests in part on circumstantial evidence only. It involves inferring that the official historians of the immediate post-rebellion

period were divided along several lines into two groups. The first group comprised Wei Shu and Liu Fang. Both had served for a long period under Hsüan tsung; Wei Shu had started his service as an official historian in 730 (*CTS* 102/3184), and Liu Fang possibly as early as 738 (see note 113 above). Both had collaborated with the rebels (*CTS* 102/3184 and 149/4008 for Wei Shu; *An Lu-shan shih chi* 3/2a for Liu Fang). Both may also have had some association with the leading intellectual of the rebellion period Fang Kuan: Liu Fang's fellow graduates Li Hua and Hsiao Ying-shih were connected with Fang (Ch. 2, note 152). Wei Shu started his escape from Ch'ang-an with Fang (*CTS* 111/3320, biog. of Fang; *Yen Lu kung wen chi* 8/7a specifies the route that Fang Kuan and others took); Liu Fang's judgement on Fang Kuan, given in his *T'ang li*, and preserved in Ssu-ma Kuang's *Tzu-chih t'ung-chien k'ao i* 15/4b, is by no means proof of his association with Fang; but it is more reflective and less hostile than the attitudes that resulted in Fang's dismissal and banishment in 758 (or than that of the historian of the second group, Ling-hu Huan, who did not even allocate Fang Kuan a biography in the *Tai tsung shih lu*; see *TFYK* 562/4a, quoted by Pulleyblank (1950), p. 458). Liu Fang referred to Fang Kuan as the patron of 'a generation of famous scholars'; it was partly as a result of Fang Kuan's role in post-rebellion politics that Su tsung came to hate 'the former ministers from Shu', that is those senior officials who had reported to Hsüan tsung first, rather than to himself, and the scholars associated with them. (See *Ch'ien chu Tu shih* 10/332; 364–5, commentary by Ch'ien Ch'ien-i, and Fu Hsüan-ts'ung (1980), pp. 182–3). The second group were official historians who had proved their loyalty to Su tsung by reporting directly to his base at Ling-wu and accepting appointment from him. It comprised Yang Wan (*CTS* 119/3430) and Yü Hsiu-lieh (*CTS* 149/4007). A third scholar, Ling-hu Huan (*CTS* 149/4011), was a protege of Yang Wan. His appointment to the history office probably dates from 763, but might just have been earlier. (He was brought in by Yang Wan when Yang was vice-president of the board of rites. The rescript appointing Yang to this office was by Chia Chih (see *WYYH* 388/6a–b). Chia was a rescript writer over the rebellion period to 758, and again, after Tai tsung's accession; see Fu Hsüan-ts'ung (1980), pp. 177, 179, 184, 189.)

The work that both these groups were involved with was the *kuo shih* in 130 *chüan* that Wei Shu had worked on (see above note 117). This is very briefly described in the Sung bibliography of 1042, the *Ch'ung-wen tsung mu*, 2/46–7, and in Liu Fang's laconic and unsatisfactory *CTS* notice (*CTS* 149/4930). The *Ch'ung-wen tsung mu* account states that 112 *chüan* of this account were by Wei Shu, 2 *chüan* by Yü Hsiu-lieh and 16 *chüan* by another hand. The addition of Yü Hsiu-lieh covered the period 756–59. (The text is here to be translated, 'As for the period [from the start of] Chih-te and Ch'ien-yüan on, the historian official Yü Hsiu-lieh further added 2 *chüan* of annals for Su tsung.' Parallels for understanding the topic in this way are supplied by, e.g. *CTS* 118/3421 (*Chih-te chih hou*); *CTS* 129/3600 (*Tzu Chih-te Ch'ien-yüan i hou*); *CTS* 17B/567

(*Chih-te Ch'ien-yüan chih hou*). All these phrases mean, 'From [at or near the start of] Chih-te (and Ch'ien-yüan).' The likelihood that Yü Hsiu-lieh was responsible for the part of the history covering Su tsung's reign is strengthened by the fact that he figured as an official historian in the detailed record of events at Su tsung's court in 757; see preceding note.

As Pulleyblank (1950), p. 546–57, notes, the *Ch'ung-wen tsung mu* account conflicts in some respects with Liu Fang's *CTS* notice. The latter gives the credit for completing and presenting the 130 *chüan* version to Liu Fang. It is, however, possible that the Liu Fang notice, in making the length of the version that he submitted 130 *chüan* and in stating that it came down to the Ch'ien-yüan period, is simply quoting the number of *chüan* and the span by which the completed work was described. It should not rule out accepting the implication of *Ch'ung-wen tsung-mu* that the version that Liu Fang presented was two *chüan* short, and that these, covering the period 756–9, were added by Yü Hsiu-lieh. In recording that Liu Fang's history was given a bad reception by official historians, however, the *CTS* notice fits into the construction proposed above. If Lui Fang were at some level a Hsüan tsung loyalist, then it would follow naturally that his account of events 'from [the start of] T'ien-pao' would have been, as the *CTS* notice implies, unacceptable to Yü Hsiu-lieh and also to Su tsung (though this would by no means have prevented Liu Fang from being critical of some of the developments of the late part of Hsüan tsung's reign. Like Wei Shu, his patron, he would have been opposed to Li Lin-fu and Yang Kuo-chung; see above note 110). Yü Hsiu-lieh, Yang Wan and others may therefore have proceeded to edit Liu Fang's version, and accentuate the pro-Su tsung bias that, as incorporated in *CTS*, it now has (cf. Levy (1960), p. 13, p. 19).

In giving exclusive credit to Liu Fang for completing and presenting the 130 *chüan kuo shih*, the *CTS* notice was broadly within the convention that permitted the T'ang composer of a biography to exaggerate his subject's contribution to a compilation. K'ung Ying-ta's sub-commentary series, which he left six years before its final completion but which subsequently bore his name, provides a near parallel.

142 *THY* 38/534, Tai tsung; *Po Hsiang-shan chi* 6/41/87, Te tsung; *THY* 29/537, Hsien tsung.

143 *THY* 56/962; *CTS* 138/3770, biog. of Chao Ching; *TFYK* 500/10a; *THY* 63/1101, of Chiang Wu, later Chiang I.

144 *Ch'üan Tsai-chih wen chi* 43/9a. Ch'üan Te-yü composed a memorial on behalf of Ch'i K'ang, attempting to decline appointment as director of the dynastic record. This reads in part, 'Again since 788, and after Li Mi, chief ministers have not combined this office. This has been because the care and weight of editing and setting forth has preoccupied your sagely mind. If a man is not what the age calls a perfect talent, how could he follow on at a distance the former precedent?' Ch'üan's spirit path stele for Ch'i K'ang, however, *Ch'üan Tsai-chih wen chi* 14/3b, makes it clear that Ch'i did direct the history. Li Mi's appointment to direct the history is confirmed by *CTS* 130/3622, biog.

145 *Ch'üan Tsai-chih wen chi* 22/8a, epitaph for Chang Chien.

146 *THY* 64/1109.

147 *CTS* 176/4569, biog. of Wei Mu; *THY* 56/965; cf. *THY* 63/1098; also *CTS* 173/4493, biog. of Cheng Lang; *TCTC* 246/7940–41, 839.8. Cf. *THY* 64/1114 for Cheng Lang's emphasis on official history. For a brief comment on the issue from this period, see *Sun Ch'iao chi* 2/5a.

148 In the first month of 796, Chiang Wu, appointed omissioner and historian compiler in the 12th month of 793, was transferred to be secretary of the board of works, while remaining a historian compiler; see *THY* 63/1101 and cf. *CTS* 149/4026 biog. of Chiang. For the much more explicit case of Chang Chien, also in 796, see *CTS* 149/4024 biog. Chang Chien's biog. attached to the *Shun tsung shih lu* (Solomon, pp. 26–7) does not mention this incident, and the account of it in *THY* 63/1101 appears garbled. It is referred to obliquely by Ch'üan Te-yü, *Ch'üan Tsai-chih wen chi* 22/7a, epitaph for Chang Chien. The removal of these two scholars from attendant posts took place in the same year as the brief revival of the *shih cheng chi*; see below, n. 150.

149 *Huang-fu Ch'ih-cheng wen chi* 3/4a; Po Chü-i's *Ts'e lin* series contains no question or answer on official history; but *Po Hsiang-shan chi* 7/48/83–84, *Ts'e lin* no. 68, brings to bear the traditional vocabulary of historical criticism, 'the straight brush', 'praise and blame'; 'reproving the evil and encouraging the good', on commemorative literature more generally.

150 *THY* 64/1109 and *CTS* 148/3995–96, biogs. of Li Chi-fu. Li's account of the *shih cheng chi* as it stands in both these texts is in error in assigning its institution by Yao Shou to the Yung-hui period; a column is probably omitted from the text. His attribution of the revival of the *shih cheng chi* under Te tsung to Chia Tan and Ch'i K'ang conflicts with *THY* 56/962, in which credit for reviving the *shih cheng chi* is given to Chao Ching. *CTS* 138/3779, biog. of Chao Ching also makes the revival Chao Ching's, adding, 'In no time Ching died and the *shih cheng chi* no longer operated.' Both *CTS* and *THY* date the revival to the 1st month of 796, the year in which two official historians were removed from their basic monitory offices. *CTS* may derive its wording from *THY* 64/1112, memorial of 838, which also attributes the revival to Chao Ching.

151 *THY* 56/962–63; cf. 64/1109, for the same text. This was in response to demands from the court diarist Yü Ching-hsiu, and with the support of the chief minister. After reproducing the text of the edict, *THY* gives lengthy explanatory glosses. Cf. *HTS* 161/4986–87, biog. of Yü Ching-hsiu.

152 *THY* 64/1111.

153 Twitchett (1985), pp. 60–61 and notes 16–20; *CTS* 17B/541; *THY* 56/965.

154 *THY* 64/1112.

155 *Li Wen-jao wen chi* 11/2b–4a. *THY* 64/1112–13 makes this one submission, does not attribute it specifically to Li Te-yü and dates it 843. T'ang Ch'eng-yeh, pp. 179–80, makes this a three-part memorial, and dates it to 841. See also *CTS* 18A/589–90.

156 *HTS* 182/5371, biog. of P'ei Hsiu. P'ei Hsiu's *CTS* biog., 177/4593–94,

does not mention this episode. There was an undated, similar proposal by Tu Mu, who held office as a historian compiler; see *Fan-ch'uan wen chi* 15/227–8.

157 *THY* 63/1102.

158 The second *shih lu* for Te tsung's reign, the *Te tsung shih lu*, (also known as the *Chen-yüan shih lu*; *THY* 64/1109) was probably first commissioned in 807, when Li Chi-fu was a chief minister (*CTS* 148/3992, biog. of Li Chi-fu; *CTS* 149/4028, biog. of Chiang I; *Liu Yü-hsi chi* 19/164, preface to the collected works of Wei Ch'u-hou). After Li Chi-fu's appointment to provincial office and P'ei Chi's appointment to direct the history in 809, the work was under P'ei's direction. The commission consisted of Wei Ch'u-hou, *Liu Yü-hsi chi* 19/164 and *CTS* 159/4183, biog.; Tu-ku Yü, *Han Ch'ang-li chi* 6/29/3b and *CTS* 168/4381, biog.; Chiang I, *CTS* 149/4028, biog.; Fan Shen and Lin Pao. P'ei Chi, however, soon became ill, and when Li Chi-fu returned to office, he was indignant that P'ei should have presented the *shih lu* while gravely handicapped. He dismissed most of the commission, reorganized the history office, and retained only Tu-ku Yü as its administrator (*THY* 64/1108). In political terms, the *shih lu* provided a vehicle for the supporters of Lu Hsüan kung and the enemies of the financial official and Te tsung favourite P'ei Yen-ling. P'ei Chi was successful in a decree examination of 794, when Ku Shao-lien, a bitter enemy of P'ei Yen-ling, was chief examiner (*Liu Yü-hsi chi* 19/163; *TKCK* 13/23b–25a; *Kuo shih pu* 1/30; *HTS* 162/4995, biog. of Ku Shao-lien). Tu-ku Yü was a son-in-law of Ch'üan Te-yü, who had opposed P'ei and who was a fervent admirer of Lu Hsüan kung (*Ch'üan Tsai-chih wen chi, pu-k'o* 3a–b and *pu i* 2a–3a). Ch'üan actually remarked of the *shih lu* that it contained a record of Lu Hsüan kung's administrative achievements (*Lu Hsüan kung han-yüan chi*, preface 3a–b). Chiang I was another of its compilers who may be presumed to have been opposed to P'ei. His own promotion was hindered by his outright opposition to P'ei (*HTS* 132/4533, biog. and note 148 above). The political outline of the account of Te tsung's reign now in *CTS* was probably thus drawn in the very earliest official records of the reign, by historians who were politically involved in the events concerned, and who lived in a community that had a common hostility to P'ei. For a rare example of a polite reference to P'ei after his death, see *Chin shih ts'ui pien* 103/32a, Ts'ui Ao, *chin shih* of 781.

159 *Po Hsiang-shan chi* 6/38/45.

160 *Han Ch'ang-li chi* 7/*Wai chi* 2/69–71; cf. Dull (1964), pp. 82–3.

161 *Liu Ho-tung chi* 31/498–500.

162 Twitchett (1985), pp. 123–8.

163 For accounts of the records of the final reigns, see Twitchett (1985), pp. 129–30. For appointment of historians very late in the T'ang, see *CTS* 20A/781; and *WYYH* 400/1b–2a, rescript appointing Cheng Lin and Lu Tse historian compilers, by Hsüeh T'ing-kuei, rescript writer in 890 and again in 898–900 (*CTS* 190C/5080, biog.). See also *THY* 63/1102, edict of 905, upgrading Chang Jung from historian compiler to supervisor of the record.

164 *Tso chuan chu shu* 35/12b; Hung (1969), p. 22, n. 40.
165 *HTS* 130/4496, biog. of Yang Ch'ang, 'If a man's actions have been of
benefit to humanity, it suffices that his name be written by the historian.
Steles, eulogies and the like simply bequeath anchor weights for
posterity.' See also *T'ang yü lin* 8/271, remark of Sui Wen ti; *Feng shih
wen chien chi* 5/11 and 13; *CTCC* epitaph for Miao Shan-wu, d. late 726
or early 727; *CTS* 158/4167, biog. of Cheng Huan. For the mercenary
aspect, *CTS* 190B/5043, biog. of Li Yung (cf. *Liu Yü-hsi chi* 39/395–96,
spirit path stele for Wang Leng); for the competition to write for great
officials, *Kuo shih pu* 2/41. Cf. also *Han Ch'ang-li chi* 4/13/15; Ch'ien Mu
(1957), p. 147; Hans Frankel (1962), p. 76, p. 82.
166 *HTS* 58/1484, the *Huan yu chi (Record of the excursions of ministers)* in
70 *chüan*. *CTS* 82/2770, biog. of Li I-fu, gives the length as 20 *chüan* and
states that the work was soon lost.
167 *CTS* 46/2004; *HTS* 58/1483; *Ho chih* p. 114, the *Wen kuan tz'u lin wen
jen chuan (Biographies of literary men for the forest of words from
literary halls)*, in 100 *chüan*.
168 *HTS* 58/1484, *Ho chih* p. 123, the *Yu ti lu (Record of friendship and
fraternal conduct)* in 15 *chüan*.
169 *CTS* 46/2006; *HTS* 58/1487; *Ho chih* p. 119, *Wu hou lieh nü chuan (The
empress Wu's biographies of illustrious women)* 100 *chüan*; (cf. *CTS*
6/123, which states 20 *chüan*).
170 *HTS* 58/1483; *Ho chih* p. 123, *Ta yin chuan (Biographies of long-term
recluses)*, in 3 *chüan*.
171 *Yen Lu kung wen chi* 8/4a, *Hsü cho chüeh (Continuation of [the record
of] outstanding [conduct])*, by Liu Fang, no note as to length; *Chu hsing
lüeh (Brief account of illustrious surnames)*, by Yin Yin, no note as to
length. For Yen Chen-ch'ing's marriage connections with the Liu and
Yin families, see e.g. *THY* 19/389, cf. also *Ch'üan Tsai-chih wen chi*
17/14b.
172 *CTS* 89/2895, biog. of Ti Jen-chieh; *HTS* 58/1484; *Ho chih* p. 124, *Ti
Jen-chieh chuan (Biography of Ti Jen-chieh)*, 3 *chüan*.
173 *HTS* 58/1484; *Ho chih*, p. 124; *Yen shih chia chuan (Family biography
for the Yen clan)*, in 1 *chüan*.
174 *HTS* 58/1484; *Ho chih* p. 124, *Chang Hsün Yao Yin chuan (Biographies of
Chang Hsün and Yao Yin)*; see also *TWT* 25/11a–13a and note 192 below.
175 *HTS* 58/1484 and *Ho chih* p. 125, *Kuo kung chia chuan (Family
biography for his excellency Kuo)*, in 8 *chüan*, by Ch'en Hung.
176 *HTS* 58/1484, *Ho chih* p. 125, *Tuan kung pieh chuan (Separate biography for his excellency Tuan)*, by Ma Yü, in 2 *chüan*. For Tuan Hsiu-shih,
see the article by Mirsky (1961).
177 *Kuo shih pu* 2/44. When P'ei Tu's slave Wang I, in the course of P'ei's
campaign in Ho-hsi, met his death, P'ei composed a sacrificial graveside
prayer for him, and 'in that year the *chin shih* candidates who composed
biographies for Wang I numbered two or three in every ten'.
178 For Chang Chien's *Tsai-hsiang chuan lüeh (Biographies of chief ministers
in brief)*, see *Ch'üan Tsai-chih wen chi* 22/8a, epitaph for Chang Chien;
CTS 149/4025, biog.; *HTS* 58/1467; *Ho chih* p. 87. For Chiang I's *Ta
T'ang tsai-fu lu (Account of the chief ministers of the great T'ang*

[dynasty]), in 70 *chüan*, see *CTS* 149/4028, biog.; *Kuo shih pu* 2/42; *HTS* 58/1467; *Ho chih* p. 87; for Chiang's *Shih ch'en teng chuan (Biographies of official historians)*, in 40 *chüan*, see *CTS* 149/4028, biog.; *HTS* 58/1467; and *Ho chih* p. 87.

179 *WYYH* 946/3a, epitaph by Li Ao.

180 *HTS* 130/4496, biog. of Yang Ch'ang, quoted above, note 165. Cf. the lament by Po Chü-i, at the age of 47 *sui*, that he had no prospect of biography in the dynastic history, *Po Hsiang-shan chi* 3/11/39, and the hope expressed by the late T'ang writer Ssu-k'ung T'u that he might 'still have a few columns in the dynastic history'; *Ssu-k'ung Piao-sheng shih chi* 4/4a.

181 *STTS* 11/11b; *STTS* 7/10a–b. Those referred to are likely to have included Fang Hsüan-ling, whose father's biog. is at *SS* 66/1561–66; Ling-hu Te-fen, whose father's biog. is in *Chou shu* 36/644 and *SS* 56/1385; Wei Cheng, whose father's biog. is at *Pei shih* 56/2039 and Tu Ju-hui, whose grandfather's biog. is at *Chou shu* 39/701; cf. *CTS* 72/2578, biog. of Ch'u Liang. For Liu's condemnation of reliance on *hsing-chuang*, see *STTS* 12/31a.

182 *Ch'ung-wen tsung mu* 2/46; Pulleyblank (1950), p. 449.

183 *TFYK* 562/4a, quoted by Pulleyblank (1950), p. 458. The criticism may refer to the omission of any record of Yen's memorials, rather than to omission of his biography, which, as Pulleyblank points out, should have been attached to the *shih lu* of Te tsung's reign. It is particularly odd that Ling-hu Huan should have failed to do Yen Chen-ch'ing justice in this way, since he composed Yen's epitaph, and claimed in it to have served on Yen's staff; see *Yen Lu kung wen chi* 14/13a–b.

184 *TFYK* 562/4a; cf. note 141 above.

185 *THY* 80/1488. *Feng shih wen chien chi* 4/23 indicates that this provision was recognized. See also Twitchett (1961), pp. 103–6.

186 *Po Hsiang-shan chi* 7/48/83–84, *Ts'e-lin* no. 68.

187 *Li Wen-kung chi* 10/75a–77b. Li listed the achievements of the reign and stated, 'Yet [for the period from the start of] the Yüan-ho period, a *shih lu* has not yet been written.' *THY* 64/1110 contains a shortened version of this memorial. For a later echo of this point, see *Sun Ch'iao chi* 2/3b–6a.

188 *Ch'üan Tsai-chih wen chi* 46/17a–b.

189 *Liu Ho-tung chi* 31/500–01.

190 *Yüan shih Ch'ang-ch'ing chi* 29/3b–4b; Dull (1964), p. 85.

191 *Li Wen kung chi* 12/97a–98b; *WYYH* 680/9b, P'ei Tu.

192 *Han Ch'ang-li chi* 4/13/4–7; Hanabusa (1964), p. 68; Hartman (1986), pp. 141–2 and notes 48–49 on p. 323. See also *CTS* 190C/5049, biog of Li Han and n. 174 above.

193 *THY* 36/666; *CTS* 149/4030 and *HTS* 132/4536, biogs. of Liu Fang; *HTS* 56/1460; *Ho chih* p. 77; *THY* 36/666, double column entry implies that the *T'ang li* was completed only after 785. This accords well with the span of the work, 617–778, as given in the *Chung-hsing shu mu*, quoted in *Yü hai* 47/27b. See Pulleyblank (1950), pp. 459–60. For the *T'ang li*, see also above, note 141; Ch. 6, note 55; Twitchett (1985), p. 65. The work was given an official continuation in 851 by a commission of scholars under Ts'ui Kuei-ts'ung as the *Hsü T'ang li*; see *CTS* 176/4573,

biog. of Ts'ui; *THY* 63/1098; *HTS* 58/1460; *Ho chih* p. 77; Twitchett (1985), p. 65. Liu's post-rebellion career included appointment as an erudit (*WYYH* 252/2b). Like his son Liu Mien, he was also a scholar of the Chi-hsien yüan; see *Liu Ho-tung chi* 12/193. (The Liu Fang of *Yin hua lu* 1/69 and 2/75 is a scribal error for Liu Ping; see *HTS* 202/5771.)

194 *HTS* 58/1461, *Ho-chih* p. 77. Cf. *Po Hsiang-shan chi* 4/23/82; for his association with Han Yü, see *Kuo shih pu* 1/31; Hartman (1986), pp. 36–40; and with Li Ao, *Li Wen kung chi* 14/120b; also, for his sceptical views, Needham Vol. 2 (1956), p. 387. Lu Ch'ang-yüan composed a commemorative text for Yen Chen-ch'ing, for erection at Hu-chou; see *Yen Lu kung wen chi* 14/7b, report of conduct by Yin Liang.

195 *Han Ch'ang-li chi* 4/16/56–58.

196 *Li Wen kung chi* 6/38b–40b.

197 *Liu Ho-tung chi* 10/164, referring to a *Han hou ch'un-ch'iu (Ch'un-ch'iu for the post-Han [period])* by Ling Chun.

198 *Po Hsiang-shan chi* 2/1/7; Waley (1949), pp. 65–69.

199 *CTS* 157/4157, biog.; *HTS* 58/1467; *Ho chih* p. 87. Another work of this period was by father and son, Kao Chün and Kao Chiung, a history in 120 *chüan*, see *HTS* 58/1458; *Ho chih* p. 68.

200 *Sun Ch'iao chi* 5/1a–3b.

201 For Ch'en Yüeh's *T'ang t'ung chi* in 100 *chüan*, see *HTS* 58/1461 and *Ho chih* p. 77; also *T'ang chih yen* 10/115; *Ch'ün-shu k'ao so* 16/431. For examples of Ssu-ma Kuang's citation of this work, see e.g. *TCTC* 203/6431, 684.31; also *Tzu-chih t'ung chien k'ao i* 15/8a and 9a. *TCTC* 207/6555, 701.4, quoting the *k'ao i*.

202 *Sun Ch'iao chi* 2/3b–6a; and especially 5/3b.

203 For references to Kuan Chung, see *Yüan Tz'u-shan chi* 6/87–90, essay by Yüan Chieh, dated 757; *CTS* 171/4455, biog. of Li Ching-chien and *TCTC* 236/7609–10, 805.6, for the reformers' comparison of themselves with him; *TT* 12/71.3, for Tu Yu's admiration of him; *HTS* 59/1532 and *Ho chih* p. 209 for Tu Yu's work, the *Kuan shih chih lüeh (Abridgement of the Kuan tzu)*, in 2 *chüan*. *TT* also contains many citations from the *Kuan tzu*. For Liang Su's dislike of him and of Chu-ko Liang, see *TWT* 92/11a, Ts'ui Kung. Han Yü associated him with Shang tzu, and asked examination candidates, 'Why is it that later generations in commending the true way are ashamed to speak of Kuan [tzu] and Shang [tzu]?'; see *Han Ch'ang-li chi* 4/14/21; and Hartman (1986), p. 130. Also the *p'an* on the topic of comparison with Kuan Chung; *WYYH* 514/5b. An official temple was maintained for him; see *THY* 22/431.

204 For references to Chu-ko Liang, see *WYYH* 128/1a–3b, rhymeprose by Hsiao Ying-shih, written in 756. I am grateful to the late Professor Wang Chung-lo for pointing this out. For the reformers' admiration of Chu-ko Liang, see preceding note. For his official temple, see *THY* 22/431; also *WYYH* 877/1, P'ei Tu. A common theme in writing on Chu-ko Liang was his comparison of himself to Kuan Chung and Yüeh I; Li Han, *WYYH* 744/1a–3a, made this the theme of an essay. For another commemorative text on Chu-ko Liang, see *WYYH* 814/6a, Lü Wen.

205 *CTS* 190B/5029–30, Chia Chih; *WYYH* 792/10a, Liang Su; *Ch'üan*

Tsai-chih wen chi 34/1a; *Ch'un-ch'iu tsuan li* 1/1b–2a, Tan Chu; *Li Wen kung chi* 4/25b–26a; *Han Ch'ang-li chi* 3/12/79–80.

206 *TT* 17/97.1, discussion by Chao K'uang; Herbert (1986a), pp. 108–11; cf. *STTS* 2/11a and 6/20b–21b. Chao K'uang, like other T'ang scholars, advocated decentralization of recruitment, but centralization of political control in all other respects; e.g. *Ch'un-ch'iu tsuan li* 1/3a and Ch. 3, note 162.

207 For Tu Yu's opposition to enfieffment and belief that Ch'in represented a culmination in Chinese history, see *TT* 31/177.1; 35/203.2, double column entry; 40/230/3; 148/773.2. For his advocacy of devolved recruitment and selection, see *TT* 15/85.1; *TT* 18/104.2; also Herbert (1986a), p. 111.

208 *Liu Ho-tung chi* 3/43–48; Gentzler (1966); William B. Crawford, in William H. Nienhauser Jr., *Liu Tsung-yüan*, New York: Twayne Publishers Inc., 1973, pp. 53–6; McMullen (1987a), at notes 50–9.

209 *WYYH* 741/10b–13b, Li Ch'i; see also his biog. at *HTS* 146/4746–47. For a late T'ang reference to Liu Tsung-yüan's essay on enfieffment, see *Ssu-k'ung Piao-sheng wen chi* 3/2a.

210 *THY* 76/1398, memorial of Yin Yu; see also *TFYK* 639/18b, edict of 634; *TFYK* 639/23b; *TFYK* 67/26a, decree examination of 660.

211 See e.g. Ch. 2, note 31;

212 *TT* 17/98.1, Chao K'uang.

213 *Yüan shih Ch'ang-ch'ing chi* 28/5b. *THY* 75/1375, however, implies that from 786, criminal law had a place in *ming ching* syllabuses in lieu of the *Erh ya* (for which the *Lao tzu* was also an alternative in this period; see *THY* 75/1374, edicts of 785 and 796).

214 *CTS* 189B/4978, biog. of Fen K'ang.

215 *THY* 76/1398, memorial of Yin Yu; *CTS* 16/502. For successful candidates, see *Teng k'o chi k'ao pu* p. 127 and *CTCC* epitaph for Chia T'ao, d. 873, aged 51 *sui*.

216 *TTCLC* 106/545 and *TKCK* 16/3b and 17/8a, decree examination sub-questions in 806 and 808.

217 *Ch'üan Tsai-chih wen chi* 40/ 16a–b, *chin shih* question of 805; *Han Ch'ang-li chi* 4/14/20, *chin shih* question; *TTCLC* 106/545, and *TKCK* 17/8b, decree examination question of 808.

218 *TTCLC* 106/543, decree examination question of 785; *Ch'üan Tsai-chih wen chi* 40/15a–b, *chin shih* question of 805; *Po Hsiang-shan chi* 7/45/38–39, *Ts'e lin* no. 15.

219 *TTCLC* 106/545 and *TKCK* 16/3b, decree examination question of 806; *WYYH* 488/5a and *TKCK* 16/24a, Tu-ku Yü; *WYYH* 488/9a, *Po Hsiang-shan chi* 5/30/45 and *TKCK* 16/28a, Po Chü-i; *WYYH* 487/12–13a and *TKCK* 16/18b, Wei Ch'un (Wei Ch'u-hou); *Yüan shih Ch'ang-ch'ing chi* 28/4a–b, *WYYH* 487/5b and *TKCK* 16/10b, Yüan Chen, for some answers.

220 *Po Hsiang-shan chi* 7/47/69–70, *Ts'e lin* no. 51.

221 *Yüan Tz'u-shan chi* 9/138–41, series of questions put to prospective *chin shih* candidates at Tao-chou, in modern Hunan, in 766. The phrasing, especially of questions 1 and 4 is echoed in *Po Hsiang-shan chi* 5/30/47, *chin shih* question of 800 set by Kao Ying though the topic is different. For another case of such repetition, see also Ch. 4, note 202.

222 *CTS* 149/4028, biog. of Chiang I; *WYYH* 887/6b–7a, spirit path stele for Chia Tan by Cheng Yü-ch'ing; *CTS* 147/3981, biog. of Tu Yu, in a proclamation issued after his death; *CTS* 148/3992, biog. of Li Chi-fu; *CTS* 165/4320, biog. of Yin Yu; *WYYH* 943/9a, Mu Yüan, of Mu Ning; *CTS* 176/4572, biog. of Ts'ui Kuei-ts'ung.

223 See above, notes 128 and 129. A large selection of *t'ing pi chi* is contained in *WYYH* 797/3b–806/3b. For an example of a replacement *t'ing pi chi*, see *Ch'üan Tsai-chih wen chi* 32/2b and *WYYH* 800/3b. Some examples that particularly concerned academic agencies are: *P'i-ling chi* 17/6b and *WYYH* 799/1b, for the vice-president of the court of sacrifices; *Ch'üan Tsai-chih wen chi* 31/4b–6a and *WYYH* 797/5a, for the senior scholars of the Hung-wen kuan or Chao-wen kuan; *Ch'üan Tsai-chih wen chi* 31/2a and *WYYH* 799/4b, for the secretaries of the imperial library; *WYYH* 797/6a, for the Han-lin yüan, by Wei Ch'u-hou; *Liu Ho-tung chi* 26/434 and *WYYH* 799/5b for the assistants of the Ssu-men hsüeh.

224 Sun Ch'iao in a letter on the compilation of histories remarked, 'Again the historian in noting offices and posts, hills and rivers and geography (*ti li*) and music and ritual should simply write in the regulations of a particular age, to enable later people to know such and such a time was like this.' See *Sun Ch'iao chi* 2/4b.

225 *CTS* 149/4016, biog. of Kuei Ch'ung-ching; *TFYK* 556/19b.

226 *CTS* 149/4016 biog. of Kuei Ch'ung-ching; *TFYK* 607/13b. Cf. the title *Li i chih (Treatise on ritual)*, entered in *CTS* 188/4937, biog. of Ting Kung-chu; see also *HTS* 57/1434, *Ho chih* p. 30.

227 *Liu Ho-tung chi* 8/125; also Ch. 6, note 170.

228 *CTS* 192/5130–31; biog; *TFYK* 560/32b. K'ung was associated intermittently for three decades with the history office: a rescript appointing him a court diarist, by Ch'ang Kun, rescript writer from 763 to 766, refers in laudatory terms to his work there; see *WYYH* 383/3a. *THY* 67/1174 indicates that K'ung was a historian compiler when retired on grounds of sickness aged 70 *sui*, in 793. Hsiao Ying-shih is said to have approved of his 'wide learning'; see *HTS* 202/5770. For another reference to K'ung at the history office, see *CTS* 149/4013, biog. of Ling-hu Huan. See also Yen Keng-wang (1959), p. 698.

229 *Ch'üan Tsai-chih wen chi* 22/2b; *TFYK* 560/29a–32a; *CTS* 138/3782–87, biog. of Chia Tan.

230 *CTS* 148/3997, biog. of Li Chi-fu.

231 *THY* 63/1095–96; *CTS* 149/4034–36; biog. of Shen Chi-chi. Shen proposed down-grading the empress Wu in T'ang official records. It is conspicuous that the group of officials represented in *CTS* ch. 91 as contributing to the restoration of the T'ang were all honoured by posthumous office at about this time; see *CTS* 91/2927–43; biogs. of Huan Yen-fan; Ching Hui; Ts'ui Hsüan-wei; Chang Chien-chih and Yüan Shu-chi.

232 For Shen Chi-chi's compilation of the *Chien-chung shih lu*, see *Yin hua lu* 2/81; *CTS* 149/4037; *TFYK* 556/20a; and *Po Hsiang-shan chi* 6/37/30. For his friendship with Tu Yu, see *Fan-ch'uan wen chi* 14/11a–b. For his banishment in 781, see *CTS* 149/4037 and Dudbridge (1983), p. 61 and n. 9, and *T'ai-p'ing kuang chi* 452/3697. In the south-east, Shen probably

met Ch'üan Te-yü; see *Ch'üan Tsai-chih wen chi* 7/3b–4a and Ts'en Chung-mien (1962a), p. 64. For Shen's *Hsüan chü chih*, see *HTS* 58/1477 and *Ho chih* p. 104.

233 *HTS* 59/1563 and *Ho chih* p. 268; Twitchett (1960), p. 86 and note 13 on p. 337.

234 *Po Hsiang-shan chi* 9/61/59, epitaph for Yüan Chen; *CTS* 166/4336, biog. *HTS* 59/1564, *Ho chih* p. 268, records a *Yuän shih lei chi* in 300 *chüan*; see also Waley (1949), p. 30.

235 *THY* 36/660; *Chin shih ts'ui pien* 103/32a, Ts'ui Ao; *Kuo shih pu* 3/54; *CTS* 163/4262, biog. of Ts'ui Hsüan. *Ch'ün-shu k'ao so* 16/472 gives a convenient account of the three stages of its compilation. Pulleyblank (1960), p. 98. The date of entries in Su Mien's compilation may be reflected in the present *THY* text; e.g. *THY* 37/672, entry for ritual commissioners (*li i shih*), states that this office had been discontinued. In fact, a ritual commissioner was appointed after the death of Te tsung in 805; see *Liu Ho-tung chi* 21/367–69. On the other hand, Su Mien's comment on the introduction of P'ei Mien's spirit tablet into the imperial ancestral temple, which took place in 809, is also included; see *THY* 18/372.

236 *THY* 78/1438–39.

237 For an expression of support for Fang Kuan, see *THY* 18/372. This was given in the context of Su Mien's objection to having Miao Chin-ch'ing as a correlative recipient of sacrifice in Su tsung's chapel in the imperial ancestral temple. Su Mien suggested that the order in which the contenders for this great honour arrived at Ling-wu was a consideration. P'ei Mien had been most prompt; Fang Kuan arrived a month later; Miao Chin-ch'ing had been fully a year later. In the event, P'ei Mien was introduced in 809 (*THY* 18/371); but Fang Kuan never was.

238 For Su Mien's denunciation of superstition, in the context of Lü Ts'ai's *Yin-yang shu*, see *THY* 36/656. *TT* 105/558.2 also incorporated examples from Lu Ts'ai's *Yin-yang shu*.

239 For condemnation of Hsü Ching-tsung and Li I-fu, see *THY* 56/961. For other expressions of the same sort of attitude, see *Li Wen kung chi* 9/5b and 10/2a; *Po Hsiang-shan chi* 2/4/55, condemning Li I-fu only; *Sui T'ang chia hua* p. 16; *Ta T'ang hsin yü* 11/171.

240 *THY* 42/763–64.

241 *THY* 74/1335.

242 Naitō (1970), pp. 226–37; (1967), pp. 78–80.; Balazs (1964), pp. 143–7; Pulleyblank (1960), pp. 99–106, p. 110. For Tu Yu's large private library, see *Fan-ch'uan wen chi* 1/9.

243 *TT* 1/9.1, preface by Tu Yu.

244 *TT* 17/96.1–18/104.2.

245 *TT* 12/71.3; *TT* 148/773.1; but cf. the list of ritual scholars at *TT* 41/234.1.

246 *TT* 185/985.1.

247 *TT* 31/177.1–2; 35/203.2, double column entry; 74/403.1; 148/773.1–3; cf. 40/230.3.

248 *TT* 12.71.2; 165/875.1.

249 One of the best tributes came from Fu Tsai, a friend of Liu Tsung-yüan: 'Anyone who reads it will be like a man in fever finding balm or a

starving man finding food. Five cartloads and 10,000 scrolls have all
become redundant. Can this be called other than "establishing words
and passing down a model?"'; see *WYYH* 783/10b. For other commendations of the *TT*, see *Ch'üan Tsai-chih wen chi* 22/5b, epitaph for Tu Yu;
Ch'üan Tsai-chih wen chi 11/4a–b, commemorative stele for Tu; also
Liu Yü-hsi chi 3/28, dated 836. Also, for briefer mentions of Tu Yu's
expertise in taxation, military policy and policy to the barbarians, see
WYYH 984/2a–3a, sacrificial graveside prayer by Cheng Yü-ch'ing; also
T'ang yü lin 2/67; *Kuo shih pu* 3/54; *Ssu-k'ung Piao-sheng wen chi*
1/6b–7a. Cf. also *Fan-ch'uan wen chi* 9/141.

250   Tu Yu's interest in Buddhism is suggested by *CTS* 148/3998, biog.; by Fu
Tsai's commemorative text, *WYYH* 783/9b; by a remark by Ch'üan
Te-yü, 'He was both put to service in this world and lodged his mind
beyond things (*shih wai*)'; see *Ch'üan Tsai-chih wen chi* 31/6a, commemorative text for Tu Yu's country estate. Cheng Yü-ch'ing also
described Tu as 'having knowledge that penetrated abstruse mysteries
(*hsüan chi*)'; *WYYH* 984/3a.

251   For Liu Tsung-yüan's Buddhism, see Gentzler (1966), pp. 145–52;
Hartman in Nienhauser (1973), pp. 56–9.

6 Attitudes to literary composition

1   The late T'ang writer Niu Hsi-chi listed 16 genres; see *WYYH* 742/10b,
essay on literature. They were poetry (*shih*); rhymeprose (*fu*); essay
(*lun*); dissertation (*ts'e*); admonition (*chen*); judgement (*p'an*); assessment (*tsan*); eulogy (*sung*); stele (*pei*); inscription (*ming*); letter (*shu*);
preface (*hsü*); prayer (*wen*); despatch (*hsi*); memorial (*piao*); note (*chi*).
Other writers made different lists, e.g. *Yen Lu kung wen chi* 5/2a,
preface to the collected works of Sun Ti, listing 13 genres. *Ch'üan
Tsai-chih wen chi* 33/9a–b, preface to the collected works of Chang Teng,
prefect of Chang-chou in modern Fukien, an otherwise obscure figure,
lists 10 genres; *Fan-ch'uan wen chi*, preface by P'ei Yen-han, p. 1, 14
genres. Cf. Hartman (1986), pp. 257–8, for a classification of Han Yü's
writings into 9 groups; also Hightower (1957), pp. 512–33; E. D.
Edwards, 'A classified guide to the thirteen classes of Chinese prose',
Bulletin of the School of Oriental and African Studies 12 (1948),
pp. 770–88; Knechtges (1982), pp. 21–52.

2   *Analects* 14/8. For examples of this phrase applied to writing in the
service of the dynasty, see *CTS* 190B/5037, of Ch'i Huan; *CTS* 190A/
4982, of Chang Yüeh and Su T'ing; *WYYH* 400/2a–b, Ch'ang Kun; *THY*
80/1477, Li Sun; *T'ang Lu Hsüan kung han-yüan chi*, pref. by Ch'üan
Te-yü, 4b; *WYYH* 840/19b, Liang Su of Yang Wan; *Ch'üan Tsai-chih
wen chi*, preface by Yang Ssu-fu, 2a; *WYYH* 384/9a, Liu Ch'ung-wang;
Liu Yü-hsi chi 19/165, of Wei Ch'u-hou. The phrase could also have a
pejorative sense, applied to writing that elevated style over substance;
P'i-ling chi 13/1b; *STTS* 6/20b; 6/2a.

3   *Chou i chu shu* 3/8b. *SS*76/1729; *WYYH* 369/2b–3a, Shang Heng; *WYYH*
701/8b, Chia Chih; *P'i-ling chi*, pref. by Li Chou, 1a; *Ch'üan Tsai-chih
wen chi* 33/4b, preface for the collected works of Ts'ui Yüan-han; *TWT*

84/1b, Liu Mien; *Lü Ho-shu wen chi* 10/3b; *Po Hsiang-shan chi* 5/28/26; *WYYH* 742/11a, Niu Hsi-chi; *TWT* 46/11b, Wei Ch'ou. See also McMullen (1973), p. 322. The cosmic aspect of *wen* was expressed in its definition as a canonization title; the first phrase defining *wen* was that it 'formed the warp of heaven and the woof of earth'; see *THY* 79/1455 and 80/1478 and *Shih chi*, appendix by Chang Shou-chieh, p. 19.

4 *Mao shih chu shu*, pref. 1a.

5 *Mao shih chu shu* 1/1/7a and 8a. The concept of 'making known the feelings of those below' was always politically important, although the closeness of its connection with specifically literary operations varied; see e.g. *SS* 76/1729; *CKCY* 5/167, 6/193; *TT* 17/96.3, Liu Chih; *Yüan Tz'u-shan chi* 3/34; *CTS* 166/4329, biog. of Yüan Chen; *Po Hsiang-shan chi* 7/48/84–5, *Tse lin* no. 69; 5/28/26; *TCTC* 299/7379–84, 783.9, Lu Hsüan kung; *WYYH* 742/11b, Niu Hsi-chi.

6 For the four divisions of Confucius's teaching, see *Analects* 11/13; for some T'ang scholars references to them, see *Ch'en shu* 34/473; *WYYH* 369/2b, Shang Heng; *WYYH* 701/7a, Li Hua; *WYYH* 703/4a, Liang Su; *TWT* 79/2b–3b, and 84/3a, Liu Mien.

7 *SS* 76/1730; *Ch'ün-shu chih yao*, pref. by Wei Cheng; *WYYH* 700/4a, Lu Ts'ang-yung; *Ho yüeh ying ling chi*, pref. and essay, pp. 40–1; *WYYH* 701/8b; *TWT* 79/2b, and 84/1a–b, Liu Mien; *Ch'üan Tsai-chih wen chi*, pu k'o 4b; *CTS* 173/449, biog. of Cheng Tan; *WYYH* 742/11a, Niu Hsi-chi; also McMullen (1973), p. 336.

8 Chang Ti-hua (1958), pp. 40–43, provides a list of pre-T'ang *lei shu* titles. T'ang scholars also mention the Sui encyclopaedia *K'uei yüan chu ts'ung (Assembly of pearls from a cassia garden)*, for which see *CTS* 46/1985; *HTS* 57/1449, and *Ho-chih* p. 56; *CTS* 189A/4945, biog. of Ts'ao Hsien; and the *Yü cho pao tien (Precious documents from candles of jade)*, by the Sui scholar Tu T'ai-ch'ing, for which see *I wen lei chü* 4/60–61; *TT* preface 3.2, Li Han; *CTS* 47/2034; *TFYK* 607/9a. To T'ang scholars, the most important pre-T'ang *lei shu* were the *Huang lan (Imperial reading)* of the San kuo Wei, cited in preface to *I wen lei chü*, p. 27; in preface to *Ch'ün-shu chih yao*, p. 2b; in pref. to *Wen ssu po yao*, *WYYH* 699/5a; the *Pien lüeh (Universal abridgement)* of the Liang, cited in *I wen lei chü* preface, in *Ch'ün-shu chih yao* preface; in *Wen ssu po yao* preface; and by Ts'ui Jung, *WYYH* 605/5a; and the *Yü lan* of the Northern Ch'i, cited in preface to *Wen ssu po yao*; by Ts'ui Jung, *WYYH* 605/5a–b; in preface to *TT*, by Li Han; and in *THY* 36/657.

9 For the *I wen lei chü*, see *CTS* 47/2046; *HTS* 59/1563; *Ho chih* p. 265; *THY* 36/651; *CTS* 189A/4947, biog. of Ou-yang Hsün; *CTS* 73/2596, biog of Ling-hu Te-fen; *CTS* 188/4922, biog. of Chao Hung-chih; *WYYH* 605/5b, Ts'ui Jung. Li Han, pref. to *TT* 3.2, listed this as among the best known *lei shu*. See also *SKCSTMTY* p. 2783; Teng and Biggerstaff (1970), pp. 85–6; Thompson (1979), p. 207; and introd. to ed. of 1965, pp. 1–16. Continuity with the Sui was provided by Yü Shih-nan who compiled the Sui *belles lettres lei shu Pei t'ang shu ch'ao (Excerpts for the Northern Hall)*. This was also widely circulated in the T'ang; see *Liu*

Pin-k'o chia hua lu p. 16; *CTS* 47/2046; *HTS* 59/1563; *Ho chih* p. 265 *SKCSTMTY* p. 2784; Teng and Biggerstaff, p. 85; Thompson, pp. 61–2.

10 For the *Wen ssu po yao*, see *WYYH* 699/4a–6a, preface by Kao Shih-lien; *CTS* 66/2462, biog. of Fang Hsüan-ling; *CTS* 65/2444, biog. of Kao Shih-lien. *WYYH* 699/5b refers to Fang Hsüan-ling as *pi shu ch'eng*; *THY* 36/656 has him as director (*chien*). *CTS* 79/2726, biog. of Lü Ts'ai has Lü participating in the commission 'at the start of Yung-hui'. This however conflicts with his designation as erudit of the court of sacrifices, a post to which he was appointed just prior to 641; see *CTS* 79/2720. See also *HTS* 82/2764, biog. of Hsü Ching-tsung; *TFYK* 607/12a–b; *CTS* 47/2046; *HTS* 59/1562; *Ho chih* p. 266–7. The *po yao* of the title is likely to be an abridgement of the characterization of the Confucian school as 'wide yet with few essentials' (*po erh kua yao*); see *Shih chi* 130/3289 and 3290.

11 *THY* 36/667.

12 Cf. the remark of Liu Hsiao-piao (Chün), 462–521: on completing the *Lei yüan (Garden of categories)* in 120 *chüan*, 'He said of it that every single thing in the world was fully represented in this book, and that not a single thing had been left out or had escaped'; Tu Pao, *Ta-yeh tsa chi (Random notes of the Ta-yeh [period])* 13b, cited by Yoshikawa (1979), p. 246. Cf. also *Ch'ün-shu chih yao*, preface 1a.

13 For the high status of the imperial library in the post-Han period, see *Ch'üan Tsai-chih wen chi* 31/2a; in the Liang, *TT* 26/155.2, double column entry.

14 *SS* 32/908; *Feng shih wen chien chi* 2/10; *HTS* 57/1422; cf. *CTS* 46/1962.

15 *SS* 32/908; *SS* 49/1297, biog. of Niu Hung; *SS* 75/1720, biog. of Liu Hsüan, *Feng shih wen chien chi* 2/9–11. The phrase used here, 'to open the road for the presentation of books' (*k'ai hsien shu chih lu*), is taken from *Han shu* 30/1701, describing the Han dynasty's efforts to recover books after the Ch'in burning. See also Lo Chen-yü (1909), 1/17a, Chao-ling stele for K'ung Ying-ta, by Yü Chih-ning.

16 *THY* 35/643; *CTS* 75/2597, biog. of Ling-hu Te-fen; *CTS* 46/1962, *Ho chih* p. 2 makes him director (*chien*) of the library.

17 *THY* 35/643; *TT* 26/155.2; *CTS* 46/1962; *CTS* 71/2548 biog. of Wei Cheng; *CTS* 190A/4996 biog. of Ts'ui Hsing-kung.

18 For Yü Shih-nan as a 'walking library', see *Kuo ch'ao tsa shih (Random incidents of the dynasty)*, quoted in *Liu t'ieh pu (Supplement to the six collections of excerpts)*, 13/6b. *CTS* 72/2566, biog. of Yü Shih-nan; *CTS* 73/2595, biog of Yen Shih-ku; *CTS* 190A/4996 biog. of Ts'ui Hsing-kung. For later T'ang praise of Chen-kuan directors of the library, see *Po Hsiang-shan chi* 5/32/66, commending Yü Shih-nan and Yen Shih-ku; *Chüan Tsai-chih wen chi* 31/2a, praising Ts'en Wen-pen, Yü Shih-nan and Ch'u Sui-liang.

19 *CTS* 190A/4996, biog. of Ts'ui Hsing-kung.

20 *THY* 64/114; *TT* 21/1242.2; *TCTC* 192/6023–24, 626.4

21 *CTS* 46/1964–65; the *Yung-hui hsin chi* is not designated here as a book title; but the editors of *Ho chih*, pp. 6–7, have marked it as one. Neither

the *Yung-hui hsin chi* nor the *Shen-lung chin shu*, for which see below at note 61, are entered as separate works in the *CTS* bibliog. monograph. This may have been because, in parallel with the pre-K'ai-yüan stages of the *kuo shih*, similarly omitted, they were considered to have been subsumed by later compilations in the same field, in this case the *Ku chin shu lu* of Wu Chiung, who had clearly seen them. See below at note 72.

22 See Yasui Kōzan and Nakamura Shōhachi (1966), p. 262. The T'ang criminal code also prohibited possession of books concerned with prognostication. For an edict of the Chen-kuan period ordering that the *Lao tzu hua hu ching (Canon of Lao tzu transforming the barbarians)* be burnt, see Lo Hsiang-lin (1954), p. 88, quoting *Chi ku-chin Fo Tao lun heng (Collection of discourses ancient and modern on Buddhism and Taoism)*. For a slightly later instance of an initiative to burn all copies of an official compilation, see *CTS* 182/2796, biog. of Li I-fu. Imperial suspicion of divinatory texts, in this case in the hands of a descendant of the Sui house, is illustrated by an incident a century later; see *TCTC* 215/6881, 747.71. For the early T'ang charge that the Sui had been responsible for massive destruction of written works, see *WYYH* 699/4b, preface by Kao Shih-lien and *SS* 75/1707, preface by Wei Cheng. Cf. the ninth-century view that Sui Wen ti relied on apocryphal books, *CTS* 176/4557–58, biog. of Yang Ssu-fu. Cf. also *TLT* 10/25b–26a, for security surrounding reporting of astronomical/astrological phenomena; students at the astrological bureau were not to read books on prognostication.

23 *THY* 36/651–56 and *TFYK* 607/12a–b include the cases of the *Lei li* and the *K'uo ti chih*; for Yen Shih-ku's *Han shu* commentary, see *TFYK* 606/15a and *CTS* 73/2595, biog. of Yen Shih-ku. See also *CTS* 72/2582, biog of Ch'u Liang, for another example. *CTS* 74/2620, biog. of Ts'ui Jen-shih gives an example of canonical commentaries that were not in the end judged acceptable.

24 *Han shu* 30/1701; see also note 15 above.

25 *CTS* 61/2362, biog. of Ch'en Shu-ta; *CTS* 70/2535–36, biog. of Ts'en Wen-pen. For T'ai tsung's esteem for Yü Shih-nan, see *CTS* 72/2565–71, biog. of Yü. For T'ai tsung's compositions in the 'palace style' see also *T'ang shih chi shih* 1/6; *Ta T'ang hsin yü* 3/67. For the origins of the style and for predominantly early T'ang characterizations of it, see *Wei Chin Nan-pei ch'ao wen-hsüeh shih ts'an-k'ao tzu-liao* vol. II, pp. 677–78.

26 *Chin shu* 54/1487–88.

27 E.g. *CTS* 77/2680, biog. of Yen Li-pen; *CTS* 80/2743, biog. of Shang-kuan I, d. 664; *T'ang yü lin* 8/134; *T'ang shih chi shih* 1/3–6, and subsequent entries for verse writers of the Chen-kuan period. Cf. the statement of Yüan Chen, *CTS* 166/4329, biog.

28 *Ch'ün-shu chih yao* preface 1a; *TFYK* 607/10a–12a.

29 *SS* 76/1730.

30 *THY* 65/1124.

31 *CTS* 72/2570, biog. of Yü Shih-nan; *TFYK* 622/4b; but cf. the similar passage in *Nan pu hsin shu* p. 112, in which calligraphy is ranked third and literary style fourth.

32 *CTS* 189A/4952, biog. of Hsiao Te-yen; cf. *Ch'en shu* 34/473, in which

the order in which Confucius ranked his four categories is, similarly, made significant. See also note 6 above.

33 *CKCY* 7/217; *CTS* 73/2600, biog. of Teng Shih-lung; cf. also *T'ang shih chi shih* 1/1, preface to *Ti ching p'ien*.

34 *CKCY* 3/93–94; *TT* 31/181.2; *CTS* 72/2576, biog. of Li Pai-yao; *TT* 18/104, Tu Yu; cf. *TWT* 79/2b–3b, letter of Liu Mien.

35 For Ch'en Shu-ta, see *CTS* 61/2363; he was involved in the proclamation transferring power from Sui to T'ang. For Yen Shih-ku and Ts'en Wen-pen see *CTS* 73/2594 and 61/2363, biogs. For later praise, see *Po Hsiang-shan chi* 5/31/56; *WYYH* 706/5b, Li Shang-yin; *Li Wen-jao pieh chi* 6/1b; *Li Wen-jao wen chi*, preface by Cheng Ya, 1b. Cf. also *T'ang shih chi shih* 4/48; *Ta T'ang hsin yü* 6/106; Li Chao, *Han lin chih* 1b. Sun Kuo-tung (1980), p. 41 analyses the function of vice-president of the central secretariat (*chung-shu shih lang*), the post that Yen Shih-ku and Ts'en Wen-pen held as rescript writers.

36 *CTS* 72/2578, biog. of Li An-ch'i. For Li Pai-yao's appointment by T'ai tsung as a grand secretary in 627, see *CTS* 72/2572.

37 *CTS* 189A/4948.

38 For Hsü Ching-tsung see *CTS* 82/2761; *Po K'ung liu t'ieh* 74/17b–18a. Li Hua, *WYYH* 799/4b, lists some celebrated holders of the office of compiler in the early T'ang, and points out that tenure of the post was often followed by appointment to that of deputy director of the imperial library or grand secretary. He mentions Yü Shih-nan, see *CTS* 72/2566; and Ts'ui Jung, *CTS* 94/2996 and two others, possibly Wei Chih-ku, *CTS* 98/3061; and Cheng Yin, *HTS* 75A/3354, *T'ang shih chi shih* 1/10 and Hung (1969), pp. 29–30, note 73.

39 *CKCY* 3/75; *TT* 15/85.2; *CTS* 66/2469, biog. of Tu Ju-hui.

40 *THY* 74/1333–34. This anecdote recurs, with differences, in a number of sources: *TT* 17/93.1, dating the incident 649; *THY* 76/1379 dating 648; *Feng shih wen chien chi* 3/1, giving the date 646. *CTS* 189A/4995, biog. of Chang Ch'ang-ling, one of the candidates, has a markedly different version, in which this incident is omitted, and in which Chang obtains T'ai tsung's appreciation and is successful in the *chin shih*. *T'ang shih chi shih* 8/111 integrates these two versions; cf. also *Nan pu hsin shu* p. 25.

41 *THY* 74/1344; *CTS* 70/3533, biog. of Tai Chou.

42 *THY* 36/656, dating 658; *TFYK* 607/12b; *CTS* 82/2764, biog. of Hsü Ching-tsung; *CTS* 189A/4955, biog. of Liu Po-chuang; *CTS* 47/2077; *HTS* 60/1621; *Ho chih* p. 368. Cf. *CTS* 46/2004 and *HTS* 58/1483, *Ho chih* p. 114; and *HTS* 60/1622, *Ho chih* p. 376, for the titles of two ancillary works. Parts of the *Wen kuan tz'u lin* were taken, with imperial permission, to Korea; see *THY* 36/667. Four *chüan*, preserved in Japan, are reprinted in Hayashi Hitoshi ed., *Isson shōsho (Collection of books preserved)*, 1799–1810.

43 *CTS* 82/2764, biog. of Hsü Ching-tsung; *CTS* 47/2046 and *HTS* 59/1563; *Ho chih* p. 266. For another anthology of which Hsü Ching-tsung was the first compiler, see *HTS* 60/1621–22, and *Ho chih* p. 368, *Fang lin yao lan (Essential reading from the fragrant forest)*.

44 Hanabusa (1951), p. 116.

45 *THY* 36/657, dating 663; *CTS* 82/2764, biog. of Hsü Ching-tsung; *CTS* 86/2828–29, biog. of Li Hung; *TFYK* 607/13a and 258/14a–b; *CTS* 190A/4997, biog. of Meng Li-chen. The *CTS* bibliography omits this compilation; *HTS* 59/1562 and *Ho chih* p. 266. For other anthologies compiled wholly or in part by Meng Li-chen see *CTS* 47/2046; *HTS* 59/1563, and *Ho chih* p. 266.

46 *CTS* 47/2080; *HTS* 60/1621, *Ho chih* p. 374.

47 *HTS* 59/1564, *Ho chih* p. 268; omitted from *CTS* bibliog.

48 For general accounts of the *San chiao chu ying*, see *THY* 36/657; *TFYK* 607/13a; *CTS* 47/2046; *HTS* 59/1563, *Ho chih* p. 267; *TCTC* 206/6546, 700.12. Participation is mentioned in the official biogs. and commemorative accounts of many of those these sources list; see e.g. *CTS* 102/3175, biog. of Hsü Chien; *CTS* 74/2622, biog. of Ts'ui Shih; *CTS* 78/2707, biog. of Chang Hsing-ch'eng; *CTS* 190B/5026, biog. of Yen Ch'ao-yin; *WYYH* 898/2a, commemorative biog. for Yüan Hsi-sheng by Ts'ui Shih; *Ch'ü-chiang Chang hsien-sheng wen chi* 19/9a, epitaph for Hsü Chien by Chang Chiu-ling. The commissioning of this encyclopaedia may have been a response to the suggestion of the crown prince drafted by Ts'ui Jung; see *WYYH* 605/5b. Fu Chen-lun (1963), pp. 54–7 supplies the fullest set of references; but cf. Pulleyblank (1961), p. 138; Guisso (1978), p. 147 and note 158 on p. 287.

49 *HTS* 60/1623; *Ho chih* p. 377; and Wang Chung-min (1978), p. 325. *Yü hai* 54/33a states that the original anthology was 276 poems by 47 scholars; *Chün chai tu shu chih* agrees that 47 scholars, rather than 26, participated. The title scholar of the pearls and blossoms (*chu ying hsüeh shih*), used under the empress Wu, may have derived from this commission; see *TLT* 9/22b. The conviviality of the commission's proceedings is suggested by the reminiscence of Chang Yüeh that they disregarded official seniority in their drinking arrangements; see *Ta T'ang hsin yü* 7/118, quoted by Ikeda (1971), p. 78.

50 Fu Chen-lun (1963), p. 55 notes that *Yü hai* 54/32a reads *fang-yü* for *fang-ch'eng; TFYK* 607/13a agrees with *Yü hai*.

51 *THY* 35/644; this entry again underlines the connection between reorganizing the imperial collections and producing large anthologies.

52 Kao Chung-wu, *T'ang chung-hsing hsien-ch'i chi (Anthology of spirit at leisure [at the time of] the T'ang dynastic revival)*, p. 302; also *Ch'üan Tsai-chih wen chi, pu k'o* 4b. The shift in perspective began before the rebellion; see pref. to *Ho yüeh ying ling chi* p. 40 and *Kuo hsiu chi (Anthology of flowering [talent])*, p. 126.

53 *CTS* 190B/5033, biog. of Ho Chih-chang. For the *Wen fu (Repository of letters)*, see *THY* 36/658; *Yü hai* 54/14b, quoting the *Chi-hsien chu chi* by Wei Shu; *HTS* 56/1622; *Ho chih* p. 376–7. A work called the *Hsü Wen hsüan (Continuation of the literary anthology)* that Chang Chiu-ling referred to in Hsü Chien's epitaph may relate to this work; see *Ch'ü-chiang Chang hsien-sheng wen chi* 19/11b; cf. *Yü hai* 54/15a, quoting *Chi-hsien chu chi*.

54 For the *Hsüan tsung shih lei*, also referred to as the *Ming huang shih lei*, see *HTS* 59/1563; also Yü Chia-hsi, *Ssu-k'u t'i yao pien cheng*, pp. 949–51.

55 For the *Ch'u hsüeh chi*, see Liu Fang, *T'ang li*, quoted by Yü Chia-hsi, *Ssu-k'u t'i yao pien cheng*, pp. 949–51; *THY* 36/658; *HTS* 59/1563; *Ho chih* p. 267; *Ta T'ang hsin yü* 9/145; *Nan pu hsin shu* p. 94; *Yü hai* 57/36b–37a, quoting the *Chi-hsien chu chi* by Wei Shu; also *Ch'u hsüeh chi*, introduction by Ssu I-tsu (1962), pp. 1–4; Teng and Biggerstaff (1971), pp. 86–7; Thompson (1979), pp. 77–8.

56 One, in 10 *chüan*, was submitted by a corrector of characters in the imperial library; see *HTS* 59/1563; cf. *Ho chih* p. 267.

57 For the Yung-hui catalogue, see *CTS* 46/1964–65, pref. to *Ku chin shu lu* by Wu Chiung; and *Ho chih* pp. 6–7.

58 *THY* 35/643.

59 *THY* 64/1114.

60 *CTS* 190B/5026, biog. of Yen Ch'ao-yin. An editing and correcting initiative, involving the canons, histories and biographies (*chuan*) and based on the imperial library, may have been made in 696; see *CTS* 183/4728, biog. of Wu Min-chih; *CTS* 191/5099, biog. of Li Ssu-chen. There is also a hint that under Chung tsung the consort Shang-kuan Chao-jung, d. 710, built up the palace collections; see *WYYH* 700/5a, preface composed on Hsüan tsung's command by Chang Yüeh. The empress Wu had a large number of works compiled on her behalf in the imperial library; see *CTS* 6/133.

61 *CTS* 46/1964–5; *Ho chih* pp. 6–7, referred to in *Ch'üan Tsai-chih wen chi* 34/1b–2a.

62 *THY* 35/644 dates this 712; *TFYK* 50/4b; *CTS* 190B/5040, memorial by Li Yung; *CTS* 99/3087, biog. of Ts'ui Jih-yung. Cf. also *CTS* 97/3050–51, biog. of Chang Yüeh and *TCTC* 207/6578, 705.2; *CTS* 189B/4970, biog. of Chu Ch'in-ming.

63 *HTS* 202/5754, biog. of Li Yung. What appears to be a different version of this story is given by Yen Chen-ch'ing, *Yen Lu kung wen chi* 5/17b; here the introduction is attributed to Ts'ui Mien.

64 *HTS* 199/5666, biog. of Wang Yüan-kan; also *TWT* 91/2b, Han Hsiu, preface for collected works of Su T'ing.

65 *CTS* 89/2901, biog. of Wang Fang-ch'ing; *CTS* 102/3184, biog. of Wei Shu; at the start of Wei's biog., the home is mentioned as having 2,000 *chüan* only. The tenfold increase was therefore Wei's own achievement. Another large collection was owned by Wu Ching, see *CTS* 102/3182, biog. His grandson, the post-rebellion official historian Chiang I, owed the start of his scholarly career to this collection, and also later built up his own; see *CTS* 149/4026 and 4028.

66 *CTS* 102/3176, biog. of Hsü Chien. *HTS* 199/5663 has rather different wording; cf. *Ch'ü-chiang Chang hsien-sheng wen chi* 19/9b and 11b, epitaph by Chang Chiu-ling.

67 *CTS* 102/3167, biog. of Ch'u Wu-liang; *CTS* 102/3164, biog. of Ma Huai-su. Ma's initiative, referring specifically to the *Sui shu ching-chi chih*, is datable to 717 on the evidence of *CTS* 102/3183, biog. of Wei Shu.

68 *CTS* 190B/5036–37, biog. of Ch'i Huan, datable to before 722, when Chang Yüeh was a book commissioner. *CTS* 190B/5033, biog. of Ho

Chih-chang. Ts'ui Mien, an official scholar and general service official, was also a commissioner for the preparation of books and pictures in the early K'ai-yüan period; see *Yen Lu kung wen chi* 5/16b; *HTS* 199/5681, biog. of Ma Huai-su.

69 *Yü hai* 52/22b quoting the *Chi-hsien chu chi* of Wei Shu; *THY* 64/118–19; *TLT* 9/22b–23a; *TT* 21/126.3; *CTS* 102/3167, biog. of Ch'u Wu-liang; *CTS* 46/1962; cf. *HTS* 57/1422; *Ho chih* p. 2. These accounts do not agree in detail. Cf. also *Ta T'ang hsin yü* 11/167; *TFYK* 50/7a; *TCTC* 211/6730, 717.17.

70 *TLT* 9/26a–b; *THY* 35/644; *CTS* 47/2081–82; *HTS* 57/1422–23; *Ho chih* pp. 3–4; Ikeda (1971), pp. 57–8.

71 *CTS* 102/3167, biog. of Ch'u Wu-liang and *CTS* 102/3178, biog. of Yüan Hsing-ch'ung and *CTS* 46/1962 suggest a date of 720; *THY* 64/1118 states 720, first month; *Chi-hsien chu chi*, quoted by *Yü hai* 52/244a–b, says 7th month of 719. There is a similar disparity over the date of the completion of the catalogue; see *TCTC* 212/6747, 721.17, *k'ao i*, citing, among other sources, the *T'ang li* of Liu Fang.

72 *CTS* 46/1964–65; *Ho chih* pp. 7–8. For the terminology used here to refer to the Yung-hui and Shen-lung catalogues, cf. *SS* 32/908, preface to bibliography monograph, referring to appending Ch'i and Liang catalogues.

73 *THY* 36/658; *CTS* 46/1964–65, preface by Wu Chiung and *TCTC* 212/6747, 721.17 gives the same figure. For an independent mention of this catalogue, see *Yen Lu kung wen chi* 10/2a, the fine epitaph for the official scholar and *Han shu* expert Yin Chien-yu.

74 *THY* 36/658; cf. *CTS* 102/3181, biog. of Wei Shu and 102/3178, biog. of Yüan Hsing-ch'ung.

75 *Yü hai* 52/25b, double column entry, citing *CTS* makes it 51,851; the text of *CTS* 46/1962 and *Ho chih* p. 3 have 51,852. *CTS* 46/1965 and *Ho chih* p. 8 reproduce Wu Chiung's preface, which also gives 51,582. For the incorporation of this catalogue and its preface into the *CTS* bibliography monograph, see van der Loon (1952), pp. 368–9; Twitchett (1985), p. 150; see also Nieh Ch'ung-chi, *I-wen chih erh-shih chung tsung-ho yin-te*, p. 38. For some examples of titles omitted from this catalogue, see Ch. 3, notes 72 and 73; Ch. 4, notes 83 and 91; and notes 21 and 47 above.

76 *TLT* 9/26a.

77 *CTS* 97/3059; *HTS* 223A/6349–50, biogs. of Ch'en Hsi-lieh.

78 *THY* 35/644; cf. *THY* 64/1119, where the total number of scrolls listed for the Chi-hsien library in 721 was 81,990.

79 For searches for Taoist books, see *T'ang shih chi shih* 2/12–13; for acceptance of a Taoist work, *WYYH* 710/5b, preface by Li Hua; *THY* 36/658. For acceptance by the library of literary works, *Meng Hao-jan chi* preface by Wei T'ao, dated 750; *TWT* 91/2b, preface by Han Hsiu. Hsüan tsung's own *Lao tzu* commentary, on the request of Hsiao Sung, was taken into the library; see *TFYK* 53/16a.

80 *Yen Lu kung wen chi* 12/2b; *TKCK* 8/4a–b.

81 *THY* 64/1119; *THY* 35/645; *HTS* 118/4270, biog. of Wei.

82 *WYYH* 130/2b; *HTS* 202/5767–68, biog. of Hsiao Ying-shih. Cf. also
   CTShih 139/1411, poem by Ch'u Kuang-hsi mentioning a book search by
   a collator which is likely to have been a pre-rebellion date. For Ch'u
   Kuang-hsi, see also *T'ang ts'ai tzu chuan* 1/18–19, *Ho yüeh ying ling chi*
   2/95, and Ch. 5, note 131.
83 *THY* 64/1119.
84 *Yü hai* 52/28b, quoting *Chi-hsien chu chi*.
85 *THY* 78/1439; *TTCLC* 51/263–64; *HTS* 223A/6350, biog. of Ch'en
   Hsi-lieh. *THY* 78/1439 gives a date of early 754.
86 *THY* 64/1119.
87 *Nien-erh shih cha chi* 20/401; Kao Ming-shih (1971), pp. 274–6. For
   translation and study of the *Wen hsüan* preface, see Hightower (1957).
88 *SS* 75/1716; *Pei shih* 82/2759, biogs. of Hsiao Kai; *SS* 35/1082; *CTS*
   47/2077; *HTS* 60/1619; *Ho chih* p. 367. See also Yoshikawa (1979), p. 259.
89 Nakatsuhama (1972), pp. 341–484, listing the authors entered in the *I*
   wen lei chü, and, against them, the titles of their compositions included
   in the encyclopaedia. All the *fu* entered in chs. 17 and 18 of the *Wen*
   hsüan, for example, are represented in the *I wen lei chü*.
90 *Liang shu* 8/165–71; cf. *Nan shih* 53/1307–13; also the remarks in *SS*
   35/1090.
91 *CTS* 189A/4945; *HTS* 198/5640–41, biogs of Ts'ao Hsien.
92 *CTS* 198A/4946; *HTS* 202/5754, biogs of Li Shan. *THY* 36/657 gives date
   of 661; Kao Pu-ying (1963), p. 1147, notes that eds. of the *Wen hsüan*
   itself make the date 658. For this commentary, see the voluminous
   modern sub-commentary to it by Kao Pu-ying (1973); also Ch'iu
   Hsieh-yu (1959), pp. 331–5; Hsü Tzu-to (1974); and Yeh Ch'eng-i (1975);
   Shiba Rokurō (1950), pp. 45–60; Knechtges (1982), pp. 52–4.
93 *Ch'ao-yeh ch'ien tsai*, quoted in *T'ai-ping kuang chi* 447/3658, shows,
   however, that the *Wen hsüan* was taught in local schools; see Kao
   Ming-shih (1971), pp. 275–6.
94 *CTS* 84/2802, biog. of P'ei Hsing-chien. A century later another P'ei,
   P'ei Lin, d. 838, canonized *Ching*, who was a clerical script (*li shu*)
   specialist, showed interest in the *Wen hsüan* by compiling a sequel
   anthology; see *CTS* 171/4448–49.
95 For example in the topic set for *fu* in 713 was the imperial ploughing
   ritual; see *WYYH* 60/1a–3a. This topic was represented in the *Wen hsüan*
   by the *Chi t'ien fu* (*Rhymeprose on ploughing the fields*) by P'an Yüeh,
   d. A.D. 300. This *fu* was included in *I wen lei chü* 39/703–04; and *Ch'u*
   hsüeh chi 14/339–41.
96 *Liu ch'en chu Wen hsüan*, pp. 1a–2b, memorial of presentation and
   imperial statement of acknowledgement. For Lü Hsiang, see *HTS*
   202/5758–59 biog.; also *CTS* 111/3320 and *HTS* 139/4625, biogs. of Fang
   Kuan; *THY* 56/963–64, and *CTS* 171/4448, biog. of P'ei Lin, for later
   praise of Lü Hsiang. See also Knechtges (1982), pp. 53–4.
97 *Yü hai* 54/15a and 54/8b quoting *Chi-hsien chu chi; Ta T'ang hsin yü*
   9/142–43; Ikeda (1971), p. 65.
98 Niimi (1937), pp. 140–5; Fujii (1970), pp. 287–301.
99 *Ho yüeh ying ling chi* pp. 40 and 116; Konishi Jinichi ed., *Bunkyō*

hifuron kō, Kōbunhen, pp. 185–6. For sequel anthologies that referred to the *Wen hsüan* in their titles see *Feng shih wen chien chi* 3/12; *HTS* 60/1622; *Ho-chih* p. 376.

100 For the interest shown in the *Wen hsüan* by the Tibetans in 731, as recorded in T'ang sources, see *THY* 36/667; *CTS* 196A/5232 and *WYYH* 694/12a. Cf. the frequency of references to it in the Japanese monk Kūkai's *Bunkyō hifuron*, e.g. pp. 16, 168, 185, 187.

101 *Han Ch'ang-li chi* 6/34/87; *CTCC* epitaph for Shen Chung-huang, d. 859 aged 67 *sui*; *CTS* 18A/602–03, Li Te-yü; cf. Waley (1949), p. 17, p. 183; Hartman (1986), pp. 122, 214 etc.

102 *TT* 17/96.3, Liu Chih.

103 *CTS* 190B/5025, biog of Sung Chih-wen; *Sui T'ang chia hua* 2/24; *T'ang shih chi shih* 11/165; also Owen (1977), pp. 271–2.

104 *T'ang ts'ai tzu chuan* 1/8; *T'ang shih chi shih* 11/192; cf. *CTS* 190B/5017, biog.; Owen (1977), pp. 339–63.

105 *WYYH* 700/5a–b, preface written on Hsüan tsung's command by Chang Yüeh; *CTS* 51/2175, biog. of Shang-kuan Chao-jung. *TCTC* 209/6622, 708.6; *T'ang shih chi shih* 13/190.

106 *THY* 77/1414.

107 *CTS* 190A/5027, biog. of Li Shih, giving number of 300; *CTS* 192/5128.

108 For the Hsiu-wen kuan, see *TCTC* 209/6622, 708.6; *CTS* 189B/4970–71, biog. of Kuo Shan-yün; *HTS* 202/5748, biog. of Li Shih; *HTS* 119/4293–95, biog. of Wu P'ing-i; also *Feng shih wen chien chi* 4/9. For the *Ching-lung wen kuan chi (Record of literary halls in the Ching-lung period)*, see *HTS* 58/1435; *Ho chih* p. 126 and *Yü hai* 57/36a–b and 165/17a. Also Andō Shunroku (1972), pp. 13–24.

109 *WYYH* 700/5a, preface to the collected works of Shang-kuan Chao-jung, by Chang Yüeh.

110 *CTS* 190B/5016–17, biog. of Li Hsien; *CTS* 190B/5028, biog. of Chia Tseng; cf. *Sui T'ang chia hua* p. 28.

111 *Yen Lu kung wen chi* 5/16b.

112 *Yen Lu kung wen chi* 8/7a.

113 *Yen Lu kung wen chi, nien-p'u* 5b.

114 For some mention of verse competition in the court of Hsüan tsung, see e.g. *CTS* 190B/5036, biog. of Hsi Yü; *HTS* 202/5760, biog. of Sun Ti; *Yen Lu kung wen chi* 8/7a, epitaph for Yen Yün-nan. Cf. records of feasts for officials leaving on provincial commissions, e.g. *CTS* 99/3092, biog. of Chang Chia-chen; *HTS* 128/4465, biog. of Hsü Ching-hsien; *CTS* 60/1622 and *Ho chih* p. 376 recording the *Ch'ao ying chi* in 3 *chüan*, for Chang Hsiao-sung, departing for service beyond the frontiers.

115 For the term 'northern gate', in the sense of a place where entertainers were gathered, see *CTS* 88/2864, biog. of Wei Ch'eng-ch'ing. As applied to the emperor's informal secretariat, it appears in Kao tsung's reign, in the period 666–8; the favourite Chang Ch'ang-tsung is referred to as a 'compiler (*hsiu-chuan*) at the northern gate'; see *T'ang shih chi shih* 8/111. The association of scholars of the northern gate with rescript writing is indicated by Li Chao, *Han lin chih*, 1b. In 688, they were consulted over the Ming-t'ang; see *CTS* 22/862; *TCTC* 204/6447, 688.2.

The ninth century scholar Niu Hsi-chi referred to northern gate scholars in T'ai tsung's reign; see *WYYH* 741/15b.

116 *CTS* 88/2877, biog. of Lu Yü-ch'ing.

117 *CTS* 190B/5010–11, biog. of Yüan Wan-ch'ing; *TCTC* 202/6376, 675.6. The other scholar mentioned with Yüan Wan-ch'ing, Liu I-chih, was concurrently a court diarist.

118 *T'ang shih chi shih* 11/165–66; cf. *CTS* 190B/5025, biog. of Sung Chih-wen.

119 *CTS* 190B/5017, biog. of Shen Ch'üan-ch'i.

120 *CTS* 102/3168, biog. of Liu Chih-chi; Fu Chen-lun (1963), pp. 64–6.

121 *CTS* 97/3050, biog. of Chang Yüeh.

122 *CTS* 94/2996, biog. of Ts'ui Jung; *CTS* 94/2992, biog. of Li Ch'iao. Ts'ui Jung and Li Ch'iao were praised in the ninth century as the outstanding rescript writers of the empress Wu's reign; see *Li Wen-jao wen chi*, preface 1b by Cheng Ya. Ts'ui Jung's two sons, Ts'ui Yü-hsi and Ts'ui Ch'iao were both rescript writers in the K'ai-yuan period, and Ts'ui Ch'iao was also a chief examiner; see *CTS* 94/3000. *CTCC* epitaph for P'ei Chien indicates that Ts'ui Yü-hsi was canonized *Chen*.

123 Li Chao, *Han lin chih* 1b, noting that her father Shang-kuan I had done the same; *CTS* 51/2175, biog.

124 *CTS* 88/2880, biog. of Su T'ing. The career of the second rescript writer mentioned here, Li I, was mainly before Hsüan tsung's reign; he was a *chin shih*, and also directed the promotion examinations; see *CTS* 101/3135–36, biog. For the practice of directing rescripts while holding a basic office other than that of grand secretary, see *HTS* 47/1211.

125 Wang Ch'iu, biog. *CTS* 100/3132–33; for his canonization see *THY* 79/1455 (here spelt Ch'iu, with posthumous enfieffment to Chiang-ling rather than Ching-chou); Han Hsiu, biog. *CTS* 98/3077–79, canonized *Wen-chung*; Chang Chiu-ling, biog. *CTS* 97/3097–3100, canonized *Wen-hsien*; Su T'ing, biog. *CTS* 88/2880–82, canonized *Wen-hsien*. For special praise for Han Hsiu's rescripts in the ninth century, see *Li Wen-jao wen chi, wai chi* 3/4b and *WYYH* 742/9a, Li Te-yü. Su Chin's biog. is at *CTS* 100/116–17, and there is no evidence that he was canonized; he was however vice-president of the board of civil office, and therefore directed examinations, in 730; see *THY* 74/1346. The remaining scholars listed, Hsü Ching-hsien, Ch'i Huan, Hsi Yü, Hsü An-chen, Sun Ti and Chia Tseng all have biogs. in the literary section of *CTS*, 190B. Sun Ti and Hsi Yü were both canonized *Wen*.

126 For ten of the eleven rescript writers listed, their *CTS* biogs. give their examination records; the exception is Chia Tseng.

127 *CTS* 190B/5033, biog. of Hsü Ching-hsien; *CTS* 190B/5035, biog. of Hsi Yü; *CTS* 100/3133, biog. of Wang Ch'iu; (cf. *CTS* 90/2921, biog. of Li P'eng-nien, in which the order was first examiner, then grand secretary).

128 *CTS* 190B/5044, biog. of Sun Ti; *Yen Lu kung wen chi* 5/1b, quoting an edict of commendation composed by Yüan Hsien. Yüan Hsien was himself a grand secretary, probably during Li Lin-fu's ministership; he was a rarity among Chinese scholars in having some knowledge of Sanskrit; *T'ang shih chi shih* 17/258.

129 *CTS* 190B/5044, biog. of Sun Ti; cf. *CTS* 102/3175, where the same remark is made of the young Hsü Chien. Cf. also *T'ang chih yen* 1/11–12.

130 *CTS* 92/2958–59, biog. of Wei Chih. Other rescript writers of the period were the official scholar Hsü Chien, his father and his son; see *HTS* 199/5663, and cf. *CTS* 102/3176, biog. of Hsü; also Chia Chih, rescript writer at the time of the rebellion and later under Su tsung and Tai tsung, and a son of the rescript writer Chia Tseng; see *CTS* 190B/5029 and Fu Hsüan-ts'ung (1981), pp. 177, 180, 189. Sun Ti's younger brother Yü, son Su, and his grandson Chien were rescript writers, while his son Ch'eng managed documents for a military commander; see *CTS* 190B/5044, and *HTS* 202/5761.

131 For this important change, see Sun Kuo-tung (1980), p. 45 and note 52 on p. 74, giving ref. to *HTS* 44/1164; see also *THY* 59/1024–25; *T'ang chih yen* 1/11; *TTCLC* 106/549, giving a date of 715, 4th month, 1st day; *Feng shih wen chien chi* 3/1; *Ta T'ang hsin yü* 10/158–59; des Rotours (1932), p. 171. Cf. *TLT* 4/4a–8a, which enters the regular examination programme under the headings of president and vice-president of the board of rites.

132 Li Chao, *Han-lin chih* 1b, using the phrase 'drafting of documents and edicts' (*ts'ao shu chao*); *HTS* 46/1183–84. For a brief sketch of the rise to political power of the Han-lin yüan, giving references to primary and secondary sources, see Sun Kuo-tung (1980), n. 67 on p. 77.

133 *WYYH* 759/1a and *TT* 15/84.1, double column passage, Shen Chi-chi; *Ch'üan Tsai-chih wen chi* 34/1b makes a very similar remark; see also *THY* 76/1379, giving date of 680, 4th month; *TTCLC* 106/549; *Feng shih wen chien chi* 3/1; *CTS* 190B/5016, biog. of Liu Hsien. See also Hsü Sung's comment at *TKCK* 2/25b–26a.

134 *CTS* 94/4007, biog. of Hsü Yen-po; *T'ang shih chi shih* 9/117–19.

135 For Shen Ch'üan-ch'i, see *CTS* 190/5017 and *TKCK* 4/23a; for Sung Chih-wen, *CTS* 190/5025 and *TKCK* 4/33b, quoting *WYYH* 978/8a. For Sung Chih-wen's love of obscure diction, see *Liu Pin-k'o chia hua lu* p. 1.

136 *TKCK* 2/21a quoting *TFYK* 645/12a. The wide range of decree examination titles was noted by Feng Yen, *Feng shih wen chien chi* 3/11; and, much more explicitly, by the Sung *pi-chi* writer Hung Mai, *Jung-chai hsü pi* 12/114. For some examples of success in the examination for instantaneous composition, (*hsia pi ch'eng chang k'o*) see *CTS* 190B/5026, biog. of Wang Wu-ching; *CTS* 149/4023, biog. of Chang Cho; *CTS* 96/3021, biog. of Yao Ch'ung. Scholars were called for examination in this category as early as 649; see *TFYK* 645/11a.

137 *TFYK* 639/20b–21a; *TFYK* 56/8b–10a.

138 *TFYK* 640/4a–b; *CTS* 9/229. For the *po hsüeh hung tz'u* examination see *T'ang yü lin* 8/275; *TKCK* 7/326; *Yü hai* 201/1a; des Rotours (1932), p. 221.

139 *TT* 17/94.3; *TCTC* 205/6481, 692.8; *CTS* 101/3138, biog. of Hsüeh Teng (also called Ch'ien-kuang). Mair (1978), pp. 48–9; this article does not mention some of the pre-rebellion instances of poem presentation: e.g. Yüan Chieh's presentation of his collection *Wen pien (Literary collection)* in 753, for which see *Yuan Tz'u-shan chi* 10/154 and Sun

Wang (1957), pp. 24–5; Hsiao Ying-shih's presentation of five poems to the official scholar Wei Shu, *WYYH* 678/12a; or Wang Ling-jan's intended presentation to Chang Yüeh, *T'ang chih yen* 6/68.

140 *TT* 17/94.1; *TCTC* 202/6374, 674.13; *THY* 74/1338; Guisso (1978), p. 96, memorial of Li Yao.

141 *TT* 17/94.1–94.3; *THY* 74/1336, memorial of Wei Hsüan-t'ung dated 685; Guisso, p. 100.

142 *TT* 17/94.3–95.1; *TCTC* 205/6481, 692.8; *CTS* 101/3138, biog. of Hsüeh Teng; Guisso, p. 101, dating 691.

143 *TT* 17/95.2–96.1; *Ch'ü-chiang Chang hsien-sheng wen chi* 16/8b, reading 'two poems and one judgement'; *THY* 74/1338; *WYYH* 676/3b; Twitchett (1979), p. 352.

144 *TT* 17/96.1–97.1. Like earlier memorials on selection, this asked for devolution of the system. It may be dated by his tenure of the post of adjutant of the watch guard of the left gates (*tso-chien men wei lu-shih ts'an-chün*), by which he is designated on submitting it. The following references, *CTS* 27/1035; *TCTC* 214/6806, 734.4; *TT* 9/52.3–53.1; *TCTC* 214/6820/736.10, indicate that he was in this post in 734–6. Liu's reference was to *Analects* 11/3.

145 *WYYH* 369/2b–3b, Shang Heng.

146 *WYYH* 678/4a–b, Hsiao Ying-shih.

147 *TCTC* 216/6921, 753.12.

148 *WYYH* 944/4b, Liang Su; *TT* 15/84.1, double column entry, and *WYYH* 759/1a, Shen Chi-chi; *CTS* 111/3328, biog. of Kao Shih; cf. also *Ch'üan Tsai-chih wen chi* 17/14a; *WYYH* 710/5b, Li Hua; *P'i-ling chi* 13/3b for variations of this remark. *Ch'üan Tsai-chih wen chi, pu k'o* 4b, makes the identification with political ambition particularly clear.

149 Cf. remark of Yüan Chieh, *Yuan Tz'u-shan chi* 5/74–75; *TT* 15/84.1, double column entry, Shen Chi-chi.

150 *T'ang chih yen* 6/65, letter of Wang Ling-jan to Chang Yüeh, listing Ts'ui Jung; Li Ch'iao; Sung Chih-wen; Shen Ch'üan-ch'i; Fu Chia-mo; Hsü Yen-po; Tu Shen-yen; and Ch'en Tzu-ang as, with Chang himself, the greatest figures in 500 years. As court writers, examination graduates and compilatory scholars, these form a remarkably homogeneous group. All nine were either *chin shih* or decree examination graduates. Only Ch'en Tzu-ang, 661–702, Ts'ui Jung, 653–706, and Fu Chia-mo, fl. *c.* 705, and Chang Yüeh were not members of the prestigious Hsiu-wen kuan, founded in 708. Only Ts'ui Jung; Tu Shen-yen, d. after 705, and Ch'en Tzu-ang did not participate in the compilation of the *San chiao chu ying*, between 699 and 701. All at some stage held academic or literary office. Cf. also the historian's comment at *CTS* 94/3007. Ts'en Chung-mien (1962b), p. 361, dates Wang Ling-jan's letter to 723. Chang Yüeh gave a rather similar list of late seventh- and early eighth-century writers; see *Ta T'ang hsin yü* 8/140, quoted by Ikeda (1971), p. 78.

151 For the phrase 'close ministers', see *Ho yüeh ying ling chi* 1/78–79, Kao Shih, dated about 723 by Liu K'ai-yang (1981), p. 1, and *nien-p'u* p. 4; and *Yüan Tz'u-shan chi* 5/65–66, dated between 750–53 by Sun Wang (1957), pp. 19–22; also Tu Fu in *Chiu chia chi chu Tu shih* 17/267.

152 *Ho yüeh ying-ling chi* 1/30, Kao shih; *Wang Mo-chieh ch'üan chi chien chu*, p. 58; *Ho yüeh ying-ling chi* 1/66, Chang Wei and 1/60, Wang Wei; *Ho yüeh ying ling chi* 2/88, Hsüeh Chü. Owen (1981), p. 143, 165–66 and *passim*, provides a detailed description of the literary climate of the later part of Hsüan tsung's reign.

153 *Chiu chia chi chu Tu shih* 2/37. Hung (1952), p. 88; cf. *Ho yüeh ying ling chi* 2/88, Hsüeh Chü, for use of timber metaphor for selection in this period.

154 *Ho yüeh ying ling chi* 3/114–15, Yen Fang; *Ho yüeh ying ling chi* 1/62–63, Liu Shen-hsü.

155 *Ho yüeh ying ling chi* 1/55–56, Li Po. For an anti-Confucian poem by Li Po, see *Li T'ai-po wen chi* 6/25/34–35; for his title as a Han-lin scholar, see *Li T'ai-po wen chi* 7/*Fu-lu* 1/61, epitaph by Li Hua, and *nien-p'u* 8/*Fu-lu* 5/54; also *WYYH* 945/1a–4b, tomb stele text by Fan Ch'uan-cheng.

156 Owen (1981), pp. 169–79; Waley (1951).

157 For Tu Fu in this period, see Hung (1952), pp. 25–89; also Hawkes (1967), pp. 1–27; Owen (1981), pp. 183–96. For Yüan Chieh's original wish for a literary post, see *Yüan Tz'u-shan chi* 7/108; for his belief that literature should represent 'the feelings of those below,' see 6/91 and his 12-poem series *Hsi yüeh-fu*, 2/18–22. See also Owen (1981), pp. 225–31, and Nienhauser (1976). For another example of *yüeh-fu* presentation, see *Ho yüeh ying ling chi* 1/74–75, Li Hsin.

158 *HTS* 202–5766–67, biog. of Cheng Ch'ien; *Feng shih wen chien chi* 5/28 and 10/7; *Chiu chia chi chu Tu shih* 14/212–13; *Liu Pin-k'o chia hua lu* p. 15; *T'ang yü lin* 2/47; also Hung (1952), pp. 66, 81–2, 107–8, 228.

159 *HTS* 202/5771–73, biog. of Su Yüan-ming; *Yüan Tz'u-shan chi* 10/154, 6/96–97; *Chiu chia chi chu Tu shih* 14/210–12; Li Shang-yin, postface to Yüan Chieh's collected works, in *Yüan Tz'u-shan chi* p. 174; Jui T'ing-chang, pref. to *Kuo hsiu chi* p. 126; *Han Ch'ang-li chi* 5/19/8 and 6/30/47; *WYYH* 972/10a, Liang Su; *Chin shih ts'ui pien* 107/21a–b, Huang-fu Shih, referring to Su by his courtesy name of Chung-hsing; *Feng shih wen chien chi* 10/7; also Hung (1952), p. 30 and pp. 81–228. *Han Ch'ang-li chi* 5/19/8.

160 For Su tsung's love of learning, see *TFYK* 40/25b. Te tsung's love of verse is clear from *CTS* 137/3762–63, biog. of Liu T'ai-chen; *TFYK* 40/26a–b and 266/27b and 34a–b; and *Kuo shih pu* 3/55. Also *HTS* 203/5785; *Yü hai* 28/3a. For Wen tsung, see *TFYK* 40/28a–29a; for Hsiuan tsung and Chao tsung, *TFYK* 40/29a. Cf. *T'ang yü lin* 2/56.

161 A. C. Graham, *Poems of the late T'ang*, Harmondsworth, Middlesex: Penguin Books Ltd., 1965, p. 141.

162 K. T. Wu (1937), pp. 259–60; for Su Pien's library, see *THY* 36/660. Cf. also Yen Keng-wang (1959), pp. 723–4. For Tu Yu's, see *Fan-ch'uan wen chi* 1/9. For the large library of the official historian Chiang I, see *CTS* 149/4028; for other examples, see *WYYH* 827/10b–11a, Li Han; Pulleyblank (1959), p. 154, Liu K'o; *T'ang chih yen* 10/117, Lu Kuei-meng.

163 *CTS* 46/1962; *Ho chih* p. 3; *HTS* 57/1423; *Ho chih* p. 4. Less serious damage to the Chi-hsien yüan collection is suggested by *THY* 64/1120 and *CTS* 149/4026, biog. of Chiang I. Cf. *Nan pu hsin shu* p. 22.

164 *THY* 63/1095; *TFYK* 560/19a–b; *CTS* 149/4008, biog. of Yü Hsiu-lieh.
165 *TFYK* 50/12a; *HTS* 57/1423; *Ho chih* p. 4. Cf. *CTS* 46/1962; *Ho chih*
p. 3. Yüan Tsai's biogs., *CTS* 118/3409–14 and *HTS* 145/4711–15,
likewise do not give him credit for this initiative. *CTS* 149/4009 shows
that Yüan Tsai brought Yü Hsiu-lieh back to high office at the start of
Tai tsung's reign, and the initiative may have been connected with this.
Miao Fa, mentioned 'with others' by *HTS* 57/1423, *Ho chih* p. 4, in
connection with initiatives under Tai tsung, was one of the 'ten talents of
the Ta-li period'. Another of these, Keng Wei, was feasted by two
others, Lu Lun and Li Tuan, before leaving for the south to search for
books and pictures; see *WYYH* 297/26; *WYYH* 275/6b; *HTS*
203/5785–86, biog. of Lu Lun. See also *T'ang ts'ai tzu chuan* 4/58, and
Yen Lu kung wen chi 12/7b–8a.
166 *WYYH* 703/3b, Liang Su, speaks of Te tsung as 'yearning to search out
the literature of the time'. *Liu Ho-tung chi* 8/125; cf. the request by Liu
T'ai-chen, as director of the library relating to copying of canonical and
historical works; see Ch. 3, note 148.
167 For examples of verse being presented to the emperor, with no record as
to where it was ultimately kept, see e.g. *CTS* 190B/5053, verse of Wang
Wei, presented to Tai tsung; *HTS* 203/5785, Lu Lun, whose writings,
presented to Tai tsung, were later admired by Te tsung, Hsien tsung and
Wen tsung. *WYYH* 703/3b shows that Li Mi's surviving works were,
however, taken into the library; as, after copying by the Chi-hsien yüan ,
were the poems of the monk Chiao-jan; see *Ch'üan T'ang wen* 919/9b
and *WYYH* 712/8b, pref. by Yü Ti; cf. *Kuo shih pu* 3/55. The Taoist Wu
Yün also had his poems accepted; see *Ch'üan Tsai-chih wen chi* 33/11b.
THY 36/659–62, covering compilations by post-rebellion scholars, enters
numbers of works and records that were submitted, but, in contrast to
the pre-rebellion coverage, pp. 651–9, with one exception, gives no note
as to their destination. The one exception was a work on the factional
history of the Yüan-ho period by the official historian Shen Ch'uan-shih,
who asked, successfully, that one copy be deposited in the history office;
see *THY* 36/661.
168 Yen Chen-ch'ing's dictionary, the *Yün hai ching yüan*, was accepted
late in 777; see *THY* 36/659; *Feng shih wen chien chi* 2/23–24; *Yen Lu
kung wen chi* 14/7b, report of conduct by Yin Liang and *Yen Lu kung
wen chi* 14/12b, spirit path stele by Ling-hu Huan, indicates that both the
imperial library and the Chi-hsien library had copies.
169 *Liu Ho-tung chi* 8/117, report of conduct for Liu Hun.
170 *Liu Ho-tung chi* 8/125; *THY* 64/1120–21. *TT* 26/155.3, double column
entry. In 792, Ch'en Ching, who administered the Chi-hsien yüan while
holding four successive basic appointments, transferred junior posts in
the library to it. It was probably in this connection that he conducted
book searches and had copies made. His catalogue, called the *Chen-yüan
yü-fu ch'ün-shu hsin lu (New catalogue of the books in the imperial
collections of the Chen-yüan period)*, was not entered in his biog., *HTS*
200/5710–16; cf. *Yü hai* 52/29b–30a.

171 For Su Yüan-ming, see *HTS* 202/5733, biog.; for Pao Chi, *HTS* 149/4798; for Hsiao Hsin, *CTS* 146/3962 biog.; in the case of Liu T'ai-chen, his biogs., *CTS* 137/3762–63 and *HTS* 203/5781, do not mention his appointment; but see *THY* 65/1124–25; *TFYK* 608/28b; *WYYH* 702/10b, pref. by Ku K'uang, and *Ch'üan T'ang wen* 538/14b, spirit path stele by P'ei Tu. For his study under Hsiao Ying-shih, see *TWT* 85/10a.

172 *Ch'üan Tsai-chih wen chi* 20/3a, report of conduct.

173 *Ch'üan Tsai-chih wen chi* 22/7a, epitaph.

174 *Liu Ho-tung chi* 8/125, report of conduct.

175 *T'ai-p'ing kuang chi* 187/1404–05 quoted by Tonami (1979), p. 184. This is made very clear in the case of an infirm, eighty-year-old scholar surnamed Ts'ui; *WYYH* 604/7b, memorial by Ch'ang Kun; also Ts'ui Ch'ün, appointed to the Lo-yang library, *Po Hsiang-shan chi* 5/34/86; also *THY* 67/1174, the case of Wei Chien in 789; *CTS* 155/4114–15, biog. of Mu Ning, in 790; *CTS* 168/4381, biog. of Tu-ku Yü; *Ch'üan Tsai-chih wen chi* 23/8b, Chou Wei about 803.

176 See *T'ang ts'ai tzu chuan* 4/58–61, entries for Ch'ien Ch'i, Hsia-hou Shen and Li Tuan. For other, later examples of young graduates being appointed to the library: *CTS* 166/4327, biog. of Yüan Chen; *CTS* 166/4340, biog. of Po Chü-i; *CTS* 164/4285, biog. of Li Chiang; *CTS* 159/4187, biog. of Ts'ui Ch'ün; *CTS* 159/4182, biog. of Wei Ch'u-hou; *CTS* 160/4205, biog. of Li Ao; *CTS* 190C/077, biog. of Li Shang-yin. For the particular prestige of these posts, see *TT* 26/55.3.

177 *CTS* 160/4213, biog.; *Han Ch'ang-li chi* 6/32/69.

178 *WYYH* 400/6b and *Po Hsiang-shan chi* 5/32/66, rescripts by Po Chü-i; *WYYH* 400/6b, rescript by Yüan Chen.

179 *THY* 65/1125.

180 *TFYK* 620/33a; this memorial spoke of holdings of over 60,000 *chüan*. This figure must, however, have been an exaggerated approximation, in view of the precise figure given in 836; see next note.

181 *THY* 65/1125; *CTS* 17B/566; *TFYK* 608/29a; *CTS* 46/1962; *Ho chih* p. 3; *HTS* 57/1423; *Ho chih* p. 4. Liu Yü-hsi, as a Chi-hsien scholar early in Wen tsung's reign, wrote of presenting over 2,000 *chüan* of new books; see *Liu Yü-hsi chi* 5/137. Cf. also *TTCLC* 51/264, edict appointing Niu Seng-ju.

182 For post-rebellion *lei shu*, see Chang Ti-hua (1958), pp. 45–6 and pp. 79–80; also *HTS* 59/1563–64, *Ho chih* p. 267–9. *CTS* 166/4356, biog. of Po Chü-i mentions a *Ching shih shih lei (Material from the canons and histories by category)* in 30 *chüan*, for which see *HTS* 59/154 and *Ho chih* p. 268, and cf. *Huang Chien Yang Wen kung t'an yüan*, in *Sung ch'ao hsiao shuo ta kuan* p. 490b and *SKCSTMTY* pp. 2787–88. For Yüan Chen's *Yüan shih lei chi* in 300 *chüan*, see Ch. 5, note 234. For another large *lei shu*, in 500 *chüan*, that was never presented, see *Kuo shih pu* 3/54; *HTS* 59/1536, *Ho chih* p. 218. For two more such *lei shu*, see *CTS* 158/4167, biog. of Cheng Huan; *TFYK* 607/18a and *CTS* 176/4571, biog. of Wei Mu. For the *Wen hsüan* sequel, presented in 834, see *THY*

36/662; *TFYK* 607/18b; *CTS* 17B/553; *CTS* 171/449, biog. of P'ei Lin. Both *TT* and *THY* were placed in this category; see *TT* preface by Li Han and *HTS* 59/1563, *Ho chih* p. 267.

183   *CTS* 46/1962–63, *Ho chih* pp. 3–4; *HTS* 57/1423, *Ho chih* p. 4; Hanabusa (1951), p. 125.

184   For the term 'outer' as applied to the imperial library, see *Han Ch'ang-li chi* 5/21/38; Han states that the Chi-hsien tien had more prestigious posts and was over twice as large as the imperial library.

185   Sun Kuo-tung (1980), pp. 47–8.

186   Kao Chung-wu, pref. to *T'ang chung-hsing hsien-ch'i chi*, pp. 302–3.

187   *CTS* 126/3559, biog. of Li K'uei; *CTS* 137/3759–60, biog. of Hsü Hao; for Chia Chih, see below, following note.

188   *Yüan Tz'u-shan chi* 6/96–97, dated 759; and *HTS* 202/5772, biog. of Su Yüan-ming; *CTS* 190C/5052, biog. of Wang Wei; *CTS* 190B/5029–31, biog. of Chia Chih. *CTS* 108/3277, biog. of Wei Chien-su refers to Chia Chih as a grand secretary at the time of the transition of power to Su tsung. He was in charge of rescripts, with the office of court diarist before the battle of Ch'en-t'ao in 756; see *CTS* 111/3321, biog. of Fang Kuan. Up till 758, he was a grand secretary and he held this post again early in Tai tsung's reign. See the detailed account of his career by Fu Hsüan-ts'ung (1980), pp. 177–89. See also *Huang-fu Ch'ih-cheng wen chi* 1/6b. For Yang Wan, see *CTS* 119/3430, biog.

189   *CTS* 119/3445–46 and *HTS* 150/4810, biogs. of Ch'ang Kun; *CTS* 119/3440, biog. of Ts'ui Yu-fu; *CTS* 118/3419, biog. of Yang Yen. For later praise, *Li Wen-jao wen chi*, pref. by Cheng Ya, 1b. For Yang Yen more generally see Pulleyblank (1960), pp. 81–82, p. 85, p. 102; Twitchett (1970), pp. 39, 112–13.

190   *CTS* 119/3440–41, biog. of Ts'ui Yu-fu; *TCTC* 225/7251, 778.6. Also the magnificently written and carved epitaph for Ts'ui now at *KFSPWK*, tr. by des Rotours (1975a), p. 99.

191   *T'ang Lu Hsüan kung han-yüan chi* 1a–5a, pref. by Ch'üan Te-yü. For Lu Hsüan kung and the wide range of his views on administration, see Twitchett (1960). For a comment on Lu Hsüan kung's role as an examiner, see *THY* 76/1384, noting that over ten of his graduates reached high office 'within a few years'. For his discussion of 'expediency' (*ch'üan*) see *T'ang Lu Hsüan kung han-yüan chi* 16/20a–b, quoting *Analects* 9/30. See also Ch. 5, note 158.

192   *CTS* 127/3581, biog. of P'eng Yen.

193   *CTS* 163/4268, biog. of Lu Lun; *T'ang ts'ai tzu chuan* 4/56. The other three were Chi Chung-fu; Han Hung and Ch'ien Ch'i, all *chin shih*, see *CTS* 163/4268–69 and *T'ang ts'ai tzu chuan* 4/57–59, and cf. note 174 above. Lu Lun's death took place after Wei Chü-mou, who had recommended him, had won Te tsung's favour. *CTS* 135/3728, biog. of Wei, indicates that he won the emperor's favour in 796.

194   *CTS* 190C/5057–58, biog. of Wu T'ung-hsüan. There was antagonism between the Wu brothers and Lu Hsüan kung; see *T'ang Lu Hsüan kung han-yüan chi*, preface by Ch'üan Te-yü, p. 3b.

195   *CTS* 147/3976–77, biog. of Kao Ying. For Te tsung's difficult approach to

administration, see e.g. *CTS* 135/3729, biog. of Wei Chü-mou. For Ch'üan Te-yü, see *CTS* 148/4003, biog. and *Ch'üan Tsai-chih wen chi*, pref. by Yang Ssu-fu, 1b. Also *Huang-fu Ch'ih-cheng wen chi* 1/6b.

196 For Kao and Ch'üan as examiners, see Ch. 3, notes 129 and 130.

197 *Sun Ch'iao chi* 2/12a; cf. *CTS* 189B/4975, biog. of Wei Piao-wei.

198 The *Ch'eng-chih hsüeh shih yüan chi (Note for the court of attendant scholars [in the Han lin])* by Yüan Chen, completed in 821, lists 15 scholars who held this office. The names from Yüan to Wei Ch'u-hou, appointed in 825, are added; see Bischoff (1963), p. 26. These appointments to the Han-lin are confirmed by the *CTS* biogs. of those concerned, though the title of attendant scholar is not specified in the cases of *CTS* 164/4286, biog. of Li Chiang; *CTS* 159/4187–88, biog. of Ts'ui Ch'ün; *CTS* 169/4401–02, biog. of Wang Yai.

199 *Po Hsiang-shan chi* 6/38/46, rescript by Po Chü-i; also *Fan-ch'uan wen chi* 17/261–2, rescript by Tu Mu.

200 Yüan Chen's reputation as a verse writer led directly to Mu tsung appointing him to direct rescripts; see *CTS* 166/4333, biog. Yüan Chen's rescript appointing Po Chü-i to direct rescripts has the emperor praising his *belles lettres* as 'remaining on mens' lips'; see *Yüan shih Ch'ang-ch'ing chi* 45/3b. For Yüan Chen's own comment on his rescripts, see 40/1a–b.

201 *Han Ch'ang-li chi* 4/13/13; *CTS* 160/4198 biog.; Hanabusa (1964) p. 379. Hartman (1986), pp. 78–80. Another example is Wang Chung-shu, *CTS* 190C/5058–59, biog. The prestige of document writing in the literary world at large is indicated by Huang-fu Shih's list of 11 great writers since Chang Yüeh. Of these, Chang Yüeh; Su T'ing; Li Yung; Chia Chih; Li Hua; Tu-ku Chi; Yang Yen; Ch'üan Te-yü; Han Yü; Li Ao; and ?Shen Ch'uan-shih, only Li Yung, Li Hua and Tu-ku Chi were not rescript writers, while Li Hua had been a grand secretary for the rebels; see *Huang-fu Ch'ih-cheng wen chi* 1/6a–b.

202 *CTS* 173/4497, biog. of Li Shen; *CTS* 166/4333, biog. of Yüan Chen; *CTS* 174/4509–10, biog. of Li Te-yü.

203 For Shen Ch'uan-shih, *Fan-ch'uan wen chi* 14/212–13, *CTS* 149/4037, biog. For the son, Shen Hsün, see *CTS* 149/4037 and *WYYH* 384/7b–8a.

204 *CTS* 160/4208, biog. of Li Ao.

205 For Tu Mu, see *CTS* 147/3986, biog., and *Fan-ch'uan wen chi*, pref. by P'ei Yen-han, p. 1 and 3. For Liu Ching, see *CTS* 149/4033; for Sun Chien, *HTS* 202/5761.

206 *CTS* 190C/5081, biog. of Li Chü-ch'uan.

207 Biogs. of late T'ang rescript writers are at *CTS* 190C/5077–85; some late T'ang rescript collections are listed at *HTS* 60/1616–17, *Ho chih* p. 363. One of the latest was that of Hsüeh T'ing-kuei, a grand secretary as late as the period 898–901; see *CTS* 190C/5080.

208 *Ou-yang Hsing-chou wen chi* 9/89b–90a. Cf. the argument that it had originated in 'middle antiquity'; *WYYH* 369/2b, Shang Heng.

209 *CTS* 119/3430–36, biog. of Yang Wan; *CTS* 190C/5029–31, biog. of Chia Chih; *THY* 76/1395–96; *TFYK* 640/4b–11a. Hsü Sung, *TKCK* 10/11b,

quotes the Sung scholar Chang Fang-p'ing, 1007–91, *Lo-ch'uan chi* 8/9b, giving an account of Yang Wan's request that the *ming ching* and *chin shih* examinations be abolished and stating that it was actually implemented, to be obstructed later by high officials.

210 *TT* 17/97.1; *WYYH* 765/6a.

211 *TT* 18/101.1–102.1, Shen Chi-chi, entering his post as supernumerary secretary of the board of rites; *TCTC* 226/7268, 779.3 includes part of this memorial, but gives Shen's post as secretary in charge of harmonizing the pitch pipes (*hsieh lü lang*). *WYYH* 759/1a and *TT* 15/84.1 enter another essay by Shen on literary values in the selection system, but calls him, as *TT* does 'supernumerary secretary of the board of rites'. *Fan-ch'uan wen chi* 14/212 and Shen's biog., *CTS* 149/4037, show that this was in fact his last post.

212 *THY* 76/1380 and 76/1374; *TFYK* 640/11b–12a, proposals of Chao Tsan; *TKCK* 11/27a–b for comment of Hsü Sung. Cf. also the remark of Kuan Po to Te tsung, *CTS* 130/3627 biog.

213 *Li Pin-k'o wen chi* 6/7b, letter to Lu Hsüan kung; *Ch'üan Tsai-chih wen chi* 39/11a; 41/1a–4a; in *Ch'üan Tsai-chih wen chi* 37/11b, Ch'üan referred to correspondence between himself and Liu Ching-feng (?Mien) and with Lu Po-ch'ung (?Ch'un) on selection policy. *Ou-yang Hsing-chou wen chi* 9/8b–90a; *Po Hsiang-shan chi* 7/48/83–84 and *Ts'e lin* no. 68; *Liu Ho-tung chi* 36/567.

214 For Lu Hsüan kung, see *Ou-yang Hsing-chou wen chi*, preface by Li I-sun, 3a, and *Liu Yü-hsi chi* 2/16. For Ch'üan Te-yü see *Han Ch'ang-li chi* 2/4/34–35. In 802, Han Yü wrote to Lu San commending candidates on the grounds of their literary ability, and commending one, Liu Shu-ku, specifically on the ground of his ability to write verse; *Han Ch'ang-li chi* 4/17/75–76. For Ch'üan Te-yü's examination question on selection policy, see *Ch'üan Tsai-chih wen chi* 40/4b; for his reflections on the place of composition skills in examinations, 41/1a–4a, letter to Liu Mien.

215 *CTS* 167/3976, biog. of Kao Ying; *Yüan shih Ch'ang-ch'ing chi* 51/1a. Yüan added that Po's *fu* on *Analects* 17/2 was among the compositions that *chin shih* candidates competed to get hold of. Kao's reputation in this respect may have derived from his use of *Analects* topics for composition; see *WYYH* 189/2b–3b and *TKCK* 14/22a, *Analects* 6/14, *Po Hsiang-shan chi* 4/21/68–69 and *TKCK* 14/27b–28a, *Analects* 17/2. Ku Shao-lien was another examiner commended in the same way; see *Liu Ho-tung chi* 30/496 and *WYYH* 988/4b–6b, Lü Wen.

216 *TT* 13/73.1. In the pre-T'ang period, Su Cho, whom Tu Yu admired, had formulated the same idea; see *Chou shu* 23/386–87. T'ai tsung had also made a similar observation; *CKCY* 3/74, entry dated 628; *TCTC* 192/6063, 627.6.

217 For Liu Mien's letter, see *TWT* 79/2b. Liu Mien's description of Tu Yu's position bears a marked verbal correspondence to the statement in *TT* 18/104.3. (Tu's tone of qualification contrasts with the laudatory tribute to Fang Hsüan-ling and Tu Ju-hui in *CTS* 66/2472. This tribute was said in the Sung to have been based on a tribute by Liu Fang, Liu Mien's

father; see *Ch'ün-shu k'ao so* 15/2b). (A brief but uninformative tribute to Fang Hsüan-ling and Tu Ju-hui by Liu Fang is included in the Yüan period commentary to *CKCY* by Ko Chih; see ed. of 1465, 2/5b.) Liu Mien excused Fang and Tu from the charge that they had failed to reform literature on the ground that literature took its quality from its age, and to revive it was always beyond the power of individual ministers.

218   *Yüan shih Ch'ang-ch'ing chi* 28/5a–b; *Huang-fu Ch'ih-cheng wen chi* 3/9a.

219   *TWT* 26A/12a, Shu Yüan-yü; *Yüan shih Ch'ang-ch'ing chi* 40/1a–b; *Shen Hsia-hsien wen chi* 8/79b–80b; *Sun Ch'iao chi* 2/11b; *WYYH* 742/10b and *WYYH* 760/13a, Niu Hsi-chi. Cf. also *TT* 15/84.1, double column entry and *WYYH* 759/1a, Shen Chi-chi; *WYYH* 936/5a–b, Chang Chiu-ling, epitaph for Chang Yüeh, *STTS* 6/18a; *Ch'ün-shu chih yao*, preface 1a.

220   *CTS* 173/4491, biog. of Cheng T'an, dating to 'the start of K'ai-ch'eng'; *CTS* 17B/551; *TTCLC* 29/106; and *TKCK* 21/5b, comment of Hsü Sung.

221   *WYYH* 704/8a, Hsü Meng-jung, attributing the phrase to Pan Ku; *WYYH* 700/5a–b, Chang Yüeh; *WYYH* 384/2a, Yüan Chen; *Po Hsiang-shan chi* 5/33/76 and 7/48/84, *Ts'e lin* no. 84; *CTS* 190A/4982, pref. for literary biogs., of the literature of the Chen-kuan period; *Yü hai* 57/36b.

222   *WYYH* 680/9b–11a, P'ei Tu; *TWT* 86/7a–b, Ts'ui Yüan-han; *TWT* 46/11a–b, Wei Ch'ou.

223   McMullen (1973), p. 337 and notes 168–73.

224   *WYYH* 701/6b, Li Hua, quoting Hsiao Ying-shih; *Yen Lu kung wen chi* 5/16a, commemorative text for Ts'ui Mien; *Yen Lu kung wen chi* 5/1a–b, preface for the collected works of Sun Ti, which modifies the praise for Ch'en Tzu-ang; *Li T'ai-po wen chi*, preface by Li Yang-ping; *P'i-ling chi* 13/2a; *WYYH* 702/9a, Li Chou, preface for collected works of Tu-ku Chi; *WYYH* 703/6b, Liang Su, preface for the collected works of Li Han; *Han Ch'ang-li chi* 5/19/8; *Liu Ho-tung chi* 21/372, preface for the collected works of Yang Ling; *Po Hsiang-shan chi* 2/1/5; 5/28/27–29; *Yüan shih Ch'ang-ch'ing chi* 30/1b; *Chin shih ts'ui pien* 107/21a–b, Huang-fu Shih; *Ssu-k'ung Piao-sheng shih chi* 1/2a–3b.

225   *TWT* 92/6b; *WYYH* 703/6b–8a reads *chen* (revival) for *pien*; *TWT* 84/1a–b, Liu Mien; *Analects* 6/24 and 19/9. The concept of *san pien* applied to literary history may have pre-dated the rebellion; *Yen Lu kung wen chi* 5/1b notes that the official scholar Sun Ti knew of the 'three changes in the transmission of *wen*' (*wen t'ung san pien*). In the Sung, the concept of 'three changes' was applied to the whole span of T'ang literature; see *HTS* 200/5725–26. Cf. also *Ts'en Chia-chou shih*, preface by Tu Ch'üeh, 1a; *Yüan shih Ch'ang-ch'ing chi* 56/3b, epitaph for Tu Fu; *WYYH* 703/5b–6a, Liang Su. *Pien* as applied to verse had the sanction of the canonical tradition; see e.g. *Tso chuan chu shu* 39/8a, K'ung Ying-ta.

226   Liu's group of letters discussing literature is at *TWT* 84/1a–4a, and 8b–9a. For an account of his views on literature, see Obi Kōichi (1962), pp. 27–37.

227 *Han Ch'ang-li chi* 5/21/28–29; *TWT* 84/2a, Liu Mien. Ch'ien Mu (1957), p. 144; Nivison (1960), pp. 182–6; Hartman (1986), p. 211–57.

228 For the meaning of *ch'i* in Liu Mien and Liang Su, as a man's moral spirit, first nurtured and then given expression in his individual style, see Obi Kōichi, pp. 36–7; also *Han Ch'ang-li chi* 4/16/58–59. Ch'ien Mu, p. 142, sees Mencian influence in Han's concept of *ch'i*.

229 *Han Ch'ang-li chi* 5/19/7–9; 4/15/43–44; 4/17/71–72; 5/20/24–25. See also Ch'en Yin-k'o (1936), pp. 39–43; Chi Chen-huai (1958), pp. 77–85; Ku I-sheng (1962), pp. 66–72; and Owen (1975), p. 119, pp. 126–8.

230 *Han Ch'ang-li chi* 4/17/74–75; cf. *Liu Yü-hsi chi* 19/166, recording Li Ao's much later reminiscence. Han was related by marriage to Li; see *Han Ch'ang-li chi* 2/4/135 and commentary.

231 *Li Wen kung chi* 8/64a–b. Li's condemnation of the idea that literature was 'a mere skill' was quoted approvingly by P'ei Tu; see *WYYH* 680/9b.

232 *Li Wen kung chi* 8/63b–64b.

233 *Ku-wen* in early and mid-T'ang usage typically had the straightforward meaning of writings in the ancient script or ancient writings; see e.g. *CTS* 189A/4945, biog. of Ts'ao Hsien; *STTS* 4/12a–b and 13/2b; *WYYH* 699/4b, Kao Shih-lien; *Feng shih wen chien chi* 2/1–2; *Han Ch'ang-li chi*, preface by Li Han, p. 1. With Li Ao's generation and in their usage, it became a literary mode that indicated distancing from current practice, a freer, more individual and imaginative medium for expressing polemical ideas; see *Li Wen kung wen chi* 7/50a; 7/55b; 11/90a; 6/43a; also *Han Ch'ang-li chi* 5/22/47. There was a process of build up to this position; see *Yüan Tz'u-shan chi*, appendix pp. 168–9, Yen Chen-ch'ing, epitaph for Yüan Chieh.

234 *Liu Ho-tung chi* 34/542; 31/371; 36/568; 34/542–43; *Han Ch'ang-li* 6/32/71. Ch'ien Mu (1957), pp. 135–37; Kuo Shao-yü (1955), pp. 116–21; Lo Ken-tse (1957), pp. 147–53; Gentzler (1966), p. 31, pp. 158–82; and Nienhauser (1973), pp. 36–8.

235 See above, note 157; also *CTS* 99/3088, biog. of Ts'ui Jih-yung; *TTKYL* 62/15a; *HTS* 14/355; *CTS* 187A/4880–81, biog. of Su An-heng; *TWT* 84/8b; *Ch'üan Tsai-chih wen chi* 37/8b; *THY* 8/121; *TTKYL* 62/15a; *HTS* 14/355; also Hu Shih (1928), pp. 357–478.

236 *Po Hsiang-shan chi* 2/1/1–2, 2/1/10; 5/28/27–28; 2/4/55–56; 5/30/52; 7/48/84–85, *Ts'e lin* no. 69. Kuo Shao-yü, pp. 98–105; Lo Ken-tse, pp. 68–74; pp. 77–80; Waley (1949), pp. 107–14; Palandri (1977), pp. 55–9.

237 Lo Ken-tse, pp. 160–3; cf. *Kuo shih pu* 3/57; *Huang-fu Ch'ih-cheng wen chi* 4/4a–b; cf 4/3a.

238 *Shen Hsia-hsien wen chi* 9/90b–91a; cf. *Han Ch'ang-li chi* 4/15/44–45, for a hint of this horticultural metaphor.

239 *Sun Ch'iao chi* 2/10a; there follows a list of individual compositions that includes Han Yü's *Chin hsüeh chieh*, and a line of transmission traced from Sun back to Han Yü; 2/10b–11a.

240 Li Shang-yin, postface to the collected works of Yüan Chieh; see *Yüan Tz'u-shan chi* appendix p. 175.

241 Lo Ken-tse (1957), pp. 174–80.

7 Conclusion

1 *TT* 18/101.1, Shen Chi-chi.
2 *TWT* 87/1a–b, Fang Kuan.
3 *WYYH* 678/6a, Hsiao Ying-shih.
4 *TWT* 85/10a, Liu T'ai-chen.
5 *Yen Lu kung wen chi* 7/12a, memorial stele; 14/2a, report of conduct by Yin Liang.
6 *Han Ch'ang-li chi* 4/17/76.
7 To cite a few examples of scholars whose names have been mentioned: *CTS* 101/3141, biog. of Hsüeh Teng (Ch'ien-kuang); *CTS* 98/3075, biog. of Li Yüan-hung; *Yüan Tz'u-shan chi* 6/82–83, tomb text for Yüan Te-hsiu; *WYYH* 703/7b, preface to anthology by Li Hua; *Liu Ho-tung chi* 8/120–21, report of conduct for Liu Hun; *HTS* 200/5707, biog. of Chung Tzu-ling; *CTS* 190B/5036, biog. of Hsi Yü; *CTS* 100/3133, biog. of Wang Ch'iu.
8 *CTS* 73/2595, biog. of Yen Shih-ku.
9 *CTS* 72/2577, biog. of Li Pai-yao.
10 *CTS* 92/2959, biog. of Wei Chih. Cf. also *CTS* 99/3092–93, biog. of Chang Chia-chen.
11 *CTS* 125/3550–51, biog. of Hsiao Fu.
12 *Ch'üan Tsai-chih wen chi* 31/6a–7b.
13 *CTS* 170/4432, biog. of P'ei Tu.
14 *Po Hsiang-shan chi* 9/61/70; Waley (1949), pp. 190–92; cf. *Po Hsiang-shan chi* 5/28/27, for claim of relative poverty in early life.
15 *Tso chuan chu shu* 35/12b; *Ch'üan T'ang wen* 175/3b, Ts'ui Hsing-kung; *Li T'ai-po wen chi* 7/*Fu-lu* 1/60, epitaph by Li Hua; *WYYH* 678/9a, Hsiao Ying-shih; *TWT* 84/40, Liu Mien. *Li-yen* (establishing words) supplied a given name in the T'ang; see *CTS* 169/4410, Lo Li-yen; *HTS* 75B/3433, K'ung Li-yen; *HTS* 75A/3320, Cheng Li-yen; also *HTS* 58/1499, Tu Hsin, courtesy name Li-yen.
16 *CKCY* 3/87–95.
17 *HTS* 202/5722, biog. of Su Yüan-ming.
18 *P'i-ling chi* 4/5a–7b; *TCTC* 223/7173, 765.5.
19 *Yen Lu kung wen chi* 2/2b–3b; *TCTC* 224/7189–90, 766.5.
20 *CTS* 82/2764–65, biog. of Hsü Ching-tsung.
21 *CTS* 136/3753–54, biog. of Lu Mai.
22 Lo Chen-yü (1909), 1/16a and 17b.
23 *Han Ch'ang-li chi* 6/33/80, epitaph for K'ung K'uei.
24 *Yen Lu kung wen chi* 7/3b; 7/11b–12a; 8/3a. The commendation was composed, at T'ai tsung's command, by Hsiao Yü as a grand secretary.
25 *Yen Lu kung wen chi* 7/12a; cf. also *Yen Lu kung wen chi* 8/6b–7a, Hsüan tsung's gift to Yen of two rubbings of his inscription for mount Hua, of which 100 only were issued.
26 *Yen Lu kung wen chi* 7/11b; also 8/4a, noting that over four generations 14 Yens had served as 'scholars' (*hsüeh shih*) and 'readers in attendance' (*ssu tu*), and citing Liu Fang's *Hsü cho yüeh*. For the friendship between Liu Fang and Yen Chen-ch'ing, see *T'ang chih yen* 7/80.
27 E.g. *Yen Lu kung wen chi* 7/12b. Highly complimentary imperial

acknowledgements of Yen Chen-ch'ing's memorials, in some cases incorporated in or referred to in Yen's own commemorative compositions for members of his family, are conveniently reprinted in *Yen Lu kung wen chi* 1/2a (Hsüan tsung as retired emperor); 1/3a–7a (Su tsung); 1/7a (Tai tsung).

28 See Ch. 6, note 168.

29 *CTS* 188/4927, biog. of Li Jih-chih; *Yen Lu kung wen chi* 9/14a; *CTS* 102/3185, biog. of Wei Shu; *WYYH* 678/7a–b, Hsiao Ying-shih; *CTS* 190B/5034, biog. of Ho Chih-chang; *CTS* 111/3321, biog. of Fang Kuan. In *Ch'üan Tsai-chih wen chi* 17/14b, Liu Fang's powers of argument were described as of great rarity.

30 *Yuan Tz'u-shan chi* 8/119–120; *TFYK* 823/10a–b, of Yang Wan; *CTS* 130/3625, biog. of Ts'ui Tsao; *Ch'üan Tsai-chih wen chi* 23/1a–3b, and *CTS* 135/3728, of Wei Chü-mou; *Liu Yü-hsi chi* 39/394; *CTS* 159/4181, biog. of Cheng Yin.

31 The *Analects* term *i tuan* was made to refer to unacceptable variants of canonical texts in *CKCY* 7/215, in the context of Yen Shih-ku's commission to redetermine the text of the *Five canons* completed in 633; by Lu Te-ming in *Ching tien shih wen* preface; or even interpretations of specific passages; *Tso chuan chu shu* preface 5b; *Tso chuan chu shu* 1/7b, referring to a Kung-yang interpretation of Confucius's attitude to death.

32 In historical scholarship, Yen Shih-ku applied the term *i tuan* to unacceptable *Han shu* exegesis; see *Han shu chi chu* pref. p. 3.

33 In ritual controversies, *i tuan* was applied to unacceptable proposals for the Feng and Shan rites, *CTS* 73/2595, biog. of Yen Shih-ku; of unacceptable suggestions for the Ming-t'ang, *THY* 11/272.

34 Yin Fan, in his preface to the *Ho yüeh ying ling chi*, p. 40 applied the term to the style of verse developed in the southern dynasties, though his phrasing here is perhaps no more than an echo of Lu Te-ming's preface cited above, note 31.

35 *Feng shih wen chien chi* 1/7.

36 *TFYK* 604/9a.

37 *Chiu chia chi chu Tu shih* 14/210.2; also *Ch'üan Tsai-chih wen chi* 25/1a–2b, epitaph for Ch'üan Tzu-i, 701–770.

38 *TT* 53/301.1, quoting *Li chi chu shu* 52/1a and 60/1a.

BIBLIOGRAPHY

A. Chinese and Japanese works written before 1900

1. Pre-T'ang works, including those with T'ang commentaries

Analects, *HYISIS* ed.

Chou i chu shu 周易注疏, with commentary by Wang Pi 王弼 and sub-commentary by K'ung Ying-ta 孔穎達 and others (T'ang), *SPPY* ed.

Chou li chu shu 周禮注疏, with commentary by Cheng Hsüan 鄭玄 and sub-commentary by Chia Kung-yen 賈公彥 (T'ang), *SPPY* ed.

Ch'un-ch'iu kuei kuo 春秋規過, by Liu Hsüan 劉炫, in Ma Kuo-han 馬國翰 comp., *Yü-han shan-fang chi i shu* 玉函山房輯佚書.

Ch'un-ch'iu kung mei 春秋攻昧, by Liu Hsüan, in Ma Kuo-han comp., *Yü-han shan-fang chi i shu.*

Ch'un-ch'iu shih li 春秋釋例, by Tu Yü 杜預, with preface by Liu Fen 劉賁 (T'ang), *Ts'ung-shu chi-ch'eng* 叢書集成 ed.

Han shu pu chu 漢書補注, with commentary by Yen Shih-ku 顏師古 (T'ang), and Wang Hsien-ch'ien 王先謙, ed. in *Kuo-hsüeh chi-pen ts'ung-shu* 國學基本叢書, reprint of Peking: Commercial Press, 1959.

Hou Han chi 後漢紀, by Yüan Hung 袁宏, ed. of 1877.

Hou Han shu 後漢書, by Fan Yeh 范曄, with monographs by Ssu-ma Piao 司馬彪, with commentary by Li Hsien 李賢 (T'ang), Peking: Chung-hua Shu-chü 中華書局, 1965.

Hsiao ching 孝經, with commentary by the emperor Hsüan tsung 玄宗 (T'ang), *SPTK* ed.

Hsün tzu 荀子, *HYISIS* ed.

I li chu shu 儀禮注疏, with commentary by Cheng Hsüan 鄭玄 and sub-commentary by Chia Kung-yen 賈公彥 (T'ang), *SPPY* ed.

Ku-liang chuan chu shu 穀梁傳注疏, with commentary by Fan Ning 范寧 and sub-commentary by Yang Shih-hsün 楊士勛 (T'ang), *SPPY* ed.

Kuan tzu 管子, with collation by Tai Wang 戴望, *Kuo-hsüeh chi-pen ts'ung-shu* ed.

Kung-yang chuan chu shu 公羊傳注疏, with commentary by Ho Hsiu 何休 and sub-commentary by Hsü Yen 徐彥 (?T'ang), *SPPY* ed.

Lao tzu 老子, with commentary by Ho-shang Kung 河上公, *SPTK* ed.

Li chi chu shu 禮記注疏, with commentary by Cheng Hsüan 鄭玄 and sub-commentary by K'ung Ying-ta 孔穎達 and others (T'ang), *SPPY* ed.

Mao shih chu shu 毛詩注疏, with commentary by Cheng Hsüan 鄭玄 and sub-commentary by K'ung Ying-ta 孔穎達 and others (T'ang), *SPPY* ed.

Meng tzu 孟子, *HYISIS* ed.

San kuo chih 三國志, compiled by Ch'en Shou 陳壽, with commentary by
P'ei Sung-chih 裴松之, Peking: Chung-hua Shu-chü, 1959.

Shang shu chu shu 尚書注疏, with commentary attributed to K'ung An-kuo
孔安國 and sub-commentary by K'ung Ying-ta 孔穎達 and others
(T'ang), *SPPY* ed.

Shang tzu 商子, *SPTK* ed.

Shen chien 申鑑, by Hsün Yüeh 荀悅, *SPTK* ed.

Shih chi 史記, by Ssu-ma Ch'ien 司馬遷, with the commentaries of P'ei Yin
裴駰, Ssu-ma Chen 司馬貞 (T'ang), and Chang Shou-chieh 張守節
(T'ang), Peking: Chung-hua Shu-chü, 1959.

Ta-yeh tsa chi 大業雜記, by Tu Pao 杜寶, ed. in *Chih hai* 指海.

T'ang yüeh ling chu, pu i 唐月令注, 補遺, with commentary by Li Lin-fu 李林甫
and others (T'ang), edited by Mao P'an-lin 茆泮林, *Ts'ung-shu chi-ch'eng*
ed.

Tso chuan chu shu 左傳注疏, with commentary by Tu Yü 杜預 and sub-
commentary by K'ung Ying-ta 孔穎達 and others (T'ang), *SPPY* ed.

Wei shu 魏書, by Wei Shou 魏收, Peking: Chung-hua Shu-chü, 1974.

Wen hsüan 文選, compiled by Hsiao T'ung 蕭統, with commentaries by
Li Shan 李善 and Lü Hsiang 呂向 and four others (T'ang), *SPTK* ed.

**2. Anthologies, collected works and compilations by T'ang scholars, and
later collections of writings wholly or partly of T'ang date**

An Lu-shan shih-chi 安祿山事蹟, by Yao Ju-neng 姚汝能, ed. in *Hsüeh-hai
lei-pien* 學海類編, Vol. 16.

Bunkyō hifuron kō Kōbunhen 文鏡祕府論考攻文篇, by Kūkai 空海, edited by
Konishi Jinichi 小西甚一. Kyoto: Kōdansha 講談社, 1953.

Chang Yen kung chi 張燕公集, by Chang Yüeh 張說, ed. in *Wu-ying tien
chü-chen pan* 武英殿聚珍版.

Chang Yüeh-chih wen chi 張說之文集, by Chang Yüeh, *SPTK* ed.

Chao-ling pei lu san chüan, fu lu i chüan 昭陵碑錄三卷附錄一卷, edited by
Lo Chen-yü 羅振玉. in *Ch'en feng ko tsung-shu* 晨風閣叢書, 1909.

Ch'ao-yeh ch'ien tsai 朝野僉載, by Chang Cho 張鷟, *Ts'ung-shu chi-ch'eng* ed.

Chen-kuan cheng yao 貞觀政要, by Wu Ching 吳兢, edited by Harada Tanishige
原田種成, and published as *Jōgan seiyō teihon* 貞觀政要定本, Tokyo:
Tōyō Bunka Kenkyūjo 東洋文化研究所, 1962.

Chen-kuan cheng yao 貞觀政要, ed. of 1465, with commentary by Ko Chih
戈直.

Chen-kuan cheng yao 貞觀政要, ed. of Shanghai: Shang-hai Ku-chi Ch'u-pan-
she 上海古籍出版社, 1978.

Ch'en shu 陳書, by Yao Ssu-lien 姚思廉 and others, Peking: Chung-hua
Shu-chü 中華書局, 1972.

Ch'en Tzu-ang chi 陳子昂集, by Ch'en Tzu-ang, edited by Sun Wang 孫望,
Peking: Chung-hua Shu-chü, 1960.

Chi ku-chin Fo Tao lun heng 集古今佛道論衡, by Tao Hsüan 道宣, ed. in
Taishō daizōkyō 大正大藏經, Vol. 52.

Ch'ien chu Tu shih 錢注杜詩, commentary by Ch'ien Ch'ien-i 錢謙益, Shanghai:
Shang-hai Ku-chi Ch'u-pan-she, 1979.

Ch'ien T'ang Chih Chai 千唐誌齋, collection of original rubbings of T'ang dynasty epitaph texts engraved in stone, in the possession of Shan-tung Ta-hsüeh 山東大學.

Chin shih hsü pien 金石續編, compiled by Lu Yao-yü 陸耀遹, reprint of edition with preface dated 1893, Taipei: Kuo-lien T'u-shu Ch'u-pan-she 國聯圖書出版社, 1965.

Chin shih ts'ui pien 金石萃編, compiled by Wang Ch'ang 王昶, preface dated 1805.

Chin shih wen tzu chi 金石文字記, by Ku Yen-wu 顧炎武, facsimile reprint of 1888 ed., [Taipei]: Chung-hua Wen-hsien Ch'u-pan she 中華文獻出版社, 1969.

Chin shu 晉書, by Fang Hsüan-ling 房玄齡 and others, Peking: Chung-hua Shu-chü, 1974.

Ching tien shih wen 經典釋文, by Lu Te-ming 陸德明, *SPTK* ed.

Chiu chia chi chu Tu shih 九家集注杜詩, ed. by Kuo Chih-ta 郭知達, with commentary by Wang Chu 王洙, Sung Ch'i 宋祁, Wang An-shih 王安石 and others, *HYISIS* ed.

Ch'u hsüeh chi 初學記, complied by Hsü Chien 徐堅 and others, edited with introduction by Ssu I-tsu 司義祖, Peking: Chung-hua Shu-chü, 1962.

Ch'un-ch'iu chi chuan pien i 春秋集傳辯疑, by Lu Ch'un 陸淳, ed. in *Ku ching chieh hui han* 古經解彙函, *Ts'e* 册 35–6.

Ch'un-ch'iu chi chuan tsuan li 春秋集傳纂例, by Lu Ch'un, ed. in *Ku ching chieh hui han, Ts'e* 30–3.

Ch'un-ch'iu wei chih 春秋微旨, by Lu Ch'un, in *Ku ching chieh hui han, Ts'e* 34.

Ch'ü-chiang Chang hsien-sheng wen chi 曲江張先生文集, by Chang Chiu-ling 張九齡, *SPTK* ed.

Chung-hsing hsien ch'i chi 中興間氣集, compiled by Kao Chung-wu 高仲武, ed. in *T'ang jen hsüan T'ang shih* 唐人選唐詩, Peking: Chung-hua Shu-chü, 1958, pp. 259–316.

Ch'üan T'ang shih 全唐詩, compiled by Ts'ao Yin 曹寅, P'eng Ting-ch'iu 彭定求 and others, ed. of Peking: Chung-hua Shu-chü, 1960.

Ch'üan T'ang wen 全唐文, compiled by Tung Kao 董誥 and others, preface dated 1814, in reduced size reprint of Taipei: Hua-wen Shu-chü 華文書局, 1965.

Ch'üan Tsai-chih wen chi 權載之文集, by Ch'üan Te-yü 權德輿, *SPTK* ed.

Ch'ün chü chieh i 群居解頤, by Kao I 高懌, ed. in *Li-tai hsiao hua chi* 歷代笑話集, Shanghai: Ku-tien Wen-hsüeh Ch'u-pan-she 古典文學出版社, 1957.

Ch'ün-shu chih yao 群書治要, compiled by Wei Cheng 魏徵, *SPTK* ed.

Ch'ün-shu k'ao so 群書考索, compiled by Chang Ju-yü 章如愚, reduced size reprint of ed. of 1508, Taipei: Hsin-hsing Shu-chü 新興書局, 1969.

Fan-ch'uan wen chi 樊川文集, by Tu Mu 杜牧, ed. of Shanghai: Shang-hai Ku-chi Ch'u-pan-she 上海古籍出版社, 1978.

Fan-nan wen chi hsiang chu 樊南文集詳注, by Li Shang-yin 李商隱, with commentary by Feng Meng-t'ing 馮孟亭 and Chu Chou-wang 朱周望, *SPPY* ed.

Feng shih wen chien chi 封氏聞見記, by Feng Yen 封演, edited by Chao Chen-hsin 趙貞信 in *HYISIS*, Supplement No. 7.

Han Ch'ang-li chi 韓昌黎集, by Han Yü 韓愈, with commentary by Chu Hsi 朱熹 and others, ed. in *Kuo-hsüeh chi-pen ts'ung-shu.*

Han-lin chih 翰林志, by Li Chao 李肇 ed. in *Pai-ch'uan hsüeh-hai* 百川學海.

Ho yüeh ying ling chi 河嶽英靈集, by Yin Fan 殷璠, ed. in *T'ang jen hsüan T'ang shih* 唐人選唐詩, Peking: Chung-hua Shu-chü, 1958, pp. 39–124.

Huang-fu Ch'ih-cheng wen chi 皇甫持正文集, by Huang-fu Shih 皇甫湜, *SPTK* ed.

Huang-fu Jan shih chi 皇甫冉詩集, by Huang-fu Jan, *SPTK San pien* 三編 ed.

Huang-fu Tseng shih chi, pu i 皇甫曾詩集, 補遺, by Huang-fu Tseng, *SPTK San pien* ed.

I wen lei chü 藝文類聚, by Ou-yang Hsün 歐陽詢 and others, edited by Wang Shao-ying 王紹楹, Peking: Chung-hua Shu-chü, 1965.

K'ai-feng Shih Po-wu-kuan 開封市博物館, collection of original T'ang dynasty epitaph texts engraved in stone, displayed in the K'ai-feng Municipal Museum.

K'an wu 干誤, by Li Fou 李涪, ed. in *Jung-yüan ts'ung-shu* 榕園叢書.

Kao Shih shih chi pien nien chien chu 高適詩集編年箋註, by Kao Shih, with commentary by Liu K'ai-yang 劉開揚, Peking: Chung-hua Shu-chü, 1981.

Kuang hung-ming chi 廣弘明集, by Tao Hsüan 道宣, *SPTK* ed.

K'uang miu cheng su 匡謬正俗, by Yen Shih-ku 顏師古, *Ts'ung-shu chi-ch'eng* ed.

Kuo hsiu chi 國秀集, compiled by Jui T'ing-chang 芮挺章, ed. in *T'ang jen hsüan T'ang shih* 唐人選唐詩, Peking: Chung-hua Shu-chü, 1958, pp. 125–89.

Kuo shih pu 國史補, by Li Chao 李肇, Shanghai: Ku-tien Wen-hsüeh Ch'u-pan-she 古典文學出版社, 1957.

K'uo ti chih chi chiao 括地志輯校, by Li T'ai 李泰 and others, edited with preface by Ho Tz'u-chün 賀次君, Peking: Chung-hua Shu-chü, 1980.

Li I-shan wen chi 李義山文集, by Li Shang-yin 李商隱, *SPTK* ed.

Li T'ai-po wen chi 李太白文集, by Li Po 李白, with commentary by Wang Ch'i 王琦, *Kuo-hsüeh chi-pen ts'ung-shu* ed.

Li Wen-jao wen chi, pieh chi 李文饒文集, 別集, by Li Te-yü, *SPTK* ed.

Li Yüan-pin wen chi 李元賓文集, by Li Kuan 李觀, *Ts'ung-shu chi-ch'eng* ed.

Liang shu 梁書, by Yao Ssu-lien 姚思廉 and others, Peking: Chung-hua Shu-chü, 1973.

Liu Ho-tung chi 柳河東集, by Liu Tsung-yüan 柳宗元, with the commentary of the Shih-ts'ai T'ang 世綵堂 ed., Shanghai: Commercial Press, 1958.

Liu Pin-k'o chia hua lu 劉賓客嘉話錄, attributed to Wei Hsün 韋詢, *Ts'ung-shu chi-ch'eng* ed.

Lo Yin chi 羅隱集, by Lo Yin, edited by Yung Wen-hua 雍文華, Peking: Chung-hua Shu-chü, 1983.

Lu Hsüan kung han-yüan chi 陸宣公翰苑集, by Lu Chih 陸贄 (Lu Hsüan kung), *SPTK* ed.

Lü Ho-shu wen chi 呂和叔文集, by Lü Wen 呂溫, *SPTK* ed.

Meng Hao-jan chi 孟浩然集, by Meng Hao-jan, *SPTK* ed.

Nan shih 南史, by Li Yen-shou 李延壽, Peking: Chung-hua Shu-chü, 1975.

Nihonkoku genzaisho mokuroku 日本國現在書目錄, compiled by Fujiwara no Sukeyo 藤原佐世, edited by Ohase Keikichi 小長谷惠吉, and published as *Nihonkoku genzaisho mokuroku kaisetsu* 解說, Tokyo: Komiyayama Shuppan Kabushiki Kaisha 小宮山出版株式會社, 1976.

Ou-yang Hsing-chou wen chi 歐陽行周文集, by Ou-yang Chan 歐陽詹, *SPTK* ed.

Pa ch'iung shih chin shih pu-cheng 八瓊室金石補正, by Lu Tseng-hsiang 陸增祥, reprint of ed. of 1925, Taipei: Wen-hai Ch'u-pan-she 文海出版社, 1967.

Pei Ch'i shu 北齊書, by Li Pai-yao 李百藥 and others, Peking: Chung-hua Shu-chü, 1972.

Pei shih 北史, by Li Yen-shou 李延壽, Peking: Chung-hua Shu-chü, 1974.

P'i-ling chi 毗陵集, by Tu-ku Chi 獨孤及, *SPTK* ed.

P'i tzu wen sou 皮子文藪, by P'i Jih-hsiu 皮日休, edited by Hsiao Ti-fei 蕭滌非, Peking: Chung-hua Shu-chü, 1959.

Po Hsiang-shan chi 白香山集, by Po Chü-i 白居易, *Kuo-hsüeh chi-pen ts'ung-shu* ed.

Po K'ung liu t'ieh 白孔六帖, compiled by Po Chü-i 白居易 and K'ung Ch'uan 孔傳, reduced size reprint of a Ming ed., Taipei: Hsin-hsing Shu-chü 新興書局, 1969.

P'u-yang Huang yü-shih chi, pieh lu fu lu 莆陽黃御史集, 別錄附錄, by Huang T'ao 黃滔, *Ts'ung-shu chi-ch'eng* ed.

Shen Hsia-hsien wen chi 沈下賢文集, by Shen Ya-chih 沈亞之, *SPTK* ed.

Shih mo chien hua 石墨鐫華, compiled by Chao Han 趙崡, *Ts'ung-shu chi-ch'eng* ed.

Shih t'ung t'ung shih 史通通釋, by Liu Chih-chi 劉知幾, with commentary by P'u Ch'i-lung 浦起龍 and P'u Hsi-ling 浦錫齡, *SPPY* ed.

Ssu-k'ung Piao-sheng shih chi 司空表聖詩集, by Ssu-k'ung T'u 司空圖, *SPTK* ed.

Ssu-k'ung Piao-sheng wen chi 司空表聖文集, by Ssu-k'ung T'u, *SPTK* ed.

Sui shu 隋書, compiled by Wei Cheng 魏徵, Ling-hu Te-fen 令狐德棻 and others, Peking: Chung-hua Shu-chü, 1973.

Sui T'ang chia hua 隋唐嘉話, by Liu Su 劉餗, Shanghai: Ku-tien Wen-hsüeh Ch'u-pan-she, 1958.

Sun Ch'iao chi 孫樵集, by Sun Ch'iao, *SPTK* ed.

Ta T'ang chiao ssu lu 大唐郊祀錄, by Wang Ching 王涇, ed. in *Shih-yüan ts'ung-shu* 適園叢書, 1915, facsimile reprint in Ikeda On 池田溫 ed., *Dai Tō Kaigen rei* 大唐開元禮, Tokyo: Koten Kenkyūkai 古典研究會, 1972.

Ta T'ang ch'uang-yeh ch'i-chü chu 大唐創業起居注, by Wen Ta-ya 溫大雅, *Ts'ung-shu chi-ch'eng* ed.

Ta T'ang hsin yü 大唐新語, by Liu Su 劉肅, Shanghai: Ku-tien Wen-hsüeh Ch'u-pan-she, 1958.

Ta T'ang K'ai-yüan li 大唐開元禮, compiled by Hsiao Sung 蕭嵩 and others, ed. in *Hung shih T'ang shih ching kuan ts'ung-shu* 洪氏唐石經館叢書, published as *Dai Tō Kaigen rei*, with introduction by Ikeda On 池田溫, Tokyo: Koten Kenkyūkai 古典研究會, 1972.

Ta T'ang liu tien 大唐六典, compiled by Chang Yüeh 張說, Hsiao Sung 蕭嵩, and others, ed. of 1724 edited by Hiroike Senkurō 廣池千九郎 and Uchida Tomoo 內田智雄, and published as *Dai Tō rikuten*, Tokyo: Hiroike Gakuen Jigyōbu 廣池學園事業部, 1973.

T'ai-p'ing kuang chi 太平廣記, compiled by Li Fang 李昉 and others, Peking: Jen-min Wen-hsüeh Ch'u-pan-she 人民文學出版社, 1959.

T'ang hui yao 唐會要, by Su Mien 蘇冕, Ts'ui Hsüan 崔鉉 and Wang Po 王溥, Peking: Chung-hua Shu-chü, 1955.

T'ang jen hsüan T'ang shih 唐人選唐詩, Peking: Chung-hua Shu-chü, 1958.

T'ang lü shu i 唐律疏義, by Chang-sun Wu-chi 長孫無忌 and others, *Ts'ung-shu chi-ch'eng* ed.

T'ang shih chi shih 唐詩紀事, by Chi Yu-kung 計有功, Peking: Chung-hua Shu-chü, 1965.

T'ang ta chao ling chi 唐大詔令集, compiled by Sung Shou 宋綬 and Sung Min-ch'iu 宋敏求, Shanghai: Commercial Press, 1959.

T'ang wen ts'ui 唐文萃, compiled by Yao Hsüan 姚鉉, *SPTK* ed.

Tou shih lien chu chi 竇氏連珠集, by Tou Ch'ang 竇常, Tou Mou 竇牟, Tou Ch'ün 竇群, Tou Hsiang 竇庠, and Tou Kung 竇鞏 ed. in *Kuan-chung ts'ung-shu* 關中叢書.

Ts'e fu yüan kuei 册府元龜, compiled by Wang Ch'in-jo 王欽若 and others, reduced size reprint of Ming ed., Peking: Chung-hua Shu-chü, 1960.

Ts'en Chia-chou shih 岑嘉州詩, by Ts'en Shen 岑參 *SPTK* ed.

T'ung li 通歷, by Ma Tsung 馬總, ed. with preface dated 1915 by Yeh Te-hui 葉德輝.

T'ung tien 通典, by Tu Yu 杜佑, *Kuo-hsüeh chi-pen ts'ung-shu* ed., in reprint of Taipei: Hsin-hsing Shu-chü 新興書局, 1962.

Wang Mo-chieh ch'üan chi chien-chu 王摩詰全集箋注, by Wang Wei 王維, with commentary by Chao Sung-chih 趙松之, reprint of Taipei: Shih-chieh Shu-chü 世界書局, 1962.

Wang Tzu-an chi 王子安集, by Wang Po 王勃, *SPTK* ed.

Wei Cheng kung chien lu 魏鄭公諫錄, by Wei Cheng 魏徵, *Ts'ung-shu chi-ch'eng* ed.

Wen yüan ying hua 文苑英華, compiled by Li Fang 李昉 and others, reduced size reprint of Sung and Ming editions, Peking: Chung-hua Shu-chü, 1966.

Wu-hsing Chou shang-jen chi 吳興晝上人集, by Chiao-jan 皎然, *SPTK* ed.

Yang Ying-ch'uan chi 楊盈川集, by Yang Chiung 楊炯, *SPTK* ed.

Yen Lu kung wen chi 顏魯公文集, by Yen Chen-ch'ing 顏眞卿 *SPTK* ed.

Yen Lu kung wen chi 顏魯公文集, by Yen Chen-ch'ing, edited by Huang Pen-chi 黃本驥, *SPPY* ed.

Yin hua lu 因話錄, by Chao Lin 趙璘, Shanghai: Ku-tien Wen-hsüeh Ch'u-pan-she, 1957.

Yu yu tzu chi 幽憂子集, by Lu Chao-lin 盧照鄰, *SPTK* ed.

Yü hai 玉海, compiled by Wang Ying-lin 王應麟, reduced size reprint of ed. of 1337–40, Taipei: Hua-wen Shu-chü, 1964.

Yü Pi-chien chi 虞祕監集, by Yü Shih-nan 虞世南, ed. in *Ssu-ming ts'ung-shu* 四明叢書.

Yüan-ho hsing tsuan 元和姓纂, compiled by Lin Pao 林寶 and edited by Sun Hsing-yen 孫星衍, with preface dated 1802.

Yüan shih Ch'ang-ch'ing chi 元氏長慶集, by Yüan Chen 元稹, *SPTK* ed.

Yüan Tz'u-shan chi 元次山集, by Yüan Chieh 元結, edited by Sun Wang 孫望, Peking: Chung-hua Shu-chü, 1960.

3. Histories, bibliographies, miscellanies and other critical works compiled after the T'ang

Chih chai shu lu chieh t'i 直齋書錄解題, by Ch'en Chen-sun 陳振孫, ed. in
   Kuo-hsüeh chi-pen tsung-shu 國學基本叢書.

Ching i k'ao 經義考, by Chou I-tsun 周彝尊, *SPPY* ed.

Chiu T'ang shu 舊唐書, by Liu Hsü 劉昫 and others, Peking: Chung-hua Shu-
   chü 中華書局, 1975.

Chün chai tu shu chih 郡齋讀書志, by Ch'ao Kung-wu 晁公武, *SPTK Hsü-pien*
   續編 ed.

Ch'ung-wen tsung mu 崇文總目, compiled by Wang Yao-ch'en 王堯臣 and
   others, *Kuo-hsüeh chi-pen ts'ung-shu* ed.

Fo tsu t'ung chi 佛祖統紀, by Chih P'an 志磐, ed. in *Taishō Daizokyō* 大正
   大藏經, Vol. 49.

Hsin T'ang shu 新唐書, by Ou-yang Hsiu 歐陽修, Sung Ch'i 宋祁 and others,
   Peking: Chung-hua Shu-chü, 1975.

Huang Chien Yang Wen kung t'an yüan 黃鑑楊文公談苑, ed. in *Sung ch'ao
   hsiao-shuo ta kuan* 宋朝小說大觀, *Ssu-pu chi yao* 四部集要 ed.

Jung chai sui-pi wu chi 容齋隨筆五集, by Hung Mai 洪邁, Peking: Chung-hua
   Shu-chü, 1959.

Kuang ch'uan shu po 廣川書跋, by Tung Yu 董逌, *Ts'ung-shu chi-ch'eng* ed.

K'ung tzu shih chia p'u 孔子世家譜, by K'ung Shang-jen 孔尚任, 1684.

Liu t'ieh pu 六帖補, by Yang Po-yen 楊伯嵒, ed. in *Ssu-k'u ch'üan-shu chen-pen
   ch'i chi* 四庫全書珍本七集.

Lo ch'uan chi 樂川集, by Chang Fang-p'ing 張方平, ed. in *Ssu-k'u ch'üan-shu
   chen-pen ch'u chi* 四庫全書珍本初集.

Nan pu hsin shu 南部新書, by Ch'ien I 錢易, *Ts'ung-shu chi-ch'eng* ed.

Nien-erh shih cha chi 廿二史札記, by Chao I 趙翼, *Ts'ung-shu chi-ch'eng* ed.

Shan-tung t'ung-chih 山東通志, Shanghai: Commercial Press, 1934.

Shih ching k'ao 石經考, by Ku Yen-wu 顧炎武, *Ts'ung-shu chi-ch'eng* ed.

Ssu-k'u ch'üan shu tsung mu t'i yao 四庫全書總目提要, *Kuo-hsüeh chi-pen
   ts'ung-shu* ed.

T'ai-p'ing huan yü chi 太平寰宇記, by Yüeh Shih 樂史, with supplement by
   Ch'en Lan-sen 陳蘭森, preface dated 1803.

T'ang chien 唐鑑, by Fan Tsu-yü 范祖禹, ed. in *Kuo-hsüeh chi-pen ts'ung-shu*.

T'ang chih yen 唐遮言, by Wang Ting-pao 王定保, Shanghai: Ku-tien Wen-
   hsüeh Ch'u-pan-she, 1957.

T'ang shu ching chi i wen ho-chih 唐書經籍藝文合志, by Liu Hsü 劉昫,
   Ou-yang Hsiu 歐陽修 and others, ed. of Shanghai: Commercial Press,
   1956.

T'ang ts'ai tzu chuan 唐才子傳, by Hsin Wen-fang 辛文房, Shanghai: Ku-tien
   Wen-hsüeh Chü-pan-she, 1957.

T'ang Yüeh ling hsü k'ao 唐月令續考, by Mao P'an-lin 茆泮林, in *Ho shou
   t'ang ts'ung-shu* 鶴壽堂叢書, 1898.

Teng k'o chi k'ao fu pu-i so-yin 登科記考附補遺索引, by Hsü Sung 徐松,
   reprint of ed. in *Nan-ching shu-yüan ts'ung shu* 南菁書院叢書, 1888, with
   supplement by Lo Chi-tsu 羅繼祖 and index, Taipei: Ching-sheng Wen-
   wu Kung-ying Kung-ssu 驚聲文物供應公司, 1972.

Tso chuan chiu shu k'ao cheng 左傳舊疏考證, by Liu Wen-ch'i 劉文淇, in

Huang Ch'ing ching chieh hsü pien 皇清經解續編.

Tsou hsien chih 鄒縣志, ed. with preface dated 1716, in *Chung-kuo fang-chih ts'ung-shu* 中國方志叢書.

Tzu-chih t'ung chien 資治通鑑, by Ssu-ma Kuang 司馬光, with commentary by Hu San-hsing 胡三省, Peking: Chung-hua Shu-chü, 1956.

Wan shan t'ung kuei lu 萬善同歸錄 by Chih-chüeh ch'an shih 智覺禪師 (Yen-shou 延壽), *Taishō daizokyō* Vol. 48.

Yen-chou t'u ching 嚴州圖經, by Ch'en Kung-liang 陳公亮 and Liu Wen-fu 劉文富, *Ts'ung-shu chi-ch'eng* ed.

Yü ti kuang chi 輿地廣記, compiled by Ou-yang Min 歐陽忞, *Ts'ung-shu chi-ch'eng* ed.

B. Works written since 1900

Andō Shunroku 安東俊六, 'Keiryū kyūtei bungaku no sōsaku kiban 景龍宮廷文學の創作基盤', *Chūgoku bungaku ronshū* 中國文學論集 3, Kyūshū Daigaku Chūgoku Bungakkai 九州大學中國文學會 (1972), pp. 13–24.

Balazs, E., 'History as a guide to bureaucratic practice', in H.M. Wright tr., *Chinese civilization and bureaucracy*, Hartford, Connecticut: Yale University Press, 1964, pp. 129–49.

Barrett, T.H. (1978), 'Buddhism, Taoism and Confucianism in the thought of Li Ao': a dissertation presented to the Faculty of the Graduate School of Yale University in candidacy for the Degree of Doctor of Philosophy, December 1978.

Barrett, T.H. (1986), 'How to forget Chinese history', *Bulletin of the British Association for Chinese Studies* (1986), pp. 12–21.

Bingham, Woodbridge (1937), 'Wen Ta-ya: the first recorder of T'ang history', *Journal of the American Oriental Society* 57 (1937), pp. 368–74.

Bingham, Woodbridge (1941), *The founding of the T'ang dynasty: the fall of Sui and rise of T'ang, a preliminary survey* (*American Council of Learned Societies Studies in Chinese and related civilizations* 4), Baltimore: Waverly Press, Inc., 1941.

Bingham, Woodbridge (1950), 'Li Shih-min's coup in A.D. 626', *Journal of the American Oriental Society* 70 (1950), pp. 89–95 and 259–71.

Bischoff, F.A., *La forêt des pinceaux, Étude sur l'académie du Han-lin sous la dynastie des T'ang et traduction du Han lin che*, Paris: Presses Universitaires de France, 1963.

Bodde, Derk, *Festivals in classical China; new year and other annual observances during the Han dynasty 206 B.C.–A.D. 220*, Princeton: Princeton University Press, 1975.

Chang Ch'ün 章群, 'Tan Chao Lu san chia Ch'un-ch'iu chih shuo 啖趙陸三家春秋之說', *Ch'ien Mu hsien-sheng pa-shih sui chi-nien lun-wen chi* 錢穆先生八十歲紀念論文集, Hong Kong: Hsin-ya Yen-chiu-so 新亞研究所, 1974, pp. 149–59.

Chang Hsi-t'ang 張西堂, *T'ang jen pien wei chi yü* 唐人辨偽集語, Peking: P'u-she 樸社, 1935.

Chang Shih-chao 章士釗, *Liu wen chih-yao* 柳文指要, Peking: Chung-hua Shu-chü, 1971.

Chang Ti-hua 張滌華, *Lei shu liu-pieh* 類書流別, Shanghai: Commercial Press, 1958.

Chavannes, Édouard, *Le T'ai chan: essai de monographie d'un culte chinois*, Paris: Ernest Leroux, 1910.

Chen Chi-yun, *Hsün Yüeh (A.D. 148–209): the life and reflections of an early medieval Confucian*, Cambridge: Cambridge University Press, 1975.

Ch'en, Kenneth 'The economic background of the Hui-ch'ang suppression of Buddhism', *HJAS* 19 (1956), pp. 67–105.

Ch'en T'ieh-fan 陳鐵凡, 'Tun-huang pen I, Shu, Shih k'ao lüeh 敦煌本易書詩考略', *K'ung Meng hsüeh-pao* 孔孟學報 17 (April, 1969), pp. 149–81.

Ch'en Yin-k'o (1936), 'Han Yü and the T'ang novel', *HJAS* 1 (1936), pp. 39–43.

Ch'en Yin-k'o (1938), 'The Shun tsung shih lu and the Hsü Hsüan-kuai lu', *HJAS* 3 (1938), pp. 9–16.

Ch'en Yin-k'o (1940), 'Sui T'ang chih-tu yüan-yüan lüeh lun kao 隋唐制度源原略論稿', reprinted in *Ch'en Yin-k'o hsien-sheng lun chi* 陳寅恪先生論集, Taipei: Chung-yang Yen-chiu Yüan Li-shih Yü-yen Yen-chiu-so 中央研究院歷史語言研究所, 1971, pp. 3–104.

Chi Chen-huai 季鎮淮 (1958), 'Han Yü ti ku-wen li-lun ho shih-chien 韓愈的古文理論和實踐', *Pei-ching Ta-hsüeh hsüeh-pao* 北京大學學報 *Jen-wen k'o-hsüeh* 人文科學 12 no. 2 (1958), pp. 77–85.

Chi Chen-huai (1959), 'Han Yü 'Shih shuo' ti ssu-hsiang ho hsieh-tso pei-ching 韓愈「師說」的思想和寫作背景', *Yü-wen hsüeh-hsi* 語文學習 (1959), pp. 16–17.

Ch'i Ssu-ho, 'Professor Hung on the Ch'un-Ch'iu', *Yenching Journal of Social Studies* I no. 1 (1938), pp. 49–71.

Chien Po-hsien 簡博賢 (1970), 'K'ung Ying-ta Ch'un-ch'iu Tso chuan cheng i p'ing i 孔穎達春秋左傳正義評議', *K'ung Meng hsüeh-pao* 20 (September, 1970), pp. 53–69.

Chien Po-hsien (1975), *Chin ts'un Nan-pei ch'ao ching hsüeh i-chi k'ao* 今存南北朝經學遺籍考, Taipei: Li-ming Wen-hua Shih-yeh Kung-ssu 黎明文化事業公司, 1975.

Ch'ien Chi-po 錢基博, *Han Yü chih* 韓愈志, revised edn., Shanghai: Commercial Press, 1958.

Ch'ien Mu 錢穆, 'Tsa lun T'ang tai ku-wen yün-tung 雜論唐代古文運動', *Hsin-ya hsüeh-pao* 新亞學報 3 no. 1 (August, 1957), pp. 123–68.

Ch'ien Tung-fu 錢冬父, *T'ang Sung ku-wen yün-tung* 唐宋古文運動, Peking: Chung-hua Shu-chü, 1962.

Ch'iu Hsieh-yu 邱燮友, 'Hsüan hsüeh k'ao 選學考', *T'ai-wan Sheng-li Shih-fan Ta-hsüeh Kuo-wen Yen-chiu-so chi-k'an* 臺灣省立師範大學國文研究所集刊 3 (June, 1959), pp. 329–96.

Ch'ü T'ung-tsu, *Law and society in traditional China*, Paris: Mouton and Co., 1961.

Cullen, C., 'A Chinese Eratosthenes of the flat earth', *Bulletin of the School of Oriental and African Studies* XXXIX (1976), pp. 106–27.

Dalby, Michael T., 'Court politics in late T'ang times', in Denis Twitchett ed., *The Cambridge history of China*, Vol. 3, *Sui and T'ang China 589–906*,

Part I, Cambridge: Cambridge University Press, 1979, pp. 561–681.

Dardess, John W., *Confucianism and autocracy: professional elites in the founding of the Ming dynasty*, Berkeley and Los Angeles: University of California Press, 1983.

de Bary, Wm. Theodore (1953), 'A re-appraisal of Neo-Confucianism', in Arthur F. Wright ed., *Studies in Chinese thought*, Chicago: University of Chicago Press, 1953, pp. 81–111.

de Bary, Wm. Theodore (1959), 'Some common tendencies in Neo-Confucianism', in David S. Nivison and Arthur F. Wright eds., *Confucianism in action*, Stanford: Stanford University Press, 1959, pp. 25–49.

de Bary, Wm. Theodore, Wing-tsit Chan and Burton Watson comp. (1960), *Sources of Chinese tradition*, New York: Columbia University Press, 1960.

Dudbridge, Glen *The tale of Li Wa*, London: Ithaca Press, 1983.

Dull, Jack L., 'Han Yü: a problem in T'ang dynasty historiography', in Yao Ts'ung-wu et al. eds., *International Association of Historians of Asia, Second Biennial Conference, Proceedings*, Taipei, 1964.

Ebrey, Patricia Buckley, *The aristocratic families of early imperial China: a case study of the Po-ling Ts'ui family*, Cambridge: Cambridge University Press, 1978.

Fang, Achilles, 'Rhymeprose on literature: the Wen-fu of Lu Chi (A.D. 261–303)', *HJAS* 14 (1951), pp. 527–66.

Frankel, Hans H., 'T'ang literati: a composite biography', in Arthur F. Wright and Denis Twitchett eds., *Confucian personalities*, Stanford: Stanford University Press, 1962, pp. 65–83.

Forte, Antonino, *Political propaganda and ideology in China at the end of the seventh century: an enquiry into the nature, authors and function of the Tunhuang document S. 6502 followed by an annotated translation*, Napoli: Istituto Universitario Orientale, Seminario di Studi Asiatici, 1976.

Fu Chen-lun 傅振倫, *Liu Chih-chi nien-p'u* 劉知幾年譜, Peking: Chung-hua Shu-chü, 1963.

Fu Hsüan-ts'ung 傅璇琮, *T'ang tai shih-jen ts'ung-k'ao* 唐代詩人叢考, Peking: Chung-hua Shu-chü, 1980.

Fujii Mamoru 藤井守, 'Monzen shūchū ni mieru Riku Zenkei chū ni tsuite 文選集注に見える陸善經注について', *Hiroshima Daigaku Bungakubu kiyō* 廣島大學文學部紀要 37 (1977, December), pp. 287–301.

Fukunaga Mitsuji 福永光司, 'Kōten jōtei to tennō taitei to genshi tenson: Jukyō no saikōshin to dōkyō no saikōshin 昊天上帝と天皇大帝と元始天尊—儒教の最高神と道教の最高神', *Chūtetsu Bungakkai hō* 中哲文學會報 2 (June, 1976), pp. 1–34.

Fung Yu-lan, tr. by Derk Bodde (1953), *A history of Chinese philosophy*, Vol. II, *The period of classical learning*, Princeton: Princeton University Press, 1953.

Gentzler, James Mason, 'A literary biography of Liu Tsung-yüan, 763–819', submitted in partial fulfilment of the requirements for the degree of Doctor of Philosophy in the Faculty of Philosophy, Columbia University, 1966.

Graham, A.C., *Poems of the late T'ang*, Harmondsworth, Middlesex: Penguin Books Ltd., 1965.

Guisso, R.W.L., *Wu Tse-t'ien and the politics of legitimation in T'ang China*, Bellingham: Western Washington University, 1978.

Hanabusa Hideki 花房英樹 (1950), 'Bun'en eiga no hensan 文苑英華の編纂', *Tōhō gakuhō* 東方學報 (Kyōto 京都) 19 (November, 1950), pp. 116–135.

Hanabusa Hideki (1964), *Kan Yu kashi sakuin* 韓愈歌詩索引, Kyoto: Kyōto Furitsu Daigaku Jimbun Gakkai 京都府立大學人文學會, 1964.

Hartman, Charles, *Han Yü and the T'ang search for unity*, Princeton: Princeton University Press, 1986.

Hawkes, David (1967), *A little primer of Tu Fu*, London: Oxford University Press, 1967.

Hawkes, David (1985), *The songs of the south*, Harmondsworth, Middlesex: Penguin Books Ltd., 1985.

Hayashi Taisuke 林泰輔, *Rongo nempu* 論語年譜, Tokyo: Ōkura Shoten 大倉書店, 1916.

Herbert, P.A. (1980), 'From shuku to tushuguan: an historical overview of the organization and function of libraries in China', *Papers on Far Eastern History* 22 (September, 1980), pp. 93–121.

Herbert, P.A. (1986), 'Civil service recruitment in early T'ang China: ideal and reality', *Studies in Language and Culture* XII (1986), Faculty of Language and Culture, Osaka University, pp. 199–211.

Herbert, P.A. (1986a), 'T'ang dynasty objections to centralized civil service selection', *Papers on Far Eastern History* 33 (March, 1986), pp. 81–112.

Herbert, P.A. (1986b), *The history of education in T'ang China (Tōdai kyōikushi no kenkyū*, by Taga Akigorō, summary translation by P.A. Herbert), Osaka: Osaka University, 1986.

Hightower, J.R., 'The Wen hsüan and genre theory', *HJAS* 20 (1957), pp. 512–33.

Ho Hsi-ch'un 何希淳, *Li chi cheng i yin i shu k'ao* 禮記正義引佚書考, [Taipei]: Chia-hsin Shui-ni Kung-ssu Wen-hua Chi-chin Hui 嘉新水泥公司文化基金會, 1966.

Honda Nariyuki 本田成之 (1935), *Shina keigakushi ron* 支那經學史論, tr. by Sun Liang-kung 孫俍工, and published as *Chung-kuo ching-hsüeh shih* 中國經學史, Shanghai: Chung-hua Shu-chü, 1935.

Hou Wai-lu 侯外廬 and Chao Chi-pin 趙紀彬 (1959), 'Lü Ts'ai ti wei-wu chu-i ssu-hsiang 呂才的唯物主義思想', *Li-shih yen-chiu* 歷史研究 9 (1959), pp. 1–21.

Hou Wai-lu (1959a), *Chung-kuo ssu-hsiang t'ung-shih* 中國思想通史, Vol. IV part 1, Peking: Jen-min Ch'u-pan-she 人民出版社, 1959.

Hsiao Kung-ch'üan 蕭公權, *Chung-kuo cheng-chih ssu-hsiang shih* 中國政治思想史, Taipei: Chung-hua Wen-hua Ch'u-pan Shih-yeh Wei-yüan-hui 中華文化出版事業委員會, 1954.

Hsü Dau-lin, 'Crime and cosmic order', *HJAS* 30 (1970), pp. 111–125.

Hsü Tzu-to 許慈多, *Wen hsüan Li Shan chu yin Li chi k'ao* 文選李善注引禮記考, [Taipei]; Wen-ching Ch'u-pan-she 文津出版社, 1974.

Hu Shih 胡適, *Pai-hua wen-hsüeh shih* 白話文學史, Shanghai: Hsin-yüeh Shu-tien 新月書店, 1928.

Hung Yeh 洪業 (1937), *Ch'un-ch'iu ching chuan yin-te, fu piao-chiao ching chuan ch'üan wen* 春秋經傳引得, 附標校經傳全文, preface by Hung Yeh (William Hung), Peking: Harvard-Yenching, 1937.

Hung, William (1952), *Tu Fu: China's greatest poet,* Cambridge, Mass.: Harvard University Press, 1952.

Hung, William (1952a), *A supplementary volume of notes for Tu Fu: China's greatest poet,* Cambridge, Mass.: Harvard University Press, 1952.

Hung, William (1957), 'A bibliographical controversy at the T'ang court, A.D. 719', *HJAS* 20 (1957), pp. 74–134.

Hung, William, (1960–1), 'The T'ang bureau of historiography before 708', *HJAS* 23 (1960–1), pp. 93–107.

Hung, William, (1969), 'A T'ang historiographer's letter of resignation', *HJAS* 29 (1969), pp. 5–52.

Ichihara Kōkichi 市原亨吉, 'Tōdai no han ni tsuite 唐代の判について', *Tōhō gakuhō* 東方學報 (Kyōto 京都) 33 (March, 1963), pp. 119–98.

Ikeda On 池田溫 (1971), 'Sei Tō no Shūken in 盛唐の集賢院', *Hokkaidō Daigaku Bungakubu kiyō* 北海島大學文學部紀要 XIX no. 2 (February, 1971), pp. 47–98.

Ikeda On 池田溫 (1972), 'Dai Tō Kaigen rei no kaisetsu 大唐開元禮の解說', in *Dai Tō Kaigen rei,* Tokyo: Koten Kenkyūkai 古典研究會, 1972, pp. 822–32.

Inaba Ichirō 稻葉一郎, 'Chū Tō ni okeru shin jugaku undō no ichi kōsatsu 中唐における新儒學運動の一考察', *Chūgoku chūseishi kenkyū. Rikuchō Sui Tō no shakai to bunka* 中國中世研究—六朝隋唐の社會と文化, Tokyo: Tōkai Daigaku Shuppankai 東海大學出版會, 1970, pp. 377–403.

Iriya Yoshitaka 入矢義高, 'Taikō kakyō kōshaku 太公家敎校釋', *Tōyō shisō ronshū: Fukui hakushi shōju kinen* 東洋思想論集福井博士頌壽紀念, Tokyo: Fukui Hakushi Shōju Kinen Ronshū Kankōkai 福井博士頌壽紀念論集刊行會, 1960, pp. 31–60.

Jan Chao-te 冉昭德, 'Kuan-yü Chin shih ti chuan-shu yü T'ang hsiu Chin shu chuan jen wen-t'i 關於晉史的撰述與唐修晉書撰人問題', *Hsi-pei Ta-hsüeh hsüeh-pao* 西北大學學報, *Jen-wen k'o-hsüeh* 人文科學 1957 no. 4 (December, 1957), pp. 71–8.

Johnson, David G., *The medieval Chinese oligarchy,* Boulder, Colorado: Westview Press, 1977.

Johnson, Wallace, *The T'ang code* Volume I, *General principles, translated with an introduction by Wallace Johnson,* Princeton: Princeton University Press, 1979.

Kanai Yukitada 金井之忠 (1939), 'Ryū Chitsu isetsu kō 劉秩遺說考', *Bunka* 6 no. 1 (1939), pp. 35–48.

Kanai Yukitada (1940), *Tōdai no shigaku shisō* 唐代の史學思想, Tokyo: Kōbundō 弘文堂, 1940.

Kao Ming-shih 高明士 (1970), 'T'ang tai kuan-hsüeh ti fa-chan yü shuai-lo 唐代官學的發展與衰落', *Yu shih-tzu hsüeh-chih* 幼獅子學誌, 9 no. 1 (March, 1970), pp. 1–74.

Kao Ming-shih (1971), 'T'ang tai ssu-hsüeh ti fa-chan 唐代私學的發展', *Kuo-li*

T'ai-wan Ta-hsüeh wen-shih-che hsüeh-pao 國立臺灣大學文史哲學報 No. 20 (June, 1971), pp. 219–89.

Kao Ming-shih (1977), 'T'ang tai 'San shih' ti yen-pien chien shu ch'i tui Tung-ya chu-kuo ti ying-hsiang 唐代三史的演變兼述其對東亞諸國的影響', *Ta-lu tsa-chih* 大陸雜誌 XXXXXIIII no. 1 (January, 1977), pp. 7–16.

Kao Pu-ying 高步瀛 (1937), *Wen hsüan Li chu i-shu* 文選李注義疏, Peking: Pei-p'ing Chih-li Shu-chü 北平直隸書局, 1937.

Kao Pu-ying (1963), *T'ang Sung wen chü-yao* 唐宋文舉要, Peking: Chung-hua Shu-chü, 1963, 3 vols.

Knechtges, David R., *Wen xuan or Selections of refined literature*, Princeton: Princeton University Press, 1982.

Kramers, K.P., 'Conservatism and the transmission of the T'ang canon: a T'ang scholar's complaint', *Journal of Oriental Studies* II no. 1 (January, 1955), pp. 119–32.

Ku I-sheng 顧易生, 'Shih t'an Han Yü ti shang ch'i chi Han wen yü tz'u-fu p'ien-wen ti kuan-hsi 試談韓愈的尚奇及韓文與辭賦駢文的關係, *Wen-hsüeh i-ch'an tseng-k'an* 文學遺產增刊 10 (1962), pp. 66–72.

Kuo Shao-yü 郭紹虞, *Chung-kuo wen-hsüeh p'i-p'ing shih* 中國文學批評史, Shanghai: Hsin Wen-i Ch'u-pan-she 新文藝出版社, 1955.

Lamont, H.G., 'An early ninth century debate on heaven' Part 1, *Asia Major* (New Series) XVIII (1973), pp. 181–208, and Part 2, *Asia Major* XIX (1974), pp. 37–85.

Levy, Howard S., *Biography of An Lu-shan*, Berkeley and Los Angeles: University of California Press, 1960.

Liu, James T.C., 'How did a Neo-Confucian school become the state ortho-doxy?', *Philosophy East and West* XXIII no. iv (October, 1973), pp. 483–505.

Liu K'ai-yang 劉開揚, *Kao Shih shi chi pien nien chien chu* 高適詩集編年箋註, Peking: Chung-hua Shu-chü, 1981.

Lo Chen-yü 羅振玉, *Chao-ling pei lu san chüan, fu lu i chüan* 昭陵碑錄三卷, 附錄一卷 in *Ch'en feng ko ts'ung-shu* 晨風閣叢書, 1909.

Lo Hsiang-lin 羅香林, 'T'ang tai san chiao chiang-lun k'ao 唐代三敎講論考', *Journal of Oriental Studies* I (1954), pp. 85–97.

Lo Ken-tse 羅根澤 (1957), *Chung-kuo wen-hsüeh p'i-p'ing shih* 中國文學批評史, Shanghai: Ku-tien Wen-hsüeh Ch'u-pan-she, 1957.

Lo Lien-t'ien 羅聯添, *Han Yü yen-chiu* 韓愈研究, Taipei: T'ai-wan Hsüeh-sheng Shu-chü 臺灣學生書局, 1977.

McMullen, D.L. (1973), 'Historical and literary theory in the mid-eighth cen-tury', in Arthur F. Wright and Denis Twitchett eds., *Perspectives on the T'ang*, New Haven: Yale University Press, 1973, pp. 307–42.

McMullen, D.L. (1984), 'A note on the Feng ritual of 742; in response to Professor Elling Eide', *T'ang Studies* 2 (Winter, 1984), pp. 37–40.

McMullen, D.L. (1987), 'Views of the state in Du You and Liu Zongyuan', in Stuart R. Schram ed., *Foundations of state power in China*, London: School of Oriental and African Studies, and Hong Kong: The Chinese University Press, 1987.

McMullen, D.L. (1987a), 'Bureaucrats and cosmology: the ritual code of T'ang China', in David Cannadine and Simon Price eds., *Rituals of royalty:*

power and ceremonial in traditional societies, Cambridge: Cambridge University Press, 1987, pp. 181–236.

McMullen, D.L. (1987b), 'T'ang attitudes to the military: the cult of Qi Taigong', article for inclusion in volume of essays for presentation to Professor E.G. Pulleyblank.

Ma Heng 馬衡, *Han shih ching chi ts'un* 漢石經輯存, Peking: K'o-hsüeh Ch'u-pan-she 科學出版社, 1957.

Mair, Victor H., 'Scroll presentation in the T'ang dynasty', *HJAS* 38 (1978), pp. 35–60.

Masui Tsuneo, 'Liu Chih-chi 劉知幾 and the Shih-t'ung 史通', *Memoirs of the Research Department of the Toyo Bunko* 34 (1976), pp. 113–62.

Mirsky, Johnathan, 'The life of Tuan Hsiu-shih based on translations of his biographies in the T'ang histories', *Journal of the China Society* I (1961), pp. 46–65.

Mou Jun-sun 牟潤孫 (1960), 'Lun ju Shih liang chia chih chiang ching yü i-shu 論儒釋兩家之講經與義疏', *Hsin-ya hsüeh-pao* 新亞學報 4 no. 2 (February, 1960), pp. 353–415.

Mou Jun-sun (1968), 'T'ang ch'u Nan-pei hsüeh-jen lun hsüeh chih i-ch'ü yü ying-hsiang 唐初南北學人論學之異趣與影響', *Hsiang-kang Chung-wen Ta-hsüeh Chung-kuo Wen-hua Yen-chiu-so hsüeh-pao* 香港中文大學中國文化研究所學報 I (1968), pp. 50–86.

Nakatsuhama Wataru 中津濱涉, *Geimon ruijū insho intoku* 藝文類聚引書引得, [Nagoya]: Saika Shorin 采華書林, 1972.

Needham, Joseph, *Science and civilization in China* Vol. 2, *History of scientific thought*, Cambridge: Cambridge University Press, 1956. Vol. 3, *Mathematics and the sciences of the heavens and the earth*, 1959.

Nienhauser, William H. Jnr. (1973), *Liu Tsung-yüan*, in Twayne's World Authors Series, No. 255, New York: Twayne Publishers Inc., 1973.

Nienhauser, William H. Jnr. (1976), '"Twelve poems propagating the music bureau ballad": Yüan Chieh's Hsi yüeh-fu shih-erh shou', *Critical essays on Chinese literature*, Hong Kong: The Chinese University of Hong Kong, 1976, pp. 135–46.

Nienhauser William H. Jnr. (1979), *P'i Jih-hsiu*, in Twayne's World Authors Series, No. 530, New York: Twayne Publishers Inc., 1979.

Niimi Hiroshi 新美寬, 'Riku Zenkei no jiseki ni tsuite 陸善經の事蹟について', *Shinagaku* 支那學 9 no. 1 (1937), pp. 131–48.

Nivison, David S., 'Protests against convention and conventions of protest', in Arthur F. Wright ed., *The Confucian persuasion*, Stanford: Stanford University Press, 1960, pp. 177–201.

Nunome Chōfū 布目潮渢 and Ōno Hiroshi 大野仁, 'Haku Kyoi hyakudō han shakugi 白居易百道判釋義', *Ōsaka Daigaku Kyōyōbu kenkyū shūroku jimbun shakaikakagu* 大阪大學教養部研究集錄人文社會科學 28 (December, 1980), pp. 21–35.

Obi Kōichi 小尾交一, 'Ryū Ben no bun ron 柳冕の文論', *Shinagaku kenkyū* 支那學研究 27 (March, 1962), pp. 27–37.

Ogawa Syōichi 小川昭一, 'Ryū On ni tsuite 呂溫について', *Tōkyō Shinagaku hō* 東京支那學報 10 (June, 1964), pp. 70–84.

Owen, Stephen (1975), *The poetry of Meng Chiao and Han Yü*, New Haven: Yale University Press, 1975.

Owen, Stephen (1977), *The poetry of the early T'ang*, New Haven: Yale University Press, 1977.

Owen, Stephen (1981), *The great age of Chinese poetry*, New Haven: Yale University Press, 1981.

P'an Chung-kuei 潘重規 (1955), 'Ch'un-ch'iu Kung-yang shu tso-che k'ao 春秋公羊疏作者考', *Hsüeh-shu chi-k'an* 學術季刊 IV no. i (1955), pp. 11–18.

P'an Chung-kuei (1965), 'Wu ching cheng i t'an-yüan 五經正義探源', *Huakang hsüeh-pao* 華崗學報 I (June, 1965), pp. 13–22.

P'ei P'u-hsien 裴普賢, *Ching hsüeh kai shu* 經學概述, Taipei: T'ai-wan K'aiming Shu-tien 臺灣開明書店, 1969.

Peterson, C.A., 'Court and province in mid- and late T'ang', in Denis Twitchett ed., *The Cambridge history of China*, Vol. 3, *Sui and T'ang China 589–906*, Part I, Cambridge: Cambridge University Press, 1979, pp. 464–560.

P'i Hsi-jui 皮錫瑞, *Ching hsüeh li-shih* 經學歷史, Shanghai: Commercial Press, 1937.

Pien Hsiao-hsüan 卞孝萱, *Liu Yü-hsi nien-p'u* 劉禹錫年譜, Peking: Chung-hua Shu-chü, 1963.

Pulleyblank, E.G. (1950), 'The Tzyjyh tongjiann kaoyih and the sources for the history of the period 730–763', *Bulletin of the School of Oriental and African Studies* XIII (1950), pp. 448–73.

Pulleyblank, E.G. (1954), 'A geographical text of the eighth century', *Silver Jubilee Volume of the Zinbun Kagaku Kenkyusyo*, Kyoto: Zinbun Kagaku Kenkyusyo, 1954, pp. 301–8.

Pulleyblank, E.G. (1955), *The background to the rebellion of An Lu-shan*, London: Oxford University Press, 1955.

Pulleyblank, E.G. (1957) 'The Shun tsung shih lu', *Bulletin of the School of Oriental and African Studies* XIX (1957), pp. 336–44.

Pulleyblank, E.G. (1959), 'Liu K'o, a forgotten rival of Han Yü', *Asia Major* VII (1959), pp. 145–60.

Pulleyblank, E.G. (1960), 'Neo-Confucianism and Neo-Legalism in T'ang intellectual life, 755–805', Arthur F. Wright ed., *The Confucian persuasion*, Stanford: Stanford University Press, 1960, pp. 77–114.

Pulleyblank, E.G. (1961), 'Chinese historical criticism: Liu Chih-chi and Ssuma Kuang'. W.G. Beasley and E.G. Pulleyblank eds., *Historians of China and Japan*, London: Oxford University Press, 1961, pp. 135–66.

Pulleyblank, E.G. (1976), 'The An Lu-shan rebellion and the origins of chronic militarism in late T'ang China', in John Curtis Perry and Bardwell L. Smith eds., *Essays on T'ang society*, Leiden: E.J. Brill, 1976, pp. 33–60.

Rideout, J.K., 'The context of the Yüan tao and the Yüan hsing', *Bulletin of the School of Oriental and African Studies* XII (1948), pp. 403–8.

Rogers, Michael C., *The chronicle of Fu Chien: a case of exemplar history*, Berkeley and Los Angeles: University of California Press, 1968.

Rotours, Robert des (1932), *Traité des examens*, Paris: Ernest Leroux, 1932.

Rotours, Robert des (1947–48), *Traité des fonctionnaires et de l'armée*, Leiden: E.J. Brill, 1947–8, 2 vols.

Rotours, Robert des (1966), 'Le culte des cinq dragons sous la dynastie des T'ang (618–907)', *Mélanges de sinologie offerts a Monsieur Paul Demiéville, Bibliothèque de l'institut des hautes études chinoises* xx, Paris: Presses Universitaires de France, 1966, pp. 261–280.

Rotours, Robert des (1975), 'Le T'ang lieou tien décrit-il exactement les institutions en usage sous la dynastie des T'ang?', *Journal Asiatique* CCLXIII (1975), pp. 183–201.

Rotours, Robert des (1975a), *Les inscriptions funéraires de Ts'ouei Mien et de Ts'ouei Yeou-fou*, Paris: École Française d'Extrême-Orient, 1975.

Schafer, E.H. (1962), 'Notes on T'ang culture', *Monumenta serica* xxi (1962), pp. 194–221.

Schafer, E.H. (1963), 'The auspices of T'ang', *Journal of the American Oriental Society* 83 (June, 1963), pp. 197–225.

Schwartz, Benjamin, 'Some polarities in Confucian thought', in David S. Nivison and Arthur F. Wright eds., *Confucianism in action*, Stanford: Stanford University Press, 1959, pp. 50–62.

Shryock, John K., *The origin and development of the state cult of Confucius*, New York and London: The Century Co., 1932.

Solomon, Bernard S., *The veritable record of the T'ang emperor Shun-tsung (February 28, 805–August 31, 805) Han Yü's Shun tsung shih lu, translated with introduction and notes*, Cambridge, Mass.: Harvard University Press, 1955.

Somers, Robert, 'The historiography of the T'ang founding', unpublished paper presented to the Yale Seminar in Chinese and Comparative Historiography, 1971.

Su Ying-hui 蘇瑩輝 (1968), 'Shang Wu ching cheng i piao chih pan-pen chi ch'i hsiang-kuan wen-t'i 上五經正義表之版本及其相關問題', *Ch'ing chu Chiang Wei-t'ang hsien-sheng ch'i-shih jung ch'ing lun-wen chi* 慶祝蔣慰堂先生七十榮慶論文集, Taipei: T'ai-wan Hsüeh-sheng Shu-chü 臺灣學生書局, 1968, pp. 345–53.

Su Ying-hui (1968a), 'Wu ching cheng i ti i tz'u p'an-hsing yü Chen-kuan nien chung 五經正義第一次頒行於貞觀年中', *Bulletin of the National Central Library, New Series* xxII (1968), pp. 29–33.

Su Ying-hui (1968b), 'Ts'ung Tun-huang pen hsien ming i yeh lun Wu ching cheng i chih k'an ting 從敦煌本銜名一頁論五經正義之刊定', *K'ung Meng hsüeh-pao* 孔孟學報 16 (September, 1968), pp. 181–93.

Sung Kuo-tung 孫國棟, 'T'ang tai chung-shu she-jen ch'ien kuan t'u-ching k'ao shih 唐代中書舍人遷官途徑考釋', in Sun Kuo-tung, *T'ang Sung shih lun ts'ung* 唐宋史論叢, Hong Kong: Lung-men Shu-tien 龍門書店, 1980.

Sun Wang 孫望, *Yüan Tz'u-shan nien-p'u* 元次山年譜, Shanghai: Ku-tien Wen-hsüeh Ch'u-pan-she, 1957.

Taga Akigorō 多賀秋五郎 (1953), *Tōdai kyōikushi no kenkyū—Nihon gakko kyōiku no genryū* 唐代教育史の研究—日本學校の源流, Tokyo: Fumeidō 不昧堂, 1953.

T'ang Ch'eng-yeh 湯承業, *Li Te-yü yen-chiu* 李德裕研究, [Taipei]: Chia-hsin Shui-ni Kung-su Wen-hua Chi-chin-hui 嘉新水泥公司文化基金會, 1973.

T'ao Hsi-sheng 陶希聖 (1972), 'Kung tzu miao-t'ang chung Han ju chi Sung ju ti wei-tz'u-shang 孔子廟堂中漢儒及宋儒的位次(上)', *Shih huo yüeh k'an* 食貨月刊 II no. i (April, 1972), pp. 9–29.

T'ao Hsi-sheng (1972a), 'K'ung tzu miao t'ang chung Han ju chi Sung ju ti wei-tz'u-hsia 孔子廟堂中漢儒及宋儒的位次(下)', *Shih huo yüeh k'an* II no. ii (May, 1972), pp. 81–85.

T'ao Hsi-sheng (1972b), 'Wu miao chih cheng-chih she-hui ti yen-pien 武廟之 政治社會的演變', *Shih huo yüeh k'an* II no. v (August, 1972), pp. 229–47.

Teng Ssu-yü and Knight Biggerstaff, *An annotated bibliography of selected Chinese reference works*, Third edition, Cambridge, Mass.: Harvard University Press, 1971.

Thompson, Paul, *The Shen tzu fragments*, London: Oxford University Press, 1979.

Tjan Tjoe Som 曾珠森, *Po hu t'ung: the comprehensive discussions in the White Tiger Hall* Vol. I, Leiden: E.J. Brill, 1949.

Toda Toyosaburō 戶田豐三郞, 'Fukuseisho no tachiba 復性書の立場', *Shinagaku kenkyū* 支那學研究 29 (March, 1963), pp. 1–9.

Tonami Mamoru 礪波護 (1975), 'Tōdai no seikō 唐代の制誥', *Tōyōshi kenkyū* 東洋史研究 XXXIV no. iii (December, 1975), pp. 348–69.

Tonami Mamoru (1979), 'Tō no sanshō rikubu 唐の三省六部', in *Zui Tō teikoku to higashi Ajia sekai* 隋唐帝國と東アジア世界, edited by the Tōdaishi Kenkyūkai 唐代史研究會, Kyoto: Kyūko Shoin 汲古書院, 1979, pp. 165–88.

Ts'en Chung-mien 岑仲勉 (1962), *T'ang jen hang-ti lu* 唐人行第錄, Peking: Chung-hua Shu-chü, 1962.

Ts'en Chung-mien (1962a), 'T'ang chi chih-i 唐集質疑', in *T'ang jen hang-ti lu*, pp. 353–481.

Tsien Tsuen-hsuin, *Written on bamboo and silk; the beginnings of Chinese books and inscriptions*, Chicago: Chicago University Press, 1962.

Tun-huang Wen-wu Yen-chiu-so 敦煌文物研究所, 'Mo-kao k'u ti 220 k'u hsin fa-hsien ti fu-pi pi-hua 莫高窟第220窟新發現的復壁壁畫', *Wen wu* 1978, no. 12, pp. 41–6.

Twitchett, D.C. (1960), 'Lu Chih (754–805): imperial advisor and court official', in Arthur F. Wright ed., *The Confucian persuasion*, Stanford: Stanford University Press, 1960, pp. 84–122.

Twitchett, D.C. (1961), 'Chinese biographical writing', in W.G. Beasley and E.G. Pulleyblank eds., *Historians of China and Japan*, London: Oxford University Press, 1961, pp. 95–114.

Twitchett, D.C. (1962), 'Problems of Chinese biography', in Arthur F. Wright and Denis Twitchett eds., *Confucian personalities*, Stanford: Stanford University Press, 1962, pp. 24–39.

Twitchett, D.C. (1970), *Financial administration under the T'ang dynasty*, 2nd ed., Cambridge: Cambridge University Press, 1970.

Twitchett, D.C. (1973), 'The composition of the T'ang ruling class: new evidence from Tun-huang', in Denis Twitchett and Arthur F. Wright eds., *Perspectives on the Tang*, New Haven: Yale University Press, 1973.

Twitchett, D.C. (1976), 'Varied patterns of provincial autonomy in the T'ang dynasty', in John Curtis Perry and Bardwell L. Smith eds., *Essays on*

T'ang society, Leiden: E.J. Brill, 1976, pp. 90–109.

Twitchett, D.C. (1976a), 'The birth of the Chinese meritocracy: bureaucrats and examinations in T'ang China', Lecture given to the China Society in London, 17 December, 1974.

Twitchett, D.C. (1979), ed., *The Cambridge history of China*, Vol. 3, *Sui and T'ang China 589–906*, Part ɪ, Cambridge: Cambridge University Press, 1979.

Twitchett, D.C. (1985), 'The writings of official history under the T'ang', unpublished typescript draft, (1985).

van der Loon, Piet, 'On the transmission of the Kuan tzu', *T'oung pao* XLI (1952), pp. 357–93.

Waley, Arthur (1949), *The life and times of Po Chü-i*, London: George Allen and Unwin, 1949.

Waley, Arthur (1960), *Ballads and stories from Tun-huang*, London: George Allen and Unwin, 1960.

Wan Man 萬曼, *T'ang chi hsü lu* 唐集叙錄, Peking: Chung-hua Shu-chü, 1980.

Wang Chung-lin 王忠林, 'Chou i cheng i yin shu k'ao 周易正義引書考', *T'ai-wan Sheng-li Shih-fan Ta-hsüeh Kuo-wen Yen-chiu-so chi-k'an* 臺灣省立師範大學國文研究所集刊 3 (June, 1959), pp. 1–111.

Wang Chung-min 王重民, *Tun-huang ku-chi hsü lu* 敦煌古籍叙錄, Kyoto: Chūbun Shuppansha 中文出版社, 1978.

Wang Shu-min 王樹民, *Shih-pu yao chi chieh t'i* 史部要籍解題, Peking: Chung-hua Shu-chü, 1981.

Wang Yün-hsi 王運熙, 'Chen Tzu-ang ho ta-ti tso-p'in 陳子昂和他的作品', *Wen-hsüeh i-ch'an tseng-k'an* 文學遺產增刊 4 (1957), pp. 92–121.

Wechsler, Howard J. (1974), *Mirror to the son of heaven: Wei Cheng at the court of T'ang T'ai-tsung*, New Haven and London: Yale University Press, 1974.

Wechsler, Howard J. (1977), 'The Confucian teacher Wang T'ung (584?–617): one thousand years of controversy', *T'oung pao* LXIII (1977), pp. 225–72.

Wechsler, Howard J. (1985), *Offerings of jade and silk*, New Haven and London: Yale University Press, 1985.

Wright, A.F. (1951), 'Fu I and the rejection of Buddhism', *Journal of the History of Ideas* XII (1951), pp. 33–47.

Wright A.F. (1976), 'T'ang T'ai-tsung; the man and the persona', in John Curtis Perry and Bardwell L. Smith eds., *Essays on T'ang society*, Leiden: E.J. Brill, 1976, pp. 17–32.

Wright, A.F. (1979), 'The Sui dynasty', in Denis Twitchett ed., *The Cambridge history of China*, Vol. 3, *Sui and T'ang China 589–906*, Part ɪ, Cambridge: Cambridge University Press, 1979, pp. 48–149.

Wu, K.T. 'Libraries and book collecting in China before the invention of printing', *T'ien Hsia Monthly* v no. iii (October, 1937), pp. 237–60.

Yang, C.K. (1957), 'The functional relationship between Confucian thought and Chinese religion', in J.K. Fairbank ed., *Chinese thought and institutions*, Chicago: Chicago University Press, 1957, pp. 269–90.

Yang, C.K. (1959), 'Some characteristics of Chinese bureaucratic behaviour', in David S. Nivison and Arthur F. Wright eds., *Confucianism in action*, Stanford: Stanford University Press, 1959, pp. 134–64.

Yang Ch'eng-tsu 楊承祖, *Chang Chiu-ling nien-p'u* 張九齡年譜, Taipei: Kuo-li T'ai-wan Ta-hsüeh Wen-hsüeh Yüan 國立臺灣大學文學院, 1964.

Yang Chia-lo 楊家駱, 'Pei shih shu yao 北史述要', reprinted as prefatory material to the Taipei: Ting-wen Shu-chü 鼎文書局, (n.d.), reprint of *Pei shih*, Peking: Chung-hua Shu-chü, 1974, pp. 1–15.

Yang Hsiang-k'uei 楊向奎, 'T'ang Sung shih-tai ti ching-hsüeh ssu-hsiang: Ching tien shih wen Shih-san ching cheng i teng shu so piao-hsien ti ssu-hsiang t'i-hsi 唐宋時代的經學思想:經典釋文十三經正義等書所表現的思想體係', *Wen shih che* 文史哲 (May, 1958), pp. 7–16.

Yasui Kōzan 安居香山 and Nakamura Shōhachi 中村璋八, *Isho no kisoteki kenkyū* 緯書の基礎的研究, Tokyo: Kan Gi Bunka Kenkyūkai 漢魏文化研究會, 1966.

Yeh Cheng-hsin 葉政欣, *Ch'un-ch'iu Tso shih chuan Tu chu shih li* 春秋左傳杜注釋例 [Taipei]: Chia-hsin Shui-ni Kung-su Wen-hua Chi-chin-hui 嘉新水泥公司文化基金會, 1966.

Yeh Ch'eng-i 葉程義 (1970), 'Li chi cheng i yin shu k'ao shu 禮記正義引書考述', *Kuo-li Cheng-chih Ta-hsüeh hsüeh-pao* 國立政治大學學報 22 (1970), pp. 313–22.

Yeh Ch'eng-i (1975), *Wen hsüan Li Shan chu yin Shang shu k'ao* 文選李善注引尚書考, Taipei: Cheng-chung Shu-chü 正中書局, 1975.

Yen Keng-wang 嚴耕望 (1953), 'Lüeh lun T'ang liu tien chih hsing-chih yü shih-hsing wen-t'i 略論唐六典之性質與施行問題', *Chung-yang Yen-chiu Yüan Li-shih Yü-yen Yen-chiu-so chi-k'an* 中央研究院歷史語言研究所集刊 XXIV (1953), pp. 69–76.

Yen Keng-wang (1959), 'T'ang jen tu shan-lin ssu-yüan chih feng-shang 唐人讀山林寺院之風尚', *Chung-yang Yen-chiu Yüan Li-shih Yü-yen Yen-chiu-so chi-k'an* 中央研究院歷史語言研究所集刊 XXX no. ii (October, 1959), pp. 689–728.

Yoshihara Fumiaki 吉原文昭 (1974), 'Tōdai Shunjū sanshi no idō ni tsuite 唐代春秋三子の異同に就いて', *Chūō Daigaku Bungakubu kiyō, tetsugakka* 中央大學文學部紀要, 哲學科, 20 (1974, March), pp. 67–104.

Yoshihara Fumiaki (1976), 'Hoku Sō Shunjūgaku no ichi sokumen: Tōdai Shunjū sanshi no bendaigi no keishō to hihan o megutte 北宋春秋學の一側面—唐代春秋三子の辨褅義の繼承と批判を回つて', *Chūgoku tetsugaku no tembō to mosaku* 中國哲學の展望と摸索, Tokyo: Sōbunsha 創文社, 1976, pp. 633–53.

Yoshikawa Tadao 吉川忠夫, 'Gan Shiko no Kanjo chū 顔師古の漢書注', *Tōhō gakuhō* 東方學報 (Kyōto 京都) 51 (March, 1979), pp. 223–319.

Yü Chia-hsi 余嘉錫, *Ssu-k'u t'i-yao pien cheng* 四庫提要辨證, Peking: K'o-hsüeh Ch'u-pan-she 科學出版社, 1958.

CHARACTER GLOSSARY AND INDEX

(Information on T'ang scholars' examinations is drawn from *TKCK, CTCC and KFSPWK*)